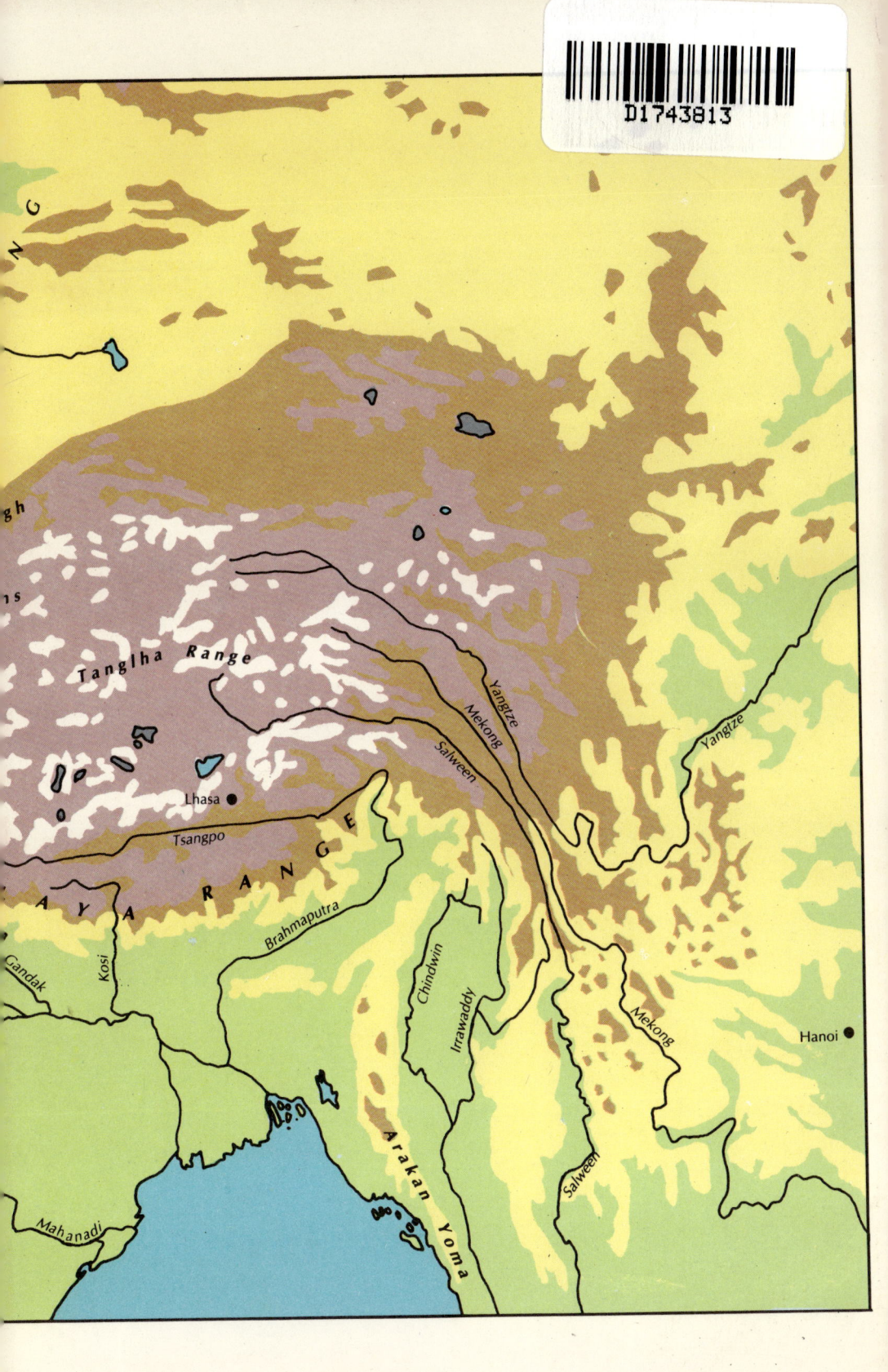

Nature Reserves of The Himalaya and the Mountains of Central Asia

Compiled by Michael J. B. Green
World Conservation Monitoring Centre

in collaboration with
IUCN Commission on National Parks and Protected Areas

IUCN–The World Conservation Union
1993

Published by Oxford University Press, New Delhi, India.

Prepared by World Conservation Monitoring Centre.

A contribution to GEMS–the Global Environment Monitoring System.

Citation: IUCN (1993). *Nature Reserves of the Himalaya and Mountains of Central Asia.* Prepared by the World Conservation Monitoring Centre. IUCN, Gland, Switzerland and Cambridge, UK.
xxiv + 458 pp.

ISBN: 0 19 562922 1 (Pbk.)

Compiled by Michael J.B. Green.

Cover photograph: Yak grazing, Kargiakh Chu, Zanskar in proposed Lung Nag Sanctuary, Jammu and Kashmir, India, by Michael J.B. Green

Cover design by IUCN.

Printed by Rekha Printers Pvt. Ltd., New Delhi 110020, India.

Available from Oxford University Press, New Delhi, Bombay, Calcutta and Madras.
IUCN Publications Services Unit, 219c Huntingdon Road, Cambridge, CB3 0DL, UK.

Contents

Contents

Foreword

The great mountains of Central Asia are one of the World's most massive features and the source of some of the most important rivers which bring life to millions of people.

In the last century, man, the great destroyer, has polluted the oceans, poisoned the rivers and lakes, made deserts of good arable land, felled the forests, and severely eroded the mountainsides. And yet there is still great beauty to be found in this world of ours. I remember the sun setting over the pinnacle of Mt. Amadablam in Nepal; the glorious low lighting across the snowy mountain peaks on Ellesmere Island in the Arctic; the shining white sand and clear blue water on the palm fringed islands in the Pacific; and the dramatic return of the sun to the Antarctic after the long dark winter.

The nature reserves of the Himalaya and associated mountain ranges seek to protect the best that remains of this superb wilderness. Much damage has already been done—in the wet monsoon season the rivers are dark with topsoil from the bare slopes, and the forests are severely denuded—but efforts are under way to control this misuse of natural resources. The Everest region of Nepal, for example, has experienced ever-mounting pressures from its resident Sherpas and from tourists. Steps are already being taken to reconcile the needs of the residents and visitors with conservation objectives—reafforestation, removal of goats, provision of hydroelectricity, and local educational and medical facilities being amongst recent initiatives, as documented in this directory.

Not only do the nature reserves remain as a symbol of what the Himalaya were like in the past, but they also serve as a living example of how to care for one of the earth's most dramatic and beautiful regions. May they long be preserved and managed for future generations to enjoy.

Sir Edmund Hillary

Introduction

As recognised by participants at the 3rd World National Parks Congress, held in Bali, Indonesia in 1982, the ready availability of comprehensive good-quality information on the world's protected areas is essential to a wide range of international organisations, governments, protected area managers, voluntary bodies and individuals. Such information is a prerequisite for assessing the coverage and status of protected areas from regional and global perspectives. Moreover, monitoring protected areas is vital to ensure that those areas allocated to conserve the world's natural resources meet the needs of society.

The World Conservation Monitoring Centre (WCMC) is expanding its capabilities as an international centre for information on protected areas. Working with the IUCN Commission on National Parks and Protected Areas, the WCMC Protected Areas Data Unit (PADU) is compiling a series of protected areas directories, with priority assigned to tropical countries where much of the world's biological diversity is to be found. Past work has been focused on the Neotropics and Afrotropics, and more recently on Indomalaya (South Asia) and Oceania, culminating in protected area directories published for each of these regions.

The present directory is thematic and covers the high mountains of Central Asia within parts of the Indomalayan and Palaearctic realms. It is the product of material first drafted for the International Workshop on the Management of National Parks and Protected Areas in the Hindu Kush–Himalaya held in Kathmandu, 6–11 May 1985, the proceedings of which were published as *People and Protected Areas in the Hindu Kush–Himalaya* by the International Centre for Integrated Mountain Development (ICIMOD) and King Mahendra Trust for Nature Conservation (KMTNC). Since then, the original material has been extensively revised and updated, and its scope extended beyond the Hindu Kush–Himalaya to include other mountain ranges which encircle the cold deserts of the Tibetan Plateau and Taklimakan.

The directory covers the Hindu Kush–Himalaya in the south, as defined by ICIMOD, and extends to the Pamir, Tien Shan, and Qilian Shan in the north. A map and gazetteer of this entire region has been compiled by the Royal Geographic Society and Mount Everest Foundation (*The Mountains of Central Asia*, 1987). The directory describes the protected areas systems of Afghanistan, Bangladesh (south-east), Bhutan, China (west), India (north), Myanmar (north), Nepal, Pakistan (north) and USSR (south-east). Summary data are presented for all protected areas known to exist within the mountains of Central Asia but only a limited number (over 120 properties) are described in detail. This is largely a reflection of the availability of information, documentation on many of the less significant properties (often the smaller properties) being non-existent or not easily obtainable.

The directory is organised into chapters for each country. Each chapter comprises a description of the national protected areas system, accompanied by a summary list and map of protected areas, and is followed by descriptions of individual properties in alphabetical order. Geographical and taxonomic indexes enable the reader to refer quickly to individual properties and plant or animal species, respectively.

Michael J. B. Green
World Conservation Monitoring Centre

Managing Information on Protected Areas at WCMC

Institutional background

The IUCN Commission on National Parks and Protected Areas (CNPPA) has been actively involved in the collection and dissemination of information on protected areas ever since it was set up in 1960 to serve as the 'leading international, scientific and technical body concerned with the selection, establishment and management of national parks and other protected areas'. Over the years CNPPA's information management role increased to the extent that in 1981 it set up the Protected Areas Data Unit to undertake this service. Support for this initiative was forthcoming from the United Nations Environment Programme (UNEP), as part of its Global Environmental Monitoring Programme. Originally part of the IUCN Conservation Monitoring Centre, PADU is now an integral part of the World Conservation Monitoring Centre, restructured in July 1988 as a joint venture between the three partners in the World Conservation Strategy, namely IUCN, World Wide Fund for Nature (WWF), and UNEP.

Objectives

WCMC aims to provide accurate up-to-date information on protected area systems of the world for use by its partners (IUCN, WWF, and UNEP) in the support and development of their programmes, other international bodies, governmental and non-governmental organisations, scientists, and the general public. Such information covers the entire spectrum of protected areas, from national parks and sanctuaries established under protected areas legislation or customary regimes to forest reserves created under forestry legislation. It also includes privately-owned reserves in which nature is protected.

PADU has an integral relationship with CNPPA. In particular, PADU is responsible to CNPPA for producing the *United Nations List of National Parks and Protected Areas* (1982, 1985, 1990), which is periodically generated from its protected areas database currently totalling some 26,000 records. This database, together with supporting documentation, includes comprehensive information on natural sites designated under international conventions and programmes, namely the Convention concerning the Protection of the World Cultural and Natural Heritage (World Heritage Convention), Convention on Wetlands of International Importance especially as Waterfowl Habitat (Ramsar Convention), and Unesco Man and Biosphere Programme. Thus, PADU co-operates closely with the Division of Ecological Sciences, Unesco, in maintaining information on biosphere reserves and World Heritage sites accorded by the MAB Secretariat and World Heritage Committee, respectively. Likewise, it has strong links with the Ramsar Bureau for managing information on Ramsar wetlands.

Information capture, management and compilation

Information is collected from official sources, that is, national agencies responsible for administering protected areas, and other sources through a global network of contacts ranging in profession from policy-makers and administrators to land managers and scientists. It is also obtained from published and unpublished literature. Regional CNPPA meetings and other relevant scientific and technical meetings provide valuable opportunities for making new contacts and collecting fresh information.

Information, ranging from books, reports, management plans, scientific papers, and maps, is stored as hard copy in manual files. Basic data on individual protected areas are extracted and, after verification, entered in a protected areas database. This computerised database can be used for generating lists of protected areas meeting predefined criteria, together with summary statistics, as well as performing more complex tasks. In addition, boundaries of protected areas are gradually being digitised, using a Geographic Information System, in order to be able to generate computerised mapped output.

The raw information is also used for compiling information sheets on national protected areas systems (*protected areas systems information sheets*) and on individual protected areas (*protected areas information sheets*). These information sheets are compiled according to standard formats developed over the years by PADU in collaboration with CNPPA, details of which are given elsewhere in this directory.

Dissemination of information

Compiled information is periodically published in the form of regional or thematic directories, with sections on individual countries comprising a *protected areas system information sheet*, a *protected areas list* with accompanying *map*, and a series of *protected areas information sheets* covering at least the more important properties. Prior to releasing or publishing documents, draft material is circulated for review by relevant government agencies and experts to help ensure that compiled information is accurate and comprehensive.

Regional and thematic directories published to date are as follows:

IUCN Directory of Neotropical Protected Areas (1982)
IUCN Directory of Afrotropical Protected Areas (1987)
IUCN Directory of South Asian Protected Areas (1990)
IUCN Directory of Protected Areas in Oceania (1991)

MAB Information System: Biosphere Reserves: Compilation 4 (1986)
Biosphere Reserves: Compilation 5 (1990)
Directory of Wetlands of International Importance (1987, 1990)
Protected Landscapes: Experience around the World (1987)

Information is also made available to a wide range of users, including international organisations, governments, protected area managers, conservation organisations, commercial companies involved in natural resource exploitation, scientists, and the media and general public. It may be consulted by arrangement. Material may be prepared under contract: for example, PADU regularly provides UNEP with summary data on protected areas for its biennial *Environmental Data Report*. PADU is experimenting with providing outside users with direct access to its protected areas database. Trials have been ongoing with the US

National Park Service since 1986 and it is hoped to be able to extend this service to other users in due course.

PADU is also able to disseminate information through the *CNPPA Newsletter* and *Parks* magazine. In the case of the latter, PADU is responsible for compiling *Clipboard* in which world news on protected areas is featured.

National Park Service since 1916 and it is hoped to be able to extend its service to other parts of the country.

PADU is also able to disseminate information through the IUCN Newsletter and IUCN magazine. In the case of the latter, IUCN is responsible for compiling four issues in which a World news on protected areas is featured.

Information Sheets: Guidelines to their Contents

Information Sheets on Protected Areas Systems

Country[1] Full name of country or political unit, as used by the United Nations (1982).

Area Area of country or political unit according to the *Times Atlas of the World* (Seventh Edition, 1986), unless otherwise stated (with full reference). Terrestrial and marine components are distinguished, if appropriate.

Population Population of country or political unit and its rate of natural increase according to the Population Reference Bureau, Washington DC, whose data is based on those of the United Nations Statistical Office. The year of census or estimate is indicated in parentheses. If another source has to be used, it is cited.

GNP Gross national product in US dollars, with year in parentheses, of country or political unit according to the Population Reference Bureau.

Policy and Legislation Information on aspects of the constitution that are relevant to protected areas.

Details of national policies that relate to nature conservation, particularly with respect to the protection of ecosystems. Policies relating to environmental impact-assessments and national/regional conservation strategies are outlined.

Brief historical account of national legislation and traditions that relate to the establishment of the protected areas system, with dates and numbers of acts, decrees, and ordinances. Legislation covering forestry and other resource sectors is included in so far as it provides for protected areas establishment. Procedures for the notification and declassification of protected areas are summarised.

Outline of legal provisions for administering protected areas.

---

[1]In the case of countries with federal systems of government, a single sheet describes the protected areas system at both federal and state levels, except in the case of geographically disjunct regions (e.g. Hawaii).

National designations of protected areas are cited and their range of provisions outlined. Their legal definitions, together with the names of the authorities legally responsible for their administration, are annexed (see below).

Reviews of protected areas policy and legislation are noted with deficiencies in prevailing provisions highlighted.

International Activities Participation in international conventions and programmes (World Heritage and Ramsar conventions, MAB Programme, UNEP Regional Seas Programme) and regional agreements (African, ASEAN, Berne, FAO, Latin American/Caribbean Technical Co-operation Network, South Asian Co-operative Environmental Programme, South Pacific, Western Hemisphere) relevant to habitat protection is summarised, with details of dates of accession or ratification, etc.

Outline of any co-operative programmes or transfrontier co-operative agreements relevant to protected areas.

Administration and Management All authorities responsible for the administration and management of protected areas are described, including a brief history of their establishment, administrative organisation, staff structure, budget, and any training programmes. Authorities responsible for different types of protected areas are clearly distinguished.

Outline of the role of any advisory boards.

Co-operative agreements between management authorities and national or foreign universities and institutes, with details of any research underway or completed.

Details of non-governmental organisations concerned with protected areas, including reference to any national directories of voluntary conservation bodies.

Effectiveness of protected areas management, noting levels of disturbance and threats to the national network. Attention is drawn to any sites registered as threatened under the World Heritage Convention, or by the IUCN Commission on National Parks and Protected Areas.

Systems Reviews Short account of physical features, biological resources, and land use patterns, including the extent and integrity of major ecosystems. (Appropriate sources of information include IUCN's *Plants in Danger*, protected areas systems reviews, and wetland and coral reef directories.)

Brief historical account of nature conservation, so far as it relates to the establishment and expansion of the national protected areas network. Emphasis is given to any systems reviews or comprehensive surveys of biological resources, with details of major recommendations arising from such studies.

Threats to the protected areas system beyond the control of the management agencies are outlined.

Other Relevant Information (optional)   Tourism and other economic benefits of the protected areas system, if applicable.

Other items, as appropriate.

Addresses   Names and addresses (with telephone, telex and Fax numbers, and cable) of authorities responsible for administering protected areas, including the title of the post of the chief executive).

Names and addresses (with telephone, telex and Fax numbers, and cable) of non-governmental organisations, including the title of the post of the chief executive, actively involved in protected areas issues.

References   Key references (including all cited works) to the protected areas system, in particular, and nature conservation, in general, are listed. Those not seen by the compiler are marked as 'unseen'.

ANNEX   Definitions of protected area designations, as legislated, together with authorities responsible for their administration

Title (English title):   Name and number of law in the original language or transliterated, with the English translation underneath, as appropriate.

Date: Day, month and year of enactment, followed by dates of subsequent major amendments.

Brief description: Summary of main provisions (often this is stated at the beginning of the legislation).

Administrative authority: Name of authority responsible for administering the law in the original language or transliterated, with the English translation underneath as appropriate. This is followed by the title of the post of the chief executive in brackets.

Designations:
National designation of protected area in the original language or transliterated, followed in brackets by the English translation as appropriate.

—Definition of designation, if given in legislation
—Summary details of activities permitted or prohibited
—Outline of penalties for offences.
—Where relevant, include reference to subsequent legislation relating to the original law.

Source: This may be 'original legislation', 'translation of original legislation', or a referenced secondary source.

Information Sheets on Protected Areas[2]

Name The name of the property or properties (including any collective name, if applicable), as designated in the original language or transliterated. Where appropriate, the English translation is given underneath. In the case of transliteration, standard systems are used.

IUCN Management Category The property is assigned to the most appropriate IUCN management category (see Annex 1) in collaboration with the IUCN Commission on National Parks and Protected Areas.

Biogeographical Province The biogeographical code, followed by the name of the province in brackets (after Udvardy 1975).

Geographical Location The general location of the property within the country, including province and/or administrative district, proximity to major towns and/or topographical features, and means and ease of access. The location of different units is described, if applicable.

The boundary of the property is briefly described, its relation to any significant political boundaries noted, and geographical co-ordinates given.

Date and History of Establishment The date of establishment, together with the act, decree or ordinance number of the original and subsequent legislative articles relating to its establishment. Proposed extensions or upgradings are detailed.

A brief chronological history of previous designations, together with details of subsequent additions (including their sizes in ha).

If applicable, dates of inscription as World Heritage Site, Biosphere Reserve, Ramsar Wetland or other appropriate international and regional designations are given.

Area The best estimate of total area in hectares (ha), together with sizes of individually gazetted units, if applicable. If this differs from the total area as notified, the discrepancy is indicated. The extent of terrestrial and marine components is specified, if appropriate.

Contiguous or otherwise associated protected areas are noted and their sizes given in hectares (ha) in parentheses, including any lying across international borders.

Land Tenure Land ownership (e.g. state, provincial, freehold, private, customary etc.), including sizes or proportions of respective areas if owned by several authorities.

Altitude Maximum and minium altitude in metres (m).

Physical Features General description of abiotic features, covering geology, topography, geomorphology, soils, and hydrology.

---

[2]Sheets contain information on individual protected areas or clusters of such properties that form discrete conservation units. 'No information' is entered under any heading for which no data are available.

Climate   Seasons, annual precipitation, and maximum and minimum temperatures, with respect to altitude if appropriate. Other outstanding climatic features are noted.

Vegetation   Main vegetation types are briefly described, including their approximate coverage and state of preservation. Characteristic species are noted.

Communities and species of particular interest, including endemic, globally threatened (see Annex 2), economically important and potentially economically important (e.g. crop relatives), and invasive or introduced species. Any nationally threatened species of direct relevance to management are also mentioned.

References to vegetation descriptions and species inventories are included in the above.

NB Names of genera and families are based on Mabberley (1987).

Fauna   Mammal, bird, reptile, amphibian, fish, and invertebrate faunas are described in relation to the different habitats, with emphasis on dominant, endemic, globally threatened (see Annex 2), economically important, and introduced or reintroduced species of particular interest. Where relevant, information is given on the use certain species make of habitats for breeding, stopover, migration, etc. Population sizes are given in the case of key species, with details of trends over specified periods of time.

References to species inventories are included in the above.

NB Scientific nomenclature of species is based on Honacki et al. (1982) for mammals, Moroney et al. (1975) for birds, Frost (1985), for amphibians, Nelson (1984) for fishes, and Parker (1982) for invertebrates. The preparation of a taxonomic reference for reptiles is being co-ordinated by The Association of Systematics Collections.

Cultural Heritage (if relevant)   Archaeological features and cultural monuments.

Ethnic groups and their traditions.

Historical features.

Local Human Population (if relevant)   Size of the human population resident, transhumant or nomadic within the property, together with details of the number and distribution of settlements.

Livelihoods of local populations are briefly described in relation to any zonation of the property, with details of land use (e.g. numbers of livestock and amount of land under permanent or shifting cultivation).

Land use is described for the area surrounding the property, particularly as it impinges on the integrity of the property.

Visitors and Visitor Facilities (if relevant)   Annual number of visitors, together with proportions of nationals and foreigners for the latest year. Total revenue accruing from tourism is also indicated. Significant trends over specified periods of time are noted.

Types of accommodation available on site (or nearby), with details of location and amount if it is particularly limited.

Availability and location of interpretation programmes, including visitor centres, educational facilities and museums.

Any other recreational facilities of particular interest.

Scientific Research and Facilities   A brief historical account of research undertaken, together with details of ongoing studies. Bibliographies, if compiled, are cited.

Laboratories and other facilities, including accommodation, available to scientists.

Conservation Value   Geological, scenic, biological, cultural, and socio-economic values of the property, and justification for its conservation.

In the case of World Heritage sites, all natural and cultural criteria are outlined, based on the IUCN evaluation of the nomination submitted to the World Heritage Committee.

Conservation Management   A brief history of the conservation of the property, including any reasons for its original establishment where these differ from its present conservation value. Any legal provisions specific to the protection of the property are mentioned, together with details of activities (e.g. hunting, fishing, grazing) specifically permitted or prohibited.

Administrative structure and management, including location of main facilities (e.g. headquarters).

Management objectives, as drawn up in the management plan, and their degree of implementation. (The existence or absence of a management plan or 'statement of objectives' is noted and, if appropriate, the authority responsible for its implementation.)

Major management activities (e.g. controlled burning, culling).

Any system of zonation, including function and size of zones.

Significant training, interpretative, and extension programmes.

Recommendations, particularly those made in the management plan, for future conservation and management of the property.

Management Constraints   Past and current problems are briefly described, such as invasive species, poaching, fire, pollution, disease, agricultural encroachment, impact of tourism, relationship between management authorities and local people, lack of trained manpower or equipment, and proposed developments (e.g. roads, dams), with emphasis on the main types of threat and their extent. Threats from within and outside the property are distinguished.

If a property is registered as threatened by the IUCN Commission on National Parks and Protected Areas or under any national or international convention (e.g. World Heritage), details are provided.

Staff Numbers of staff allocated to each position and, if applicable, details of voluntary staff for the latest year, with trends if significant.

Budget Annual budget for the latest year (in parentheses) in local currency, and in US dollars for ease of comparison. Capital (e.g. construction of facilities) and recurrent (e.g. salaries) costs are distinguished. Significant trends are noted.

Financial support from outside sources.

Local Addresses Names and addresses (with telephone, telex, Fax numbers, and cable) of the local authorities responsible for the day-to-day administration and management of the property, including the title of the post of the chief executive (i.e. park warden or equivalent).

Names and addresses (with telephone, telex, Fax numbers, and cable) of any local non-governmental organisations directly involved in the protection and management of the property, including the title of the post of the chief executive.

References Key references, including management plans, reports, scientific monographs, bibliographies, and handbooks, in addition to other scientific papers or popular articles and books specifically about the property. Particularly relevant references not available for consultation are also listed and cited as 'unseen'.

References

Frost, D.R. (Ed.) (1985). *Amphibian species of the world: a taxonomic and geographical reference.* Allen Press and The Association of Systematics Collections, Lawrence, Kansas, USA. 735 pp.

Honacki, J.H., Kinman, K.E., and Koeppl, J.W. (1982). *Mammal species of the world: a taxonomic and geographic reference.* Allen Press and The Association of Systematics Collections, Lawrence, Kansas, USA. 694 pp.

IUCN (1984). Categories and criteria for protected areas. In: McNeely, J.A. and Miller, K.R. (Eds.), *National parks, conservation, and development. The role of protected areas in sustaining society.* Smithsonian Institution Press, Washington. Pp. 47-53.

IUCN (1990). *1990 IUCN Red List of threatened animals.* IUCN, Gland, Switzerland and Cambridge, UK. 192 pp.

Mabberley, D.J. (1987). *The plant-book.* Cambridge University Press, Cambridge. 706 pp.

Morony, J.J. Jr., Bock W.J., and Farrand Jr. (1975). *Reference list of the birds of the world.* American Museum of Natural History, New York. 207 pp.

Nelson, J.S. (1984). *Fishes of the world.* John Wiley, New York.

Parker, S.P. (1982). *Synopsis and classification of living organisms.* 2 vols. McGraw Hill, New York.

Udvardy, M.D.F. (1975). A classification of the biogeographical provinces of the world. *IUCN Occasional Paper* no. 18, Morges, Switzerland. 48 pp.

United Nations (1982). Names of countries and adjectives of nationality. *Terminology Bulletin* no. 327.

ANNEX 1

Categories and management objectives of protected areas

I **Scientific Reserve/Strict Nature Reserve:** to protect nature and maintain natural processes in an undisturbed state in order to have ecologically representative examples of the natural environment available for scientific study, environmental monitoring, education, and for the maintenance of genetic resources in a dynamic and evolutionary state.

II **National Park:** to protect natural and scenic areas of national or international significance for scientific, educational and recreational use.

III **Natural Monument/Natural Landmark:** to protect and preserve nationally significant natural features because of their special interest or unique characteristics.

IV **Managed Nature Reserve/Wildlife Sanctuary:** to assure the natural conditions necessary to protect nationally significant species, groups of species, biotic communities, or physical features of the environment where these require specific human manipulation for their perpetuation.

V **Protected Landscape or Seascape:** to maintain nationally significant natural landscapes which are characteristic of the harmonious interaction of man and land while providing opportunities for public enjoyment through recreation and tourism within the normal life style and economic activity of these areas.

VI **Resource Reserve:** to protect the natural resources of the area for future use and prevent or contain development activities that could affect the resource pending the establishment of objectives which are based upon appropriate knowledge and planning.

VII **Natural Biotic Area/Anthropological Reserve:** to allow the way of life of societies living in harmony with the environment to continue undisturbed by modern technology.

VIII **Multiple-Use Management Area/Managed Resource Area:** to provide for the sustained production of water, timber, wildlife, pasture, and outdoor recreation, with the conservation of nature primarily oriented to the support of economic activities (although specific zones may also be designed within these areas to achieve specific conservation objectives).

IX **Biosphere Reserve:** to conserve for present and future use the diversity and integrity of representative biotic communities of plants and animals within natural ecosystems, and to safeguard the genetic diversity of species on which their continuing evolution depends.

X **World Heritage Site:** to protect the natural features for which the area was considered to be of World Heritage quality, and to provide information for world-wide public enlightenment.

Abridged from IUCN (1984).

ANNEX 2

IUCN threatened species categories

Species identified as threatened by IUCN are assigned a category indicating the degree of threat. Definitions are as follows:

(Ex) Extinct: species not definitely located in the wild during the past 50 years.

(E) Endangered: taxa in danger of extinction and whose survival is unlikely if causal factors continue operating.

(V) Vulnerable: taxa believed likely to move into the 'Endangered' category in the near future if causal factors continue operating.

(R) Rare: taxa with small world populations that are not at present 'Endangered' or 'Vulnerable' but are at risk.

(I) Indeterminate: taxa known to be 'Endangered', 'Vulnerable' or 'Rare' but where there is insufficient information to say which of these categories is appropriate.

(K) Insufficiently known: taxa that are suspected, but not definitely known, to belong to any of the above categories because of lack of information.

(T) Threatened: threatened is a general term to denote species which are 'Endangered', 'Vulnerable', 'Rare', 'Indeterminate', or 'Insufficiently known'. It is used to identify taxa comprised of several sub-taxa which have differing status categories.

(C) Commercially Threatened: taxa not currently threatened with extinction but most or all of whose populations are threatened as a sustainable resource, or will become so unless their exploitation is regulated.

Adapted from IUCN (1990).

Acknowledgements

Preparation of this directory has been achieved largely due to a tremendous amount of co-operation from within the South–Central Asian region. Many people have contributed to the preparation of the directory through reviewing or compiling material and providing new information. Their assistance is greatly appreciated. Those who come to mind in the last stages of its preparation are listed below under respective country chapters (some individuals have helped with a number of countries but they are listed only once). To others, whose contributions may have been overlooked inadvertently in the course of time, sincere apologies are due.

Afghanistan   Dr Tahir Enayat (Afghan National MAB Committee), J. A. Sayer (IUCN).

Bangladesh   Abdul Wahab Akonda (Department of Forests-Wildlife, Government of Bangladesh), Dr Monowar Hossain (Multidisciplinary Action Research Centre, Bangladesh), Dr Zakir Hussain (Department of Forests, Government of Bangladesh), Dr Md Ali Reza Khan (Al Ain Zoo and Aquarium, Abu Dhabi), Dr M. Salar Khan (Bangladesh National Herbarium), M. Nazneen Mansur-Azim (IUCN, Bangladesh), S. A. Rahman (Department of Forests-Wildlife, Government of Bangladesh), Dr Sultan H. Rahman (Bangladesh Institute of Development Studies), Mr Haroun Er Rashid (Polli Unnayan Sangstha, Bangladesh), Mr S. M. Saheed (Soil Resources Development Institute, Bangladesh).

Bhutan   John Blower (formerly FAO), G. S. Child (Forestry Department, Wildlife and Protected Areas Management, FAO), Dr C .W. Holloway (World Bank), Peter Jackson (WWF-International), T. B. Mongar (Wildlife Division, Royal Government of Bhutan), Dr Caroline Sargent (International Institute for Environmental Development), M. N. Sherpa (WWF-USA), Dr Hartmut Wollenhaupt (formerly Forest Management and Conservation Project, Royal Government of Bhutan).

China   Dr W. A. Laurie (University of Cambridge, UK), Dr John MacKinnon (WWF-International), Han Qunli (Unesco/MAB Secretariat, Dr D. Taylor-Ide (Woodlands Mountain Institute, USA).

India   J. S. Asthana (Nanda Devi National Park), M. S. Bacha (Department of Wildlife Protection, Jammu & Kashmir), Sultana Bashir (Environmental Studies Division, Indian Institute of Public Administration), H. Adams Carter (American Alpine Journal), Dr Kalyan Chakrabarti (Wildife Preservation, Eastern Region, Government of India), Alok Chandola (Abercrombie & Kent, India), Andrew Clark (formerly University of East Anglia, UK), J. E. David (WWF-India Data Centre for Natural Resources), Dr J. L. Fox (University of Trønso,

Norway), Dr P. J. Garson (University of Newcastle-upon-Tyne), Dr A. J. Gaston (Canadian Wildlife Service), Ashish Kothari (Environmental Studies Division, Indian Institute of Public Administration), Dr B. S. Lamba (formerly Zoological Survey of India), David Mallon (formerly University of Manchester, UK), Thomas Mathew (WWF-India), J. K. Mehta (Arunachal Pradesh Forest Corporation), I. U. Mir (formerly Department of Wildlife Protection, Jammu & Kashmir), A. G. Oka (Department of Environment, Forests & Wildlife, Government of India), W. L. Oliver (formerly Jersey Wildlife Preservation Trust), Sanjeeva Pandey (Department of Forest Farming and Conservation, Himachal Pradesh), H. S. Panwar (Wildlife Institute of India), Dr M. K. Ranjitsinh (Department of Environment, Forests and Wildlife, Government of India), Dr T. M. Reed (Nature Conservancy Council, UK), Dr W. A. Rodgers (formerly Wildlife Institute of India), Graham Scott (University of Newcastle Kashmir Expedition 1988), Dr M. P. Searle (formerly University of Leicester, UK), Johara Shahabuddin (Environmental Studies Division, Indian Institute of Public Administration), M. P. Sharma (Department of Forest Farming and Conservation, Himachal Pradesh), R. C. Sharma (Department of Forest Farming and Conservation, Himachal Pradesh), R. P. Sharma (Wildlife Preservation Organisation, Uttar Pradesh), Virinder Sharma (Simla), Ashok Singh (Corbett National Park), Dr Kh Shamungou Singh (D. M. College of Science, Manipur), N. Shamungou Singh (Department of Science, Technology and Environment, Government of Manipur), Dr Shekhar Singh (Environmental Studies Division, Indian Institute of Public Administration), R. C. Thanga (Department of Environment and Forests, Mizoram), Shane Winser (Expedition Advisory Service, UK).

Myanmar   Ron Cooksy (US National Park Service), the late H. G. Hundley (retired Conservator of Forests), Joanne Michalovic (US National Park Service), U Saw Han (formerly Wildlife and Sanctuaries Division, Forest Department, Myanmar), U Thein Lwin (Wildlife and Sanctuaries Division, Forest Department, Myanmar).

Nepal   Dr D. J. Bell (University of East Anglia, UK), Dr B. W. Bunting (WWF-USA), Professor S. Chalise (International Centre for Integrated Mountain Development, Nepal), R. J. Dobias (King Mahendra Trust for Nature Conservation, Nepal), Dr J. M. Eddington (University College, Cardiff, UK), Carol Inskipp (UK), R. M. Jackson (California Institute of Environmental Studies, USA), B. E. Jeffries (formerly HMG/UNDP/FAO National Parks and Wildlife Conservation Project, Nepal), Dr A. R. Joshi (National Planning Commission, HMG Nepal), B. Kattel (Department of National Parks and Wildlife Conservation, HMG Nepal), A. D. Lelliott (formerly World Pheasant Association), P. H. C. Lucas (IUCN Commission on National Parks and Protected Areas), Dr H. R. Mishra (King Mahendra Trust for Nature Conservation, Nepal), Dr N. Picozzi (Institute of Terrestrial Ecology, UK), Mathew Rowntree (Coventry Polytechnic, UK), Dr C. D. Schaaf (Zoo Atlanta, USA), I. S. Thapa (Department of Forest, HMG Nepal), G. P. Upadhyay (Department of National Parks and Wildlife Conservation, HMG Nepal), B. N. Upreti (Department of National Parks and Wildlife Conservation, HMG Nepal), P. Wegge (Institute for Nature Conservation, Norway), Dr C. M. Wemmer (National Zoological Park, Conservation and Research Center, USA).

Pakistan   M. Hamid Ali (formerly National Council for Conservation of Wildlife, Government of Pakistan), James Burt (formerly World Pheasant Association-Pakistan), Guy Duke (International Council for Bird Preservation), Mazhar Hussain (Capital Development Authority-Environment Directorate, Islamabad), Abeedullah Jan (Ministry of Food, Agriculture and Co-operatives), Aban Marker Kabraji (IUCN, Pakistan), Mumtaz Malik North-West Frontier Province Forest Office), Dr Yasin J. Nasir (National Herbarium, Islamabad), Abdul Latif Rao (National Council for Conservation of Wildlife, Government of

Pakistan), Ghulam Rasul (Wildlife Warden, Northern Areas and compiler of a directory entitled *National Parks and Equivalent Reserves in Northern Areas of Pakistan*).

USSR Dr N. G. Dobrynina (USSR Research Institute for Nature Conservation and Reserve Management), Baiba Klince (Ecological Centre, Latvian State University), Dr Roman Zlotin (Institute of Geography, USSR Academy of Sciences).

A number of past and present staff of PADU have been involved in preparing this directory. The preliminary draft, presented at the International Workshop on the Management of National Parks and Protected Areas in the Hindu Kush–Himalaya, Kathmandu, 6–11 May 1985 was prepared by Sally Ward. Chapters on Afghanistan, Burma, China and USSR were prepared by Sara Day, James Paine, Peter Gorbutt, and Zbigniew Karpowicz, respectively, with secretarial support provided by Alison Suter and Deborah Rothera. Particular thanks are due to Jeremy Harrison in his role as Head of the Unit, Alison Suter for help with proof reading, and to Mike Adam, Simon Blyth, and Gillian Bunting for preparing the maps. Others who have contributed their expertise include Mark Collins, Steve Davis, Brian Groombridge, Tim Inskipp, Martin Jenkins, Duncan Mackinder, and Christina Smith from WCMC; Richard Grimmett and Tim Johnson from the International Council for Bird Preservation; and Derek Scott from the International Waterfowl and Wetlands Research Bureau. The support of our colleagues at IUCN headquarters, notably Vitus Fernando, Jeffrey McNeely, Jeffrey Sayer, and James Thorsell, is also acknowledged. Notwithstanding the significant contributions of those mentioned above, errors and omissions must remain the responsibility of the compiler.

This directory is not a final statement but a review of the current conservation status of the mountains of Central Asia. There is a continual need to maintain and update this information as national protected areas networks change and as more documentation becomes available. With this directory goes a plea for corrections, comments and additional material to help WCMC carry out its mission as effectively as possible. By the same token, WCMC offers an information service that covers an increasingly wide range of topics concerned with nature conservation. All parties, from private individuals to state departments, are invited to contact WCMC with their enquiries at the address below.

WCMC Protected Areas Data Unit
219 c Huntingdon Road
Cambridge CB3 ODL
United Kingdom

Tel. 0223 277314
Fax 0223 277316
Tlx 817036 SCMU G

AFGHANISTAN

Area 636,265 sq. km.

Population 16,557,000 (1990 estimate)   Natural increase 2.6% per annum

GNP No information.

Policy and Legislation Conservation began in Afghanistan around 1900 with the establishment of hunting reserves for use by royalty (Rahim and Larsson, 1978).

There is no enabling legislation to provide for the establishment and management of protected areas. A number of protected areas, such as Ab-i-Estada and Dashte-Nawar waterfowl sanctuaries, have been gazetted through government orders in response to petitions submitted to the Head of State (Sayer and van der Zon, 1981).

A draft forests law exists but has not been legislated. It has been proposed that this draft forest law be revised to incorporate provisions for the establishment and management of a system of protected areas, with different management categories clearly defined (Sayer and van der Zon, 1981).

International Activities Afghanistan ratified the Convention concerning the Protection of the World Cultural and Natural Heritage (World Heritage Convention) on 20 March 1979. To date no sites have been inscribed.

Administration and Management The Department of Forests and Range, Ministry of Agriculture and Land Reform, established in 1957, is responsible for the management and protection of the country's protected areas and wildlife. A Directorate of Wildlife and National Parks was established within the Department in 1973, then staffed by an administrative officer and two assistants to supervise a number of field officers. To date it lacks any specific and approved jurisdictional powers (FAO, 1978).

Jurisdiction over Afghanistan's only national park, Band-e Amir, is held by the Afghan Tourist Organisation which promoted its creation in 1973. Under a protocol agreement between this organisation and the Department of Forests and Range signed in June 1977, conservation and management became the prerogative of the Department, while all forms of economic utilisation were allocated to the Afghan Tourist Organisation (FAO, 1978).

1

The Republican Guard, a cadre of the Afghan army directly linked to the presidential office, was given charge of former royal hunting reserves, such as Ajar Valley and Kole Hashmat Khan, when the monarchy was abolished in 1973. Its management activities have been limited (Shank, Petocz and Habibi, 1977).

A training programme for wardens and conservation officers was established through a bilateral agreement with Iran in 1974. Some 34 students were trained prior to this programme being discontinued. A number of post-graduates have been trained in forestry and range management (FAO, 1978).

Systems Reviews There is good evidence that the natural vegetation of large parts of Afghanistan was originally woodland and forest, the present steppes reflecting the cutting of wood by man and grazing and browsing by his domestic animals over millenia. According to Sayer and van der Zon (1981), approximately 54.7 million ha (84%) of the country are rangeland, 7.9 million ha (12%) arable and only 2.2 million ha (3.4%) forest. Rangeland, on which the majority of Afghans depend directly or indirectly, is being degraded and abused. In more arid regions dryland farming has exhausted soils and led to erosion. The few remaining forested areas are being destroyed at an alarming rate to meet the fuel requirements of the major cities, while shrubs and dried herbs meet the needs of the rural population and even those of quite large towns.

The government requested the assistance of UNDP and FAO in the conservation and management of its wildlife and protected areas. Under a project running from 1972 to 1979, assistance was given to establish a system of protected areas, strengthening the Department of Forests and Range and contributing towards a conservation strategy (FAO, 1980). Some assistance was also received from the World Wildlife Fund for infrastructure developments in Ab-i-Estada and Dashte Nawar waterfowl sanctuaries. Conservation activities were brought to an abrupt halt in 1979 due to political unrest.

Addresses

Department of Forests and Range, Ministry of Agriculture and Land Reform, Kabul (Tel. 408415).

References

Rahim, A. and Larsson, J. (1978). *A preliminary study of Lake Hashmat Khan with recommendations for management.* UNDP/FAO, Kabul. 17 pp. (Unseen)

Shank, C. C., Petocz, R. G., and Habibi, K. (1977). *A preliminary management plan for the Ajar Valley wildlife reserve.* UNDP/FAO/Department of Forests and Range, Kabul. 35 pp.

FAO (1978). *National parks and utilization of wildlife resouces. Afghanistan. Project findings and recommendations.* UNDP/FAO, Rome. 32 pp.

FAO (1980). *National parks and wildlife management. Afghanistan. Project findings and recommendations.* UNDP/FAO, Rome. 22 pp.

Sayer, J.A. and van der Zon, A.P.M. (1981). *National parks and wildlife management. Afghanistan. A contribution to a conservation strategy.* 2 vols. UNDP/FAO, Rome. 107 and 153 pp.

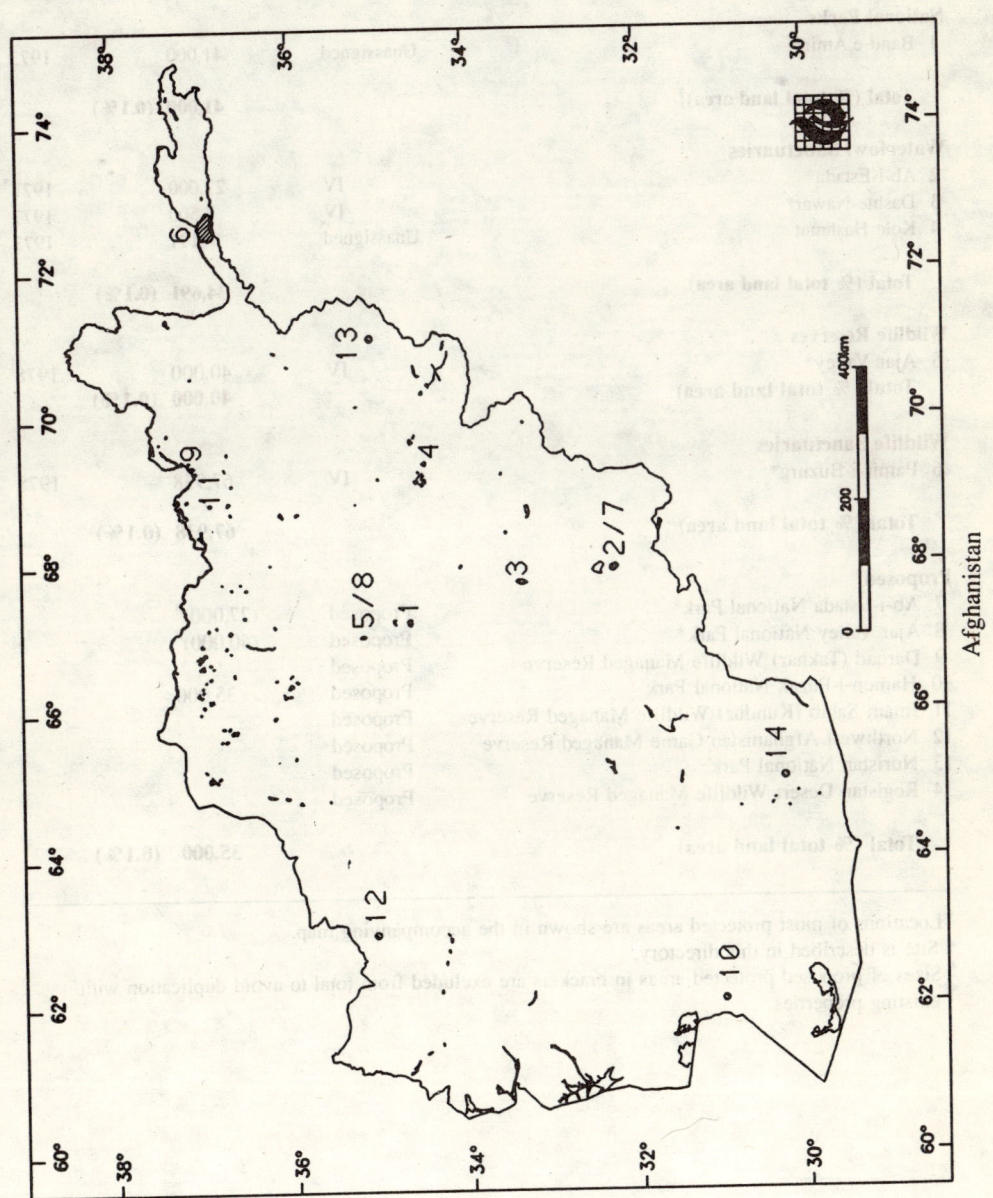

Afghanistan

Summary of Protected Areas of Afghanistan

National designation Name of area and map reference+	IUCN Management Category	Area (ha)	Year notified
National Parks			
1 Band-e Amir*	Unassigned	41,000	1973
Total (% total land area)		**41,000 (0.1%)**	
Waterfowl Sanctuaries			
2 Ab-i-Estada*	IV	27,000	1977
3 Dashte-Nawar*	IV	7,500	1977
4 Kole Hashmat	Unassigned	191	1973
Total (% total land area)		**34,691 (0.1%)**	
Wildlife Reserves			
5 Ajar Valley*	IV	40,000	1978
Total (% total land area)		**40,000 (0.1%)**	
Wildlife Sanctuaries			
6 Pamir-i-Buzurg*	IV	67,938	1978
Total (% total land area)		**67,938 (0.1%)**	
Proposed			
7 Ab-i-Estada National Park*	Proposed	(27,000)[#]	
8 Ajar Valley National Park*	Proposed	(40,000)[#]	
9 Darqad (Takhar) Wildlife Managed Reserve	Proposed		
10 Hamun-i-Puzak National Park	Proposed	35,000	
11 Imam Sahib (Kunduz) Wildlife Managed Reserve	Proposed		
12 Northwest Afghanistan Game Managed Reserve	Proposed		
13 Nuristan National Park	Proposed		
14 Registan Desert Wildlife Managed Reserve	Proposed		
Total (% total land area)		**35,000 (0.1%)**	

[+] Locations of most protected areas are shown in the accompanying map.

* Site is described in this directory.

[#] Sizes of proposed protected areas in brackets are excluded from total to avoid duplication with existing properties.

AB-I-ESTADA WATERFOWL SANCTUARY

IUCN Management Category IV (Managed Nature Reserve)

Biogeographical Province 2.37.12 (Hindu Kush Highlands)

Geographical Location Lies in south-east Afghanistan in Ghazni Province, approximately 130 km south of Ghazni Town. Access from Ghazni is via Noqur and Korawaddin, the latter lying 3 km from the western shore of the lake. Approximately 32°50′N, 67°50′E

Date and History of Establishment Approved a wildlife sanctuary on 20 December 1977 (Order no. 707) by the Head of State, based on Petition no. 1765 dated 6 June 1977. In 1974, boundaries were drawn up and the area was declared a national flamingo and waterfowl sanctuary by the Directorate of Wildlife and National Parks (Shank and Roderburg, 1977). Proposed as a national park (FAO, 1981).

Area Approximately 27,000 ha, including mud-flats but not cultivated land within a 2 km-wide belt of land (Shank and Rodenburg, 1977). (NB An area of 10,000 ha, with a 2 km-wide border, is given in the original declaration.)

Land Tenure State. Semi-nomadic people have traditional grazing rights (Shank and Roderburg, 1977).

Altitude The lake lies at 2,100 m.

Physical Features The lake lies on a gently rolling plateau in the southern foothills of Kohe Baba and Kohe Paghman ranges. It is a shallow, alkaline lake of about 13,000 ha, measuring 16 km at its broadest point. Its size and shape vary within and between years. During a normal year, the lake's volume ranges from 270 million cu. m in spring to about 140 million cu. m in autumn, which results in a 1 m change in depth (Forstner and Bartsch 1970). Mud-flats surround the lake; these extend for 7 km in the east and less than 0.5 km on the western shore. The north-eastern shore is marshy around the mouth of an unnamed river formed by the confluences of the Gandez, Ghazni and Nahara rivers. Once a year there is an influx of water from this river, but during the rest of the year the water level of Ab-i-Estada is very much dependent on ground water. There are two small islands in the lake (Shank and Rodenburg, 1977).

Climate Summers are dry and hot, and winters cold. Mean annual precipitation at Moqur, 40 km to the north-west of the lake, is 216.4 mm (1967–75), of which 92% falls as snow during the winter months of December through April inclusive. Mean monthly maximum temperature remains above freezing point year-round, but the lake freezes in winter, with only tiny pools remaining where waterfowl may concentrate (Shank and Rodenburg, 1977).

Vegetation The only higher plant to be found in the lake itself is pondweed *Ruppia maritima*. The mud-flats are almost entirely devoid of plant life, the only conspicuous vegetation being colonies of *Taraxacum monochlamydeum*. Beyond the mud-flats is a sparsely vegetated transition zone before the steppe proper. This zone contains a diversity of small herbs such as common mat-forming *Psylliostachys beldushistanica*, which is usually associated with a *Ranunculus* sp., clumps of *Asperugo procumbens* in sheltered areas, and such common and widely dispersed species as *Valerianella cymbicarpa*, *Veronica* sp., *Eremopyrum orientala*, *Papaver* spp., and many species of the families Crucifereae and Papillionaceae. The steppe zone is represented by an *Amygdalus* shrubland community, with scattered, thorny shrubs and dispersed grasses with a ground cover of 15–25%. Shrubs such as *Amygdalus* sp., *Cousinia* sp., *Tamarix laxa* and *Artemisa* sp. are predominant. *Bromus gracillimus*, *B. tectorum*, *B. danthoniae* and *Boissiera squarrosa* are common grasses. Stream banks support a lush growth of *Carex* sp. (Shank and Rodenburg, 1977).

Fauna   Small mammals are numerous around Ab-i-Estada. Ground squirrel *Citellus fulvus* and jird *Meriones libycus* are common (Shank and Rodenburg, 1977). Red fox *Vulpes vulpes*, long-eared hedgehog *Hemiechinus auritus* and the only record of marbled polecat *Vormela peregusna* in the area are reported by Niethammer (1971).

The lake is a very important breeding and feeding site for migratory waterfowl and waders. Greater flamingo *Phoenicopterus roseus* breeds at the site, arriving in spring (late March to April) and departing in early autumn (late September to early October). Other breeding species include avocet *Recurvirostra avosetta*, black-winged stilt *Himantopus himantopus*, slender-billed gull *Larus genei*, gull-billed tern *Gelochelidon nilotica*, shelduck *Tadorna tadorna*, Kentish plover *Charadrius alexandrinus*, and greater sandplover *Charadrius leschenaultii* (Niethammer, 1971). The lake is thought to be an important stop-over site for the very rare Siberian crane *Grus leucogeranus* (E).

Amphibians are apparently absent, but several reptile species occur, including tortoise *Testudo horsfieldii*, lizard *Agama agills*, and a small skink *Ablepharus* sp. (Shank and Rodenburg, 1977). There are no fish in the lake, but invertebrate and other aquatic organisms are various and periodically numerous.

Cultural Heritage   Ab-i-Estada is an important archaeological site, exhibiting intact stratigraphic sequences. Several mounds representing early dwellings have been discoverd with accompanying artefacts, which suggest occupation from Palaeolithic to Buddhist times (Shank and Rodenburg, 1977).

Local Human Population   Several modern villages are located nearby, with major population concentrations about 8 km to the north-east of the lake and 2 km from its western shore. There are more than 15 villages within 10 km of the lake, with a total human population of about 2,500. In addition, there are some 200–300 people living in scattered settlements and about 300 semi-nomadic people (muldar or kuchis), who temporarily reside on the rolling plains in summer to graze their livestock (Shank and Rodenburg, 1977).

Visitors and Visitor Facilities   No information

Scientific Research and Facilities   The presence of vast flocks of greater flamingos at Ab-i-Estada was perhaps first documented in the memoirs of the Moghul Emperor, Babur the Great, who observed tens of thousands in 1504, since when research has been focused mainly on the ecology of this species (Akhatar, 1947; Niethammer, 1970; Nogge, 1971; Petocz and Habibi, 1975). More extensive work on the avifauna was conducted by Niethammer (1971) and Nogge (1974)

Conservation Value Together with Dashte-Nawar to the north, Ab-i-Estada is a vital staging ground for migratory waterfowl and waders of the Siberian–Kazakhstan/Pakistan–India population, in particular Siberian crane, as well as an essential breeding ground for certain of these species, notably greater flamingo. The international importance of the two sites was recognised at the 1971 Conference of the Contracting Parties to the Ramsar Convention, following which the Government of Afghanistan responded to pleas to protect both these areas. Ab-i-Estada is also an important archaeological site.

Conservation Management Following its legal protection, a management plan was prepared (Shank and Rodenburg, 1977). Principal objectives outlined in the plan include protecting birds from adverse influences of human origin and initiating a monitoring programme upon which to base future management decisions. In 1975, assistance was received from WWF to provide quarters for a resident warden and research facilities. Work was subsequently interrupted in May 1979 (FAO, 1980).

Management Constraints The greatest threat is from irrigation projects diverting water from the Ghazni and Gandez rivers which flow into the lake. The volume of water in the lake is thereby decreased, resulting in increased salinity levels. Should diversions continue, Ab-i-Estada might well become a sterile wasteland. Extensive grazing by domestic stock on the lake shores destroys the vegetation and disturbs the waterfowl. Egg collection, disturbance during the breeding season and hunting throughout the year are significant problems (Shank and Rodenburg, 1977).

Staff Game guards in summer months (1974 onwards)

Budget No information

Local Addresses No information

References
Akhtar, S.A. (1947). Ab-i-Estadah, a breeding place of the flamingo (*Phoenicopterus ruber roseus*) (Pallas) in Afghanistan. *Journal of the Bombay Natural History Society* 47: 308–14. (Unseen)
FAO (1980). *National parks and wildlife management, Afghanistan. Project findings and recommendations.* UNDP/FAO, Rome. 22 pp.
Forstner, U. and Bartsch, G. (1970). Die Seen von Banda-Amir, Datscht-i- Nawar, Ob-i-Istada and Humun-i-Puzak (Zentral und Südwestafghanistan). *Science, Kabul* 6: 19–23. (Unseen)
Klockenhoff, H. and Madel, G. (1970). Uber di Flamingos (*Phoenicopterus ruber*) der Dasht-i-Nawar in Afghanistan. *Journal für Ornithologie* 111: 78–84. (Unseen)
Niethammer, G. (1971). Vogelleben am Ab-i-Estada (Afghanistan). *Die Vogelwarte* 26: 221–7. (Unseen)
Niethammer, J. (1970). Die Flamingos am Ab-i-Estada in Afghanistan. *Natur und Museum* 100: 201–10. (Unseen)
Nogge, G. (1971). Afghanistan—the Ab-i-Estada: a vanishing breeding place of flamingos. *IWRB Bulletin* 31: 28–38. (Unseen)
Nogge, G. (1974). Beobachtungen an den Flamingobrutplätzen Afghanistans. *Journal für Ornithologie* 115: 142–51. (Unseen)
Petocz, R.G. and Habibi, K. (1975). The flamingos (*Phoenicopterus ruber roseus*) of Ab-i-Estada and Dashte-Nawar, Ghazni Province, Afghanistan. UNDP/FAO, Department of Forests and Range, Kabul. (Unseen)

Shank, C.C. and Rodenburg, W.F. (1977). *Management plan for Ab-i-Estado and Dashte-Nawar flamingo and waterfowl sanctuaries.* UNDP/FAO/Department of Forests and Range, Kabul. 43 pp.

AJAR VALLEY WILDLIFE RESERVE

IUCN Management Category   IV (Managed Nature Reserve)

Biogeographical Province   2.37.12 (Hindu Kush Highlands)

Geographical Location   Lies 55 km north-west of Bamiyan in Bamiyan Province, central Hindu Kush. Access to the area is from Kabul via Charikan, Doabi Mekh-i-Zarin and Karmard. Approximately 67°37′E, 36°40′N

Date and History of Establishment   Established as a wildlife reserve on 10 September 1978, but proposed as a national park (FAO, 1981). Previously used as a hunting reserve by royalty since the turn of the century and protected as such since the early 1950s, first by the former king and subsequently by the Republican Guard. Following the Revolution of July 1973, the area has been under the jurisdiction of the Guard-i-Jamhuriat, a cadre of the Afghan army, directly attached to the presidential office (Shank et al., 1977).

Area   40,000 ha

Land Tenure   State

Altitude   Ranges from approximately 2,000 m to 3,800 m.

Physical Features   The terrain is mountainous and typical of the central Hindu Kush. East~west oriented ridges with precipitous peaks rise to 3,800 m and are interspersed with gently rounded vegetated mountain tops up to 3,200 m in elevation. Bisecting the reserve from east to west is the sheer-sided Jawzari Canyon (Darre Jawzari), formed aeons ago when the Ajar River eroded its way downwards through the soft limestone. In the recent geological past, the river became subterranean, leaving Darr Jawzari dry. The Ajar River now flows directly out of the rock wall into the canyon at the spring of Chiltan, located in the eastern portion of the reserve. The river flows out through the spectacular eastern extension of Darre Jawzari into the broad Ajar Valley. A major earthquake in the early 1960s caused the canyon sides to collapse, creating the tiny Lake Chiltan (Shank et al., 1977).

There are five major geological formations. The youngest and overlying layer is the Lower Eocene Gazak Formation which consists of marly limestone shales, and bituminous shales. This formation is found along an east-west syncline which runs through Lachakhana and the western portion of Darre Jawzari as well as at the higher elevations of Kohe Jawzari. Underlying it are the massive limestones of the Badjgah Formation which are of Danian to Paleocene age and occur throughout much of the reserve. Beneath the Badjgah lies the Hajar Formation which contains marlstones and limestones. It is found only in a thin band surrounding the underlying terrestrial Red-Grit Formation of Lower Cretaceous age. The reddish conglomerates and sandstones of this formation are evident in the Kohe Surkhob

Bowl and along the main Ajar Valley near the lodge. Lastly, the Saighan Formation of Jurassic age outcrops only along the stream draining the Ghawgasar Bowl in the extreme south-east. This formation consists of sandstones, conglomerates and shales. Tectonically, the mountains are of Oligocene and Miocene age (Weippert, 1964).

Climate The closest meteorological station is at Bamiyan (2,500 m), which is probably representative of conditions in the central Hindu Kush. Data for 1969–75 indicate that the coldest month is January with mean minimum and maximum temperatures of −12.8 °C and 0.9 °C, respectively. The warmest month is July with mean minimum and maximum temperatures of 9.6 °C and 26.4 °C, respectively. Conditions are dry with a mean annual precipitation of 162 mm, most of which falls between February and May. Because of its vertical relief and higher elevation, conditions at Ajar Valley will generally be colder and wetter than at Bamiyan (Shank et al., 1977).

Vegetation The flora corresponds roughly to the *Amygdalus* community type (Freitag, 1971a). Skogland (1976) recognises five associations within this community type: *Carex stenophylla* (Gilli, 1969), with a ground cover of 25–100% in moist areas; *Stipa szowitsiana* (Gilli, 1969), with a cover of 50–100% in slightly drier areas; *Artemisia* (Gilli, 1969), with a cover of 15–50% in yet drier areas; pure *Amygdalus communis* in very dry areas; and an association dominated by *Cousinia polyneurae* (Gilli, 1969) above 3,000 m. Along the Ajar River is a distinctive plant community dominated by willow *Salix* spp. The high proportion of shrubs and geophytic herbs present in all the plant communities is considered evidence that species assemblages have been greatly modified by overgrazing in the Ajar area (Skogland, 1976).

Fauna This is an important area for ibex *Capra ibex*, urial *Ovis orientalis* and an introduced population of Bactrian deer *Cervus elaphus bactrianus* (E). Petocz counted 1,190 ibex in 1974 in the eastern part of the reserve but the total population is likely to be nearer 5,000 (Shank et al., 1977). The urial occurs mainly in the west where there is more typical sheep habitat with fewer cliffs and canyons (Shank et al., 1977). Bactrian deer were introduced in about 1955. From an original two there are now about 42 deer (FAO, 1981). Other large mammals include a population of about 70 feral yak *Bos grunniens* (E), snow leopard *Panthera uncia* (E), leopard *P. pardus* (T), lynx *Lynx lynx* , which locals report is present, wolf *Canis lupus* (V), which is evidently common, jackal *C. aureus*, fox *Vulpes vulpes*, otter *Lutra lutra*, marten *Martes foina* and long-tailed marmot *Marmota caudata* (Shank et al., 1977).

The avifauna is the most diverse yet recorded in the Hindu Kush, with 60 species identified so far (Shank et al., 1977). Chukar partridge *Alectoris chukar*, marsh warbler *Acrocephalus palustris*, isabelline wheatear *Oenanthe isabellina*, redstart *Phoenicurus phoenicurus*, rock nuthatch *Sitta tephronota* and red-fronted serin *Serinus pusillus* breed in the Ajar Valley, and an additional 22 species are presumed to breed here. Other notable species are black stork *Ciconia nigra,* and a wide variety of warblers (Sylviidae) and chats, wheatears and redstarts of the family Turdidae.

Amphibians and reptiles include the frog *Rana ridibunda*, common toad *Bufo viridis*, two species of racerunners *Eremias velox persica* and *Eremias* sp., skink *Ablepharus* sp., lizard *Agama* sp., and a piscivorous snake *Natrix tessellata* (Shank et al., 1977).

Brown trout *Salmo trutta* was introduced into Lake Chiltan, probably about 15 years ago, and has successfully colonised the Ajar River to its mouth where the species comes into contact with the native milk fish (sher mohi) or carp of the family Cyprinidae (Shank et al., 1977).

Cultural Heritage   The spring of Chiltan, where the Ajar River flows out of the canyon wall is an important shrine. Long ago, according to local belief, it was entered by a famous saint who found himself in a large subterranean room among 40 people reading the Holy Koran. The shrine attracts many visitors from nearby areas (Shank et al., 1977).

Local Human Population   The people of the Ajar Valley are primarily of Tajik extraction and speak Dari. There are no permanent settlements, except for the village of Dehkan Qala inhabited by reserve staff and farmers. In Darre Jawzari, just east of the Surkhob Bowl, a family farms the canyon bottom during summer and fall while living in a cliff niche (Shank et al., 1977). East of the reserve, along the Ajar River, is a cluster of villages known as Dehe Tajik and Khargoshak, with a population of some 340 people, while 4 km to the west lies the village of Podinatu inhabited by 33 people.   Domestic livestock, belonging to an undetermined number of semi-nomadic kuchis and the people of Saighan and Kahmard Woleswalis south and east of the reserve, respectively, are grazed along the reserve border on the Kohe Tabaqsar, Haftnawa and Zardnawa mountain slopes (Shank et al., 1977).

Visitors and Visitor Facilities   Prior to the 1973 revolution, there were about 500 visitors per year. Hunting safaris and other excursions, organised by the Afghan Tourist Organisation, attracted foreign visitors. Subsequently, there were plans to launch a trekking programme. A hunting lodge, built in the early 1900s by Amir Habibullah, is now in ruins (Shank et al., 1977).

Scientific Research and Facilities   Most research has been concentrated on the ibex population (Skogland, 1976; Shank et al., 1977). Other work includes status surveys of the Afghan urial (Shank et al., 1977), Bactrian deer (Habibi, 1976; Shank et al., 1977) and avifauna (Shank et al., 1977). There are no scientific facilities.

Conservation Value   Ajar Valley represents the largest tract of land in Afghanistan with a history of effective environmental protection. Thus, it still supports large wildlife populations and a diverse avifauna.

Conservation Management   There is a preliminary management plan in which the primary objective is to ensure that the wildlife can thrive with as little interference from man as possible (Shank et al., 1977). Management practice follows the general pattern established in the 1950s: local people continue to refrain from hunting and grazing their domestic livestock in the reserve. Farmland, totalling 90 ha in the reserve, is leased by the Government for a percentage of the crop. Some 100 donkeys and cattle, owned by caretakers and farmers, and 200–300 sheep owned by the reserve authorities are grazed in the reserve.The Guard-i-Jamhuriat tends the 70 feral yak.

Management Constraints   Some livestock are grazed within the reserve and compete with wildlife for grazing. The position of the endangered Bactrian deer is particularly serious, with grazing competition from domestic livestock and, in winter, from feral yak. There is some illegal hunting and grazing (Shank et al., 1977; **FAO, 1981**). **Management activities** have been limited since 1979.

Staff   No information

Budget   No information

Local Addresses   No information

References
Freitag, H. (1971a). In: Davies, P.H. , Harper P.C. and Hedge I.C. (Eds.), *Study in the natural vegetation of Afghanistan. On plant life in south-west Asia*. University Press, Aberdeen. Pp. 80–106. (Unseen)

Freitag, H. (1971b). Die natürliche Vegetation Afghanistans. *Vegetatio* 22: 285–344. (Unseen)

Gilli, A. (1969). Afghanischen Pflanzengesellchaften. *Vegetatio* 16: 307–75. (Unseen)

Petocz, R.G. (1973). The Bactrian deer (*Cervus elaphus bactrianus*) : A report of the March 1973 field survey in northern Afghanistan. Afghan Tourist Organisation, Kabul. Unpublished. 8 pp. (Unseen)

Shank, C.C., Petocz, R.G., and Habibi, K. (1977). *A preliminary management plan for the Ajar Valley Wildlife Reserve*. UNDP/FAO/Department of Forests and Range, Kabul. 35 pp.

Skogland, T. (1976). *Ecological reconnaissance of the Hindu Kush ibex* (Capra ibex) *in Ajar Valley. Bamiyan Province, Afghanistan*. UNDP/FAO/Department of Forests and Range, Kabul. (Unseen)

Weippert, D. (1964). Zur geologie des gebietes Doab-Saighan-Hajar (Nord-Afghanistan). *Beih. geol. Jb* 70: 153–84.

BAND-E AMIR NATIONAL PARK

IUCN Management Category   Unassigned

Biogeographical Province   2.37.12 (Hindu Kush Highlands)

Geographical Location   Lies in the Hazarajat mountains of the western Hindu Kush, Bamiyan Province, some 60 km west of Bamiyan Town. It is inaccessible from November to late April. The boundaries encompass the entire catchment area of the headwaters of the Band-e Amir. 67°05′–67°20′E, 34°45′–34°55′N

Date and History of Establishment   Declared a national park on 30 September 1973 in response to a petition from the Afghan Tourist Organisation. This declaration has not been published in the official Government Gazette by the Ministry of Justice and, therefore, has no legal status (Sayer and van der Zon, 1981).

Area   41,000 ha.

Land Tenure   Lalmi (wheat fields) surrounding the lakes are state-owned, but farming rights are passed on by patrilineal descent. In 1974, the Yakowland waleswali decreed that no lalmi could be sold. Much of the land is considered *de facto* common land and is used to graze domestic livestock.

Altitude   The lakes lie at approximately 2,900 m, and surrounding peaks rise to 3,832 m.

Physical Features   Consists of a chain of six lapis lazuli lakes nestled between 300 m-high magenta rock walls in the Band-e Amir Valley. From west to east these are: Gholaman, Qambar, Haibat, Panir, Pudina and Zulfiqar. Travertine dams, about 10 m high and 3 m thick, and formed by the precipitation of calcium carbonate, separate the lakes from each other in a series of terraces. The combined surface area of the lakes is 600 ha, of which the two largest comprise 490 ha and 90 ha, respectively. Band-e Panir is the smallest (100 m in diameter). Band-e Qambar is also of limited extent, but gastropod shells found beyond its present water level indicate that it used to be larger. After clearing the final travertine dam of Band-e Gholaman, the Band-e Amir flows down the slopes of the Hindu Kush to the burning wastes of the north where it peters out near the USSR border (Shank and Larsson, 1977; Matthews, 1988). The lakes' waters are oligotrophic and calcareous with a pH of 7.8 (Foerstner and Bortsch, 1970). Their deep blue colour is a result of the water's purity and high lime content. Surface water temperatures reach 14–17 °C during summer (Shank and Larsson, 1977). Around the lakes, the high rolling steppe rises steeply in the west to rugged limey schist and conglomerate peaks. Soils are shallow (usually 10–30 cm and rarely exceeding 60 cm) and have a pH of 7.0–7.9. They are essentially grey semi-desert types with little evidence of leaching (Jux and Kempf, 1971).

Climate   Conditions are strongly continental, with low air humidity, high evaporation, and extreme temperature variations. Annual precipitation reaches 400 mm, all of which falls between October and May, with 50% falling in April alone (Freitag, 1971). More extensive data are available from the nearest metereological stations at Bamiyan, Panjaw and Lal (see Shank and Larsson, 1977).

Vegetation   Located in the central highlands of Afghanistan, Band-e Amir belongs to the Irano-Turanian floral region, characterised by high steppes and deserts. The area contains four of eleven species endemic to Bamiyan Province. There are three types of plant community: lake shore, creek bank and steppe. Shorelines, where vegetated, are dominated by reeds *Phragmites australis, Carex* spp. and *Scirpus* spp., and cattail *Typha laxmannii*. Between the lake shore proper and the steep cliffs, the ground is covered in dense herb and grass meadows. These meadows have been invaded by nitrophilous plants due to grazing practices. Common meadow plants of more natural origin are mint *Mentha longifolia*, plantain *Plantago gentianoides*, gentians *Gentiana* spp., small reeds *Calamagnostis* spp., and sedges and rush. The Darae Sabzel and Darae Band-e Amir creeks downstream from the lakes are flooded each spring as a result of snow-melt. Vegetation on the creek banks, therefore, is dominated by pioneer species. Below spring water level, sedges and rush *Juncus turkestanicus* are found. Above normal spring water level, where flooding is only occasional, are shrubs, notably *Myricaria germanica,* willows *Salix* spp., and sea buckthorn *Hippophae rhamnoides*. The alpine steppe is mainly of the *Artemisia-Acantholimon* dwarf-shrub types, believed to be of secondary origin due to centuries of over-grazing. The natural vegetation is believed to be grass-steppe with *Stipa, Festuca, Herdeum* and *Poa* species. Within the steppe community, three plant associations can be recognised. *Artemisia* occurs on the plateau of Dashte Menabard and Kutshe Mohammadjan. Characteristic species are *Artemisia codringtonii, Eremostachys baminanica, Scariola orientalis* and larkspur *Delphinium latisquamatum*. Vegetation cover is 30–60%. Soils remain moist underneath the dry surface and have a high humus content of 2–3%. These soils are favoured for dry cultivation. Semi-desert replaces the sage community on dry south-facing slopes. This community is characterised by two species, ***Krascheninnikovia** pungens* and *Jurinea mallophora*. Soils are of a whitish-grey semi-desert type and vegetation cover is 10–40%. On exposed ridges and hill tops, where snow is blown away in the winter, occurs a community of drought- and frost-resistant plants, notably *Astragalus microphypti* and *Fibigia membrancea*. Vegetative cover varies from 10% to 80% (Dieterle, 1973; Shank and Larsson, 1977).

Fauna   The fauna is impoverished. No large mammals occur in the immediate vicinity of the lakes, due to the overwhelming presence of man. Nearby, Kohe Burocinal and Kohe Argosa, are seasonally inhabited by urial *Ovis orientalis* and ibex *Capra ibex* in summer. Populations have remained stable since at least the mid-1950s, according to local reports (Shank and Larsson, 1977). Wolf *Canis lupus* (V) and fox *Vulpes vulpes* are reportedly common in the Hazarajat mountains (Habibi, 1977). Small mammals include Afghan pika *Ochotona rufescens*, long-tailed marmot *Marmota caudata* and jerboa *Allactaga williamsi* (Niethammer, 1965; Habibi, 1977).

A total of 46 bird species have been recorded around the Band-e Amir lakes, including little bittern *Ixobrychus minutus*, black-winged stilt *Himantopus himantopus*, common sandpiper *Tringa hypoleucos*, rock and water pipit *Anthus spinoletta* and masked shrike *Lanius nubiscus*.

A species of carp Cyprinidae, known locally as milk fish or *shir moi*, is abundant in the lakes.

Cultural Heritage   The creation of the lakes is attributed to Ali, son-in-law of Mohammed, the founder of Islam. There are several versions of this legend (Shank and Larsson, 1977; Matthews, 1988). A small mosque, built in 1904, commemorates the spot where Ali recited two ragats (cycles) of prayer on the shores of Band-e Haibat.

Local Human Population   The immediate banks of the lakes are quite densely inhabited by a predominantly Hazara population, estimated at 3,000–5,000 residents. Land surrounding the lakes is extensively farmed, while the outlying steppe is heavily stocked with 10,000 sheep and goats, 1,500 cattle and 200 horses belonging to residents, and a further 1,500–3,000 sheep owned by semi-nomadic kuchis and mulclan. The latter arrive from Jalalabad in May and remain for three or four months. The Bamiyan Provincial Government has recognised the grazing rights of three tribes, the Tanaki with about 100 families, the Amorkhil with 100 families and the Nurzai with about 60 families. Small numbers of Shinwari and Safis also use the area seasonally (Shank and Larsson, 1977).

Visitors and Visitor Facilities   For almost two decades, Band-e Amir has been a popular tourist attraction. Day tours from Bamiyan were operated by the Afghan Tourist Organisation. Present facilities are limited to local hotels in the bazaar (Shank and Larsson, 1977).

Scientific Research and Facilities   Preliminary surveys of the geology (Jux and Kemof, 1971), vegetation (Dieterle, 1973) and wildlife (Petocz and Skogland, 1974) have been carried out.

Conservation Value   Band-e Amir is without doubt one of the most beautiful natural landscapes in Afghanistan.

Conservation Management   Lack of legislation, planning and management make the continued existence of Band-e Amir as a place of beauty and national significance precarious. The Afghan Tourist Organisation maintains *de facto* control, although the Directorate of National Parks and Wildlife is willing to be responsible for conservation in national parks. No protocol agreement has yet been reached. A strategy for the establishment and development of the national park has been drawn up (Shank and Larsson, 1977). Long-term objectives are to conserve the natural landscapes through a system of zonation and to develop the tourist potential of the area. Traditional land-use practices will continue within a buffer area which surrounds an inner core zone protecting the lakes and their immediate uplands.

Management Constraints The national park lacks any legal status, and as yet there is no protocol agreement between the Afghan Tourist Organisation and the Directorate of National Parks and Wildlife over its jurisdiction. Unlimited grazing and uprooting of shrubs has lead to serious range degradation and soil erosion. Cultivation is excessive. Reeds are harvested and grazed, thus destroying waterfowl nesting habitat. The poor visitor facilities detract from the beauty of the park (Petocz and Skogland, 1974; Shank and Larsson, 1977).

Staff In 1977 there was one park superintendent posted at Bamiyan and a soldier/policeman responsible for enforcement measures in the park.

Budget No information.

Local Addresses No information

References
Dieterle, A. (1973). *Vegetationskundliche Untersuchungen im Gebiete von Band-i-Amir (Zentral-Afghanistan)*. Dissness bot. 24 pp.

Sayer, J.A. and van der Zon, A.P.M. (1981). *National parks and wildlife management. Afghanistan. A contribution to a conservation strategy*. Vol. 1. UNDP/FAO, Rome. 107 pp.

Freitag, H. (1971). Die natürliche Vegetation Afghanistans. *Vegetatio* 22: 283–344. (Unseen)

Habibi K. (1967). Fading natural splendor of Bande Amir lakes. *Kabul Times*, 30 September. (Unseen)

Jux, U. and Kempf (1971). Stauseen durch Travertinabsatz im Zentralen Afghanischen Hochgebirge. Z. *Geomorphological*. Supplement 12: 107–37. (Unseen)

Matthews R.O. (1988). Band-e-Amir Lakes. Jewels in the foothills of the Hindu Kush. *The atlas of natural wonders*. Facts on File Publication, New York. Pp. 85–7.

Niethammer, J. (1965). Die Säugetiere Afghanistans (Teil II) Insectivora, Lagomorpha, Rodentia. *Journal of the Faculty of Science, Kabul*: 18–41. (Unseen)

Petocz, R.G. and Skogland, T. (1974). *Report on the status of Band-e Amir National Park*. Department of Forests and Range, Kabul. Unpublished. (Unseen)

Shank, C.C. and Larsson, S.Y. (1977). *A strategy for the establishment and development of Band-e Amir national park*. UNDP/FAO/Department of Forests and Range, Kabul. 37 pp.

DASHTE-NAWAR WATERFOWL SANCTUARY

IUCN Management Category IV (Managed Nature Reserve)

Biogeographical Province 2.37.12 (Hindu Kush Highlands)

Geographical Location Lies in south-east Afghanistan, Ghazni Province, some 55 km north-west of Ghazni Town. Access from Ghazni is via Nawar. Dashte-Nawar is relatively isolated and accessible only in summer. Approximately 33°50'N, 67°45'E

Date and History of Establishment Approved a wildlife and waterfowl sanctuary on 20 December 1977 (Order no. 707) by the Head of State, on the basis of Petition no. 1765 dated 6 June 1977. This followed its declaration as a national flamingo and waterfowl sanctuary by the Directorate of Wildlife and National Parks in 1974 (FAO, 1978).

Area 7,500 ha, including a 1 km-wide peripheral strip of land (Shank and Rodenburg, 1977). (NB An area of 7,000 ha, including a 1 km-border of land, is given in the original declaration).

Land Tenure State. Semi-nomadic people have traditional grazing rights.

Altitude The lake lies at 3,200 m.

Physical Features Dashte-Nawar is a high desert in the Kohe Baba Range of the Hindu Kush Plain. It is surrounded on all sides by mountains which rise above 4,800 m. Contained within Dashte-Nawar is a shallow, brackish lake, Ab-i-Nawar, which is approximately 14 km by 3 km and 3,500 ha in area. There are about 40 islands, varying in size from 35 sq. m to 500 sq. m, situated in the lake (Shank and Rodenburg, 1977). Ab-i-Nawar's water volume may drop typically from nearly 20 million cu. m in spring to 2 million cu. m in autumn (Nogge, 1974) and completely dry up in winter. The water supply comes primarily from spring snow melt from the surrounding mountains.

Climate Summers are hot and dry and winters cold. Mean annual precipitation at Nawar, 20 km west of Dashte-Nawar, is 184 mm (1967–75), 72% of which falls during the winter months. The temperature regime is harsh, with only three months of the year having a mean minimum temperature above freezing point (Shank and Rodenburg, 1977).

Vegetation The lake bottom supports a dense cover of a higher alga belonging to the family Characeae. The mud flats surrounding Ab-i-Nawar are mostly devoid of vegetation, except at the outer edge where the herbs *Glaux maritima*, *Crypsis aculeata* and *Polygonum sibiricum* become common. The dashte consists of an extensive meadow of low grasses and herbs with a ground cover of up to 40%. Common grasses in this zone include *Bromus gracillimus*, *Puccinellia stapfiana* and *Aelunopus littoralis*. Herbs commonly encountered are *Halocharis clavata*, *Polygonum paronychioides*, *Potentilla komaroviana*, *Gentiana kaufmanniana*, *Tragopogon* sp. and *Artemisia* sp. Throughout the dashte are shallow, dry stream beds which support distinctive communities, with *Taraxacum bessarabicum*, *Triglochin palustre*, *Ranunculus* sp., *Juncus bufonius* and the grass *Eremopoa bellula* present. Where the dashte rises into the surrounding mountains, the terrain becomes rocky and the plant community correspondingly sparse, with *Acantholimon* spp. predominant (Shank and Rodenburg, 1977).

Fauna Mammals recorded in and around Dashte-Nawar include long-tailed marmot *Marmota caudata*, ground squirrel *Citellus fulvus*, jackal *Canis aureus*, wolf *Canis lupus* (V) and fox *Vulpes vulpes*. The birds have not been intensively studied, but greater flamingo *Phoenicopterus roseus*, avocet *Recurvirostra avosetta*, redshank *Tringa totanus*, greater sandplover *Charadrius leschenaultii* and common tern *Sterna hirundo* breed here (Klockenhoff and Madel, 1970). There are no fish in the lake. Aquatic organisms are varied and periodically numerous. A toad *Bufo andersoni* and a skink *Ablepharus* sp. are the only cold-blooded vertebrates recorded (Shank and Rodenburg, 1977).

Cultural Heritage Dashte-Nawar is an important archaeological site, exhibiting intact stratigraphic sequences. Several mounds representing early dwellings have been discovered with accompanying artefacts, which suggest occupations from Palaeolithic to Buddhist times (Shank and Rodenburg, 1977).

Local Human Population   Dashte-Nawar is sparsely inhabited. Some 25 villages, with an estimated 1,200–1,500 residents, lie within the dashte. In addition, an estimated 1,300 semi-nomadic people (260 families) traditionally use the area as summer grazing grounds for approximately 5,000–7,000 sheep and goats and 700 camels (Shank and Rodenburg, 1977).

Visitors and Visitor Facilities   No information

Scientific Research and Facilities   The avifauna, particularly greater flamingo, has been studied by Klockenhoff and Madel (1970) and Nogge (1974).

Conservation Value   Dashte-Nawar is an important breeding and feeding site for migratory waterfowl and waders. Its international importance was recognised at the 1971 Conference on the Contracting Parties to the Ramsar Convention, following which the Government of Afghanistan responded to pleas to protect this area.

Conservation Management   Following its legal protection, a management plan was prepared (Shank and Rodenburg, 1977). Principal objectives outlined in the plan include protecting birds from adverse influences of human origin and initiating a monitoring programme upon which to base future management decisions. In 1975, assistance was received from WWF to provide quarters for a resident warden and research facilities.

Management Constraints   Grazing by domestic livestock disrupts almost all shore breeding by migratory birds. Egg collection and disturbance of nests by humans is a problem (Shank and Rodenburg, 1977).

Staff   Game guards in summer months only (1974 onwards)

Budget   No information

Local Addresses   No information

References

FAO (1978). *National parks and utilization of wildlife resources. Afghanistan. Project findings and recommendations.* UNDP/FAO, Rome. 43 pp.

Forstner, U. and Bartsch, G. (1970). Die Seen von Banda-Amir, Datscht-i-Nawar, Ob-i-Istada and Humun-i-Puzak (Zentral und Südwestafghanistan). *Science, Kabul* 6: 19–23. (Unseen)

Klockenhoff, H. and Madel, G. (1970). Uber di Flamingos (*Phoenicopterus ruber*) der Dasht-i-Nawar in Afghanistan. *Journal für Ornithologie* 111: 78–84. (Unseen)

Nogge, G. (1974). Beobachtungen an den Flamingobrutplätzen Afghanistans. *Journal für Ornithologie* 115: 142–51. (Unseen)

Petocz, R.G. and Habibi, K. (1975). The flamingos (*Phoenicopterus ruber roseus*) of Ab-i-Estada and Dashte-Nawar, Ghazni Province, Afghanistan. Department of Forests and Range, Kabul. (Unseen)

Shank, C.C. and Rodenburg, W.F. (1977). *Management plan for Ab-i-Estada and Dashte-Nawar flamingo and waterfowl sanctuaries.* UNDP/FAO/Department of Forests and Range, Kabul. 43 pp.

KOLE HASHMAT KHAN WATERFOWL SANCTUARY
LAKE HASHMAT KHAN WATERFOWL SANCTUARY

IUCN Management Category   Unassigned

Biogeographical Province   2.37.12 (Hindu Kush Highlands)

Geographical Location   Situated on the south-eastern outskirts of Kabul, in Kabul Province, just south of the Kabul-Gardez Highway. Approximately 34°30'N, 69°12'E

Date and History of Establishment   Not yet formally gazetted, the lake has been under the jurisdiction of the Department of Forests and Range since 1978. Formerly (from 1973 to 1978), the area was under the jurisdiction of the Guard-i-Jamhouriat (Republican Guard). This jurisdiction implies a ban on all hunting except by a privileged few. The lake has been used as a hunting ground since Moghul times. During the reign of Amin Habibullah Khan (1901–19) the lake was closed to all but the few privileged to hunt. In the 1930s, King Mohammed Zahir Shah took a personal interest in the area and declared it a waterfowl reserve. The area came under the protection of the royal garrison but has received little attention (Rahim and Larsson, 1978; Sayer and van der Zon, 1981).

Area   The lake extends over an area of 191 ha.

Land Tenure   The lake proper is state property and administered by the Department of Ceremonies of Arg-i-Jamjhouriat (Presidential Office). Fields to the south belong to the Public Bath, those to the north are privately owned.

Altitude   The lake itself lies at an elevation of 1,793 m.

Physical Features   Lake Hashmat Khan lies in a small basin on a large shelf in the Hindu Kush foothills. It is surrounded by hills on two sides and opens up into the Logar Valley to the north-east. The lake is fed by a tributary of the Logar River; it has no outlet except when the water level is exceptionally high. The lake is L-shaped, about 2.5 km in length and 0.3–1 km in width, and shallow (no more than 1.5 m in depth). The water level has been reduced due to the development of irrigation systems which have tapped the Logar River. The lake level fluctuates seasonally, being high in winter and early spring and nearly drying up in summer. Some of its water is used to irrigate the surrounding fields. High evaporation creates slightly saline conditions (Rahim and Larsson, 1978).

Climate   Meteorological data are from Kabul for the period 1967–76. Mean annual precipitation is 295 mm, with most occurring from February to April. August is usually the driest month. Precipitation normally falls as snow from December to March. Mean annual temperature is 11.8 °C. The warmest month is July with a mean of 24.9 °C; the coldest month is February with a mean of –2.6 °C. The lake is usually frozen for two to three months of the year (Rahim and Larsson, 1978).

Vegetation   The lake is strongly eutrophic and the open water is abundant with algae, *Utricularia* and *Ranunculus* spp. Approximately half of the lake is covered with high reeds *Phragmites australis*. A meadow-type halophytic plant community dominates the ground cover. It is strongly modified by grazing and fertilisation from animal droppings, presenting an impression of a semi-cultivated pasture. Among the plants recorded are meadow buttercup *Ranunculus arvensis*, brome grass *Bromus danthoniae*, knapweed *Centaurea* sp., *Eleocharis* and several species belonging to the families Cyperaceae, Crucifera and Compositae (Rahim and Larsson, 1978).

Fauna   Voles *Alticola roylei* and *Microtus afghans*, jackal *Canis aureus* and fox *Vulpes vulpes* have been recorded from the lake surrounds (Niethammer, 1967). Other mammals known to occur in the general area are wolf *Canis lupus* (V), marbled polecat *Vormela peregusna*, Euphrate's jerboa *Allactaga euphratica* and grey hamster *Cricetulus migratorius* (Niethammer 1965; Rahim and Larsson, 1978).

The majority of birds are migratory (over 30,000), although several species actually breed on the lake, for example, pochard *Aythya ferina*, coot *Fulica atra*, moorhen *Gallinula chloropus*, black-necked grebe *Podiceps nigricollis*, little grebe **Tachybaptus** *ruficollis* and black kite *Milvus migrans*. Thousands of ducks, coots and waders have been recorded. Rare sightings include greater flamingo *Phoenicopterus roseus*, spoonbill *Platalea leucorodia*, glossy ibis *Plegadis falcinellus*, ruddy shelduck *Tadorna ferruginea* and marbled teal *Anas angustirostris*. To date some 157 species have been identified from the lake and its surroundings (Rahim and Larsson, 1978).

The lake itself contains a typical aquatic community of crustaceans, insects and some amphibians, notably toad *Bufo viridis* and frogs *Rana* spp. Golden carp has been introduced and thrives, together with common carp of the family Cyprinidae (Rahim and Larsson, 1978).

Cultural Heritage   Near Kole Hashmar Khan is the shrine of Jubur Ansar, built in AD 645 in memory of soldiers killed in the effort to convert the Afghan population from Buddhism and Hinduism to Islam. It remains a prominent site among Kabul residents for performing religious rites. Remains of an old fort built during the reign of Amir Habibullah Khan lie in the lake itself, and nearby is the Quala-i-Hashmat Khan, formerly used as a royal guest house (Rahim and Larsson, 1978).

Local Human Population   A small Tujik village (300 houses) lies to the west of the lake. North-west of the lake are about 200 houses occupied mainly by Pansjirs and Sujis. Residents from both villages are mostly skilled workers. Between the lake and the Kabul-Gardez Highway are a dozen houses owned by farmers. In addition, there are a dozen houses near the cemetery occupied by religious men and caretakers, and a public bath (haman) where ten Hazara families live and work. At the base of the Khwaja Safa mountains are some 300 houses built by the Tara Khal tribals. Kuchis (nomadic pastoralists) utilise the area for one or two months in spring en route to the central Hindu Kush mountains (Rahim and Larsson, 1978).

Visitors and Visitor Facilities   Local people visit the shrines and the cemetery and come for purely recreational purposes. An environmental education centre has been proposed (Rahim and Larsson, 1978).

Scientific Research and Facilities   A two-year study of the avifauna was conducted by Niethammer (1967). This was followed by an ecological survey of the lake to assess its conservation importance (Rahim and Larsson, 1978).

Conservation Value   The lake lies on the Hindu Kush flyway and is a major staging ground for western Siberian waterfowl. Furthermore, it is the only remaining water body and marsh area of the formerly expansive marshlands of Kabul. It is also an important recreational site for the city population and is of religious and historical importance (Rahim and Larsson, 1978).

Conservation Management   In 1978 the lake was placed under the Department of Forests and Range, but effective control remained with the Republican Guard. It has been recommended that the lake and its surrounds (up to high water level) be legally gazetted as a waterfowl sanctuary and placed under the administration of the Department of Forests and Range. The lake and its vicinity should be secured as a breeding/nesting area for waterfowl and steps should be taken to relieve human pressure on the habitat (Rahim and Larsson, 1978).

Management Constraints   The lake's ecology is much affected by the surrounding human population. The Logar River is polluted. Domestic animals graze among the reeds and disturb the waterfowl whenever the water level is low. Reeds are cut and birds hunted. The shore is used as a playground by children. Clothes are laundered in the lake. Water channelled from the Logar River and lake for irrigation purposes contributes to the low lake level during drought periods (Rahim and Larsson, 1978; Sayer and van der Zon, 1981). Since 1979 the area has been restricted and management activites have not been sustained (FAO, 1980).

Staff   No information

Budget   No information

Local Addresses   No information

References

FAO (1980). *National parks and wildlife management, Afghanistan. Project findings and recommendations.* UNDP/FAO, Rome. 22 pp.

Sayer, J.A. and van der Zon, A.P.M. (1981). *National parks and wildlife management, Afghanistan. A contribution to a conservation strategy.* Vol. 1. UNEP/FAO, Rome 105 pp.

Niethammer, J. (1965). Die Säugetiere Afghanistans (Teil II) Insectivora, Lagomorpha, Rodentia. *Journal of the Faculty of Science, Kabul*: 18–41. (Unseen)

Niethammer, J. (1967). Zwei Jahre Vogelbeachtungen an stehenden Gewässern bei Kabul in Afghanistan. *Journal für Ornithologie* 108: 119–64. (Unseen)

Rahim, A. and Larsson, J.Y. (1978). *A preliminary study of Lake Hashmat Khan with recommendations for management.* FAO/UNEP/Department of Forest and Range, Kabul. 17 pp.

PAMIR-I-BUZURG WILDLIFE SANCTUARY
BIG PAMIR WILDLIFE SANCTUARY

IUCN Management Category   IV (Managed Nature Reserve.)

Biogeographical Province   2.37.12 (Hindu Kush Highlands)

Geographical Location   Lies in the western part of the Wakhan Corridor on the border with the USSR, in Badakhshan Province. It is approximately 250 km east of Fayzabad. Access is from Kabul via Kunduz and Fayzabad to Zebak and Qala-i-Pandja and then by horse and yak to the Big Pamir. A description of the boundaries is given in Petocz (1978b). Approximately 73°00′E, 37°10′N

Date and History of Establishment   Gazetted as a wildlife sanctuary on 10 September 1978. Originally what was established as a royal hunting reserve in the late 1950s in Tulibai Valley was enlarged by the Afghan Tourist Organisation following recommendations by Petocz (1971, 1973). It has been recommended that the wildlife sanctuary be designated a national park and World Heritage site (Petocz 1978b; FAO, 1981).

Area   67,938 ha

Land Tenure   State

Altitude   Ranges from 3,250 m to 6,103 m (Petocz, 1978b; FAO, 1981).

Physical Features   The term 'Pamir' itself refers to a mountain valley of glacial formation differing from adjacent or other mountain valleys in its superior altitude, and in the greater degree to which the trough has been filled up by glacial debris and alluvium. Its appearance approximates to a plain owing to the inability of the central stream to secure itself a deeper channel (Curzon, 1896). There are four main rivers (Sargaz, Tulibai, Manjulah, and Abakhan), all of which flow north-west into the Darya-i-Pamir on the northern border. The landscape has been shaped by frost shattering and heaving, glacial scouring and plucking, together with wind and stream erosion. The dominant rocks forming the mountains of the Wakhan are metamorphics and igneous intrusives. Sulphurous hot springs emanate from igneous rocks. Moist valley bottoms are composed of an alluvium with shallow (10–40 cm) but widespread peat deposits. A small icefield remains in the highest area of the Big Pamir whose generally retreating glaciers spill out into the heads of tributary valley floors above 4,600 m (Matthews, 1975; Petocz, 1978a).

Climate   Meteorological data are all but absent from the Pamir. The nearest government weather station is located at the provincial capital of Faizabad. Here the warmest temperatures occur from June to August, which can also be correlated with the period of lowest precipitation. This trend is believed analogous to the situation in the Pamir. Most precipitation in Faizabad falls largely as rain during March, April and May. In the Pamir, however, snow accumulation begins towards the end of October, probably peaks in late January to early February then

20

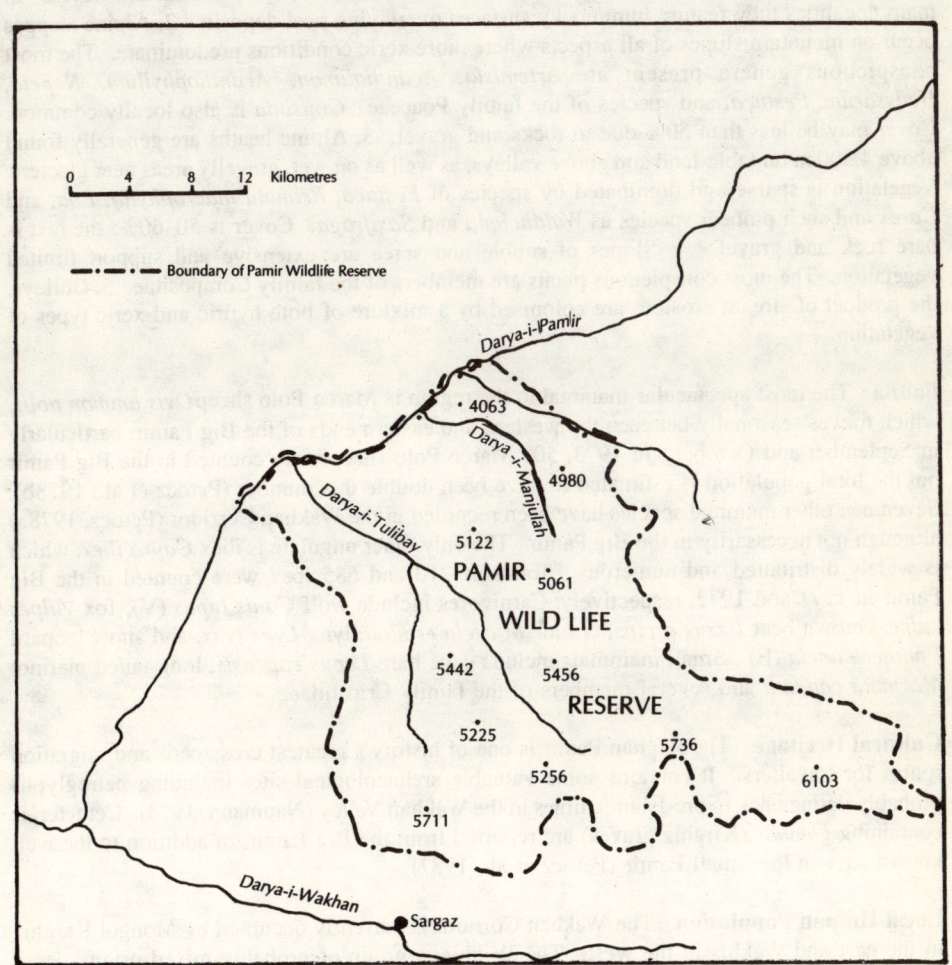

Pamir-i-Buzurg Wildlife Sanctuary

declines towards the end of March. Snow covers the Pamir region for six or seven months of the year, and is by and large the most important form of moisture. According to local people several metres may accumulate in the valleys of the Big Pamir (Petocz, 1978a).

Vegetation   The flora of the high Pamir belongs to the alpine vegetation community of Freitag (1971). Five habitat types are recognised by Petocz (1978b). 1. Sedge meadows occur on well-watered flats or depressions and are dominated by *Kobresia* and *Carex*. In many localities they feature hummocky surfaces overlaying peat deposits. 2. Alpine steppes occur on mountain slopes of all aspects where more xeric conditions predominate. The most conspicuous genera present are *Artemisia*, *Acantholimon*, *Acanthophyllum*, *Nepeta*, *Hedysarum*, *Festuca*, and species of the family Poaceae. *Cousinia* is also locally common. Cover may be less than 50% due to rocks and gravel. 3. Alpine heaths are generally found above 4,300 m on table-land and above valleys, as well as on wet, gravelly areas near glaciers. Vegetation is sparse and dominated by species of *Festuca*, *Primula macrophylla*, *Poa*, and *Carex* and such pioneer species as *Waldheimia* and *Saxifraga*. Cover is 50–60%; the rest is bare rock and gravel. 4. Slopes of rubble and scree are extensive and support limited vegetation. The most conspicuous plants are members of the family Compositae. 5. Gulleys, the product of stream erosion, are colonised by a mixture of both hydric and xeric types of vegetation.

Fauna   The most spectacular mammal in the region is Marco Polo sheep *Ovis ammon polii*, which moves seasonally between the western and eastern ends of the Big Pamir, particularly in September and October. In 1973, 500 Marco Polo sheep were counted in the Big Pamir but the total population is estimated to have been double this number (Petocz et al., 1978b). Seventeen other mammal species have been recorded in the Wakhan Corridor (Petocz, 1978a) although not necessarily in the Big Pamir. The only other ungulate is ibex *Capra ibex*, which is widely distributed and numerous. Totals of 210 and 685 ibex were counted in the Big Pamir in 1971 and 1972, respectively. Carnivores include wolf *Canis lupus* (V), fox *Vulpes vulpes*, brown bear *Ursus arctos*, ermine *Mustela ermina*, lynx *Lynx lynx*, and snow leopard *Panthera uncia* (E). Small mammals include cape hare *Lepus capensis*, long-tailed marmot *Marmota caudata* and several members of the family Cricetidae.

Cultural Heritage   The Afghan Pamir is one of history's greatest crossroads and migration routes for travellers. It contains some valuable archaeological sites including petroglyphs probably dating back to pre-Islamic times in the Wakhan Valley (Naumann, 1973). Cemeteries containing *gumbaz* (Kirghiz graves) are reported from the Big Pamir, in addition to the well known sites in the Small Pamir (Petocz et al., 1987).

Local Human Population   The Wakhan Corridor is currently occupied by Mongol Karghiz in the east and Wakhis in the west. The Wakhis, a group of probably mixed origin, occur throughout the sanctuary. They have established permanent villages along the Wakhan River up to Sarhad, with about 4,000 inhabitants. The Wakhis are both agricultural and pastoral. They grow wheat, barley and peas in the Wakhan Valley and in spring and summer move up to the alpine pastures of the Big Pamir to graze their yaks, sheep and goats (Petocz, 1978a). An estimated 75 people, with a total of 3,550–4,550 sheep and goats, and 920 yaks and cows, are encamped inside the sanctuary in summer (Petocz et al., 1978). Apart from settlements along the Wakhan Valley, the main population centres are the villages of Qala-i-Panja and Khundud, located 38 km and 65 km, respectively, from the reserve (Petocz, 1978b).

Visitors and Visitor Facilities   Entry to the entire Pamir region is restricted; foreigners require special permits from the Ministry of Interior. Tourism is limited mainly to guest clients participating in the hunting programme of the Afghan Tourist Organisation, which maintains a fully equipped base camp in the Tulibai Valley during the hunting season. Many of the recommendations proposed by Petocz (1973) have been incorporated into the organisation of the programme, including provision of medical facilities and a qualified doctor for tourists and free to local people.   At Sargaz, in the Wakhan Valley, overnight accommodation is available for visitors *en route* to the sanctuary (Petocz 1978b).

Scientific Research and Facilities   Geological reconnaissance and mineral exploration have been carried out in the Wakhan Corridor by Russian scientists (Petocz, 1978b). The Big Pamir was included in an ecological reconnaissance of the entire Afghan Pamir (Petocz, 1978b). As part of this project the flora of the Tulibai Valley (Petocz, 1978a) and the biology of the Marco Polo sheep (Petocz, 1978b) were studied. Other work includes observations on mammals (Naumann and Niethammer, 1973; Naumann and Nogge, 1973) and avifauna (Neithammer and Nogge, 1973).

Conservation Value   The Pamirs are among the most spectacular landscapes of central Asia, with high mountains and beautiful rivers and lakes. The Wakhis still lead a traditional pastoral life. Archaeological sites include petroglyphs and graves.

Conservation Management   The sanctuary was established to protect Marco Polo sheep. Hunting restrictions were first imposed in the late-1950s by order of the former king. Part of the area was converted to a tourist hunting site in the mid-1960s and later enlarged, whereby protection of the rangeland from grazing by livestock was extended from the upper Tulibai Valley to other main headwaters. The Afghan Tourist Organisation has been involved in the management of the area since 1968, when the former king Mohammed Zahir Shah granted sole use of the then royal hunting reserve for hunting Marco Polo sheep. *De facto* control of the sanctuary rests with the Afghan Tourist Organisation. A protocol concerning the jurisdiction of wildlife concerns has since been agreed between the Afghan Tourist Organisation and the Department of Forests and Range, whereby hunting quotas are set by the latter authority. The primary objective outlined in the management plan is to ensure that the wildlife, particularly Marco Polo sheep and ibex, thrive in an ecological framework, in harmony with the local human population (Petocz, 1978b).

Management Constraints   The main problem is socio-economic: competition between livestock and Marco Polo sheep is severe, resulting in the deterioration of rangeland. While protection of rangeland in valley heads has benefited plant production there, it has served to concentrate and isolate livestock on the more fragile alpine steppes in the lower parts of valleys. Various remedial actions to eliminate or reduce domestic stock, while maintaining the status quo of the local people, have been suggested (Petocz, 1978b).

Staff   No information.

Budget   No information

Local Addresses   No information

References

Anderson, S.C. and Leverton, A.E. (1969). Amphibians and reptiles collected by the Street expedition to Afghanistan, 1969. *Proceedings of the California Academy of Sciences.* 4th series, 37(2): 25–56. (Unseen)

Curzon, G.N. (1896). The Pamirs and the source of the Oxus. *Bulletin of the Royal Geographical Society,* London. 83 pp.

Freitag, H. (1971). In: Davies, P.H., Harper, P.C. and Hedge, I.C. (Eds.), *Studies on the natural vegetation of Afghanistan: On Plant life in South-west Asia.* University press, Aberdeen. Pp. 89–106. (Unseen)

Matthews, J.V. Jr. (1975). *Arctic Steppe*—an extinct biome. Terrain Sciences Division, Geological Survey of Canada, Ottawa. Unpublished. (Unseen)

Naumann, C.M. (1973). Ein ehemaliges Wildyak-Vorkommen im Afghanischen Pamir. *Bonn Zool. Beitr.* 24: 254–69. (Unseen)

Petocz, R.G. (1978a). *Report on the Afghan Pamir: ecological reconnaissance.* UNDP/FAO/Department of Forests and Range, Kabul. 33 pp.

Petocz, R.G. (1978b). *Report on the Afghan Pamir: a management plan for the Big Pamir wildlife reserve.* UNDP/FAO/Department of Forests and Range, Kabul. 33 pp.

Petocz, R.G., Habibi, K., Jamilt, A. and Wassey, A. (1978). *Report on the Afghan Pamir: biology of the Marco Polo sheep.* UNDP/FAO/Department of Forests and Range. Kabul. 42 pp.

Shor, J.B. (1955). *After you, Marco Polo.* McGraw-Hill Book Co., New York. (Unseen)

Skogland, T. and Petocz, R.G. (1975). *Ecology and behavior of Marco Polo Sheep (Ovis ammon poli) in the Pamir during winter.* Report to the Government of Afghanistan. Unpublished. (Unseen)

Wood (1941). *Source of the River Oxus.* Blackwood and Son, London. (Unseen)

BANGLADESH

Area 144,000 sq. km

Population 114,800,000 (1990)   Natural increase 2.5% per annum

GNP US $ 170 per capita (1988).

Policy and Legislation Environmental policy in Bangladesh is based on the following three broad principles: precautionary, whereby harm to the environment is avoided; originator, whereby the costs of ameliorating damage to the environment are borne by those responsible; and co-operation, whereby relevant bodies are involved in planning for environmental protection (Rahman, 1983).

The need for an explicit national policy on environmental protection and management has been repeatedly highlighted (BARC, 1987), and is presently under consideration by the government. The objectives of such a policy will be as follows: to create, develop, maintain and improve conditions under which man and nature can thrive in productive and enjoyable harmony with each other; to fulfill the social, economic and other requirements of present and future generations; and to ensure the attainment of an environmental quality that is conducive to a life of dignity and well-being (Rahman, 1983).

An environmental impact assessment for anticipating any adverse impacts has not yet been incorporated into the development planning process, nor is it a mandatory requirement of project-approving agencies. According to government policy, sanctioning agencies should ensure that project proposals contain adequate environmental safeguards but, in practice, this is not strictly followed (BARC, 1987).

Bangladesh has completed the first phase of a national conservation strategy aimed at integrating conservation goals with national development objectives and overcoming identified obstacles to sustainable development (BARC, 1987). Some twenty sectors in the current Third Five Year Plan are identified for critical analysis during a second phase, including the conservation of genetic resources, wildlife management and protected areas. The Bangladesh Agricultural Research Council, Ministry of Agriculture is the lead agency for the implementation of Phase II which began in October 1989.

There is no national wildlife conservation policy. The Bangladesh Wildlife (Preservation) Order 1973, promulgated under Presidential Order no. 23 on 27 March 1973 and subsequently enacted and amended in two phases as the Bangladesh Wildlife (Preservation) (Amendment)

Act 1974, provides for the establishment of national parks, wildlife sanctuaries, game reserves and private game reserves (see Annex). Under Article 23, wildlife sanctuaries enjoy a greater degree of protection than national parks. For example, entry or residence, introduction of exotic or domestic species of animals and lighting of fires is prohibited in wildlife sanctuaries, but not national parks. No specific rules are detailed for game reserves. The Article makes provision, however, for the government to relax any of these prohibitions for scientific, aesthetic or other exceptional reasons, and to alter the boundaries of protected areas. Under Article 24, provision is made for the establishment of private game reserves upon application by the landowner. The owner of a private game reserve may exercise all the powers of an officer provided under the Act. Proposals are being drawn up to strengthen the existing legislation, largely through raising fines and terms of imprisonment for offences.

Conservation, use and exploitation of marine resources are provided for under the Territorial Water and Maritime Zones Act 1974. According to provisions in this Act conservation zones may be established to protect marine resources from indiscriminate exploitation, depletion or destruction. At present, there is no legal provision for the management of coastal zones.

The Forest Act 1927 enables the government to declare any forest or waste land to be reserved forest or protected forest (see Annex). Activities are generally prohibited in reserved forests; certain activities, such as removal of forest produce, may be permitted under license in protected forests while others, such as quarrying of stone and clearing for cultivation, may be prohibited. The rights of government to any land constituted as reserved forest may be assigned to village communities, with conditions for their management prescribed by government. Such forests are called village forests. Under the Forest (Amendment) Ordinance, 1989, penalties for offences committed within reserved and protected forests have been increased from a maximum of six months imprisonment and a fine of Tk 500 to five years imprisonment and a Tk 5,000 (US $ 1,700) fine. In accordance with the National Forest Policy, adopted in 1979, effective measures will be taken to conserve the natural environment and wildlife resources. The Policy does not, however, deal explicitly with the need to set aside special areas as protected forests, as distinct from productive forests, to preserve genetic diversity and maintain ecological processes within the context of sustainable development (BARC, 1987).

Other environmental legislation less specifically related to protected areas is reviewed elsewhere (DS/ST, 1980; Rahman, 1983).

International Activities   Bangladesh is party to the Convention concerning the Protection of the World Cultural and Natural Heritage (World Heritage Convention) which it accepted on 3 August 1983. No natural sites have been inscribed to date. Bangladesh participates in the Unesco Man and Biosphere Programme. Apart from a couple of reserved forests proposed as candidate sites by the Bangladesh MAB National Committee in the late 1970s, there does not appear to have been any significant development in recent years. A proposal to become a party to the Convention on Wetlands of International Importance especially as Waterfowl Habitat (Ramsar Convention) was submitted to the erstwhile Ministry of Agriculture and Forestry by the Forest Department and awaits approval. It is proposed to nominate the Sundarbans mangrove forests as a wetland of international importance, in partial fulfilment of the requirements of the Convention (Rahman and Akonda, 1987).

Administration and Management   Wildlife conservation, including the management of protected areas, is the responsibility of the Forest Directorate within the new Ministry of

Environment and Forests formed in 1989. Previously, the Forest Directorate came under the Ministry of Agriculture and Forests while the former Department of Environmental Pollution Control, concerned largely with environmental pollution, was under the Ministry of Local Government and Rural Development.

In 1976 a Wildlife Circle was established within what was then known as the Forest Department, with specific responsibility for wildlife matters under the charge of a Conservator of Forests responsible directly to the Chief Conservator of Forests. A $ 13.3 million scheme, entitled 'Development of Wildlife Management and Game Reserves', was incorporated within the country's First Five Year Plan, but reduced to $ 92,000 in the subsequent Two Year Approach Plan (Olivier, 1979). The Wildlife Circle was subsequently abolished in June 1983, allegedly in the interests of economy and following the recommendations of the Inam Commission. The post of Conservator of Forests (General Administration and Wildlife) remains but the incumbent has many other administrative duties unrelated to wildlife. Following its general down-grading within the Forest Department, wildlife conservation has become the theoretical responsibility of the various divisional forest officers (Blower, 1985; Husain, 1986). Separate staff are deployed for protection purposes in a number of national parks and wildlife sanctuaries (Sarker and Fazlul Huq, 1985).

The Bangladesh Wildlife (Preservation)(Amendment) Act 1974 also provides for the establishment of a Wildlife Advisory Board, which was set up in 1976 under the chairmanship of the Minister of Agriculture. The Board is supposed to approve important wildlife management decisions and directives (Olivier, 1979). Although it still exists, it does not appear to be a dynamic force (Blower, 1985; BARC, 1987).

In view of the low priority accorded to protected areas, a Task Force was formed by the Ministry of Agriculture in 1985 to identify institutional and other measures needed to improve current provisions for wildlife conservation. Recommendations of the Task Force, submitted to the government in July 1986, await approval by the competent authority. They include a plan to immediately revive the erstwhile Wildlife Circle, review Phase II of the Wildlife Development Project and secure protection of 5% of the total land area of the country for conservation purposes (Rahman and Akonda, 1987).

The principal non-governmental conservation organisations within the country are the Society for Conservation of Nature and Environment (SCONE), which is mainly concerned with environmental pollution, and the Wildlife Society of Bangladesh. Pothikrit, based in Chunati, and Polli Unnayan Sangstha (POUSH), founded in 1984, are both involved in promoting the adoption of sound management practices in and around protected areas. Their efforts are presently focused on Chunati Wildlife Sanctuary and Teknaf Game Reserve. IUCN–The World Conservation Union has a project office in Dhaka.

Given that wildlife resources are vested largely in reserved forests, their conservation has in the past been diametrically opposed to forest management practices. Few, if any, protected areas are effectively managed and protected. Lack of personnel trained in wildlife conservation is a further handicap (Olivier, 1979; Gittins and Akonda, 1982; Khan, 1985). The very low priority apparently now accorded to wildlife conservation is reflected in the recent abolition of the Wildlife Circle, the reassignment of staff to normal duties, the lack of any separate financial provision within the Forest Directorate's budget and the now moribund Wildlife Advisory Board (Blower, 1985).

Systems Reviews   Some 80% of Bangladesh is lowland, comprising an alluvial plain cut by the three great river systems (Ganges-Padma, Brahmaputra-Jamuna and Meghna) that flow into the Bay of Bengal. Typically, at least one-half of the land is inundated annually, with one-tenth subject to severe flooding. The entire flood plain was well-vegetated, but much of the forest has been replaced by cultivations and plantations in recent decades due to mounting pressure from human populations. Here, the only extensive tract of forest remaining is the Sundarbans. Hills are confined chiefly to the east and south-east, notably the Chittagong Hills where forest cover is among the most extensive in the country.

According to the 1987 Statistical Yearbook of Bangladesh, forests cover 2.1 million hectares or 14.7% of total land area but this represents neither the area under forest nor that under the control of the Forest Department (Rashid, 1989). In 1980, Gittins and Akonda (1982) estimated remaining natural forest to be 4,782 sq. km (3.3%) and scrub forest 9,260 ha (6.5%). Actual forest cover is presently estimated to be 1 million hectares or 6.9% of total land area, a reduction of more than 50% over the past 20 years (WRI/CIDE, 1990).

The major forest types are mangrove, moist deciduous or sal *Shorea robusta*, restricted to the Madhupur Tract and northern frontier with Meghalaya, and evergreen forests found in the eastern districts of Sylhet, Chittagong and Chittagong Hill Tracts. A small amount of freshwater swamp occupies the basins of the north-east region.

Wetlands, variously estimated as covering between seven and eight million hectares or nearly 50% of total land area, support a variety of wildlife, as well as being of enormous economic importance (Scott, 1989).

The only known coral reef is around Jinjiradwip (St Martin's Island) in the Bay of Bengal. It is reputed to be a submerged reef but little is known about it (UNEP/IUCN, 1988).

Conservation efforts began in 1966, prior to independence, when the Government of Pakistan invited the World Wildlife Fund to assess its wildlife resources and recommend measures to arrest their depletion. Two expeditions were mounted (Mountfort and Poore, 1967, 1968) and the severity of the situation confirmed, whereupon the Government was urged to appoint its own Wildlife Enquiry Committee. The committee was established in 1968 and by 1970 had drafted a report. That part relating to East Pakistan was published as a separate report (Government of East Pakistan, 1971). Considerable progress was made with the establishment of several protected areas (Mountfort, 1969), research undertaken on the Sundarbans tiger population of East Pakistan (Hendrichs, 1975), and technical input from UNDP/FAO (Grimwood, 1969). Then, in 1971, came the War of Liberation which inevitably disrupted subsequent progress. In spite of political instability, however, the Bangladesh Wildlife (Preservation) Order was promulgated in 1973 and an ambitious programme of wildlife management developed, followed by the formation of a Wildlife Circle in 1976 and further technical assistance from UNDP/FAO (Olivier, 1979). Economic constraints, however, have subsequently been responsible for the loss of much of this initiative (Blower, 1985).

The existing system of protected areas has recently been reviewed (Green, 1989). It is not comprehensive, having been established with little regard to ecological and other criteria, and falls well below the target of 5% recommended by the erstwhile Ministry of Agriculture Task Force. Some effort has been made to include representative samples of the major habitats but, for example, marine and freshwater areas have been largely neglected (Olivier, 1979; Gittins and Akonda, 1982; Khan, 1985; Rahman and Akonda, 1987). Priorities to develop the present network of protected areas are identified in the IUCN systems review of the Indomalayan Realm (MacKinnon and MacKinnon, 1986) and further recommendations are made in the Corbett Action Plan (IUCN, 1985), many of which are based on earlier recommendations by Olivier (1979). More recently, wetlands of conservation value have been identified (Scott, 1989). Of outstanding importance is the need to prepare a plan for the development of the country's protected areas network.

Addresses

Office of the Chief Conservator of Forests (Conservator of Forests, General Administration and Wildlife), Bana Bhawan, Gulsham Road, Monakhali, Dhaka 12 (Cable FORESTS; Tel. 603537).

Forest Directorate (Chief Conservator of Forests), Ministry of Environment and Forests, Bana Bhaban, Gulshan Road, Monakhali, Dhaka 12 (Cable FORESTS)

IUCN–The World Conservation Union (Country Representative), 35 B/2 Indira Road, Dhaka 1215 (Tlx 671054 FRCBJ; Fax 813466; Tel. 815601)

Polli Unnayan Sangstha, 43 New Eskaton Road, Dhaka (Tlx 642639 OCNBJ; Tel. 402801, 406628).

Pothikrit, Chunati Village, Chittagong District

The Society for Conservation of Nature and Environment (Secretary General), 146 Shanti Nagar, Dhaka 17 (Cable ENVIRON DHAKA; Tel. 409119)

Wildlife Society of Bangladesh (General Secretary), c/o Department of Zoology, University of Dhaka, Dhaka 1000

References

BARC (1987). National conservation strategy for Bangladesh. Draft prospectus (Phase I). Bangladesh Agricultural Research Council/IUCN, Gland, Switzerland. 154 pp.

Blower, J.H. (1985). *Sundarbans Forest Inventory Project, Bangladesh. Wildlife conservation in the Sundarbans*. Project Report 151. ODA Land Resources Development Centre, Surbiton, UK. 39 pp.

DS/ST (1980). Draft environmental profile on Bangladesh. Science and Technology Division, Library of Congress. Washington, DC. 98 pp.

Gittins, S.P. and Akonda, A W. (1982). What survives in Bangladesh? *Oryx* 16: 275–81.

Government of East Pakistan (1971). Report of the Technical Sub-committee for East Pakistan of the Wildlife Enquiry Committee. Dacca.

Green, M.J.B. (1989). Bangladesh: an overview of its protected areas system. World Conservation Monitoring Centre, Cambridge, UK. 63 pp.

Grimwood, I.R. (1969). Wildlife Conservation in Pakistan. *Pakistan National Forestry Research and Training Project* Report No. 17. FAO, Rome. 31 pp.

Hendrichs, H. (1975). The status of the tiger *Panthera tigris* (Linne, 1758) in the Sundarbans mangrove forest (Bay of Bengal). *Saugetierkundliche Mitteilungen* 23: 161–99.

Husain, K.Z. (1986). Wildlife study, research and conservation in Bangladesh. *Eleventh Annual Bangladesh Science Conference* Section 2: 1–32.

IUCN (1985). *The Corbett Action Plan for protected areas of the Indomalayan Realm*. IUCN, Gland, Switzerland and Cambridge, UK. 23 pp.

Khan, M.A.R. (1985). Furture conservation directions for Bangladesh. In: Thorsell, J.W. (Ed.), *Conserving Asia's natural heritage*. IUCN, Gland, Switzerland. Pp. 114–22.

MacKinnon, J. and MacKinnon, K. (1986). *Review of the protected areas system in the Indo-Malayan Realm*. IUCN, Gland, Switzerland Cambridge, UK. 284 pp.

Mountfort, G. (1969). Pakistan's progress. *Oryx* 10: 39–43.

Mountfort, G. and Poore, D. (1967). The conservation of wildlife in Pakistan. World Wildlife Fund, Morges, Switzerland. Unpublished report. 27 pp.

Mountfort, G. and Poore, D. (1968). Report on the Second World Wildlife Fund Expedition to Pakistan. World Wildlife Fund, Morges, Switzerland. Unpublished. 25 pp.

Olivier, R.C.D. (1979). *Wildlife conservation and management in Bangladesh*. UNDP/FAO Project No. BGD/72/005. Forest Research Institute, Chittagong. 121 pp.

Rahman, S. (1983). Country monograph on institutional and legislative framework on environment, Bangladesh. UN/ESCAP and Government of Bangladesh. 76 pp.

Rahman, S.A. and Akonda, A.W. (1987). Bangladesh national conservation strategy: wildlife and protected areas. Department of Forestry, Ministry of Agriculture and Forestry, Dhaka. Unpublished. 33 pp.

Rashid, H. Er (1989). Land use in Bangladesh: selected topics. Bangladesh Agriculture Sector Review. UNDP Project No. BGD/87/023. Pp. 106–55.

Sarker, N.M. and Fazlul Huq, A.K.M. (1985). Protected areas of Bangladesh. In: Thorsell, J.W. (Ed.), *Conserving Asia's natural heritage*. IUCN, Gland, Switzerland. Pp. 36–8.

Scott, D.A. (Ed.) (1989). *A directory of Asian wetlands*. IUCN, Gland, Switzerland and Cambridge, UK. 1,181 pp.

UNEP/IUCN (1988). *Coral reefs of the world*. Vol. 2: *Indian Ocean, Red Sea and Gulf*. UNEP Regional Seas Directories and Bibliographies. IUCN, Gland, Switzerland and Cambidge, UK/UNEP, Nairobi, Kenya. 389 pp.

WRI/CIDE (1990). Bangladesh environment and natural resource assessment. Draft for review. World Resources Institute/Centre for International Development and Environment, Washington DC. 86 pp.

ANNEX   Definitions of protected area designations, as legislated, together with authorities responsible for their administration.

Title (English title):
Bangladesh Wildlife (Preservation) (Amendment) Act

Date: 1974

Brief description:
Provides for the preservation, conservation and management of wildlife in Bangladesh.

Administrative authority:
Forest Directorate, Ministry of Environment and Forests

Designations:
National park
— A comparatively large area of outstanding scenic and natural beauty, in which the protection of wildlife and preservation of the scenery, flora and fauna in their natural state is the primary objective, and to which the public may be allowed access for recreation, education and research.

— Hunting, killing or capturing any wild animal within a national park or one mile (1.6 km) of its boundaries, causing any disturbance (including firing of any gun) to any wild animal or its breeding place, felling, tapping, burning or in any other way damaging any plant or tree, cultivation, mining or breaking up any land, and polluting water flowing through a national park are not allowed. Such prohibitions may be relaxed for scientific purposes, aesthetic enjoyment of the scenery or any other exceptional reason.

— Construction of access roads, rest houses, hotels and public amenities should be planned so as not to impair the primary objective of the establishment of a national park.

Wildlife sanctuary

— An area closed to hunting and maintained as an undisturbed breeding ground, primarily for the protection of wildlife including all natural resources such as vegetation, soil and water.

— Entry or residence, cultivation, damage to vegetation, killing or capturing wild animals within one mile (1.6 km) of its boundary, introduction of exotic or domestic species of animals, lighting of fires, and pollution of water are notallowed, but any of these prohibitions may be relaxed for scientific reasons, or for the improvement or aesthetic enjoyment of the scenery.

Game reserve

— An area in which the wildlife is protected to enable populations of important species to increase. Capture of wild animals is prohibited.

— Hunting and shooting may be allowed on a permit basis.

Private game reserve

— Area of private land set aside by the owner for the same purpose as a game reserve. On application by the owner, such an area may be notified as a private game reserve.

— The owner shall excercise all the powers of an officer under this Act.

Source: Original legislation

Title (English title):
Forest Act

Date: 1927

Brief description:
An Act to consolidate the law relating to forests, the transit of forest produce and the duty leviable on timber and other forest produce.

Administrative authority:
Forest Directorate, Ministry of Environment and Forests

Designations:
Reserved forest

— Any forest land or wasteland belonging to the Government, or to which it has proprietary rights, may be constituted a reserved forest subject to completion of notification and settlement procedures provided under the Act.

— Prohibited activities include: making fresh clearings or breaking up land for cultivation; kindling or carrying fire; trespass and cattle grazing; felling or otherwise damaging any tree; quarrying stone, burning lime or charcoal; removing forest produce; and hunting, shooting, fishing, trapping and poisoning water.

Village forest

— Any land constituted as reserved forest that has been assigned to a village community by the Government.
— Rules for regulating the provision of timber, other forest produce or pasture to the community, and their duties for protecting and improving such forest may be prescribed by the Government.
— All provisions of the Act relating to reserved forest apply to village forest, in so far as they are consistent with the rules.

Protected forest

— Any forest land or wasteland not included in a reserved forest and belonging to the Government, or to which it has proprietary rights, may be declared a protected forest provided that the nature and extent of rights of Government and of private persons in or over such land have been recorded.
— Any trees or class of trees may be reserved; any portion of forest may be closed for up to 30 years; and quarrying of stone, burning of lime or charcoal, collection and removal of any forst produce, and breaking up or clearing of any land for any purpose may be prohibited.
— Rules may be made to regulate collection and removal of forest produce, granting of licences to inhabitants of nearby settlements to remove forest products for domestic consumption, granting of licences for commercial extraction of forest products, clearing or breaking up of land for cultivation or other purposes, and the protection from fire of timber lying in such forests and of trees reserved under the Act.

Source: Original legislation

32

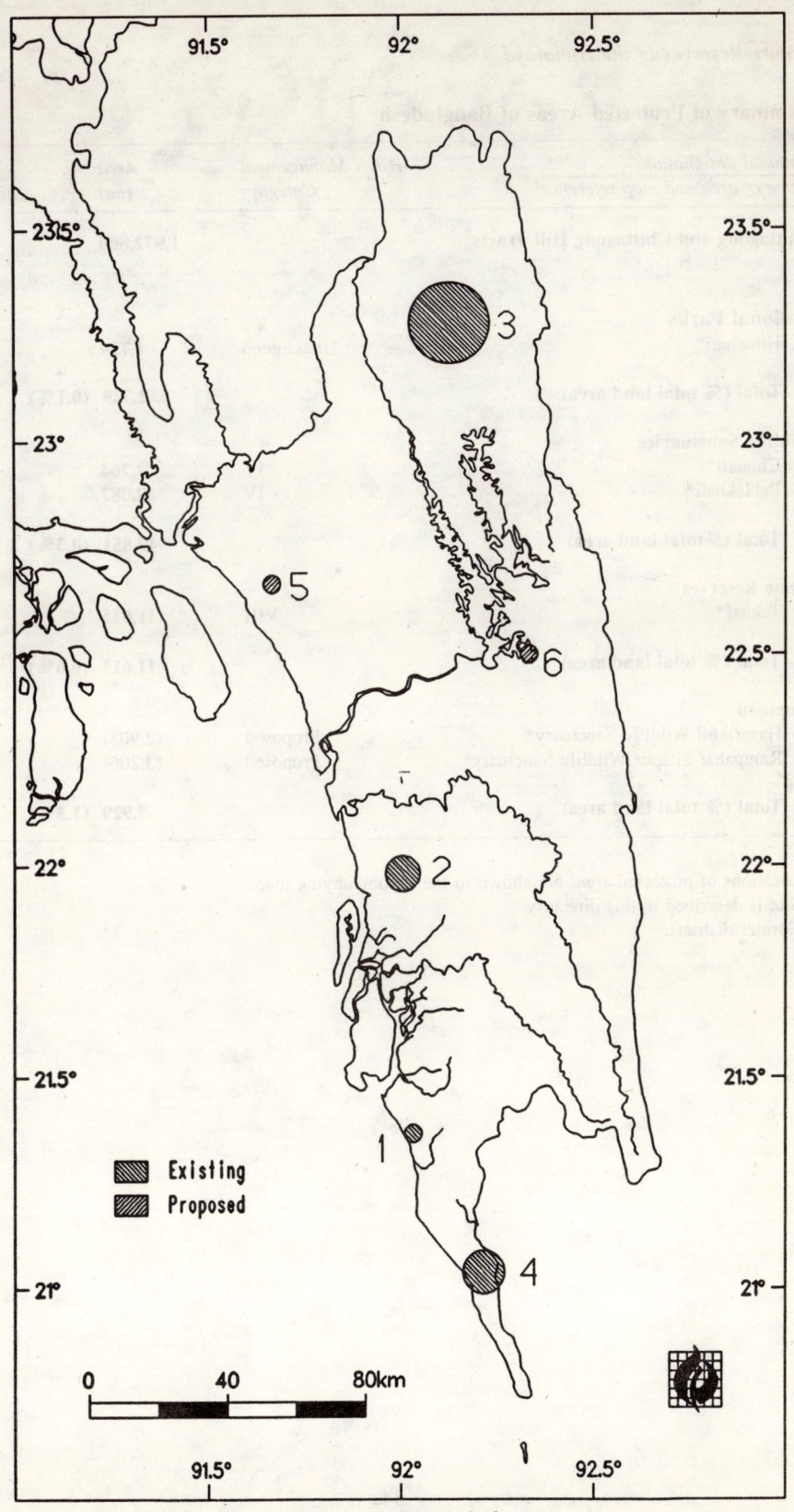

Eastern Bangladesh

Summary of Protected Areas of Bangladesh

National designation Name of area and map reference[+]	IUCN Management Category	Area (ha)	Year notified
Chittagong and Chittagong Hill Tracts[#]		**1,972,800**	
National Parks			
1. Himchari*	Unassigned	1,729	1980
Total (% total land area)		**1,729 (0.1%)**	
Wildlife Sanctuaries			
2. Chunati*	IV	7,764	1986
3. Pablakhali*	IV	42,087	1938
Total (%total land area)		**49,851 (0.3%)**	
Game Reserves			
4. Teknaf*	VIII	11,615	1983
Total (% total land area)		**11,615 (0.6%)**	
Proposed			
5. Hazarikhil Wildlife Sanctuary*	Proposed	(2,903)	
6. Rampahar-Sitapur Wildlife Sanctuary*	Proposed	(3,206)	
Total (% total land area)		**5,929 (1.5%)**	

[+] Locations of protected areas are shown in the accompanying map.
* Site is described in this directory.
[#] Former districts.

CHUNATI WILDLIFE SANCTUARY

IUCN Management Category   IV (Managed Nature Reserve)

Biogeographical Province   4.04.01 (Burman Rainforest)

Geographical Location   Lies about 70 km south of Chittagong Port, Chittagong and Cox's Bazaar districts. The eastern boundary is formed by the Chittagong–Cox's Bazaar Highway. 22°08′–22°53′N, 91°58′–92°05′E

Date and History of Establishment   Formerly part of the reserved forests of Chittagong Forest Division, the area was designated a wildlife sanctuary on 8 March 1986 (Notification no. XII/For-I/84/174).

Area   7,763.97 ha

Land Tenure   State

Altitude   Up to 90 m

Physical Features   The sanctuary is bisected along its north–south axis by a range of hills, some 60–90 m high. Spurs projecting from this range are separated by deep ravines. The area is drained by four major streams.

Climate   No information

Vegetation   The area used to support subtropical semi-evergreen forest, dominated by garjan *Dipterocarpus* spp. Associates were ratkan *Lophopetalum* spp., jam *Syzygum* spp., uriam *Mangifera* spp., chapalish *Artocarpus* spp., simul *Salmalva* spp., korai *Albizia* spp. and toon *Cedrela* spp. Bamboos and grasses were profuse. Much of the original vegetation has been heavily disturbed through commercial exploitation, illegal felling and encroachment (Jalil, n.d.).

Fauna   Wildlife populations are depleted due to heavy disturbance to the habitat. Some 26 species of mammals are reportedly present, including rhesus macaque *Macaca mulatta*, common langur *Presbytis entellus*, Hoolock gibbon *Hylobates hoolock* (V), dhole *Cuon alpinus* (V), fox *Vulpes bengalensis*, leopard *Panthera pardus* (T), tiger *P. tigris* (E), Indian elephant *Elephas maximus* (E), Indian muntjac *Muntiacus muntjak* and sambar *Cervus unicolor* (Ahmed, n.d.). A resident herd of 15 to 30 elephant is present, as well as a dozen of the nationally rare serow *Capricornis sumatraensis*. Tiger *Panthera tigris* (E), last recorded in 1983, may also be present (IUCN, 1990).

Some 40 species of birds have been recorded, including a variety of birds of prey, pheasants and fish-eating species (Ahmed, n.d.).

Cultural Heritage 'Chuna' means chosen and, according to legend, Chunati was chosen by members of Shah Shuja's caravan who remained in the area while the Prince continued his journey to Arakan to flee from his brother, Aurangzeb. The history of the region has since been recorded in Persian by scholars from the region (Rahman, 1989).

Local Human Population Surrounding areas are settled. About 500 households distributed among 10–12 villages depend on the sanctuary's wood resources as a source of income (IUCN, 1990).

Visitors and Visitor Facilities No information

Scientific Research and Facilities A preliminary inventory of the mammals and birds has been compiled (Ahmed, n.d.).

Conservation Value Chunati lies at the northern edge of one of the most dense tropical rain forests in Bangladesh. It supports a rich flora and fauna and its diminishing resources are vital for the poor and landless (Rahman, 1989; IUCN, 1990).

Conservation Management A citizens committee, known as Pothikrit, was responsible for persuading the government to declare the area a wildlife sanctuary. Since then, Pothikrit has been raising the level of awareness among the poor and landless farmers about the need to conserve forest resources. For example, poor people dependent on the sanctuary's wood resources have been engaged in forestry activities in peripheral areas to plant and raise trees. In time, this may ease pressure on the sanctuary and adjacent forests (Anon., 1990; IUCN, 1990).

Chunati has not been subject to any management regime since its inception. Plans have been drawn up, however, to restore the sanctuary to its original condition but await sanctioning. Priorities include the provision of adequate staffing and quarters, development of pastures and waterholes for wildlife, and construction of visitor facilities (Jalil, n.d.).

Management Constraints Encroachment has been a persistent problem in and around the sanctuary. The forest has been cleared for cultivation by wealthy land-owners. Timber and firewood resources have been legally and illegally extracted for many years, this being the major cause of depletion and loss of wildlife habitat. Timber traders represent a strong vested-interest group and are located near the sanctuary. Impoverished fuelwood gatherers have also traditionally depended on the resources of the sanctuary, as it represents their major source of income, particularly outside the agricultural season. In addition, wildlife is under constant threat from chronic hunting and poaching. The Forest Department has so far proved to be ineffective in arresting deforestation and the decline of wildlife within the sanctuary and, at present, there is no management plan. Unless new management measures are implemented soon, it is anticipated that the sanctuary will be destroyed within 15 years. These constraints are addressed in a project proposed by IUCN (1990) to assess the forest resources in Chunati and the dependence of the local people on them, and to prepare a management plan.

Staff Presently staffed by one honorary wildlife warden but one assistant conservator of forests, one forest ranger, one forester, forest guards and honorary wildlife wardens are proposed (Jalil, n.d.).

Budget No information

Local Addresses Divisional Forest Officer, Chittagong Forest Division

References
Ahmed, M. (n.d.). Introducing the Chunati Wildlife Sanctuary. Forest Research Institute, Chittagong. Unpublished report. 6 pp.
Anon. (1990). Participatory forestry. *Bangladesh Environmental Newsletter* 1(1): 5.
IUCN (1990). Applied research and management plan for Chunati Wildlife Sanctuary, Chittagong. Bangladesh. Project Proposal. 8 pp.
Jalil, S.M. (n.d.). Chunati Game Sanctuary. Chittagong Forest Division. Unpublished report. 4 pp.
Rahman, S.H. (1989). About Pothikrit and Chunati. Unpublished paper presented at the Seminar on Forest Resources Management, Chittagong, February 1989. 4 pp.

HAZARIKHIL WILDLIFE SANCTUARY

IUCN Management Category Proposed

Biogeographical Province 4.04.01 (Burman Rainforest)

Geographical Location Lies in the Ramgarh-Sitakunda forests, 45 km north of Chittagong Port in south-east Bangladesh. 91°40′E, 22°40′N

Date and History of Establishment Proposed as a wildlife sanctuary in 1967. Maintained since the mid-1970s by the Forest Directorate.

Area 2,903 ha. According to a report by the Divisional Forest Officer, the proposed area is 2,033 ha (Olivier, 1979).

Land Tenure State

Altitude Mean altitude is 350 m.

Physical Features The terrain is irregular, comprising ridges from which numerous spurs protrude in various directions. Soils vary from clay to clay-loam on level ground, and from sandy loam to coarse sand on the hills. The sandy soil is often impregnated with iron.

Climate Conditions are moist tropical. Mean annual rainfall is 3000 mm, falling mainly between June and September (Sarker and Fazlul Huq, 1985).

Vegetation Comprises evergreen and semi-evergreen forests. Predominant tree species are *Dipterocarpus* spp., *Artocarpus chaplasha*, *Tetrameles nudiflora*, *Cedrela toona*, *Mesua ferrea*, *Eugenia* spp., *Ficus* spp., and *Albizia procera*. The undergrowth is dominated by bamboos and *Eupatorium odoratum* (Sarker and Fazlul Huq, 1985).

Fauna   Mammals known to be present include rhesus macaque *Macaca mulatta*, capped langur *Presbytis pileata*, dhole *Cuon alpinus* (V), sloth bear *Melursus ursinus* (I), wild boar *Sus scrofa*, and Indian muntjac *Muntiacus muntjak* (Sarker and Fazlul Huq, 1985). Hoolock gibbon *Hylobates hoolock* (V), leopard *Panthera pardus* (T), and Phayre's leaf monkey *Presbytis phayrei* may also be present (Olivier, 1979), as may sambar *Cervus unicolor* (S.M. Saheed, pers. comm., 1989). Indian python *Python molurus* (V) is reported to be present but low in number (Sarker and Fazlul Huq, 1985).

Cultural Heritage   No information.

Local Human Population   No information.

Visitors and Visitor Facilities   No information.

Scientific Research and Facilities   Limited census of the wildlife has been undertaken (Olivier, 1979).

Conservation Value   The area is reportedly rich in wildlife (Olivier, 1979).

Conservation Management   Though not yet notified a wildlife sanctuary, forestry operations have been suspended (Sarker and Fazlul Huq, 1985) and some 12 km of the boundary demarcated (Olivier, 1979).

Management Constraints   No information.

Staff   Quarters for staff have been constructed (Olivier, 1979) but the present level of staffing is not known.

Budget   No information

Local Addresses   No information.

References
Olivier, R.C.D. (1979). *Wildlife conservation and management in Bangladesh*. UNDP/FAO Project BGD/72/005. FAO, Forest Research Institute, Chittagong. 121 pp.
Sarker, N.M. and Fazlul Huq, A.K.M. (1985). Country report on national parks, wildlife sanctuaries and game reserves of Bangladesh. Prepared for the 25th Working Session of IUCN's Commission on National Parks and Protected Areas. Corbett National Park, India. 4–8 February 1985. 5 pp.

HIMCHARI NATIONAL PARK

IUCN Management Category   Unassigned.

Biogeographical Province   4.04.01   (Burman Rainforest).

Geographical Location Lies 1.5 km to the south of Cox's Bazar township in the Chittagong Hill Tracts. Forms part of Cox's Bazaar Peninsular Reserved Forest. 21°22'N, 92°02'E

Date and History of Establishment Declared a national park in 1980 under the Bangladesh Wildlife (Preservation) (Amendment) Act 1974. Previously established as a reserved forest under the Forest Act 1927 and subsequently declared a game reserve, with an area of 2,331 ha.

Area 1,729 ha

Land Tenure State

Altitude No information

Physical Features The terrain is irregular with steep-sided hills aligned in a north-to-south direction, and bounded on the west by the Bay of Bengal. Soils comprise clay loams and loams on hills, and sands along beaches.

Climate Conditions are moist, humid and maritime, with little temperature variation. Rainfall is high, falling mainly between May and October.

Vegetation Characteristically comprises tropical semi-evergreen forest, which is dense and multi-storeyed. Deciduous trees predominate in the upper canopy, common species including *Albizia procera*, *Artocarpus chaplasha*, *Salmalia malabarica* and *Sterculia alata*. The sub-canopy is dominated by a great variety of evergreen species including *Quercus*, *Castanopsis*, *Eugenia*, *Lannea*, *Lagerstroemia* and *Amoora* spp. The undergrowth consists mainly of bamboo (Sarker and Fazlul Huq, 1985).

Fauna Mammals include gibbon *Hylobates hoolock* (V), capped langur *Presbytis pileatus*, rhesus macaque *Macaca mulatta*, leopard *Panthera pardus* (T), dhole *Cuon alpinus* (V), leopard cat *Felis bengalensis*, jungle cat *F. chaus*, fishing cat *F. viverrina*, sloth bear *Melursus ursinus* (I), elephant *Elephas maximus* (E), Indian muntjac *Muntiacus muntjak*, and wild boar *Sus scrofa* (Sarker and Fazlul Hug, 1985). Hog-badger *Arctonyx collaris* and pangolin *Manis* sp. may also be present (S.M. Saheed, pers. comm., 1989). There are many species of birds. The reptile fauna is rich and includes Indian python *Python molurus* (V) (Sarker and Fazlul Huq, 1985).

Cultural Heritage No information.

Local Human Population No information

Visitors and Visitor Facilities No information

Scientific Research and Facilities No information

Conservation Value Limited due to the poor quality of the habitat and its isolation (Olivier, 1979).

Conservation Management Blocks 34, 35 and 37 (totalling 2,331 ha) were originally recommended as a 'Class A' national park (Government of East Pakistan, 1971). In the event,

Blocks 35 and 37, which still contained commercially valuable forest, were rejected in favour of Blocks 30, 32 and 33, which consisted of poor-stature, partially-logged, semi-swamp forest whose further exploitation had been abandoned. Thus, not only does the area afford poor habitat for wildlife, but it is isolated from all other forests within the division (Oliver, 1979). A development scheme prepared for the park and to be executed by the Divisional Forest Officer has not yet been approved (Sarker and Fazlul Huq, 1985).

Management Constraints   The park is encroached by hundreds of villagers entering daily to cut timber (Rashid, 1990).

Staff   No information

Budget   No information

Local Addresses   Divisional Forest Officer, Cox's Bazaar Forest Division

References
Government of East Pakistan (1971). Report of the Technical Sub- committee for East Pakistan of the Wildlife Enquiry Committee. Dacca.
Olivier, R.C.D. (1979). *Wildlife conservation and management in Bangladesh*. UNDP/FAO Project BGD/72/005. FAO, Forest Research Institute, Chittagong. 121 pp.
Rashid, H. Er (1990). Note on an environmental study visit to Cox's Bazar in February 1990. Unpublished. Polli Unnayan Sangstha, Dhaka. 5 pp.
Sarker, N.M. and Fazlul Huq, A.K.M. (1985). Country report on national parks, wildlife sanctuaries and game reserves of Bangladesh. Prepared for the 25th Working Session of IUCN's Commission on National Parks and Protected Areas. Corbett National Park, India. 4–8 February 1985. 5 pp.

PABLAKHALI WILDLIFE SANCTUARY

IUCN Management Category   IV (Managed Nature Reserve)

Biogeographical Province   4.09.04 (Burma Monsoon Forest)

Geographical Location   Lies at the northern end of Kaptai Reservoir in the south-eastern part of Kassalong Reserve Forest in the Chittagong Hill Tracts, some 112 km from Rangamati Town. The western boundary is formed by Kassalong River. 23°08′N, 92°16′E

Date and History of Establishment   Declared a wildlife sanctuary in 1983 under the Bangladesh Wildlife (Preservation) (Amendment) Act 1974. First established as a game sanctuary in June 1962.

Area   42,087 ha

Land Tenure   State

Altitude   Ranges from 100 m to 300 m.

Physical Features   The topography comprises a complex of hills and valleys aligned north–south, with spurs branching from the ridges. The hills are rugged and steeply sloping to the north, and smaller with gentler slopes to the south. Some 3,885 ha in Working Unit I have been under water since 1963, following the construction of a dam at Kaptai as part of the Karnafuli hydro-electric project (Olivier, 1979). Soils are typically clay or clay loams in the valleys, and pale brown to yellow-red (acidic) clay loams and loams in the hills with localised concretions of iron-manganese.

Climate   Conditions are typically sub-tropical with a long dry season lasting from November to May. Mean annual rainfall is 2500 mm. Mean temperature ranges from 23 °C in December to 35 °C in May. Humidity is high throughout the year.

Vegetation   Three forest types can be distinguished. Tropical wet evergreen forest commonly occurs in valleys and on sheltered slopes with a plentiful water supply. The irregular canopy, characterised by emergent trees, is dense and rich in species. Typical trees include civit *Swintonia floribunda*, garjan *Dipterocarpus* spp., *Pterygota alata*, *Quercus* spp. and *Castanopsis* spp. Tropical semi-evergreen forest, the most extensive forest type in the sanctuary, includes a significant proportion of deciduous canopy species. The predominant tree genera are *Dipterocarpus*, *Mangifera*, *Amoora*, *Cinnamomum*, *Syzygium*, *Tetrameles*, *Artocarpus*, *Salmalia*, and *Albizia*. Tropical moist deciduous forest is confined to new alluvial areas near rivers and streams. The trees are scattered and interspersed with extensive patches of *khagra* and *nal* grassland and stands of wild banana. Characteristic tree genera include *Albizia*, *Salmalia*, *Terminalia* and *Ficus*. Bamboo grows beneath the canopy of all three forest types (Sarker and Fazlul Huq, 1985).

Fauna   According to reports in old district gazetteers, Kassalong Valley used to be rich in wildlife, with tiger *Panthera tigris* (E), two species of rhinoceros Rhinocerotidae spp., gaur *Bos gaurus* (V) and banteng *B. javanicus* (V) present in the 19th and early 20th centuries. Tiger, gaur and banteng were last seen in the early 1970s (Khan, 1985), but tiger and also leopard *Panthera pardus* (T) are reported to still occur (Sarker and Fazlul Huq, 1985). Most important is the small population of Asian elephant *Elephas maximus* (E) that commonly uses the southern part of the sanctuary, probably because of the mosaic of habitats and permanent water supply (Olivier, 1979). Many other large mammals are present, including rhesus macaque *Macaca mulatta*, capped langur *Presbytis pileata*, Hoolock gibbon *Hylobates hoolock* (V), dhole *Cuon alpinus* (V), small cats, otters and wild boar *Sus scrofa* (Sarker and Fazlul Huq, 1985), and also Indian muntjac *Muntiacus muntjak*, and sambar *Cervus unicolor* (Olivier, 1979). Hague (1989) lists 61 species of mammals recorded in the late 1970s.

Some 133 bird species have been recorded from the sanctuary (Husain, 1975). This total includes 25 species previously reported by Mountfort (1969). Following the formation of Kaptai Reservoir and with the continuing reduction of former wintering grounds in Sylhet and Mymensingh, the sanctuary supports increasing numbers of resident and migratory waterfowl (Olivier, 1979), notably little grebe *Tachybaptus ruficollis*, a variety of herons and egrets, common moorhen *Gallinula chloropus*, common coot *Fulica atra* and Asian openbill stork *Anastomus oscitans* (Scott, 1989). White-winged wood duck *Cairina scutulata* (V) used to be common but the population has declined in recent years, most probably due to systematic clear-felling of primary forest and its replacement with commercially viable timber species (Khan, 1986). Some five pairs were present up to 1979, but the status of the species has since become uncertain owing to political disturbances (Khan, 1985). Khan (1986) estimates there to be some 20 pairs within an area of 240 sq. km in and around the sanctuary.

Of the reptiles, Indian python *Python molurus* (V) is common (Sarker and Fazlul Huq, 1985).

Cultural Heritage   No information.

Local Human Population   Part of the sanctuary has been allotted to settlers from the plains. Rebel tribal groups operate in the area (Khan, 1985).

Visitors and Visitor Facilities   Access to the Chittagong Hill Tracts has been restricted since 1982 for security reasons. There are two rest houses.

Scientific Research and Facilities   The elephant population was surveyed by the Forest Directorate in 1978 (Olivier, 1979; Sarker and Fazlul Huq, 1985). The status of white-winged wood duck was first investigated by Husain (1975, 1977) and subsequently by Khan (1986) between 1978 and 1981. Its population dynamics and breeding behaviour were examined by an university student in 1976–7 (Sarker and Fazlul Huq, 1985).

Conservation Value   Pablakhali contains some of the finest lowland forest remaining in Bangladesh and is also an important wetland site (Scott, 1989).

Conservation Management   Under the working plan, due to expire in 1988-9, the sanctuary is divided into two working units. Some 25,900 ha are allotted to Working Unit I, in which wildlife is protected and forestry operations are prohibited. In the remaining area allotted to Working Unit II, it is intended that wildlife preservation proceed alongside normal forestry operations. Working Unit I comprises some 3,885 ha of reservoir, 1,554 ha of teak plantation and 20,461 ha of natural forest. This is nowhere more than 5 km wide and runs north–south along the eastern edge of Working Unit II; to the east is unclassed state forest, which has been heavily disturbed by local hill tribesmen. Conversion of Working Unit II to plantations has been proceeding steadily (Olivier, 1979).

Some 7,770 ha (Compartments 23–30) within Working Unit I were proposed as an elephant sanctuary, but the area was considered far too small and devoid of much suitable habitat. This proposal is thought to have arisen as a result of the Technical Sub-Committee of the Wildlife Enquiry Committee having originally proposed Compartments 23–30 as Pablakhali Wildlife Sanctuary (Olivier, 1979).

Management prescriptions include strict protection of the wildlife and provision of artificial feeding sites, waterholes and salt-licks. It was planned to limit forestry operations to thinning of existing plantations and impose a three-year cycle for the collection of bamboo (Olivier, 1979).

Management Constraints   Few of the original management prescriptions have proved possible to implement. Rice was cultivated beside the reservoir, grass cut for fodder and thatching material, and cattle roamed freely inside the sanctuary. Most serious is the encroachment on the narrow strip of natural forest running north–south. In many places, this had either gone or been reduced to a few hundred metres in width, thereby isolating the smaller southern part of the sanctuary from the rest and threatening the free movement of elephants to and from preferred feeding areas (Olivier, 1979). In the mid-1980s the government began to lease out forest lands, both within the sanctuary and neighbouring areas, to plains-dwellers for settlement at the rate of 2.5 ha per family, as a counter-measure to tribal insurgency. This policy is very detrimental to wildlife, and much encroachment has resulted. Locals hunted white-winged wood ducklings with dogs in 1981 and this practice may be continuing (Khan, 1986).

Staff No information

Budget No information

Local Addresses Divisional Forestry Officer, Chittagong Hill Tracts (North) Forest Division.

References
Haque, M.N. (1989). The mammalian fauna of Pablakhali Wildlife Sanctuary. In: Karim, G.M.M.E., Akonda, A.W. and Sewitz, P. (Eds.), *Conservation of wildlife in Bangladesh*. German Cultural Institute/Forest Department/Dhaka University/Wildlife Society of Bangladesh/Unesco, Dhaka. Pp. 133–9.
Husain, K.Z. (1975). Birds of Pablakhali Wildlife Sanctuary. (The Chittagong Hill Tracts). *Bangladesh Journal of Zoology* 3: 155–7.
Husain, K.Z. (1977). The white-winged wood duck. *Tiger paper* 4(1): 6–8.
Khan, M.A.R. (1985). Future conservation directions for Bangladesh. In: Thorsell, J.W. (Ed.) *Conserving Asia's natural heritage: the planning and management of protected areas in the Indomalayan Realm*. IUCN, Gland, Switzerland and Cambridge, UK. Pp. 114–22.
Khan, M.A.R. (1986). The threatened white-winged wood duck *Cairina scutulata* in Bangladesh. *Forktail* 2: 97–101.
Mountfort, G. (1969). *The vanishing jungle*. Collins, London. 286 pp.
Olivier, R.C.D. (1979). *Wildlife conservation and management in Bangaladesh*. UNDP/FAO Project BGD/72/005. FAO, Forest Research Institute, Chittagong. 121 pp.
Sarker and Fazlul Huq, A.K.M. (1985). Country report on national parks, wildlife sanctuaries and game reserves of Bangladesh. Prepared for the 25th Working Session of IUCN's Commission on National Parks and Protected Areas. Corbett National Park, India. 4–8 February 1985. 5 pp.

RAMPAHAR-SITAPAHAR WILDLIFE SANCTUARY

IUCN Management Category Proposed

Biogeographical Province 4.04.01 (Burman Rainforest)

Geographical Location Lies 48 km north-east of Chittagong Port. Approximately 22°30'N, 92°20'E

Date and History of Establishment Presently classified as reserved forest, Rampahar-Sitapahar has not yet been designated a wildlife sanctuary under the Bangladesh Wildlife (Preservation)(Amendment) Act 1974 but has been maintained as such by the Forest Department since 1973 (Sarker and Fazlul Huq, 1985).

Area 3,026 ha

Land Tenure State

Altitude   No information.

Physical Features   Comprises low, gently sloping hills which are steeper in Sitapahar block than Rampahar block. The Karnaphuli River flows through the area. Soils are clays or clayey loams in valley bottoms and mostly pale brown (acidic) clay loams and loams on hills (Sarker and Fazlul Huq, 1985).

Climate   Conditions are typically sub-tropical with a long dry season from October to May. Mean temperatures vary from 24 °C in December to 35 °C in May. Mean annual rainfall is 2500 mm.

Vegetation   Comprises evergreen and semi-evergreen forests. Predominant tree species are *Dipterocarpus* spp., *Artocarpus chaplasha*, *Tetrameles nudiflora*, *Cedrela toona*, *Mesua ferrea*, *Eugenia* spp., *Ficus* spp., and *Albizia procera* (Sarker and Fazlul Huq, 1985).

Fauna   Mammals include capped langur *Presbytis pileatus*, sloth bear *Melursus ursinus* (I), Indian muntjac *Muntiacus muntjak* and sambar *Cervus unicolor*. Reptiles include python *Python molurus* (V) (Sarker and Fazlul Huq, 1985).

Cultural Heritage   No information

Local Human Population   No information.

Visitors and Visitor Facilities   No information

Scientific Research and Facilities   No information

Conservation Value   No information

Conservation Management   Maintained as virgin forest by the Forest Department.

Management Constraints   No information.

Staff   No information

Budget   No information

Local Addresses   No information

References
Sarker, N.M. and Fazlul Huq, A.K.M. (1985). Country report on national parks, wildlife sanctuaries and game reserves of Bangladesh. Prepared for the 25th Working Session of IUCN's Commission on National Parks and Protected Areas. Corbett National Park, India. 4–8 February 1985. 5 pp.

TEKNAF GAME RESERVE

IUCN Management Category   VIII (Multiple Use Management Area)

Biogeographical Province   4.04.01 (Burman Rainforest)

Geographical Location   Lies 80 km south of Cox's Bazaar in the Teknaf Peninsula of south-eastern Bangladesh. Stretches from Thainkhali in the north to Teknaf township in the south, all of which is within Cox's Bazaar Forest Division. 21°00'N, 92°20'E

Date and History of Establishment   Teknaf is a reserved forest which was declared a game reserve in 1983 under the Bangladesh Wildlife (Preservation) (Amendment) Act 1974. It includes an area formerly referred to as the Thainkhali Game Reserve (7,770 ha) (Government of Bangladesh, 1973).

Area   11,615 ha

Land Tenure   State

Altitude   Ranges from 5 m to 700 m.

Physical Features   The terrain is rugged, with undulating hills aligned in a north-to-south direction and bordering the Bay of Bengal to the west. Soils on the hills are predominantly pale brown (acidic) clay loams and loams developed from shales and siltstones. Perennial water courses, known as 'charas', in the forested hilly areas are the only dependable source of water for elephants in the vicinity.

Climate   Moist tropical maritime conditions prevail, with a mean annual rainfall of 4060 mm and mean humidity of 81.2% (Khan and Rashid, 1983).

Vegetation   Comprises evergreen and semi-evergreen secondary forests, which have regenerated following clear-felling, and teak *Tectona grandis* plantations. The tropical wet evergreen forest is characterised by chapalish *Artocarpus chaplasha*, telsur *Hopea odorata*, chundul *Tetrameles nudiflora*, pitraj *Amoora wallichii*, uriam *Mangifera longipes*, civit *Swintonia floribunda*, toon *Toona ciliata* and jam *Syzygium* spp. It is now confined to deep valleys and shaded slopes with good water supplies. The dense multi-storeyed semi-evergreen forest, typical of the peninsula, ranges in height from 20 m to 45 m. The top canopy, which includes several deciduous species, is characterised by baitta garjan *Dipterocarpus scaber*, telya garjan *D. turbinatus*, dulya garjan *D. alatus*, koroi *Albizia procera*, chukka k'oroi *A. chinensis*, chapalish, uriam, civit, shimul *Bombax ceiba* and *B. insigne*, bandarholla *Duabanga grandiflora*, and narikeli *Sterculia alata*. The second storey is dominated by evergreens, such as batna *Quercus* sp., jam, *Castanopsis* sp., jarul *Lagerstroemia speciosa*, bena *Macaranga denticulata*, kamdeb *Calophyllum polyanthum*, hargoza *Dillenia pentagyna*, dharmara *Pterospermum personatum*, moos *P. paniculata*, *Sterculia villosa*, *S. colorata*, konak *Schima wallichii*, nageshwar *Mesua ferrea*, bahera *Terminalia bellerica*, haritaki *T. chebula*, champa *Michelia champaca*, gamar *Gmelina arborea*, and bot *Ficus* spp. Saplings predominate below the second storey, together with adaliya *Meliosma pinnata*, naricha *Musa ramentacea*, dormala *Callicarpa arborea*, goda *Vitex glabrata*, kestoma and kechua *Glochidion* spp., sheora *Streblus asper*, jalpai *Elaeocarpus* spp. and bela *Semicarpus anacardium*. The undergrowth of both evergreen and semi-evergreen forests is dominated by bamboo, the commonest species being muli *Melocannia bambusoides*, mitenga *Bambusa tulda*, kaliserri *Oxytenanthera auriculata*, daloo *Teinostachyum dulooa* and orah *Dendrocalamus longispathus* (Khan and Rashid, 1983).

Fauna   Teknaf Peninsula still has quite a rich fauna. Moreover, it provides a vital refuge for elephant *Elephas maximus* (E), estimated in 1982–3 to number 101, of which 71 resided within an area of 55,000 ha and the rest came from the Arakan area of Burma (Reza Khan and Rashid, 1983). Other mammals include rhesus macaque *Macaca mulatta*, capped langur *Presbytis pileata*, Hoolock gibbon *Hylobates hoolock* (V), sloth bear *Melursus ursinus* (I), hog-badger *Arctonyx collaris*, crab-eating mongoose *Herpestes urva*, civets (Viverridae), small cats *Felis* spp., flying squirrel *Petaurista* sp. and Malayan giant squirrel *Ratufa bicolor* (Khan, 1985a). Ungulates present in that part of the park which used to be known as Thainkhali Game Reserve include Indian muntjac *Muntiacus muntjak*, sambar *Cervus unicolor* and wild boar *Sus scrofa* (Olivier, 1979). Leopard *Panthera pardus* (T) and possibly dhole *Cuon alpinus* (V), are also present (Olivier, 1979).

The avifauna is diverse and includes kalij pheasant *Lophura leucomelana*, fruit pigeons, hornbills and woodpeckers (Khan, 1985a).

Reptiles include Malayan box turtle *Cuora amboinensis*, uncommon in Bangladesh, Indian python *Python molurus* (V), and monitor *Varanus* sp. (Khan, 1985a).

Cultural Heritage   No information

Local Human Population   There are 25 to 30 villages within the forests of the Peninsula and some 50 villages on their peripheries. Local people, who are largely dependent on forest resources for their livelihood, grow rice, millet, vegetables and pan in the valleys (Khan and Rashid, 1983).

Visitors and Visitor Facilities   The reserve has potential for tourism, particularly since Cox's Bazaar, renowned as being the only health resort in the country, is a tourist centre (Khan and Rashid, 1983). There are two rest houses in the vicinity, at Inoni and Teknaf (Olivier, 1979).

Scientific Research and Facilities   The elephant population was studied between May 1982 and April 1983 (IUCN/WWF Project 3038) and a management strategy developed to conserve the species (Khan and Rashid, 1983).

Conservation Value   Teknaf Peninsula contains the most important tracts of evergreen and semi-evergreen forests in south-eastern Bangladesh (Khan and Rashid, 1983) and about one third of the country's total elephant population, estimated at 300 animals (Khan, 1985b). The Peninsula is also an important wetland site (Scott, 1989), although the wetlands themselves lie outside the reserve.

Conservation Management   The reserve was established to protect the elephant population, but the Forest Department continues its operations in the area. Preliminary recommendations for elephant management include: replacing clear-felling with selective felling; replanting cleared areas with indigenous species of trees; establishing corridors to facilitate movement of elephants and other wildlife between cleared areas; and controlling encroachment, grazing by livestock and extraction of bamboo (Khan and Rashid, 1983).

Management Constraints   There has been considerable pressure on minor forest products from the coastal people who either fished or grew pan *Piper betle*. Removal of the forest understorey, to meet local demands for timber, firewood and bamboo, has interfered with natural regeneration. Large areas of forest have been turned into plantations (teak) and, since 1976, Burmese refugee camps have had a severe local impact on forests (Womersley, 1979). Most accessible areas on the Peninsula have been clear-felled or subjected to shifting cultivation, with the result that little virgin forest remains. Regeneration is hindered, due to the pressure of livestock and other forms of disturbance, and the vegetation is changing towards a drier scrub-forest or savannah, characterised by sungrass *Imperata cylindrica*, bhat *Clerodendrum infortunatum*, *Lantana camara*, *Eupatorium odoratum*, *Melostoma* sp. and others. The main elephant food, bamboo, has largely been extracted and replaced by unpalatable plants, such as *Lantana* and *Eupatorium*. This has probably been responsible for the increased raiding of crops, particularly by solitary elephants. Oil palm has recently been introduced to a 4,000 ha area but is damaged by migratory elephants and, to a much greater extent, by porcupines. In 1978–83, over 400 ha of forested land was encroached by villagers with the authority of the Forest Department and others. Bamboo is extracted at an estimated rate of 10,000 canes per week, and some 8,000 cattle and water buffalo are taken daily into the forests for grazing, except possibly from January to April (Khan and Rashid, 1983).

Staff   Forest guards.

Budget   No information

Local Addresses   No information

References
Government of Bangladesh (1973). Development of wildlife management and game reserves. Forest Department, Dacca.

Olivier, R.C.D. (1979). *Wildlife conservation and management in Bangladesh*. UNDP/FAO Project BGD/72/005. FAO, Forest Research Institute, Chittagong. 121 pp.

Khan, M.A.R. (1985a). Future conservation directions for Bangladesh. In: Thorsell, J.W. (Ed.) *Conserving Asia's natural heritage: the planning and management of protected areas in the Indomalayan Realm*. IUCN, Gland, Switzerland and Cambridge, UK. Pp. 114–24.

Khan, M.A.R. (1985b). *Mammals of Bangladesh*. Nazma Reza, Dhaka. 92 pp.

Khan, M.A.R. and Rashid, S.M.A. (1983). Development of an elephant management plan for the Cox's Bazar Forest of Bangladesh. Report to WWF/IUCN, Gland. Unpublished. 13 pp.

Sarker, N.M. and Fazlul Huq, A.K.M. (1985). Country report on national parks, wildlife sanctuaries and game reserves of Bangladesh. Prepared for the 25th Working Session of IUCN's Commission on National Parks and Protected Areas. Corbett National Park, India. 4–8 February 1985. 5 pp.

Scott, D.A. (Ed.) (1989). *A Directory of Asian wetlands*. IUCN, Gland, Switzerland and Cambridge, UK.

Womersley, J.S. (1979). *Botanic Garden Dacca, commercial horticultural forest botany and national parks*. UNDP/FAO Project BGD/72/005. FAO, Forest Research Institute, Chittagong. 71 pp.

WWF/IUCN (n.d.) Project No. 3033. Bangladesh, Cox's Bazar Forest, elephant management plan.. Unpublished.

BHUTAN

Area   46,620 sq. km

Population   1,600,000 (1990)   Natural increase 2.1% per annum

GNP   US $ 150 per capita (1988)

Policy and Legislation   Government policy on environmental conservation is strong, with the emphasis consistently given to nature conservation and careful management of natural resources.   National development plans have stressed the potential for ecological damage from exploitation of the nation's natural resources, particularly its forests (World Bank, 1988; Blower, 1989). A National Conservation Strategy is being formulated by the newly created National Environment Secretariat, formed under the National Planning Committee (MacKinnon, 1991).

The existing National Forest Policy of 1974 emphasises the importance of maintaining adequate forest cover, with a minimum of 60%, in order to prevent soil erosion and maintain climatic equilibrium.   It recognises the problems caused by grazing and shifting cultivation, and the need to regulate both practices.   A new National Forest Policy was prepared in 1985 at the express command of His Majesty the King, but this has yet to be adopted.   The new policy lays even greater stress on conservation, its basis being that the nation's forest resources should be regarded more in terms of their conservation value and less as a source of revenue. Prescriptions include: designation of all forest land above 2,700 m or on slopes exceeding 60° as protection forest; establishment of a protected areas network (including biosphere reserves) to conserve representative samples of the diverse fauna and flora in their pristine state; control of shifting cultivation and its prohibition on slopes of 45° and more; and the total banning of grazing in forests reserved for protection or conservation (Blower, 1986, 1989).

The Bhutan Forest Act of 1969 is the only legislation covering environmental conservation. Under this Act, all forested land other than any privately owned, is declared as government reserved forest.   Activities prohibited within reserved forest are annexed.   The maximum penalty for any offence under the Forest Act is one month's imprisonment or a fine of Nu. 200 (US $ 13) or both.   There is no specific provision in the Forest Act for the establishment or management of any other category of protected area, although it is mentioned that 'nothing shall be done to fell or damage trees or clear forests in the area of a National Park or Game Sanctuary or the shooting grounds of His Majesty the King.'   Protected areas, other than reserved forests, have been established by notification, notably no. TIF-11/74 of 1 November

1979 under which three wildlife sanctuaries, one game reserve, one national park and three reserved forests were designated. A further six sites were declared under Notification no. TIF/FAO/111-8/83/7049. The provisions of the Forest Act apply to these areas (see Annex), together with additional restrictions. These include: prohibition of entry except for Bhutanese officials or visitors with written permission from the Divisional Forest Officer; felling of trees or cutting of other vegetation, except under the provision of a Forest Department Working Plan; no use of land for agricultural, horticultural or other purposes; and no grazing by domestic cattle without permission from the Forest Department. Penalties prescribed for infringements are up to six months' imprisonment or a fine of up to Nu. 1,000 (US $ 65).

While the present forestry legislation covers many of the essential requirements for conservation, there are serious omissions with respect to such matters as the criteria for different categories of protected area and procedures for their establishment and management. New legislation entitled the Bhutan Wildlife (Protection) Act, based on the Indian Wild Life (Protection) Act, was drafted in 1985 but it was considered to be unnecessarily lengthy and complicated. Blower (1986) recommended that new conservation legislation be formulated to provide the basis for an effective conservation programme. This should take the form of a basic enabling act with more emphasis on the broader aspects of environmental conservation, rather than merely on the protection of wildlife and control of hunting. A new Forest and Nature Conservation Act has since been prepared which will replace the Forest Act of 1969. The new law expands on the forestry policy to include related aspects of wildlife and biological diversity (Adams, 1989). It was due to have been presented to the National Assembly in 1988 (H. Wollenhaupt, pers. comm., 1988).

International Activities   Bhutan is not as yet party to any international convention concerned with protecting natural areas, such as the Convention Concerning the Protection of the World Cultural and Natural Heritage (World Heritage Convention) and Convention on Wetlands of International Importance especially as Waterfowl Habitat (Ramsar Convention), nor does it participate in the Unesco Man and Biosphere Programme.

Administration and Management   The Forest Department, under the Ministry of Agriculture, is responsible for the management of reserved forests in particular. It is headed by a Director-General and divided into various functional divisions (e.g. planning, management) at its headquarters in Thimphu and a number of territorial divisions. These coincide with the administrative districts or Dzongkhags and are headed by a divisional forest officer (Blower, 1989). Forestry has a recent origin in Bhutan, beginning in 1952 with the establishment of the first administrative unit at Samchi. Further divisions were established at Sarbhang in 1961 and Thimphu in 1967 but funding was very limited until the Third Development Plan (1971–6) when forest development activities gathered momentum. A forest guard school was established at Kalikhola in 1971, later shifted to Taba in 1977 and upgraded in 1982 for training foresters. Officials and rangers are trained in India (Tenzing, 1989).

Nature conservation is the responsibility of the Wildlife Division established within the Forest Department in 1984. The Division consists of two wildlife circles, each under the charge of a deputy director. The Northern Wildlife Circle, with its headquarters at Thimphu, is nominally responsible for the whole of northern Bhutan including the vast Jigme Dorji Wildlife Sanctuary. With a staff of only one forest ranger and three guards, this is obviously an impossible task. The Southern Wildlife Circle, based at Sarbhang, is responsible for southern Bhutan, including the management of 10 protected areas. Staff include two forest rangers, nine foresters and 36 guards under the charge of a deputy director. The budget for the

Northern and Southern Wildlife Circles in 1988–9 was Nu. 420,000 (US $ 27,300) and Nu. 1,708,000 (US $ 110,000), respectively. In addition, WWF has contributed US $ 300,000 for the development of Manas Wildlife Sanctuary over a three-year period (Blower, 1989).

The Royal Society for the Protection of Nature is the first non-governmental conservation organisation in the country, established in 1987 with assistance from WWF. Its principal aim is to promote conservation and wise management of natural resources through raising public awareness, instituting programmes and acting as an information centre. Due to the Society's efforts, two areas (Phobjikah Valley and Bomdiling) have been declared by the government as sanctuaries for cranes (Adam, 1989; Bunting, 1989).

The Forest Department is short of trained personnel and this has led to a reduction of field staff in its Wildlife Division from 66 in 1986 to 53 in 1989. The Wildlife Division is so inadequately staffed as to be virtually ineffective as far as the country as a whole is concerned (Blower, 1989).

Systems Reviews   Bhutan is a small kingdom in the Eastern Himalaya similar in size to Switzerland, but with a much wider altitudinal range (200 m to over 7,500 m) and only one-fifth of the population density. There has been almost no industrial development in the country: about 95% of the population is primarily dependent on agriculture and animal husbandry. The Himalayan chain runs along the northern border and the interior of the country is made up of a series of six major north–south aligned mountain ranges. The largest of these, the Black Mountains, rise to nearly 5,000 m and form a substantial physical barrier between eastern and western Bhutan. Four of the seven river valleys merge to form the Manas and all of them flow southwards across the plains of West Bengal and Assam into the Brahmaputra. The enormous altitudinal range and varied climatic conditions are reflected in the country's great ecological diversity, ranging from tropical moist deciduous forest along the southern foothills, through extensive temperate broad-leaved and coniferous forests across the middle of the country, to alpine scrub and meadows up to the permanent snow-line to the north.

Bhutan's most valuable natural resources are its forests and its major river systems. Most of the original forest remains. Analysis of LANDSAT 2 imagery for 1978 shows that some 53% of Bhutan is forested, of which 19% is broad-leaved evergreen forest and 34% coniferous and deciduous. The remaining landcover comprises snow/water/scree (19%) and pasture/scrub/arable (28%) (Sargent, 1985; Sargent et al., 1985). This is lower than the official estimate of 64% forest cover (Negi, 1983), which is based on visual inspection of LANDSAT images without recourse to objective ground surveys (Sargent et al., 1985). There was extensive commercial exploitation of forest resources up until 1979, when logging operatives were nationalised and severe restrictions imposed on the export of timer in the interests of sound forestry management and ecological stability (World Bank, 1984, 1986).

The conservation importance of major rivers (Torsa/Ammo Chu, Paidak/Wong Chu, Sankosh/Mo Chu and Manas) are reviewed by Scott (1989). Rivers are generally rocky and fast-flowing, with marshes restricted to flat valley bottoms in the inner valleys. Most marshes have been drained for agricultural purposes but some of those remaining are internationally important for black-necked crane.

Isolated for centuries by its remote geographic location and latterly by its resistance to outside influence, Bhutan has maintained a relatively pristine environment along with a strong cultural heritage. Following its membership of the United Nations in 1971, a more open foreign policy has emerged but, acutely aware of mistakes made in neighbouring countries and elsewhere, the government has proceeded cautiously with its development programme. Recognising the need to promote economic growth while sustaining the natural resource base, the government has maintained a strong traditional conservation ethic as the basis of its forest and other policies (Bunting, 1989; Tenzing, 1989). In the case of tourism, for example, the number of foreign visitors is strictly limited to minimise erosion of the Bhuddhist culture (Hickman and Edmunds, 1988; Singh, 1989).

Bhutan's oldest protected area is Manas, maintained as a royal hunting reserve for many years prior to being notified a wildlife sanctuary in 1966 and more recently (1988) upgraded to a national park. The bulk of the protected areas network, covering nearly 19% of the country, was established in 1974 and subsequently expanded by a further 2% in 1984. The entire north of Bhutan, comprising nearly 17% of the total area, is protected within the 790,495 ha Jigme Dorji Wildlife Sanctuary. While such provisions are impressive, exceeding those of all other countries in South Asia and many elsewhere, the protected areas system is unevenly distributed, with inadequate representation across the middle of the country. Moreover, the relative conservation value of protected areas varies enormously, as does the effectiveness of their protection (Blower, 1985). The only areas considered to be under any form of effective management in 1986 were Manas and the adjacent Nangyal Wangchuk (now combined within Royal Manas National Park), and Mochu Wildlife Sanctuary (Blower, 1986). These deficiencies are being addressed, partly through various internationally assisted development projects. WWF is presently financing a co-operative nature conservation programme to the extent of Nu. 9,120,000 for the period 1988–93 (Bunting, 1989; Tenzing, 1989). This includes assistance for the institutional development of the Wildlife Division and infrastructural support for Royal Manas National Park. Under the UNDP/FAO Integrated Forest Management and Conservation Project (1987–91), priorities for nature conservation have been identified, including the strengthening of the protected areas system through the establishment of two large protected areas in the middle of the country (Blower, 1989). These and other priorities have been incorporated within a national conservation plan, recently formulated as part of the Master Plan for Forestry Development (MacKinnon, 1991).

Bhutan's natural resources are becoming increasingly threatened. While less pronounced than in other parts of the Himalaya, there is substantial evidence that uplands in Bhutan are being degraded at accelerating rates (Thinley, 1989; Denholm, 1990). The main conservation problem is the conversion of forests to other forms of land use as a result of human settlement, high domestic consumption of fuelwood and timber, shifting cultivation, overgrazing and encroachment, all of which reflect the rising human population (Jackson, 1981; Blower, 1985; Mahat, 1985; Sargent, 1985). Forests are grazed by excessive numbers of domestic livestock and are burnt, while the wildlife is declining due to habitat destruction, grazing competition with domestic livestock and, in some southern areas, organised poaching (Blower, 1985). The southernmost forest belt has been almost completely cleared for human settlement (Mahat, 1985). People are concentrated in the fertile valleys and, in the south-western foothills, at densities approaching an upper limit given present production methods, which are unlikely to change in the near future (Jackson, 1981).

Addresses

Northern Wildlife Circle (Deputy Director of Wildlife), Forest Department, Thimphu (Cable: BHUFOREST; Tel. 22452; Fax: 22395).

Forest Department (Director-General of Forests), Ministry of Agriculture, Royal Government of Bhutan, PO Box 130, Thimphu (Cable: BHUFOREST; Tel. 22487; Fax: 22395).

Royal Society for the Protection of Nature (President), Thimphu (Tel. 22056; Fax: 22578).

References

Adams, J. (1989). Bhutan: right from the start. *World Wildlife Fund Letter* 1989(6): 1–8.

Blower, J.H. (1985). Nature conservation and wildlife management in Bhutan. FAO, Rome. Unpublished. 23 pp.

Blower, J.H. (1986). *Nature conservation in Bhutan: project findings and recommendations.* FO: DP/BHU/83/022. FAO, Rome. 55 pp.

Blower, J.H. (1989). *Nature conservation in northern and central Bhutan.* FO: BHU/85/016. FAO, Rome. 48 pp.

Bunting, B. (1989). A strategy for environmental conservation in Bhutan: a WWF/RGOB cooperative programme. *Tiger Paper* 16(4): 5–12.

Denholm, J. (1990). Bhutan must protect its green health. *Himal* 3(1): 24.

Hickman, K. and Edmunds, T.O. (1988). Tourism in Bhutan: 'The serpent in paradise'. *The Geographical Magazine* 60(11): 18–23.

Jackson, P. (1981). Conservation in Bhutan. Unpublished. 15 pp.

Mahat, G. (1985). Protected areas of Bhutan. In: Thorsell, J.W. (Ed.), *Conserving Asia's natural heritage.* IUCN, Gland, Switzerland. Pp. 26–9.

MacKinnon, J. (1991). National conservation plan for Bhutan. Annex report no.1. *Master Plan for Forestry Development.* Department of Forestry, Royal Government of Bhutan, Thimphu. 94 pp

Sargent, C. (1985). The forests of Bhutan. *Ambio* 14: 75–80.

Sargent, C., Sargent, O., and Parsell, R. (1985). The forests of Bhutan: a vital resource for the Himalaya? *Journal of Tropical Ecology* 1: 265–86.

Scott, D.A. (Ed.) (1989). *A directory of Asian wetlands.* IUCN, Gland, Switzerland and Cambridge, UK. 1,181 pp.

Singh, M.M. (1989). Controlled growth in Bhutan. *Himal* 2(3): 11.

Tenzing, D. (1989). Forestry in Bhutan: policies and programmes. *Forest News* 3(4): 5–9.

Thinley, S. (1989). Upland conservation in Bhutan. *Forest News* 3(4): 10–15.

World Bank (1984). Bhutan, development in a Himalayan kingdom. World Bank, Washington, DC. (Unseen)

World Bank (1986). Bhutan Forestry II Development Project. Preparation Mission Report. FAO/World Bank Co-operative Programme Investment Centre, FAO, Rome. (Unseen)

World Bank (1988). Bhutan, development planning in a unique environment. Report No. 7189-BHU. World Bank, Washington DC. (Unseen)

ANNEX Definitions of protected area designations, as legislated, together with authorities responsible for their administration.

Title (English title): The Bhutan Forest Act

Date: 1 November 1969

Brief description: To amend the law relating to forests, forest produce and the duty leviable on timber and other forest produce.

Administrative authority:
Forest Department (Director-General of Forests)

Designations:
  Reserved forest:
  — Any land under forest to which no person has acquired a permanent, heritable and transferable right of use and occupancy is declared as government reserved forest.
  — Prohibited activities include: any fresh clearing or breaking up of land for cultivation or other purpose; burning or leaving a fire unattended; felling; girdling; tapping, lopping or otherwise injuring any tree; quarrying of minerals, rocks and sand; poisoning water; hunting and fishing, or setting traps or snares; grazing cattle in new plantations, regeneration areas, catchments reserved for supply of drinking water and hydro-electric projects, and such areas as may be restricted by His Majesty's Government.
  — Shifting cultivation is allowed in areas where it was practised prior to issue of this Act, but this concession may be withdrawn if highways or public property are endangered. Fresh clearance for shifting cultivation is strictly prohibited.
  — All forest operations are prohibited within catchments that supply water to townships or are sites of hydro-electric projects.
  — Only His Majesty the King of Bhutan may grant a 'special permit for any forest produce'.
  —Rights and concessions of the local people include: cattle grazing (except in areas defined above., subject to payment of taxes; collection of timber for domestic consumption from dead, dying and fallen trees (or from thinnings aad cuttings if such firewood is not available); and collection of leaf-litter, boulders, stones and sand for domestic consumption provided their removal does not accelerate erosion.

Source: Original legislation.

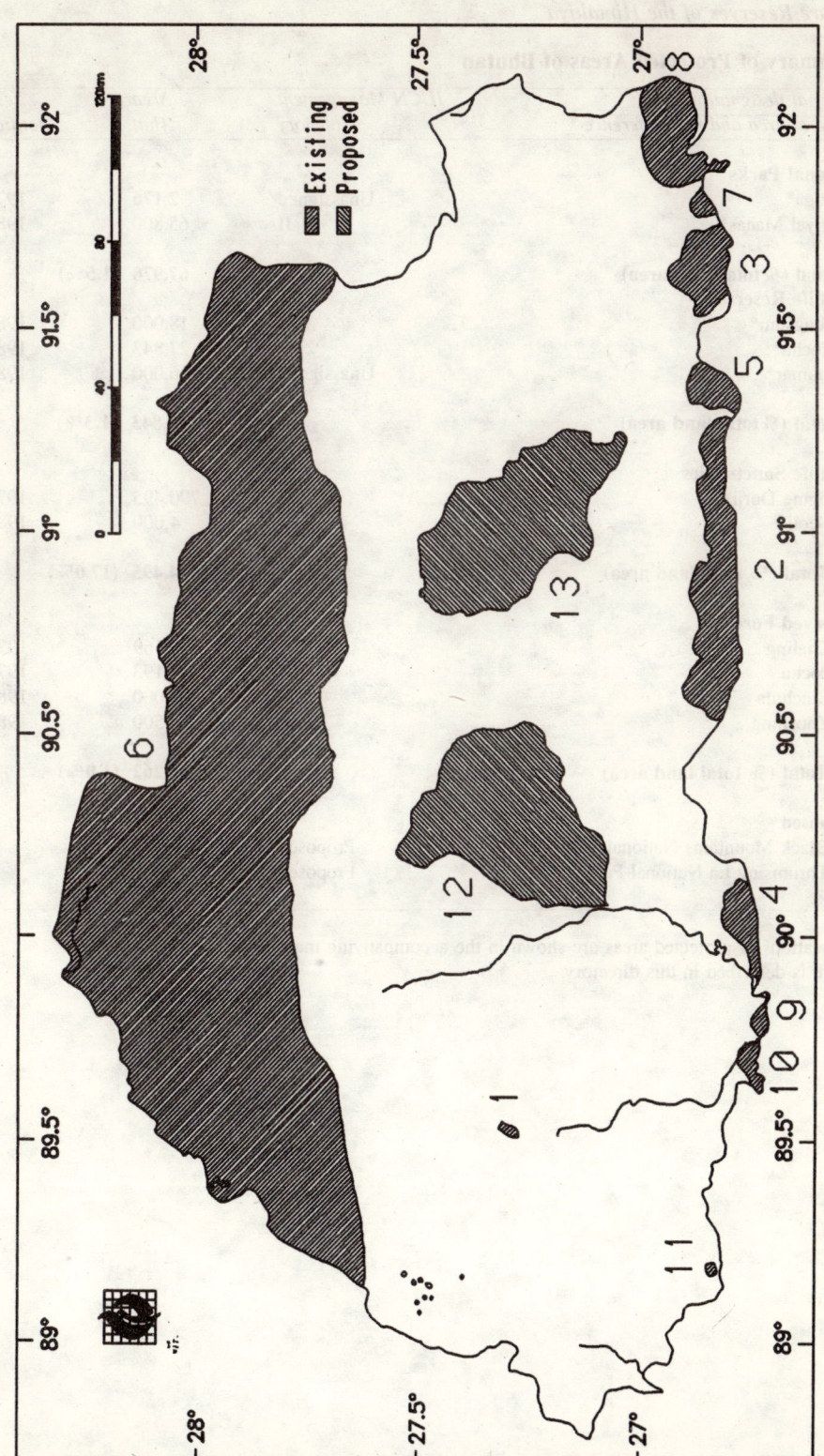

Bhutan

Existing
Proposed

Summary of Protected Areas of Bhutan

National designation Name of area and map reference +	IUCN Management Category	Area (ha)	Year notified
National Parks			
1 Doga*	Unassigned	2,176	1974
2 Royal Manas*	II	65,800	1988
Total (%total land area)		**67,976 (1.5%)**	
Wildlife Reserves			
3 Dungsum*	IV	18,000	1984
4 Mochu*	IV	27,843	1984
5 Shumar*	Unassigned	16,000	1984
Total (%total land area)		**61,843 (1.3%)**	
Wildlife Sanctuaries			
6 Jigme Dorji*	IV	790,495	1974
7 Neoli*	IV	4,000	1984
Total (% total land area)		**794,495 (17.0%)**	
Reserved Forests			
8 Khaling	VIII	23,569	1974
9 Pochu	VIII	14,193	1974
10 Sinchula	VIII	8,000	1984
11 Zhoshing	VIII	500	1984
Total (% total land area)		**46,262 (1.0%)**	
Proposed			
12 Black Mountains National Forest*	Proposed		
13 Thrumsing La National Park	Proposed		

+ Locations of protected areas are shown in the accompanying map.

* Site is described in this directory.

BLACK MOUNTAINS NATIONAL FOREST

IUCN Management Category   Proposed

Biogeographical Province   2.38.12   (Himalayan Highlands)

Geographical Location   Lies in central Bhutan between the Sankosh Chu in the west and the Tongsa in the east. Approximately 27°20'N, 90°25'E

Date and History of Establishment   Mostly classed as reserved forest.

Area   No information

Land Tenure   Land is mostly state owned, but subject to customary rights of grazing and collection of forest produce?

Altitude   Ranges from about 1,500 m to 4,925 m.

Physical Features   The Black Mountains are a southern spur of the main Himalayan range, forming the watershed between the Sankosh to the west and the Mangde Chu to the east. The highest part of the range includes a series of rocky peaks from 3,800 m to over 4,900 m, with some areas of permanent snow (Blower, 1989). The proposed area includes Phobsikha Valley, a wide glacial valley. The entire valley floor is an extensive marsh, perhaps the largest in Bhutan (Scott, 1989).

Climate   Conditions are dry temperate, with a mean annual rainfall of 1000 mm and temperatures ranging from −7 °C to 20 °C. Frosts, low cloud and fog are frequent in winter; snowfall is moderate in winter. Strong winds are common in summer; the rainy season is from June to September (Scott, 1989).

Vegetation   The main vegetation types are broad-leaved semi-evergreen forest on the lower slopes, coniferous forest (blue pine *Pinus wallichiana* is predominant), mixed with birch *Betula* sp. and rhododendron *Rhododendron* sp. on the middle slopes, and extensive alpine pasture and scrub above the tree-line. There is a small amount of subtropical forest rich in palms and *Pandanus* (Blower, 1989). The marsh vegetation of Phobsikha Valley is dominated by *Arundinaria maling* (Scott, 1989).   Wollenhaupt (1988) provides a vegetation map (1:250,000) for Phobsikha Valley.

Fauna   The high altitude fauna is not as varied as that of the main Himalayan range but it includes musk deer *Moschus chrysogaster* and serow *Capricornis sumatraensis*. Other large mammals include Himalayan black bear *Selenarctos thibetanus*, golden leaf monkey *Trachypithecus geei* (R), leopard *Panthera pardus* (T), the occasional tiger *Panthera tigris* (E), numerous wild boar *Sus scrofa*, Indian muntjac *Muntiacus muntjak* and sambar *Cervus unicolor* (Blower, 1989).

Phobsikha Valley is important as one of Bhutan's three known wintering grounds for black-necked crane *Grus nigricollis* (R), with about 100-140 over wintering from October to March. Temminck's tragopan *Tragopan temminckii*, not previously recorded from Bhutan, has been seen in the Upper Hara Chu on the western flanks of the Black Mountains (Blower, 1989).

Cultural Heritage   Gangte Gompa, towards the head of Phobsikha Valley, is an important religious centre (Blower, 1989).

Local Human Population   There are a few settlements in the Phobsikha, Hara and Shiligung valleys.   Terraced (at lower altitudes) and shifting (at higher altitudes) cultivation, and pastoralism are the main forms of land use.   Large numbers of cattle from Bumthang winter in the upper Shiligung Valley.

Visitors and Visitor Facilities   Gangte Gompa attracts large numbers of devotees (Scott, 1989).   There is a guest house in the Phobsikha Valley (Wollenhaupt, 1988).

Scientific Research and Facilities   Observations of black-necked crane have been made by Gole (1987), and Clements and Bradbear (1986).

Conservation Value   The existing protected areas network does not cover the subtropical, temperate and subalpine forests of central Bhutan, which are well-represented in the Black Mountains.   The area also includes important feeding grounds of black-necked crane (Blower, 1989; Scott, 1989).

Conservation Management   The black-necked crane population in Phobsikha Valley is legally protected.   Under the proposed new legislation, it is recommended that the Black Mountains be established as a strictly protected national forest in which limited exploitation of timber and other forest produce would be allowed (Blower, 1989).

Management Constraints   The main problem is overgrazing which in many areas is preventing natural regeneration.   Biga yak pasture in the north-west, for example, is seriously degraded, with severe surface and gully erosion.   Shifting cultivation is spreading up the Hara Valley.   The chir pine *Pinus roxburghii* forest between the lower Hara Chu and Chirang is slowly being destroyed by burning and excessively severe resin tapping (Blower, 1989).

Staff   None.

Budget   None.

Local Addresses   None

References
Blower, J.H. (1989). *Nature conservation in northern and central Bhutan.* FO: BH/85/016. FAO, Rome. 48 pp.
Clements, F.A. and Bradbear, N.J. (1986). Status of wintering black-necked cranes (*Grus nigricollis*) in Bhutan. *Forktail* 2:103–7.
Gole, P. (1981). *Status survey of the black-necked crane wintering in Bhutan: February 1981.* WWF-India Report. Unpublished.

Scott, D.A. (Ed.) (1989). *A directory of Asian wetlands*. IUCN, Gland, Switzerland and Cambridge, UK. 1,181 pp.

Wollenhaupt, H. (1988). Report of a field trip to the wintering area of the black-necked crane (*Grus nigricollis*) in the Phubjekha region (14.3.88–15.3.88). UNDP/FAOForest Management and Conservation Project, Thimphu. Unpublished. 6 pp.

DOGA NATIONAL PARK

IUCN Management Category   Unassigned

Biogeographical Province   4.03.01 (Bengalian Rainforest)

Geographical Location   Lies immediately south of the confluence of the Paro Chu and Thimphu Chu, adjacent to the main Thimphu–Phumtsholing road which follows the Wang Chu and forms the eastern boundary. The western boundary is formed by the road from Ha, via Sira Gampa Chu, to the Paro/Thimphu confluence, and the southern boundary by the Susuna Chu. 27°13′–27°18′N, 89°30′–89°33′E

Date and History of Establishment   1 November 1974

Area   2,176 ha

Land Tenure   State

Altitude   2,000 m to 2,600 m

Physical Features   Occupies part of the west bank of the Wang Chu Valley.

Climate   No information.

Vegetation   Apart from a few scattered patches of blue pine *Pinus wallichiana* forest, the area is largely deforested from burning and overgrazing, and comprises mostly grassland and scrub. Wollenhaupt (1988) provides a vegetation map (1:250,000).

Fauna   Well-known for its population of goral *Nemorhaedus goral*, the park no longer provides a permanent refuge for this species (Wollenhaupt, 1988).

Cultural Heritage   No information

Local Human Population   There are a number of small settlements and timber yards inside the park and much of the landscape is terraced for cultivation.

Visitors and Visitor Facilities   None

Scientific Research and Facilities   None.

Conservation Value   Doga was declared a national park ostensibly for the protection of goral. Why it was designated a national park rather than a wildlife sanctuary, which might have been more appropriate, is not known. The park, which is undemarcated and has no staff, is so degraded as to be of doubtful conservation value. It has been recommended that it should be redesignated as reserved forest and reafforested under the Forest Department's planting programme (Blower, 1986).

Conservation Management   There is no management (Wollenhaupt, 1988).

Management Constraints   The park is almost completely degraded and exploitation of its natural resources remains uncontrolled (Blower, 1986). Logging, cultivating and grazing by livestock are excessive (Wollenhaupt, 1988).

Staff   None

Budget   The total budget for the Northern Wildlife Circle, which is responsible for Doga NP and Jigme Dorji Wildlife Sanctuary, was Nu. 384,000 (US $ 32,000) in 1984–5.

Local Addresses
Deputy Director of Forests, Northern Wildlife Circle, Department of Forestry , Thimpu.

References
Blower, J.H. (1986). *Nature conservation in Bhutan: project findings and recommendations.* FO: DP/BHU/83/022. FAO, Rome. 55 pp.
Wollenhaupt, H. (1988). *Report of a field trip to Doga National Park.* UNDP/FAO Forest Management and Conservation Project, Thimphu. Unpublished. 3 pp.

DUNGSUM WILDLIFE RESERVE

IUCN Management Category   IV (Managed Nature Reserve)

Biogeographical Province   4.09.04 (Burma Monsoon Forest)

Geographical Location   Lies on the Indian border and extends from the Samdrup Jongkhar–Tashingang road in the west to the valley of the Bar Nadi in the east. It is bisected by the Deothang–Bhangtar road. Approximately 26°49′–26°54′N, 91°32′–91°42′E

Date and History of Establishment   13 February 1984

Area   18,000 ha. Lies adjacent to Shumar Wildlife Reserve (16,000 ha).

Land Tenure   State

Altitude   Rises from about 200 m on the Indian border in the south to 1,800 m on the northern boundary.

Physical Features   The terrain is broken and hilly.   A number of perennial streams drain the reserve in a north–south direction, often through steep rock gorges.

Climate   No information.

Vegetation   Moist evergreen/semi-evergreen forest and dry mixed deciduous woodland are extensive on the southernmost foothills (Blower, 1986).

Fauna   The area provides good wildlife habitat for tiger *Panthera tigris* (E), Indian elephant *Elephas maximus* (E), wild boar *Sus scrofa*, Indian muntjac *Muntiacus muntjak*, sambar *Cervus unicolor*, gaur *Bos gaurus* (V), and other large mammals which are reported to be present (Blower, 1986; Mahat, n.d.).

Cultural Heritage   No information.

Local Human Population   There is extensive settlement, particularly along the recently completed Deothang–Bhangtar road (Blower, 1986; Mahat, n.d.).

Visitors and Visitor Facilities   No information.

Scientific Research and Facilities   None.

Conservation Value   The area has good potential for a small national park in view of its fairly extensive areas of excellent forest, large mammals and easy road access from Deothang, provided that it can be saved from further encroachment (Blower, 1986).

Conservation Management   No information.

Management Constraints   Extensive settlement, shifting cultivation and livestock grazing have caused serious damage to parts of the reserve.   Boundaries are undemarcated and no staff are available to protect the area.   The Forest Department is apparently undertaking a timber extraction and land clearance project in the reserve (Blower, 1986).

Staff   None.

Budget   The total budget for the Southern Wildlife Circle in 1984–5, which then administered 10 (including Dungsum) of Bhutan's 12 protected areas, was   Nu. 1,278,000 (US $ 107,350).

Local Addresses
Deputy Director of Forests, Southern Wildlife Circle, Department of Forestry, Sarbhang

References
Blower J.H. (1986). *Nature conservation in Bhutan: project findings and recommendations.* FO: DP/BHU/83/022. FAO, Rome. 55 pp.
Mahat, G. (n.d.).   A study tour of forest belt in southern Bhutan.   Department of Forestry, Thimphu. Unpublished. 10 pp.

JIGME DORJI WILDLIFE SANCTUARY
(INCLUDES LAYA AND GASA WILDLIFE SANCTUARIES)

IUCN Management Category   IV (Managed Nature Reserve)

Biogeographical Province   2.38.12 (Himalayan Highlands)

Geographical Location   Extends over the whole of northern Bhutan up to the border with Tibet in China. The boundaries of the three wildlife sanctuaries are described in the original notification (Royal Government of Bhutan, 1974). 27°30′–28°21′N, 89°08′–91°41′E

Date and History of Establishment   1 November 1974 (Notification no. TIF-11/74). Originally declared as three separate but contiguous wildlife sanctuaries (Laya, Gasa and Jigme Dorji) which later became known collectively as Jigme Dorji Wildlife Sanctuary (Blower, 1986).

Area   790,495 ha. Comprises Laya Wildlife Sanctuary (147,708 ha), Gasa Wildlife Sanctuary (271,795 ha) and Jigme Dorji Wildlife Sanctuary (370,992 ha).

Land Tenure   State

Altitude   Ranges from about 2,000 m to 7,554 m.

Physical Features   Forming part of the Great Himalaya, the sanctuary includes Chomo Lhari (7,314 m) and Kula Kangri (7,554 m) and all other high peaks along the border with China. Perpetual snow, glaciers and barren land above the tree-line constitute 70–80% of the area (Blower, 1985). Bhutan's major rivers rise in the area and flow southwards, eventually draining into the Brahmaputra River south of the border with India.

Climate   There is no meteorological data. In general, rainfall is known to increase eastwards in the Himalaya due to the effects of the south-east monsoon.

Vegetation   Forests, comprising 20–30% of the sanctuary, are found in the upper catchments of the major river systems in the southern sector (Blower, 1985). It is not certain if the area extends into the subtropical zone. Temperate forests, extending from about 2,000 m to 3,000 m, are dominated by blue pine *Pinus wallichiana* with evergreen oak *Quercus semecarpifolia* in the west and appear to be replaced by deciduous oak *Quercus griffithii* east of 90° E. Xeric montane forests, which extend up to approximately 4,000 m, consist of fir *Abies densa* or spruce *Picea spinulosa*, giving way to and often in association with juniper *Juniperus pseudosabina*. Mesic forests of the montane zone are dominated by spruce, with hemlock *Tsuga dumosa* and larch *Larix griffithiana*, in the west; fir with hemlock and birch *Betula alnoides* is common in the east. Hemlock with birch and maple *Acer* spp., which occurs in slightly lower drier areas, and evergreen oak are also present (Sargent et al., 1985). Above 4,000 m there are extensive areas of alpine pasture. Further details of the vegetation are given by Wollenhaupt (1988a, 1988b), including vegetation maps (1:250,000) for the Upper Mo Chu and Pho Chu catchments.

Fauna The area is important for Himalayan wildlife, with Palaearctic and Indomalayan elements represented. Notable species include snow leopard *Panthera uncia* (E), Himalayan musk deer *Moschus chrysogaster*, Himalayan tahr *Hemitragus jemlahicus*, takin *Budorcas taxicolor*, and blue sheep *Psuedois nayaur* (Blower, 1985). Brown bear *Ursus arctos*, Himalayan black bear *Selenarctos thibetanus* and serow *Capricornis sumatraensis* (Blower, 1989), and sambar *Cervus unicolor*, Indian muntjac *Muntiacus muntjak*, and wild boar *Sus scrofa* are also present (Wollenhaupt, 1988b). Wolf *Canis lupus* (V), kiang *Equus kiang (hemionus)* (V) and Tibetan gazelle *Procapra picticaudata* are reported to have been seen in the extreme north (Jackson, 1981), but the presence of kiang and Tibetan antelope is considered unlikely (J.H. Blower, pers. comm.; H. Wollenhaupt, pers. comm.). Both shou *Cervus elaphus wallichi* (E) and great Tibetan sheep *Ovis ammon hodgsoni* (I) occurred in northern Bhutan (and hence the sanctuary) until comparatively recently (Blower, 1989). The sanctuary is probably the most secure area in the Himalaya for snow leopard, although some are poisoned by yak herdsmen in retaliation for stock lifting (Jackson, 1981). The catchment basins of the Mo Chu include both the summer and winter ranges of one of Bhutan's few known takin populations (Blower, 1986); a second population occurs in the Lunana region (Blower, 1989). The avifauna is rich, particularly in pheasants which include blood pheasant *Ithaginis cruentus*, Himalayan monal *Lophophorus impejanus* and satyr tragopan *Tragopan satyra* (Blower, 1989).

Cultural Heritage Among the numerous holy mountains is Masang Khang, sacred to the legendary Masang people who may have originated from southern Tibet. The inhabitants of Laya differ significantly in their language and costume from other Bhutanese peoples, and practise the Bön religion (Wollenhaupt, 1988a).

Local Human Population There are numerous human settlements within the sanctuary. Permanent settlements occur up to about 3,800 m in some parts of the sanctuary, notably in Gasa District to the north of Thimphu. There are no roads, villages being connected by a network of paths. Large numbers of yak and other domestic livestock are grazed on the alpine pastures in the summer months (Blower, 1986; Wollenhaupt, 1988a).

Visitors and Visitor Facilities There is a limited amount of trekking, the main destinations being Chila La and Chomo Lhari (Gibbons and Ashford, 1982). There are no visitor facilities.

Scientific Research and Facilities The vegetation has been sampled at a number of sites within the sanctuary, as part of a survey of the forests of Bhutan (Sargent et al., 1985). Preliminary reconnaissances of the Mo Chu and Pho Chu catchments have been carried out by Blower (1989) and Wollenhaupt (1988a, 1988b). There are no scientific facilities.

Conservation Value This northern region of Bhutan is unique and merits highest priority in conservation planning because: it includes the upper catchment areas of all the country's major rivers, the maintenance of forest cover being of vital importance to agricultural communities downstream; some of its valleys still contain areas of pristine montane and subalpine forest of a richness and beauty unparalleled elsewhere in the entire Himalaya; and it provides habitat for certain species of Himalayan wildlife, such as the snow leopard, musk deer, blue sheep and takin, which could become seriously threatened in the foreseeable future unless more effectively protected (Blower, 1986, 1989).

Conservation Management   It has been recommended that the sanctuary be given the highest priority in conservation planning, with two or three smaller areas of outstanding ecological value and scenic beauty selected and managed as effective national parks or nature reserves. One such area is the upper catchment of the Mo Chu, which fulfils all the criteria for a superb national park, and has only a few small settlements, with which it should be unnecessary to interfere, and which is a nationally important area for takin (Blower, 1986, 1989). Another is the area immediately north of Punakha, between the Mo Chu and Pho Chu, which is virtually uninhabited and largely undisturbed because of its difficult access. Boundaries would need to be readjusted because only the northern part of this area presently lies within the sanctuary (Wollenhaupt, 1988b). Jigme Dorji is not managed at present (H. Wollenhaupt, pers. comm., 1988).

Management Constraints   None of the people living in the area seems to be aware of its special status, although the prohibition on hunting appears to be respected. Over-grazing, burning and damage to trees are widespread, resulting in serious degradation of the habitat in some areas. There are only a few Forest Department staff to control such activities. Consequently, the majority of trees at higher altitudes are over-mature, many are fire-damaged, and regeneration in many areas is almost totally absent (Blower, 1985, 1986). Numbers of livestock are increasing (10% per annum in the case of yak), leading to degradation of existing grazing grounds and extension of pastures through deforestation (Wollenhaupt, 1988a; Blower, 1989).

Staff   One deputy director, three guards and one administrative staff, all of whom are stationed at the headquarters in Thimphu (H. Wollenhaupt, pers. comm., 1988).

Budget   The total budget for the Northern Wildlife Circle (which administers both Jigme Dorji Wildlife Sanctuary and Doga National Park) for 1984–5 was Nu. 384,000 (US $ 32,000).

Local Addresses
Deputy Director, Northern Wildlife Circle, Department of Forestry, Thimphu

References

Blower, J.H. (1985). Nature conservation and wildlife management in Bhutan. Preliminary report. FAO, Rome. 23 pp.

Blower, J.H. (1986). *Nature conservation in Bhutan: project findings and recommendations.* FO: DP/BHU/83/022. FAO, Rome. 55 pp.

Blower, J.H. (1989). *Nature conservation in northern and central Bhutan.* FO: BH/85/016. FAO, Rome. 48 pp.

Gibbons, B. and Ashford, B. (1982). *The Himalayan kingdom: Nepal, Bhutan and Sikkim.* B.T. Batsford Ltd, London. Pp. 139–41.

Jackson, P. (1981). Conservation in Bhutan. Unpublished. 15 pp.

Royal Government of Bhutan (1974). *Creation of wildlife sanctuaries, parks/forest reserves.* Department of Forestry, Thimphu. 12 pp.

Sargent, C., Sargent, O., and Parsell, R. (1985). The forests of Bhutan: a vital resource for the Himalayas? *Journal of Tropical Ecology* 1: 265–86.

Wollenhaupt, H. (1988a). Report of a field trip to the upper catchment area of the Mo Chu (26.3.1988–12.4.1988) . UNDP /FAO Forest Management and Consvation Project, Thimphu. Unpublished. 19pp.

Wollenhaupt, H. (1988b). Report of a field trip to the upper catchment area of the Pho Chu. UNDP /FAO Forest Management and Conservation Project, Thimphu. Unpublished. 8 pp.

ROYAL MANAS NATIONAL PARK

IUCN Management Category   II (National Park)

Biogeographical Province   4.03.01 (Bengalian Rainforest)

Geographical Location   Lies on the southern international border with the Indian state of Assam, and extends from the Aigunmari River on the east to the Sukuntaklai River in the west. 26°47′–26°56′N, 90°30′–91°22′E

Date and History of Establishment   Established as a national park in 1988 by the amalgamation and upgrading of the former Manas Wildlife Sanctuary and Namgyal Wangchuk Wildlife Reserve. Manas was originally declared a wildlife sanctuary on 11 July 1966 (Government Order no. F-13(4)/MWL/66/4549), having previously been protected for many years as a royal hunting reserve. It was subsequently enlarged to 4,385 ha following the notification of an eastern extension of 2,000 ha on 13 February 1984 (vide TIF/FAO/111-8/83/7049). Namgyal Wangchuk (19,709 ha, of which 1,200 ha was allocated to the Army Welfare Association for cultivation of sugarcane) was originally established on 1 November 1974 as Goley Game Reserve (Notification no. TIF-11/74) and subsequently renamed in memory of His Royal Highness, Namgyal Wangchuk, then Minister of Trade, Industry and Forests.

Area   65,800 ha. To the east, Manas is separated from Shumar Wildlife Reserve (16,000 ha) by a strip of settled land several kilometres in width. Across the international border with India to the south, the park abuts Manas Sanctuary (39,100 ha) which is both a World Heritage Site and part of a tiger reserve.

Land Tenure   State

Altitude   Ranges from about 200 m to 2,310 m.

Physical Features   Lying in the Outer Himalaya, the park has a variety of habitats ranging from forested hills in the north to open savannah in the south. It is well-watered by the Manas River itself and various smaller perennial rivers flowing southwards through it. In the west, the Kanamakra River cuts through the northern hills as a deep narrow valley and emerges in the lowlands as a broad stony bed several hundred metres wide. The main geological formations are: the Siwalik series (Miocene-Pliocene) consisting of bedded sandstones and grey to green claystones along the southern boundary; the Phuntsholing series (mid-Palaeozoic), comprising mostly folded successions of purple phyllites, quartzites and silicon limestones with epidiozite sills along the length of the park; and the Buxa series (Permo-Triassic), represented by isolated formations of feldspar, sandstone, phyllites and slates with coal. Soil of the Bhabar formation lies over mixed layers of boulders and gravels along the foothills. Recent alluvial deposits cover the floodplain, above which are older soils of brown loam and sandy loam (Lahan, 1986).

Climate   The climate is governed by the south-east monsoon which lasts from late May until mid-September. Annual rainfall is about 3000 mm. Mean monthly temperatures range from 4°C to 28°C (Lahan, 1986).

Vegetation   Three zones can be recognised: tropical (below 1,000 m), subtropical (1,000–2,000 m) and montane (2,000–3,000 m), within which occur a variety of vegetation types (Lahan, 1986). Tropical semi-evergreen forests are found in the foothills along the southern boundary and occur in well-drained soils of the hill slopes up to altitudes of 760 m or more. Important species are *Phoebe hainesiana*, *Eugenia* spp., *Castanopsis* spp., *Michelia* spp., *Elaeocarpus* spp., *Tetrameles nudiflora*, *Ailanthus grandis*, *Quercus* spp., and *Schima wallichii*. East Himalayan moist mixed deciduous forests occur between 500 m and 650 m in lower areas. Typical species are: *Lagerstroemia parviflora*, *L. reginae*, *Sterculia villosa*, *Bombax ceiba*, *Schima wallichii*, *Careya arborea*, *Amoora wallichii*, *A. rohituka*, *Terminalia myriocarpa*, *Pterospermum acerifolium*, *Duabanga sonneratioides*, *Ailanthus grandis* and *Chukrasia tabularis*. Subtropical wet forests cover the hill slopes from about 1,000 m to 2,000 m. Typical species are: *Betula alnoides*, *Castanopsis* spp., *Cedrela toona*, *Albizia* spp., *Schima wallichii*, *Alnus nepalensis* and *Engelhardtia spicata*. Fresh alluvial deposits along the river banks are colonised by grasses, such as *Saccharum spontaneum*, *S. arundinaceum*, *Imperata cylindrica*, *I. arundinacea*, *Erianthus filifolius*, and succeeded by woody pioneer species, such as *Acacia catechu* and *Dalbergia sissoo*. The drier soils of the Bhabar formation support tall reed grasses, such as *Phragmites karka*, *Saccharum ravennae* and *Typha elephantina*. A preliminary list of the flora is given by Lahan (1986). The former Namgyal Wangchuk sector contains evergreen and semi-evergreen forest and extensive areas of fire climax savannah woodland in the south. Dry mixed deciduous hill forest and evergreen/semi-evergreen forest occurs along the watercourses in the north. Much of the forest in the south is degraded as a result of past exploitation and fire (Blower, 1986).

Fauna   Manas contains an interesting variety of mammals including golden leaf monkey *Trachypithecus geei* (R), recently discovered and endemic to the Bhutan/India border region, wolf *Canis lupus* (V), wild dog *Cuon alpinus* (V), tiger *Panthera tigris* (E), leopard *P. pardus* (T), clouded leopard *Neofelis nebulosa* (V), golden cat *Felis temmincki* (I), Indian elephant *Elephas maximus* (E), Indian rhinoceros *Rhinoceros unicornis* (E), water buffalo *Bubalus bubalis* (V) and nowhere else present in Bhutan (Blower, 1986), gaur *Bos gaurus* (V) and hispid hare *Caprolagus hispidus* (E). Otter *Lutra sp.*, wild boar *Sus scrofa*, Indian muntjac *Muntiacus muntjak*, hog deer *Cervus porcinus*, spotted deer *C. axis*, sambar *C. unicolor*, and serow *Capricornis sumatraensis* are also present (Jackson, 1981). Ganges dolphin *Platanista gangetica* is still reported to occur in the Manas River. Populations of golden leaf monkey, wild boar, muntjac, sambar and gaur appear to be healthy but little sign of tiger and rhinoceros was found in 1985–6 (Blower, 1986). In 1988 there were reported to be 30 tigers in the park (Dorji and Santiapillai, 1989). The golden leaf monkey population is estimated to total at least 100 individuals (Santiapillai, 1988; Subba, 1989). A small herd of water buffalo was seen by the Gobarkunda River in September 1985 (J.H. Blower, pers. comm.). Elephant occurs in small groups, which are subject to seasonal movements and are probably to be found mostly in the hills to the north in the dry season (Blower, 1986). Pygmy hog *Sus salvanius* (E) has not been recorded (Blower, 1986) although it does occur on the Indian side of the international border. Gharial *Gavialis gangeticus* (E) used to be present but is now probably extinct. An apparently unsuccessful attempt was made to reintroduce this species a few years ago (Blower, 1986). Santiapillai (1988) provides tentative estimates of certain large mammal populations based on a limited survey.

The avifauna is rich and includes both plains and hill species, as well as migrants (Jackson, 1981). A wide variety of waterfowl has been recorded, including cormorant *Phalacrocorax carbo*, great white egret *Egretta alba*, grey heron *Ardea cinerea*, black stork *Ciconia nigra*, ruddy shelduck *Tadorna ferruginea*, teal *Anas crecca*, mallard *Anas platyrhynchos*, and merganser *Mergus merganser*. Ibisbill *Ibidorhyncha struthersii* is a regular winter visitor in small numbers. Resident birds include Asiatic stork *Ephippiorhynchus asiaticus*, lesser adjutant stork *Leptoptilos javanicus*, water cock *Gallicrex cinerea*, great stone-curlew *Esacus recurvirostris*, and spur-winged lapwing *Vanellus spinosus*.

Faunal lists are given in Lahan (1986) but that for the avifauna is based on records for Manas Tiger Reserve in India.

Cultural Heritage   No information

Local Human Population   About 100 people resided in the former Manas Wildlife Sanctuary (Jackson, 1981). There are old established settlements on the Kakulong River in the south, and at Udigaon and Shilingtot in the north. There is more recent encroachment in the valley of the Udang Nadi, near the northern boundary, and on the Chaimari River in the eastern extension, where a further area of about 100 ha was recently cleared and settled by Sharchops people. They have apparently been permitted to remain there, together with their livestock which are grazed further into the sanctuary. There is one village, Chengba, in the former Namgyal Wangchuk Wildlife Reserve. This lies on the Sukuntaklai River (Blower, 1986).

Visitors and Visitor Facilities   Manas has considerable tourist potential but receives few visitors and hardly any foreign tourists due to the difficulty of access, which involves a lengthy detour through India for which Restricted Area Permits are requested. To obviate this difficulty, the Wildlife Division has begun constructing a fair-weather road between Galypug and Manas Headquarters to provide direct access. The Bhutan Tourist Corporation manages an attractively-sited, three-bedroomed guest house at Manas Headquarters (Blower, 1986; Santiapillai, 1988).

Scientific Research and Facilities   Scientific studies are limited to preliminary status surveys of the wildlife (Dorji and Santiapillai, 1989; Subba, 1989). There are no scientific facilities.

Conservation Value   Manas is the richest of Bhutan's protected areas and, together with India's Manas Sanctuary, forms a trans-frontier reserve of immense importance for the conservation of many rare and threatened plants and animals (Blower, 1986). It is also an important staging and wintering area for waterfowl (Scott, 1989).

Conservation Management   Agreement was reached in 1974 between Bhutan and India for joint management of the adjacent Bhutanese and Indian Manas properties. Under the aegis of the Directorate of Project Tiger, India, a management plan for Bhutan's Manas was prepared for the period from 1975–6 to 1978–9 (Anon., 1979) but the joint management agreement has since been allowed to lapse (Jackson, 1981).

Subsequently, a master development plan was prepared under an FAO consultancy (Lahan, 1986), in which it was recommended that Manas should be amalgamated with Namgyal Wangchuk and developed as a national park. This recommendation has since been implemented. The establishment of an intensive use zone, covering 5% of the area, buffer zones on the eastern and western flanks, and a wilderness zone, covering the rest, has been proposed as the basis of management (Lahan, 1986). Removal of shifting cultivation and agricultural settlement (including the sugarcane plantation on the Kakumari River, the recent settlement on the Chaimari River and in the Udang Nadi), boundary adjustments (e.g. to exclude Chengba Village) and demarcation, an increase in staff and the provision of essential equipment (including vehicles and radios), are all urgent requirements (Blower, 1986), some of which are receiving attention (Santiapillai, 1988). Other recommendations are outlined by Santiapillai (1988).

Management Constraints   Owing to its original establishment as a royal hunting reserve, the former Manas Wildlife Sanctuary is the only protected area in the south of Bhutan which has not been extensively exploited and where the natural ecosystem remains relatively intact. Nevertheless, there has been some encroachment, particularly in the north. To date, the Army Welfare Association has cleared 500 ha of forest on the west bank of the Kanamakra River for a sugarcane plantation. This is in direct contravention of the National Forest Policy and, apart from the serious damage to the habitat, the sugarcane inevitably attracts elephants, which the army then wants to shoot to protect its crop (Blower, 1988). This project is running at a loss and the Army Welfare Association would consider abandoning it if adequately compensated (Santiapillai, 1988). Other problems include poaching (mainly from across the Indian border but also from the Sharchops settlements), the deliberate setting of fires, and theft of timber, particularly the valuable agar wood *Aquilaria agallocha* which is used in medicine and for making incense (Blower, 1986). A proposal by the Indian Government to build two dams in the upper reaches of the Manas and Sankosh rivers for flood control and electricity production has been rejected. The former dam would have had a serious impact on the whole Manas ecosystem, completely altering the hydrology of the region at the expense of the wildlife (Jackson, 1981; CNPPA, 1985).

Staff   Prior to the amalgamation of Manas and Namgyal, the total complement was 55 field staff. Manas had a warden of forest ranger rank, two foresters and 16 wildlife guards, in addition to mahouts, boatmen and other administrative personnel. Namgyal Wangchuk was under the charge of the warden at Manas, with a field staff consisting of a forester and three guards stationed at Kanamakra (Lahan, 1986).

Budget   The total budget for the Southern Wildlife Circle in 1984–5, which administered 10 (including Manas and Namgyal Wangchuk) of Bhutan's 12 protected areas, was Nu. 1,287,000 (US $ 107,350). Additional support is being received from WWF (Santiapillai, 1988).

Local Addresses
Warden, Manas Wildlife Sanctuary, c/o Forest Department, PO Box 130, Thimphu.

References
Anon. (1979). A management plan of Bhutan Manas Tiger Reserve 1975–6 to 1978–9. Director of Forests, Royal Government of Bhutan, Thimphu. Unpublished.
Blower, J.H. (1986). *Nature conservation in Bhutan: project findings and recommendations.* FO: DP/BHU/83/022. FAO, Rome. 55 pp.
CNPPA (1985). Another dead dam. *IUCN Commission on National Parks and Protected Areas Members Newsletter* 33.
Dorji, D.P. and Santiapillai, C. (1989). The status, distribution and conservation of the tiger *Panthera tigris* in Bhutan. Biological Conservation 48: 311–19.

Jackson, P. (1981). Conservation in Bhutan. Unpublished. 15 pp.

Lahan, P. (1986). *Report on ecological reconnaissance of Manas Wildlife Sanctuary, Namgyal Wangchuk Wildlife Reserve, and Phipsoo Wildlife Reserve and an outline master development plan for the reserves.* FO: DP/BHU/83/022. Field Document no. 9. FAO, Rome. 110 pp.

Royal Government of Bhutan (1974). *Creation of wildlife sanctuaries, parks/forest reserves.* Department of Forestry, Thimphu. 12 pp.

Santiapillai, C. (1988). Management of the proposed Royal Manas National Park, Bhutan. WWF, Gland, Switzerland. 24 pp.

Scott, D.A. (Ed.) (1989). *A directory of Asian wetlands.* IUCN, Gland, Switzerland and Cambridge, UK. 1,181 pp.

Subba, P.B. (1989). The status and conservation of the golden langur (*Presbytis geei* Khajuria, 1956) in the Manas National Park, Bhutan. *Tiger paper* 16(4): 16–18.

WWF/IUCN Project no. 1022. Operation tiger, Bhutan, Manas Tiger Reserve.

MOCHU WILDLIFE RESERVE

IUCN Management Category   IV (Managed Nature Reserve)

Biogeographical Province   4.03.01 (Bengalian Rainforest)

Geographical Location   Lies on the Indian border, from where it extends northwards to the crest of the first range of Himalayan foothills. It is bounded by the Samatung and Sankosh rivers to the east and west, respectively, (Royal Government of Bhutan, 1974). 26°42′–26°51′N, 89°56′–90°12′E

Date and History of Establishment   Established as Mochu Reserved Forest on 1 November 1974 (Notification no. TIF-11/74) but, subsequently, referred to in all official communications the area as the Phipsoo Wildlife Reserve (Lahan, 1986). Created a wildlife reserve in 1984.

Area   27,843 ha. Contiguous with Kachugaon Game Reserve in Assam, India (Lahan, 1986).

Land Tenure   State

Altitude   Ranges from 180 m to 400 m on the south and south-eastern portions to 600 m to 1,200 m in the north.

Physical Features   The southern portion is undulating, rising abruptly northwards to steep ridges separated by deep rocky gorges that drain either north and west to the Sankosh or southward. A prominent feature of these watercourses is the number of natural salt licks, where mineralised soil has been exposed by erosion of the river banks. The main geological formations are: the Siwalik series (Miocene-Pliocene), consisting of bedded sandstones and grey to green claystones along the southern boundary; the Phuntsholing series (mid-Palaeozoic), comprising mostly folded successions of purple phyllites, quartzites and silicon limestones with epidiozite sills along the length of the reserve; and the Buxa series (Permo-Triassic), represented by isolated formations of feldspar, sandstone, phyllites and slates with coal. Soil of the Bhabar formation lies over mixed layers of boulders and gravels along the foothills. Recent alluvial deposits cover the floodplain, above which are older soils of brown loam and sandy loam (Lahan, 1986).

Climate   Conditions are tropical monsoonal, governed by the south-east monsoon which lasts from late May until mid-September. Annual rainfall is about 3000 mm. Mean monthly temperatures vary from 4 °C to 28 °C (Lahan, 1986).

Vegetation   Three zones can be recognised: tropical (below 1,000 m), subtropical (1,000–2,000 m) and montane (2,000–3,000 m), within which occur a variety of vegetation types (Lahan, 1986). Tropical semi-evergreen forests are found in the foothills along the southern boundary and occur in well-drained soils of the hill slopes up to altitudes of 760 m or more. Important species are *Phoebe hainesiana, Eugenia* spp., *Castonopsis* spp., *Michelia* spp., *Elaeocarpus* spp., *Tetrameles nudiflora, Ailanthus grandis, Quercus* spp., and *Schima wallichii*. Sal forests occur along the lower slopes in the southern boundary. East Himalayan moist mixed deciduous forests occur between 500 m and 650 m in lower areas. Typical species are: *Lagerstroemia parviflora, L. speciosa, Sterculia villosa, Bombax ceiba, Schima wallichii, Careya arborea, Amoora wallichii, A. rohituka, Terminalia myriocarpa, Pterospermum ascerifolium, Duabanga sonneratioides, Ailanthus grandis* and *Chikrassia tabularis*. Sub-tropical wet forests cover the hill slopes from about 1,000 m to 2,000 m. Typical species are: *Betula alnoides, Castanopsis* spp., *Cedrella toona, Albizia* spp., *Schima wallichii, Alnus nepalensis* and *Engelhardtia spicata*. Fresh alluvial deposits along the river banks are colonised by grasses, such as *Saccharum spontaneum, S. munja, Imperata cylindrica, I. arundinacea, Erianthus filifolius*, and succeeded by woody pioneer species, such as *Acacia catechu* and *Dalbergia sissoo*. The drier soils of the Bhabar formation support tall reed grasses, such as *Phragmites karka, Brianthus ravanae* and *Typha elephantina*. A preliminary list of the flora is given by Lahan (1986).

The southern part was heavily logged some 20 years ago when there was a sawmill at Phipsoo. Accessible slopes have been denuded and sal *Shorea robusta* trees of exploitable girths have been removed. There are some 800 ha of forest plantations owned by the Forest Department (Blower, 1986; Lahan, 1986).

Fauna   Large mammals include substantial numbers of the locally endemic golden leaf monkey *Trachypithecus geei* (R) at the western extremity of its range, rhesus macaque *Macaca mulatta*, wild dog *Cuon alpinus* (V), tiger *Panthera tigris* (E), leopard *P. pardus* (T), Asiatic black bear *Selenarctos thibetanus*, wild boar *Sus scrofa*, Indian muntjac *Muntiacus muntjak*, hog deer *Cervus porcinus*, sambar *C. unicolor*, and gaur *Bos gaurus* (V). Spotted deer *C. axis* is reportedly an infrequent visitor from the Indian side of the border. There is also a rich avifauna (Blower, 1986). Faunal lists are given by Lahan (1986) but that for the avifauna is based on records from Manas Tiger Reserve in India. A wide variety of waterfowl is found in the flood plains of the Sankosh River. Species include cormorant *Phalacrocorax carbo*, great white egret *Egretta alba*, grey heron *Ardea cinerea*, black stork *Ciconia nigra*, ruddy shelduck *Tadorna ferruginea*, teal *Anas crecca*, mallard *A. platyrhynchos* and merganser *Mergus merganser*. Resident waterbirds include Asiatic stork *Ephippiorhynchus asiaticus*, lesser adjutant stork *Leptoptilos javanicus*, water cock *Gallicrex cinerea*, great stone-curlew *Esacus recurvirostris*, and spur-winged lapwing *Vanellus spinosus* (Scott, 1989).

Cultural Heritage   No information

Local Human Population   There are several villages, mostly in the south-west near the Sankosh River, but including Pinkhua with 25 houses on the southern border and Phipsoo with 17 houses. All of these communities cultivate land and graze cattle extensively in the reserve (Blower, 1986).

Visitors and Visitor Facilities   No information

Scientific Research and Facilities   None

Conservation Value   The reserve contains viable populations of several large mammal species and is also important as habitat for the golden leaf monkey. The marshes of the Sankosh River are an important staging and wintering area for waterfowl (Scott, 1989).

Conservation Management   Although not meriting national park or nature reserve status, Mochu (Phipsoo) has traditionally been protected as a royal hunting reserve. Mochu warrants protection as a wildlife sanctuary, subject to revision of its western boundary to exclude those villages near the Sankosh River (Blower, 1986). At present, cattle are allowed to be grazed within a 1 km radius of villages (Lahan, 1986), but this concession would appear to be infringed.

Management Constraints   In addition to various forms of exploitation by local communities, there is reported to be extensive poaching by armed gangs from the Indian side of the border. This probably accounts for the apparent paucity of wildlife in the lowland areas (Blower, 1986).

Staff   The present complement is 42 field staff, consisting of one warden of forest ranger rank, four foresters and 16 wildlife guards, plus mahouts and other administrative personnel (Lahan, 1986).

Budget   The total budget for the Southern Wildlife Circle in 1984–5, which then administered 10 (including Mochu) of Bhutan's 12 protected areas, was Nu. 1,287,000 (US $ 107,350).

Local Addresses   Deputy Director of Forests, Southern Wildlife Circle, Department of Forestry, Sarbhang

References
Blower, J.H. (1986). *Nature conservation in Bhutan: project findings and recommendations.* FO: DP/BHU/83/022. FAO, Rome. 55 pp.
Lahan, P. (1986). *Report on ecological reconnaissance of Manas Wildlife Sanctuary, Namgyal Wangchuk Wildlife Reserve and Phipsoo Wildlife Reserve and an outline master development plan for the reserves.* FO: DP/BHU/83/022. Field Document no. 9. FAO, Rome. 110 pp.
Royal Government of Bhutan (1974). *Creation of wildlife sanctuaries, parks/forest reserves.* Department of Forestry, Thimphu. 12 pp.

NEOLI WILDLIFE SANCTUARY

IUCN Management Category   IV (Managed Nature Reserve)

Biogeographical Province   4.09.04 (Burma Monsoon Forest)

Geographical Location   Extends from the valley of the Bar Nadi, near Bhangtar township, eastwards along the border with India to the Neoli Khola, and northwards to the valley of the Dighlai Nadi. Approximately 26°49′–26°53′N, 91°32′–91°38′E

Date and History of Establishment   13 February 1984

Area   4,000 ha. Contiguous with Barnadi Sanctuary (2,622 ha) in Assam, India..

Land Tenure   State

Altitude   Approximately 200 m to 700 m

Physical Features   The area is very broken, with steep-sided ridges separated by narrow winding stream valleys and rocky gorges. Most streams are seasonal although some, including the southward-flowing Nalpara and Koila Kata, are perennial. There are some natural salt licks to which the wildlife is attracted.

Climate   No information

Vegetation   Forest cover consists of dry mixed deciduous hill forest with much bamboo in some areas, and semi-evergreen forest along the watercourses (Blower, 1986).

Fauna   Pygmy hog *Sus sylvanius* (E), which is not known from elsewhere in Bhutan, is reported to occur in Neoli and the adjacent Barnadi Sanctuary. Other large mammals are reported to include langur *Presbytis entellus*, tiger *Panthera tigris* (E), leopard *P. pardus* (T), Himalayan black bear *Selenarctos thibetanus*, Indian elephant *Elephas maximus* (E), Indian muntjac *Muntiacus muntjak*, sambar *Cervus unicolor*, gaur *Bos gaurus* (V), and wild boar *Sus scrofa* (Blower, 1986).

Cultural Heritage   No information

Local Human Population   There are three small villages in the western and southern parts of the sanctuary and a number of cattle camps both in the south, along the Indian border, and in the north. The sanctuary is heavily settled on all sides (Blower, 1986).

Visitors and Visitor Facilities   No information

Scientific Research and Facilities   None

Conservation Value   The sanctuary was established primarily for the protection of the rare pygmy hog (Blower, 1986).

Conservation Management   In view of its importance for pygmy hog, it is essential that Neoli be maintained as a wildlife sanctuary and protected more effectively than at present. Demarcation of boundaries, removal of cattle camps, the provision of an adequate guard force and a status survey of the pygmy hog and other wildlife, are all priorities (Blower, 1986).

Management Constraints   There is some encroachment and other forms of human disturbance, with extensive poaching from the Indian side of the border and illegal felling of timber. The forest is much degraded in areas near settlements (Blower, 1986).

Staff   None

Budget   The total budget for the Southern Wildlife Circle in 1984–5, which then administered 10 (including Neoli) of Bhutan's protected areas, was Nu. 1,287,000 (US $ 107,350).

Local Addresses
Deputy Director of Forests, Southern Wildlife Circle, Department of Forestry, Sarbhang.

References
Blower, J.H. (1986). *Nature conservation in Bhutan: project findings and recommendations.* FO: DP/BHU/83/022. FAO, Rome. 55 pp.

SHUMAR WILDLIFE RESERVE

IUCN Management Category   Unassigned

Biogeographical Province   4.09.04 (Burma Monsoon Forest)

Geographical Location   Lies on the Indian border about 10 km east of the eastern boundary of Manas Wildlife Sanctuary and extends as far east as Samdrup Jongkhar township. Approximately 26°46′–26°57′N, 91°20′–91°32′E.

Date and History of Establishment   13 February 1984

Area   16,000 ha. Lies adjacent to Dungsum Wildlife Reserve (18,000 ha).

Land Tenure   State

Altitude   Ranges from about 300 m on the Indian border in the south to over 2,000 m in the north.

Physical Features   Broken hilly country

Climate   No information

Vegetation   Little of the original forest remains, apart from a few remnants on hilltops (Blower, 1986).

Fauna   Tiger *Panthera tigris* (E), Indian elephant *Elephas maximus* (E), wild boar *Sus scrofa*, sambar *Cervus unicolor*, and gaur *Bos gaurus* (V) are present and there is an interesting variety of birdlife (Blower, 1986; Mahat, n.d.).

Cultural Heritage   No information.

Local Human Population   Several villages and cattle camps occur within the boundaries, and shifting cultivation is practised extensively.

Visitors and Visitor Facilities   No information

Scientific Research and Facilities   None

Conservation Value   There seems to be little justification for Shumar's designation as a wildlife reserve rather than reserved forest, in view of the degraded state of most of the remaining forest and the extensive encroachment (Blower, 1986).

Conservation Management   It has been recommended that Shumar should be redesignated as reserved forest and be given high priority for demarcation and reafforestation under the Forest Department's planting programme (Blower, 1986).

Management Constraints   Encroachment from shifting cultivation and domestic livestock is widespread. The Indian Army artillery range at Parkejuli, on the southern boundary, adds further to the general disturbance (Blower, 1986).

Staff   One beat officer and two guards are stationed at a guard post on the southern boundary (Blower, 1986).

Budget   The total budget for the Southern Wildlife Circle in 1984–5, which then administered 10 (including Shumar) of Bhutan's 12 protected areas, was Nu. 1,287,000 (US $ 107,350).

Local Addresses
Deputy Director of Forests, Southern Wildlife Circle, Department of Forestry, Sarbhang

References
Blower, J.H. (1986). *Nature conservation in Bhutan: project findings and recommendations.* FO: DP/BHU/83/022. FAO, Rome. 55 pp.
Mahat, G. (n.d.). A study tour of forest belt in southern Bhutan. Department of Forestry, Thimphu. Unpublished. 10 pp.

THRUMSING LA NATIONAL FOREST

IUCN Management Category   Proposed

Biogeographical Province   2.38.12 (Himalayan Highlands)

Geographical Location   Lies south of Jakar in east-central Bhutan and comprises several watersheds between the Mangda Chu in the west and Kuru Chu in the east. Thrumsing La (3,780 m) is the pass by which the road from western Bhutan to Mongar and Tashigang crosses the watershed. Approximately 27°20′ N, 90°55′E.

Date and History of Establishment   Mostly classed as reserved forest

Area   No information

Land Tenure   Land is mostly state owned, but subject to customary rights of grazing and collection of forest produce(?).

Altitude   Up to about 5,000 m.

Physical Features   In the west, the area is drained by the Ghizam Chu which, below its confluence with the Bumthang Chu, flows through a deep gorge. The watershed between the Bumthang Chu and Mangda Chu rises to a series of rocky peaks at 4,000 m to 5,000 m. Eastwards from the crest of the main watershed on which lies Thrumsing La, the terrain falls away steeply to the beautiful valley in which lies Sengor village and beyond it the valley of the Kuru Chu.

Climate   No information

Vegetation   The higher slopes of the Thrumsing La watershed are mostly covered with fir *Abies* sp., and rhododendron *Rhododendron* sp. understorey. Lower down are mixed conifers including *Cupressus*, blue pine *Pinus wallichiana*, spruce *Picea* sp., and hemlock *Tsuga dumosa*. Relatively undisturbed broad-leaved forest occurs along both sides of the Bumthang Chu (Blower, 1989).

Fauna   Little specific information is available. Wild boar *Sus scrofa* and Indian muntjac *Muntiacus muntjak* are present, and probably Himalayan black bear *Selenarctos thibetanus*, musk deer *Moschus chrysogaster*, and sambar *Cervus unicolor* (Blower, 1989).

Cultural Heritage   No information

Local Human Population   There is no settlement in the main watershed itself, which is too high. The nearest villages are Ura on the western slope and Sengor on the eastern slope, both lying at about 3,350 m. There are pastures on the Wantha La (3,750 m), a western spur of the main watershed between the Ura and Ghizam valleys, and in the lower Ghizam Valley.

Visitors and Visitor Facilities   None.

Scientific Research and Facilities   None

Conservation Value   Contains relatively undisturbed tracts of coniferous and temperate broad-leaved forest which, in central Bhutan, is not represented in the existing protected areas network (Blower, 1989).

Conservation Management   Under the proposed new legislation, it is recommended that Thrumsing La be established as a strictly protected national forest in which limited exploitation of timber and other forest produce would be allowed (Blower, 1989).

Management Constraints   There is a proposal to log the Thrumsing La area under a project to be financed by the Austrian government. This forest lies on a major watershed at 3,500 m to 3,800 m where the soil is relatively unstable, as is evident from the unhealed erosion scars and landslips remaining from the construction of the road there some 20 years ago (Blower, 1989).

Staff   None.

Budget   None.

Local Addresses   None

References
Blower, J.H. (1989). *Nature conservation in northern and central Bhutan*. FO: BH/85/016. FAO, Rome. 48 pp.

CHINA

Area 9,597,000 sq. km

Population 1,119.9 million (1990)   Natural increase 1.4% per annum

GNP US $ 300 per capita (1988)

Policy and Legislation Nature conservation is incorporated in Articles 9, 10, 22 and 26 of the new constitution adopted on 12 December 1982 in which it is stipulated that, 'The State protects the environment and natural resources and prevents and eliminates pollution and other hazards to the public'. The Environmental Protection Law of the People's Republic of China, adopted in principle as Decree no. 2 at the eleventh meeting of the Standing Committee of the Fifth National People's Congress on 13 September 1979, was passed on 26 December 1989 by China's National People's Congress (Anon., 1990). The law comprises seven chapters and 33 articles covering nature conservation areas, forests, grasslands, historic sites and scenic spots. In Article 15 the need to protect, develop and rationally utilise wildlife and wild plant resources is noted, and protection extended to rare animals and precious trees. Articles 6 and 7 of the law make provision for environmental impact assessments to be instigated by the Environment Protection Bureau and other relevant departments.

The first nature reserves were declared in 1956 under Proposal no. 92 passed at the Third Conference of the First National People's Congress (Yuging, 1987). Under this proposal both the State Council and the provinces and autonomous regions may designate nature reserves, and declare non-hunting areas and closed seasons within them. National and provincial nature reserves are classified into six types according to the administrative system, ecological character of the area and the objectives of protection. The first type is directed towards preservation of natural ecosystems; the second towards protection of rare or endangered fauna; the third towards protection of rare relict plants and special types of vegetation; the fourth towards conservation of natural landscapes; the fifth towards preservation of special geological sections and geomorphological features; and the sixth towards protection of the natural environment and natural resources of the coastline (Wenhua and Xianying, 1989). The criteria used in the selection of nature reserves include the degree of naturalness, biological diversity, rarity and size of the area. Lucas (1987) differentiates between national nature reserves and provincial nature reserves, the latter being created at the provincial level of government (see Annex). Of the national nature reserves, a selected number have historically held an additional title which is more precisely transliterated from the Chinese as 'key' national nature reserves, a practice which continues to date. This tends to cover those under the jurisdiction of the

77

Ministry of Forestry and entitles them to obtain central government funding. National nature reserves can be zoned into core, buffer and experimental areas.

Articles 4, 11, 20 and 21 of the Forest Law of 1979 provides for the establishment of forest reserves and reserves (see Annex), the management and administration of forests and prevention of hunting in forests (Richardson, 1990).

In 1982, a Marine Environmental Protection Law was adopted, covering a wide range of issues and is administered by the Environmental Protection Department under the State Council. In 1983, there were proposals for coastal zone protection legislation, aimed at conserving mangrove forests in south-east China (UNEP/IUCN, 1988).

International Activities The Convention concerning the Protection of the World Cultural and Natural Heritage (World Heritage Convention) was ratified on 12 December 1985 and three natural sites have since been inscribed on the World Heritage List. There are currently seven Unesco Man and Biosphere reserves, three designated in 1979, one in 1986, two in 1987 and one in 1990. Co-operative efforts in nature conservation were agreed between the US and China under a special protocol signed in 1986. Earlier, in 1979, WWF signed an agreement on co-operative activities including natural resources management, environmental policy and legislation. There is also a bilateral agreement (1981) covering migratory species between China and Japan. China and Nepal have both established protected areas on their respective sides of Mount Everest (Sagarmatha/Chomolangma). Management plans are being formulated under co-operative agreements with the Woodlands Mountain Institute in the case of both countries.

Administration and Management The Ministry of Urban and Rural Reconstruction and Environmental Protection (an amalgamation of various offices and commissions, including the Environmental Protection Office) shares responsibility with the Ministry of Forestry for the management of nature reserves (Ratcliffe, 1982). The Environmental Protection Office (also referred to as the Environmental Protection Bureau or Agency) was set up by the State Council under the Environmental Protection Law in 1979 and covers nature conservation and protected areas, while the Bureau of Surveying and Mapping deals with research. The Environmental Protection Office supervises the implementation of legislation concerning environmental protection as well as having scientific and educational roles. In 1986 it had 10 divisions, with bureaux in 324 cities, employing 30,000 people, of which 7,000 were research workers (Thornback, 1986). The Chairman of the Environmental Protection Office is the Vice-President of the Republic. The Commission for Nature Conservation (a part of the Environmental Protection Office) is responsible for the coordination of national and international conservation activities, and for reviewing nature conservation resources. The People's governments of the 22 provinces, five autonomous regions and three municipalities are obliged to establish environmental protection bureaux under the Law. In the counties, autonomous counties and prefectures, environmental protection organisations may be set up (Anon., n.d.).

The Ministry of Forestry retains responsibility for co-ordinating protection of all protected areas located on forest lands (estimated to be 90% of the total). The Ministry of Forestry functions as an economic ministry operating at state level below the planning and economic commissions. The Ministry is responsible for research (through the Academy of Forestry), education (at three universities and four colleges), and the administration of state forestry throughout China. It administers nature reserves and 'forest farms' (through the Forest

Department) covering 50 million ha. The provincial arm of the Ministry replicates that at the centre, including research and training activities, which is maintained in simplified form at district (prefecture and county) levels. In Heilongjiang, forest production is overseen by a quasi-autonomous Forest Industries Bureau (Richardson, 1990).

A master plan has been prepared for the entire 29,500 sq. km range of the giant panda (MacKinnon, 1989a) and management plans for major reserves under a WWF/China joint agreement, which also provides training for Chinese reserve staff. In addition, there is specialist training in wetland management and education project work. Datian Nature Reserve was added to the IUCN Commission on National Parks and Protected Areas List of Threatened Protected Areas of the World in November 1990 due to the declassification of 25% of the reserve for cattle ranching purposes. Fu Tien Nature Reserve was removed from the list in 1988 after the proposal for a new airport had been dropped. Nature reserves are maintained in near natural conditions as far as possible and are extensively used for research and as resources of plant genetic material (Ratcliffe, 1982), but many lack adequate funding and trained personnel (MacKinnon, 1989b).

Systems Reviews China's topography ranges from high mountains, undulating plateaux and rolling hills to broad basins and plains. In the west, the relief is high and steep, while in the east it is low and flat. The Qinghai-Tibet plateau in the west comprises a series of east–west aligned mountains ranging in altitude between 5,000 m and 8,848 m, and includes the Himalaya of which Qomolangma (Mount Everest) is a part. The three main rivers flowing across China are the Yellow (Huang), Yangtze (Chang) and Amur (Heilong). Much of China experiences a monsoon climate due to its proximity to the Pacific Ocean, but conditions become much drier in the west (Ji et al., 1990).

Tropical evergreen rain forest occurs in the lowlands of Yunnan and Guangdong Provinces and on the eastern side of Hainan Island. Along the southern coast of China are mangrove forests. Temperate deciduous forests and subtropical broad-leaved deciduous forests exist on limestone in the tropical and subtropical zones of the south. Various types of subarctic coniferous forests (taiga) and cold temperate mixed forests are found in the north. The most extensive tracts of natural forest are in the north-east and in the south-western provinces of Sichuan and Yunnan. Much of western China, the vast plains of the north-east and Inner Mongolia, is arable land. Northern Dongbei is mostly steppe grassland. Fuelwood cutting, overgrazing and deforestation has left little primary forest, even in remote areas and steep terrain. In 1980, forests and woodlands accounted for 58 million ha, grassland and pasture 778 million ha, and croplands 134 million ha (Repetto, 1988). According to FAO (1988) natural forest covers 115,047,000 ha (12% of total land area). Smil (1983) estimates that China has lost 24% of its forested area since 1949. Other comparisons between natural forest cover in the 1950s and the 1980s reflect decreases from 52% to 35% in north-eastern provinces; from 54% to 21% in southern Yunnan Province; and from 20% to 12.5% in mid-western Sichuan Province (ADB, 1987).

Initiatives to establish a wildlife preservation programme were interrupted during the Cultural Revolution from 1966 to 1976, when conservation practices were abandoned and protected areas misused. The protected areas network has expanded progressively from 45 nature reserves in 1979 (Wang Huen-pu, 1980), to 73 in 1981 and 273 in 1984 (Boswell, 1983). According to Forest Department statistics, by 1986 there were 333 nature reserves covering a total area in excess of 19,330,000 ha (2.0%) of China. Of these, 31 are 'key' national nature reserves. By the end of 1989, there were 600 protected areas of various kinds covering

3% of the country (Chongqi, 1991). Much of the work associated with developing the protected areas network has been carried out at the local level through universities or local branches of the National Academy (Lucas, 1987).

Soil erosion is a major problem in China with 50 billion tons of soil washed away annually due to the degradation of the natural vegetation. An associated problem is desertification, which is increasing at a rate of 6,660 sq. km per year. Another problem facing China is pollution from improper discharge of waste water, waste gas and industrial residues (Ji et al., 1990). Acid rain in the south is being caused by coal burning (Smil et al., 1982). A comprehensive national plan to improve land management and increase afforestation, drafted in 1985, has led to extensive planting schemes covering nearly four million sq. km in the border desert regions (Richardson, 1990).

Addresses

Division of Nature Conservation (Director), National Environmental Protection Agency, Ministry of Urban and Rural Construction and Environmental Protection, 115 Xizhimennei Nansciaojie, Beijing (Tel. 86 1 8992211; Tlx: 22477)

Forest Department (Director), Ministry of Forestry, Hepingh, Beijing (Tel. 86 1 22237)

References

Anon. (n.d.). *The Environmental Protection Law of the People's Republic of China (For Trial Implementation)*. 32 pp.

ADB. (1987). *Environmental and natural resources briefing profile, People's Republic of China*. Asian Development Bank, Manila. 11 pp.

FAO. (1988). An interim report on the state of forest resources in the developing countries. FAO, Rome. 18 pp.

Anon. (1990). Governments: China.. *Bruntland Bulletin*. P. 33.

Boswall, J. (1983). *Visit to China*. Unpublished. 10 pp.

Chongqi, L. (1991). Nature reserves in China. *Tiger Paper* 18: 2–5.

Ji, Z., Guangmei, Z., Huadong, W., and Jialin, X. (1990). *The Natural History of China*. Collins, London. 224 pp.

Lucas, B. (1987). Notes on trip to China. IUCN, Gland, Switzerland. Unpublished. 4 pp.

MacKinnon, J. (1989a). *National conservation management plan for the giant panda and its habitat*. China Alliance Press, Hong Kong. 157 pp.

MacKinnon, J. (1989b). The selection of nature reserves in China. Paper prepared for Beijing Pheasant Symposium. 4 pp.

Ratcliffe, D.A. (1982). Philosophy and practice of nature conservation in China. Nature Conservancy Council, London. Unpublished. Pp. 34–44.

Repetto, R. (1988). *The forest for the trees ? Government policies and the misuse of forest resources*. World Resources Institute, Washington, DC. P. 4.

Richardson, S.D. (1990). *Forests and forestry in China*. Island Press, Washington, DC. 352 pp.

Smil, V., Goodland, R., and Toh, G. (1982). *The People's Republic of China: Environmental Aspects of Economic Development*. World Bank, Washington, DC. 76 pp.

Smil, V. (1983). Deforestation in China. *Ambio* 12: 226–31.

Thornback, J. (1986). Report of a visit to China 22 June–5 July. IUCN Conservation Monitoring Centre, Cambridge, UK. Unpublished. 7 pp.

UNEP/IUCN (1988). *Coral Reefs of the World. Vol. 3: Central and Western Pacific*. UNEP Regional Seas Directories and Bibliographies. IUCN, Gland, Switzerland and Cambridge, UK/UNEP, Nairobi, Kenya. 329 pp.

Wang Huen-pu (1980). Nature Conservation in China: the present situation. *Parks* 5(1): 1–10.

Wenhua, L. and Xianying, Z. (1989). *China's nature reserves*. Foreign Languages Press, Beijing. Pp. 11–16.

Xuezhi, X. (1987). *Wildlife management in China*. Paper presented at International Conference on Wildlife Conservation in China, 14–19 July, Beijing. Pp. 153–61.

Yuging, W. (1987). Natural conservation regions in China. *Ambio* 16: 326–31.

ANNEX Definitions of protected area designations, as legislated, together with authorities responsible for their administration.

Title (English title):
Proposal no. 92 passed at the Third Conference of the First National People's Congress.

Date: 1956

Brief description:
Provides for the declaration and classification of nature reserves.

Administrative authority:
Division of Nature Conservation, Ministry of Urban and Rural Reconstruction and Environmental Protection

Designations:
— National nature reserve -Preserves the flora and fauna in their original state.
— Designated by the State Council
Provimcial nature reserve
— Designated by the provincial government

Source: Yuging 1987

Title (English title):
Forestry Act.

Date: 1979, amended 1984

Brief description:
Provides for the establishment and administration of forest reserves.

Administrative authority:
Forest Department, Ministry of Forestry

Designations:
Forest reserve
— Designated for the protection of typical forest ecosystems and forests of great value.
Reserve
— Designated areas for the protection of rare and precious animals, as well as their habitats and breeding grounds.

Source: Richardson (1990)

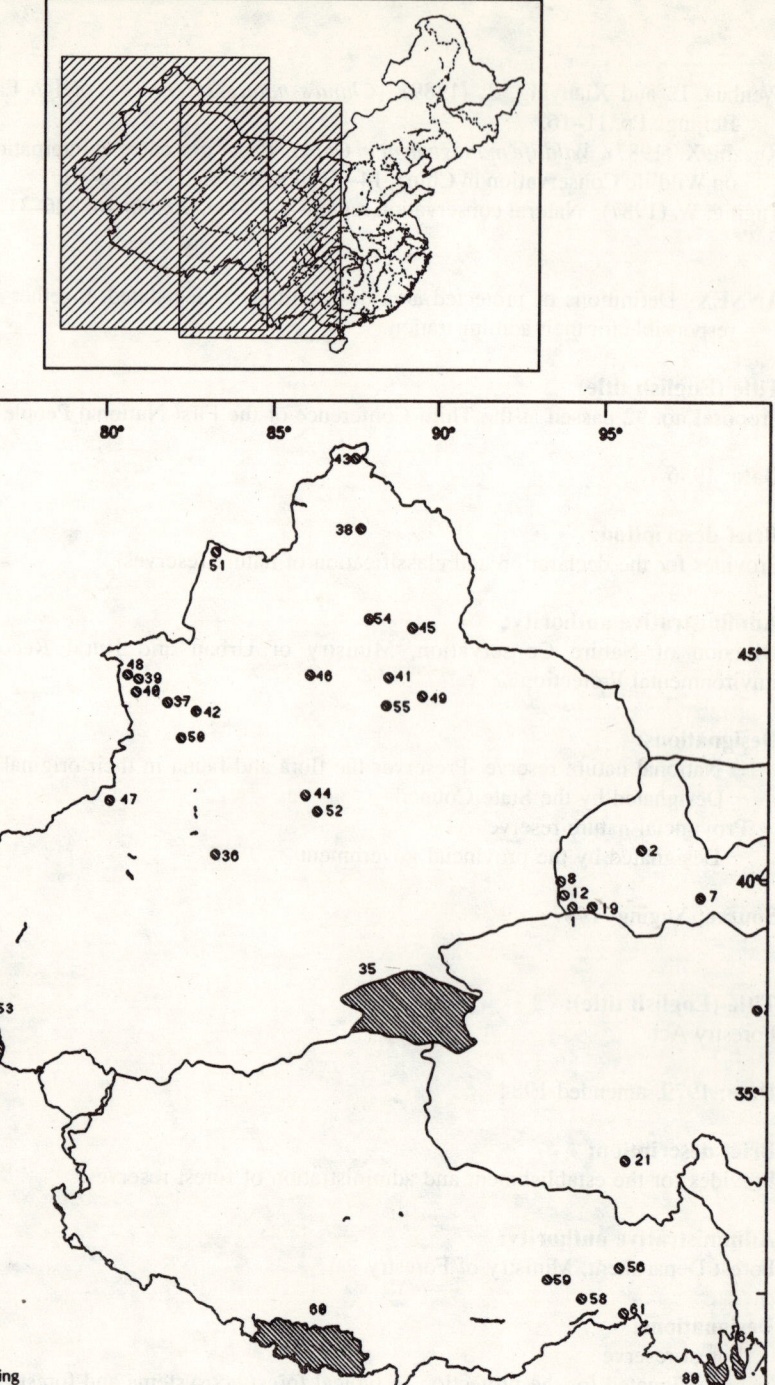

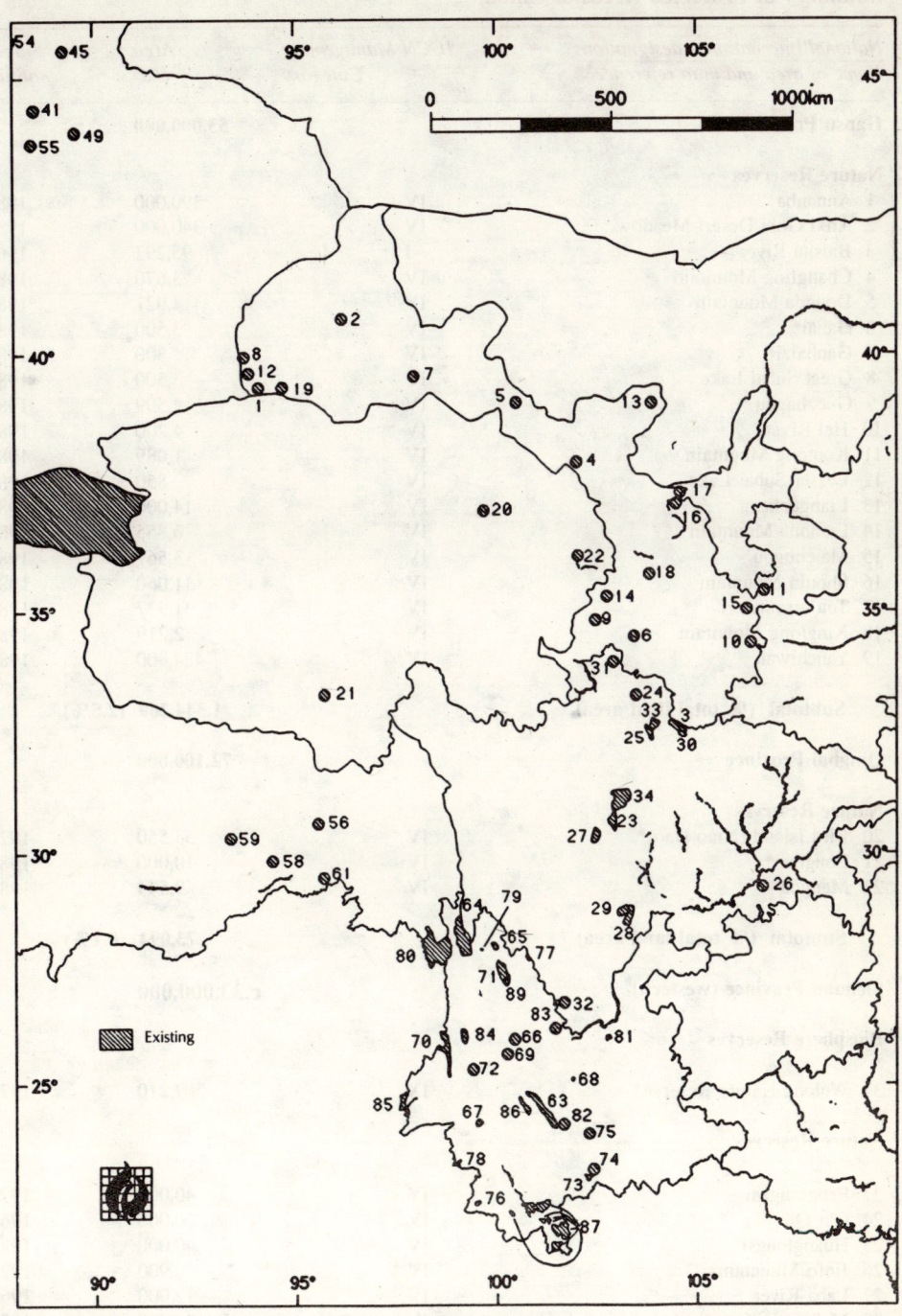

China

Summary of Protected Areas of China

National/International designation Name of area and map reference[+]	IUCN Management Category	Area (ha)	Year notified
Gansu Province		**53,000,000**	
Nature Reserves			
1 Annanba	IV	390,000	1982
2 Anxi Gobi Desert Meadow	IV	340,000	1985
3 Baishu River	I	95,292	1963
4 Changling Mountain	IV	3,670	1980
5 Dongda Mountain	IV	4,921	1980
6 Gahai*	IV	3,500	1982
7 Ganhaizi*	IV	300	1982
8 Great Suhai Lake	IV	3,500	1982
9 Guozhagou	IV	2,509	1982
10 Hei River	IV	4,200	1982
11 Kontong Mountain	IV	1,089	1982
12 Lesser Suhai Lake	IV	850	1982
13 Liangucheng	IV	14,000	1982
14 Lianhua Mountain	IV	6,855	1982
15 Maichogou	IV	3,567	1982
16 Shoulu Mountain	IV	11,060	1980
17 Tou'ersantan	IV	31,937	1982
18 Xinglong Mountain	IV	2,219	1982
19 Yanchiwan	IV	424,800	1982
Subtotal (% total land area)		**1,344,269 (2.5%)**	
Qinghai Province		**72,100,000**	
Nature Reserves			
20 Bird Island (Niao Dao)*	IV	53,550	1975
21 Longbao*	IV	10,000	1984
22 Mengda	IV	9,544	1980
Subtotal (% total land area)		**73,094 (0.1%)**	
Sichuan Province (western)[#]		**c.33,000,000**	
Biosphere Reserves			
34 Wolong Nature Reserve*	IX	207,210	1979
Nature Reserves			
23 Fengtongzai	IV	40,000	1978
24 Gar Qu	IV	20,000	1963
25 Huanglongsi	IV	40,000	1983
26 Jinfo Mountains	IV	900	1979
27 Laba River	IV	12,000	1963
28 Mabian Dafengding	IV	30,000	1978
29 Meigu Dafengding	IV	16,000	1978
30 Tangjiahe*	IV	28,000	1978

National/International designation Name of area and map reference[+]	IUCN Management Category	Area (ha)	Year notified
31 Tiebu	IV	23,000	1965
32 Tukou Cycas	IV	310	1983
33 Wanglang*	IV	27,700	1963
34 Wolong*	IV	200,000	1975
Subtotal (% total land area)		**457,910 (1.4%)**	
Xinjiang Uygur Zizhiqu Autonomous Region		**164,680,000**	
Biosphere Reserve			
54 Bogdhad Mountain Biosphere Reserve*	IX	217,000	1990
Nature Reserves			
35 A Er Jin Shan (Arjin Mountains)*	IV	4,512,000	1985
36 Bayanbulak*	IV	100,000	1980
37 Black Bees	IV	—	1980
38 Bulgan River	IV	5,000	1980
39 Bunge Ash	IV	1,400	1983
40 Chinese Walnut	IV	1,180	1983
41 Fuhai Jengsetas	IV	9,767	1986
42 Ganjia Lake	IV	1,042,000	1983
43 Hanas*	IV	250,000	1980
44 Huocheng	IV	35,000	1983
45 Kalamaili Mountain	IV	1,700,000	1982
46 Lake of Heaven	IV	38,069	1980
47 Mount Tomur	IV	100,000	1980
48 Naz-Quelute	IV	16,400	1986
49 Qitai	IV	12,333	1986
50 Schrenk Spruce	IV	28,000	1983
51 Tacheng	IV	1,500	1980
52 Tarim	IV	387,000	1980
53 Taxkorgan*	IV	1,500,000	1984
54 Tianchi	IV	38,063	1980
55 Urumqi Geological	IV	200,000	1986
Subtotal (% total land area)		**9,978,612 (6.1%)**	
Xizang Zizhiqu Autonomous Region		**122,160,000**	
Nature Reserves			
56 Gang	IV	4,600	1985
57 Jiangcun* (now part of 60)	IV	—	1985
58 Medog*	IV	62,620	1985
59 Pagyi	IV	8	1985
60 Qomolangma*	IV	3,500,000	1989
61 Zayu	IV	101,400	1985
62 Zham (now part of 60)	IV		1985
Subtotal (% total land area)		**3,668,628 (3%)**	

National/International designation Name of area and map reference[+]	IUCN Management Category	Area (ha)	Year notified
Yunnan Province		**43,620,000**	
Nature Reserves			
63 Ailao Mountain	IV	50,360	1986
64 Baima Mountain	IV	180,000	1983
65 Bitahai*	IV	14,133	1984
66 Cangshan Erhai	IV	70,000	1981
67 Daxue Mountain	IV	15,787	1986
68 Dialin Mountain	IV	613	1984
69 Erhai Lake	IV	24,976	—
70 Gaoligong Mountain	IV	123,333	1983
71 Haba Mountain	IV	21,907	1984
72 Heaven Lake	IV	6,667	1983
73 Huanglian Mountain	IV	13,835	1983
74 Jizu Mountain	IV	2,000	1983
75 Kunming	IV	143,000	1981
76 Long Mountain	IV	54	1986
77 Lugu Lake	IV	8,127	1986
78 Nangun River	IV	7,000	1980
79 Napahai*	IV	2,067	1984
81 Pudu River	IV	11	1984
82 Songhuaba	IV	60,000	1981
83 Stone Grove	IV	9,000	1981
84 Tianchi	IV	7,000	1981
85 Tongbiguan	IV	34,160	1986
86 Wuliang Mountain	IV	23,353	1986
87 Xishuangbanna*	IV	207,000	1958
88 Yulong Mountain	IV	26,000	1984
Subtotal (% total land area)		**1,425,816 (3.3%)**	
TOTAL			
Nature reserves (% total land area)		**16,989,241 (3.5%)**	

+ Locations of most protected areas are shown in the accompaning map.
* Site is described in this directory.
# Comprises Aba (Ngawa) Zangzu Zizhizhou, Garze Zangzu Zizhizhou, Leshan, Wenjiang, Xichang and Yaan counties.

A ER JIN SHAN (ARJIN MOUNTAINS) NATURE RESERVE

IUCN Management Category   Absolute Conservation Zone: I (Strict Nature Reserve)
Relative Conservation Zone: IV (Managed Nature Reserve)

Biogeographical Province   2.23.08 (Tibetan)

Geographical Location   The reserve is located within the Bayan Gor Autonomous District of Ruoqiang County. It is situated in the extreme south-east corner of the region bordering Xizang Zizhiqu Autonomous Region (Tibet) to the south and Qinghai Province to the east. The northern border follows the Chimen Tagh Mountains and the western border extends to the Chimen Tagh mountains. The nearest town is Ruoqiang, approximately 150 km to the north (340 km by road). 36°14′–37°53′N, 87°22′–91°20′E.

Date and History of Establishment   Declared a national nature reserve in March 1985 by the State Council, Beijing. Previously notified a nature reserve by the State Council of Xinjiang Uygur Zizhiqu Autonomous Region in May 1983, having first been proposed as a conservation zone in 1979.   In July 1983 the Environmental Protection Agency (EPA) established a regional administration office in Ruoqiang and a first checkpost at Duckspring.

Area   4,512,000 ha.

Land Tenure   State

Altitude   Ranges from 3,100 m in the northern valleys of the reserve to 7,725 m at the summit of Mount Muztag in the south-west corner. There are more than 100 peaks over 5,000 m.

Physical Features   The reserve consists of a series of mountain ranges, generally rising to 5,000–6,000 m, and intervening valleys lying at 3,100–4,600 m. The major mountain ranges are Chimen Tagh in the north and a section of the Kunlun Shan, stretching from Achik Lake in the central-west to the south-east of the reserve. Large alluvial fan and apron deposits are extensive in the valleys; Aeolion deposits in the form of sand dunes and blankets are also common. There are active dunes south of Yixiekepati Lake and eastwards from there to Karquka Lake; these rise 300 m above the valley floor. The geology of the reserve is poorly known and geological maps are not available. In other parts of the reserve, such as the Karton area, dunes have been stabilised by vegetation. The reserve is located on the nothern edge of the Tibetan Plateau, which was formed during orogenic events beginning in the Mesozoic period 120 million years ago. Being furthest north, the reserve was one of the first areas to emerge from the Tethys Sea and it continues to rise at perhaps several centimetres per year. A band of limestone bedrock, containing early-stage karst features, extends south-east from Achik Lake along the Arka Tagh. Igneous intrusions are noted in the Karton Karquka areas. It has been suggested that Muztag is a volcanic peak, although this is disputed. Hot springs, which are usually associated with igneous activity, may occur in the southern part of the reserve. Drainage is primarily into two internal basins: Achik Lake in the west and the other, including Ayak Kum Lake, in the east and north.   Smaller drainage basins occur in the south-east and along the northern boundary. River and stream flow is seasonal, with daily variation occurring when influenced by glacial melt. There are five large lakes in the reserve: Achik and Ayak Kum are brackish, Yixiekepati and Karquka are fresh, and the fifth, on the south-central border, is partly fresh and partly salt. The two salt lakes are shrinking, probably having attained a maximum size during the Pleistocene. There are many glaciers at high altitudes in the Chimen Tagh and Kunlun Shan, those on Mount Muztag being the most extensive and spectacular (Butler et al., 1986).

Climate Conditions are continental, arid and cold. Mean annual temperature at lower altitudes is probably about 0 °C. Summers are cool, typically with daily maxima of 7–9 °C and daily minima of –2 °C to 2 °C in July at the lowest altitudes. Winters are very cold. Total annual precipitation, which occurs mostly in summer, is estimated to be 100–200 mm at the lowest altitudes (Butler et al., 1986).

Vegetation Ten vegetation types have been recognised. 1. Wet saline meadow is dominated by *Elymus secalinus* and *Achnatherum splendus*. These meadows occur near springs, lakes and rivers in the northern and eastern parts of the reserve. 2. Wet marshland meadow occurs around springs, lakes and rivers in eastern and southern parts. Dominant species are *Carex* spp. and *Blysmus* sp. 3. Sand hills vegetation is found in the central part and is dominated by *Carex moorcroftii*, *Trisetum spicatum*, *Stipa basiplumosa*, and *Elymus* spp., with *Salsola* spp. on moist lower slopes. 4. Low semi-shrub desert is found at 4,050–4,200 m in northern and eastern valleys and is dominated by *Salsola abrotanoides*. 5. Cold desert, dominated by *Salsola abrotanoides* and *Ceratoides compacta*, occurs on low hills at 4,200–4,350 m in the north and north-east parts. This is a transition zone between low semi-shrub desert below and very cold desert above. 6. Very cold desert occurs on mountain slopes above 4,350 m and is dominated by *Ceratoides compacta*. 7. Desert grassland, dominated by *Stipa glareosa* and *Salsola abrotanoides,* is found in eastern and central parts on low hills and valley bottoms at 4,050–4,200 m. 8. Cold, dry grassland (steppe) is dominated by *Stipa glareosa* and occurs in the central region at 4,200–4,350 m. 9. Very cold grassland occurs in central and eastern parts, at 4,200–4,400 m and is dominated by *Stipa glareosa*, *Carex* spp., *Leontopodium* sp., *Potentilla* sp., *Artemisia* sp., and *Astragalus* sp. 10. High mountain herb mat occurs at 4,400–5,000 m on mountain slopes in the central part. It is dominated by *Leontopodium* sp., *Potentilla* sp., *Aster* sp., *Astragalus* sp., *Poa* sp., *Gogen* sp., and *Arenaria monticola* (Butler et al., 1986). The flora currently consists of more than 240 species and contains elements of both Central Asian Desert and Tibetan Plateau floras, but taxonomists have found possibly half a dozen new species in the reserve and more are likely. A preliminary list of vascular plans is given in Butler et al., 1986. A more complete list is available from Professor Cui Nai Ran at Xinjiang Normal University, Urumqi. No studies have been made of lichens or bryophytes.

Fauna Consists of Central Asian species, most prominent in the north, and Tibetan Plateau species which are most common in the south. Of the ungulates, the most numerous species are: Tibetan antelope *Pantholops hodgsoni*, with an estimated 70,000–100,000 distributed throughout the reserve; Tibetan wild ass *Equus hemionus* (V), with an estimated 30,000 fairly evenly distributed; and wild yak *Bos grunniens* (E), with over 10,000 mostly in the south. There are also some 10,000 bharal *Pseudois nayaur*, and similar numbers (less than 10,000) of Tibetan gazelle *Procapra picticaudata* and argali *Ovis ammon hodgsoni*. The presence of ibex *Capra sibirica* has not been confirmed although the species occurs just to the north in the Chimen Tagh. Carnivores include wolf *Canis lupus* (V), brown bear *Ursus arctos*, snow leopard *Panthera uncia* (E), steppe cat *Felis manul*, and lynx *F. lynx*. Other mammals include

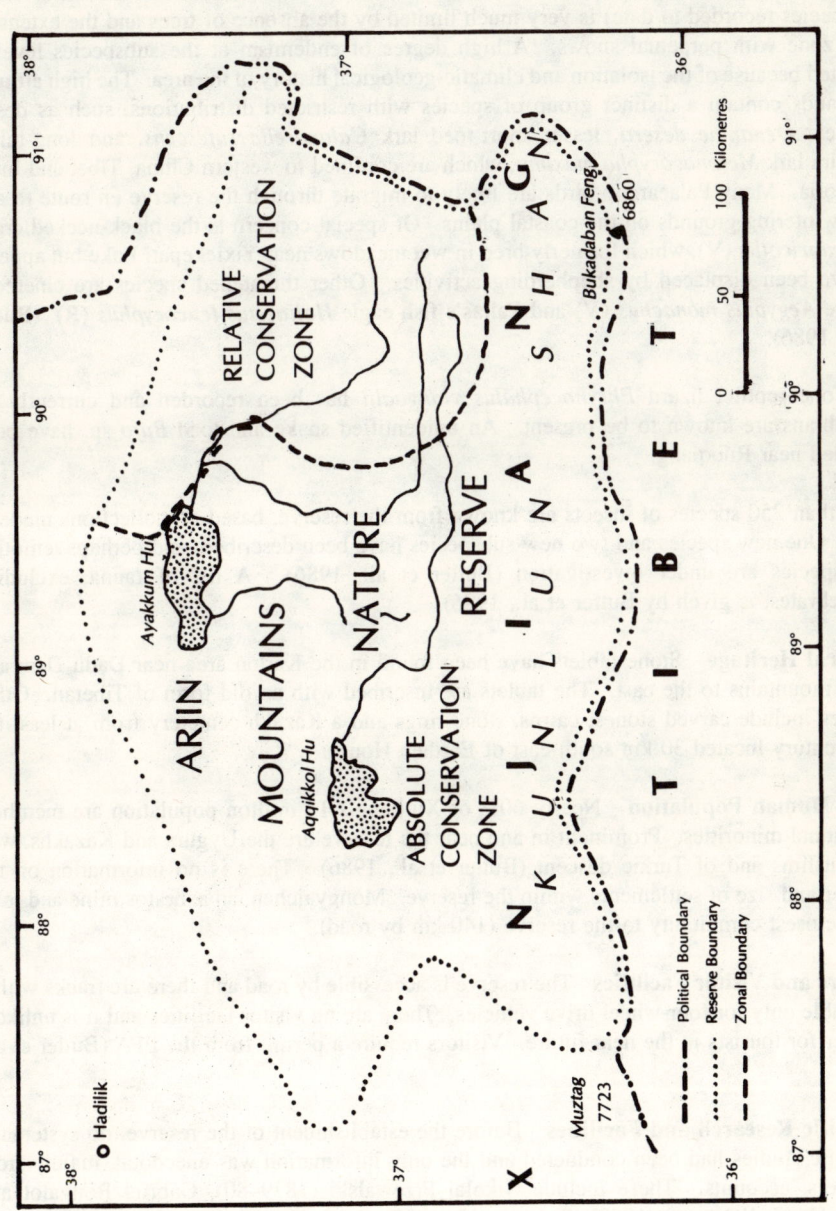

A er Jin Shan (Arjin Mountain) Nature Reserve

four species of pika *Ochotona* spp., Himalayan marmot *Marmota bobak,* and five species of smaller rodents (Butler et al., 1986).

The avifauna is similar to that of other east–west mountain ranges in Central Asia; its diversity (42 species recorded to date) is very much limited by the absence of trees and the extensive nival zone with perpetual snows. A high degree of endemism at the subspecies level is expected because of the isolation and climatic-geological history of the area. The high altitude grasslands contain a distinct group of species with restricted distributions, such as desert wheatear *Oenanthe deserti,* lesser short-toed lark *Calandrella rufescens,* and long-billed calandra lark *Melonocorypha maxima,* which are confined to western China, Tibet and Inner Mongolia. Many Palaearctic birds are likely to migrate through the reserve en route to and from wintering grounds on the coastal plains. Of special concern is the black-necked crane *Grus nigricollis* (V), which formerly bred in wet meadows near Yixiekepati Lake but appears to have been displaced by shepherding activities. Other threatened species are cinereous vulture *Aegypius monachus* (V) and Pallas's fish eagle *Haliaeetus leucoryphus* (R) (Butler et al., 1986).

Only one reptile, lizard *Phrynocephalus vlangaalii* has been recorded and currently no amphibians are known to be present. An unidentified snake and toad *Bufo* sp. have been recorded near Ruoqiang.

More than 250 species of insects are known from the reserve, based on collections made in 1984. One new species and two new subspecies have been described, and perhaps ten other new species are under investigation (Butler et al., 1986). A list of fauna, excluding invertebrates, is given by Butler et al., 1986).

Cultural Heritage   Stone tablets have been found in the Karton area near Dadu Dam and in the mountains to the east. The tablets are inscribed with an old form of Tibetan. Other features include carved stones, cairns, stone rings and a Kazakh cemetery from at least the 19th century located 30 km south-east of Earthen House.

Local Human Population   Nearly 60% of Xinjiang's 13 million population are members of national minorities. Prominent in and near the reserve are the Uygurs and Kazakhs, who are Muslims and of Turkic descent (Butler et al., 1986). There is no information on the number and size of settlements within the reserve. Mongyaichen, an asbestos mine and mill, is the closest community to the reserve (140 km by road).

Visitors and Visitor Facilities   The reserve is accessible by road and there are tracks within it suitable only for four-wheel drive vehicles. There are no visitor facilities and it is unlikely to cater for tourists in the near future. Visitors require a permit from the EPA (Butler et al., 1986).

Scientific Research and Facilities   Before the establishment of the reserve, no systematic scientific studies had been conducted and the only information was anecdotal, mainly from travellers' accounts. These include Nikolai Przewalski (1879–80), Gabriel Bonvalot and Prince Henri d'Orleans (1889), Roborovski (1890), Jules Dutriel de Rhins (1893), George Littledale (1895–6), Sven Hedin (1900–1) and Ella Maillart and Peter Fleming (1935). Following its establishment, the EPA made at least one field trip each summer. Extensive collections and observations were made in 1984 by scientists from universities and institutes; a film 'Scenes of the Arjin Mountains Nature Reserve' was also made that year. The breeding biology of the bar-headed goose in the reserve has been studied by Liu Wei, based at Ruoqiang EPA office in 1986. In July 1986, an IUCN/WWF China joint expedition made an inventory of the resources in the reserve and advised on planning and management (Butler et al., 1986). Planned studies include research on the vegetation, animal numbers and migration patterns, rodents, karst landform distribution, collection of climatic data and cultural sites.

Conservation Value The reserve is the highest and largest protected area in China, with a wide range of physical and biological features that are of international significance. Furthermore, the area has been little disturbed by human activities. To date, it is the only protected area in the northern region of the Tibetan Plateau (Butler et al., 1986).

Conservation Management The reserve is currently divided into two zones: a large absolute conservation zone, in which all types of use, except authorised scientific research, are prohibited; and a smaller relative conservation zone, in which a variety of human uses are permitted, in addition to resource protection. The main resource use in the relative conservation zone, in the north-eastern corner of the reserve, is pastoralism. This occurs primarily in the Yixiekapati Lake area where there were an estimated 20,000 animals in July 1986. Steps are being taken to reduce this population, in view of possible conflict with native species. It has been recommended that the reserve should be nominated as a biosphere reserve (Butler et al., 1986).

Management Constraints Grazing by domestic livestock, the primary impact, needs to be properly controlled in the relative conservation zone. Vast areas of the reserve are not patrolled regularly due to the limited administrative facilities. Given the difficult access, this is not a major deficiency at present.

Staff No precise information.

Budget No information.

Local Addresses
Managing Bureau, Arjin Mountains Nature Reserve, Xinjiang EPA, Ruoqiang, Xinjiang Uygur Autonomous Region

References
Butler, J., Achuff, P. and Johnston, J. (1986). *Arjin Mountains Nature Reserve, Xinjiang Management Recommendations and Resource Summary*. IUCN/WWF China Joint Expedition, 1986. IUCN/WWF Gland, Switzerland. 59 pp.

BAYANBULAK NATURE RESERVE

IUCN Management Category IV (Managed nature reserve)

Biogeographical Province 2.36.12 (Pamir-Tian-Shan Highlands)

Geographical Location   Located in the Yurdus Basin of Hejing County, 200 km north-west of Kuerle.   The reserve is difficult to reach, being accessible only by two rough trails. 42°50′N, 84°00′E

Date and History of Establishment   Approved as a nature reserve in 1980 by the Regional People's Government in Document 101 (Anon., n.d.), and officially established in 1981 (Xiyang, 1988).

Area   100,000 ha

Land Tenure   State

Altitude   Ranges from 2,430 m to 4,800 m.

Physical Features   Occupies the Yurdus Basin which is surrounded by the snow-capped Tian Shan whose peaks rise up to 4,800 m.   The basin is vast and flat, and includes a complex of small freshwater lakes, ponds and marshes fed by numerous rivers and streams from the surrounding hills which drain east through a gorge into Bosten Hu and Bo Hu marshes (Jianjian, 1989).

Climate   The climate is distinctly influenced by the topography of the basin and the Tian Shan, with cold air currents descending from the mountains.   Summers are short (June to August) but warm, with temperatures averaging 10 °C and reaching 20 °C in July (Yusheng, 1984).   Mean annual temperature is −4.7 °C, with no more than 12 frost-free days during the year.   Winters are long and extremely cold with temperatures as low as −20° C (Xiyang, 1988).   Mean annual rainfall is 276 mm (Yusheng, 1984).

Vegetation   The lakes support reed-beds dominated by *Phragmites communis* and sedge marshes dominated by *Carex muliensis* (Jianjian, 1989).   Other species found near the waters edge include *Typha latifolia*, bulrush *Scirpus validus*, and sorrel *Rumex* spp; submerged plants occur in the lake (Xiyang, 1988).   In the surrounding areas, the vegetation is predominantly grassland (Yusheng, 1984) because trees and shrubs are unable to tolerate the extreme climatic conditions.   Notable species include *Scirpus tabernaemontani* and nut grass, on which swans feed (Xiyang, 1988).

Fauna   Mammals include grey wolf *Canis lupis* (V), and corsac fox *Vulpes corsac* (K) which preys on the waterfowl.   The avifauna totals 72 species including, cinereous vulture *Aegypius monachus* (V), whistling swan *Cygnus columbianus*, mute swan *Cygnus olor*, whooper swan *Cygnus cygnus* which occurs in large numbers, white-bellied sea eagle *Haliaeetus leucogaster*, black stork *Ciconia nigra*, bar-headed goose *Anser indicus*, brown-headed gull *Larus brunnicephalus*, mallard *Anas platyrhynchos*, common redshank *Tringa totanus*, great egret *Egretta alba*, and common crane *Grus grus* which uses the reserve as a breeding, staging and wintering area (Xiyang, 1988).

Cultural Heritage   About 200 years ago the area was inhabited by a Mongolian tribe.   The swans are believed by the local people to be angelic symbols of loyalty and good fortune, which is an important factor in their protection.

Local Human Population   Due to the inaccessibility of the reserve, the area is sparsely populated mostly by Mongolian herdsmen (Yusheng, 1984).

Visitors and Visitor Facilities No information.

Scientific Research and Facilities A team of scientists from Xinjiang Institute of Biology, Sand and Soil Sciences surveyed the avifauna in 1987 (Yusheng, 1984). There are no scientific facilities.

Conservation Value The reserve provides an important source of freshwater for the surrounding area, as well as for waterfowl, particularly swans (Jianjian, 1989).

Conservation Management There are regulations against the hunting and removal of swans from the reserve (Xiyang, 1988). The Environmental Protection Agency supervises the running of the reserve but it is administered by the Bazhou Forestry Department (Jianjian, 1989). Regular patrols are made around the lake to ensure that swans are not disturbed by either human activity or predators, especially during the moulting period (Yusheng, 1984). The local police are actively involved in the protection of swans by generating publicity and by investigating cases of harrassment (Xiyang, 1984).

Management Constraints There have been a number of cases in which cygnets have been removed from within the boundaries of the reserve (Xiyang, 1984).

Staff No information

Budget No information.

Local Addresses No information.

References
Jianjian, L. (1989). In: Scott, D.A. (Ed.), *A directory of Asian wetlands*. IUCN, Gland, Switzerland and Cambridge, UK. Pp. 249–50.
Wenhua, L. and Xianying, Z. (1989). *China's nature reserves*. Foreign Languages Press, Beijing. P. 185.
Xiyang, T. (1988). *Living Treasures. An odyssey through China's extra ordinary nature serves*. Pp. 95–106.
Yusheng, W. (1984). The real swan lake—a bird sanctuary. *China Reconstructs,* August: 8–11.

BIRD ISLAND (NIAO DAO) NATURE RESERVE

IUCN Management Category IV (Managed Nature Reserve).

Biogeographical Province 2.22.08 (Takla-Makan-Gobi Desert)

Geographical Location The reserve is one of five islets lying furthest in the west in Qinghai Lake, which is situated on the Qinghai-Tibet plateau of Gangchu County, 90 km west of Xining. 36°59′N, 99°51′E

Date and History of Establishment Niao Dao Nature Reserve was approved in 1975 by the Provincial Revolutionary Committee (Orr, n.d.).

Area   The reserve was enlarged from 7,850 ha to its present size of 53,550 ha in 1975.

Land Tenure   Provincial government

Altitude   3,185 m

Physical Features   Bird Island is connected to the mainland by a narrow isthmus of marshes and salt flats.   The reserve incorporates part of the lake in an inland drainage system surrounded by bare salt flats, shingle and sand beaches.   Along the south-western shore are brackish marshes and extensive wet meadows (Dehao et al., 1989).   The lake is fed by the Boha and Shalu rivers, numerous streams and hot springs.   Its soil is barren with pebbles and gravel deposits predominant (Wenhua and Xianying, 1989).   The lake has a high salinity of 12.49 grams per litre (Ji et al., 1990).

Climate   The influence of the Qinghai-Tibet plateau gives rise to arid, cold, windy conditions with little rainfall and high variations in daily temperatures (Wenhua and Xiangying, 1989). Winters are long and cold with temperatures falling to −35 °C in January but little snowfall. Summers are short and hot, with most of the precipitation occurring during this period (Dehao et al., 1989).

Vegetation   Due to the climatic conditions, the vegetation is sparse and of low stature as the growing season is extremely short (Wenhua and Xianying, 1989).   There is no aquatic vegetation in the lake other than algae, while adjacent marshes are brackish with halophytic vegetation, or fresh with an abundant growth of emergents, such as *Typha* sp.   Bordering the marshes are wet grasslands and a rich alpine meadow plant community, with low *Salix* scrub growing along the rivers.   The surrounding area is grassy steppe, with some stunted woodland on north-facing slopes (Dehao et al., 1989).

Fauna   Bird Island is an extremely important breeding area for a number of waterfowl including 500 pairs of great cormorant *Phalacrocorax carbo*, 2,300 pairs of bar-headed goose *Anser indicus*, 6,500 pairs of brown-headed gull *Larus brunnicephalus*, several hundred pairs of ruddy shelduck *Tadorna ferruginea*, common coot *Fulica atra*, Kentish plover *Charadrius alexandrinus*, great black-headed gull *Larus ichthyaetus*, and smaller numbers of great-crested grebe *Podiceps cristatus*, gadwall *Anas strepera*, mallard *A. platyrhynchos*, spotbill duck *A. poecilorhyncha*, northern shoveller *A. clypeata*, red-crested pochard *Netta rufina*, pochard duck *Aythya nyroca*, northern lapwing *Vanellus vanellus*, common redshank *Tringa totanus* and common tern *Sterna hirundo*.   Small numbers of migranting black-necked crane *Grus nigricollis* (R) spend the summer in the wet meadows by the lake and there is a breeding population of Pallas's sea-eagle *Haliaeetus leucoryphus* (R).   The reserve also supports 1,000–1,250 whooper swans *Cygnus cygnus*, teal duck *Anas falcata*, tufted duck *Aythya fuligula*, and goosander *Mergus merganser*.   Swans arrive in October and stay until late March and early April.   The lake is also used as a stop-over by migratory birds during spring and autumn; for example, in April 1986 over 1,000 bar-headed geese, 400 northern pintail, 150 common goldeneye, 600 ruddy shelduck, 2,000 tufted duck, and 25 smew were recorded. Migrants present during mid-May 1987 included lesser sand plover *Charadrius mongolus*, wood sandpiper *Tringa glareola* and Temminck's stint *Calidris temminckii*, plus small numbers of six other species of shorebirds (Dehao et al., 1989).   The only known species of fish in the lake is naked carp *Gymnocypris przewalskii* (Wenhua and Xianying, 1989).

Cultural Heritage   No information

Local Human Population   Several villages occur on the lakeshore. The area is also used by nomadic pastoralists from the region. Fishing and domestic livestock grazing takes place inside the reserve. Outside the reserve, hunting and the removal of birds eggs for human consumption is widespread (Dehao et al., 1989).

Visitors and Visitor Facilities   The reserve attracts a large number of both national and foreign visitors each year. Extensive new visitor facilities, including observation hides, were built in 1987 (Dehao et al., 1989).

Scientific Research and Facilities   Biologists from the North-West Plateau Institute of Biology in Xining have been involved in research on the lake, its meadows and wildlife. In 1983, the National Bird Banding Centre began ringing waterfowl, especially *Anser indicus* and *Larus brunnicephallus*. Liao et al. (1984) have studied the behaviour of *Larus ichthyaetus*. Located at the reserve headquarters is the Bird Island Management Research Station, constructed in 1987 (Dehao et al., 1989).

Conservation Value   Bird Island is an important wetland for waterfowl, as well as being a valuable natural laboratory for scientific research (Wenhua and Xianying, 1989). It is economically important for fishery and tourism (Dehao et al., 1989).

Conservation Management   The reserve is supervised by the Environmental Protection Agency in Beijing, but is administered locally by the Agriculture and Forest Department of Qinghai Province (Anon., 1986), who maintain a Wildlife Management Office on site (Dehao et al., 1989). No management plan currently exists.

Management Constraints   Overgrazing of marshes and meadows has reduced nesting habitat for waterfowl (Dehao et al., 1989). The lake is over-fished: all unlicensed fishing needs to be stopped (Wenhua and Xianying, 1989).

Staff   No information

Budget   No information

Local Addresses   Agriculture and Forestry Department, Xining, Qinghai Province

References
Anon. (1986). *Chinese wetland inventory.* China Wildlife Conservation Association, Beijing. Unpublished. 2 pp.

Dehao, L., Jianjian, L., Olsson, U., Robson, C., Scott, D.A., Xiao-di, Y. and Zhi-yen, Z. (1989). In: Scott, D.A. (Ed.), *A directory of Asian wetlands.* IUCN, Gland, Switzerland and Cambridge, UK. Pp. 236–8.

Ji, Z., Guangmei, Z., Huadong, W. and Jialin, X. (1990). *The natural history of China.* Collins, London. P. 106.

Orr, I. (n.d.). *Some Chinese reserves.* Unpublished report. P. 3.

Wenhua, L. and Xianying, Z. (1989). *China's nature reserves.* Foreign Languages Press, Beijing. Pp. 106–7.

BITAHAI NATURE RESERVE

IUCN Management Category IV (Managed Nature Reserve).

Biogeographical Province 2.39.12 (Szechwan Highlands)

Geographical Location Situated in the Hengduan Mountains of Zhongdian county, 20 km east of Zhongdian and 245 km north of Xiaguan. 27°46′N, 99°54′E

Date and History of Establishment Established in 1984 as a nature reserve.

Area 14,133 ha, of which 159 ha comprises a lake and associated marshes.

Land Tenure Provincial government

Altitude 3,540 m

Physical Features Bitahai is a small, shallow, freshwater lake with associated marshes, fed by streams and run-off from the north–south orientated Hengduan Mountains (Scott, 1989).

Climate Conditions are temperate and montane, with a mean annual precipitation of 620 mm and a mean annual temperate of 5.4 °C (Scott, 1989).

Vegetation The lake and marshes are surrounded by mountains which support coniferous forests (Scott, 1989). Species include spruce *Picea asperata*, firs *Abies* sp., and *Rhododendron* spp. (Ji et al., 1990).

Fauna The avifauna includes black-necked crane *Grus nigricollis* (R), with over 100 recorded, ruddy shelduck *Tadorna ferruginea*, common pochard *Aythya ferina*, and tufted duck *A. fuligula* which uses the lake as a wintering area. Fish species found in the lake include *Brachymystax lenok* (Scott, 1989).

Cultural Heritage No information

Local Human Population The lake is fished and surrounding pastures, both inside and outside the reserve, are grazed (Scott, 1989).

Visitors and Visitor Facilities No information

Scientific Research and Facilities Studies on the fauna and flora have been carried out by biologists from Yunnan Forest Department (Scott, 1989).

Conservation Value The reserve's alpine coniferous forests and waterfowl are characteristic of the region (Wenhua and Xianying, 1989). The lake is an important source of water for surrounding areas. It also provides opportunities for scientific research, conservation education and nature tourism (Scott, 1989).

Conservation Management   Bitahai was initially set up to protect the coniferous forests in the region, but it now includes the wetland.   Hunting is prohibited.   The reserve is locally administered by the Yunnan Forest Department.   A comprehensive management plan is being prepared.   Proposals include the setting up of an environmental education centre in the reserve (Scott, 1989).

Management Constraints   Excessive fishing and grazing are threatening the wetlands within the reserve (Scott, 1989).

Staff   No information

Budget   No information

Local Addresses   Yunnan Provincial Forestry Bureau, Kunming, Yunnan Province

References
Ji, Z., Guangmei, Z., Huadong, W. and Jialin, X. (1990). *The natural history of China*. Collins, London. Pp. 144–6.
Scott, D.A. (Ed.) (1989). *A directory of Asian wetlands*. IUCN, Gland, Switzerland and Cambridge, UK. P. 233.
Wenhua, L. and Xianying, Z. (1989). *China's nature reserves*. Foreign Languages Press, Beijing. P. 187.

BOGHDAD MOUNTAIN BIOSPHERE RESERVE

IUCN Management Category   IX   (Biosphere Reserve)

Biogeographical Province   2.36.12   (Pamir-Tian-Shan Highlands)
2.22.08   (Takla-Makan-Gobi Desert)

Geographical Location   Lies in Fukang County, Changji Hui Autonomous Prefecture, about 50 km north-east of the city of Urumqi.   43°50′–44°30′N, 87°45′–88°05′E.

Date and History of Establishment   Designated as a biosphere reserve in 1990.   It comprises Tian Chi Nature Reserve, *Reaumuria* Reserve and part of *Haloxylon ammodendron* Reserve. Various parts of the reserve are protected under national or provincial legislation (MAB China, 1990).

Area   217,000 ha, comprising a core area of 15,000 ha, a buffer zone of 173,000 ha and a transition area of 29,000 ha (MAB China, 1990).

Land Tenure   Tian Chi Nature Reserve is state owned and an area is also owned by the Academia Sinica (MAB China, 1990).

Altitude   Ranges from 450 m to 5,445 m.

Physical Features   The altitude decreases fairly uniformly from south to north, with the snow- and ice-covered Boghdad Mountain at one extreme and the Kurbantonket and Sacsaoul deserts on the lower, northern edge. Boghdad is the highest peak in the eastern part of the Tian Shan and is on the edge of the Zhungeer Basin desert. Three main rivers drain the area, including the Sangonghe River which flows from Tian Chi (heavenly) Lake. These rivers peter out in a number of distributaries at the edge of the desert. The region was glaciated four times during the Quaternary. Rocks have also been subjected to strong upwarping in the Permian, Jurassic, Cretaceous and Quaternary. Quaternary deposits, at least 300 m thick, have accumulated on the plains and there are also deposits of loess. The plains have mainly saline and desert soils (MAB China, 1990).

Climate   Conditions are arid, continental of the temperate zone. Annual precipitation is over 700 mm in the mountains but only 150 mm in the plains. At 1,911 m a mean annual precipitation of 530 mm has been recorded. Evaporation can be as high as 1960 mm per annum. Maximum mean temperature of the warmest month is 25.8°C and minimum mean temperature of the coldest month is −19 °C (MAB China, 1990).

Vegetation   Below the snow and ice region of the peak there are alpine meadows with *Festuca*, *Stipa*, *Rosa alberti*, and *Artemisia*. Forests below this are dominated by *Picea schrenkiana*. The main species planted or managed for forestry are poplar *Populus diversifolia*, elm *Ulmus pumila,* and *Eleagnus angustifolia*. Desert vegetation is sparser but includes *Reaumuria*, and *Haloxylon ammodendron* in areas of dunes. Nationally threatened species which have been recorded include *Saussurea involucrata*, *Fritillaria walujewii*, *Haloxylon ammodendron*, and *H. persicum* (MAB China, 1990).

Fauna   An estimated 21 species of mammals have been recorded. Internationally or nationally threatened species include brown bear *Ursus arctos*, marten *Martes foina*, otter *Lutra lutra*, lynx *Felis lynx*, Pallas's cat *F. manul*, snow leopard *Panthera uncia* (E), Sikkim stag *Cervus elaphus*, Asiatic wild ass *Equus hemionus* (V), *E. przewalskii* (Ex?), *Gazella subgutturosa*, *Capra sibirica*, argali *Ovis ammon*, and saiga antelope *Saiga tatarica*. Among the birds are black stork *Ciconia nigra*, black kite *Milvus migrans*, long-legged buzzard *Buteo rufinus*, European sparrowhawk *Accipiter nisus*, booted eagle *Hieraaetus pennatus,* griffon vulture *Gyps fulvus*, European hobby *Falco subbuteo*, common kestrel *F. tinnunculus*, and Himalayan snowcock *Tetraogallus himalayensis* (MAB China, 1990).

Cultural Heritage   No information

Local Human Population   Very few people live in the core area but there are several hundred in the buffer zone, some of whom are nomadic. About 120,000 live in the transition area (MAB China, 1990).

Visitors and Visitor Facilities   There are about 500,000 visitors per year (MAB China, 1990).

Scientific Research and Facilities   There are 30 research staff supported by eight technical staff. Academia Sinica has the Fukang Desert Ecosystem Research Station which is managed by Xinjiang Institute of Biology, Pedology and Desert. Foreign scientists also participate in research at this site. An integrated study involving the effects of population and resource use on the environment in the Sangonghe Valley is planned. Sustainable grazing and artificial improvement of grassland is being studied in the buffer zone. It is hoped that a botanic garden of economically useful desert plants can be set up, as well as a facility for breeding wild animal species, particularly *Saiga tatarica* and *Equus przewalskii*, for return to the wild (MAB China, 1990).

Conservation Value   The reserve is typical of the eastern part of the Tian Shan Mountains and extends over a wide altitude range (5,000 m), from snow and ice zones, through alpine meadows and various forest communities to desert at the foot of the mountains. The fauna is varied and includes several threatened species.

Conservation Management   The reserve is zoned into core, buffer and transition areas (MAB China, 1990).

Management Constraints   Wood-cutting and animal husbandry, particularly grazing of the alpine meadows, are the major disturbances in the core area and grazing by domesticated sheep, cattle, goats, pigs, and camels in the desert areas. A variety of crops (cereals, melons, alfalfa, and hops), are cultivated in the desert, contributing to the destruction of *Haloxylon ammodendron* and *Reaumuria*, the former species being scarce in Xinjiang. There is tourist activity in the forested parts, and oil and gas developments in the buffer zone (MAB China, 1990).

Staff   Total of 60, including 30 for administration, protection and resource management, six for education and training, and 30 for research (MAB China, 1990).

Budget   RMB 6 million

Local Addresses
Boghdad Mountain Biosphere Reserve, Xinjiang Institute of Biology, Pedology and Psammology, Beijing Road, Urumqui, Xinjiang 830011

References
MAB China (1990). Boghdad Mountain Biosphere Reserve. Biosphere Reserve Nomination Form.

GAHAI NATURE RESERVE

IUCN Management Category   IV (Managed Nature Reserve)

Biogeographical Province   2.39.12 (Szechwan Highlands)

Geographical Location   Situated on the eastern edge of the Qinghai-Tibetan plateau, 240 km south-west of Lanzhou, in the extreme south of Gansu Province. 34°12′N, 102°20′

Date and History of Establishment   Established as a nature reserve in 1982.

Area   3,500 ha

Land Tenure   The wetland is state owned; surrounding areas are under collective ownership.

Altitude   Ranges from 1,200 m to 3,320 m

Physical Features   The wetland lies on a small plain almost entirely surrounded by peaks, some of which attain 4,150 m. Local run-off and ten springs feed a complex of shallow, freshwater lakes and marshes which drain north into the Tao He, a tributary of the Yellow River (Huang Ho). Water levels remain stable throughout the year, with a maximum depth of 1.2 m and pH of 8.6 (Jianjian, 1989). Soils are mostly podzolic with alpine meadow soils occurring at higher elevations (Richardson, 1990).

Climate   Mean annual temperatures is 1.1 °C, ranging from 10.5°C in July to –9.9 °C in January. Mean annual rainfall is 637 mm (Jianjian, 1989).

Vegetation   The area surrounding the wetland is covered in steppe vegetation. The wetland supports algae and wet alpine meadows (Jianjian, 1989).

Fauna   The reserve, and especially the wetland, supports a large number of mammals, avifauna and fish species. Mammals comprise European otter *Lutra lutra* (V) and marmot *Marmota* sp. Birds include great cormorant *Phalacrocorax carbo* (400 recorded), whooper swan *Cygnus cygnus* (110), greylag goose *Anser anser*, bar-headed goose *A. indicus*, *Anas* spp., common crane *Grus grus*, black-necked crane *Grus nigricollis* (R), and ruddy shelduck *Tadorna ferruginea* (1,000) (Jianjian, 1989).

Cultural Heritage   No information.

Local Human Population   Land is not used inside the reserve but domestic livestock graze in the surrounding areas (Jianjian, 1989).

Visitors and Visitor Facilities   No information.

Scientific Research and Facilities   Studies have been made on the behaviour of black-necked crane. The reserve has basic research facilities (Jianjian, 1989).

Conservation Value   The reserve is an important wetland, noted for its birds. Of botanical interest is the rich alpine meadow flora (Jianjian, 1989; Wenhua and Xianying, 1989).

Conservation Management   A number of regulations have been drawn up by the local government to control waterfowl hunting and protect their habitats (Jianjian, 1989). The Environmental Protection Agency in Beijing supervises the running of the reserve (Achuff et al., 1986) but it is administered locally by the Gansu Forest Department (Anon, 1986). A number of measures have been proposed for the management of the reserve by the Zhangzhu Autonomous Prefecture Congress, which include the improvement of research facilities and the development of a summer resort for the encouragement of nature tourism (Jianjian, 1989).

Management Constraints   None (Jianjian, 1989)

Staff   No information

Budget   No information

Local Addresses   Gansu Forest Department, Lanzhou, Gansu Province

References

Achuff, P., Butler, J., Maw, R. and Johnson, J. (1986). *Heilongjiang, China–Alberta Canada, Scientific Exchange 1986, concerning: Wildlife, parks and nature reserves*. University of Alberta. P. 5.

Anon. (1986). Chinese wetland inventory. China Wildlife Conservation Association, Beijing. Unpublished. 2 pp

Jianjian, L. (1989). In: Scott, D.A. (Ed.), *A directory of Asian wetlands D*. IUCN, Gland, Switzerland and Cambridge, UK. Pp. 235–6.

Richardson, S.D. (1990). *Forests and forestry in China*. Island Press. Pp. 80–3.

Wenhua, L. and Xianying, Z. (1989). *China's nature reserves*. Foreign Languages Press. P. 162.

GANHAIZI NATURE RESERVE

IUCN Management Category   IV (Managed Nature Reserve)

Biogeographical Province   2.22.08 (Takla-Makan-Gobi Desert)

Geographical Location   Lies on the Qinghai-Tibet plateau, 75 km north-east of Yumen City in north-western Gansu Province. 40°24′N, 98°03′E

Date and History of Establishment   Ganhaizi Nature Reserve was established in 1982.

Area   300 ha

Land Tenure   Provincial government

Altitude   1,203 m.

Physical Features   The reserve is part of an inland drainage system amidst sandy plains and consists of a small, permanent, brackish lake and riverine marshes. The lake is fed by a small river. It is maintained at a mean depth of 1 m for most of the year by local run-off and underground water sources, but during the wet season the water level rises by 1 m to 2 m. The pH of the lake is 9.0 (Jianjian, 1989).

Climate   Conditions are semi-arid and continental, with a mean annual precipitation of 618 mm falling mostly during the wet summer season. Summers are usually hot with a maximum temperature of 36.7 °C, while winters are cold with a minimum temperature of −28.7 °C (Jianjian, 1989).

Vegetation   Reed beds of *Phragmites communis* are predominant, with *Salix* and other shrubs in the surrounding areas (Jianjian, 1989).

Fauna   Feeding species of waterfowl include great crested grebe *Podiceps cristatus*, ruddy shelduck *Tadorna ferruginea*, great egret *Egretta alba*, grey heron *Ardea cinerea*, spotbill duck *Anas poecilorhyncha*, and common pochard *Aythya ferina* (Jianjian, 1989). The goitred gazelle *Gazella subgutturosa* (E) is present.

Cultural Heritage   No information

Local Human Population   The reserve is uninhabited (Jianjian, 1989).

Visitors and Visitor Facilities   No information

Scientific Research and Facilities   There are no research facilities (Jianjian, 1989).

Conservation Value   The reserve is an important breeding area for over 20 species of waterfowl, as well as gazelle (Wenhua and Xianying, 1989).

Conservation Management   The reserve is administered locally by Yumen City Forestry Department under the supervision of the Environmental Protection Agency in Beijing. Hunting and cultivation are prohibited. Proposals include plans for the construction of research facilities. There is no management plan (Jianjian, 1989).

Management Constraints   Illegal hunting occurs within the reserve (Jianjian, 1989).

Staff   No information

Budget   No information

Local Addresses   Yumen City Forestry Department, Yumen City, Gansu Province

References
Jianjian, L. (1989). In: Scott, D.A. (Ed.), *A directory of Asian wetlands*. IUCN, Switzerland and
    Cambridge, UK. P. 236.
Wenhua, L. and Xianying, Z. (1989). *China's nature reserves*. Foreign Languages Press,
    Beijing. P. 162.

HANAS NATURE RESERVE

IUCN Management Category   IV (Managed nature reserve)

Biogeographical Province   2.30.11 (Mongolian-Manchurian steppe)

Geographical Location   Centred on the Altay Mountains in Burqin County, approximately 130 km north of Burqin. 48°25'N, 86°50'E

Date and History of Establishment   Established in 1980 on approval by the Regional People's Government in Document 167 (Orr, n.d.).

Area   250,000 ha

Land Tenure   State

Altitude   Ranges from 1,500 m to 3,000 m.

Physical Features Comprises the southern slopes of the Middle Range, formed by the continuous process of faulting and upheaval. Glaciation has created a number of lakes within the reserve, including Hanas Lake in the north-west of the Altay Mountains formed during the Quaternary period (Ji et al., 1990). Soils include chestnut and grey forest types, depending on altitude (Richardson, 1990).

Climate Conditions are generally cold, with mean annual air temperature between 3 °C and 4 °C. Summers are short. Annual precipitation ranges from 250–350 mm at 1,500 m to 500 mm at 1,500–3,000 m, creating fairly humid conditions (Ji et al., 1990).

Vegetation Due to severe conditions, a coniferous deciduous forest (light taiga) predominates (Richardson, 1990). Species include many Siberian representatives such as Siberian larch *Larix subirica*, Siberian spruce *Picea obovata*, Siberian pine *Pinus sibirica*, and Siberian fir *Abies sibirica*. Other broad-leaf species are Swedish birch *Betula verrucosa*, David poplar *Populus davidiana*, and bay-leaf willow *Salix pentandra*, being of both commercial and scientific value (Wenhua and Xianying, 1989).

Fauna Mammal species include snow leopard *Panthera unica* (E), lynx *Felis lynx*, red deer *Cervus elaphus*, sable *Martes zibellina*, ibex *Capra ibex*, argali sheep *Ovis ammon*, and Arctic hare *Lepus timidus*. Birds include capercaillie *Tetrao* spp., Eurasian hazel grouse *Bonasia bonasia,* and European black grouse *Tetrao tetrix* (Wenhua and Xianying, 1989).

Cultural Heritage No information

Local Human Population The reserve is largely inaccessible (Ji et al., 1990) and, therefore, has not been exploited (Richardson, 1990).

Visitors and Visitor Facilities The reserve has been virtually untouched by tourism due to its relative inaccessibility (Ji et al., 1990).

Scientific Research and Facilities No information.

Conservation Value The reserve lies in the main glacial region of China, and includes features such as Hanas Lake (Wenhua and Xianying, 1989). It contains valuable examples of Siberian flora and fauna (Xiyang, 1988).

Conservation Management The aim of the reserve is to preserve the natural ecosystem (Yuqing, 1987). Administration of the reserve is supervised by the Environmental Protection Agency in Beijing (Achuff et al., 1986).

Management Constraints No information.

Staff No information.

Budget No information

Local Addresses
Chief, Division of Nature Conservation, National Environmental Protection Agency, Beijing.

References

Achuff, P., Butler, J., Maw, R. and Johnson, J. (1986). Heilongjiang, China–Alberta, Canada. Scientific exchange 1986 concerning: wildlife, parks and nature reserves. University of Alberta, Alberta. Unpublished. P. 5.

Ji, Z., Guangmei, Z., Huadong, W. and Jialin, X. (1990). *The natural history of China.* Pp. 40–1, 137.

Orr, I. (n.d.). Some Chinese reserves. Unpublished. P. 4.

Richardson, S.D. (1990). *Forests and forestry in China.* Island Press, Washington DC. Pp. 78–9.

Wenhua, L. and Xianying, Z. (1989). *China's nature reserves.* Foreign Languages Press, Beijing. P. 76.

Xiyang, T. (1988). *Living treasures. An odyssey through China's extraordinary nature reserves.* P. 170.

Yuqing, W. (1987). Natural conservation regions in China. *Ambio* 16: 326.

JIANGCUN NATURE RESERVE

IUCN Management Category   IV (Managed Nature Reserve)

Biogeographical Province   2.38.12 (Himalayan Highlands)

Geographical Location   Located on the southern slopes of the Himalaya in Gyirong County. Access is by road from Lhasa to Gyirong and by track. 28°57′N, 85°12′E

Date and History of Establishment   Established as a nature reserve in 1985 but now forms part of Qomolangma Nature Reserve.

Area   34,060 ha

Land Tenure   State

Altitude   Ranges from 1,850 m to 3,000 m.

Physical Features   The reserve is bisected by the Gyirongzangbo River which runs from west to east and flows into Nepal. Yellow-brown soils are predkminant but at higher altitudes (2,000–3,000 m) medium humus-brown soil and soils formed from micacite, shale and gneiss are present (Wenhua and Xianying, 1989).

Climate   Wet and warm conditions prevail, with a mean annual temperature of 10 °C. Annual precipitation ranges between 900 mm and 1700 mm. Annual relative humidity exceeds 60% (Wenhua and Xianying, 1989).

Vegetation   Long-leaf pine *Pinus palustris* predominates at 1,850–2,600 m, being best suited to yellow-brown soils, and is mixed with Bhutan pine *Pinus griffithii*, oak *Quercus tungmaiensis*, and poplar *Populus ciliata*. On the forest floor, species are sparse with rhododendron, *Lyonia ovalifolia*, sumac *Rhus punjabensis*, cotoneaster *Cotoneaster microphyllus*, *Elaeagnus umbellata*, *Desmodium*, jasmine *Jasminium humile*, and bamboo.

The herbaceous layer is poorly developed, with *Apluda mutica* and *Streptolirion* being the most common. Other less common herbs include, *Asparagus filicinus*, *Polygonatum cirrhifolium*, *Smilacina oleracea*, and *Galium triflorum*.

Himalayan spruce occurs at 2,000 m to 3,000 m, mixed with oak and Bhutan pine. The lower forest layer is well-developed, with maples *Acer caesium*, *A. campbellii*, *A. tetramerum*, and *Toxicodendron succedaneum*. Shrubs include honeysuckle *Lonicera japonica*, jasmine *Jasminium humile*, *Desmodium cotoneaster*, *Spiraea bella*, *Berberis* sp., *Pieris formosa*, bamboo, and *Viburnum*. **Herbs include *Thalictrum macrorhynchum*,** *Asparagus cochinchinensis*, *Geranium*, *Ophiopogon japonicus*, and violet *Viola philippica*. Climbing vines include Himalayan creeper *Parthenocissus himalayana*, *Smilax* sp., *Schisandra grandiflora*, and ivy *Hedera nepalensis* (Wenhua and Xianying, 1989).

Fauna Mammals include Himalayan black bear *Selenarctos thibetanus* (V) and masked palm civet *Paguma larvata*. Birds include rufous-vented tit *Parus rubidiventris*, grey-crested tit *P. dichrous*, Tibetan snowcock *Tetraogallus tibetanus*, and sunbirds Nectariniidae. Amphibians include tree frogs Rhacophoridae (Ji et al., 1990).

Cultural Heritage No information

Local Human Population Gyirong lies within the reserve (Wenhua and Xianying, 1989).

Visitors and Visitor Facilities No information

Scientific Research and Facilities Wenhua and Xianying (1989) have made a preliminary study of the flora. There are no scientific facilities.

Conservation Value The reserve is now part of Qomolangma Nature Reserve. It is important for long-leaf pine, a commercially valuable timber species (Wenhua and Xianying, 1989).

Conservation Management The reserve was supervised by the Environmental Protection Agency in Beijing and administered locally by the Ministry of Forestry (Achuff et al., 1986). Overall authority now lies with the Working Commission of the Qomolangma Nature Reserve. A management plan is due to be completed in 1991 (Working Commission, 1991).

Management Constraints Indiscriminate felling has taken place (Wenhua and Xianying, 1989).

Staff No information

Budget No information

Local Addresses Director, Qomolangma Nature Preserve, Shigatse, Xizang Zizhiqu Autonomous Region.

References
Achuff, P., Butler, J., Maw, R. and Johnson, J. (1986). Heilongjiang, China–Alberta, Canada. Scientific Exchange 1986 concerning: wildlife, parks and nature reserves. University of Alberta, Alberta. Unpublished. P. 5.

Ji., Z., Guangmei, Z., Huadong, W. and Jialin, X. (1990). *The natural history of China*. Collins, London. Pp. 70, 149.

Wenhua, L. and Xianying, Z. (1989). *China's nature reserves*. Foreign Languages Press, Beijing. Pp. 125–7.

Working Commission. (1991). The Qomolangma Nature Preserve of the Tibet Autonomous Region of China. The Working Commission, Qomolangma Nature Preserve, Tibet Autonomous Region of China. Unpublished. 61 pp.

LONGBAO NATURE RESERVE

IUCN Management Category   IV (Managed Nature Reserve)

Biogeographical Province   2.23.08 (Tibetan).

Geographical Location   Situated on the Qinghai-Tibet plateau in Yushu County, 40 km west-north-west of Yushu, southern Qinghai Province. 33°10′N, 96°35′E

Date and History of Establishment   Established as a nature reserve in 1984 by the local government of Qinghai (Anon., n.d.).

Area   10,000 ha.

Land Tenure   Provincial government.

Altitude   4,200 m

Physical Features   Longbao is a marsh (25 km by 2–3 km) lying in a high east-west oriented mountain valley, with adjacent peaks rising to 5,270 m. The marsh lies in an upper tributary of the Tongtian River, itself a tributary of the Chang Jiang (Yangtze River). Numerous springs and streams supply the marsh. There are a number of freshwater ponds contain grassy islands formed by wave action. The maximum depth of the ponds is 2.5 m, their bottoms being covered by a deep layer of silt (Zhi-yen, 1989).

Climate   Conditions are cold and dry due to the influence of the Qinghai-Tibet plateau. Diurnal variations in temperature are large, with temperatures in May and June varying from −12 °C to 19 °C. Mean annual temperature is 5.0 °C. Mean annual rainfall is less than 300 mm and mean relative humidity is 55% (Zhi-yen, 1989).

Vegetation The alpine marshes and meadows support *Cartex* spp., *Eleocharis* sp., *Polygonum sibiricum, Kobresia reyleana, K. tibetica, Primulailla amscrina*, and *Taraxacum* spp. (Zhi-yen, 1989).

Fauna The marsh has a rich fish and arthropod fauna, and is an important breeding area for waterfowl. Over 1,000 black-necked cranes *Grus nigricollis* (R) use the reserve as a breeding and staging area (Anon, n.d.). Some eight breeding pairs and ten non-breeding pairs remain in the reserve throughout the summer, while the others move to other breeding sites in the vicinity. The marsh is also an important breeding area for bar-headed goose *Anser* *indicus*: the population increased from several dozen breeding pairs in 1980 to 2,000 pairs in 1986. Other breeding species include great-crested grebe *Podiceps cristatus*, ruddy shelduck *Tadorna ferruginea*, goosander *Mergus merganser*, common coot *Fulica atra*, common redshank *Tringa totanus*, and common tern *Sterna hirundo* (Zhi-yen, 1989).

Cultural Heritage   No information.

Local Human Population   No information.

Visitors and Visitor Facilities   No information.

Scientific Research and Facilities   A number of studies have been carried out on the breeding of black-necked crane (Zhi-yen, 1989).

Conservation Value   The reserve is particularly important for the protection of black-necked crane, and other species of waterfowl and their habitats (Wenhua and Xianying, 1989).

Conservation Management   The reserve is administered locally by the Agriculture and Forestry Department in Qinghai Province under the supervision of the Environmental Protection Agency in Beijing (Anon, 1986). No management plan exists for the reserve.

Management Constraints   None (Zhi-yen, 1989)

Staff   No information.

Budget   No information

Local Addresses   Agriculture and Forestry Department, Xining, Qinghai Province.

References
Anon. (n.d.). Fifteen new nature reserves for Qinghai Province. *Xinhua*.
Anon. (1986). Chinese wetland inventory. China Wildlife Conservation Association, Beijing. Unpublished. P. 1.
Wenhua, L. and Xianying, Z. (1989). *China's nature reserves*. Foreign Language Press, Beijing. P. 178.
Zhi-yen, Z. (1989). In: Scott, D.A. (Ed.), *A directory of Asian wetlands*. IUCN, Gland, Switzerland and Cambridge, UK. Pp. 240–1.

MEDOG NATURE RESERVE

IUCN Management Category   IV   (Managed Nature Reserve).

Biogeographical Province   2.38.12   (Himalayan Highlands)

Geographical Location   Situated at the eastern edge of the Qinghai-Tibet plateau, south-west of Mainling in Medog County.   29°20'N, 95°23'E

Date and History of Establishment Designated as a nature reserve in 1985.

Area 62,620 ha

Land Tenure State

Altitude Ranges from 600 m in the valley bottoms to 7,756 m on the peaks over a distance of 45 km, with an mean altitude of 4,000 m on the Qinghai-Tibet plateau.

Physical Features The reserve encompasses Mount Namcha Barwa and part of the Yarlungzangbo River on the windward slopes of the Himalaya. The valley of the Yarlungzangbo River lies below 800 m and is flanked by mountain slopes. Scree slopes formed near the mountain peaks and ridges by continual erosion and weathering are devoid of soil (Wenhua and Xianying, 1989). Elsewhere, soils are predominantly podzolic, merging with alpine meadow soils (including lithosols and tundra soils) at higher altitudes (Richardson, 1990).

Climate Temperature and precipitation are influenced by the windward slopes of the Himalaya exposed to the south-west monsoon, radiation from the Qinghai-Tibet plateau and the east-west mountain range to the north of the plateau acting as a buffer to cold air currents. The terrain influences temperature within the valleys: for every 100 m rise in altitude there is a corresponding decrease of 0.58 °C in the mean annual temperature. The temperature is generally higher than other areas at the same latitude and altitude in south-east China. Below 800 m, the mean annual temperature reaches 20 °C, while that for the coldest month does not fall below 13 °C. Between 2,400 m and 3,800 m the mean annual temperature ranges between 3 °C and 11 °C, conditions being cool and wet. Annual precipitation exceeds 2000 mm, mostly brought by humid air currents from the Gulf of Bengal. Winter rainfall is scarce but mists occur in the river valleys (Wenhua and Xianying, 1989).

Vegetation Four altitudinal zones can be distinguished. Below 800 m, river valleys support tropical forest, including groves of bananas and wild citrus trees. Adjacent slopes support tropical forest, with a canopy of *Terminalia myriocarpa*, *Lagerstroemia subcostata*, *Homalium cochinchinense*, *Sloanea sinensis*, *Garcinia morella*, *Fissistigma oldhamii*, and tall broad-leaf evergreens such as figs. A second tree layer consists of *Actinodaphne laucifolia*, *Altingia* sp. and *Cryptocarya chinensis*. On the forest floor are shrubs and small trees such as *Psychotria rubra* and *Lasianthus chinensis*, and herbaceous plants and pteriodophytes such as *Phrynium capitatum*, *Alpinia japonica*, and *Anglopteris* sp. Climbers include arums (Araceae), orchids (Orchidaceae) , peppers (Piperaceae), and palms (Palmae). *Epipremnum pinnatum* grows alongside (Leguminosae) and bottle gourds *Lagenaria* spp. At 2,400 m, there is a central zone of montane subtropical evergreen broad-leaf forest comprising *Cyathea spinulosa*, *Podocarpus* sp., *Amentotaxus argotaenia*, magnolia, *Tetracentron sinense*, laurel, ginseng, and witch-hazel (Hamamelidaceae). Shrubs and herbaceous plants include *Eurya japonica*, and *Myrsine semiserrata*, interspersed with dense bamboo groves. Commercially important trees are pine *Pinus griffithii*, camphor *Cinamomum camphora*, *Castanopsis* sp., and *Phoebe* spp. The montane temperate zone (2,400–3,800 m) comprises coniferous forest, with Chinese hemlock *Tsuga chinensis* and, at higher altitudes, fir *Abies fabri* and spruce *Picea asperata*. Other woody species include Japanese honeysuckle *Lonicera japonica*, maple, bird cherry *Prunus padus*, raspberry *Rubus* sp., currant *Ribes* sp., and the endemic fountain bamboo *Sinarundinaria nitida*. Alpine scrub and meadow occur between 3,800 m and 4,700 m, above which is perpetual snow. Alpine shrubs include rhododendrons and willows, growing alongside dwarf clubmoss *Cassiope selaginoides*, *Potentilla fruticosa*, *Sibiraea* sp., blueberry *Vaccinium bracteatum*, wintergreen *Gaultheria cumingiana*. Herbs include *Primula* spp., *Saxifraga stolonifera*, Japanese buttercup *Ranunculus japonicus*, gentian *Gentiana scabra*, poppies *Mecanopsis* spp., mountain sorrel *Oxyria* sp., and *Leontopodioides*. On alpine scree slopes are found *Saussurea involucrata*, *Mecanopsis* sp., monkshood *Aconitum carmichaeli*, stone crop *Hylotelephium erythrostictum*, and sandwort *Arenaria serpyllifolia*. Rare species include *Hodgsonia macrocarpa*, *Gynocardia odorata*, *Cordia* sp., and *Pyrularia edulis*. Details of medicinal and economically important plants are given by Wenhua and Xianying (1989).

Fauna   Forty-two species of mammals have been recorded. Nationally threatened species include leopard *Panthera pardus* (T), snow leopard *P. uncia* (E), clouded leopard *Neofelis nebulosa* (V), lynx *Felis lynx*, large Indian civet *Viverra zibetha*, small Indian civet *Viverricula indica*, Assam macaque *Macaca assamensis*, rhesus macaque *M. mulatta*, lesser panda *Ailurus fulgens* (K), red deer *Cervus elaphus*, tufted deer *Elaphodus cephalophus*, musk deer *Moschus chrysogaster*, serow *Capricornis sumatraensis*, takin *Budorcas taxicolor* (R), langur *Presbytis entellus*, bharal *Pseudois nayaur*, and hare *Lepus timidus*.

Birds include Sclater's monal *Lophophorus sclateri* (I), Blyth's tragopan *Tragopan blythii* (I), Cabot's tragopan *T.caboti* (R), crimson-bellied tragopan *T. temminckii*, white-eared pheasant *Crossoptilon crossoptilon*, grey peacock-pheasant *Polyplectron bicalcaratum*, Tibetan snowcock *Tetraogallus tibetanus*, golden pheasant *Chrysolophus pictus*, blood pheasant *Ithaginis cruentus*, and hornbills **Bucerotidae** spp. (Wenhua and Xianying, 1989).

Cultural Heritage   No information

Local Human Population   Medog Village lies within the reserve (Wenhua and Xianying, 1989).

Visitors and Visitor Facilities   No information.

Scientific Research and Facilities   No information.

Conservation Value   Medog contains the most northerly tropical ecosystem in the world, with a number of species of flora and fauna from the South Asian tropics. Many species are economically important, such as medicinal plants (Wenhua and Xianying, 1989).

Conservation Management   The main aim is to protect the montane forest and its fauna. The reserve is supervised by the Tibetan Environmental Protection Agency and is administered locally by the responsible management agency (Achuff et al., 1986).

Management Constraints   No information.

Staff   No information

Budget   No information

Local Addresses   No information

References

Achuff, P., Butler, J., Maw, R. and Johnson, J. (1986). Heilongjiang, China–Alberta, Canada. *Scientific* exchange 1986 concerning: wildlife, parks and nature reserves. University of Alberta, Edmonton. Unpublished. P. 5.

Richardson, S.D. (1990). *Forests and forestry in China*. Island Press, Washington, DC. Pp. 80–3.

Wenhua, L. and Xianying, Z. (1989). *China's nature reserves*. Foreign Languages Press, Beijing. Pp. 67–74.

NAPAHAI NATURE RESERVE

IUCN Management Category   IV (Managed Nature Reserve)

Biogeographical Province   2.39.12 (Szechwan Highlands)

Geographical Location   Lies in the Hengduan mountains, 250 km north-north-west of Xiaguan in Zhongdian county. 27°49′–27°55′N, 99°37′–99°40′E

Date and History of Establishment   Designated in 1984 as a provincial nature reserve.

Area   2,067 ha

Land Tenure   The wetland is state-owned with surrounding areas under the control of the local communities.

Altitude   Ranges from 3,255 m to 3,260 m.

Physical Features   Napahai comprises a complex of fresh water ponds, marshes and swamps in the north–south oriented Hengduan mountains (Ji et al., 1990). Eight small streams from the surrounding hills feed the marshes. A shallow lake is formed during the rainy season but gradually dries out during the dry season. Water drains out of the system into the Chang Jiang (Yangtze River) through nine natural sink holes. The size of the lake has decreased from 1,000 ha in the 1950s to several hundred hectares at present (Lan and Jianjian, 1989).

Climate   A temperate montane climate predominates with a rainy season lasting from May to August. Mean annual precipitation is 620 mm. Mean annual temperature is 5.4 °C, with a maximum of 25.1 °C and a minimum of −25.4 °C. There are 125 days of frost every year and occasional snow from September to May (Lan and Jianjian, 1989).

Vegetation   Coniferous forests surround the lake and its marshes (Lan and Jianjian, 1989). Species include spruce *Picea asperata*, fir *Abies* sp., bamboo and *Rhododendron* spp. (Ji et al., 1990).

Fauna   The wetland is an important wintering area for black-necked crane *Grus nigricollis* (R). There were 63 present in the 1984–5 winter and 58 in the 1985-6 winter, but as many as 130 have been recorded in the past. Japanese crane *Grus japonensis* (V) and common crane *Grus grus* occur in small numbers. Other bird species include bar-headed goose *Anser* *indicus* (maximum of 800 in December 1985), ruddy shelduck *Tadorna ferruginea* (up to 315), mallard *Anas platyrhynchus*, northern pintail *A. acuta*, and goosander *Mergus merganser* (Lan and Jianjian, 1989).

Cultural Heritage   No information

Local Human Population   The reserve is used for grazing by domestic livestock during the dry winter season. The surrounding areas are cultivated and grazed (Lan and Jianjian, 1989).

Visitors and Visitor Facilities   No information

Scientific Research and Facilities   Studies include preliminary research on the waterfowl, especially cranes, by biologists from the Yunnan Forest Department and Kunming Institute of Zoology (1984–6). There are no scientific facilities (Lan and Jianjian, 1989).

Conservation Value   Napahai is an important wetland for the protection of black-necked crane and other rare birds (Wenhua and Xianying, 1989).

Conservation Management   The reserve is administered locally by Yunnan Forest Department under the supervision of the Environmental Protection Agency in Beijing (Achuff et al., 1986). Hunting is prohibited and measures have been taken to prevent pollution. It has been proposed that several small dams be constructed to manipulate water levels and improve the water supply to the marshes (Lan and Jianjian, 1989).

Management Constraints   The diversion of water supplies for other uses is resulting in a lowering of the water level and the loss of wetland habitat. The marsh vegetation is overgrazed (Lan and Jianjian, 1989).

Staff   No information

Budget   No information

Local Addresses
Yunnan Provincial Forestry Bureau, Kunming, Yunnan Province

References
Lan, Y. and Jianjian, L. (1989). In: Scott, D.A. (Ed.), *A directory of Asian wetlands*. IUCN, Gland, Switzerland and Cambridge, UK. P. 234.
Ji, Z., Guangmei, Z., Huadong, W. and Jialin; X. (1990). *The natural history of China*. Collins, London. Pp. 144–6.
Wenhua, L. and Xianying, Z. (1989). *China's nature reserves*. Foreign Languages Press, Beijing. P. 188.

QOMOLANGMA NATURE RESERVE[1]

IUCN Management Category   IV (Managed nature reserve)

Biogeographical Province   2.38.12 (Himalayan Highlands)

Geographical Location   Lies in the Rikize (Shigote) Prefecture of southern Tibet. The reserve includes Dingri (Tingri), Nelamu (Nyelam) and part of Dingjie (Dinggue) and Jilong (Kyirong) counties. It extends from the easternmost bend of the Pengqa (Punychu or Arun) River near Dingqye to the Jilongzangbu (Trisuli) River near Jilong in the west. The reserve is accessible by the Friendship Highway linking Lhasa with Kathmandu, Nepal. The northern boundary roughly parallels the 29°N latitude line just south of Lhasa, and the southern boundary is delimited by the international border with Nepal. 28°30′N, 86°10′E

Date and History of Establishment   Established in 1989 by the Government of the Xizang Zizhiqu Autonomous Region. Two regions within Jilong and Zhangmu valleys had previously been gazetted as nature reserves in 1985, namely Jiangcun and Zham.

Area   3,500,000 ha. The reserve is part of a 4,008,800 ha protected areas complex, being contiguous to Nepal's Langtang and Sagarmatha national parks, as well as the Makalu-Barun National Park and Conservation Area.

Land Tenure   State

Altitude   Range from 1,433 m to 8,848 m.

Physical Features   The southernmost boundary comprises the High Himalaya which is an east–west oriented, geologically young and seismically active range formed through the collision of the Indian shield and Eurasian mainland plate at the beginning of the Tertiary (BP 63 million years). The presence of antecedent rivers, such as the Pengqu, glacial advances and retreats, and physical and chemical weathering processes have created the present topography, with schist, gneiss, granite and limestone peaks. The rate of uplift of the High Himalayan and Tibetan Plateau is estimated to be 0.7–10 mm per year. Five valleys penetrate the Himalaya: these are, from east to west, Pengqu (Chentang), Rongxia (Rongshan), Poqu (Nielamu), Jilong and Gongdang. North of the High Himalayan chain is a plateau with numerous lakes, such as the 26,800 ha Peikucuo, Meteli Tso and Duqian Tso. Large lake basins occur from west to east, including Jilong, Selong, Jenmu, Dingri, Dingjie and Takexun. Extensive plains are found along the northern slopes of Mount Xixiabangma (Shishapangma), the basin surrounding Peikucuo and the river valley of the Yarlung Tsangpo. To the west are steeply dissected mountains. The southern region is drained by the Pengqu River, which flows 275 km river westward from its headwaters near Siling and the northern slopes of Mount Xixiabangma to become the Arun River as it cuts southwards through the High Himalaya (Woodlands Mountain Institute, 1991).

Climate   Conditions are influenced by the Himalaya which acts as a meteorological barrier to the south-west monsoon. Mean annual precipitation ranges from 2,000–2,500 mm on the

[1]See map on p. 363.

southern aspects of the Himalaya exposed to the monsoon and 600–800 mm in the Pengqu catchment to less than 250 mm in the northern plateau region, where conditions are continental and semi-arid. There is a north–south temperature gradient, with lower mean annual air temperatures of 2–3 °C north of the Himalayan chain (Woodlands Mountain Institute, 1991).

Vegetation   The vegetation is summarised by Jackson (1991c) and comprises: an upper subtropical zone evergreen broad-leaf forest, dominant species including *Castanopsis hystrix*, *Engelhardia* sp., and *Machilus* sp.; lower temperate zone of mixed evergreen oak forest, with *Quercus oxydon*, *C. hystrix*, *Engelhardia* sp., and *Machilus* sp.; upper temperate zone of oak, hemlock *Tsuga dumosa*, blue pine *Pinus wallichiana*, and chir pine *P. roxburghii*; subalpine zone of spruce *Picea smithiana*, silver fir *Abies spectabilis*, larch *Larix griffithiana*, birch *Betula utilis*, perennial grassland *Stipa/Pennisetum* spp., and riverine scrub *Hippophae* spp.; alpine zone of grassland *Orinus thoroldii*, low sage *Artemisia* spp., rhododendron *Rhododendron* spp., juniper *Sabina* spp., birch/willow *Betula/Salix* spp. and wet meadow *Kobresia-Carex* spp.; and a nival zone of pincushion plants, dominated by species of *Androsace* and *Arenaria*. In the southern region, subtropical forests occur between 1,100 m and 1,800 m, dominated by *Castanopsis hystrix*, *C. tribuloides*, *Lithocarpus* spp., *Schima* sp., *Machilus* sp., *Michelia* sp., *Engelhardia* sp., and *Olea* sp. Understorey shrubs include *Ardisia* sp., *Vaccinium* sp., *Symplocos* sp., and *Viburnum* sp. Some areas support rich stands of laurel *Machilus yunnanensis*. Where oaks have adapted to moist conditions, species include *Quercus oxydon* and *Q. annulata*. The Kama Valley in the south-west is renowned for its coniferous forests, dominated by blue pine *Pinus wallichiana*, spruce *Picea smithiana*, and silver fir *Abies spectabilis*. Chir pine *Pinus roxburghii* occurs in the forests of Jilong, while at Chentang deciduous larch *Larix griffithiana* is found as high as 4,000 m. Hemlock *Tsuga dumosa* occurs in the more humid valleys and mountain slopes. In the northern region, vegetation in the semi-arid plateau consists of steppe grassland and shrub trees, dominated by grasses such as *Stipa purpurea*, *Orinus thoroldii*, and *Pennisetum flaccidum*, and shrubs such as *Artemisia* spp., *Potentilla fruticosa*, and *Caragana versicolor*. River valleys and high mountain basins support a lush growth of the sedges *Kobresia pymaea*, *Carex moorcroftii*, and *C. montis-everestii*.

Fauna   Primates include langur *Presbytis entellus*, Assam macaque *Macaca assamensis*, and rhesus macaque *M. mulatta*. Carnivores include Himalayan black bear *Selenarctos thibetanus* (V), brown bear *Ursus arctos*, snow leopard *Panthera uncia* (E), leopard *Panthera pardus* (T), clouded leopard *Neofelis nebulosa* (V), Pallas's cat *Felis manul*, wolf *Canis lupus* (V), Asiatic cat *Felis temmincki* (I), jungle cat *Felis chaus*, wild dog *Cuon alpinus* (V), leopard cat *Felis bengalensis*, and jackal *Canis aureus*. Lynx *Felis lynx* is found in lower forested valleys, while fox *Vulpes vulpes* and Tibetan fox *Vulpes ferrilata* are widespread. Mountain weasel *Mustela altaica*, Siberian weasel *M. sibirica*, beech marten *Martes foina*, and yellow-throated marten *M. flavigula* are present, and European otter *Lutra lutra* (V) occurs in rivers at lower elevations (Jackson, 1991c). Herbivores include red panda *Ailurus fulgens* (K) and Asiatic wild ass *Equus hemionus* (V), of which 50 now roam the plains surrounding Pegu Tso (Jackson, 1991b), Tibetan gazelle *Procapra piticaudata*, bharal *Pseudois nayaur*, serow *Capricornis sumatraensis* which is common in forested gorges, goral *Nemorhaedus goral*, Himalayan tahr *Hemitragus jemlahicus*, Indian muntjac *Muntiacus muntjak*, and musk deer *Moschus chrysogaster*. Other species include Himalayan marmot *Marmota bobak*, black-lipped pika *Ochotona curzoniae*, Moupin pika *O. thibetana*, Royle's pika *O. roylei*, Stoliczka's mountain vole *Alticola stoliczkanus*, Sikkim vole *Pitymys sikkimensis*, Blyth's vole *P. leucurus*, Hodgson's flying squirrel *Petaurista magnificus*, and Himalayan striped squirrel

Callosciurus macclellandi. Orange-bellied Himalayan squirrel *Dremomys lokriah* is found in low elevation forests, together with wild boar *Sus scrofa* (Jackson, 1991c).

Birds are distributed according to habitat and altitude. Species include peregrine falcon *Falco peregrinus*, lammergeier *Gypaetus barbatus*, Eurasian griffon vulture *Gyps fulvus*, Himalayan monal pheasant *Lophophorus impejanus*, satyr tragopan *Tragopan satyra*, blood pheasant *Ithaginis cruentus*, koklass pheasant *Pucrasia macrolopha*, Tibetan snowcock *Tetraogallus tibetanus*, and Himalayan snowcock *T. himalayensis*. West of Peku Tso a small freshwater lake supports oriental white stork *Ciconia ciconia boyciana* (R), blacked-necked crane *Grus nigricollis* (R), and brown-headed gull *Larus brunnicephalus*. Python *Python molurus* (V) is present (Jackson, 1991c).

Cultural Heritage   Qomolangma is rich in cultural sites and artifacts, human activities having been traced back 50,000 years with the discovery of Palaeolithic stone tools near Dingri. Recorded history in the region dates back to before AD 700, based upon the mention of the Xiangxiong culture in Tibetan literature. Several monasteries *(gompas) occur within the reserve, including Lapchi, Tho-sam-ling, the 575-year old Laangkhor, Ronbuk (Dzasong) and Milarepa's hermitage in the village of Changdong (Woodlands Mountain Institute, 1991).*

Local Human Population   Tibetan is the major ethnic group, accounting for 99% of the population (Working Commission, 1991). Approximately 12,000 families (total population 67,468) live within the reserve, involved mainly in agriculture and animal husbandry. The livestock population totalled 182,518 animals in 1989, with yak grazed seasonally in summer pastures by semi-nomadic groups of pastoralists (Woodlands Mountain Institute, 1991).

Visitors and Visitor Facilities   Since 1985, tourism has expanded significantly, with lodges and hotels now located in Dingri, Neilamu, Pazhuo (Paljor), Rongbu, Xegar, and Zhangmar (Woodlands Mountain Institute, 1991).

Scientific Research and Facilities   A number of scientific surveys have been carried out, including floral studies by Zhang et al. (1988). Scientific expeditions have been conducted by the Chinese Academy of Sciences. Surveys have been instigated by the participating agencies and include a socio-economic survey by the Tibet Academy of Social Sciences, vegetation mapping and geographical surveys by the Chinese Academy of Sciences, a cultural survey by the Culture Department, a health survey by the Health Department, an education survey by the Education Department, a tourism survey by the Tibet Mountaineering Association, an environmental pollution survey by the Environmental Protection Bureau, and a management survey by the Management Bureau, resulting in a number of reports being published in 1989 (Working Commission, 1991).

Conservation Value   Qomolangma is among the world's largest protected areas and, together with three adjacent protected areas in Nepal, protects much of the Everest ecosystem. It has a high biological diversity due to its location at the juxtaposition of the Palaearctic and Oriental biogeographical realms. Species diversity is particularily high in the temperate forests of the Karma and Kyirong valleys, and pristine forests occur in Chentang and Kyirong valleys. Other habitats range from grassland to wetland and alpine shrubland, and from cliffs to large lakes and rivers. Its spatial continuity with three Himalayan parks in Nepal enhances the long-term genetic viability of otherwise isolated plant and animal populations. The reserve also presents an opportunity to implement management using a participatory model of land management which integrates the needs of local people with the protection of the environment (Woodlands Mountain Institute, 1991; Jackson, 1991c).

Conservation Management The reserve was established through the efforts of the Working Commission of the Qomolangma Nature Reserve and Woodlands Mountain Institute, in conjunction with the Chinese Academy of Sciences and the Tibet Academy of Social Sciences, under a co-operative agreement signed on 26 October 1989 and effective until 31 December 2000. Overall authority lies with the Working Commission which includes representatives from 13 governmental departments holding executive powers. An eight-member 'Expert Group' of key scientists, planners and administrators, appointed by the Working Commission, is responsible for the project's applied research and planning needs. A management bureau, established in Xikeze Prefecture, is responsible for the administration of the reserve. Officials from the Bureau of Agriculture, Animal Husbandry and Forestry, run the management bureau through each county government. Two branch offices have been established: one in Xegar, the administrative centre of Dingri County, and one in Jilong (Working Commission, 1991). In Kyirong a system of recruiting village leaders as forest and wildlife guards has been successfully employed to protect the forests. Other employment opportunities include training Tibetans and Chinese as tour guides and support staff (Jackson, 1991c).

A management plan is due to be completed in 1991 and will cover management, research, community development, cultural conservation and tourism development. Six core zones of minimally disturbed and largely intact ecosystems are proposed within the reserve: Shishapangma (Xixiabangma), Xuebugang, Jiangum, Gongdang (Guntan), and Qomolangma (Jackson, 1991c). Immediate management objectives include regulating hunting by terminating all predator bounty programmes, banning the hunting of snow leopard and lynx, and protecting native ungulate populations.

Management Constraints Hunting is a major problem and has led to the decimation of populations of snow leopard, lynx, wolf, argali, and brown bear. This is partly due to financial incentives: for example, a snow leopard is worth 400 yuan (US $ 85). Also herdsmen protect their livestock from predation, and from crop damage by wildlife such as wild boar, black bear, monkey, and pheasant (Jackson, 1991c).

Staff Over 40 people were employed during 1989–90.

Budget In 1989 the allocated budget was US $ 224,821 (838,582 yuan), of which capital costs accounted for US $ 61,293 (228,623 yuan) and recurrent costs US $ 163,528 (609,959 yuan). In 1990 the planned budget totalled US $ 428,700 (1,599,051 yuan) with capital costs of US $ 131,000 (488,630 yuan) and recurrent costs US $ 297,700 (1,110,421 yuan). The budget for 1991 is US $ 604,000 (2,252,920 yuan), with capital costs of US $ 192,500 (715,025 yuan) and recurrent costs US $ 425,000 (1,585,250 yuan). The reserve has received funding from international donors such as International Development Research Centre (Canada), Funding Exchange, Needmor Foundation, Sequoia Foundation, International Fund for Animal Welfare (England), and the Miflin Trust (Working Commission, 1991).

Local Addresses
Director, Qomolangma Nature Reserve, Shigatse, Xizang Zizhiqu Autonomous Region

References
Jackson, R. (1991a). Snow leopards on the roof of the world. *Cat News* (14): 16–17.

Jackson, R. (1991b). Snow leopards and other wildlife in the Qomolanga Nature Preserve of Tibet. *Snow Line* 9(1): 9–12.

Jackson, R. (1991c). A wildlife survey of the Qomolangma Nature Preserve, Tibet Autonomous Region, People's Republic of China. Report prepared for Working Commission, Qomolangma Nature Preserve and Chinese Academy of Sciences, Beijing. 15 March. 35 pp.

Woodlands Mountains Institute (1991). The Qomolangma Nature Preserve physical setting, culture, and contemporary environmental and community issues. Woodlands Mountain Institute, Franklin , USA. Unpublished.10 pp.

Working Commission. (1991). The Qomolangma Nature Preserve of the Tibet Autonomous Region of China. The Working Commission, Qomolangma Nature Preserve, Tibet Autonomous Region of China. Unpublished. 61 pp.

TANGJIAHE NATURE RESERVE

IUCN Management Category IV (Managed Nature Reserve)

Biogeographical Province 2.39.12 (Sichuan Highlands)

Geographical Location Located in Qingchuan County, north-central Sichuan Province, and bordered by Gansu Province to the north. It lies some 360 km from the provincial capital, Chengdu. The borders of the reserve follow the watersheds of large rivers, and make excellent natural boundaries. 32°32′–32°41′N, 104°37′–104°53′E.

Date and History of Establishment Ratified as a nature reserve by the provincial government in December 1978 and, subsequently, as a national nature reserve by the State Council in July 1986.

Area 28,000 ha. Some 40,000 ha were included under the original proposals but the boundaries were later revised, due to extensive damage by farmers to the southern Majiagou and Pinggouli valleys and the shortage of agricultural land in the county. The reserve borders on Baishu River Nature Reserve (95,292 ha) in Gansu Province.

Land Tenure Central Government

Altitude Ranges from about 1,200 m in valley bottoms to 3,837 m in the Dacaoping area.

Physical Features Lying at the eastern end of the Min Shan, the main mountain range separating the fertile Sichuan basin to the south from the drier ranges of Gansu Province to the north, the reserve comprises a series of rugged ridges and narrow valleys of two main drainages, the Beilu and Motiangling rivers. Tributary valleys are steep and V-shaped, with streams falling in a series of rapids and waterfalls. Lower down are gorges, while higher up the valleys broaden out and their floors are covered with accumulated fallen rocks and alluvium. Rock strata consist primarily of granite, exposed as high peaks along the Gansu border and surrounded by a great variety of metamorphic rocks and limestone. Bedrock is commonly exposed on ridges and valley sides, and soil development is poor. Four soil types

116

are recognised by Seidensticker et al. (1984), namely: mountain yellow, mountain brown, mountain green, and mountain grassland.

Climate   The area falls within the Qinghai-Tibetan climatic belt, which is characterised by a long winter, with snow falling from November to March, and a relatively cool summer. Recordings taken at Baixiongping Meteorological Station (1,790 m) indicate that January is the coldest month, with mean daily maximum and minimum temperatures of 1.8 °C and −5.3 °C, respectively, and an absolute range from 8 °C to −11 °C. The warmest months are June to August, with mean daily maximum and minimum temperatures of 22.6–24.7 °C and 13.1–14.2 °C, respectively, and an absolute range from 30° C to 10° C. Mean annual precipitation is 1,100–1,200 mm, with over 90% of precipitation falling in the rainy season of the south-east monsoon between May and October (Bi et al., 1986).

Vegetation   Much of the original vegetation has been affected by extensive logging up to 2,200 m and some selective logging above that. Five main types of vegetation are recognised by Bi et al., (1986), namely: areas cleared for pasture and cultivation that now support early seral communities, with colonisers including poplars *Populus* spp. and shrubs such as *Salix*, *Spiraea*, *Deutzia*, *Rosa*, *Rubus* and *Buddleia*; evergreen and deciduous broad-leaved forest (up to 1,700 m) dominated by the evergreen trees *Lindera communus* and *Cyclobalanopsi oxyodon*, together with deciduous oak *Quercus glandulifera* and beech *Fagus longipetiolata* mixed coniferous and deciduous broad-leaved forest (1,700–2,100 m), with pine *Pinus armandii* favouring dry southern slopes, and hemlock *Tsuga chinensis* and spruce *Picea brachtyla* found mainly on moist northern ones; subalpine coniferous forest (from 2,100–2,300 m to the tree-line at 3,200–3,300 m), dominated by fir *Abies faxoniana* at higher altitudes, and with birch *Betula utilis* and rhododendrons *Rhododendron* spp. as the main broad-leaved trees; and alpine tussock grassland up to 3,500–3,800 m, where it merges with rock outcrops on the highest peaks. Bamboo, which is of particular importance to the ecology of the giant panda, occurs in extensive patches in the temperate and subalpine zones. *Fargesia scabrida* and, at higher altitudes, *F. denudata*, are predominant, but few mature stands remain after a period of mass-flowering and die-off in the 1970s (Bi et al., 1986).

The flora is diverse owing to the varying topography, climate, soil and hydrology. The reserve has an estimated 2,000 species of plants. Of interest are some relics of the Tertiary Palaeotropical flora of the Western Chinese Mountains. These include the katsura tree *Cercidiphyllum japonicum.*, dove tree *Davidia involucrata*, rhododendrons *Rhododendron* spp., *Xylosma japonicum*, and *Abies fabri* (Bi et al., 1986; MOF, 1989).

Fauna   Tangjiahe straddles the border between subtropical lowlands and temperate uplands, hence its fauna is allied to both the Oriental and Palaearctic regions. The forest fauna at low-to-medium altitudes is mainly Oriental in origin (e.g. stump-tailed macaque *Macaca speciosa*, giant panda *Ailuropoda melanoleuca* (R), clouded leopard *Neofelis nebulosa* (V), tufted deer *Elaphodus cephalophus*, serow *Capricornis sumatraensis*, bamboo rat *Rhizomys sinensis*, and golden pheasant *Chrysolophus pictus*), while that of the subalpine coniferous forest and particularly that above the tree-line is characterised by Palaearctic species (e.g. musk deer *Moschus berezovskii*, blue sheep *Pseudois nayaur*, pika *Ochotona thibetana*, and Tibetan snowcock *Tetraogallus tibetanus*). Some 90 species of mammals and 200 species of birds have been recorded (Bi et al., 1986). Of these, 25 are nationally protected species, which include golden snub-nosed monkey *Rhinopithecus roxellanae* (V), Sichuan takin *Budorcas taxicolor tibetana* (I), giant panda, red panda *Ailurus fulgens* (K), blue-eared pheasant *Crossoptilon auritum*, and Temminck's tragopan *Tragopan temminckii*.

Evidence of some 100–140 giant pandas was found during a census conducted in 1975 by the Rare Animal Resources Investigation Team, an estimate which is considered by Bi et al. (1986) to be more realistic than that of 200 based on a previous survey (Seidensticker et al., 1984). The giant panda population has since declined to an estimated 50–60 (Hu et al., 1980) following the flowering of much of reserve's bamboo in the mid-late 1970s. The red panda, formerly scarce in the reserve, may have died out as a result of the bamboo flowering but could still exist in Motianling Valley. Otter *Lutra lutra* is very rare with possibly only one family in the whole reserve. While much of the large mammal fauna (e.g. macaques and leopard) has been disturbed by past hunting and other activities, human disturbance has favoured other species such as takin, which feeds in abandoned agricultural land, and Himalayan black bear *Selenarctos thibetanus* (V), which feeds on *Rubus* berries in secondary clearings and raids old apple orchards (Bi et al., 1986).

Other groups have not been systematically surveyed but show great richness. In particular, the butterfly fauna appears to be extemely varied (Bi et al., 1986).

Cultural Heritage   Motianling Valley has been used as a travel route across the mountains separating Gansu and Sichuan provinces for hundreds of years. Historical records go back to the Three Kingdom Period (AD 220–80) when General Deng Ali rode the Yangping Trail through Motianling Valley (MOF, 1989).

Local Human Population   It was not until early this century that farmers settled in the lower Beilu and Motianling valleys to extract timber and cultivate the less steep slopes. Large-scale logging commenced in 1965, with the construction of a highway to the area, and a sawmill was built at Maoxiangba, now the reserve headquarters.

There are no longer any settlements in the reserve. In 1986, the residential population (61 farmers and their families totalling 301 people) was resettled and absorbed into local communities in return for compensation paid by the Ministry of Forestry both to the local government and to the villagers to relinquish their rights to orchards, trees and other natural resources left behind in the reserve (Bi et al., 1986).

Visitors and Visitor Facilities   The reserve is becoming increasingly popular among visitors. The exact number of visitors is not known but in 1983 there were 600 in May, 400 in June and 300 in July. Over a thousand students visit it each year for practical botanical and other studies. A few foreigners come on specialised bird-watching tours or to see the home of the giant panda. New visitor accommodation, with provision for 50 beds, is being constructed at the reserve's headquarters at Maoxiangba, at 1,430 m (Bi et al., 1986).

Scientific Research and Facilities   Research conducted under a joint agreement made between the Department of Forestry and World Wide Fund for Nature in 1983 includes ecological studies of the giant panda, bear and takin by G.B. Schaller and the regeneration of bamboo after flowering (Taylor, 1984). Work continues in all of these fields (Bi et al., 1986). A scientific research camp was established at Baixiongping (1,790 m) in 1984. Training courses for protection and research staff are held regularly (Laurie, 1986).

Conservation Value   Tangjiahe is of great importance for its biological variety, with a number of threatened mammals, a rich avifauna and a diverse flora that is high in regional endemics and species of medicinal and horticultural value to man. Furthermore, in terms of immediate economic rationale, the hydrological importance of the reserve as a water catchment is one of the strongest justifications for protecting the area, reforesting bare slopes and removing human settlements. The reserve also has a rare scientific facility, being strategically located in a site of key biological significance.

Conservation Management In the wake of the great concern aroused over the fate of the panda as a result of the mass-flowering of bamboo and subsequent die-off of both bamboo and giant pandas, during which 138 panda corpses were found in the Min Shan, the area was selected as one of the first panda reserves with the stated management objective, '... to conserve the giant panda, takin, and golden monkey—the rare and precious animals of China.' Tangjiahe probably still holds the second largest protected giant panda population after Wolong, with nearly 10% of the entire world population.

In view of the logging that occurred in 1965–78 over most of the reserve up to an altitude of about 2,200 m and its fairly small size, it is recommended in the draft management plan that as much lost habitat as possible be returned to the giant panda and that all remaining giant panda habitat be linked by bamboo corridors and given reserve status. In particular, Tangjiahe should be extended eastwards to Sanguo and Haoxi communes, where some national forest remains, in line with the originally proposed area of 40,000 ha (Bi et al., 1986, Wang and Hu, 1989). A system of zonation is proposed, with the bulk of the reserve designated as a fully protected area or sanctuary zone. Furthermore, current pressure on the reserve for fuelwood should be reduced by establishing fuelwood plantations in peripheral buffer zones. The management plan, first drafted in November 1986, has still to be approved. The government is considering the creation of one large reserve in the Minshan by connecting Tangjiahe, Baishu River (95,292 ha), Jiuzhaigou (60,000 ha), and Wanglang (27,700 ha) nature reserves through the creation of the proposed 90,000 ha Wujiao reserve (Schaller et al., 1985, MacKinnon and Qiu, 1986), and modified in the light of recent proposals for a reserve system in the northern Minshan (Wang and Hu, 1989). Villagers living adjacent to the reserve are encouraged to sign a joint contract with the reserve authority to protect the panda and its habitat (MOF, 1989).

Management Constraints   The biggest constraint to reserve management has been the damage to giant panda habitat from logging and the activities of former residents. This has reduced the amount of habitat available for giant pandas as well as destroyed corridors of habitat linking the different parts of the population. It probably also contributed to the severity of flooding experienced in Sichuan in 1981. The mass-flowering and die-off of bamboo in the 1970s has placed additional hardship on the giant panda population, considerably reducing its size, but this is a natural effect from which the species should recover in the absence of added human pressures. The small size of the reserve is a further constraint, making it difficult to maintain a giant panda population of viable size but this can be overcome by maintaining links with adjacent populations. Poaching, largely for musk deer, is a continuing but minor problem (Bi et al., 1986).

Staff The reserve is managed for the provincial Department of Forestry by a director and an assistant-director, who direct 33 employees, including 28 'work' staff (1987).

Budget The annual allocation from Sichuan Provincial Government is Yuan 40,000 to 50,000 (US $10,800 to US $13,500) for recurrent expenditure (1987).

Local Addresses

Director, Tangjiahe Natural Reserve Headquarters, Maoxiangba, Qingchuan County, Sichuan Province

References

Bi Fengzhou, Jiang Mindas, Qiu Minjang, Laurie, A., and Reid, D. (1986). Draft Management plan for Tangjiahe Natural Reserve. Sichuan Forest Bureau/World Wildlife Fund. Unpublished.

Hu Jinchu, Deng Qixang, Yu Zhiwei, Zhou Shoude and Tian Zhixiang (1980). Biological studies of giant panda, golden monkey, and some other rare and prized animals. Journal of Nanchong Teachers' College 1980(2): 1–39.

Laurie, W.A. (1986). Training for panda reserves staff. *WWF Monthly Report* November 1986: 313–16.

MOF (1989). The habitats of the giant panda: Wolong, Tangjiahe, Wanglang nature reserves. World Heritage nomination. Ministry of Forestry, People's Republic of China. 60 pp.

Schaller, G.B., Teng, Q., Johnson, K., Wang, X., Shen, H. and Hu Jinchu (1989). Feeding ecology of giant panda and Asiatic black bear in Tangjiahe Reserve, China. In: Gittleman, J. (Ed.), *Carnivore behaviour, ecology and evolution*. Cornell University Press, Ithaca, New York.

Seidensticker, J., Eisenberg, J.F., and Simons, R. (1984). The Tangjiahe, Wanglang, and Fengtongzhai giant panda reserves and biological conservation in the People's Republic of China. *Biological Conservation* 28: 217–51.

Taylor, A.H., (1984). The ecology of bamboos and their role in forest dynamics in the Wolong and Tangjiahe nature preserves, Northern Sichuan Province, China. World Wildlife Fund, Gland. Unpublished.

Wang, M. and Hu, T. (Eds.) (1989). National conservation management plan for the giant panda and its habitat: Sichuan, Shaanxi and Gansu provinces, The People's Republic of China. Ministry of Forestry, Beijing and WWF, Gland, Switzerland. 157 pp.

WWF/IUCN (n.d.) Project 3027. Ecology of giant panda, Tangjiahe Reserve.

TAXKORGAN NATURE RESERVE

IUCN Management Category   IV (Managed Nature Reserve).

Biogeographical Province   2.38.12 (Himalayan Highlands).

Geographical Location   Situated in the south-west corner of the Xinjiang Uygur Autonomous Region, at the juncture of the China, Pakistan, USSR and Afghanistan borders. The centre of the reserve lies about 265 km south of Kashi (Kashgar). The south-western boundary follows the Pakistan border from the vicinity of Kilik Pass south-eastwards to just beyond K2. The northern and eastern boundaries trace various tributaries of the Yarkant River (Schaller et al., 1987). 35°40′N–37°25′N, 74°30′E–76°50′E

Date and History of Establishment   Established as a nature reserve in 1984.

Area   1,500,000 ha. According to Schaller (1987), the area is 1,400,000 ha. Taxkorgan is contiguous to Khunjerab National Park (226,913 ha) in Pakistan.

Land Tenure   State.

Altitude   Ranges from below 3,000 m to the peak of K2 at 8,611 m.

Physical Features   The reserve is mountainous, about half of it is above 4,500 m, including the northern flanks of the Karakoram, the western edge of the Kunlun Shan, and eastern rim of the Pamir Mountains. It is drained by the Yarkant River and its tributaries. This flows north through the eastern part of the reserve. The western part is drained by the Chalachigu River, a branch of the Taxkorgan River which meets the Yarkant River north of the reserve. The south-eastern section of the reserve includes the Karakoram and extensive glaciers, the Aghil Range and the Oprang (Shaksgam) Valley, a region well described by Shipton (1938). This area is very remote, whereas the west has been an international travel route for centuries. Flat and in places more than 5 km wide, the Taxkorgan Valley was part of the ancient Silk Road which continues into the Chalachigu Valley and over the Mintaka Pass into Pakistan. The westernmost part of the reserve represents mainly 'pamirs', broad valleys and steeply rolling hills above 3,500 m and flanked by rugged ranges. Between the eastern rim of the Taxkorgan Valley and the Yarkant River is a complex of mountains, broken cliffs and sharp ridges cut by gorges. Near the junction with the Yarkant River, the Raskam, Mariang and other drainages lie below 3,000 m, the lowest part of the reserve. On the eastern bank of the Yarkant are the Taxkuzuke Mountains, a discrete, rough range (Schaller et al., 1987).

Climate   Conditions are cool and dry. Mean monthly minimum temperature at Taxkorgan Town (3,090 m) to the north of the reserve was −16 °C to 17 °C during the coldest months of December and January in 1984, and mean daily maximum reached 22 °C to 23 °C during the warmest months from June to August. Only 75.4 mm of precipitation fell in 1984, 81% of it between May and September (Schaller et al., 1987).

Vegetation   Much of the terrain is too high or arid to support much vegetation. Below 3,000–3,200 m there are usually cliffs, screes, sand and silt, a desert that is so dry that few plants survive except along streams. The only native trees are found in low-lying valleys: willow *Salix* and tamarisk *Tamarix* below 3,400 m, and cottonwood *Populus*, and birch *Betula* below 3,300 m, a few being as tall as 10 m. At 4,400 m, near the upper vegetation limit, plants grow mainly along seepages and rivulets, and at 4,500 m bare rock dominates, although hardy species of *Rhodiola*, *Saussurea* and *Tanacetum* may occur as high as 4,600–4,700 m. Vegetation has been greatly modified by human and livestock use (Schaller et al., 1987).

Fauna   Three wild ungulate species inhabit the reserve; a fourth, Asiatic wild ass *Equus hemionus* (V), once occurred along the upper Yarkant and Oprang rivers, but has not been seen since the 1950s (Schaller et al., 1987). The presence of the species on the Pakistan side of the border has recently been confirmed (Wegge, 1988). According to Schaller et al. (1987), the last known viable population of Marco Polo sheep *Ovis ammon polii* in China is confined to the western part of Chalachigu Valley, where 48 were recorded in June 1986, but more recent reports suggest that 100–200 winter in the Chopdur area, 2 km east-south-east of the Khunjerab Pass (Wegge, 1988). Schaller et al. (1987) estimates the total population in the area, which extends north of the reserve boundary, to be below 150, but more recent information presented by Wegge (1988) suggests that this figure may be too low. Ibex *Capra ibex* is found in the west of the reserve, where there are an estimated 1,000 animals. Bharal *Pseudois nayaur* is present in all eastern and south-eastern ranges of the reserve, its distribution overlapping with that of ibex in the north. A few thousand bharal are thought to be present. Among carnivores, brown bear *Ursus arctos* and wolf *Canis lupus* (V) are rare. Some 50 to

75 snow leopard *Panthera uncia* (E) are thought to frequent the reserve (Schaller et al., 1987, 1988). Information on the avifauna is not available.

Cultural Heritage   Part of the Silk Road, an ancient travel route, follows the Chalachiga Valley along the northern border of the reserve and over the Mintaka Pass into Pakistan. The Karakoram Highway, completed in the 1960s, now follows this route.

Local Human Population   In 1985, four communes and a breeding farm, totalling about 7,750 Kirgiz and Tajik people with 70,000 head of livestock, used the reserve at least seasonally in 1985. About 80% of the livestock is sheep and goats and the rest comprises donkeys, horses, cattle, camels and yaks. Where land is flat and irrigation possible, barley and a few other crops are grown. Most fields are at low elevations, although a few occur as high as 3,900 m (Schaller et al., 1987).

Visitors and Visitor Facilities   The western part is accessible by the Karakoram Highway. There are no visitor facilities.

Scientific Research and Facilities   A status survey of large mammals in the western half of the reserve was conducted by Schaller et al. (1987, 1988) in May–June 1985 and June–July 1986. The more remote south-eastern part has been visited only twice by foreign expeditions (Younghusband, 1896; Shipton, 1938)–.

Conservation Value   Taxkorgan and the adjacent Khunjerab National Park in Pakistan constitute one of the most important wildlife areas in the mountains of Asia. Their establishment provides the foundation for an international peace park in the region. Taxkorgan has important populations of large ungulates and carnivores, notably Marco Polo sheep and snow leopard (Schaller et al., 1987).

Conservation Management   Management is in its infancy. In 1987 two guards were posted at Mintaka to protect Marco Polo sheep. There are plans to set up a committee of commune, county and forest department representatives to propose, execute and enforce conservation measures (Schaller et al., 1987).

Management Constraints   Taxkorgan cannot become a viable reserve until the activities of human residents and their livestock are modified, and hunting is controlled. Overgrazing by livestock and the removal of shrubs and trees for fuelwood has greatly reduced the carrying capacity of the land, and turned low-lying slopes and valley flats into desert. Traditionally, ibex, blue sheep and Marco Polo sheep were hunted to supplement the diet, but this has intensified with the construction of the Karkoram Highway. Predators, particularly wolves and snow leopards, kill large numbers of livestock (partly a reflection of depleted wild ungulate populations) and are in turn killed in retribution (Schaller et al., 1987, 1988).

Staff   No precise information.

Budget   No information

Local Addresses
Forest Department, Kashi, Xinjiang Uygur Autonomous Region

References

Schaller, G.B., Talipu, L.H., Hua, L., Junrang, R., Mingjiang, Q., and Haibin, W. (1987). Status of large mammals in the Taxkorgan Reserve, Xinjiang, China. *Biological Conservation* 42: 53–71.

Schaller, G.B., Talipu, L.H., Junrang, R., Mingjiang, Q. (1988). The snow leopard in Xinjiang, China. *Oryx* 22: 197–204.

Shipton, E. (1938). *Blank on the map*. Hodder and Stoughton, London. (Unseen)

Wegge, P. (1988). Assessment of Khunjerab National Park and environs, Pakistan. IUCN, Gland, Switzerland. Unpublished. 25 pp.

Younghusband, F. (1896). *The heart of a continent*. John Murray, London. (Unseen)

WANGLANG NATURE RESERVE

IUCN Management Category   IV (Managed Nature Reserve)

Biogeographical Province   2.39.12 (Sichuan Highlands)

Geographical Location   Lies in Pingwu County of northern Sichuan, about 430 km north of the provincial capital of Chengdu. Mountain ridges provide natural boundaries on all sides of the reserve. 32°49′–33°02′N, 103°55′–104°10′E

Date and History of Establishment   Ratified as a nature reserve by the People's Committee (provincial government) of Sichuan in September 1963.

Area   27,700 ha. The reserve borders on Jiuzhaigou Nature Reserve (60,000 ha) in the north-west.

Land Tenure   Provincial government

Altitude   Ranges from about 2,400 m to 4,983 m.

Physical Features   Situated on the north-eastern escarpment of the Min Shan, the reserve is a steep-sided basin encompassing the headwaters of the Fu Chiang, a major tributary of the Chang Jiang (Yangtze). The main river is the Baima Ho, which drains to the south-east. Rock formations date back mainly to the Devonian, Carboniferous and Permian periods. Parent rock material is limestone. Soils are described as yellow-brown, grey and meadow. Earthquakes are a frequent if irregular occurrence at the edge of the Tibetan Plateau, the last serious one in 1976 (7.2 on the Richter scale) being responsible for extensive landslides in the reserve. Sometimes, where streams have been blocked by landslides, lakes have been formed.

Climate   The reserve lies in the subtropical monsoon climatic belt. Annual precipitation is up to 1800 mm, most of which falls in summer. Mean monthly temperatures range between approximately −7° C in January and 18–20 °C in July.

Vegetation   The vegetation is vertically distributed. Below 2,600 m are mixed montane forests, the main conifers being hemlocks *Tsuga chinensis* and *T. yunnanensis* and pine *Pinus*

armandii, and broad-leaved trees represented by birch *Betula* spp., beech *Fagus longipetiolata*, rhododendrons *Rhododendron* spp., and oak *Quercus aquifolioides*. Between 2,600 m and 3,800 m are coniferous forests of fir *Abies fabri*, spruce *Picea asperata* and larch *Larix potanini*, and broad-leaved forests of birches *Betula platyphylla*, *B. albo-sinensis*, rhododendrons, and *Lonicera tangutica*. Above 3,800 m are alpine shrubs and herbs. The bamboos *Fargesia denudata* and *F. nitida*, which are the staple food of the giant panda, are plentiful in the mixed montane and coniferous forests. *F. scabrida*, another favoured species, is regenerating following mass flowering and die-back in 1975. According to Seidensticker et al. (1984), forest covers 44%, mountains 19% and rocks 37% of the surface area.

Of the tree flora, *Tetracentron sinense*, *Cercidiphyllum japonicum*, and *Larix mastersiana* are nationally protected on account of their rarity. Over 150 species of medicinal plants have been recorded (MOF, 1989).

Fauna   Some 63 species of mammals, 89 species of birds, eight species of reptiles, and eight species of amphibians are reported to be present. Those legally protected at national level include golden snub-nosed monkey *Rhinopithecus roxellanae* (V), Pallas's (steppe) cat *Felis manul*, Asiatic golden cat *F. temmincki*, clouded leopard *Neofelis nebulosa* (V), giant panda *Ailuropoda melanoleuca* (R), red panda *Ailurus fulgens* (K), musk deer *Moschus berezovskii*, Sichuan takin *Budorcas taxicolor tibetana* (I), and several of the 11 species of pheasant in the reserve (e.g. Temminck's tragopan *Tragopan temminckii*, Chinese monal pheasant *Lophophorus lhuysii* (E), blue-eared pheasant *Crossoptilon auritum*, and golden pheasant *Chrysolophus pictus*).

The Giant Panda Expedition (1974) estimated that in 1968–9 there were 196 pandas in 122.5 sq. km, but ten years later only 10–20 remained. Of those that had disappeared, some had starved with the mass-flowering of bamboo in over 80% of the reserve in 1975–6 (13 were found dead), some may have emigrated and others may have been killed in landslides during the 1976 earthquake (Schaller et al., 1985). Evidence of 20 pandas was found during a survey conducted in 1984 (MOF, 1989).

Cultural Heritage   The people of the ancient Longan Prefecture (now Pingwu County) are said to have presented a giant panda to King Yu who saved Cathay from a catastrophic deluge some 4,000 years ago. Wanglang is named after a legendary Tibetan youth who settled down and became a hermit (MOF, 1989).

Local Human Population   Although no longer inhabited, the reserve is surrounded by settlements, including the Beima commune for Tibetan minorities, with a total population in excess of ten thousand people. Traditional activities include collection of medicinal herbs and hunting both in and around the reserve.

Visitors and Visitor Facilities   Information about visitor numbers is not available. Roads provide access to two valleys and, in 1983, a hotel was under construction (Schaller, 1983).

Scientific Research and Facilities   The mammals and birds of Pingwu County were first surveyed by naturalists and missionaries from Russia, France and Great Britain in 1870–85. A census of the reserve's giant panda population was undertaken in 1968–9 (Giant Panda Expedition, 1974). Brief surveys have also been carried out by Schaller (1983) and Seidensticker et al. (1984).

Conservation Value   The reserve was established for the protection of the giant panda and several other rare and nationally prestigious animal species (Seidensticker et al., 1984).

Conservation Management   Logging ceased in the 1950s, since when secondary forest has regenerated on most slopes (Schaller, 1983). Following the mass-flowering of bamboo in 1983, a giant panda rescue operation was launched. Giant pandas found starving were captured, taken to villages to be fed and, subsequently, transferred to a holding centre built inside the reserve by the Chinese authorities. The usefulness of this operation is difficult to assess as details are not readily available, but it is doubtful if it made a significant contribution to saving the species (MacKinnon and Qiu, 1986). A management plan is being prepared by the Sichuan Forest Department and reserve authority. Villagers living near the reserve are encouraged to sign a joint agreement with the reserve authority to protect the panda and its habitat.

Management Constraints   The giant panda population within the reserve has declined markedly, largely due to habitat removal and disturbance but more recently exacerbated by the mass-flowering of bamboo in 1975–6 (80% die-back) and again in 1983. Hunting and the collection of minor forest products are minor constraints.

Staff   The reserve is managed by a staff of 15 persons, three in management and 12 'work' staff.

Budget   Sichuan Provincial Government allocates Yuan 30,000 (US $ 8,000) annually for recurrent expenditure (1987).

Local Addresses   No information

References
Giant Panda Expedition (1974). A survey of the giant panda (*Ailuropoda melanoleuca*) in the Wanglang Natural Reserve, Pingwu, northern Szechuan, China. *Acta Zoologica Sinica* 20: 162–73. (In Chinese.)

MacKinnon, J., and Qiu, M. (1986). Masterplan for saving the giant panda and its habitat. Preliminary draft. Ministry of Forestry, People's Republic of China/World Wildlife Fund.

MOF (1989). The habitats of the giant panda: Wolong, Tangjiahe, Wanglang nature reserves. World Heritage nomination, Ministry of Forestry, People's Republic of China. 60 pp.

Schaller, G.B. (1983). Panda Project. Report to World Wildlife Fund. P. 8.

Schaller, G.B., Hu Jinchu, Pan Wenshi and Zhu Jing (1985). *The giant pandas of Wolong*. University of Chicago Press, Chicago. 298 pp.

Seidensticker, J., Eisenberg, J.F. and Simons, R. (1984). The Tangjiahe, Wanglang and Fengtongzhai giant panda reserves and biological conservation in the People's Republic of China. *Biological Conservation* 28: 217–51

WOLONG NATURE RESERVE

IUCN Management Category   IV   (Managed Nature Reserve)

Biogeographical Province   2.39.12   (Sichuan Highlands)

Geographical Location   Lies in Wenchuan County, Sichuan, some 130 km from the provincial capital of Chengdu. Mountain ridges provide natural boundaries on all sides. 30°45′–31°25′N, 102°52′–103°24′E

Date and History of Establishment   Ratified as a national nature reserve by the State Council in March 1975. Dashuigou and other tributary valleys of the upper Pitiao in Wolong were first designated as a nature reserve in March 1963 and covered an area of 20,000 ha. Wolong was accepted as a biosphere reserve in November 1979.

Area   200,000 ha. Extended from its original area of 20,000 ha in the same year (1975) that it was designated a national nature reserve. Almost continuous with Fengtongzhai Nature Reserve (40,000 ha) to the south.

Land Tenure   Land is under Government ownership except for 434 ha along the Pitiao and Erher rivers which are owned and cultivated by the communities of Gengda and Wolong.

Altitude   Ranges from about 1,200 m at Mujiangping to 6,250 m (Mt. Siguniang).

Physical Features   Lying between the Sichuan Basin and the Tibetan Highlands, the mountains of Wolong have been so warped, crumbled and folding during the Tertiary, when the Himalaya and neighbouring ranges began to be uplifted, that the topography is spectacular. Mountains and rivers generally run parallel with the Longmen Mountain Fault, which transects the area in a north-east to south-west direction. The terrain descends progressively from the north-west to south-east, with the Pitiao River forming a natural dividing line. Peaks to the east of the Pitiao are mostly below 3,200 m, those to the west mostly over 4,000 m and about 60 are over 5,000 m. Intense tectonic activity and erosion have created deep, V-shaped valleys, flanked either by cliffs or steep river banks, where landslides and mud floors are common. Other features including hanging valleys and cirques. The gradient of rivers is steep and the water turbulent, often laden with silt in the summer rains. The river water is slightly saline (mean pH 8.2, range 7.7 to 8.6), low in salinity (mean 160.4 mg/l, range 102.0 to 265.7) and generally soft (mean 6.4, range 3.7 to 11.2, German system).

According to the Chengdu Geographic Institute of Academica Sinica, the rock strata consist primarily of sandstone, slate, schist, siltstone, gneiss, quartzite, dolomite, limestone, and phyllite and they range in age from Silurion to Triassic. Limestone and phyllite are most abundant. There are also igneous intrusions of serpentine, granite, and granodiorite. Soils are typical of those developed in subtropical, glacial conditions. On the slopes between 2,000 m and 3,100 m are many small plateaux or stripped plains (horizontal strata from which weaker rocks have been eroded) where deep brown and dark brown soils provide excellent conditions for forest and bamboo growth.

Climate   Wolong lies in the Qinghai-Tibetan climatic belt, characterised by a long winter, with snow lasting from November to March, and relatively cool wet summers. The south-east monsoon lasts from June until October. According to recordings from Shawan Meteorological Station at 1,920 m within the reserve, mean annual maximum and minimum temperatures are 29°C and –8 °C, respectively. Mean annual precipitation is 888 mm and relative humidity 80.3% (MOF, 1989). Conditions are more extreme at higher altitudes. Total annual precipitation recorded by Schaller et al. (1985) at Wuyipeng (2,520 m) in 1981 was 1511 mm, of which 37.9% fell as snow between late October and April. Mean daily minimum temperature was below freezing point from November through March, the coldest day

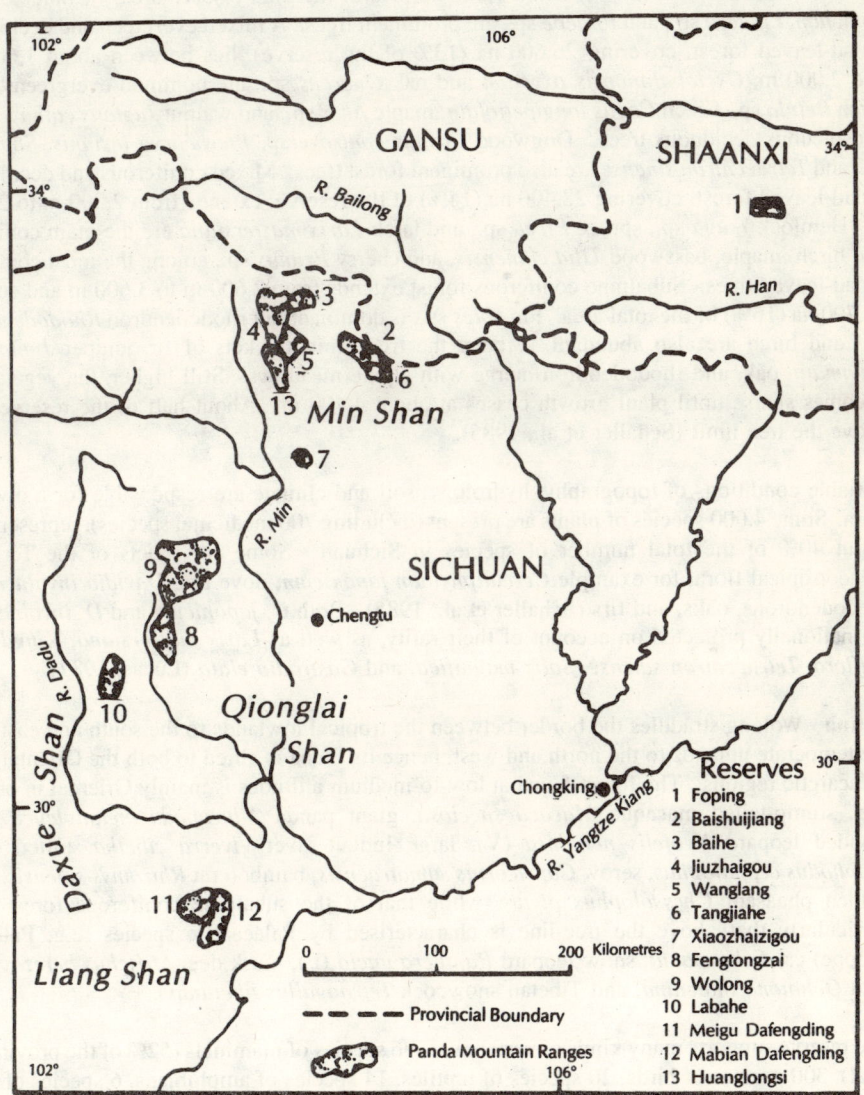

Wolong Nature Reserve and associated panda reserves

registering −12.5 °C. The warmest months were June, July and August when mean daily maxima reached 16 °C–29 °C.

Vegetation The vegetation is altitudinally distributed into a number of zones that have been described by Hu (1981). Subtropical evergreen broad-leaved forest grows below 1,600 m in the south-east and extend over some 3,300 ha (2% of the total reserve area). *Cinnamomum inunctum*, *Lindera* sp., and *Phoebe* sp., are prominent trees. A mixed evergreen and deciduous broad-leaved forest, covering 26,600 ha (13% of the reserve), lies between about 1,600 m and 2,000 m. *Cyclobalanopsis oxyodon* and oak *Quercus* sp., are common evergreens, and birch *Betula* sp., beech *Fagus longipetiolata*, maple *Acer* sp., and walnut *Juglans cathayensis*, conspicuous deciduous trees. Dogwood *Cornus controversa*, *Pterocarya insignis*, *Sophora* sp., and *Tetracentron sinense* are also prominent forest trees. Mixed coniferous and deciduous broad-leaved forest, covering 28,400 ha (14%) of the reserve, extends from 2,000 m to 2,600 m. Hemlock *Tsuga* sp., spruce *Picea* sp., and larch *Larix mastersiana* are the main conifers, and birch, maple, basswood *Tilia chinensis*, and cherry *Prunus* sp., among the most common broad-leaved trees. Subalpine coniferous forest extends from 2,600 m to 3,600 m and covers 31,700 ha (16%) of the total area. Fir *Abies* sp., is dominant but rhododendron *Rhododendron* sp., and birch are also abundant. Above the tree limit, thickets of fir, juniper *Juniperus squamata*, oak, and rhododendron merge with alpine meadows. Still higher, the vegetation becomes sparse until plant growth ceases at about 4,400 m. About half of the reserve lies above the tree limit (Schaller et al., 1985).

Variable conditions of topography, hydrology, soil and climate are responsible for a diverse flora. Some 4,000 species of plants are present (including 700 medicinal species), representing about 40% of the total number of species in Sichuan. Some are relicts of the Tertiary palaeotropical flora, for example *Cercidiphyllum japonicum*, dove tree *Davidia involucrata*, rhododendrons, oaks, and firs (Schaller et al., 1985). Both *C. japonicum* and *D. involucrata* are nationally protected on account of their rarity, as well as *Larix mastersiana*, *Kingdonia uniflora*, *Tetracentron sinense*, *Salix magnifica*, and *Gastrodia elata* (Lucas, 1987).

Fauna Wolong straddles the border between the tropical lowlands to the south and east and the temperate uplands to the north and west, hence its fauna is allied to both the Oriental and Palaearctic regions. The forest fauna at low-to-medium altitudes is mainly Oriental in origin (e.g. stump-tailed macaque *Macaca speciosa*, giant panda *Ailuropoda melanoleuca* (R), clouded leopard *Neofelis nebulosa* (V), large Indian civet *Viverra zibetha*, tufted deer *Elaphodus cephalophus*, serow *Capricornis sumatraensis*, bamboo rat *Rhizomys sinensis*, and golden pheasant *Chrysolophus pictus*, while that of the subalpine coniferous forest and particularly that above the tree-line is characterised by Palaearctic species (e.g. Pallas's (steppe) cat *Felis manul*, snow leopard *Panthera uncia* (E), musk deer *Moschus berezovskii*, pika *Ochotona thibetana*, and Tibetan snowcock *Tetraogallus tibetanus*).

The reserve supports many kinds of vertebrates, 96 species of mammals (52% of the provincial total), 300 species of birds, 20 species of reptiles, 14 species of amphibians, 6 species of fish and 1,700 species of insects having been noted so far. Among these are 30 species that China prizes and to which it has given complete legal protection, including Chinese monal *Lophophorus lhuysii* (E) and Temminck's tragopan *Tragopan temminckii*, golden snub-nosed monkey *Rhinopithecus roxellanae* (V), white-lipped deer *Cervus albirostris* (I), Sichuan takin *Budorcas taxicolor tibetana* (I), snow leopard *Panthera uncia* (E), red panda *Ailurus fulgens* (K), and, of course, giant panda *Ailuropoda melanoleuca* (K), for whom the reserve was established and whose presence has assured the survival of all other species there.

Evidence for 145 giant pandas was found during a census conducted in 1974 by the Rare Animal Resources Investigation Team. Based on independent data for 1981–2, Schaller et al. (1985) concluded that these census results are of the correct order of magnitude and, in the Choushuigou study area, at an estimated the ecological density to be 1.25 sq. km per animal. Numbers have since declined to an estimated 72 pandas, based on a census conducted in 1986 (MacKinnon and Qiu, 1986).

Cultural Heritage   No information

Local Human Population   The forests of Wolong were in virgin condition prior to the 20th century, with only a small number of Tibetans subsisting on farming and hunting. Immigrants entered in the early part of this century to grow opium in Pitiao Valley and in 1916 timber merchants began logging, primarily along the banks of rivers and streams which were used for transporting the timber. A highway to Wolong was opened up in the 1960s to improve access for timber production (MOF, 1989).

There are two townships, Wolong and Gengda, and six villages within the reserve, which has a residential population of some 3,854 farmers distributed among 675 households. Many of them are Qiang of Tibetan stock, but other national minorities include Tibetan, Han and Hui. Divided into two communes, most of them inhabit the main valley of Wolong, where they grow potatoes, maize, beans and other crops within a cultivated area of 434 ha. Many mountainsides have been denuded below an altitude of 2,400 m, the forest converted into fields and pasture or reduced to scrub. Villagers penetrate even higher up the slopes to collect wood for fuel and to cut timber for house beams and roof shingles.

Visitors and Visitor Facilities   There is a visitor centre with exhibition hall, which is used extensively by students. Tourist accommodation is needed.

Scientific Research and Facilities   Following a census of the giant panda conducted throughout the reserve from April to July 1974 by the Expedition of Rare Animal Species in Sichuan (1977), the Chinese initiated panda research in the Choushuigou Valley in March 1978. The original breeding station at Yingxionggou was abandoned after several fruitless years and a new complex, fully equipped with research laboratories and veterinary facilities, was established at Hetauping. There are 11 resident pandas (five males, six females), including the first captive-born panda, born on 12 August 1986. Late in December 1980 a collaborative China–World Wildlife Fund panda research project began its work in the same valley. The first two and a half years of work have been summarised by Hu et al. (1980) and Hu (1981), while research undertaken between January 1981 and June 1982 is reported on by Schaller et al. (1985). Since 1984, an investigation into the life cycle of the giant panda's main food plant, bamboo, has been underway (Taylor, 1984). The effects of selective cutting on forest regeneration to meet local needs for wood products has also been examined in panda habitat (Taylor and Qin, 1989). Training courses for protection and research staff are held regularly (Laurie, 1986).

Conservation Value   Wolong is of great importance for its biological diversity, having a particularly rich flora and avifauna. It holds the world's largest protected population of giant panda. It is considered to be an outstanding natural area which merits inscription on the World Heritage List on the basis of criterion (iv) as a significant area of natural habitat for the best known of the world's endangered species, the giant panda (IUCN Technical

Evaluation, 1987). Inscription has been deferred, however, until the management plan is fully operational.

Conservation Management Wolong was established for the protection of the giant panda and a number of other rare and nationally prestigious animal species. Extensive areas within the reserve have been logged during this century, beginning in 1916 and reaching a peak after the establishment of the Wolong Forest Industry Bureau at Shawan in 1961. In 1975 it was stopped abruptly to preserve giant panda habitat (Schaller et al., 1985). Subsequently, in 1983, the provincial government approved the establishment of the Wolong Special Administration Zone in which tree-felling, hunting and land reclamation are strictly prohibited (Chen, 1985). Together with the Wolong Nature Reserve Authority, this administration is responsible for conserving natural resources within the reserve and meeting the livelihood requirements of its resident human population. A management plan has been drafted (MacKinnon et al., 1988) but still awaits approval. At present, a core area of some 50,000 ha is strictly protected from all activities other than scientific research. The remaining 150,000 ha constitutes a buffer zone.

Various conservation initiatives are underway. Two hydropower stations have been installed over the Pitiao and Gengda rivers to make available cheap electricity to replace the former vast consumption of fuelwood (MOF, 1989). One commune, totalling about 1,900 people, is scheduled to be moved out of the upper Pitiao Valley and, in view of the reserve's designation as a biosphere reserve, resettled in a multiple-use enclave further downstream in the reserve's Gengda Valley. However, it is now considered more appropriate to resettle these people completely outside the reserve, together with the 2,000 already living at Gengda. If this cannot be done, it is recommended that 20,000 ha of forest and village land be excised from the reserve and returned to the management of Wenchuan County government (Wang and Hu, 1989).

Management Constraints The main constraint to reserve management has been the damage to giant panda habitat from logging and the activities of the resident human population. The mass-flowering and die-off of bamboo in the mid-1970s and again in 1983 has imposed additional hardship on the giant panda population, but this is a natural phenomenum with which the species is able to cope in the absence of added human pressures.

A major discontinuity exists between giant pandas north and east of the Zheng/Gengda Valley and those south of the Pitiao Valley. A quiet corridor, in which no further cultivation or wood cutting is permitted, needs to be created to link these populations. Moreover, as the Wolong population cannot be regarded as viable in the long-term, it needs to be linked with other populations in the Qionglai Mountains through extensions to the panda reserve system (see Wang and Hu, 1989). Hunting and the collection of forest products are minor constraints.

Staff 330 staff, comprising 176 supervisory/management staff and 154 'working' staff (1987).

Budget Being a 'key' national nature reserve, funding is provided by the Ministry of Forests, Central Government. The allocation for recurrent expenditure in 1987 was Yuan 0.8–0.9 million (US $ 0.215 to US $ 0.240 million).

Local Addresses
Wolong Nature Reserve, Management Office, Wenchuan Country, Sichuan 623006.

References

Chen Gengtao (1985). China establishes more nature reserves. *Biological Conservation* 31: 1-5.

Expedition of Rare Animal Species in Sichuan (1977). A report on the rare animal species in Sichuan. The Sichuan Forest Bureau. (In Chinese.)

Hu Jinchu (1981). Ecology and biology of the giant panda, golden monkey and takin. Sichuan People's Publishing House. (In Chinese.)

Hu Jinchu, Deng Qixang, Yu Zhiwei, Zhou Shoude and Tian Zhixiang (1980). Biological studies of giant panda, golden monkey, and some other rare and prized animals. *Journal of Nanchong Teachers' College* 1980(2): 1–39.

Laurie, W.A. (1986). Training for panda reserves staff. *WWF Monthly Report* November 1986: 313–16.

Lucas, B. (1987). Notes on trip to China. IUCN, Gland, Switzerland. Unpublished. 7 pp.

MacKinnon, J., Qiu Minjang, Bi Fengzhou and Zhang Kewen (1988). Draft management plan for Wolong Natural Reserve. World Wildlife Fund, Gland, Switzerland.

MOF (1989). The habitats of the giant panda: Wolong, Tangjiahe, Wanglang nature reserves. World Heritage nomination, Ministry of Forestry, People's Republic of China. 60 pp.

Schaller, G., Hu Jinchu, Pan Wenshi and Zhu Jing (1985). *The giant pandas of Wolong*. University of Chicago Press, Chicago. 298 pp. (Contains an extensive bibliography.)

Taylor, A.H., (1984). The ecology of bamboos and their role in forest dynamics in the Wolong and Tangjiahe nature reserves, northern Sichuan Province, China. World Wildlife Fund. Unpublished.

Taylor, A.H. and Qin Zisheng (1989). Structure and composition of selectively cut and uncut *Abies-Tsuga* forest in Wolong Nature Reserve and implications for panda conservation in China. *Biological Conservaton* 47: 83–108.

WWF/IUCN (n.d). Project no. 1929.China, giant panda research.

XISHUANGBANNA NATURE RESERVE (INCLUDES MENGYANG, MENGLA, SHANGYONG, MENGAO AND MENGLUN NATURE RESERVES)

IUCN Management Category   IV   (Managed Nature Reserve)

Biogeographical Province   2.39.12   (Szechwan Highlands)

Geographical Location   The Xishuangbanna Nature Reserve is divided into a network of five separate nature reserves isolated from each other.   They are Mengyang, Mengla, Shangyong, Mengao, and Menglun, all within Xishuangbanna Prefecture in Yunnan Province. Mengyang is in northern Jinghong County, Menglun is in the centre of the Prefecture, Mengla and Shangyong are in Mengla County in the south-east, and Mengao is in Menghai County in the north-west.   Access to the reserves is limited to roads, small trails and paths. 21°10′–22°24′N, 100°16′–101°55′E

Date and History of Establishment   Mengyang, Menghin, Mengla and Menglong were established as nature reserves by the Provincial People's Government in 1958.   Their total area was 6,000 ha, but in 1980 they were combined with Shangyong Nature Reserve to form Xishuangbanna Nature Reserve for administrative purposes (Wenhua and Xianying, 1989).

Area   The total area is officially cited as 200,000 ha, but that of the constituent reserves is 207,000 ha (Anon., 1985a):Altitude   Ranges from 420 m to 2,300 m.

Mengyang: 90,000 ha
Mengla and Shangyong: 100,000 ha
Mengao: 8,000 ha
Menglun: 9,000 ha

Land Tenure   Provincial government

Physical Features   Xishuangbanna Nature Reserve lies in the Lancang (Mekong) River basin. The terrain is mostly (95%) mountainous (Wachtel, 1984). Limestone formations account for 18,000 ha. Mengla is a limestone mountain, formed during the Permain and subsequently weathered to form a karst landscape. The geology of the remaining area comprises granites and sandstones. Soils covering 60% of the area are mostly leached and acidic with a marked lack of phosphorus. On better soils, the pH range is 4.5 to 5.4 (Anon., 1985a).

Climate   Conditions are tropical monsoonal due to the warm and wet air currents created by the south-western monsoon from the Indian Ocean and the south-eastern monsoon from the Pacific Ocean. Cold air from the north is intercepted by mountain ranges (Wenhua and Xianging, 1989). There is a distinct wet and dry season: the dry season lasts from November to March, and the wet season from April to October. Annual precipitation ranges from 1194 mm to 2492 mm, of which 80% falls during the wet season (Anon., 1985a). There are 170–195 rainy days each year. Mean annual temperature is 15.1 °C to 21.7 °C, depending on altitude (Qinsong, 1985). Fog (115 to 145 days per year) occurs mostly in the dry season (Wenhua and Xianging, 1989).

Vegetation   The flora is diverse with more than 60 species of trees per 100 sq. m of tropical forest. There are 3,500 species of higher plants of which 300 species are rare. There are 200 species of food plants, 100 species of oil plants, 20 species of aromatic oil plants, 100 species of rapid-growing trees, 50 species of bamboo, 300 species of medicinal plants, and 30 species of 'living fossils'. Valuable genetic resources include wild types of rice, wild tea *Camellia sinnensis*, wild litchi *Litchi sinnensis*, and wild tea-oil *Camellia confusa*. Four main types of vegetation are distinguished by the North-East Forestry Institute. Tropical rain forest (13,900 ha) is found below 800 m. Dominant species include *Parashorea sinnensis, Cattica fleuryana, Tetrameles nudiflora, Pometia tomentosa, Nephelium chryseum, Terminalia myriocarpa, Knema surfuracea, Horsfieldia glabra, Cryteronia paniculata, Homalium laoticum, Garuga pinnata, Gironniera subaequalis* and *Bacaurea ramiflora*. Above 800 m is tropical monsoon rain forest (3,000 ha), with *Stereospermun tetragonum, Pterospermum acerifolium, Dolichandrons stipulata, Mayodendron igneum, Chukrasia tabularis, Gmelina arborea, Bombax insigne, Anthocephalus sinnensis, Bauhinia variegata, Bischofia javanica, Cleistanthus sumatranus, Duabanga grandiflora*. Bamboo has emerged where the forest has been destroyed. Above 1,000 m are 179,830 ha of south subtropical monsoon broad-leaved evergreen forest. The main components of woody flora are Lauraceae, Fagaceae, Magnoliaceae and Theaceae. Species include *Castonopsis mekongensis, C. hystrix, C. argyrophylla, C. ferox, Lithocarpus fenestratus, L. mohaiensis, Pygium topengii, Erythroxyllum kunthianum, Magnolia hennji*, and *Elaeocarpus austro yunnanensis*. Mossy broad-leaved evergreen forest is found above 1,800 m on Nangang Mountain. Predominant tree species include *Cyclobalanopsis rex, Lithocarpus inuensis, Lindera moghaiensis, Phoebe* *macrocarpus*, *Heliciopsis terminalis*, *Caryota urens*, and *Podocarpus wallichii* (Qinsong, 1985). The Yunnan Institute of Tropical Botany classifies the vegetation into wet seasonal rain forest, dry seasonal rain forest, monsoon forest, and a monsoon forest limestone sub-type. Shifting cultivation has lead to a fire-climax grassland (Anon., 1985a).

Fauna   Mammals total 102 species and include tiger *Panthera tigris* (E), leopard *Panthera pardus* (T), binturong *Arctictis binturong*, slow loris *Nycticebus coucang*, gibbon *Hylobates concolor* (V), grey langur *Presbytis pileata*, Asian elephant *Elephas maximus* (E), gaur *Bos gaurus* (V), pangolin *Manis pentadactyla*, and sambar *Cervus unicolor*.   Since the establishment of the reserve, elephant and gaur populations have increased (Anon., 1985b).

Birds total 427 species and include rufous-necked hornbill *Aceros nipalensis* (R), green peacock *Pavo muticus* (V), great barbet *Megalaima virens*, thick-billed green pigeon *Treron curvirostra nipalensis*, thick-billed flowerpecker *Dicaeum agile*, crimson sunbird *Aethopyga siparaja*, peacock-pheasant *Polyplectron bicalcaratum*, olive-backed sunbird *Nectarinia jugularis*, silver pheasant *Lophura nycthemera*, red jungle fowl *Gallus gallus*, melodious laughing thrush *Garrulax canorus*, eastern blossom-headed parakeet *Psittacula roseata*, coppersmith barbet *Megalaima haemacephala*, and silver-eared mesia *Leiothrix argentauris* (Qinsong, 1985).   Other species include Asian barred owl *Glaucidium cuculoides*, beach stone-curlew plover *Esacus magnirostris*, black-crested bulbul *Pycononotus melanicterus*, blue-throated barbet *Magalaima asiatica*, baya weaver *Ploceus philippinus*, *Pitta* spp., and *Zoothera* spp. (Watt, 1990).

Amphibians total 38 species and reptiles 60 species, including python *Python molurus* (V), fish salamander *Icthyophis glutinous*, black-webbed tree frog *Rhacophorus rainwardtii*, flat-breated tortoise *Platysternon meacephalus*, naked-eared flying dragon *Draco blanford*, flying lizard *D. maculatus*, and water monitor *Varanus salvator*.   Over 1,437 different species of insects exist, the dominant genera being Lepidoptera, Colepteroidae and Hemipteroidae. White ant nests 3 m tall have also been recorded (Qinsong, 1985).

Cultural Heritage   The reserve is home to a number of minority groups, including Han (30%) and Dai (30%).   The remainder belong to Hani, Lagu, Bulang, Jimio, Yao, Bai, Miao, Hui, Zhuang, Va, and Yi. They live in the more hilly areas, using slash and burn techniques to cultivate land.   These groups have strong cultural identities, maintaining traditional beliefs and customs (Bamford, 1988).

Local Human Population   The resident population has increased from 12,000 in 1980 to 20,000 in 1985, due to both natural growth and immigration.   Some 93 villages are distributed throughout the reserve (Anon., 1985a). Shifting cultivation and permanent agriculture extend over 13,000 ha, while 30% of the reserve is forested (Anon., 1989).   Other activities include hunting, grazing and tea cultivation.   The surrounding areas have been used for shifting cultivation, rubber plantations and fuelwood (Santiapillai, 1990).

Visitors and Visitor Facilities   Between 3% to 5% of foreign visitors to Kunming (Yunnan Province) visit the reserve (3,000 or more per year), whilst nationals number at least 6,000 per year.   Accommodation and other tourist facilities are available at the ranger stations. Accommodation at Kunming and Jinghong includes hotel facilities (Bamford, 1988).

Scientific Research and Facilities   Studies of the vegetation have been made by the Yunnan Institute of Tropical Botany and the North-Eastern Forestry Institute.   The South-Western

Forestry College (1982) has inventoried the fauna. Santiapillai (1990) has studied of the management of elephants. A team from WWF-International and WWF-Hong Kong (1990), led by John MacKinnon, carried out a survey of bird numbers and their relationship to forest of various sizes. Human impact on the reserve and its flora and fauna was also examined. The Botanical Gardens at Menglun have carried out research into tropical rain forests. Tourism has been examined by Bamford (1988). Facilities include field management stations for each reserve.

Conservation Value   Xishuangbanna is an extremely important reserve complex which supports a rich and diverse flora and fauna, representative of tropical, subtropical and temporate zones. It provides a refuge for a number of threatened species such as Asian elephant, gaur, green peacock and tiger, and supports a wealth of economically important plant species (Wenhua and Xiangying, 1989).

Conservation Management   Hunting is prohibited and a permit from the reserve bureau must be obtained before visiting or conducting scientific research. The reserve is administered by the Protection Division of the Prefectual Forestry Bureau, responsible to the Prefectual Government and Yunnan Provincial Forestry Bureau under the supervision of the Ministry of Forestry in Beijing. A statement of objectives has been issued jointly by the authorities and includes: the total protection of 'core areas' within each component reserve; removal and resettlement of 10,000 people (1,700 families) living in the proposed core areas; improvement of living standards; removal of a further 10,000 people from within the boundaries of the reserve; planting economic crops in areas of shifting cultivation within and adjacent to the reserve; registration of all firearms; demarcation of boundaries of each component reserve; and construction of additional forest management stations and control posts, access roads and paths to facilitate control and administration of the separate units. Beijing has formulated a two-stage project: Stage 1 (duration two-three years) includes the development of management plans for the separate reserves; and Stage 2 (duration five years) covers resettlement, road and path construction, boundary demarcation and the improvement of agricultural land. It is proposed to upgrade Xishuangbanna to a national reserve to facilitate funding from outside the province (Anon., 1985a). The reserve headquarters are located in Jinghong.

A one-month training course for reserve guards and managers was held in Xishuangbanna in 1988 and a draft management plan for Mengyang Reserve has been prepared. Butterfly farming and agroforestry developments were initiated in 1990. The road joining Menglun, Menglan and Jinghong is currently under construction (Bamford, 1988).

Management Constraints   Xishuangbanna Nature Reserve is in a fairly remote and politically sensitive area due to its proximity to Laos, Myanmar and Vietnam. This will impede foreign assistance to some reserves. The above average population growth has led to increased pressure on land in and around the reserve. Prevention of shifting cultivation, the traditional form of agriculture practised by minority groups, has caused further problems due to shortage of flat agricultural land. Effective control of the reserve is unlikely until the resident agricultural population is resettled. Major constraints are the very limited development funds and lack of technical staff. Enforcement of existing regulations on hunting and grazing is inadequate due to the shortage of field staff (Anon., 1985a).

Staff   The Protection Division has 90 personnel, including both technical staff and labourers of whom only four are forestry graduates.

Budget   The annual budget for 1985 was 420,000 Yuan (US $ 112,600) of which 70% was provided by the Provincial Government and 30% by the Ministry of Forestry.   Most of the budget was assigned to salaries and wages.

Local Addresses
Protection Division, Xishuangbanna Forestry Bureau, Jinghong, Yunnan

References
Anon. (1985a). Xishuangbanna. Consultant's report. IUCN, Gland, Switzerland. Unpublished. 11 pp.
Anon. (1985b). Elephant herds increase in China. *Oryx* 19: 241.
Anon. (1989). WWF Project no. 3194. Xishuangbanna Reserve, Tropical Forest Conservation. *WWF-Year Book*. Pp. 53–4.
Bamford, D. (1988). WWF Project no. 3194. China, Xishuangbanna reserves nature tourism consultancy. Tourism Resource Consultants (New Zealand). 28 pp.
Qinsong, K. (1985). In: Thorsell, J.W. (Ed.), *Conserving Asia's natural heritage*. IUCN, Gland, Switzerland and Cambridge, UK. Pp. 32–5.
Santiapillai, C. (1990). Management of elephants in the Xishuangbanna Nature Reserve. People's Republic of China: a case study (Abstract). FAO Regional Office For Asia And The Pacific, Bangkok. 2 pp.
Wachtel, P. (1984). Trip report to Xishuangbanna, Yunnan Province, China. WWF-International, Gland, Switzerland. Unpublished. 7 pp.
Watt, N. (1990). The Dragon Hills of Xishuangbanna. *WWF Features* February: 1–4.
Wenhua, L. and Xianging, Z. (1989). *China's nature reserves*. Foreign Languages Press, Beijing. Pp. 52–67.

INDIA

Area   3,166,830 sq. km

Population   853,400,000 (1990)   Natural increase 2.1% per annum

GNP   US $ 330 per capita (1988)

Policy and Legislation   A commitment to protect and enhance the environment is enshrined within India's Constitution (Forty-Second Amendment) Act 1977, as follows:

'The State shall endeavour to protect and improve the environment and to safeguard the forests and wildlife of the country.' (Article 48A); and

'It shall be the duty of every citizen of India . . . (g) to protect and improve the natural environment including forests, lakes, rivers and wildlife, and to have compassion for living creatures.' (Article 51A).

There is no provision, however, which enables the Union to enact legislation pertaining to environmental issues that is uniformly applicable to all states and union territories. In addition to the separate federal and state jurisdiction, there exists a Concurrent List of legislative powers which includes *inter alia* forests and the protection of wild animals and birds. The Concurrent List gives over-riding power to the Union but executive authority lies with the state governments (Dwivedi and Kishore, 1984). Among the recommendations of the Tiwari Committee, a high-powered committee appointed by the government in February 1980 to suggest administrative and legislative reforms to improve environmental protection in the country, was the introduction of environment protection in the Concurrent List of the Constitution. The constitutional directives have provided a strong basis for the enactment of legislative measures for environmental protection. The need to integrate environmental considerations with economic development was explicitly articulated for the first time in the Fourth Five-Year Plan, 1969–74 (Biswas and Bannerjee, 1984).

The National Environment Policy envisages conservation and development, as well as equity among the people sharing the environment, but these aims tend to be mutually incompatible under much of the existing legislation (Singh, 1985). There is no statutory requirement for environmental impact assessment at present but a mechanism has been initiated whereby assessment is an integral part of the planning process, with appraisals of major projects being the responsibility of the Department of Environment, Forests and Wildlife (Dwivedi and Kishore, 1984).

137

The protection of wildlife has a long tradition in Indian history. Wise use of natural resources was a prerequisite for many hunter-gatherer societies which date back to at least 6000 BC.The most notable of such traditions are sacred groves, totally inviolate to any human interference, and village groves where only limited use by members of the community is permitted. Many of these are still in existence. Extensive clearance of forests accompanied the advance of agricultural and pastoral societies in subsequent millenia, but an awareness of the need for ecological prudence emerged and many so-called pagan nature conservation practices were retained (Gadgil, 1989). Among the earliest provisions for the establishment of protected areas are those codified in the *Arthasashtra, Indica* (321–300 BC), written by Kautilya, reputedly the Prime Minister of King Chandra Gupta Maurya. Prescriptions included rules for the administration and management of forests, and provisions for three classes of forests, namely those reserved for the king, those allocated for ascetics and those for the public which could be used only for hunting purposes. Kautilya is also the first-recorded person to have advocated the creation of *Abhayaranyas*, or sanctuaries for wildlife. The following century, during the reign of Emperor Ashoka, the first-recorded conservation measures for wildlife were enacted, and reserves were established for wild animals (Singh, 1986; Mitra, 1989). Hindu, Moslem and, latterly, British rulers continued these traditions in subsequent centuries, setting up reserves for privileged hunting over much of India. As more and more land became settled or cultivated, so these hunting reserves increasingly became refuges for wildlife. Many of these reserves were subsequently declared as national parks or sanctuaries, mostly after Independence in 1947. Examples include Gir in Gujarat, Dachigam in Jammu & Kashmir, Bandipur in Karnataka, Eravikulum in Kerala, Madhav (now Shivpuri) in Madhya Pradesh, Simlipal in Orissa, and Keoladeo, Ranthambore and Sariska in Rajasthan. The fact that the great majority of the Indian population is vegetarian (devout Hindus and Jains) has undoubtedly helped to preserve that part of India's natural heritage which remains today (Singh, 1985; Gadgil, 1989).

Following independence, a number of states (Goa, Haryana, Himachal Pradesh, Jammu & Kashmir, Madhya Pradesh, Maharashtra, Mysore, Punjab, Rajasthan and Tamil Nadu) enacted wildlife preservation acts, while others (Assam, Uttar Pradesh and West Bengal) continued to enforce the Government of India Wild Birds and Animals Protection Act 1912. National park acts were enacted by a few states but only five national parks were established under these acts, namely Kanha, Bandhavgarh and Shivpuri in Madhya Pradesh, Tadoba in Maharashtra and Hailey (now Corbett) in Uttar Pradesh. The Hailey National Park Act of 1936 was probably the first law in India intended for the exclusive protection of wildlife and its habitat (IBWL, 1970; Kothari et al., 1989).

A National Wildlife Policy for India was first formulated by an Expert Committee of the Indian Board for Wildlife in 1970 (IBWL, 1970). A major aim was to reserve at least 4% of the total land area   for wildlife, both plants and animals—an objective which has recently been exceeded. Much of this policy was subsequently enshrined in the Wild Life (Protection) Act 1972. The Act provides the necessary uniform legislation for the establishment of protected areas and has since been adopted by all states and union territories. Provisions include *inter alia* the constitution of state wildlife advisory boards and the notification of sanctuaries, national parks, game reserves and closed areas by state governments (see Annex). Setting up a sanctuary involves settling all private rights, either allowing them to continue or acquiring them after adequate compensation. Only a completely unencumbered area, in which all rights have become vested in the government, may be declared a national park. Once established, its boundaries may not be altered except through a resolution passed by the state legislature.

The basis to present nature conservation policy in India is the National Wildlife Action Plan (Department of Environment, n.d.). Drawing on the World Conservation Strategy launched by IUCN in March 1980, the Bali Action Plan arising from the 3rd World Parks Congress in October 1982, and the World Charter for Nature proclaimed by the United Nations General Assembly in October 1982, it was adopted by the Government of India in October 1983 on the recommendation of the Indian Board for Wildlife. Objectives include the establishment of a representative network of protected areas and development of appropriate management systems (together with the restoration of degraded habitats), and the adoption of a National Conservation Strategy, which is now being formulated.

The Indian Forest Act, first enacted in 1865 and succeeded by a more comprehensive act in 1927, provides significant protection to wildlife through the provision of reserved and protected forests which may be established in any forest or waste lands belonging to the government, or over which the government has proprietary rights (see Annex). Some states enacted their own forest legislation after the National Forest Policy was announced in 1952, while others amended the Act to suit their own requirements. The Act also makes provision for the rights of government over land constituted as reserved or, in the case of a few states, protected forest to be assigned to village communities. The Forest (Conservation) Act was promulgated in 1980 (and later amended in 1988) to stem the indiscriminate diversion of forest land to non-forestry purposes. Under this Act, no forest land can be de-reserved or diverted to non-forestry purposes without the approval of Central Government. Enforcement of this Act has had a salutary effect, the annual rate of diversion of forests having been reduced from about 140,000 ha pre-1980 to 6,500 ha in the 1980s (Panwar, 1990). Other initiatives include a moratorium imposed since 1983 on the felling of trees at altitudes of 1,000 m and above (Ministry of Environment and Forests, 1985). The 1952 National Forest Policy was superseded by a new National Forest Policy (Resolution no. 3-1/86 FP) on 7 December 1988. The objectives include the maintenance of environmental stability, conserving the nation's natural heritage by preserving the remaining natural forests, preventing soil erosion and the denuding of catchment areas, and creating a people's movement, involving women, to achieve such aims, and to minimise pressure on existing forests. A target has been set for one-third of the total land area of the country to be under forest, as originally stipulated in the 1952 National Forest Policy, but in the hills and mountainous regions the target is two-thirds. In addition, forest management must provide 'corridors' to link protected areas and thereby maintain genetic continuity between artificially separated sub-populations of migrant wildlife. Also, full protection of the rights and concessions of tribals and poor people dependent on forests is advocated (Government of India, 1988).

A selected list of other environmental legislation is given in *A Second Citizen's Report* (CSE, 1985). Of particular note is the Environment (Protection) Act 1986, which provides a focus for environmental issues in the country and plugs loopholes in the existing legislation (Ministry of Environment and Forests, 1987a).

Inadequacies in the existing nature conservation legislation are reviewed by Dwivedi and Kishore (1984) and by Singh (1986). The recognition of only wild animals and birds, without reference to plants, is an important omission from both the Wild Life (Protection) Act and the Constitution. Uniform and comprehensive forest legislation is urgently needed, with emphasis on forest conservation rather than the existing system of resource exploitation. Both acts are currently under revision.

International Activities　India ratified the Convention concerning the Protection of the World Cultural and Natural Heritage (World Heritage Convention) on 14 November 1977. Five natural sites have been inscribed on the World Heritage List to date, namely Kaziranga, Keoladeo, Sundarbans, and Nanda Devi national parks, and Manas Sanctuary

India acceded to the Convention on Wetlands of International Importance especially as Waterfowl Habitat (Ramsar Convention) on 1 October 1981, at which time Chilka Lake and Keoladeo National Park were designated as wetlands of international importance. Four more sites (Harike, Logtak, Sambhar, and Wular lakes) were designated on 23 March 1990.

Participation in the Unesco Man and Biosphere Programme began in 1972 with the constitution of the Indian National MAB Committee. The Indian Biosphere Reserves Programme will operate within the ambit of existing state and federal legislation; separate legislation for biosphere reserves is not envisaged (Ministry of Environment and Forests, 1987b). Thirteen potential biosphere reserves have been identified, of which the Nilgiri Biosphere Reserve is the first to have been established but has yet to be nominated for inclusion in the international biosphere reserve network.

Administration and Management　The Department of Environment, Forests and Wildlife within the Ministry of Environment and Forests was created in September 1985. It serves as the administrative focus within Central Government for planning, promoting and co-ordinating environmental and forestry programmes, including the preservation and protection of wildlife and the biosphere reserve programme (Ministry of Environment and Forests, 1987a). Previously, wildlife management was the responsibility of the Forest Department within the Ministry of Agriculture. Following recommendations made by the Tiwari Committee, a separate Department of Environment was constituted on 1 November 1980 to which wildlife management was transferred in September 1982. This Department became part of a new Ministry of Environment and Forests, constituted under Presidential Notification no. 74/2/1/85-Cab. dated 4 January 1985. At that time, the Ministry consisted of two departments, namely Environment, and Forests and Wildlife, but these were merged later that year (Government of India, n.d.; Ministry of Environment and Forests, 1986, 1987a). Departments of Environment have also been set up in a number of states (Biswas and Bannerjee, 1984).

Wildlife, together with forestry, has traditionally been managed under a single administrative organisation within the forest departments of each state or union territory, with the role of Central Government being mainly advisory. There have been two recent developments. Firstly, the Wild Life (Protection) Act has provided for the creation of the posts of chief wildlife wardens and wildlife wardens in the states in order to exercise statutory powers under the Act. This has largely been responsible for the creation of wildlife wings within each state headed by a chief wildlife warden. Under this Act it is also mandatory for the states to set up state wildlife advisory boards. Secondly, the inclusion of protection of wild animals and birds in the Concurrent List of the Constitution has provided the Union with some legislative control over the states in the conservation of wildlife (Pillai, 1982). Guidelines specifying that the management of protected areas should be under the remit of the wildlife wings were issued by Central Government in 1975, but progress in implementing them was slow. This prompted Central Government to threaten cessation of financial assistance to states which had not transferred protected areas to their respective wildlife wings. The situation has since improved, all states and union territories with national parks or sanctuaries having set up wildlife wings. However, by 1987, three states (Andhra Pradesh, Punjab, and Tamil Nadu) had not transferred control over any protected area to their respective wildlife wings, while eight others (Bihar, Gujarat, Karnataka, Maharashtra, Madhya Pradesh, Orissa, Uttar Pradesh and West Bengal) had transferred only some of their national parks and sanctuaries (Ministry of Environment and Forests, 1987a; Kothari et al., 1989). The management of protected areas in individual states and union territories is summarised by Pillai (1982).

The Indian Board for Wildlife, under the chairmanship of the Prime Minister, is the main advisory body to the Government of India on wildlife matters. First constituted in 1952 as the Central Board for Wildlife, it was later redesignated as the Indian Board for Wildlife. Among its various achievements, it has been instrumental in the formulation of the Wild Life (Protection) Act the establishment of many new protected areas (including tiger reserves), and in the formation of separate departments for wildlife conservation both at the Centre and in the states. State wildlife advisory boards have been constituted under statutory provisions of the Wild Life (Protection) Act to advise state governments (Saharia and Pillai, 1982).

The administration of Project Tiger, initiated as a Central Sector Scheme in 1973, is overseen by a Steering Committee headed by the Minister of State for Environment and Forests. The Director is responsible for co-ordinating the Project within Central Government. The execution of the Project is the responsibility of the chief conservators of forests in the relevant states, with tiger reserves managed by field directors. The Project's present status is that of a centrally-sponsored scheme, with costs shared equally between the union and state governments (Panwar, 1982).

Training in wildlife management is undertaken at the Wildlife Institute of India, which became an autonomous institution of the Ministry of Environment and Forests with effect from 1 April 1986. Its objectives include training in protected areas management, research and extension services, building a computerised wildlife information system, and providing advisory services. The Institute offers a one-year post-graduate diploma course for forest officers, a three-month certificate course for forest rangers and an M.Sc. Wildlife Biology course (WII, 1987).

There are many non-governmental organisations involved in nature conservation. The oldest is the Bombay Natural History Society, established in 1883 and currently comprising about 3,000 members. Whereas work undertaken in its early years was concentrated on collecting, identifying and documenting India's flora and fauna, the emphasis has shifted to conservation-oriented research in recent decades, particularly that of threatened species and habitats. Long-term field studies are based in a number of protected areas, such as Keoladeo National Park (Rajasthan), Mudumalai Sanctuary (Tamil Nadu), and Dalma Sanctuary (Bihar). The Society's *Journal of the Bombay Natural History Society* is widely circulated in India and overseas.

World Wide Fund for Nature-India (formerly World Wildlife Fund-India), established in 1969, has quickly developed to become the largest non-governmental nature conservation organisation in India, with 20 branches and a total staff of about 130. Its activities include ecological research and surveys, policy reviews, conservation projects, nature education and responsibility to the Ministry of Environment and Forests for environmental information relating to federal and state legislatures, NGOs and the media. Two recent initiatives underway are the establishment of the Indira Gandhi Conservation Monitoring Centre and the launch of a Community Biodiversity Conservation Movement.

The Indian National Trust for Art and Cultural Heritage, constituted in January 1984, has rapidly emerged as one of the most progressive and influential conservation bodies in India. It has 150 regional chapters spread over India's 32 states and union territories, the ultimate goal being to establish a chapter in each district. Its aim is to develop an awareness among the public of India's cultural and natural heritage and to promote its conservation. The Trust set up a Natural Heritage Cell in May 1985 which promotes land-use planning and management in areas of critical conservation importance.

The Centre for Science and Environment aims to publicise topical environmental issues, as well as to promote people's participation in environmentally-sound rural development. Its findings are documented in its citizens' reports, two of which have been published to date (CSE, 1982, 1985).

Other national conservation organisations include the Wildlife Preservation Society of India, founded in 1958 and publisher of the journal *Cheetal*, and the Indian Society of Naturalists, which publishes *Environmental Awareness*. Details of some 700 environmental non-governmental organisations can be found in a directory produced by WWF-India.

Protected areas are often poorly managed, with little consideration given to the local people living in and around them (Singh, 1986). The legal, ecological and management status of protected areas has recently been examined by the Environment Studies Division, Indian Institute of Public Administration (Kothari et al., 1989). The study was commissioned by the National Committee on Environmental Planning in 1984 and sponsored by the Ministry of Environment and Forests. The survey shows, for example, that only 40% of 52 national parks and 8% of 209 sanctuaries have completed legal procedures for their establishment. Only 43% of national parks and 28% of sanctuaries surveyed have management plans; in many cases they are cursory documents and have never been approved by the state government. Many of the deficiencies in protected areas management reflect a lack of commitment of resources on the part of state governments. For example, in 1983–4, expenditure on protected areas was 1.5% of forest department budgets. The Environmental Studies Division is currently engaged in a series of in-depth studies of management issues in a selection of India's major protected areas.

Systems Reviews   India is a nation of extraordinary diversity, the seventh largest and second most populous in the world. Its relief can be conceptualised in terms of three well-defined regions: the Himalayan mountain system along its northern margin; the Gangetic Plain, which extends some 2,400 km from Assam in the east to the Punjab in the west and southwards to the Rann of Kutch in Gujarat; and the Deccan Plateau which is flanked on either side by the Western Ghats and Eastern Ghats (Mani, 1974). Its rich diversity of ecosystems, which range from tropical rain forests to deserts, and from marine and coastal systems to high mountains, support an estimated 5–8% of the world's known flowering plant and animal species, of which a significant proportion are endemic (Gadgil and Meher-Homji, 1986b). Important centres of biological diversity, particularly for plants, are the Western Ghats, north-eastern India, and the Andaman and Nicobar Islands (Nayar, 1989).

Forest once covered most of India but much of it has been destroyed or severely degraded as a result of human population pressures, particularly in the fertile lowlands which are among the most densely populated areas in the world. For example, 4.1 million hectares of forest were cleared mainly for agriculture between 1951 and 1980 (Vedant, 1986; Singh, 1986). Probably less than 1% of the total land area is covered by primary forest (Mani, 1974). Forests are estimated to have covered 64.01 million hectares in 1985–7, or 19.5% of total land area comprising 11.5% dense forest (at least 40% crown density), 7.8% open forest (at least 10% crown density) and 0.1% mangrove forest (FSI, 1989).

The total area of wetlands (excluding rivers) in India is 58,286,000 ha, or 18.4% of the country, 70% of which comprises areas under paddy cultivation. A total of 1,193 wetlands, covering an area of 3,904,543 ha, were recorded in a preliminary inventory co-ordinated by the Department of Science and Technology, of which 572 were natural. In a recent review of India's wetlands, 93 are identified as being of conservation importance (Scott, 1989).

Coral reefs occur along only a few sections of the mainland, principally the Gulf of Kutch, off the southern mainland coast, and around a number of islands opposite Sri Lanka. This is due largely to the presence of major river systems and the sedimentary regime on the continental shelf. Elsewhere, corals are also found in the Andaman, Nicobar and Lakshadweep groups, although their diversity is reported to be lower than in south-east India (UNEP/IUCN, 1988).

Historically, conservation in India stems mainly from the creation of large forest reserves in the late 19th and early 20th centuries to safeguard timber, soil and water resources. Superimposed on this network of reserved forests has been a much smaller number of national parks and sanctuaries where the value of the biological resource has persuaded authorities to reduce the level of forest product utilisation (Rodgers, 1985). Both the adoption of a National Policy for Wildlife Conservation in 1970 and the enactment of the Wild Life (Protection) Act in 1972 lead to significant growth in the protected areas network, from 5 national parks and 60 sanctuaries in 1960 to 69 and 410, respectively, in 1990 (Panwar, 1990). The network was further strengthened by a number of national conservation projects, notably Project Tiger, initiated on 1 April 1973 by the Government of India with support from WWF (IBWL, 1972; Panwar, 1982), and the Crocodile Breeding and Management Project, launched on 1 April 1975 with technical assistance from UNDP/FAO (Bustard, 1982). Project Tiger has been acclaimed as an internationally outstanding conservation success story. The number of tiger reserves has increased from 9 (covering a total area of 13,723 sq. km) at the time of its launch to 18 (covering 28,017 sq. km) by 1990 (Panwar, 1990). Its achievements and shortcomings are reviewed by Panwar (1984) and Singh (1986). The Government of India subsequently initiated a Snow Leopard Conservation Scheme along the lines of Project Tiger, but with the emphasis on resolving conflicts between wildlife and resident human populations without having to relocate villagers from within protected areas (Ministry of Environment and Forests, 1987a). This has yet to be implemented.

In fulfilment of one of the major objectives of the National Wildlife Action Plan (Department of Environment, n.d.), the existing protected areas system has been reviewed and plans formulated for a comprehensive network which covers the full range of biological diversity in the country (Rodgers and Panwar, 1988). In mid-1987, there were 426 national parks and sanctuaries covering a combined area of 109,652 sq. km, or 3.3% of the country. Major gaps in the network include inadequate representation (1%) of the following biotic provinces: Ladakh, South Deccan, the Gangetic Plain, Assam Hills, and the Nicobars. The recommendations in the systems plan bring the total number of protected areas to 651, covering 151,342 sq. km or 4.6% of the country. Particular emphasis is given to protecting sites of high species diversity and endemism, as well as ecologically fragile areas. This plan for a national network of protected areas has been accepted by Central Government and commended to the states for implementation. Proposals in the plan supercede previous recommendations emanating from the Corbett Action Plan (IUCN, 1985) and the IUCN systems review of the Indomalayan region (MacKinnon and MacKinnon, 1986). They also endorse the earlier work of Gadgil and Meher-Homji (1986b), in which representation of the main vegetation types of India within the protected areas network is assessed. A number of states are now implementing many of the recommendations made in the systems plan, to the extent that total coverage by national parks and sanctuaries is nearly 4%. There are financial provisions under the Eighth Five-Year Plan (1991–5) to enhance the protected areas network in accordance with the systems plan, and to improve management of protected areas and to promote ecodevelopment in the areas surrounding them, with emphasis on at least 20 important national parks and sanctuaries (Panwar, 1990).

Wildlife conservation in India has met with tremendous success but protected areas management is beset with problems of inadequate fund allocation, a reluctance on the part of the states to establish national parks and sanctuaries because the land is lost forever for other uses (moreover, industries are not permitted within 30 km of the boundary of a sanctuary), insufficient magisterial powers for wildlife staff to deal with poachers, difficulties of communication in often remote areas, and lack of trained manpower at lower levels (Chandha, 1989).

Other Relevant Information

Arunachal Pradesh State
The total forest area is 51,540 sq. km., of which 12,606 sq. km. is reserved forest, 251 sq. km. *anchal* reserved forest, and 7 sq. km. protected forest (Mehta, n.d.).

The Wild Life (Protection) Act 1972 came into force on 15 May 1973 (Notification no. G.S.R. 272(E)). There is no separate wildlife wing. There are six wildlife divisions under a Conservator of Forests, ex officio Chief Wildlife Warden (Pillai, 1982). Each national park and sanctuary is under the charge of a Divisional Forest Officer (Mehta, n.d.).

Himachal Pradesh State
The Department of Forest and Conservation is headed by a Principal Chief Conservator of Forests. In 1990 the total staff complement was 6,627, of which 255 were gazetted officers. Total revenue in 1986–7 was Rs 213.7 million and expenditure Rs 356.4 million (DFFC, 1990).

Forest covers 21,325 sq. km. of the state and is mostly of the subtropical, temperate and subalpine types. Reserved forest covers 1,896 sq. km. and protected forest 33,350 sq. km. (of which 31% is demarcated and the rest undemarcated) (DFFC, 1990). From an examination of forest department records, it seems likely that forest cover has not changed greatly over the past 50 years, despite periods of rapid forest destruction. The destruction of the forest understorey as a result of overgrazing by domestic livestock is more likely to account for accelerating siltation rates and flooding along Himalayan rivers (Gaston, 1983).

The Wildlife (Protection) Act 1972 has been enforced since 2 April 1973 (Notification no. G.S.R. 19 (E)). The State Wildlife Advisory Board was constituted in 1975 but it is not active. A separate wildlife wing, headed by a Chief Wildlife Warden of the rank of Additional Chief Conservator of Forests, has been created but it is not fully fledged because the administration of protected areas is still vested with territorial staff. There are four wildlife divisions, each headed by a divisional forest officer (Arya, n.d.). Revenue in 1987–8 totalled Rs 168,000 and expenditure Rs 19.8 million, or 4.5% of total expenditure within the Department (DFFC, 1990). The Government of Himachal Pradesh has banned the commercial felling of trees within both national parks and in 21 of 29 sanctuaries. Legal procedures have been completed in the case of only two sanctuaries (Bandli and procedures have been completed in the case of only two sanctuaries (Bandli and Shikari Devi). Neither of the two national parks have been finally notified. Further details of the management status of protected areas are given by Singh et al. (1990).

Jammu & Kashmir State
The Forest Department, created in 1891, is headed by a Chief Conservator of Forests. The total staff complement in 1986 was 5,920 (234 gazetted officers and the rest ungazetted). Revenue in 1986–7 totalled Rs 400.0 million and expenditure Rs 217.5 million (J & K Forest Department, 1987). Forests, predominantly of temperate and sub-tropical types, cover 20,182 sq. km or 15% of the State (52% if the cold deserts of Ladakh and Zanskar are excluded) (J & K Forest Department, 1987).

Jammu & Kashmir has enacted separate legislation known as the Jammu & Kashmir Wildlife Act 1978, modelled on the Wild Life (Protection) Act 1972, which has been enforced since late January 1979. Full details of the Act are given by Ganhar (1979). Legislation also exists for the establishment of biosphere reserves. A Wildlife Advisory Board has been constituted under the provisions of the Act. A separate wing of the Forest Department, known as the Directorate of Wildlife Protection, came into existence in 1978. This was upgraded to departmental status in 1982 with the establishment of the Department of Wildlife Protection (Bacha, 1986). This is headed by a Chief Wildlife Warden of the rank of Chief Conservator of Forests. There are three wildlife divisions at present, each managed by a Deputy Conservator of Forests. The conservation importance of Ladakh, India's largest district and administratively part of Jammu & Kashmir, was first officially recognised in 1978, since when a network of conservation areas has been identified and given protected status (Bacha, 1985)

Manipur State
Forest covers 15,021 sq. km (67.3%) of the state (Government of Manipur 1990).

The Wild Life (Protection) Act 1972 has been enforced since 15 May 1973 (Notification no. G.S.R. 269 (E) and wildlife rules since 1974. A State Wildlife Advisory Board has been constituted but there is no separate wildlife wing (Pillai, 1982).

Meghalaya State
Forest covers 15,690 sq. km (69.8%) of the state (FSI, 1989) but only 3% of total land area is state-controlled forest, the remaining forest being controlled by district councils, local villages and clans and under private ownership (Rodgers and Gupta, 1989).

The Wild Life (Protection) Act has been enforced in the state since 1976 and the wildlife rules since 1977. A State Wildlife Advisory Board has been constituted. There is only one Wildlife Division functioning in the State (Pillai, 1982).

Mizoram State

The scientific management of the forest estate was a low priority in the 1970s, as reflected in the small staffing levels (155 personnel under a Conservator of Forests) within the former Department of Forests in 1973. Considerable progress has been made since the creation of the post of Principal Chief Conservator of Forests in 1987. The Department of Environment and Forests now comprises 10 territorial forest divisions and 6 functional divisions. of which one is the Wildlife Division. The total staff compliment in 1990 was 1,238, with 47 in the Wildlife Division. Revenue for the Department in 1989–90 totalled Rs 7.7 million, of which Rs 2.7 million was collected by the Wildlife Division, and expenditure Rs 67.6 million (Government of Mizoram, 1989, 1991).

Mizoram has vast natural forest resources but extensive tracts have been degraded due to shifting cultivation. Forest covers 18,178 sq. km (86.2%) of the state (FSI, 1989). Reserved forests cover about 6,400 sq. km, protected forests (in which utilisation of any land is prohibited and cutting of trees not allowed without permission) 1,447 sq. km, and village safety and supply forests 1,485 sq. km. An important landmark in the protection of forests was the notification of the Inner Line Reserve (1,320 sq. km) in 1877, to which access by outsiders was prohibited (Government of Mizoram, 1989, 1991).

The Wild Life (Protection) Act 1972 has been enforced since 1974. A Wildlife Advisory Board has been constituted and is active (Pillai, 1982). A Wildlife Division was created in 1986 and began functioning the following year. The Conservator of Forests, Northern Circle was appointed Chief Wildlife Warden, and all territorial Divisional Forest Officers as Wildlife Wardens of their respective territories in 1986 (Government of Mizoram, 1991).

Nagaland State

Forest covers 14,356 sq. km (86.8%) of the state. A unique feature is that 88% of the total recorded forest is under private ownership (FSI, 1989). Deforestation is estimated to be currently about 180 sq. km per year (Thakkar, 1987).

The Wild Life (Protection) Act 1972 has been enforced since the 1970s. There is a State Wildlife Advisory Board. The Conservator of Forests (Wildlife) is designated as the Chief Wildlife Warden since no separate wildlife wing has yet been created. There is only one Wildlife Division (Pillai, 1982).

Sikkim State

Forest covers 3,124 sq. km (42.8%) of the state (FSI, 1989). Alpine pastures and permanent snow-covered areas occupy a further 30% (Ali, 1981). A disturbing situation is that of the 2,650 sq. km of recorded forest, only 1,577 sq. km are reserved forest; the rest is of nebulous legal status (FSI, 1989).

The Wild Life (Protection Act 1972 and wildlife rules have been enforced since 1976, following the integration of Sikkim within the Indian Union in 1975. There is no separate wildlife wing. The Chief Conservator of Forests is designated as the Chief Wildlife Warden. A State Wildlife Advisory Board has been constituted and is active on conservation policy matters (Pillai, 1982).

Tripura State

Forest covers 5,325 sq. km (50.1%) of the state (FSI, 1989). Only about 8% is dense natural forest, the rest having been much depleted by clearance for shifting cultivation and, recently, for settlement of refugees from Bangladesh (Paxton, 1985).

The Wild Life (Protection) Act 1972 was enforced on 2 October 1973 (Notification no. G.S.R. 465 (E). There is no wildlife wing but a Conservator of Forests is ex officio Chief Wildlife Warden. A State Wildlife Board has been constituted. No honorary wildlife wardens have been appointed (Pillai, 1982).

Uttar Pradesh State

Forest covers 33,844 sq. km (11.5%) of the state (FSI, 1989).

The Wild Life (Protection) Act 1972 has been enforced since 1 February 1973 (Notification no. G.S.R. 44 (E)) and the wildlife rules since 1974. The Wildlife Preservation Organisation was originally set up in 1956, with the introduction of a Wild Life Preservation Scheme under the Second Five-Year Plan (Srivastava, 1969), and later reorganised in 1958. It is now headed by a Chief Wildlife Warden of the rank of Additional Chief Conservator of Forests. There are five wildlife divisions. Honorary wildlife wardens have been appointed. A State Wildlife Advisory Board has been constituted (Pillai, 1982).

West Bengal State

Forest covers 8,394 sq. km of the state (FSI, 1989). Notified forest extends over 11,830 sq. km (Ministry of Environment and Forests, 1986).

The Wild Life (Protection) Act 1972 has been enforced since 1 May 1973 (Notification no. G.S.R. 224 (E)). The wildlife rules were also enforced in 1973. No separate wildlife wing has yet been created. The Chief Conservator of Forests is designated as the Chief Wildlife Warden and wildlife management duties are the responsibility of the territorial staff of the Forest Department. A State Wildlife Advisory Board has been constituted (Pillai, 1982).

Addresses

Department of Environment, Forests and Wildlife (Joint Secretary, Wildlife),
Ministry of Environment and Forests, Paryavaran Bhawan, CGO Complex, Lodi Road, New Delhi 110 003 (Cable: PARYAVARAN, NEW DELHI; Tlx: 3163015 WILD IN; Tel. 306156)
Department of Environment, Forests and Wildlife (Inspector-General of Forests), Ministry of Environment and Forests, Paryavaran Bhawan, CGO Complex, Lodi Road, New Delhi 110 003 (Cable: AGRINDIA, NEW DELHI).
Project Tiger (Director), Bikaner House, New Delhi 110 011

Wildlife Institute of India (Director), PO New Forest, Dehra Dun 248 006 (Cable: WILDLIFE; Tlx 585238 PRES IN, 585258 FRIC IN; Tel. 27021-8, 28760, 27724)
Government of Arunachal Pradesh (Chief Wildlife Warden), Itanagar, Arunachal Pradesh 791 111
Department of Forest Farming and Conservation (Chief Conservator of Forests, Wildlife and Chief Wildlife Warden), Talland, Simla, Himachal Pradesh 171 002
Department of Wildlife Protection (Chief Wildlife Warden), Tourist Reception Centre, Srinagar, Jammu & Kashmir 190 001
Government of Manipur (Chief Wildlife Warden), PO Sanjenthong, Imphal, Manipur 795 001
Government of Meghalaya (Chief Wildlife Warden), Risa Colony, Shillong, Meghalaya 793 003

Department of Environment and Forests (Chief Wildlife Warden), Aizawal, Mizoram 796 001

Government of Nagaland (Chief Conservator of Forests, Wildlife), Dimapur, Nagaland 797 112

Forest Secretariat (Chief Wildlife Warden), Gangtok, Sikkim 737 101

Government of Tripura (Chief Conservator of Forests and Chief Wildlife Warden), PO Kunjaban, Agartala, Tripura 799 006

Wildlife Preservation Organisation (Chief Wildlife Warden), 17 Rana Pratap Marg, Lucknow, Uttar Pradesh 226 001

Office of the Chief Conservator of Forests, West Bengal (Chief Wildlife Warden), P-16 India Exchange Place Extension, New CIT Building, Calcutta, West Bengal 700 073

Bombay Natural History Society (BNHS) (Curator), Hornbill House, Shahid Bhagat Singh Road, Bombay 400 023 (Cable: HORNBILL; Tel. 243869, 244085)

Centre for Science and Environment (CSE) (Director), F6 Kailash Colony, New Delhi (Tel. 6438109)

Indian National Trust for Art and Cultural Heritage (INTACH) (Director-Natural Heritage), 71 Lodi Estate, NEW DELHI 110 003 (Tel. 611362, 618912, 616581)

Indian Society of Naturalists (INSONA), Oza Building, Salatwada, Baroda 390 001 Wildlife Preservation Society of India (Honorary Secretary), 7 Astley Hall, Dehra Dun (Tel. 5392)

Worldwide Fund for Nature-India (WWF-India) (Secretary General), Secretariat, 172-B Lodi Estate, New Delhi 110 003 (Fax 626837; Tel. 616532, 693744)

References

Ali, Mohammad S. (1981). Ecological reconnaissance in eastern Himalaya. *Tiger Paper* 8(2): 1–3.

Arya, S.R. (n.d.). *Status of the wildlife protection areas and their management in Himachal Pradesh*. Department of Forest Farming and Conservation, Simla. 7 pp.

Bacha, M.S. (1985). *Ecological cum management plan for Hemis High Altitude National Park, Jammu and Kashmir State, 1985–90*. Department of Wildlife Protection, Srinagar. 31 pp.

Bacha, M.S. (1986). *Snow leopard recovery programme for Kishtwar High Altitude National Park, Jammu and Kashmir State, 1986–87 to 1989–90*. Department of Wildlife Protection, Srinagar. 51 pp.

Biswas, D.K. and Bannerjee, P.K. (1984). Environmental programmes of the Government of India. In: Singh, Shekhar (Ed.), *Environmental policy in India*. Indian Institute of Public Administration, New Delhi. Pp. 97–115.

Bustard, H.R. (1982). Crocodile breeding project. In Saharia, V.B. (Ed.), *Wildlife in India*. Natraj Publishers, Dehra Dun. Pp. 147–63.

Chandha, C.M. (1989). National parks and sanctuaries in India. In: *Proceedings of the International Conference on National Parks and Protected Areas*. 13–15 November 1989, Kuala Lumpur. Department of National Parks, Peninsular Malaysia. Pp. 111–14.

CSE (1982). *The state of India's environment 1982. A first citizens' report*. Centre for Science and Environment, New Delhi.

CSE (1985). *The state of India's environment 1984–85. A second citizens' report*. Centre for Science and Environment, New Delhi. Pp. 343–51.

Department of Environment (n.d.). *National Wildlife Action Plan*. Government of India, New Delhi. 28 pp.

DFFC (1990). *H.P. statistics 1990*. Department of Forest Farming and Conservation, Simla . 257 pp.

Dwivedi, O.P. and Kishore, B. (1984). India's environmental policies: a review. In: Singh, Shekhar (Ed.), *Environmental policy in India*. Indian Institute of Public Administration, New Delhi. Pp. 47–84.

FSI (1989). *The state of forest report 1989*. Forest Survey of India, Government of India, Dehra Dun. 50 pp.

Gadgil, Madhav (1989). The Indian heritage of a conservation ethic. In: Allchin, B., Allchin, F.R. and Thapar, B.K. (Eds.), *Conservation of the Indian Heritage*. Cosmo Publishers, New Delhi. Pp. 13–21.

Gadgil, Madhav and Meher-Homji, V.M. (1986a). Role of protected areas in conservation. In: Chopra, V.L. and Khoshoo, T.N. (Eds.) *Conservation for productive agriculture*. Indian Council of Agricultural Research, New Delhi. Pp. 143–59.

Gadgil, Madhav and Meher-Homji, V.M. (1986b). Localities of great significance to conservation of India's biological diversity. *Proceedings of the Indian Academy of Sciences (Animal Sciences/Plant Sciences) Supplement* 1986: 165–80.

Ganhar, J.N. (1979). *The wildlife of Ladakh*. Haramukh Publications, Srinagar.

Gaston, A.J. (1983). Forests and forest policy in northwest India since 1800. Paper presented at Bombay Natural History Society Centenary Symposium. Powai, Bombay. 30 pp.

Government of India (n.d.). *Department of Environment: a profile*. Government of India, New Delhi. 23 pp.

Government of India (1988). *National Forest Policy 1988*. Ministry of Environment and Forests, Government of India, New Delhi. 13 pp.

Government of Manipur (1990). Report on land use/land cover, Manipur State (Bishnupur, Chandel, Churachandarpur, Imphal, Senapati, Tamenglong, Thoubal and Ukhrul districts). State Remote Sensing Centre, Government of Manipur, Imphal and National Remote Sensing Agency, Government of India, Hyderabad. Unpublished.

Government of Mizoram (1989). Mizoram forests. *Forest Extension Series* 89(2): 1–35.

Government of Mizoram (1991). *Progress report of forestry in Mizoram 1990*. Department of Environment and Forests, Government of Mizoram, Aizwal. 73 pp.

IBWL (1970). *Wildlife conservation in India*. Report of the Expert Committee. Indian Board for Wildlife, Government of India, New Delhi. 149 pp.

IBWL (1972). *Project Tiger. A planning proposal for preservation of tiger (Panthera tigris tigris Linn.) in India*. Indian Board for Wildlife, Government of India, New Delhi. 114 pp.

IUCN (1985). *The Corbett Action Plan for protected areas of the Indomalayan Realm*. IUCN, Gland, Switzerland and Cambridge, UK. 23 pp.

J&K Forest Department (1987). A digest of forest statistics 1987. *J&K Forest Record* no. 1. 199 pp.

J&K Forest Department (1989). *Jammu & Kashmir Forest Department. Activities and future strategies*. 24 pp.

Kothari, A., Pande, P., Singh, S., Variava, D. (1989). Management of national parks and sanctuaries in India: a status report. Environmental Studies Division, Indian Institute of Public Administration, New Delhi. 298 pp.

Kothari, A., Pande, P., and Singh, S. (Eds.) (1990). *Directory of national parks and sanctuaries in Himachal Pradesh*. Environmental Studies Division, Indian Institute of Public Administration, New Delhi.

MacKinnon, J. and MacKinnon, K. (1986). *Review of the protected areas system in the Indo-Malayan Realm*. IUCN, Gland, Switzerland and Cambridge, UK. 284 pp.

Mani, M.S. (Ed.)(1974). Ecology and biogeography in India. Junk, The Hague.

Mehta, J.K. (n.d.). Status paper on the protected areas and their management in Arunachal Pradesh. Government of Arunachal, Itanagar. Unpublished. 9 pp.

Ministry of Environment and Forests (1985). India. Country Report 1985. Presented to IX World Forestry Congress. Government of India, New Delhi. 53 pp.

Ministry of Environment and Forests (1986). *Annual report 1985–86*. Government of India, New Delhi. 57 pp.

Ministry of Environment and Forests (1987a). *Annual report 1986–87*. Government of India, New Delhi. 73 pp.

Ministry of Environment and Forests (1987b). *Biosphere reserves*. Government of India, New Delhi. 250 pp.

Mitra, D.K. (1989). A note on the ancient history of nature and wildlife conservation in India. *Zoo's Print* 4(12): 13.

Nair, S.C. (n.d.). *Natural resources conservation and development in Andaman and Nicobar islands*. Department of Environment, New Delhi. 76 pp.

Nayar, M.P. (1989). *In situ* conservation of wild flora resources. Paper presented at National Symposium on the Conservation of India's Genetic Estate, New Delhi, 3–4 November 1989. 19 pp.

Panwar, H.S. (1982). Project Tiger. In: Saharia, V.B. (Ed.), *Wildlife in India*. Natraj Publications, Dehra Dun. Pp. 130–7.

Panwar, H.S. (1984). What to do when you've succeeded: Project Tiger, ten years later. In: McNeely, J.A. and Miller, K.R. (Eds.), *National parks, conservation and development: the role of protected areas in sustaining society*. Smithsonian Institution Press, Washington DC. Pp. 183–9.

Panwar, H.S. (1990). Status of management of protected areas in India: problems and prospects (revised). Regional Expert Consultation on Management of Protected Areas in the Asia-Pacific Region, 10–14 December 1990. FAO Regional Office for Asia and Pacific, Bangkok. Unpublished. 21 pp.

Paxton, J. (Ed.)(1985). *The Stateman's year-book*. The Macmillan Press, London. Pp. 669–71.

Pillai, V.N.K. (1982). Status of wildlife conservation in states and union territories. In: Saharia, V.B. (Ed.), *Wildlife in India*. Natraj Publishers, Dehra Dun. Pp. 74–91.

Ram, A. (1991). Slippery slope for project controls. *Panoscope* 22: 6–7.

Rogers, W.A. (1985). Biogeography and protected area planning in India. In: Thorsell, J.W. (Ed.), *Conserving Asia's natural heritage*. IUCN, Gland, Switzerland and Cambridge, UK. Pp. 103–13.

Rodgers, W.A. and Gupta, S. (1989). The Pitcher Plant (*Nepenthes khasiana* HK.F.) Sanctuary of Jaintia Hills, Meghalaya: lessons for conservation. *Journal of the Bombay Natural History Society* 86: 17–21.

Rodgers, W.A. and Panwar, H.S. (1988). *Planning a wildlife protected area network in India*. 2 vols. Project FO: IND/82/003. FAO, Dehra Dun.

Saharia, V.B. and Pillai, V.N.K. (1982). Organisation and legislation. In: Saharia, V.B. (Ed.), *Wildlife in India*. Natraj Publishers, Dehra Dun. Pp. 53–73.

Scott, D.A. (Ed.) (1989). *A directory of Asian wetlands*. IUCN, Gland, Switzerland and Cambridge, UK. 1,181 pp.

Singh, Chhatrapati (1985). Emerging principles of environmental laws for development. In: Bandopadhyay, J., Jayal, N.D., Schoettli, V., Singh, Chhatrapati (Eds.), *India's environment: crises and responses*. Natraj Publishers, Dehra Dun. Pp. 247–75.

Singh, Samar (1985). Protected areas in India. In: Thorsell, J.W. (Ed.), *Conserving Asia's natural heritage*. IUCN, Gland, Switzerland and Cambridge, UK. Pp. 11–18.

Singh, Samar (1986). *Conserving India's Natural Heritage*. Natraj Publishers, Dehra Dun. 219 pp.

Singh, S., Kothari, A. and Pande, P. (1990). *Directory of national parks and sanctuaries in Himachal Pradesh: management status and profiles*. Indian Institute of Public Administration, New Delhi. 164 pp.

Srivastava, T.N. (1969). *Wildlife of Uttar Pradesh, India*. Wild Life Preservation Organisation, Lucknow. Unpublished. 21 pp.

Thakkar, Natwar (1987). Deforestation and Nagaland—a layman's observations. Views from keepers of the forests. Paper presented at Asia-Pacific NGOs Conference on Deforestation and Desertification. New Delhi, 23–25 October 1987. 5 pp.

UNEP/IUCN (1988). *Coral Reefs of the World. Vol. 2: Indian Ocean, Red Sea and Gulf.* UNEP Regional Seas Directories and Bibliographies. IUCN, Gland, Switzerland and Cambridge, UK/UNEP, Nairobi, Kenya. 389 pp.

Variava, D. and Singh, S. (1985). *Directory of national parks and sanctuaries in India.* Directorate of Wildlife Preservation, Government of India, New Delhi.

Vedant, C.S. (1986). Comment: afforestation in India. *Ambio* 15: 254–5.

WII (1985). The Biogeography Project of the Government of India. First Report. Wildlife Institute of India, Dehra Dun. 23 pp.

WII (1986). The Biogeography Project of the Government of India. Third Report. Wildlife Institute of India, Dehra Dun. 14 pp.

WII (1987). *Annual report 1986–87.* Wildlife Institute of India, Dehra Dun. 58 pp.

ANNEX Definitions of protected area designations as legislated, together with authorities responsible for their administration

Title (English title): Wild Life (Protection) Act

Date: 1972, last amended 1987

Brief description:
An Act to provide for the protection of wild animals and birds, and related or ancillary matters.

Administrative authority:
Central Government (Director of Wild Life Preservation) State Government (Chief Wild Life Warden).

Designations:
Sanctuary[1]
— An area of 'adequate ecological, faunal, floral, geomorphological, natural or zoological significance' may be declared a sanctuary for the protection and propagation of its wildlife[2] or environment.
— Permission to enter or reside in a sanctuary may be granted by the Chief Wildlife Warden for purposes of photography, scientific research, tourism and transaction of lawful business with any resident. Entry is restricted to a public servant on duty, a person permitted by the Chief Wildlife Warden to reside in a sanctuary or who has any right over immovable property within a sanctuary, a person using a public highway, or dependents of any of the above.
— Hunting without a permit, entry with any weapon, causing fire, and using substances potentially injurious to wildlife are prohibited. Fishing and grazing by livestock may be allowed on a controlled basis.

[1] State-owned land leased or otherwise transferred to Central Government may be declared as a sanctuary or national park by the federal authority.
[2] Wildlife is defined in the Act as including any animal, bee, butterfly, crustacean, fish, and moth, and aquatic or land vegetation which forms part of any habitat.

National park
— An area of 'ecological, faunal, floral, geomorphological, or zoological importance' may be declared a national park for the protection, propagation or development of its wildlife or environment once all rights have become vested in the State Government.

— No alteration of boundaries may be made except by resolution passed by the state legislature.
— Entry, unless used as a vehicle by an authorised person, and grazing of any cattle is prohibited.
— Restrictions on entry, in so far as they apply, are the same as those for a sanctuary.
— Destruction, exploitation or removal of any wildlife or its habitat is prohibited, except with permission from the Chief Wildlife Warden and provided it is necessary for the improvement and better management of wildlife. Other prohibited activities, in so far as they apply, are the same as those for a sanctuary.
Game Reserve
— An area in which only licensed hunting is permitted.
Closed area
— An area closed to hunting for such periods as may be specified in the notification.

Source: Original legislation.

Title (English title): Indian Forest Act.

Date: 1927, amended 1930, 1933, 1948 (Central Legislation).

Brief description:
An Act to consolidate the law relating to forests, the transit of forest produce and the duty leviable on timber and other forest produce.

Administrative authority:
Central Government (Inspector General of Forests).
State Government (Chief Conservator of Forests).

Designations:
Reserved forest
— Any forest land or wasteland belonging to the Government, or to which it has proprietary rights, may be constituted a reserved forest once all lands within the proposed forest have become invested in the Government.
— Prohibited activities include: making fresh clearings or breaking up land for cultivation; kindling or carrying fire; trespass and cattle grazing; felling or otherwise damaging any tree; quarrying stone, burning lime or charcoal; removing forest produce; and hunting, shooting, fishing, trapping and poisoning water.
Village forest
— Any land constituted as reserved forest that has been assigned to a village community by the State Government. Such an assignment may be cancelled.

152

— Rules for regulating the provision of timber, other forest produce or pasture to the community, and their duties for protecting and improving such forest may be prescribed by the State Government.
— All provisions of the Act relating to reserved forest apply to village forest, in so far as they are consistent with the rules.

Protected forest
— Any forest land or wasteland not included in a reserved forest and belonging to the Government, or to which it has proprietary rights, may be declared a protected forest provided that the nature and extent of rights of Government and any private persons in or over such land have been recorded.
— Activities prohibited within reserved forests are subject to regulations in protected forests. In addition, in protected forests, any trees, class of trees or portion of forest may be temporarily closed to all forms of exploitation, including the quarrying of stone and burning of lime.

Source: Original legislation

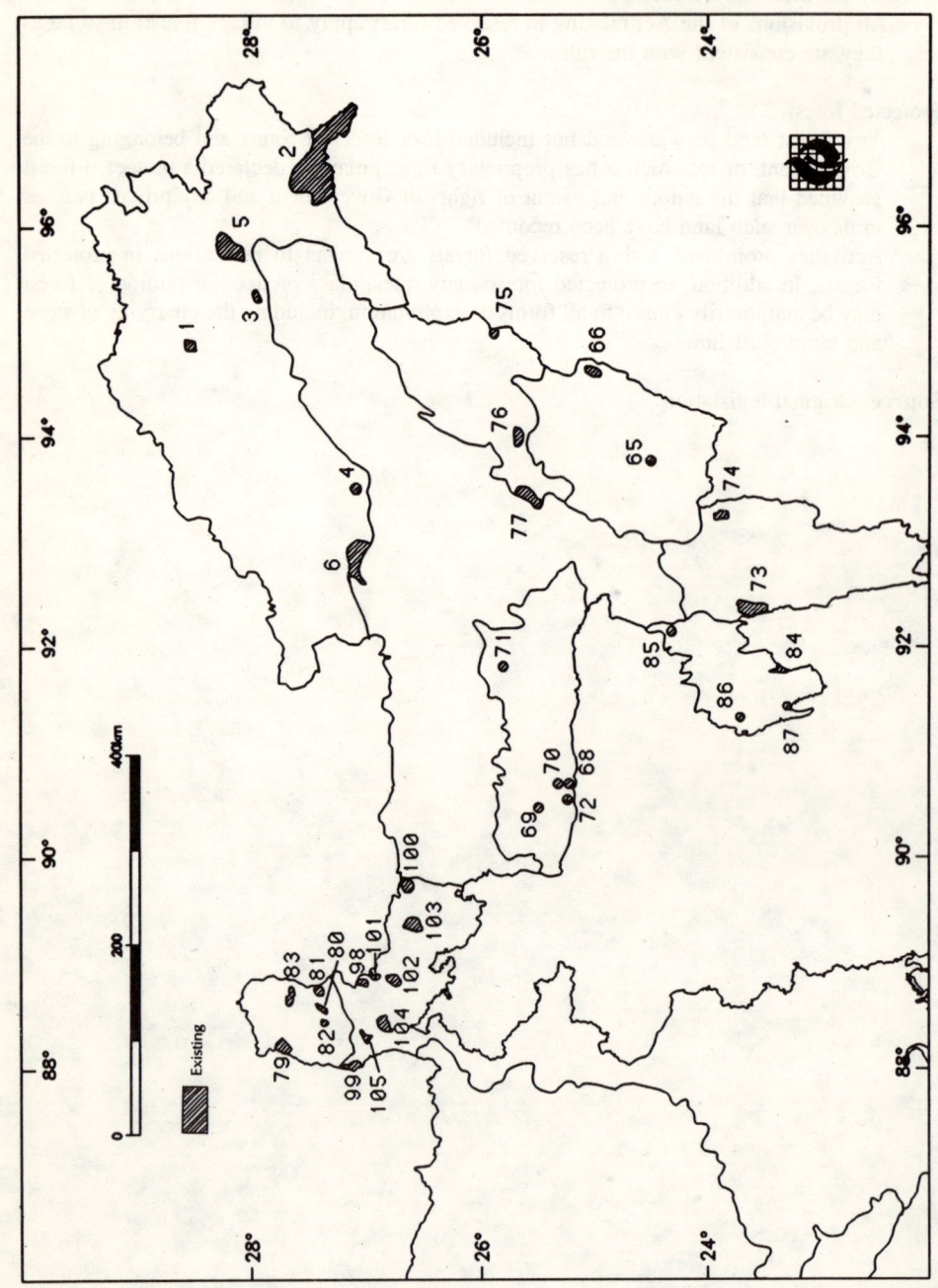

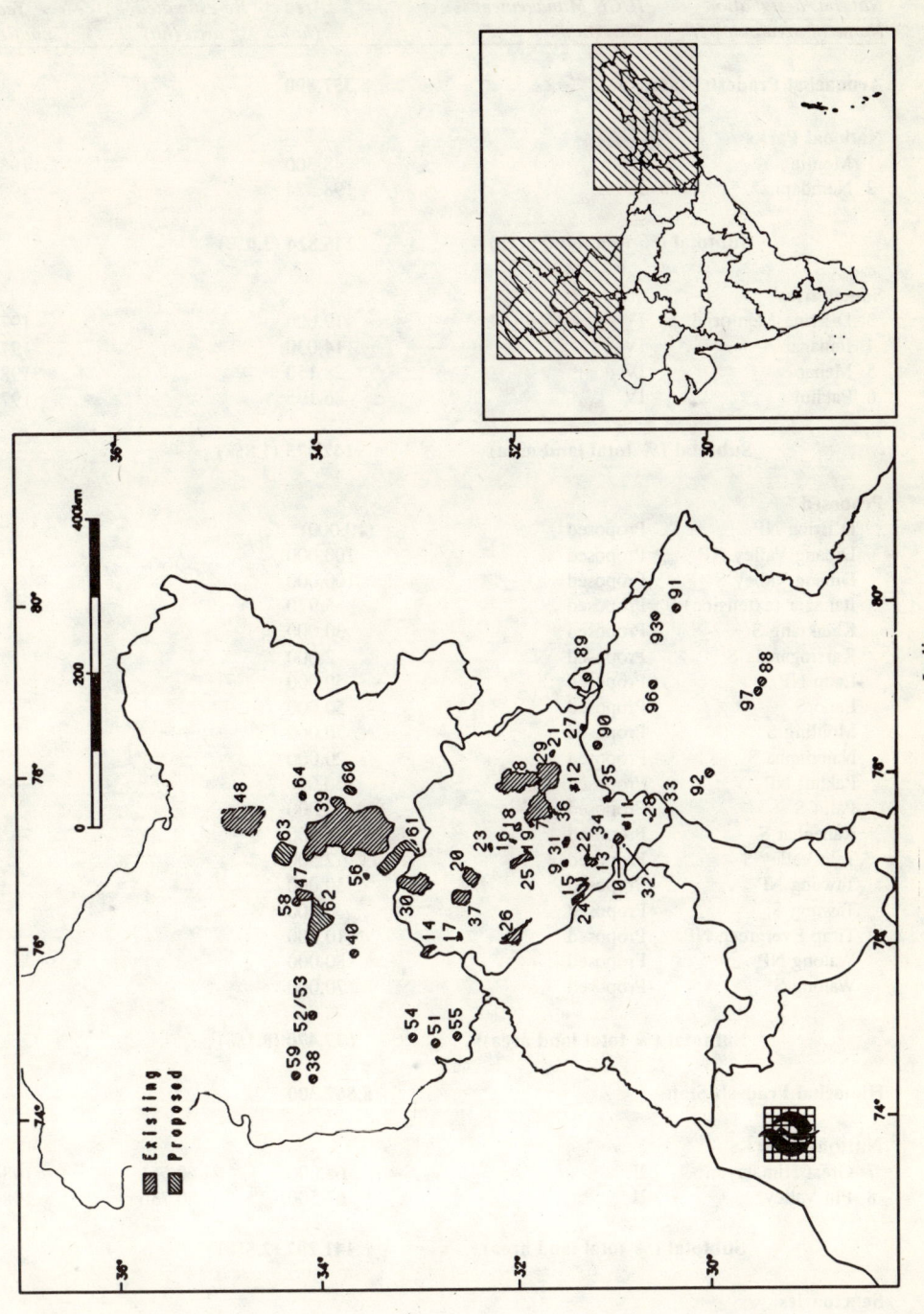

India

Summary of Protected Areas of India

Nat./Int. designation Name of area/map ref[+]	IUCN Management Category	Area (ha)	Re-estimated area (ha)[#]	Year notified
Arunachal Pradesh State		**8,357,800**		
National Parks				
1 Mouling	II	48,300		1986
2 Namdapha*	II	198,524		1983
Subtotal (% total land area)		**246,824 (3.0%)**		
Sanctuaries				
3 D'Ering Memorial	IV	19,000		1978
4 Itanagar	IV	14,030		1978
5 Mehao	IV	28,150		1980
6 Pakhui	IV	86,195		1977
Subtotal (% total land area)		**147,375 (1.8%)**		
Proposed				
D'Ering NP	Proposed	(10,000)[@]		
Dibang Valley NP	Proposed	100,000		
Dibang Valley S	Proposed	100,000		
Itanagar (extension) S	Proposed	5,970		
Kalaktang S	Proposed	30,000		
Karsinganala S	Proposed	2,000		
Lado NP	Proposed	50,000		
Lado S	Proposed	50,000		
Mouling S	Proposed	70,000		
Namdapha S	Proposed	20,000		
Pakhui NP	Proposed	(50,000)[@]		
Palin S	Proposed	25,000		
Raneghat S	Proposed	2,000		
Tale Valley S	Proposed	2,500		
Tawang NP	Proposed	30,000		
Tawang S	Proposed	30,000		
Tirap Evergreen NP	Proposed	10,000		
Walong NP	Proposed	80,000		
Walong S	Proposed	70,000		
Subtotal (% total land area)		**677,470 (8.1%)**		
Himachal Pradesh State		**5,567,300**		
National Parks				
7 Great Himalayan*	II	62,000	60,561	1984
8 Pin Valley*	II	67,500	80,736	1987
Subtotal (% total land area)		**141,297 (2.5%)**		
Sanctuaries				
9 Bandli	IV	4,133	3,947	1962
10 Chail*	IV	10,854	11,004	1976

Nat./Int. designation Name of area/map ref[+]	IUCN Management Category	Area (ha)	Re-estimated area (ha)	Year notified
11 Churdhar*	IV	5,615	5,659	1985
12 Daranghati*	IV	16,740	2,701	1962
13 Darlaghat	IV	9,227	9,871	1962
14 Gamgul Siahbehi*	IV	10,885	10,546	1949
15 Gobind Sagar*	IV	10,034	12,067	1962
16 Kais*	IV	1,419	1,220	1954
17 Kalatop & Khajjiar*	IV	2,027	3,069	1949
18 Kanawar*	IV	6,070	6,157	1954
19 Khokhan	IV	1,405	1,760	1954
20 Kugti*	IV	37,887	33,000	1962
21 Lippa Asrang*	IV	3,090	2,953	1962
22 Majathal*	IV	3,939	3,164	1962
23 Manali*	IV	3,180	3,127	1954
24 Naina Devi*	IV	12,268	3,719	1962
25 Nargu	IV	27,837	24,313	1962
26 Pong Dam*	IV	30,729	32,270	1983
27 Raksham Chitkul	IV	3,411	3,827	1962
28 Renuka	IV	403	478	1964
29 Rupi Bhabha*	IV	26,915	85,414	1982
30 Sechu Tuan Nala*	IV	10,295	65,532	1962
31 Shikari Devi	IV	7,200	7,119	1962
32 Shilli	IV	213	202	1963
33 Simbalbara	IV	1,903	1,720	1958
34 Simla Water Catchment*	I	1,025	951	1958
35 Talra	IV	4,049	3,616	1962
36 Tirthan*	IV	6,112	6,825	1976
37 Tundah	IV	6,422	41,948	1962

Subtotal (% total land area)   **388,179 (7.0%)**

Proposed

Sechu Tuan Nala NP	Proposed	(10,300)@	
Spiti NP	Proposed	50,000	
Spiti S	Proposed	50,000	

Subtotal (% total land area)   **100,000 (1.8%)**

Jammu and Kashmir State   **13,894,200**

National Parks

38 Dachigam*	II	14,100	1981
39 Hemis*	II	410,000	1981
40 Kishtwar*	II	42,500	1981

Subtotal (% total land area)   **466,600 (3.4%)**

Sanctuaries

41 Baltal	IV	20,300	1987
42 Changthang	IV	400,000	1987
43 Gulmarg*	V	18,600	1987
44 Hirapora*	IV	11,000	1987

Nat./Int. designation Name of area/map ref[+]	IUCN Management Category	Area (ha)	Re-estimated area (ha)	Year notified
45 Hokarsar*	IV	1,000		
46 Jasrota	IV	406		1987
47 Kanji*	IV	25,000		1988
48 Karakoram	IV	180,000		
49 Lachipora*	IV	8,000		1987
50 Limber*	IV	2,600		1987
51 Nandini	IV	3,372		1981
52 Overa*	IV	3,237		1981
53 Overa-Aru*	IV	42,500		1987
54 Ramnagar	IV	1,290		1981
55 Surinsar-Mansar	IV	3,958		1981
56 Tongri	IV	2,000		
57 Trikuta	IV	310		1981
Subtotal (% total land area)		**723,573 (5.2%)**		
Game Reserves				
Bohu	Unassigned	1,974		1981
58 Boodkharbu	Unassigned	1,200		1981
Brain	Unassigned	1,870		
Chashul	Unassigned	1,500		1981
Daksum	Unassigned	5,000		
Dara	Unassigned	3,000		
Gaurana	Unassigned	80		1981
Honlei	Unassigned	700		1981
59 Hygam*	Unassigned	1,400		
Jawahar Tunnel	Unassigned	1,799		1981
Khangurd	Unassigned	4,910		
Khirram	Unassigned	2,800		
Khrew	Unassigned	4,410		
Kokarian	Unassigned	2,023		1981
Koritaroh	Unassigned	1,166		
Mirgrind	Unassigned	300		
Nadoora	Unassigned			
Nangachantar	Unassigned	1,529		1980
Noorichang	Unassigned	200		1981
Pampore-Kranchoo	Unassigned	500		
Panyar	Unassigned	1,600		
Pargawal	Unassigned	4,918		1981
Sabu	Unassigned	1,500		1981
Sangral	Unassigned	696		1981
Shallabug	Unassigned	700		1981
Shikargah	Unassigned	2,800		
Sudh Mahadev	Unassigned	10,165		1981
Thain	Unassigned	1,889		1981
Tsomarari	Unassigned	1,000		1981
Subtotal (% total land area)		**61,629 (0.4%)**		
Proposed				
Boniyar S	Proposed	6,500		

Nat./Int. designation Name of area/map ref[+]	IUCN Management Category	Area (ha)	Re-estimated area (ha)	Year notified
Brako S	Proposed	6,000		
Chang-Chenmo NP	Proposed	50,000		
Dachigam (extension) NP*	Proposed	20,400		
Daultbeg-Depsang NP	Proposed	30,000		
Gurgurdoo S	Proposed	22,500		
60 Gya-Miru S*	Proposed	13,000		
Hajibal (Kanzalwan) S	Proposed	5,500		
Hemis (extension) NP*	Proposed	65,000		
Indus Valley S	Proposed	2,000		
Kargil-Leh Road S	Proposed	5,000		
Khandadhar S	Proposed	5,000		
Kishtwar-Lahul S	Proposed	50,000		
Lower Suru S	Proposed	10,000		
61 Lung Nag S*	Proposed	40,000		
Mindum S	Proposed	8,000		
Nambla S	Proposed	2,000		
Nunkun Mt. S	Proposed	30,000		
Pir-Panjal S	Proposed	10,000		
62 Rangdum S*	Proposed	20,000		
63 Rizong S*	Proposed	10,000		
Rupshu NP	Proposed	300,000		
64 Sabu S	Proposed	4,000		
Shiang (Saichen)-Shyok NP	Proposed	400,000		
Shimsha Kharbu S	Proposed	20,000		
Umba S	Proposed	7,000		
Subtotal (% total land area)		**1,141,900 (8.2%)**		
Manipur State		**2,232,700**		
National Parks				
65 Keibul Lamjao*	II	4,010		1977
66 Siroi	II	4,130		1982
Subtotal (% total land area)		**8,140 (0.4%)**		
Sanctuaries				
67 Yagoupokpi Lokchao	IV	18,480		1989
Subtotal (% total land area)		**18,480 (0.8%)**		
Proposed				
Dzuko NP	Proposed	30,000		
Dzuko S	Proposed	10,000		
Imphal Botanic Garden S	Proposed	1,300		
Kaihlam S	Proposed	26,000		
Siroi (extension) NP	Proposed	20,000		
Taret Lakhao S	Proposed	10,000		
Subtotal (% total land area)		**97,300 (4.4%)**		

Nat./Int. designation Name of area/map ref[+]	IUCN Management Category	Area (ha)	Re-estimated area (ha)	Year notified
Meghalaya State		**2,249,000**		
National Parks				
68 Balphakram*	II	22,000		1986
69 Nokrek*	II	6,801		1985
Subtotal (% total land area)		**28,801 (1.3%)**		
Sanctuaries				
70 Baghmara	IV	2		1984
71 Nongkhyllem	IV	2,900		1981
72 Siju	IV	518		1979
Subtotal (% total land area)		**3,420 (0.2%)**		
Proposed				
Garampani S	Proposed	1,000		
Mawsmai S	Proposed	1,000		
Nongkhyllem (ext.) S	Proposed	15,100		
Nongkhlaw NP	Proposed	15,000		
Rongrengri S	Proposed	20,000		
Saipung Link S	Proposed	30,000		
Shillong Peak NP	Proposed	1,000		
Tura Arabella NP	Proposed	3,000		
Subtotal (% total land area)		**86,100 (3.8%)**		
Mizoram State		**2,109,000**		
Sanctuaries				
73 Dampa*	IV	48,000		1985
74 Murlen	IV	5,000		1989
Subtotal (% total land area)		**53,000 (2.5%)**		
Proposed				
Dampa NP	Proposed	(30,000)[@]		
Murlen NP	Proposed	20,000		
Ngengpui S	Proposed	110,000		
Palak S	Proposed	20,000		
Phawngpui NP	Proposed	3,500		
Rengdil S	Proposed	1,000		
Twai S	Proposed	10,400		
Subtotal (% total land area)		**164,900 (7.8%)**		

Nat./Int. designation Name of area/map ref[+]	IUCN Management Category	Area (ha)	Re-estimated area (ha)	Year notified
Nagaland State		1,653,000		
Sanctuaries				
75 Fakim	IV	642		1983
76 Intanki	IV	20,202		1975
77 Puliebadze	IV	923		1979
78 Rangapahar	IV	470		1986
Subtotal (% total land area)		**22,237 (1.3%)**		
Proposed				
Dzuko-Puliebadze S	Proposed	7,000		
Intanki NP	Proposed	(5,000)[@]		
Kisa S	Proposed	3,000		
Macaque S	Proposed	3,000		
Shiloi S	Proposed	10,000		
Subtotal (% total land area)		**23,000 (1.4%)**		
Sikkim State		729,900		
National Parks				
79 Khangchendzonga*	II	84,950		1977
Subtotal (% total land area)		**84,950 (11.6%)**		
Sanctuaries				
80 Fambong Lho	IV	5,176		1984
81 Kyongnosla	IV	401		1984
82 Maenam	IV	3,534		1987
83 Shingba	IV	3,250		1984
Subtotal (% total land area)		**12,361 (1.7%)**		
Proposed				
Dzongri S	Proposed	46,800		
Khangchendzonga (ext.) NP	Proposed	9,700		
Kitam S	Proposed	1,300		
Kyongnosla (ext.) S	Proposed	2,100		
Nimphu S	Proposed	16,700		
Pangola NP	Proposed	10,000		
Tolung S	Proposed	23,000		
Subtotal (% total land area)		**109,600 (15.0%)**		
Tripura State		1,048,000		
Sanctuaries				
84 Gumti	IV	38,954		1988
85 Roa	IV	858		1988
86 Sepahijala	IV	1,853		1987

Nat./Int. designation Name of area/map ref[+]	IUCN Management Category	Area (ha)	Re-estimated area (ha)	Year notified
87 Trishna	IV	17,056		
Subtotal (% total land area)		**58,721 (5.6%)**		
Proposed				
Trishna NP	Proposed	(12,300)[@]		
Central Catchment S	Proposed	5,000		
Subtotal (% total land area)		**5,000 (0.5%)**		
Uttar Pradesh State (northern[0])		**4,834,500**		
World Heritage Sites				
91 Nanda Devi National Park*	X	63,033		1988
National Parks				
88 Corbett*	II	52,082		1936
89 Gangotri	II	155,273		1991
90 Govind*	II	47,208		1991
91 Nanda Devi*	I	63,033		1982
92 Rajaji*	II	83,153		1988
93 Valley of Flowers*	II	8,950		1982
Subtotal (% total land area)		**409,699 (8.5%)**		
Sanctuaries				
94 Askot	IV	600		1986
95 Binsar	IV	4,559		1988
90 Govind Pashu Vihar*	IV	48,104		1954
96 Kedarnath*	IV	97,524		1972
97 Sonanadi	IV	30,118		1987
Subtotal (% total land area)		**180,905 (3.7%)**		
Proposed				
Banog S	Proposed	2,000		
Chakrata Deodar S	Proposed	5,000		
Dodital S	Proposed	10,000		
Dudhatoli S	Proposed	16,600		
Kedarnath NP*	Proposed	(30,000)@		
Ladhiya Valley S	Proposed	20,000		
Nainital Oak S	Proposed	5,000		
Pindari S	Proposed	20,000		
Ranikhet Pine S	Proposed	2,000		
Yamunotri S	Proposed	20,000		
Subtotal (% total land area)		**100,600 (2.1%)**		

Nat./Int. designation Name of area/map ref[+]	IUCN Management Category	Area (ha)	Re-estimated area (ha)	Year notified
West Bengal State (Darjeeling District)		**307,500**		
National Parks				
98 Neora Valley	II	8,689		1986
99 Singalila	II	7,860		1986
Subtotal (% total land area)		**16,549 (0.3%)**		
Sanctuaries				
100 Buxa*	IV	31,452		1986
101 Chapramari	IV	960		1976
102 Gorumara	IV	862		1984
103 Jaldapara*	IV	11,563		1941
104 Mahananda	IV	12,722		1976
105 Senchal	IV	3,860		1976
Subtotal (% total land area)		**61,419 (20.0%)**		
Proposed				
Badamtan S	Proposed	100		
Baxiganj S	Proposed	1,400		
Birik-Rongpo S	Proposed	100		
Buxa (ext.) S*	Proposed	4,548		
Dalka S	Proposed	700		
Jaldapara NP*	Proposed	(10,000)@		
Jaldapara (ext.) S*	Proposed	15,737		
Mal 13 S	Proposed	100		
Teesta S	Proposed	1,800		
Subtotal (% total land area)		**24,485 (8.0%)**		
TOTALS				
National parks (% total land area)		**1,402,860 (3.3%)**		
Sanctuaries (% total land area)		**1,669,670 (3.9%)**		
Game reserves (% total land area)		**61,629 (0.1%)**		
Proposed areas (% total land area)		**2,530,355 (5.9%)**		

+ Locations of most protected areas are shown in the accompanying maps.

* Site is described in this directory. In the case of Himachal Pradesh, further information on these and all other sites can be found in Singh et al. (1990).

Preliminary data provided courtesy of IIPA/Environmental Study Division. Estimates generated by computer from digitized maps using Autocad 2.6 software.

@ Sizes of proposed protected areas in brackets are excluded from subtotals to avoid duplication with existing properties.

0Comprises Almora, Chamoli, Dehra Dun, Garhwal, Nainital, Pithoragarh, Tehri Garhwal and Uttar Kashi districts.

BALPHAKRAM NATIONAL PARK

IUCN Management Category   II (National Park)

Biogeographical Province   4.09.04 (Burma Monsoon Forest)

Geographical Location   Lies in the West Garo Hills and West Khasi Hills districts of southern Meghalaya, about 200 km by road south-west of Shillong. Approximately 25°19′N, 90°58′E.

Date and History of Establishment   Notification of the intention to declare Balphakram a national park was issued on 15 February 1986.

Area   22,000 ha.

Land Tenure   Provincial government

Altitude   Ranges from 50 m to 1,026 m (Kaylash or Chutmang Peak).

Physical Features   Comprises a plateau at 797 m of about 700 ha, from where a number of rivers originate that have cut deep gorges (up to nearly 800 m) and valleys in various directions. Mahadeo, for example, is a spectacular canyon. Geological formations date back to the Archaen group, represented by a gneissic complex of granite, magnetite, pyroxene, granulite and amphibolite. Tertiary sediments include the following formations: Shella, with sandstone, limestone, lithomeric clay, shale and coal seams; Kopili, comprising alternate beds of sandstone, shale and fossiliferous limestone; Simsang, with seltstone and sandstone; and Baghmara, with field spathic sandstone and pebble conglomerate. Whereas there is a belt of limestone in the southern portion of the park, there is a belt of granite, schist and gneiss in the Lengta and Nawa catchments to the north. The area is rich in minerals, notably coal (with possible reserves of 107 million tonnes), limestone, mica, feldspur and bery. Soils vary from sandy to clayey and pH from 5.6 to 6.5. Forest soils have about 10% organic content (Kumar and Rao, 1985).

Climate   Conditions are hot for most of the year (February to October) due to the relatively low altitude of southern Meghalaya. Mean maximum temperature ranges from 25 °C in winter (November to January) to 32 °C in June. Mean minimum temperature in winter is about 10 °C. The south–east monsoon lasts from May to October, the wettest months being June, July and August. Rainfall is negligible from November to February. Mean annual rainfall is 6,136 mm (Kumar and Rao, 1985).

Vegetation   The vegetation is fairly undisturbed due to the area's relative inaccessibility. Eight types of tropical moist forest are distinguished, as follows: tropical moist evergreen forest (almost virgin), which is confined to gorges and moderately sloping limestone areas and dominated by members of the Ebenaceae, Fagaceae, Lauraceae and Clusiaceae; tropical semi-evergreen (mixed evergreen) forest, occupying depressions in the plateau and surrounded by grassland or secondary forest; riverine forest in areas subject to periodic inundation;

grassland and tree-savanna, which are confined to the Rongcheng and Lumsorjong areas and maintained through browsing and burning; tropical deciduous forest, which is a successional type, man-made and tends to be heavily disturbed; bamboo forest, dominated by *Bambusa* spp. and *Melocanna bambusifolia*; and secondary formations in areas of shifting agriculture. Full details of species composition for the different forest types, and a vegetation map, are given by Kumar and Rao (1985).

Fauna The area supports a diverse fauna and, in particular, is an important refuge for elephant *Elephas maximus* (E) and tiger *Panthera tigris* (E), populations of which are estimated to total 860 and 10, respectively (Government of Meghalaya, 1981). Four species of primates are present, namely: Assam macaque *Macaca assamensis*, rhesus macaque *M. mulatta*, capped langur *Presbytis pileata*, and hoolock gibbon *Hylobates hoolock* (V), and possibly also slow loris *Nycticebus coucang* (Ghosh and Biswas, 1977). Carnivores include wild dog *Cuon alpinus* (V), Himalayan black bear *Selenarctos thibetanus* (V), leopard *Panthera pardus* (T), clouded leopard *P. nebulosa* (V), Asiatic golden cat *Felis temmincki* (I), and a number of other small felids. Ungulates include wild boar *Sus scrofa*, sambar *Cervus unicolor*, Indian muntjac *Muntiacus muntjak*, water buffalo *Bubalus bubalis* (E), gaur *Bos gaurus* (V), goral *Nemorhaedus goral*, and serow *Capricornis sumatraensis*. Water buffalo and gaur are confined largely to the grasslands, savannas and adjacent evergreen forests of the plateau. Further details, including preliminary estimates of population sizes, are given by Kumar and Rao (1985).

Information on the avifauna is limited. Good numbers of red jungle fowl *Gallus gallus* and grey peacock-pheasant *Polyplectron bicalcaratum* are present (Kumar and Rao, 1985).

Cultural Heritage Balphakram, literally meaning 'wind blows continuously', is believed by the Garo tribals to be the land of the departed soul (Kumar and Rao, 1985). Further details of the mythological importance of Balphakram are given by Gogoi (1981).

Local Human Population There are about 500 inhabitants (mostly Garos) distributed among six villages within the park (Ghosh and Biswas, 1977; Kumar and Rao, 1985).

Visitors and Visitor Facilities No information.

Scientific Research and Facilities Wildlife studies, including an elephant census, were undertaken by the Zoological Survey of India (Ghosh and Biswas, 1977) as part of a multi-disciplinary project to survey the vegetation, flora, fungal and insect pathogens, and ma mmals of Balphakram Forest (Kumar and Rao, 1985). There are no scientific facilities.

Conservation Value Balphakram is well-known for its beautiful scenery and contains expansive tracts of relatively undisturbed forest that support an extraordinary biological diversity, including the bulk of the elephant population in the region (Kumar and Rao, 1985; Rodgers and Panwar, 1988).

Conservation Management Original proposals by the Government of Meghalaya to designate the area as a sanctuary (Kumar and Rao, 1985) were superceded by its establishment as a national park. The park was to be 37,000 ha in extent but negotiations for land purchase are incomplete in the eastern part. This extension is essential to the long-term integrity of the park (Rodgers and Panwar, 1988).

Management Constraints   Elephants visit nearby villages and cause considerable damage to crops, particularly during the dry season (Kumar and Rao, 1985).

Staff   No information

Budget   No information

Local Addresses
Forest Ranger, Mahadeo Village

References
Ghosh, A.K. and Biswas, S. (1977). A preliminary report on wildlife in 'Balphakram', a proposed sanctuary in Meghalaya, India. *Tiger Paper* 4(1): 24–5.
Gogoi, P.C. (1981). *Tura Ridge Biosphere Reserve (Citrus Gene Sanctuary).* Department of Forests, Government of Meghalaya, Shillong. 99 pp
Government of Meghalaya (1981). Report of elephant census of Balphakram. Forest Department, Government of Meghalaya, Shillong.
Kumar, Y. and Rao, R.R. (1985). Studies on Balphakram Wildlife Sanctuary in Meghalaya—3: general account, forest types and fauna. *Indian Journal of Forestry* 8: 300–9
Rodgers, W.A. and Panwar, H.S. (1988). *Planning a wildlife protected area network in India.* 2 vols. Project FO: IND/82/003. FAO, Dehra Dun.

BUXA SANCTUARY

IUCN Management Category   IV (Managed Nature Reserve)

Biogeographical Province   4.03.01 (Bengalian Rainforest)

Geographical Location   Lies in the hills of Jalpaiguri District. Approximately 26°37′N, 91°53′E

Date and History of Establishment   Notified a sanctuary in 1986. Designated the core of Buxa Tiger Reserve which was established in 1982–3.

Area   The sanctuary covers 31,452 ha, which forms the core of the 74,500 ha tiger reserve.

Land Tenure   Provincial government.

Altitude   Up to 3,000 m at Sinchula

Physical Features   The Buxa Hills are the southern outspurs of the hills of Bhutan. The tiger reserve lies in the Western Duars, floodplains comprising alluvium with deposits of coarse gravels near the hills, sandy clay and sand along river courses, and fine sand and clay elsewhere. The beds of the Buxa Hills consist of variegated slates, quartzites and dolomites, and the low hills to the south are representative of the upper Tertiary strata. The Sankis River forms the eastern boundary of the tiger reserve, while other rivers include the Rydak, Jainti,

Bala, Dima and Pana. Rivers, which are erratic in flow and ever-changing in course, characteristically deposit huge amounts of rock debris.

Climate The summer is hot, with maximum temperatures in April. Mean annual rainfall is 5,323 mm, considerably higher than the average of 3,925 mm for the district (Jain and Sastry, 1983).

Vegetation Much of the tiger reserve contains a combination of natural and man-made forests. The former includes tropical semi-evergreen, moist sal, riverine khair-sissoo, deciduous and pockets of evergreen forests. Of the savanna types, a dense growth of tall grasses (e.g. *Phragmites karka, Saccharum procerum, S. spontaneum, Erianthus elephantinus*, and *Anthistiria gigantea*), with scattered trees of *Albizia procera, Salmalia malabarica, Syzygium cerasoides*, and *Butea monosperma* occurs in low-lying moist areas. In the riverine alluvial savannas *Dalbergia sissoo* is dominant. High-level savannas occur on well-drained soils and are dominated by *Narenga porphyrocoma*. Other grasses are *Saccharum arundinaceum, Cymbogon nardus*, and *Imperata cylindrica*. The high-level savannas also favour the growth of sal *Shorea robusta*. Where silt is deposited on the riverbeds, *Dalbergia sissoo* and *Acacia catechu* predominate; associates include *Salmalia malabarica, Randia dumentorum*, and *Albizia* spp. Savannas are gradually colonised by fire-resistant species, such as *Shorea robusta, Careya arborea, Dillenia pentagyna, Syzygium cerasoides*, and *Salmalia malabarica*, eventually leading to the formation of mixed deciduous forest. In areas with sufficient moisture, deciduous forest is replaced by evergreen forest. Further details are given by Mukherjee (1965) and Jain and Sastry (1983).

Fauna Mammals include rhesus macaque *Macaca mulatta*, common langur *Presbytis entellus*, sloth bear *Melursus ursinus* (I), tiger *Panthera tigris* (E), leopard *Panthera pardus* (T), leopard cat *Felis bengalensis*, civets Viverridae spp., elephant *Elephas maximus* (E), wild boar *Sus scrofa*, Indian muntjac *Muntiacus muntjak*, spotted deer *Cervus axis*, sambar *Cervus unicolor*, gaur *Bos gaurus* (V), and porcupine *Hystrix* spp. Clouded leopard *Neofelis nebulosa* (V) may still be present. Avifauna includes peafowl *Pavo cristatus*, red jungle fowl *Gallus gallus*, and great hornbill *Buceros bicornis*. Mahseer *Barbus putitora* are found in the rivers (Anon., n.d.).

Cultural Heritage No information.

Local Human Population There are eight villages with 25,000 cattle in the sanctuary, and a total of 10,000 people with 50,000 cattle in the entire tiger reserve (Sen, 1987).

Visitors and Visitor Facilities Accommodation is available in forest rest houses.

Scientific Research and Facilities No information.

Conservation Value Buxa, together with the nearby Jaldapura Sanctuary, is one of the most important conservation areas in northern India, providing a refuge for potentially viable populations of several threatened species (tiger, elephant, rhinoceros, swamp deer, gaur, and wild buffalo, as well as certain lesser cats and hispid hare) and critical as a corridor for wildlife moving between Bhutan and Assam (Rodgers and Panwar, 1988).

Conservation Management The sanctuary or core area is surrounded by a buffer zone, in which livestock grazing, exploitation of forest products and other practices need to be rationalised (Anon., n.d.). It is proposed that the sanctuary be linked to Jaldapura Sanctuary via a corridor and extended to the east to connect with forest in Assam (Rodgers and Panwar, 1988).

Management Constraints   There is mounting pressure on natural resources, both from resident human populations (Sen, 1987) and the heavily populated adjacent lands (Anon., n.d.). There are four large dolomite mines in the tiger reserve which are the cause of considerable disturbance to the habitat and wildlife (Sen, 1987).

Staff   The tiger reserve is under the administration of a field director.

Budget   No information

Local Addresses
Field Director, Buxa Tiger Reserve, Alipurduar, District Jalpaiguri, West Bengal.

References
Anon. (n.d.). Project Tiger 1973–83 Department of Environment, Government of India.
Jain, S.K. and Sastry, A.R.K. (1983). *Botany of some of the tiger habitats of India*. Botanical Survey of India, Howrah. Pp. 3–4.
Mukherjee, S.K. (1965). A sketch of the vegetation of Jalpaiguri District of West Bengal. *Bulletin of the Botanical Survey of India* 8: 252–63.
Rodgers, W.A. and Panwar, H.S. (1988). *Planning a wildlife protected area network in India*. 2 vols. Project FO: IND/82/003. FAO, Dehra Dun.
Sen, S. (1987). Digging the tiger's grave. *Calcutta Magazine* July: 13–15.

CHAIL SANCTUARY

IUCN Management Category   IV (Managed Nature Reserve)

Biogeographical Province   2.38.12 (Himalayan Highlands)

Geographical Location   Lies in Solan District some 45 km by road south of Simla. Bounded by a tributary of Giri River to the north–west and south–west, by Solan/Simla District boundary to the north and by Giri River to the south–east. 30°54′–31°01′N, 77°07′–77°17′E

Date and History of Establishment   Notifed a sanctuary on 21 March 1976, having been a private hunting reserve of the erstwhile Maharaja of Patiala.

Area   Notified as 10,855 ha, but re-estimated by IIPA/Environmental Studies Division (pers. comm.) as 11,004 ha using digitised maps. Chail is connected by a forest corridor to Simla Water Catchment Area, a 951 ha sanctuary to the north.

Land Tenure   Provincial government. Local people exercise certain rights to land resources. Some 3,446 ha are cultivated and only 100 ha of forest are free from such rights, other than right of access (Singh et al., 1990).

Altitude   Ranges from 701 m to 2,180 m (Singh et al., 1990).

Physical Features   Comprises part of the catchment area of a tributary of Giri River.

Climate   Mean annual rainfall is 1,603 mm. Temperatures range from -4 °C to 28 °C (Singh et al., 1990).

Vegetation   In general, the northern slopes are forested while the southern slopes support grasslands, usually with patches of forest or scrub in gullies and depressions. Grasslands are probably maintained by regular burning and cutting. The dominant forest tree is ban oak *Quercus incana*, mixed at lower altitudes with chir pine *Pinus roxburghii*. Rhododendron *Rhodedendron arboreum* forms pure stands in places, and cedar *Cedrus deodara* and blue pine *Pinus wallichiana* have been sown in some areas. There is little mature forest and much secondary growth due to disturbance (Gaston and Joginder Singh, 1980). Reference to the habitat map in Garson (1983) shows that forest is largely confined to the northern half of the sanctuary. Some 418 ha had been planted with pine, oak, cedar, and *Robinia* sp. up to 1984 (Singh et al., 1990).

Fauna   Large mammals include rhesus macaque *Macaca mulatta*, leopard *Panthera pardus* (T), Indian muntjac *Muntiacus muntjak*, goral *Nemorhaedus goral* (numerous), and crested porcupine *Hystrix indica* (Gaston et al., 1981, 1983). Other species listed by Singh et al. (1990) include Himalayan black bear *Selenarctos thibetanus* (V), wild boar *Sus scrofa*, common langur *Presbytis entellus*, sambar *Cervus unicolor* (its northernmost distribution), and black-naped hare *Lepus nigricollis*. European red·deer *Cervus elaphus* were introduced half a century ago by the former Maharaja of Patiala (Singh et al., 1990), but none were sighted during a census in 1988 (S. Pandey, pers. comm.).

Singh et al. (1990) provide a list of birds. Cheer pheasant *Catreus wallichii* (E) and kalij pheasant *Lophura leucomelana* populations may have declined in the period 1979–83. The cheer population in March 1983 is estimated to have numbered at least 32 pairs, at a density of about 7 pairs per sq. km (Garson, 1983). A cheer pheasant breeding and rehabilitation progra mme was initiated in 1988 (Singh et al., 1990).

Cultural Heritage   Of historic interest are the former palace of the Maharaja of Patiala (now a hotel) and Siddh Baba temple.

Local Human Population   There are 121 villages (including Chail township) inside the sanctuary, with a total population of 8,627 people. There are also 18 private industries, including sawmills, inside the sanctuary. The surrounding area is also densely populated (Singh et al., 1990).

Visitors and Visitor Facilities   Accommodation is available at Chail (Hotel Palace, and forest and PWD rest houses) and Gaura (forest rest house).

Scientific Research and Facilities   The cheer pheasant population was censused in April 1979 (Gaston and Joginder Singh, 1980) and March 1983 (Garson, 1983). There are no scientific facilities, but a small laboratory is located nearby at Kufri.

Conservation Value   Formerly a private hunting reserve of the Maharaja of Patiala, Chail is now severely degraded (Singh et al., 1990). Nevertheless, it holds an internationally important population of cheer pheasant (Gaston and Joginder Singh, 1980; Garson, 1983).

Conservation Management   Local people have rights to graze livestock, collect timber, firewood and other forest produce, quarry, cultivate, and perform religious rites, including the burial of the dead. There is no management plan. It has been reco mmended that extraction of timber should be stopped altogether, or at least during the breeding season for the benefit of the cheer pheasant population (Garson, 1983). Electric fencing has been installed to keep out livestock.

Management Constraints   Much of the area is heavily degraded and local activities are largely uncontrolled. Forest fires affected 1,364 ha in 1984–5. Colonisation by the weed *Lantana camara* is becoming a problem (Singh et al., 1990).

Staff   Two range officers, five deputy range officers, 20 forest guards.

Budget   Rs 700,000 in 1987–8 for works and protection

Local Addresses
Range Officer, Chail Sanctuary, Chail 173217, Tehsil Kondaghat, District Solan, Himachal
   Pradesh

References
Garson, P.J. (1983). The cheer pheasant *Catreus wallichii* in Himachal Pradesh, Western
   Himalayas: an update. *World Pheasant Association Journal* 8: 29–39.
Gaston, A.J. and Joginder Singh (1980). The status of the cheer pheasant *Catreus wallichii*, in
   the Chail Wildlife Sanctuary Himachal Pradesh. *World Pheasant Association Journal* 5:
   68–73.
Gaston, A.J., Hunter, M.L. Jr., and Garson, P.J. (1981). The wildlife of Himachal Pradesh,
   Western Himalayas. *University of Maine School of Forest Resources Technical Notes* no.
   82. 159 pp.
Gaston, A.J., Garson, P.J. and Hunter, M.L. Jr. (1983). The status and conservation of forest
   wildlife in Himachal Pradesh, Western Himalayas. *Biological Conservation* 27: 291–314.
Singh, S., Kothari, A. and Pande, P. (Eds.) (1990). *Directory of national parks and sanctuaries
   in Himachal Pradesh.* Indian Institute of Public Administration, New Delhi. 164 pp.

CORBETT NATIONAL PARK

IUCN Management Category   II (National Park)

Biogeographical Province   4.08.04 (Indus-Ganges Monsoon Forest)

Geogaphical Location   Lies in the foothills of the Outer Himalaya within the districts of Nainital and Pauri Garhwal, and occupies the middle reaches of the Ram Ganga. The park is bounded to the east by the Ramnagar–Ranikhet road, to the south and south–west by the Kotdwara–Ramnagar forest road, to the north–west by Ramganga Reservoir and to the north–east by various topographical features within the catchment area of the Ram Ganga. The boundaries are defined in Notification no. 4229/ZIV-A-867-62 of 24 August 1966. 29°25′–29°39′N, 78°44′–79°07′E.

Date and History of Establishment   Established as India's first national park on 8 August 1936, being the date on which the Uttar Pradesh National Parks Act came into force, and named Hailey National Park after Sir William Malcolm Hailey, then Governor of Uttar Pradesh who was instrumental in its creation. Following independence, its name was changed to Ramganga National Park in 1954 and then in 1957 to its present name, Corbett National Park, in memory of Jim Corbett, the legendary hunter and naturalist who had helped in marking out its boundaries and setting it up. With the launching of Project Tiger on 1 April 1973, Corbett National Park was selected as one of the nine tiger reserves, and has the distinction of being chosen as the venue for the inauguration of this project on 1 February 1974.

Area   52,082 ha. The area of the national park was increased from 32,375 ha to its present size in 1966 to enhance its integrity, and to compensate for the land later submerged by the construction of a hydel dam at Kalagarh. The park is contiguous with Sonanadi Sanctuary (30,118 ha) along its western boundary.

Land Tenure   Provincial government. Villages on the boundary enjoy grazing rights within the park.

Altitude   Ranges from about 400 m to the peak of Kanda at 1,210 m on the northern extremity.

Physical Features   The park extends from the Outer Himalaya, locally represented by the Siwaliks which run through its middle in an east–west direction, across Patli Dun to the foothills of the Middle Himalaya. The Siwaliks are distinct from the Himalaya, being formed from the latter's erosion products of sand, gravel and conglomerates, but are scarcely distinguishable here in western Kumaon because they abut directly onto the Himalayan chain. Patli Dun is an elevated valley with a virtually level floor through which flows the Ram Ganga, the only source of perennial water. This river flows westwards and widens beyond Khinanauli, giving rise to 'sheesum islands' colonised by sheeshum *Dalbergia sissoo*. West of Dhikala, the sheeshum islands give way to winding strips of alluvial grassland or 'chaurs', being land that was cultivated in historic times. The chaurs provided important grazing for wildlife but, with the completion of the Kalagarh Dam in 1974, they and the sheeshum islands have been inundated as far back as Khinanauli. The reservoir, which was filled to capacity by 1979–80, covers 4,220 ha of prime wildlife habitat. The geological strata consist of: recent alluvial and slightly older 'bhabar' deposits; Siwalik Series, with conglomerate, sandrock and Nahan sandstone; and older Himalayan rocks, mostly of dark blue-grey limestone with a few grits and shales and confined to part of Kanda Block. Soils tend to be sandy and shallow on the southern slopes of the Siwaliks, sandy or sandy with loam on northern slopes, and deep, fresh and stony in the duns (Singh, 1974; Singh, 1986; Lamba, n.d.).

Climate   There are three distinct seasons: cold (November to February), hot (March to mid-June) and rainy (mid-June to October). Mean monthly maximum temperatures range from 26 °C in January to 44 °C in June, and minimum temperatures from 2 °C in January to 21 °C in August, based on data for 1980–4. Annual rainfall varies from 1,400 mm in the outer hills to 2,800 mm in the upper hills, with 1,500–1,600 mm in the main Ram Ganga

Valley (Singh, 1985). Conditions are humid throughout the year, relative humidity rising to 98% in the monsoon and seldom falling below 57% even in the driest period (November). A wind locally known as 'dadu' blows down the valley from about 9 p.m. to 8 a.m., lowering the night temperature. In the hot season, it is followed by a hot wind blowing up-valley from 10 a.m. to 8 p.m. During this season a thick haze of suspended dust develops which is only cleared by thunderstorms (Lamba, n.d.). There are 13 meteorological stations in the park, with recordings dating back to 1978 (Singh, 1985).

Vegetation   The park is notable for its extensive sal *Shorea robusta* forests which cover nearly 73% of its entirety (Singh, 1985). A frequent associate of sal is haldu *Adina cordifolia*. On higher ridges bakli *Anogeisus latifolia* is predominant, and other other associates are khetwa *Piliostigma malabaricum*, gurial *Bauhinia racemosa*, pula *Kydia calycina*, dhauri *Lagerstroemia parviflora*, amaltas *Cassia fistula*, bhilawa *Semicarpus anacardium*, amla *Emblica officinalis*, and ber *Zizyphus mauritiana*. Less common species are papri *Holoptelea integrifolia*, kumbhi *Carya arborea*, and mahwa *Madhuca indica*. Trichoniya *Wendlandia heynei*, rohni *Mallotus philippinensis*, and jamun *Syzygium cumini* occur along dry river beds in exposed areas. The *Dalbergia sissoo-Acacia catechu* association along the Ram Ganga is a notable feature. Amongst the shrubs *Clerodendrum viscosum*, *Colebrookea oppositifolia*, *Adhatoda vasica*, *Helicteres isora* and *Woodfordia fruticosa* are predominant, while climbers such as *Milletia auriculata*, *Cryptolepis buchanani*, *Porana paniculata*, *Phanera vahlii*, and *Vallaris solanacea* are common. Bamboos are common in some areas. Palms include *Phoenix acauliea* and the rare *Wallichia densiflora*. The only indigenous conifer is chir pine *Pinus roxburghii*. Grasses such as *Themeda arundinacea*, *Thysanolena maxima*, and *Vetiveria zizanioides* are abundant in the chaurs of Patli Dun, while on burnt soil they are associated with herbs such as *Vicoa indica*, *Trichodesma indicum*, *Lactuca* sp., *Crotalaria* sp., *Desmodium* sp., and *Polygala* sp. In the other open areas common grasses include *Eulaliopsis binata*, *Apluda mutica*, *Oplismenus compositus*, and *Eragrostis uniloides*. The comparatively rare ground orchids *Zeuxine* sp., and *Eulophia* sp., and also the dwarf understorey shrub *Pygmae opremna herbacea* have a scattered distribution. Common weeds are *Lantana* sp., *Acanthospermum hispidum*, and *Xanthium strumericum* (Lamba, n.d.). A more detailed description of the vegetation is given by Singh (1974), Pant (1977), and Jain and Sastry (1983).   A total of 488 species of plants has been recorded in the park (Pant, 1976; Pant et al., 1981).

Fauna The Park is noted for its rich and diverse fauna, which includes 50 species of mammals (Lamba, n.d.), 575 species of birds (Lamba, n.d.), 33 species of reptiles (Bedi, 1985), 7 species of amphibians (Bedi, 1985), 7 sepecies of fish (Bedi, 1985), and 37 species of dragonflies (Singh and Prasad, 1977).

Corbett is an important refuge for Indian elephant *Elephas maximus* (E).*Also notable among the large mammals are leopard cat *Felis bengalensis*, tiger *Panthere tigris* (E), wild dog *Cuon alpinus* (V), hog deer *Cervus porcinus*, and Indian pangolin *Manis crassicaudata*, all of which used to exist in large numbers throughout the terai of Uttar Pradesh but are now rarely seen outside the park. Swamp deer *Cervus duvauceli* (E) became locally extinct about 20 years ago. Spotted deer *Cervus axis*, hog deer and Indian porcupine *Hystrix indica* populations were severely affected by the inundation of much of the grassland. Although spotted deer and hog deer populations dispersed elsewhere, the former showed a fall in birth rate from 22.2 to 4.1 fawns per 100 females in three years.   Worst affected was the porcupine population. By 1978 its relative density had dropped to 20% of that recorded in 1976–7. The creation of a reservoir also denied access to an important traditional imigration route (Lamba, n.d.).

Estimates of population sizes for large mammals in 1987 are: 90 tiger, 42 leopard, 178 elephant, 16,801 spotted deer, 2,485 sambar, 188 hog deer, 993 Indian muntjac *Muntiacus muntjak*, 27 sloth bear *Melursus ursinus* (V), 1,907 wild boar *Sus scrofa*, and 340 goral *Nemorhaedus goral* (Ashok Singh, pers. comm., 1988). Census data are also available for 1983–4 (Singh, 1985). The common otter *Lutra lutra* population is estimated to be about 400 animals (Sharma and Ashok, 1988).

The avifauna is particularly interesting on account of the overlap between high altitude and plains, and eastern and western races of a number of species. The park attracts a large number of migratory birds. The river is a source of attraction to many winter migrants. A number of high altitude species visit during winter, and the summer also sees many visitors. Being situated on a migratory route, the park is also visited by quite a few passage migrants. Among the birds that have suffered heavily on account of the large-scale inundation are the passerines that roost and breed in smaller trees, bushes and reed-beds, notably red ardvart *Estrilda amandava*, spotted munia *Lonchura punctulata*, weaver bird *Ploceus philippinus*, black-throated baya *P. bengalensis*, and common myna *Acridotheres tristis*. These changes in habitat, however, have benefited a large number of resident and migratory water birds. Populations of Cormorants *Phalacrocorax* spp., darter *Anhinga rufa*, herons and egrets (Ardeidae), storks (Ciconidae), fishing eagles *Haliaeetus leucoryphus* and *Icthyophaga nana*, and kingfishers (Alcedinidae) have increased many fold, while gulls *Larus* spp. and moorhen *Gallinula chloropus* have since become residents (Lamba, n.d.).

Of the reptiles, both mugger *Crocodylus palustris* (V) and gharial *Gavialis gangeticus* (E) are present. Populations had increased from an estimated 16 mugger and four gharial in 1974 (Whitaker 1974), to 37 and 17, respectively, by 1983 (Singh, 1985). The increase in the gharial population was due to the release of 12 young reared in captivity. By 1987 there were an estimated 43 mugger and 47 gharial (Ashok Singh, pers, comm., 1988).

Cultural Heritage   Patli Dun was formerly part of the princely state of Tehri Garhwal. At that time its forests were cleared to make the area less vulnerable to attacks from the Rohilas, Later, the Raja of Tehri ceded part of his state to the British in return for their assistance in driving out the Gurkhas. Boksas, tribals from the *terai*, settled in the area and practised shifting cultivation, but they were evicted in the early 1860s under Major Ramsay (Singh, 1974; Bedi, 1985; Singh, 1985).

Local Human Population   There are no settlements within the national park. Some seven or eight villages on the boundary have grazing rights inside the park. A large settlement has been established at Kalagarh under the Ramganga Dam project (Singh, 1985).

Visitors and Visitor Facilities   The park has become increasingly popular among tourists, both national and foreign. Numbers have increased from just over 5,000 in 1971–2 to nearly 20,000 in 1983–4, with the proportion of nationals increasing progressively from about 80% to over 90% during this period (Singh, 1985). Corbett is accessible via Ramnagar, the main entrance at Dhangarhi being 19 km to the north and the tourist complex at Dhikala a further 32 km. It is open from 15 November to 15 June, being inaccessible during the monsoon. Accommodation is available at Dhikala and there are a number of forest rest houses elsewhere in the park. There is also provision for caravans and tents. The park information centre and Project Tiger Office are located at Ramnagar. A Jim Corbett Museum has been established in his former home at Kaladhungi, 32 km from Ramnagar on the Nainital road.

Scientific Research and Facilities Early research includes studies of predator-prey relations (Schaller, 1965) and of the ungulate populations, principally spotted deer (De and Spillet, 1966). Hog deer (Tak and Lamba, 1981) and spotted deer (Tak and Lamba, in press) populations have been studied more recently. The first stage (1976–9) of an assessment of the impact of the Ramganga Dam on the fauna has been completed (Lamba, n.d). Populations of the large mammals and reptiles are censused annually (Singh, 1985). Recent studies include elephant and spotted deer ecology, effects of burning on grasslands, and *Lantana* eradication (Ashok Singh, pers. Comm., 1988).

Conservation Value Corbett is India's oldest national park. It supports extensive sal forests and a rich and diverse flora and fauna, including large and important populations of tiger and elephant. Moreover, it is free from human settlements.

Conservation Management Forestry operations continued under prescriptions of the working plans until 1975 when the entire territorial jurisdiction of the park was transferred to Project Tiger, leaving only wildlife tourism under the control of the State's Wild Life Preservation Organisation. Following recommendations made in the first managment plan (Singh, 1974), the park has been zoned into core and buffer areas of 32,998 ha and 19,084 ha, respectively. The core zone is strictly protected for research, while tourism is confined to the buffer zone. Grazing and lopping has been stopped throughout the park and is restricted to a narrow strip along the periphery where villagers have rights under the Indian Forest Act. Attempts are underway to relocate peripheral villages to forests some 30–40 km from the park (Singh, 1985).

In a recent examination of management requirements, the two essential needs in the long-term are considered to be the enlargement of existing core and buffer zones, and protecting the corridor of uninterrupted forest between Corbett and Rajaji national parks to enable elephants to migrate between the two areas (Panwar, 1985). This priority is addressed in the latest management plan by A. Singh and R.N. Pandey and the urgent need to maintain the corridor is highlighted by Johnsingh et al. (1990).

Management Constraints The Ramganga River Project at Kalagarh has led to a significant change in the character of the park, with wetland replacing a largely grassland habitat over an extensive area. Long-term changes, particularly with regard to to the fauna, are being monitored (Lamba, n.d.). Fires are a perennial problem, commonly occurring from early March until the start of the monsoon sometime in June. Attempts to control fires date back to 1865, but met with little success until 1876–7 with the creation of a network of fire-lines (Singh, 1974). With the establishment of a radio network and fire-fighting squads under Project Tiger, serious damage from summer fires is now a relatively rare occurrence. The last extensive fires were in 1980 and 1984 when 29% and 17% of the park, respectively, was affected, but with little damage to trees (Singh, 1985). Fire is an important management tool, both in the maintenance of grasslands for herbivores and in controlling the accumulation of inflammable material on forest floors (Panwar, 1985).

The biggest problem in the core area is infestation by weeds, notably *Lantana* and *Cannabis* (Panwar, 1985). Trained elephants are being used to remove the former, pulling plants out by the root stock and replanting with narkul *Arundo donax*. This has proved very successful, with almost complete suppression of *Lantana* over 3 to 4 years (Ashok Singh, pers. comm., 1988). Being an annual, the eradication of *Cannabis* is more easily achieved by repeated cutting prior to flowering (Panwar, 1985). The tourist complex at Dhikala, in the heart of the park, is not only a major source of disturbance but also appropriates a sizeable chunk of prime grassland habitat. Its relocation has been mooted (Panwar, 1985). Visitors can be a menace, behaving in a manner that is incompatible with viewing wildlife (Kaur, 1985). Poaching is not a significant problem, although dynamiting and the illicit netting of fish in the Ram Ganga is frequent (Singh, 1985). Water is a limiting factor in the dry season, shortages sometimes causing animals to move to peripheral areas of the park where they are more at risk from hunting. Artificial waterholes of various types have been constructed in various localities throughout the park (Panday and Singh, 1985).

Recently proposed developments, which would add to the existing pressures on the park, include the construction of a tunnel to connect Kosi with the Ramganga and the establishment of a BHEL factory at Kalabagh in quarters previously used by Irrigation Department staff. The latter has been sanctioned by the State Industries Department but is not permissible under either the Wildlife (Protection) Act or the Forest Conservation Act (Singh, 1985).

Staff Field director, wildlife warden, four range officers and 176 other staff (1987–8).

Budget Rs 56.61 lakh, of which Rs 31.12 lakh is from the State Government and the rest from Central Government (1987–8).

Local Addresses

Field Director, Project Tiger, Corbett National Park, PO Ramnagar 244 715, District Nainital, Uttar Pradesh.

References

Bedi, R. (1985). *Corbett National Park*. Clarion Books, Delhi. 388 pp.

Burton, R.W. Lt.-Col. (1950). Wildlife reserves in India: Uttar Pradesh. *Journal of the Bombay Natural History Society* 49: 749–54.

Hewett, J. (1938). *Jungle trails in northern India*. Methuen and Co., London. (Unseen)

Jain, S.K. and Sastry, A.R.K. (1983). *Botany of some tiger habitats in India*. Botanical Survey of India, Howrah. Pp. 5–8.

Johnsingh, A.J.T., Narendra Prasad, S. and Goyal, S.P. (1990). Conservation status of the Chila–Motichur corridor for elephant movement in Rajaji–Corbett National Parks area, India. *Biological Conservation* 51: 125–38.

Kaur, J. (1985). *Himalayan pilgrimages and the new tourism*. Himalayan Books, New Delhi. Pp. 158–65.

Lamba, B.S. (n.d.). *Impact assessment of bio-ecological changes in the faunal patterns (selected groups) brought about by the partial submersion of Corbett National Park, as a result of Ramganga Multipurpose Hydel Project Dam. 1st Stage 1976–1979*. Department of Environment, Government of India. 150 pp.

Pandey, R.N. and Singh, A. (1986). Management of water resources in Corbett National Park. *Tiger Paper* 13(3): 12–18.

Pant, P.C (1976). Plants of Corbett National Park, Uttar Pradesh. *Journal of the Bombay Natural History Society* 78: 287–95.

Pant, P.C., Uniyal, B.P. and Prasad, R. (1981). Additions to the plants of Corbett National Park. Uttar Pradesh. *Journal of the Bombay Natural History Society* 78: 50–3.

Panwar, H.S. (1985). A study of management requirements in Corbett National Park, In: Thorsell, J.W. (Ed.), *Conserving Asia's natural heritage*. IUCN, Gland, Switzerland and Cambridge, UK. Pp. 169–76.

Schaller, G.B. (1967). The deer and the tiger. Chicago University Press, Chicago.

Sharma, R.P. and Ashok (1988). Status report on the otters in Uttar Pradesh. *Asian Otter Specialist Group Newsletter* 1: 18.

Singh, A. (1985) Corbett national park. An overview. Paper submitted at 25th Working Session of IUCN's Commission on National Parks and Protected Areas, 4–8 February, 1985. Corbett National Park, India. 35 pp.

Singh, A. and Prasad, M. (1977). Odonata (Insecta) of Corbett National Park (Uttar Pradesh, India). *Journal of the Bombay Natural History Society* 73: 419–21.

Singh, V.B. (1974). Management plan of Tiger Reserve, Corbett National Park, U.P. 131 pp.

Tak, P.C. and Lamba, B.S. (1981). Some observations on hog-deer, *Axis porcinus porcinus* (Artiodactyla: Cervidae) at Dhikala, Corbett National Park. *Indian Journal of Forestry* 4: 296–9.

Tak, P.C. and Lamba, B.S. (in press). Ecology and ethnology of the spotted-deer, *Axis axis axis* (Erxleben).

Whitaker, R. (1974). The crocodilians of Corbett National Park. *Indian Journal of Forestry* 38–40.

CHURDHAR SANCTUARY

IUCN Management Category   IV (Managed Nature Reserve)

Biogeographical Province   2.38.12 (Himalayan Highlands)

Geographical Location   Lies in Sirmaur and Shimla districts. The nearest town is Nohra (1 km distant). 30°48′–30°54′N, 77°23′–77°29′E

Date and History of Establishment   Notified as a sanctuary on 15 November 1985 (Notification no. 6–24/73-SF).

Area   Notified as 5,615 ha, but re-estimated by IIPA/Environmental Studies Division (pers. comm.) as 5,659 ha using digitised maps.

Land Tenure   Provincial government. Residents enjoy certain rights.

Altitude   Ranges from 2,000 m to 3,647 m.

Physical Features   The sanctuary gets its name from Chur Peak, on top of which sits a majestic statue of Lord Shiva co mmanding a breathtaking view of the valleys and forests below.

Climate   No information.

Vegetation   Forest types include Western mixed coniferous, Kharsu oak and alpine pastures. Plantations of deodar, oak and other species have been established by the Forest Department. A preliminary list of flora is given in Singh et al. (1990).

Fauna   Mammals include common langur *Presbytis entellus*, rhesus macaque *Macaca mulatta*, leopard *Panthera pardus* (T), Himalayan black bear *Selenarctos thibetanus* (V), wild boar *Sus scrofa*, Indian muntjac *Muntiacus muntjak*, musk deer *Moschus chrysogaster*, goral *Nemorhaedus goral*, Royle's pika *Ochotona roylei*, and Indian porcupine *Hystrix indica*. The musk deer population has reportedly been severely depleted by hunting and it is uncertain if it survives. Singh et al. (1990) provide a preliminary list of 30 bird species recorded in the sanctuary.

Cultural Heritage   Churdhar and the nearby temples are an important pilgrimage site.

Local Human Population   Twenty-three villages and six temporary settlements (possibly all Gujjar camps) are located within the sanctuary. In addition, there is one temple complex where a handful of priests and assistants stay most of the year (Singh et al., 1990).

Visitors and Visitor Facilities   No record of visitor numbers is kept but several thousand pilgrims visit Chur Peak and the temple every year. There are two rest houses, one inside and one outside the sanctuary. The temple complex near Chur Peak also offers accommodation (Singh et al., 1990).

Scientific Research and Facilities   No information.

Conservation Value   Churdhar has one of the last good patches of forest left in southern Himachal Pradesh (Singh et al., 1990).

Conservation Management   Residents have rights to habitation, agriculture, extraction of timber, fuelwood and minor forest produce, grazing and collection of fodder. Gujjars are given permits for grazing and periodically bring large numbers of livestock into the sanctuary. A management plan is under preparation. Some labourers were employed in 1988–9 to make inspection paths. Entry into the sanctuary is not regulated (Singh et al., 1990).

Management Constraints   Poaching of animals and removal of wood has been reported (Singh et al., 1990).

Staff   One range officer, one deputy range officer and six forest guards.

Budget   Rs 335,000 have been allocated for development work in 1989–90, and additional funds have been allocated for salaries and plantations.

Local Addresses
Range Officer (Wildlife), Nohra 173 104, District Sirmaur, Himachal Pradesh

References
Singh, S., Kothari, A. and Pande, P. (1990). *Directory of national parks and sanctuaries in Himachal Pradesh: management status and profiles*. Indian Institute of Public Administration, New Delhi. Pp. 20–2.

DACHIGAM NATIONAL PARK

IUCN Management Category   II (National Park)

Biogeographical Province   2.38.12 (Himalayan Highlands)

Geographical Location   Lies 21 km north-east of Srinagar, summer capital of the State of Jammu & Kashmir. It comprises the catchment area of the Dagwan River. The boundary follows the watershed of the river and its tributaries. Approximately 34°05′N, 74°28′E.

Date and History of Establishment   Declared a national park on 4 February 1981 (State Order no. FST/20). The area was a hunting reserve or 'rakh' of the Maharaja of Jammu & Kashmir from 1910 until 1947, when its management was handed over to the Fisheries Department and subsequently the Forest Department. It was declared a sanctuary by State Order no. 276/C in 1951 (Holloway, 1970; Holloway and Wani, 1970). The enlargement of the park has been recommended (Rodgers and Panwar, 1988).

Area   14,100 ha.

Land Tenure   Provincial government.

Altitude   Ranges from 1,690 m at the national park entrance to 4,290 m.

Physical Features   The mountain ranges enclosing Dachigam are a part of the great Zanskar Range which forms the north-west branch of the central Himalayan axis, bifurcating near Kulu and terminating in the high twin peaks of Nun and Kun. The fold of this range is thrown into a number of undulations enclosing narrow gullies, and broader outflanked gullies locally known as 'Nar'. Two steep ridges, one rising from near Harwan Reservoir and another to the east of New Thir form the natural boundaries of the sanctuary. The series of undulations presents a variety of slope aspects, supporting an array of vegetational types. A number of rocky cliffs and scree slopes break the uniformity of the main slopes. The main Dagwan River originates from Marsar Lake and flows into Harwan Reservoir; it is fed throughout its course by a network of mountain streams draining through the numerous gullies. Complex crystalline rocks, granites, gneisses and schists form the core of the Zanskar Range. Sedimentary rocks consist of slates, phyllites, and schists with embedded crystalline limestone Kurt, 1978).

Climate   Dachigam experiences an irregular climate, with much variation in annual precipitation and in the seasonal occurrence and the length of dry periods. Conditions are sub-Mediterranean, with two dry periods in June and September–November, and high precipitation during the winter and, to a lesser extent, summer seasons. Mean annual precipitation for the period 1892–1971 is 664 mm. Mean monthly temperatures range from about 20 °C in summer to 3 °C in winter for evergreen forests at 1,700 m (Singh and Kachroo, 1977). Meteorological data for Srinagar is given in the current management plan (Department of Wildlife Protection, 1985).

Vegetation   A summary and map of the main vegetation types are given by Kurt (1978), based on the work of Singh and Kachroo (1977, in press). Climax co mmunities are: riverine forest (1,600–1,800 m), with Kashmir elm *Ulmus wallichiana* (E), poplar *Populus ciliata*, willow *Salix caprea*; *Morus alba* co mmunity (1,700–1,900 m), with *Rhus succedanea*; blue pine *Pinus griffithii* forest (1,700–3,000 m) with *Rosa brunonii*, *Parrotiopsis jacquemontiana*, *Viburnum cotinifolium* and *Staphylea emodi*; silver fir *Abies pindrow* forest (2,300–3,200 m), with birch *Betula utilis*, spruce *Picea smithiana*, *Rhus succedanea*, and Kashmir elm; birch forest (2,900–3,700 m) with *Rhododendron campanulatum*; tall evergreen shrub (3,200–3,400 m) with *R. campanulatum* and *Syringa emodi*; dwarf evergreen shrub (3,500–3,700 m), with *Rhododendron anthopogon* and *Juniperus recurva*; and alpine pastures. Many of the riverine forest associates were introduced by the Maharaja and other former occupants of the valley (Holloway and Wani, 1970). *Parrotiopsis jacquemontiana* scrub (1,700–2,400 m), with *Rosa webbiana*, *Indigofera heterantha*, and *Isodon plecantranthoides* predominates on northern slopes, while deciduous thorn scrub (1,700–2,400 m) characterised by *R. webbiana*, *Berberis lycium* and *I. heterantha* occurs on southern slopes in Lower Dachigam. The other main scrub community at 1,700–2,400 m comprises *Chrysopogon echinulatus*, *Themeda anthera*, and *Artemesia vesitita* (Kurt, 1978). Further details of the vegetation are given in the current management plan (Department of Wildlife Protection, 1985).

Fauna   Dachigam contains the only known truly viable population of hangul (Kashmir stag) *Cervus elaphus hanglu* (E), along with some 15 other known species of ma mmals (Holloway, 1970; Department of Wildlife Protection, 1985). These include common langur *Presbytis entellus*, good numbers of leopard *Panthera pardus* (T), and Himalayan black bear *Selenarctos thibetanus* (V) (Kurt, 1979), brown bear *Ursus arctos*, which occurs in Upper Dachigam but appears to be rare (Kurt, 1979; Gruisen, 1983), Himalayan musk deer *Moschus chrysogaster* (Green, 1986), serow *Capricornis sumatraensis*, and long-tailed marmot *Marmota caudata*. Wild boar *Sus scrofa* was introduced by the late Maharaja for hunting but it appears to have died out, having been last recorded in 1987 (Mansoor, 1989). It is thought unlikely that Snow leopard *Panthera uncia* (E) still occurs within the park (Green, 1988), although Holloway (1970) reports seeing one. Due largely to poaching, the hangul population declined drastically from a crudely estimated 1,000–2,000 in 1947 (Gee, 1966) to under 200 in 1965–70 (Gee, 1966; Schaller, 1969; Holloway, 1970). Concomitant with the effective implementation of conservation measures, the population has steadily increased, with 250 estimated in 1976–7 (Kurt, 1978), 320 in 1978 (Kurt, 1979) and, based on censuses carried out by the Wildlife Protection Department, 347, 430, 482 and 554 in 1980, 1982, 1983 and 1984, respectively (Mir, n.d.).

The avifauna is rich (Kurt et al., 1978). Some 112 species of birds are listed by the Department of Wildlife Protection (1985), and 145 species recorded by Katti (1989). Of the pheasants, Himalayan monal *Lophophorus impejanus* and koklass *Pucrasia macrolopha* are present. Although within their ranges, Himalayan snowcock *Tetraogallus himalayensis* and western tragopan *Tragopan melanocephalus* (E) have not been recorded (Rodgers and Panwar, 1988).

Brown trout *Salmo trutta* was introduced to the Dagwan River at the turn of this century (Holloway and Wani, 1970).

Cultural Heritage   No information.

Local Human Population   There is no longer any permanent settlement within the park. An estimated 10,000 sheep and 5,000 water buffalo belonging to Chopans, Gujjars, Bakarwals and Banyaris used to graze the alpine pastures in summer, and wood and grass was collected by local villagers (Kurt, 1978, 1979). Such practices have since been stopped, although livestock from a government sheep-breeding farm, established on land excised from the former sanctuary in 1961, continue to occupy the Dagwan pastures of Upper Dachigam in summer (Department of Wildlife Protection, 1985).

Visitors and Visitor Facilities   Dachigam can be visited with special permission from the Chief Wildlife Warden. There is a VIP lodge for visiting dignitaries at Draphama. This was built on the site of the Maharaja's shooting lodge, burned down in 1969. There are rest houses at Pahlipora in Lower Dachigam, and Gratnar, Sangagolu and Nagaberan in Upper Dachigam. A nature interpretation centre has recently been built near the main entrance.

Scientific Research and Facilities   Detailed plant ecological studies have been carried out by Singh and Kachroo (1977, in press). The interrelationships between microclimate and altitude, topography and vegetation cover were examined by Singh and Kachroo (1978). The status of the hangul population has received considerable attention following a report by Gee (1968), since when censuses have been carried out by Schaller (1969), Holloway (1970), Kurt (1978, 1979) and more recently by the Department of Wildlife Protection (Mir, n.d.). Schaller (1969) made some preliminary observations of hangul rutting behaviour; Kurt (1978, 1979) undertook a detailed ecological study, and Shah et al. (1983) examined the winter diet of the species. An ornithological survey was conducted by Kurt et al. (1978). Recently, a number of ecological studies have been carried out by students at the Wildlife Institute of India, including bear ranging and feeding behaviour (Saberwal, 1989; Manjrekar, 1989) and bird co mmunity structure (Katti, 1989). Acco mmodation is available for visiting scientists.

Conservation Value   Dachigam is vital not only as a refuge for hangul, but also as an undisturbed catchment area for the Harwan Reservoir, which is the main freshwater supply for Srinagar. Lower Dachigam contains the only extensive patch of riverine forest remaining in the State (Ranjitsinh, 1979). Here occurs the endangered Kashmir elm (Lucas and Synge, 1978), the only naturally reproducing population that is currently protected (Maunder, 1988).

Conservation Management   Holloway and Wani (1970) give an historical resum of the conservation and management of the area. With the construction of the reservoir in the 1920s, people living within the catchment area were evicted. The last eviction is said to have occurred at Pahlipora in 1934. While a hunting reserve, the area was policed by a force of game guards and laws were strictly enforced. After independence, responsibility for the area reverted to the State Government and its administration passed successively to the Fisheries Department (1947–54), Forest Department (1954–60), Tawaza Entertainment Department (1960–4), Forest Department (1964–72), Fisheries Department (1972–77), and finally back to the Forest Department (Directorate of Game Preservation) in 1978. The protection of wildlife deteriorated in the period of upheavals following the accession of Kashmir to India. A block of some 1,036 ha was excised from the western edge of Lower Dachigam as compensation to villagers who had formally occupied the sanctuary.

The first management plan was prepared for the period 1970–5 (Holloway and Wani, 1970). Poaching and many other management problems continued unabated, however, until the effective implementation of control measures from 1975 onwards (Kurt, 1978). In a subsequent management plan, the need to restore the habitat and regulate human activities was highlighted (Forest Department, 1980). In the present management plan (Department of Wildlife Protection, 1985), emphasis is given to developing the education programme, both for local people and visitors, and initiating a research progra mme. According to this plan, it is ultimately planned to notify as protected all areas buffering the park. It has been reco mmended that the park be enlarged to 34,500 ha to the north and east, as far as Nun and Kun in the Zanskar Range of Ladakh (Rodgers and Panwar, 1988). In an award scheme organised by the Government of India in 1986, Dachigam was selected as the best-managed national park in the country.

Management Constraints Numerous problems existed in the past (see Holloway and Wani, 1970; Kurt, 1978, 1979) but many of these have since been overcome, as is evident from the increasing hangul population. The presence of the government sheep breeding farm is recognised as the main and long outstanding problem, which, ultimately, can only be solved by its removal (Department of Wildlife Protection, 1985). In the meantime, with funds from the Dal Development Board, a chain-link fence has been erected around the farm to prevent sheep from grazing the southern slopes of Lower Dachigam. However, large quantities of grass are still cut from within the park for winter fodder (Gruisen, 1983). Other problems include the lack of co-ordination between the many different departments having interests in the park (e.g. Animal Husbandry, Hospitality and Protocol, PWD, Irrigation and Water Works, Electricity, Telephones, Agriculture and Fisheries), and the disturbance to wildlife caused by visitors driving noisily along the 5 km stretch of road to the VIP lodge at Draphama (Gruisen, 1983).

Staff The present level of staffing is unknown. One director, one range officer, four foresters, thirty wildlife guards, one research officer, one ecologist, one veterinary surgeon and supporting staff are proposed (Department of Wildlife Protection, 1985).

Budget The capital expenditure for 1985–90 is estimated at Rs 26.42 lakhs and annual recurrent expenditure at Rs 4.49 lakhs (Department of Wildlfe Protection, 1985).

Local Addresses
Supervisor, Dachigam National Park, PO Box Theed (Harwan), Srinagar, Jammu & Kashmir.

References
Department of Wildlife Protection (1985). *Ecological cum management plan for Dachigam National Park, Jammu and Kashmir State 1985–90*. Department of Wildlife Protection, Srinagar. 56 pp.
Forest Department (1980). *Ecological cum management plan for Dachigam National Park, Jammu and Kashmir State 1980–85*. Forest Department, Srinagar.
Gee, E.P. (1966). Report on the status of the Kashmir stag: October 1965. *Journal of the Bombay Natural History Society* 62: 1–15.
Green, M.J.B. (1986). The distribution, status and conservation of the Himalayan musk deer (*Moschus chrysogaster*). *Biological Conservation* 35: 347–75.
Green, M.J.B. (1988). Protected areas and snow leopards: their distribution and status. In: Freeman, H. (Ed.), *Proceedings of the Fifth International Snow Leopard Symposium*. International Snow Leopard Trust, Seattle, USA and Wildlife Institute of India, Dehra Dun, India. Pp. 3–20.
Gruisen, J. van (1983). The hangul, Dachigam's endangered deer. *Sanctuary (Asia)* 3: 114–31.
Holloway C. (1970). The hangul in Dachigam: a census. *Oryx* 10: 373–82.
Holloway, C.W. and Wani, A.R. (1970). Management plan for Dachigam Sanctuary, Jammu & Kashmir, India 1971–5. IUCN, Morges, Switzerland and Forest Department, Srinagar. Unpublished. 22 pp.

Katti, M.V. (1989). Bird communities of lower Dachigam Valley, Kashmir. M. Sc. Thesis, Saurashtra University, Rajkot. 58 pp.

Kurt, F. (1978). Kashmir deer (*Cervus elaphus hanglu*) in Dachigam. In: *Threatened deer*. IUCN, Morges, Switzerland. Pp. 87–109.

Kurt, F. (1979). IUCN/WWF Project no. 1103 (22–4): Hangul, India—ecological study to identify conservation needs. Final report (draft). WWF, Gland, Switzerland. 23 pp.

Kurt, F. et al. (1978). Bericht einer Beobachtungsreise nach Kashmir. WWF–Switzerland, Zürich. Unpublished. 149 pp.

Lucas, G. and Synge, H. (1978). *The IUCN plant red data book*. IUCN, Morges, Switzerland. Pp. 527–8.

Manjrekar, N. (1989). Feeding ecology of the Himalayan black bear (*Selenarctos thibetanus* Cuvier) in Dachigam National Park. M.Sc. Thesis, Saurashtra University, Rajkot. 55 pp.

Mansoor, M. (1989). Extinction of wild boar (*Sus scrofa*) from Dachigam National Park, Jammu & Kashmir State. *Zoo's Print* 4 (10): 19–20.

Maunder, M. (1988). Plants in peril, 3. *Ulmus wallichiana* Planchon (Ulmaceae). *The Kew Magazine* 5: 137–40.

Mir, I.U. (n.d.). Hangul (*Cervus elaphus hanglu*). Department of Wildlife Protection, Srinagar. Unpublished. 8 pp.

Ranjitsinh, M.K. (1979). Conservation in Kashmir. A brief note with recommendations. UNEP, Bangkok. Unpublished. 17 pp.

Rodgers, W.A. and Panwar, H.S. (1988). *Planning a wildlife protected area network in India*. 2 vols. Project FO: IND/82/003. FAO, Dehra Dun.

Saberwal, V. (1988–9). Distribution and movement patterns of the Himalayan black bear (*Selenarctos thibetanus cuvier*) in Dachigam National Park, Kashmir. In: Johnsingh, A.J.T. (Ed.), Dissertation submitted to the Saurashtra University, Rajkot. In partial fulfilment of Master's degree in wildlife science. 18pp.

Schaller, G.B. (1969). Observations on the hangul or Kashmir stag (*Cervus elaphus hanglu* Wagner). *Journal of the Bombay Natural History Society* 66: 1–7.

Shah, G.M., Gadri, M.Y. and Yousuf, A.R. (1983). Winter diets of hangul-deer (*Cervus elaphus hanglu*, Wagner) at Dachigam National Park, Kashmir. *Journal of Indian Science* 64 (C): 129–36.

Singh, G. and Kachroo, P. (1976). Microclimatic variations in Dachigam Sanctuary, Kashmir. *The Indian Forester* 102: 841–8.

Singh, G. and Kachroo, P. (1977). *Forest flora of Srinagar*. Dehra Dun.

Singh, G. and Kachroo, P. (in press). Plant community characteristics in Dachigam Sanctuary (Kashmir). (Unseen)

WWF/IUCN. Project no. 1103 (22–4). Hangul, India—ecological study to identify conservation needs.

DAMPA SANCTUARY

IUCN Management Category   IV (Managed Nature Reserve)

Biogeographical Province   4.09.04 (Burma Monsoon Forest)

Geographical Location   Lies at the north-western tip of the Mizo Hills, 10 km from Phaileng township. 23°20′–24°27′N, 92°20′–93°29′E.

Date and History of Establishment   Notified a sanctuary on 25 March 1985 (Notification no. 11011/14/84-FST). In fact the property was first declared a sanctuary on 20 January 1976 but the notification was subsequently deemed to be technically defective.

Area   48,000 ha (GoM, 1991). According to records held by the Government of India and IIPA/Environmental Studies Division, the area is 68,700 ha.

Land Tenure   Union territory

Altitude   Ranges from 500 m to 1,090 m.

Physical Features   The terrain is hilly and cut by several wet and dry nullahs. The gradient ranges from gentle slopes to steep precipices. The area is drained by the Dhaleswar River and its tributaries.

Climate   Total annual rainfall is 2,300 mm. Maximum and minimum temperatures are 35 °C and 6 °C, respectively.

Vegetation   Consists of tropical semi-evergreen forest (80%) interspersed with bamboo (20%). Prominent genera include *Dipterocarpus, Dubanga, Artocarpus, Michelia, Schima, Mesua, Amoora, Albizia, Bischofia, Tetrameles, Calophyllum* and *Bambusa* (Israel and Sinclair, 1988).

Fauna   Large mammals include hoolock gibbon *Hylobates hoolock* (V), elephant *Elephas maximus* (E), tiger *Panthera tigris* (E), leopard *P. pardus* (T), Himalayan black bear *Selenarctos thibetanus* (V), sambar *Cervus unicolor*, goral *Nemorhaedus goral*, and pangolin *Manis crassicaudata*. Swamp deer *Cervus duvauceli* (E) are reported to occur in the lower areas (Israel and Sinclair, 1987). It would appear from the 1989 census data that hoolock gibbon (38), tiger (4) and elephant (2) populations are small (GoM, 1991). Other mammals recorded by the Department of Environment and Forests include rhesus macaque *Macaca mulatta*, common langur *Presbytis entellus*, large jungle cat *Felis chaus,* sloth bear *Melursus ursinus* (V), serow *Capricornis sumatraensis* (GoM, 1991). The avifauna includes a variety of phasianids, namely black partridge *Francolinus francolinus*, black-breasted quail *Coturnix coromandelica*, jungle bush-quail *Perdicula asiatica*, and pheasants. Among the reptiles is python *Python molurus* (V).

Cultural Heritage   No information

Local Human Population   There were 17 villages (851 households) within the sanctuary but some of these have already been relocated. Another six villages (635 households, 5,800 people) are located within a 10 km radius of the sanctuary (IIPA/Environmental Studies Division, pers. comm., 1990).

Visitors and Visitor Facilities   There are two rest houses.

Scientific Research and Facilities   The first wildlife census was conducted by the Department of Environment and Forests (GoM, 1991) in February 1989.

Conservation Value   Dampa has excellent evergreen forest and lowland bamboo communities and a viable elephant population (Rodgers and Panwar, 1988).

Conservation Management The main activity has been the eviction of 480 families from the sanctuary and their relocation elsewhere at a cost of Rs 31.57 lakhs (GoM, 1991). It has been proposed that the entire Dampa area bordering Bangladesh be established as a protected area complex with a core national park buffered by sanctuary (Rodgers and Panwar, 1988).

Management Constraints Residents practise shifting cultivation.

Staff One range officer, four foresters, four forest guards, four gamewatchers, one game tracker (1988).

Budget No information.

Local Addresses
Range Officer, Teiri Range Office, PO Teiri, via Phaileng, Aizawl, District Mizoram

References
GoM (1991). *Progress report of forestry in Mizoram 1990*. Department of Environment and Forests, Government of Mizoram. 73 pp.
Israel, S. and Sinclair, T. (Eds.) (1987). *Indian wildlife*. APA Productions (HK), Singapore. 363 pp.
Rodgers, W.A. and Panwar, H.S. (1988). *Planning a wildlife protected area network in India*. 2 vols. Project FO: IND/82/003. FAO, Dehra Dun.

DARANGHATI SANCTUARY

IUCN Management Category IV (Managed Nature Reserve)

Biogeographical Province 2.38.12 (Himalayan Highlands)

Geographical Location Comprises two separate units situated 60 km immediately east of Rampur Bushahr in Simla District. 31°22′–31°28′N, 77°47′–77°51′E

Date and History of Establishment First notified a sanctuary in March 1962 and renotified on 27 March 1974, having originally been a private hunting reserve of the former Raja of Bushahr State.

Area Notified as 16,740 ha, but re-estimated by IIPA/Environmental Studies Division (pers. comm.) as 2,701 ha using digitised maps. According to Pandey (1990), Part I is 2,373 ha and Part II is 2,284 ha but this conflicts with the much larger size of Part II figured in Singh et al. (1990).

Land Tenure Provincial government, but local people exercise traditional rights.

Altitude Ranges from 2,100 m to 3,315 m.

Physical Features The two units of the sanctuary lie either side of Dhaula Dhar, an intervening range of hills that forms part of the Middle Himalaya. Part I to the north forms the southern catchment area of the Manglad Gad. Three main rivers, including Wajadi Gad and Gharat Gad, flow northwards into Manglad Gad. Part II to the south encompasses the southern catchment area of the Nogli Gad. Main rivers flowing northwards through Part II into the Nogli Gad include Bankdari Nala, Rigir Gad and Setlu Nala. Manglad and Nogli are eastern tributaries of the Sutlej River. The area between the two units is settled and cultivated (Singh et al., 1990).

Climate   Conditions are temperate, with cool summers and severe winters. Annual precipitation is 625–900 mm, with heavy monsoonal rains from July to September and frequent snow falls from January to March. Temperatures range from –8 °C in winter to 28 °C in summer (Pandey, 1990).

Vegetation   There are five main forest types. Moist cedar forest (1,900–3,000 m) comprises *Cedrus deodara*, mixed with blue pine *Pinus wallichiana* on ridges and an understorey of oaks *Quercus* spp., rhododendrons *Rhododendron* spp. and holly *Ilex dipyrena*. Common shrubs include *Indigofera* sp., honeysuckles *Lonicera* spp., *Prinsepia utilis*, and *Berberis* spp. Western mixed coniferous forest occurs on northern and eastern slopes above 2,000 m. Main species are blue pine, silver fir *Abies spectabilis*, and spruce *Picea smithiana*, with cedar on well-drained sites. Broadleaf species include Indian horse chestnut *Aesculus indica*, walnut *Juglans regia*, maples *Acer* spp., and rhododendrons. Shrubs include *Viburnum* spp., willow *Salix* spp., *Indigofera* spp., *Cotoneaster* spp., *Rubus* spp., and *Rosa moschata*. Moist temperate deciduous forest extends up to 2,700 m along streams and moist hollows, with Indian horse chestnut, walnut, bird cherry *Prunus cornuta*, elm *Ulmus wallichiana*, and maples predominant. Oak *Quercus semecarpifolia* forest occurs in sheltered locations between 2,500 m and 3,500 m, and is replaced at higher altitutes by birch *Betula utilis*, *Juniperus* spp., and *Rhododendron campanulatum*. Common associates in oak forest are maples, bird cherry, yew **Taxus baccata**, and pears *Pyrus* **spp. West Himalayan subalpine forest, with silver fir and some *Quercus semecarpifolia*, occurs above 3,000 m** (Pandey, 1990).

Fauna   Records of mammals by Gaston et al. (1981a, 1983) are limited to small carnivores, namely red fox *Vulpes vulpes*, Himalayan weasel *Mustela sibirica*, yellow-throated marten *Martes flavigula*, Himalayan palm civet *Paguma larvata*, and jungle cat *Felis chaus*. Among ungulates, ibex *Capra ibex* and bharal *Pseudois nayaur* are reported as present by Fox (1987), but according to Pandey (1991) ibex does not occur east of the Sutlej River. Other mammals reported by Singh et al. (1991) include Himalayan black bear *Selenarctos thibetanus* (V), brown bear *Ursus arctos*, Himalayan musk deer *Moschus chrysogaster*, Indian muntjac *Muntiacus muntjak*, and goral *Nemorhaedus goral*, serow *Capricornis sumatraensis*, and Himalayan tahr *Hemitragus jemlahicus*. In February 1990, the musk deer population was estimated to total 15 animals, Himalayan tahr 45 (at a density of 2.3 animals per sq. km), goral 28 (1.2 animals per sq. km), and the serow population was very small (Pandey, 1990, 1991).

Gaston et al. (1981a) recorded some 88 species of birds from two main localities in the Sutlej Valley, namely Saharan (Kulu District), to the north-west of Rampur, and Rampur itself. Singh et al. (1990) provide a list of birds reported from the sanctuary. Most important is the presence of western tragopan *Tragopan melanocephalus* (V), estimated at 22 individuals in February 1990. Himalayan monal *Lophophorus impejanus*, with a population estimated at 166, occurs at densities of 2.1–5.0 individuals per sq. km and koklass pheasant *Pucrasia macrolopha*, estimated at 75, at densities of 0.9–2.3 individuals per sq. km. Kalij pheasant *Lophura leucomelana*, with a total population of 35 individuals, is less numerous (Pandey,

1991). No evidence of cheer pheasant *Catreus wallichii* (E) was found by Gaston et al. (1981a, 1981b), although the species used to occur in this area (Winter-Blyth, 1951).

Cultural Heritage There are several wooden temples in the vicinity featuring a unique architecture (Singh et al., 1990).

Local Human Population There are two villages, one *logri* (farmstead) and one *thach* (summer settlement) within the sanctuary. The surrounding area is heavily populated with 26 villages and other settlements. Over 7,500 cattle, sheep and goats graze inside the sanctuary, of which 5,000 are from surrounding villages. Nomadic Gujjars also bring livestock into the sanctuary on the basis of permits issued by the Forest Department.

Visitors and Visitor Facilities There are four rest houses inside the sanctuary, including one at Daranghati, and an inspection hut at Kashaport.

Scientific Research and Facilities Daranghati was visited for three days in March 1980 during a survey of the wildlife of Himachal Pradesh and its pheasant populations censused (Gaston et al., 1981a). Systematic censuses of ungulate and pheasant populations have subsequently been conducted on a regular basis by the Wildlife Wing since 1987, the most recent being February 1990 (Pandey, 1990). There are no scientific facilities.

Conservation Value Daranghati, a former hunting reserve of the Raja of Bushahr State, shows signs of degradation but it remains particularly important for pheasants, notably western tragopan, and supports a variety of Himalayan ungulates (Pandey, 1990; Singh et al., 1990).

Conservation Management The sanctuary has been actively managed since the adoption of the first management plan for the period 1985–6 to 1989–90. The current management plan (1990–1 to 1994–5) has been submitted to the Wildlife Wing by the range officer (Pandey, 1990). Local people have rights for grazing, cultivation, habitation, and extracting stone for house construction. The collection of timber, fuelwood, and minor forest products is allowed on a concessional basis (Singh et al., 1990).

Management Constraints The forest shows many signs of disturbance (Gaston et al., 1981a). Forest fires are common and poaching frequent (Singh et al., 1990).

Staff One range officer, two deputy ranger officers and eight forest guards (1990).

Budget Rs 234,000 (1989–90).

Local Addresses
Range Officer, Daranghati Sanctuary, Mashnoo, Tehsil Rampur Bushahr, District Simla, Himachal Pradesh.

References
Fox, J.L. (1987). Caprini of northwestern India. *Caprinae News* 2(1): 6–8.
Gaston, A.J., Hunter, M.L. Jr. and Garson, P.J. (1981a). The wildlife of Himachal Pradesh, Western Himalayas. *University of Maine School of Forest Resources Technical Notes* no. 82. 159 pp.

Gaston, A.J. Garson, P.J. and Hunter, M.L. Jr. (1981b). Present distribution and status of pheasants in Himachal Pradesh, Western Himalayas. *World Pheasant Association Journal* 6: 10–30.

Gaston, A.J., Garson, P.J. and Hunter, M.L. Jr (1983). The status and conservation of forest wildlife in Himachal Pradesh, Western Himalayas. *Biological Conservation* 27: 291–314.

Pandey, S. (1990). Management plan of Daranghati Sanctuary (1990–1 to 1994–5). Department of Forest Farming and Conservation, Simla. (Unseen)

Pandey, S. (1991). Species accounts. Report to Wildlife Institute of India, Dehra Dun. Unpublished. 4 pp.

Singh, S., Kothari, A. and Pande, P. (Eds.) (1990). *Directory of National Parks and sanctuaries in Himachal Pradesh*. Indian Institute of Public Administration, New Delhi. 164 pp.

Winter-Blyth, M.A. (1951). A naturalist in the Northwest Himalaya. *Journal of the Bombay Natural History Society* 50: 344–54.

GAMGUL SIAHBEHI SANCTUARY

IUCN Management Category   IV (Managed Nature Reserve)

Biogeographical Province   2.38.12 (Himalayan Highlands)

Geographical Location   Lies in Chamba District, 75 km from Chamba, the nearest town. The northern boundary of the sanctuary adjoins the state of Jammu and Kashmir. 32°49′–32°52′N, 75°52′–75°57′E

Date and History of Establishment   First notified as a sanctuary in 1949 and renotified on 27 March 1974.

Area   Notified as 10,885 ha, but re-estimated by IIPA/Environmental Studies Division (pers. comm.) as 10,546 ha using digitised maps.

Land Tenure   State. Local people enjoy certain rights.

Altitude   Ranges from 1,800 m to 3,919 m.

Physical Features   The Siul Nal flows along the western boundary of the sanctuary.

Climate   Temperatures range between –10 °C and 35 °C. Mean annual rainfall is 1,430 mm, and mean annual snowfall 1,143 mm (Singh et al., 1990).

Vegetation   Forest types include moist deodar, western mixed coniferous, and alpine pastures. Between 1981 and 1983, 174 ha were planted with robinia *Robinia pseudoacacia*, deodar *Cedrus deodara*, kail *Pinus wallichiana*, ash *Fraxinus* sp., willow *Alnus* spp., poplar *Salix* sp., and walnut *Juglans regia*, primarily for commercial use. A preliminary list of the flora is given in Singh et al. (1990).

Fauna   Gamgul Siahbehi is the only sanctuary in Himachal Pradesh in which Kashmir stag *Cervus elaphus hanglu* (E) is reported to occur, although none has been observed in the last few years. Other mammals include common langur *Presbytis entellus*, rhesus macaque *Macaca mulatta*, Himalayan black bear *Selenarctos thibetanus* (V), brown bear *Ursus arctos*, fox *Vulpes vulpes*, Himalayan weasel *Mustela sibirica*, jungle cat *Felis chaus*, leopard cat *Felis bengalensis*, leopard *Panthera pardus* (T), jackal *Canis aureus*, wolf *C. lupus* (V), goral *Nemorhaedus goral*, ibex *Capra ibex*, long-tailed marmot *Marmota caudata*, yellow-throated marten *Martes flavigula*, Royle's pika *Ochotona roylei*, Himalayan palm civet *Paguma larvata*, Indian muntjac *Muntiacus muntjak*, musk deer *Moschus chrysogaster*, serow *Capricornis sumatraensis*, Himalayan tahr *Hemitragus jemlahicus*, Indian porcupine *Hystrix indica*, and common giant flying squirrel *Petaurista petaurista* (Singh et al., 1990). According to Cavallini (1990), goral is either absent or very scarce. Singh et al. (1990) provide a preliminary list of 90 bird species recorded in the sanctuary, which includes all four species of pheasants occurring in Himachal Pradesh.

Cultural Heritage   No information

Local Human Population   Three villages (with a total population of 400 people) are located inside the sanctuary, together with several Gujjar settlements. There are 55 villages, with a total population of 4,953, surrounding the sanctuary.

The number of livestock from adjoining areas grazing inside the sanctuary is 9,000; the corresponding number from villages inside is not known. Gujjars bring in an additional 11,639 ha cattle (Singh et al., 1990).

Visitors and Visitor Facilities   Tourists rarely visit the sanctuary. There are two Public Works Department rest houses inside the sanctuary, and one outside (Singh et al., 1990).

Scientific Research and Facilities   No information

Conservation Value   Gamgul Siahbehi contains a diverse temperate and alpine flora and fauna. It could be particularly important for a remnant population of Kashmir stag if this still exists.

Conservation Management   Local people have rights or leases for collection of timber, fuelwood and minor forest produce, quarrying, habitation, and cultivation. Gujjars are also issued grazing permits by the Department of Forest Farming and Conservation. A management plan is under preparation (Singh et al., 1990).

Management Constraints   The sanctuary is under severe human pressure and is heavily grazed. The Public Works Department is constructing a road through the sanctuary. Commercial felling by the Forest Department was carried out until 1986 but has now been stopped (Singh et al., 1990).

Staff   One range officer (with additional charge of Tundah and Kugti sanctuaries), one deputy range officer and four forest guards. The deputy range officer, located at Bhandal, is in charge locally.

Budget   Rs 125,400 (1987–8)

Local Addresses
Deputy Range Officer (Wildlife), P O Bhandal, Tehsil Chauraha, District Chamba, Himachal
    Pradesh.

References
Cavallini, P. (1990). Status of the goral (*Nemorhaedus goral*) in Himachal Pradesh, India.
    Caprinae News 5(1): 4–6.
Singh, S., Kothari, A. and Pande, P. (1990). *Directory of national parks and sanctuaries in
    Himachal Pradesh: management status and profiles*. Indian Institute of Public
    Administration, New Delhi. Pp. 30–2.

GOBIND SAGAR AND NAINA DEVI SANCTUARIES

IUCN Management Category   IV (Managed Nature Reserve).

Biogeographical Province   4.08.04 (Indus Ganges Monsoon Forest)

Geographical Location   Gobind Sagar is in Bilaspur and Mandi districts, Naina Devi in
Bilaspur District. Access is via Bilaspur which is 1 km from Gobind Sagar and 31 km from
the adjoining Naina Devi Sanctuary. Gobind Sagar: 31°14′–31°26′N, 76°26′–76°51′E. Naina
Devi: 31°16′–31°24′N, 76°25′–76°35′E

Date and History of Establishment   Both sites were first notified as sanctuaries on 5
December 1962 and renotified on 27 March 1974.

Area   Gobind Sagar Sanctuary was notified as 10,034 ha, but re-estimated as 12,067 ha
using digitised maps. Naina Devi Sanctuary was notified as 12,268 ha, but re-estimated as
3,719 ha (IIPA/Environmental Studies Division, pers. comm.).

Land Tenure   Provincial government. Local people enjoy certain rights.

Altitude   Gobind Sagar Sanctuary: 350 m to 500 m.
             Naina Devi Sanctuary: 500 m to 1,019 m.

Physical Features   Gobind Sagar comprises the Bhakra Dam, fed by the Sutlej River, and
is primarily a wetland. Naina Devi is located in the inner Siwaliks and harbours flora and
fauna more akin to that found in the forests of the northern plains of India than in the Himalaya.

Climate   Temperatures range from –2 °C to 45 °C in Gobind Sagar and from –1 °C to 40
°C in Naina Devi. Mean annual rainfall is 1,155 mm in both sanctuaries (Singh et al., 1990).

Vegetation   Forest types on the periphery of Gobind Sagar include northern dry mixed
deciduous. Forest types in Naina Devi include northern dry mixed deciduous (covering 3,000
ha) and chir pine (spread over 1,550 ha). There are also some dry bamboo brakes. Commercial
plantations of chir and *Acacia* spp. were established in Naina Devi over 1,427 ha between

189

1979 and 1984. *Eucalyptus* sp. has been introduced. Preliminary lists of the flora are available for both sanctuaries (Singh et al., 1990).

Fauna   Fish fauna recorded from Gobind Sagar include chilwa *Barilius bendilisis*, jhalli *Clupisona montana*, gid *Labeo dero*, kuni *Labeo dyocheilus*, ticto *Puntius ticto*, sarena *P. sarana*, gungli *Schizothorax richardsonii*, mahseer *Tor putitora*, and a number of introduced species. The avifauna is poorly recorded (Singh et al., 1990).

Mammals in the Naina Devi Sanctuary reportedly include common langur *Presbytis entellus*, rhesus macaque *Macaca mulatta*, leopard *Panthera pardus* (T), jungle cat *Felis chaus*, Bengal fox *Vulpes bengalensis*, Indian hare *Lepus nigricollis*, yellow-throated marten *Martes flavigula*, mongoose *Herpestes edwardsi*, Indian muntjac *Muntiacus muntjak*, goral *Nemorhaedus goral*, wild boar *Sus scrofa*, sambar *Cervus unicolor*, possibly serow *Capricornis sumatraensis*, Indian porcupine *Hystrix indica*, and common giant flying squirrel *Petaurista petaurista*. Reptiles include Indian cobra *Naja naja*, northern house gecko *Hemidactylus flaviviridis*, common Indian krait *Bungarus caeruleus*, Indian monitor *Varanus bengalensis*, and ratsnake *Ptyas mucosus*. Singh et al. (1990) provide a preliminary list of 15 bird species recorded in the sanctuaries.

Cultural Heritage   Places of interest include Naina Devi temple adjacent to the sanctuary.

Local Human Population   Gobind Sagar is uninhabited but the towns of Bilaspur and Nangal are located in the surrounding area, as are several villages. Fourteen villages and hamlets are located within Naina Devi Sanctuary and the surrounding area is heavily settled. There is also some private agricultural land in the sanctuary. Livestock (3,902 head) belonging to residents graze inside the sanctuary. Gaddi nomads are also permitted to bring in their livestock numbering 2,500 (Singh et al., 1990).

Visitors and Visitor Facilities   There is no information on visitors to Gobind Sagar, but there are 10 rest houses on the outskirts of the sanctuary. No record is kept of the number of visitors to Naina Devi, but entry is controlled by the Bhakra Dam Project authorities. There are two guest houses in the sanctuary and two on the outskirts.

Scientific Research and Facilities   The Central Fisheries Research Organisation has a research centre at Bilaspur on the edge of Gobind Sagar.

Conservation Value   Gobind Sagar provides habitat for several native species of fish and a winter refuge for migratory waterfowl (Singh et al., 1990).

Conservation Management   Local people have rights or leases in relation to grazing, collection of timber, fuelwood and minor forest produce, fodder extraction, and religious activities. Neither sanctuary has a management plan. Administration is the responsibility of the Wildlife Wing of the Forest Department, but the Bhakra Management Board has control over Gobind Sagar Sanctuary. The Public Works Department has control over the 20 km stretch of road inside Naina Devi Sanctuary (Singh et al., 1990).

Management Constraints   Bhakra Dam is polluted, the main sources being nearby cement and match factories, quarrying and Bilaspur Town. The weed *Lantana camara* is spreading throughout Naina Devi. Forest fires occur in the western part of Naina Devi: in the period

1979 to 1982, 6.3 ha of land were affected by fire. Soil erosion and landslides have also been recorded (Singh et al., 1990).

Staff Gobind Sagar is not staffed. Naina Devi has one range officer (also in charge of Naina Devi Sanctuary), three deputy range officers, nine forest guards and one peon.

Budget No budget has been specifically allocated for Gobind Sagar. Rs 4,00,000 is budgeted for protection staff and habitat development at Naina Devi.

Local Addresses
Range Officer (Wildlife), P O Naina Devi 174 310, District Bilaspur, Himachal Pradesh

References
Singh, S., Kothari, A. and Pande, P. (1990). *Directory of national parks and sanctuaries in Himachal Pradesh: management status and profiles.* Indian Institute of Public Administration, New Delhi. Pp. 33–5, 60–2.

GOVIND NATIONAL PARK AND GOVIND PASHU VIHAR SANCTUARY

IUCN Management Category   II (National Park).
IV (Managed Nature Reserve)

Biogeographical Province   2.38.12 (Himalayan Highlands)

Geographical Location Govind Pashu Vihar lies in Uttarkashi District, some 225 km north of Dehra Dun, and comprises the whole of Supin Range in the Tons Forest Division. It is bound to the north by the interstate boundary with Himachal Pradesh, to the east by a chain of mountain peaks and to the south by the Tons/Yamuna watershed. 31°01′–31°17′N, 78°00′–78°38′E

Date and History of Establishment The entire area was notified a sanctuary in 1954 when its name was changed from Tons to Govind Pashu Vihar (meaning Govind Animal Park). The government of Uttar Pradesh notified its intention to constitute part of the sanctuary as a national park on 9 January 1991.

Area The original area of the sanctuary was 95,312 ha, of which 47,208 ha has since been declared a national park.

Land Tenure Provincial government but some land is still under private ownership.

Altitude Ranges from 1,290 m to 6,387 m.

Physical Features Comprises the catchment area of the tributaries of the Tons River, which flows south-westwards to its confluence with the Yamuna River. It is thought that this catchment contributes the largest volume of water to the Yamuna, on whose banks lies Delhi, Agra and other urban centres in the Gangetic Plain (A. Chandola, pers. comm.). An account of the area is given by Hewlett (1938), being extracts from the diary of B.B. Osmaston of the Forest Service.

Climate Conditions are monsoonal, with most rain falling in July and August. The sanctuary is snow-bound for 3–4 months in winter, following heavy snowfalls in December. Meteorological data is not available.

Vegetation Forests are dominated by chir pine *Pinus roxburghii*, cedar *Cedrus deodara*, oaks *Quercus* spp. and other broad-leaved species up to about 2,600 m, above which blue pine *Pinus wallichiana*, cedar, silver fir *Abies pindrow*, spruce *Picea smithiana*, yew *Taxus baccata*, and broad-leaved species such as oaks *Quercus* spp., maples *Acer* spp., walnut *Juglans regia*, Indian chestnut *Aesculus indica*, hazel *Corylus jacquemontii*, and rhododendrons *Rhododendron* spp. are predominant (Anon., 1986).

Fauna The large mammal fauna is diverse and includes common langur *Presbytis entellus*, Himalayan black bear *Selenarctos thibetanus* (V), brown bear *Ursus arctos*, common leopard *Panthera pardus* (T), snow leopard *P. uncia* (E), wild boar *Sus scrofa*, Himalayan musk deer *Moschus chrysogaster*, Indian muntjac *Muntiacus muntjak*, sambar *Cervus unicolor*, goral *Nemorhaedus goral*, serow *Capricornis sumatraensis*, Himalayan tahr *Hemitragus jemlahicus*, and bharal *Pseudois nayaur*. About 50 blue sheep were recorded in the upper valleys in April 1986 (Anon., 1986; Fox et al., 1986).

Among the game birds, cheer phesant *Catreus wallichii* (E) and western tragopan *Tragopan melanocephalus* (E) are reputedly present (Seshadri, 1986) but this needs to be reliably confirmed. In 1986 Himalayan monal pheasant *Lophophorus impejanus* and koklass pheasant *Pucrasia macrolopha* were commonly seen above Harki Dun, as well as an occasional Kalij pheasant *Lophura leucomelana*, common hill partidge *Arborophila torqueola*, and Himalayan snowcock *Tetraogallus himalayensis* (J.L. Fox, pers. comm.).

Cultural Heritage No information

Local Human Population There are about 47 villages within the sanctuary (Anon., 1986). That portion above and including Sankri Village contains 21 villages, with a total human population of 7,060, within an area of approximately 53,000 ha. Livestock in this area includes 10,100 goats, 24,700 sheep and 5,500 cattle. Of the 12,326 ha under village ownership, 2,764 ha (22%) is cultivated. Apart from this, locally-owned livestock, sheep and goats from lower down the valley are brought up to graze the alpine pastures in summer. In addition, Gujjars used to bring in several thousand buffalo from outside the sanctuary but, under pressure from local inhabitants, they were banned from entering the areas above Harki Dun in the Supin Valley in 1984 (Fox et al., 1986).

Visitors and Visitor Facilities Harki Dun, in the east of the sanctuary and three days walk from the road head near Sankri, is a popular tourist trekking destination. There are forest rest houses at Naitwar, Taluka, Osla and Harki Dun.

Scientific Research and Facilities The wildlife was briefly surveyed in April 1986 as part of an Indo-US snow leopard project (Fox et al., 1986).

Conservation Value   The sanctuary is important for its temperate forests, spectacular alpine meadows (comparable to the Valley of Flowers) and diverse mammalian fauna (Kandari, 1985–6; Fox et al., 1986).

Conservation Management   There is no management plan. Wildlife staff have recently been increased in response to the need to manage the sanctuary more effectively (Fox et al., 1986). There is considerable potential for extending the sanctuary eastwards (A. Chandola, pers. comm., 1986) which, together with integrating its management with that of the nearby Raksham Chitkul Sanctuary in Himachal Pradesh, would enhance the conservation value of the whole area. The recommendation to upgrade a core zone to national park status (Rodgers and Panwar, 1988) has recently been implemented with the initial notification of a 47,208 ha national park.

Management Constraints   The high degree of exploitation of natural resources is not compatible with the area's protected status, particularly in view of the increased pressure this places on residents trying to maintain a subsistence-level economy. The Uttar Pradesh Timber Corporation harvests substantial quantities of timber, mostly cedar, from the lower portions of the sanctuary; minor forest products (including medicinal plants) are collected by up to 1,000 Nepali labourers on hire to local contractors; and large flocks of sheep and goats are brought in from other parts of Garhwal. There is substantial hunting in the area, most commonly for musk deer and goral, and every village has at least one regular hunter. The total number of licensed guns exceeds 150, with probably a similar number of unlicensed firearms (A. Chandola, pers. comm., 1986; Fox et al., 1986).

Staff   No information

Budget   No information

Local Addresses   No information

References

Anon. (1986). Indo-U.S. snow leopard project. Progress report for Spring 1986. *Snow Line* 10: 4–5.

Fox, J.L., Sinha, S.P., Chundawat, R.S. and Das, P.K. (1986). A survey of snow leopard and associated species in the Himalaya of northwestern India. Project Completion Report. Wildlife Institute of India/U.S. Fish and Wildlife Service/International Snow Leopard Trust, Dehra Dun. 51 pp.

Hewlett, Sir J. (1938). Jungle trails in northern India. (Unseen)

Kandari, G.P. (1985–6). A note on the national parks and wildlife sanctuaries of Garhwal Himalaya. *Journal of Himalayan Studies and Development* 9 & 10: 31–5.

Rodgers, W.A. and Panwar, H.S. (1988). *Planning a wildlife protected area network in India.* 2 vols. Project FO: IND/82/003. FAO, Dehra Dun.

Seshadri, B. (1986). *India's wildlife and wildlife reserves.* Sterling Publishers, New Delhi. Pp. 92–5.

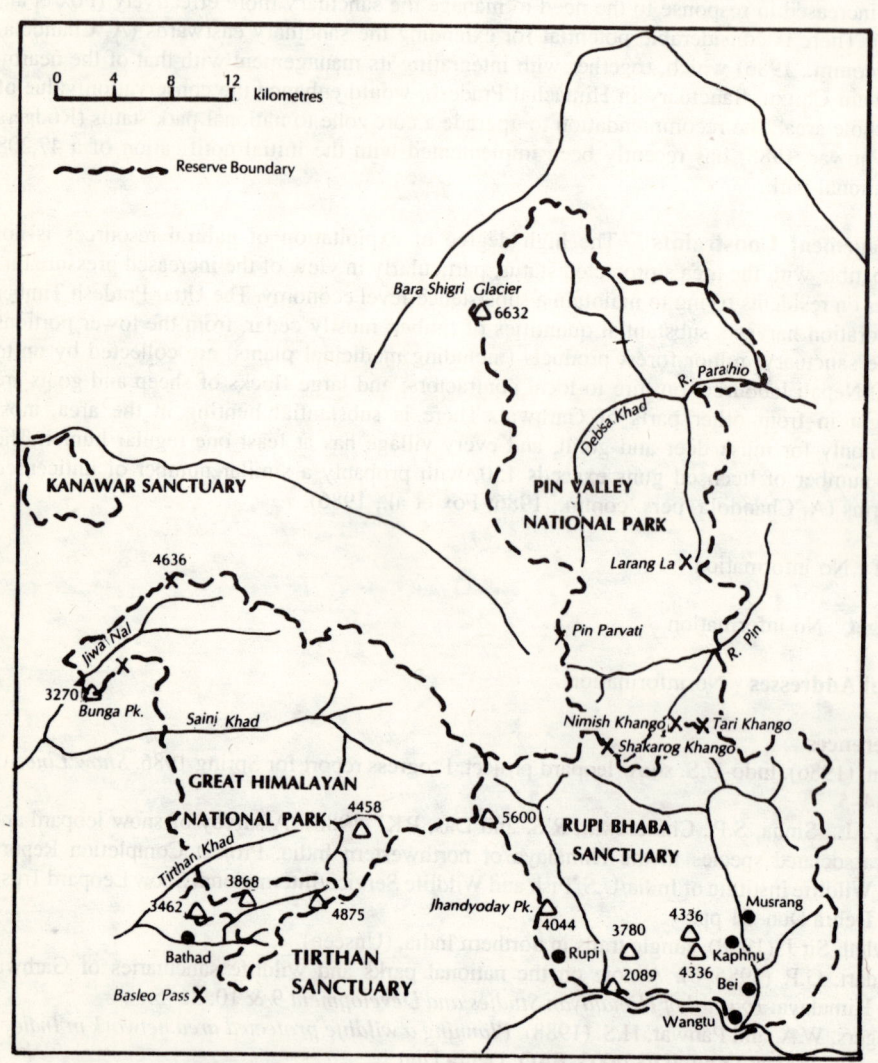

Great Himalayan National Park, Pin Valley National Park, Kanawar Sanctuary,
Rupi Bhaba Sanctuary, and Tirthan Sanctuary

GREAT HIMALAYAN NATIONAL PARK,
INCLUDING TIRTHAN SANCTUARY

IUCN Management Category   Great Himalayan National Park: II (National Park)
Tirthan Sanctuary: IV (Managed Nature Reserve)

Biogeographical Province   2.38.12 (Himalayan Highlands)

Geographical Location   Lies in Seraj Forest Division, Kulu District, some 60 km by road
south-west of Kulu Town. Tirthan Sanctuary adjoins the southern boundary of the park. The
park is bounded by mountain ridges on all but its western side, notably Mathaun Dhar/Rakti
Dhar to the north-east and Sirikand Dhar to the south-east. 31°38'–31°55'N, 77°20'–77°46'E
(park) 31°34'–31°40'N, 77°28'–77°37'E (sanctuary)

Date and History of Establishment   Tirthan was notified a sanctuary on 17 June 1976.
Part of this was subsequently included in Great Himalayan National Park. Intention to declare
the park was issued on 1 March 1984 (Notification no. 6–16/73–SF–11), but the settlement
of rights and the final notification are outstanding. Some 111,600 ha adjoining the park has
been notified as a buffer zone. The park was renamed Jawaharlal Nehru Great Himalayan
National Park in mid-1989, but its original name is still commonly used (Singh et al., 1990).

Area   Great Himalayan National Park: 62,000 ha (re-estimated as 60,561 ha)
Tirthan Sanctuary: 6,113 ha (re-estimated as 6,825 ha)

Tirthan was originally notified as 17,800 ha in 1976 but the northern part was incorporated
within Great Himalayan Natinal Park in 1984. The park and sanctuary form part of a much
larger protected areas complex that includes Rupi Bhaba Sanctuary and Pin Valley National
Park, and covers a total notified area of 161,528 ha, re-estimated by IIPA/Environmental
Studies Division (pers. comm.) as 233,536 ha using digitised maps.

Land Tenure   Provincial government. Local people still have rights of access and use of
land resources.

Altitude   Ranges from 1,500 m to 5,805 m in Great Himalaya National Park, and from 2,100
m to 4,875 m in Tirthan Sanctuary.

Physical Features   The park comprises the upper catchment areas of the Jiwa, Sainj and
Tirthan rivers in the inner Seraj. These rivers flow west into the Beas River. The Sainj and
Tirthan valleys are narrow and steep-sided throughout their length, showing little sign of
glaciation. The upper section of the Sainj Valley abuts on the upper Parbati Valley to the
north, while the upper Tirthan forms part of the watershed separating the Beas and Sutlej
catchments. The eastern part of the park is permanently under snow and ice. Tirthan Sanctuary
is drained by Palachan Gad, a tributary of Tirthan Gad.

Climate   Compared to the rest of the upper Beas area, conditions are more akin to those for
Simla and the front ranges, with less snowfall in winter, more rainfall during the summer

monsoon and probably higher temperatures. Simla, at 2,200 m, receives in excess of 1,500 mm annual precipitation and experiences mean monthly maximum and minimum temperatures ranging from 8.6 °C to 24.1 °C and from 1.9 °C to 15.7 °C, respectively (Gaston et al., 1981a). Mean annual precipitation in Tirthan Sanctuary is 1500 mm, and temperature ranges from −5 °C to 30 °C (Singh et al., 1990).

Vegetation   The vegetation of Saini and Tirthan valleys is similar, with northerly aspects clothed in dense forest, dominated below 2,000 m by blue pine *Pinus wallichiana*, and higher up by a diverse deciduous broad-leaved forest on moderately sloping areas and fir *Abies pindrow* on steep areas. Tirthan Valley, between Bandal and Rolla, also supports small areas of oak forest (*Quercus dilatata* and *Q. incana*). Southerly aspects are generally more open; stands of blue pine and cedar *Cedrus deodara* are interspread among grass and shrub-clad hillsides, with a zone of kharsu oak *Q. semecarpifolia* forest above 2,800 m. Extensive meadows occur above the tree-line, particularly on the south side of Sainj Valley above Shangarh and at Dela Thach, above Lopah. Much of the forest on the northern slopes contains a dense understorey of bamboo *Arundinaria spathiflora*, which forms impenetrable thickets in some places, particularly at 2,200–2,800 m. At lower altitudes the forest, even close to villages, supports a well-developed understorey containing a wide variety of shrubs. Vegetation on the high altitude meadows is also diverse, including many attractive herbaceous plants not seen elsewhere; among them are species of *Iris, Frittillaria, Gagea*, and *Primula* (Gaston et al., 1981a). There is a patch of yew *Taxus baccata* near Manjhan Village in Jiwa Valley, the only known locality for this species in the park and surrounding areas. Within the park, 52,602 ha are demarcated as reserved forest and the rest is unclassed forest, pasture, permanent snow, cultivated, or settled. In the buffer belt, 94,897 ha are demarcated as reserved forest, the rest being unclassed forest, or cultivated or settled (Singh et al., 1990).

Fauna   The area supports diverse large mammal and avifaunal communities and is particularly noted for its prolific pheasant populations. Species lists are given by Gaston et al. (1981a). Both rhesus macaque *Macaca mulatta* and common langur *Presbytis entellus* are present. Carnivores include *Panthera pardus* (T), and both Himalayan black bear *Selenarctos thibetanus* (V) and brown bear *Ursus arctos*. Himalayan tahr *Hemitragus jemlahicus* and goral *Nemorhaedus goral* occur in reasonable numbers, and Indian muntjac *Muntiacus muntjak* and serow *Capricornis sumatraensis* in smaller numbers. Himalayan musk deer *Moschus chrysogaster* has been recorded in Tirthan Valley (Gaston et al., 1981a). Bharal *Pseudois nayaur* is present in good numbers (Fox, 1987; Pandey, 1991). The occurrence of ibex *Capra ibex* remains uncertain (Pandey, 1991). Several other mammals are reported by Singh et al. (1990).

Avifaunal diversity is much higher than elsewhere in the upper Beas Valley. Of the 152 species of birds recorded in the area, 68 are residents and 49 summer visitors (Gaston et al., 1981a). Five species of pheasant are present, namely: western tragopan *Tragopan melanocephalus* (E), recorded more frequently than elsewhere in the upper Beas; cheer *Catreus wallichii* (E), with a small population near Bandal; koklass *Pucrasia macrolopha* and Himalayan monal *Lophophorus impejanus*, both of which are numerous; and kalij *Lophura leucomelana*, which is uncommon (Gaston et al., 1981a, 1981b; Garson, 1983).

Cultural Heritage   Places of religious importance in and around the park include the hot springs at Khirganga and Mantalai Rakti Sar (source of the Rakti Nal) and Hans Kund (source of Tirthan River) (Singh et al., 1990).

Local Human Population   There are four small villages in the park, all of which are in Sainj, namely Sakti, Maror, Kunder and Manjhan. These villages are inhabited by 114 families. The surrounding buffer belt has 75 villages. Livestock grazing inside the park includes 570 from park villages, 1,015 from adjacent villages and 6,611 brought from the south (Tirthan Valley) and north-west (Kanawar) (Singh et al., 1990). Large numbers of local people visit the forests of Tirthan Valley in spring to collect morel *Morchella esculenta*. Similarly, medicinal plants are collected from the alpine meadows of Sainj Valley (Gaston et al., 1981a). Tirthan Sanctuary is uninhabited but it is permitted to graze livestock inside its boundaries (Singh et al., 1990).

Visitors and Visitor Facilities   Tourists are few. There are 13 rest houses in the vicinity of the park and 7 on the outskirts of the sanctuary.

Scientific Research and Facilities   A multi-disciplinary survey of Inner Seraj was conducted in 1979–80, with particular emphasis on wildlife and the impact of human disturbance and livestock on the structure and composition of the vegetation (Gaston et al., 1981a, 1983). A number of sites with cheer pheasant have subsequently been identified (Garson, 1983). Cavallini (1990) assessed the status of goral in the park in late-1989. There are no scientific facilities.

Conservation Value   Inner Seraj was considered the best site for establishing a national park in the Kulu-Manali area because its forests were relatively undisturbed, despite large-scale fellings in easily accessible parts during World War II, and there were few signs of development. Moreover, the area has a near-complete complement of large mammal and pheasant species known to occur in Himachal Pradesh, as well as a more diverse avifauna than recorded elsewhere in the state (Gaston et al., 1981a, 1983). The park supports the largest known population of Himalayan tahr in the state (Gaston, 1986) and is one of only two places in India where anything more than a remnant population of western tragopan is known to survive (Garson and Gaston, 1989). Some spectacular scenery complements the biological richness of the area.

Conservation Management   Local people have rights to grazing, collection of timber, fuelwood, fodder and minor forest products, agriculture, habitation, religious monuments and burial grounds in both the park and sanctuary. In addition, permits are issued to Gaddis to graze livestock in the entire park, except for Rolla Forest in Tirthan Valley (Singh et al., 1990). The park's first management plan was prepared on 22 July 1987 and approved in 1988 (Anon., 1987). It is proposed to relocate the four villages in Sainj Valley to the buffer belt. There are also provisions in the plan for a tourist zone. Settlement of existing rights, boundary demarcation and final notification of the park are matters of outstanding priority. There is a proposal to extend the park to the north to include that part of the Parvati catchment lying between Pulga and Pin Parvati Pass. A management plan for Tirthan Sanctuary was drawn up for the period 1983–4 to 1987–8. There is no current plan (Singh et al., 1990).

Management Constraints   There are plans to extend the road along the Sainj Valley by a further 10 km to Shangarh, and plans have been mooted in the past to build a road from Gushaini to Rolla as part of a scheme for a national park. Any extension of the road network is likely to result in increased lumbering and possibly other forms of disturbance. Musk deer are hunted in Tirthan Valley by outside poachers (Gaston et al., 1981a). Approximately 7,000 dead or dying trees in the upper Sainj Valley were earmarked for felling in spring 1986. Exploitation would probably lead to serious disturbance of the habitat (A. Chandola, pers.

comm.). Forest fires sometimes occur over large areas (Singh et al., 1990), and in 1987 a large expanse of forest in Rolla was burnt in one of the worst fires in living memory (A.J. Gaston, pers. comm.).

Staff The park is staffed by one divisional forest officer (park director), two range officers, four deputy range officers, and fifteen forest guards. One honorary wildlife warden has been appointed to the park. Tirthan Sanctuary is staffed by one range officer, two deputy range officers and fifteen forest guards (Singh et al., 1990).

Budget Rs 1,000,000 (1988–9) for the park. No budget has been allocated for the sanctuary.

Local Addresses

Director, Great Himalaya National Park, Shamshi 175125, District Kulu, Himachal Pradesh.

Range Officer (Wildlife), Tirthan Wildlife Range, Banjar 175123, District Kulu, Himachal Pradesh.

References

Anon. (1987). Management plan for the Great Himalayan National Park, Kulu District, Himachal Pradesh, 1987–8 to 1996–7. Department of Forest Farming and Conservation, Simla. (Unseen)

Cavallini, P. (1990). Status of the goral (*Nemorhaedus goral*) in Himachal Pradesh, India. *Caprinae News* 5(1): 4–6.

Fox, J.L. (1987). Caprini of northwestern India. *Caprinae News* 2(1): 6–8.

Garson, P.J. (1983). The cheer pheasant *Catreus wallichii* in Himachal Pradesh, Western Himalayas: an update. *World Pheasant Association Journal* 8: 29–39.

Garson, P.J. and Gaston, A.J. (1989). The conservation of forests and wildlife in Himachal Pradesh In: Allchin B., Allchin, F. R., and Thapar, B.K. (Eds.), *The Conservation of the Indian heritage. Cosmo Publications, New Delhi. Pp. 39–54.*

Gaston, A.J. (1986). West Himalayan wildlife survey: report on activities in 1985. Unpublished. 8 pp.

Gaston, A.J., Hunter, M.L. Jr., and Garson, P.J. (1981a). The wildlife of Himachal Pradesh, Western Himalayas. *University of Maine School of Forest Resources Technical Notes* no. 82. 159 pp.

Gaston, A.J., Garson, P.J., Hunter, M.L. Jr. (1981b). Present distribution and status of pheasants in Himachal Pradesh, Western Himalayas. *World Pheasant Association Journal* 6: 10–30.

Gaston, A.J., Garson, P.J. and Hunter, M.L. Jr. (1983). The status and conservation of forest wildlife in Himachal Pradesh, Western Himalayas. *Biological Conservation* 27: 291–314.

Pandey, S. (1991). Species accounts. Report to Wildlife Institute of India, Dehra Dun. Unpublished. 4pp.

Singh, S., Kothari, A. and Pande, P. (Eds.) (1990). *Directory of National Parks and sanctuaries in Himachal Pradesh* . Indian Institute of Public Administration, New Delhi. Pp. 5–8.

GULMARG SANCTUARY

IUCN Management Category V (Protected Landscape)

Biogeographical Province 2.38.12 (Himalayan Highlands)

Geographical Location   Lies on the north-eastern side of the Pir Panjal Range, some 50 km south-west of Srinagar. It encompasses the upper catchment area of Ferozpur Nala and the forests that surround the Gulmarg basin. It is bounded to the north by Jhelum Valley Forest Division, south by Poonch and Pir Panjal forest divisions, east by Drang Village and to the west by Jhelum Valley and Poonch forest divisions. Approximately 34°05'N, 74°25'E.

Date and History of Establishment   Notified a sanctuary in 1987, having originally been declared a game reserve in 1981. Declared a biosphere reserve by the State Government on 4 February 1981, but not nationally or internationally recognised as such.

Area   18,600 ha

Land Tenure   Provincial government

Altitude   Ranges from 2,400 m to 4,300 m.

Physical Features   The terrain is steep, becoming precipitous in the upper reaches of Ferozpur Nala. Underlying rocks are predominantly Panjal volcanics, with well-exposed acidic lava flows. Shales, limestone, slates and quartzites occur throughout the tract (Department of Wildlife Protection, 1987).

Climate   Conditions are temperate, with cold winters and warm summers. Most precipitation falls as snow during winter (Department of Wildlife Protection, 1987).

Vegetation   Forests surrounding the resort at Gulmarg consist predominantly of silver fir *Abies pindrow*, with spruce *Picea smithiana*, pine *Pinus griffithii*, and occasionally maple *Acer caperdocicum* and *Padus cornuta*. The shrub layer, which sometimes occurs as dense thickets but in most places has been thinned or cleared, is almost entirely of *Ski mmia laureola* and *Viburnum cotinifolium*. Alpine pastures occur above 3,000 m (Green, 1979).

Fauna   The area is not noted for its wildlife. Large mammals recorded during a brief survey in 1979 include rhesus macaque *Macaca mulatta*, bear (probably *Ursus arctos*), fox *Vulpes vulpes*, leopard *Panthera pardus* (T), and Himalayan musk deer *Moschus chrysogaster* at a low density of less than 0.4 animals per sq. km (Green, 1979, 1986). No pheasants were recorded during that survey, but Himalayan monal *Lophophorus impejanus* is present (Rodgers and Panwar, 1988). A variety of other mammals and birds appears in official lists (Department of Wildlife Protection, 1987) but these records need to be confirmed.

Cultural Heritage   No information

Local Human Population   There are no permanent settlements, apart from a tourist resort in the centre of the sanctuary which depends on the surrounding forests for fuelwood. Gujjars bring their livestock into the sanctuary during the summer (Department of Wildlife Protection, 1987).

Visitors and Visitor Facilities   Gulmarg is a very popular tourist resort, receiving up to 3,000 visitors per day during summer (Green, 1979). It boasts of having one of the highest golf courses in the world and provides for skiing in winter. Accommodation is available in the form of government rest houses and hotels.

Scientific Research and Facilities The wildlife was briefly surveyed in 1979 (Green, 1979). Behavioural studies of bumble bees were conducted in 1985 and 1986 (Williams, 1986). There are no scientific facilities.

Conservation Value Gulmarg is noted for its scenic, landscaped setting in the Pir Panjal Range and is an important recreational area.

Conservation Management There is no management plan.

Management Constraints The flora, with the exception of trees, and fauna are depleted due to unrestricted grazing practices and collection of forest produce. Tourism is uncontrolled and exerts additional pressure on forest resources, notably fuelwood (Green, 1979; Department of Wildlife Protection, 1987).

Staff No information

Budget No information

Local Addresses No information

References
Department of Wildlife Protection (1987). Status survey report of the proposed Gulmarg Wildlife Sanctuary. Department of Wildlife Protection, Srinagar. Unpublished. 3pp.
Green, M.J.B. (1979). Himalayan musk deer, India. Progress Report no. 2. WWF, Gland, Switzerland. Pp. 12–14.
Green, M.J.B. (1986). The distribution, status and conservation of the Himalayan musk deer (*Moschus chrysogaster*). *Biological Conservation* 35: 347–75.
Rodgers, W.A. and Panwar, H.S. (1988). *Planning a wildlife protected area network in India*. 2 vols. Project FO: IND/82/003. FAO, Dehra Dun.
Williams, P.H.C. (1986). Kashmir Bumble Bee Survey 3, India 1986. In: *Expedition Yearbook* Expedition Advisory Centre, London. Pp. 97–9.

GYA-MIRU SANCTUARY

IUCN Management Category Proposed.

Biogeographical Province 2.38.12 (Himalayan Highlands)

Geographical Location Lies on the east side of the central mountains of Ladakh, some 50 km south-east of Leh in part of the catchment area of the Miru Nala (Chhabe Name). The proposed area occupies the east bank of the Miru Nala, extending from Miru Village in the north to Taglang La in the south. A high mountain ridge forms the eastern boundary, and the Leh–Himachal Pradesh road runs parallel to the western boundary. Approximately 33°34′–33°45′N, 77°44′E

Date and History of Establishment Proposed as a sanctuary by the Department of Wildlife Protection.

Dry alpine habitat, looking towards Gompa Ranchen in the proposed Lung Nag Sanctuary, Zanskar, Ladakh. India. (*M. J. B. Green*)

Temperate zone oak forest, Kedarnath Sanctuary, Garhwal, Uttar Pradesh, India. (*M. J. B. Green*)

Subtropical zone chir pine forest, Kedarnath Sanctuary, Garhwal, Uttar Pradesh, India. (*M. J. B. Green*)

Subalpine meadows, pre-monsoon season, Kedarnath Sanctuary, Garhwal, Uttar Pradesh, India. (*M. J. B. Green*)

Mixed moist deciduous and evergreen forest, Puliebadze Sanctuary, Nagaland, India.   (*Ashish Kothari*)

Higher altitude mixed deciduous-fir forest, mid-Manalsu Nala valley, Manali Sanctuary, Uttar Pradesh, India.
(*M. J. B. Green*)

Lower alpine zone habitat in the glacier-formed Langtang Valley, Langtang National Park, Nepal.
(*M. J. B. Green*)

Area 13,000 ha

Land Tenure No information

Altitude Ranges from about 3,500 m to 5,960 m.

Physical Features Miru Nala is a tributary of the Indus River, with its confluence at Upshi Village, about 8 km north of Miru Village. At the head of the north–south oriented Miru Valley at 5,100 m is Taglang La, a pass. Steep mountains rise from the Miru Valley, with a mixture of rocky and open slopes. Rocks are mainly of slate, phyllite, schist, quartzite, crystalline limestone, and dolomite (Department of Wildlife Protection, n.d.; Mallon, 1989).

Climate The climate of Ladakh is one of extremes, with considerable daily and seasonal fluctuations. Precipitation is scanty, with only 76 mm per year. During winter, when night temperatures fall to −30 °C and below, the Miru Nala becomes iced over (Department of Wildlife Protection, n.d.; Osborne et al., 1983).

Vegetation Vegetation is typical of eastern Ladakh, with large areas dominated by *Caragana* spp. Other species include *Artemisia* spp., *Ephedra gerardiana,* and *Acantholimon lycopodioides* (Mallon, 1989). Along river beds are patches of scrub, with *Rosa webbiana*, *E. gerardiana*, and *Lonicera* spp. *E. gerardiana* scrub covers the lower slopes, above which are alpine pastures (Department of Wildlife Protection, n.d.).

Fauna Eleven species of mammals have been recorded, and wild dog *Cuon alpinus* (V) and stone marten *Martes foina* may also be present (Mallon, 1989). The Miru catchment area lies in the easternmost part of the distribution of the urial *Ovis orientalis vignei* in Ladakh and forms the western limit of the world range of the Tibetan argali *Ovis ammon hodgsoni* (Mallon, 1983, 1985; Osborne et al., 1983). The two populations were censused for the first time in 1984 when a total of 121 urial and 57 argali was recorded (Department of Wildlife Protection, n.d.). Other mammals include fox *Vulpes vulpes*, wolf *Canis lupus* (V), lynx *Felis lynx*, snow leopard *Panthera uncia* (E), bharal *Pseudois nayaur*, Himalayan marmot *Marmota bobak*, Royle's pika *Ochotona roylei*, and woolly hare *Lepus oiostolus*.

Less is known about the avifauna but 28 species were recorded during a short winter visit by Mallon (1989), including three species typical of eastern Ladakh and the Tibetan Plateau: Tibetan snowcock *Tetraogallus tibetanus*, Tibetan sandgrouse *Syrrhaptes tibetanus*, and Blanford's snowfinch *Montifringilla blanfordi*.

Cultural Heritage No information.

Local Human Population There are no permanent settlements within the proposed sanctuary, but villagers from Miru, Gya and Rumtse graze their livestock in the area (Department of Wildlife Protection, n.d.).

Visitors and Visitor Facilities No information

Scientific Research and Facilities Surveys of the wildlife, notably urial, were first carried out by Mallon (1983) during three visits in 1981–2. Subsequently, the urial and argali populations were censused by the Department of Wildlife Protection in 1984 (Department of Wildlife Protection, n.d.).

Conservation Value   The proposed sanctury is of prime importance in protecting the remaining populations of urial and argali in Ladakh (Mallon, 1989). The latter population is particularly important because the species' distribution in Ladakh is limited to the extreme east.

Conservation Management   None

Management Constraints   The urial and argali populations have suffered from hunting in the past but may now be recovering (Mallon, 1989).

Staff   None

Budget   None

Local Addresses None

References

Department of Wildlife Protection, (n.d.). Survey and census report of the proposed Gya-Miru Wildlife Sanctuary for the nayan and shapu Department of Wildlife Protection, Srinagar. Unpublished. 6 pp.

Mallon, D. (1983). The status of Ladakh urial *Ovis orientalis vignei* in Ladakh, India. *Biological Conservation* 27: 373–81.

Mallon, D.P. (1985). Status report on wild sheep in India. In: Hoefs, M. (Ed.), *Wild sheep: distribution, abundance, management and conservation of the sheep of the world and closely related mountain ungulates.* Northern Wild Sheep and Goat Council, Whitehorse, Canada. Pp. 164–78.

Mallon, D.P. (1989). An ecological survey of the protected area network in Ladakh. Report to the Department of Wildlife Protection, Jammu & Kashmir Government, Srinagar. Unpublished. 13pp.

Osborne, B.C., Mallon, D.P. and Fraser, S.J.R. (1983). Ladakh, threatened stronghold of rare Himalayan mammals. *Oryx* 17: 182–9.

HEMIS NATIONAL PARK

IUCN Management Category   II (National Park)

Biogeographical Province   2.38.12 (Himalayan Highlands)

Geographical Location   Lies in the Transhimalayan district of Ladakh on the west bank of the Indus River and extends from the southern side of the Indus Valley southwards across the Zanskar Range as far as the Tsarap Chu. 33°38′–34°11′N, 77°00′–77°44′E

Date and History of Establishment   Hemis was notified a national park on 4 February 1981 (Government Order no. FST/20), when it was known as Hemis High Altitude National Park and named after Hemis Gompa, the most important Buddhist monastery in Ladakh which lies just outside the park's northern boundary. At that time, the park encompassed the catchments of the Markha, Rumbak, and Sumdah Nalas, an area of 60,000 ha. It has since been considerably expanded through the addition of three blocks comprising the Alum Nullah and lower Chang Chu catchments (which now constitute the core area of the park), upper Chang Chu, and Shun-Shadi, as well as the Shang extension to the Markha Block following recommendations by Mallon (1986, 1987). Shang was originally notified a game reserve (8,000 ha) in 1981, and both this reserve and Shun-Shadi were recommended for sanctuary status (Rodgers and Panwar, 1988). Further extensions to the park have been recommended through the addition of Zanskar Gorge (38,000 ha) and Zangla (15,000 ha) blocks adjacent to the western boundary to buffer the core area, and Alehi Block (12,000 ha) in the north (Mallon, 1989).

Area   410,000 ha, comprising a 125,000 ha core area and 285,000 ha buffer zone. Further extensions to the park totalling 65,000 ha are recommended (Mallon and Bacha, 1989).

Land Tenure   Provincial government. Local people enjoy traditional rights.

Altitude   Ranges from 3,300 m to 6,400 m according to Mallon and Bacha (1989), but there is a 6,930 m peak at the head of the Markha Valley marked on some maps.

Physical Features   Hemis is wholly mountainous in character. The core area (Alam Nullah and lower Chang Chu) lies in a band of hard limestones and other sediments that have been raised and tilted almost vertically, then deeply incised by a series of river gorges. The terrain is extremely rugged with a high proportion of cliffs, screes and exposed rocks. It is isolated, with few passes crossing the main watersheds. The Markha and adjacent Sumdah blocks comprise the catchments of the Markha, Rumbak, Shang, and Sumdah rivers, all of which drain north into the Indus. The area covered by these two blocks consists of steep, V-shaped valleys with short gorge sections. The terrain is rough and often rocky, with a mixture of open slopes, cliffs and screes. Gently sloping alluvial fans form a short section of stone desert along the south bank of the Indus between the Zanskar and Rumbak confluences. The upper Chang Chu (or Karnak) Block lies above 4,000 m. It has a landscape that is different from the rest of the park and typical of the eastern plateau of Ladakh. The valley is broad, with a level floor up to 1 km wide, and bounded by open hills with relatively few cliffs. Shun-Shadi, which encompasses the Niri Chu and Shun catchments, is a remote and sparsely inhabited block lying above 3,800 m. The terrain is exceptionally rugged, with deep gorges, cliffs and steep broken slopes. There are two small lakes, unusual features in the mountains of central Ladakh (Mallon and Bacha, 1989).

Climate   The nearest meteorological station is Leh, 15 km north-east of the park's northern border. Mean annual precipitation in Leh is 10 mm. The mean minimum temperature in January, the coldest month, is −14 °C. Precipitation in the Shun-Shadi Block is probably higher, given its closer proximity to the main Himalayan Range, and the eastern parts of the park are drier (Mallon and Bacha, 1989). The Zanskar River and its tributaries become frozen during winter (Bacha, 1985), when temperatures drop typically to −15 °C to −20 °C at night and rise to near freezing point in daytime (Fox et al., 1986).

Vegetation   Much of central Ladakh is high altitude desert (Dhar and Kachroo, 1983) characterised by sparse grassland and herbaceous vegetation on mountain slopes, with shrublands and patchy forest in the valley bottoms (Hartmann, 1983). The park's vegetation is described by Mallon and Bacha (1989), and further details of that found in the Chang Chu are given by Fox et al. (1986).

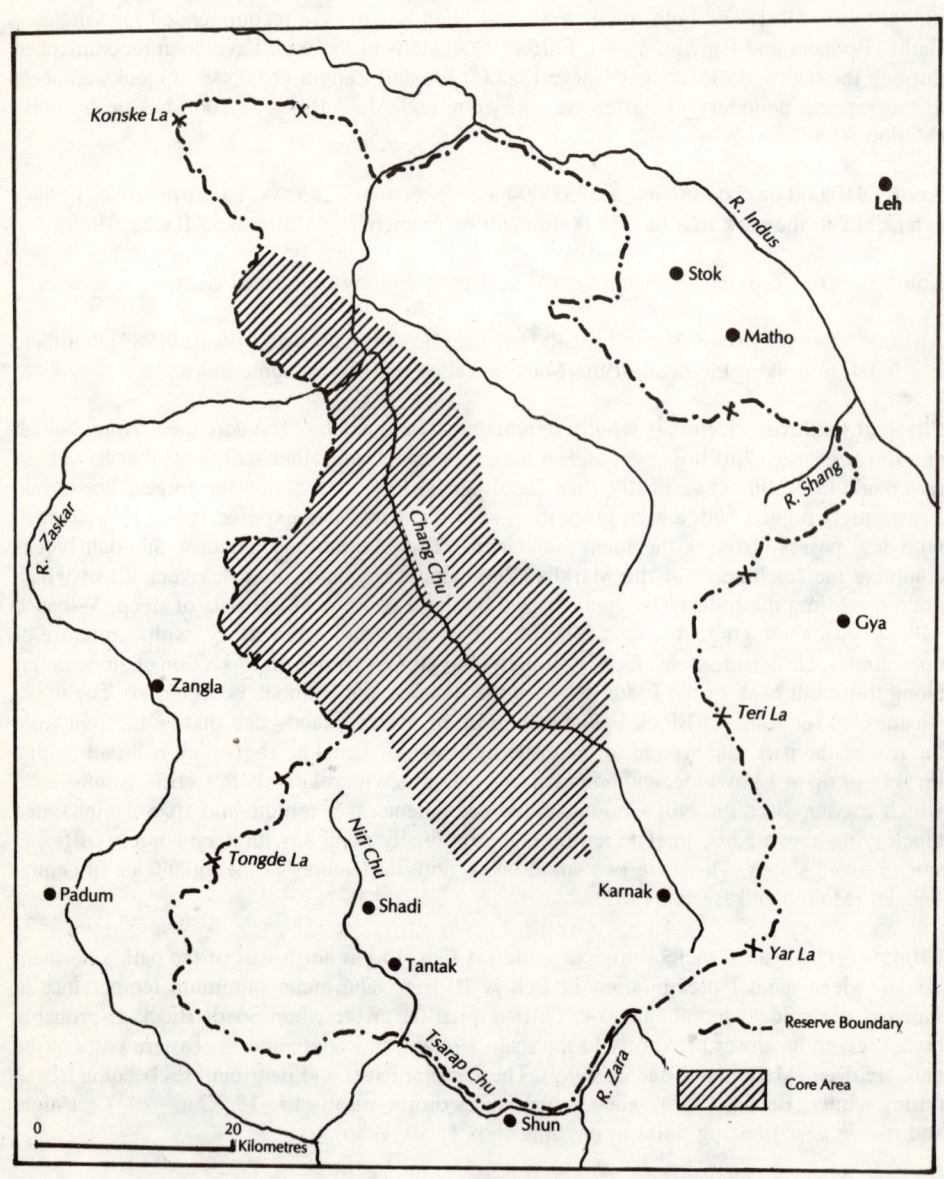

Hemis National Park

Trees are sparse, in common with the rest of Ladakh, and occur as isolated specimens, or as remnant open assemblies on hill slopes, and thin strips of riverine woods. The core area and the proposed Zanskar Gorge Block contain some of the best remaining fragments of a type of steppe juniper forest formerly common to many parts of central Asia. Characteristic species are *Juniperus macropoda* and *J. indica*, which occur as scattered trees on cliffs and high slopes up to 4,250 m, and form patches of open scrub in a few localities. Thin strips of riverine woodland are most extensive in the Chang Chu catchment. Principal species are *Salix karelinii* and *Myricaria squamosa*, with a few poplars *Populus euphratica*, birch *Betula utilis*, juniper, and other *Salix* species. Associated shrubs include *Hippophae rhamnoides*, *Rosa webbiana*, *Lonicera glauca*, and *Ribes alpestre*. Trees are cultivated in all settlements except in the upper Chang Chu. The species grown are chiefly willows, poplars *Hippophae* spp., apricot, and apple. The commonest arid steppe species in the park are *Artemisia* spp., *Caragana* spp., *Astragalus* spp., *Acantholimon lycopodioides*, *Aconogonum tortuosum*, *Krascheninnikovia ceratoides*, *Lonicera spinosa*, *Stachys tibetica*, *Ephedra gerardiana*, and *Cotoneaster* sp. Other associates include *Tanacetum gracile*, *Heracleum pinnatum*, *Crepis flexuosa* and *Nepeta* spp., *Rosa webbiana*, *Lonicera glauca*, and *Berberis* sp. form patches of scrub in a few places. A particularly arid community occurs along the northern edge of the park between the lower Zanskar and lower Rumbak valleys. This is characterised by *Ephedra gerardiana*, *Capparis spinosa*, and *Echinops cornigerus*. Common species occurring in damper locations on rocky slopes, alpine pastures, or in river valleys are *Inula obtusifolia*, *Saussurea jacea*, *Lindelofia anchusoides*, *Thermopsis inflata*, *Bergenia stracheyi*, *Biebersteinia odora*, *Nepeta glutinosa*, *Arnebia euchroma*, *Aquilegia moorcroftiana*, and species of *Taraxacum, Leontopodium, Gentiana, Gentianella,* and *Eritrichium,* along with species of *Carex, Stipa, Bromus,* and other grasses and sedges. In the wettest areas are *Euphrasia* sp., *Pedicularis longiflora*, *P. bicornuta* and, rarely, the Himalayan purple orchid *Dactylorhiza hatagirea*. The vegetation thins out above 4,500 m, with snow-patch plants and a few alpine species persisting to 5,000 m and above. These include *Delphinium cashmerianum*, *Glechoma tibetica*, *Silene longicarpophora*, *Saussurea gnaphalodes*, *Potentilla fruticosa*, *Thylacospermum caespitosum*, and *Nepeta* spp. (Mallon and Bacha, 1989). A list of 314 plant species recorded in the catchment of Rumbak Nallah is given by Chundawat (1990).

Fauna Hemis is a stronghold for Ladakh's mammals, most species of which are threatened elsewhere in their range. Some 16 species have been recorded, including wolf *Canis lupus* (V) (widespread), wild dog *Cuon alpinus* (V), lynx *Felis lynx* (rare), snow leopard *Panthera uncia* (E), Tibetan wild ass *Equus (hemionus) kiang* (V), ibex *Capra ibex*, bharal *Pseudois nayaur*, Tibetan argali *Ovis ammon hodgsoni*, and Ladakh urial *O. orientalis vignei*. Smaller mammals are large-eared pika *Ochotona macrotis,* woolly hare *Lepus oiostolus,* Himalayan marmot *Marmota bobak,* altai weasel *Mustela altaica,* stone marten *Martes foina* and otter *Lutra lutra* (Mallon and Bacha, 1989). Snow leopard occurs at a low density. The total population is estimated at 75–120 individuals, being densest in the Chang Chu catchment of the core area. Bharal is widespread throughout the park, with the highest density of 1.3 animals per sq. km recorded in Shang Valley. The total population is estimated at 2,600–5,300 (Mallon and Bacha, 1986). Urial is restricted to the northern part of the park where 226 animals were recorded in 1984. The distribution of ibex in the park is limited to the high parts of Sumdah Valley and Shun-Shadi Block. An isolated herd of 6–12 argali still lives in the vicinity of Ganda La, the pass between the Rumbak and Markha valleys. These are descendants of a small group which wandered into the area 15–20 years ago, the limit of the normal range of this species being some 75 km to the north-east (Bacha, 1985; Fox et al., 1986; Mallon and Bacha, 1989).

A total of 73 bird species has been recorded of which 47 are known or presumed to breed in the park. All breeding species common to the mountains of Ladakh are present; less common breeding species include great rosefinch *Carpodacus rubicilla*, eastern great rosefinch *C. rubicilloides*, red-mantled rosefinch *C. rhodochlamys*, and Guldenstadt's redstart *Phoenicurus erythrogaster*. Thick stands of *Hippophae rhamnoides* and other vegetation provide important habitat for large numbers of wintering passerines such as some of the above species, as well as black-throated thrush *Turdus ruficollis*, Stoliczka's tit-warbler *Leptopoecile sophiae*, robin accentor *Prunella rubeculoides*, and brown accentor *P. fulvescens*. Unusual passage migrants include the first recordings in Ladakh of great grey shrike *Lanius excubitor*, spotted flycatcher *Muscicapa striata*, and red-flanked bluetail *Tarsiger cyanurus*. There are no extensive wetlands in the park but a few species of ducks have been seen on the Zanskar River in spring and migrating teal *Anas crecca* sighted in the Markha and Chu valleys (Mallon and Bacha, 1989).

Amphibians are absent, but reptiles are represented by three species of lizard: *Agama himalayana* (numerous), *Scincella ladacensis* (sparsely distributed), and *Phrynocephalus theobaldi*, which is restricted to stony desert in the north of the park (Mallon and Bacha, 1989).

Cultural Heritage   The local residents are Buddhists. There is a monastery at Markha Village. Hemis Gompa, reputedly the largest and weathiest monastery in Ladakh, lies just outside the northern boundary.

Local Human Population   The park has some 1,600 residents distributed among 23 settlements, but there are no permanent settlements in the core area. In addition, people from outside the park use its resources, particularly for grazing. Most residents are engaged in both agriculture and pastoralism, while those in the upper Chang Chu follow a semi-nomadic existence typical of the eastern plateau of Ladakh. Less than 1% of the park's total area is cultivated, the main crops being barley and peas. All families own some domestic livestock. Traditional grazing rights are respected, preventing degradation of pastures from overgrazing trees, where available, and shrubs are used for timber, fuel, and winter fodder. *Artemisia*, *Caragana* and *Acantholimon* shrubs are commonly used for fuel, and *Aconogonum tortuosum* and *Stachys tibetica* as winter fodder. Animal dung is also used for fuel, precluding its use as fertiliser on fields or pastures (Mallon and Bacha, 1989). A breakdown of the numbers of families and livestock for each village in the Rumbak and Markha valleys is given by Department of Wildlife Protection (n.d.), and further details of resource use in this part of the park are provided by Fox et al. (1986).

Visitors and Visitor Facilities   Many tourists visit the park for trekking in summer. Most of these follow the popular route through the Markha, Shang and Rumbak valleys. Visitors to Sumdah are expected to increase following the construction of a road up the Zanskar Valley (Mallon and Bacha, 1989). There are no facilities but some dormitory and tented accommodation has been proposed (Bacha, 1985).

Scientific Research and Facilities   Censuses of the large mammal populations were conducted by the Department of Wildlife Protection in 1979 (Department of Wildlife Protection, n.d.) and 1984 (Bacha, 1985). In particular, research has focused on snow leopard and its prey species, with studies carried out in 1980–6 by Mallon (1983, 1984, 1987b, 1991), in 1986 by Fox et al. (1986), and in 1988–90 by Chundawat (1990). There are no scientific facilities.

Conservation Value   Hemis is the largest protected area in the Indian Himalaya. Its large size and maximal altitudinal range, from valley floors to mountain peaks, ensure that it is fully representative of the Transhimalayan ecosystem of central Ladakh. Important features are the remnant patches of juniper scrub and riverine woodland, snow leopard and associated prey populations, and an uninhabited and little-disturbed core area (Mallon and Bacha, 1989). It has been earmarked as one of several snow leopard reserves under a project launched by Central Government and aimed at conserving the species, its prey populations, and its fragile mountain habitat (MEF, 1988).

Conservation Management   The first management plan for the period 1986–7 to 1989–90 relates to the original park area as notified in 1981 (Bacha, 1985). Emphasis is given to developing ways to enable residents to continue living in the park that are compatible with conservation objectives, but confining their activities to buffer areas. Subsequently, the Chang Chu catchment was identified as an ideal core of a much larger park because of the prime snow leopard and bharal habitat that is relatively inaccessible and subject to low intensities of human use (Fox et al., 1986). Following the extension of the park, a management plan was outlined by Mallon and Bacha (1989). Immediate objectives are to develop the park infrastructure, eliminate current land use and disturbance in the core area, and to develop strategies in consultation with local people for managing resources in the buffer zone for the benefit of residents but without detriment to the habitat. A reduction in grazing and the establishment of fuelwood plantations are also priorities. Recommendations have also been made to extend both the core and buffer zones, and to designate the park as a biosphere reserve.

Management Constraints   In general, the human population in and around the park is low, most pressure on natural resources being in the Markha and Sumdah blocks to the north, where 60% of the resident population is concentrated and where land use is most intensive. An additional 5,000 people live in the area adjacent to the northern border between Martselang and Stok. It is along this border that the park is most vulnerable to hunting (Mallon and Bacha, 1989). There is substantial interaction between local people and wildlife with, for example, some competition between domestic sheep and goats and bharal for food. Snow leopards and wolves commonly prey on livestock. Between March 1985 and March 1986, these two species are reported to have killed about 130 sheep and goats, and 10 yak and yak–cow hybrids. The routine killing of livestock by snow leopard is generally accepted without complaint because carcasses can usually be retrieved and used as meat, but when a snow leopard gets into a closed pen and kills 30–40 sheep and goats it is killed (Fox et al., 1986).

A major threat to the core area is the proposed continuation of the new road up the Zanskar Valley through to Padum. This would involve blasting a route through the core area and Zanskar Gorge (proposed as an extension to the park), bringing road access to the remotest and least-disturbed part of Ladakh (Mallon and Bacha, 1989).

Staff   The park infrastructure is negligible (Mallon and Bacha, 1989). A director, supported by one range officer, three block officers, thirty wildlife guards, and seven administrative and other staff, were proposed for 1985.

Budget   A capital outlay of Rs 28 lakhs, shared on a 50:50 basis by State and Central Government, was proposed for the four-year period beginning in 1986–7. Recurrent expenditure was estimated at Rs 458,765 per year.

Local Addresses   Range Officer (Wildlife), Department of Wildlife Protection, Leh

References

Bacha, M.S. (1985). *Ecological cum management plan for Hemis High Altitude National Park, Jammu and Kashmir State, 1985–90*. Department of Wildlife Protection, Jammu & Kashmir Government, Srinagar. 31 pp.

Chundawat, R.S. (1990). The ecological studies of snow leopard and its associated prey species in Hemis High Altitude National Park, Ladakh. *Technical Report* no. RR-1. Wildlife Institute of India, Dehra Dun. 27 pp.

Dhar, U. and Kachroo, P. (1983). *Alpine flora of Kashmir Himalaya*. Scientific Publisher, Jodhpur.

Department of Wildlife Protection (n.d.). *Status survey report of notified and proposed national parks, sanctuaries and reserves in Ladakh region*. Department of Wildlife Protection, Jammu & Kashmir Government, Srinagar. 29pp.

Department of Wildlife Protection (1987). Proposal for extension of the Hemis High Altitude National Park. Department of Wildlife Protection, Jammu & Kashmir Government, Srinagar. Unpublished. 7 pp.

Fox, J.L., Sinha, S.P., Chundawat, R.S. and Das, P.K. (1986). A survey of snow leopard and associated species in the Himalaya of northwestern India. Project Completion Report. Wildlife Institute of India, Dehra Dun. Unpublished. 51 pp.

Hartmann, H. (1983). Pflanzengesellschaften entlang der Kashmirroute in Ladakh. *Jahrbuch Verein zum Schutz der Bergwelt* 1983: 131–73.

Mallon, D. (1983). The status of Ladakh urial *Ovis orientalis vignei* in Ladakh, India. *Biological Conservation* 27: 373–81.

Mallon, D. (1984). The snow leopard in Ladakh. *International Pedigree Book of Snow Leopards* 4: 23–37.

Mallon, D.P. (1986). Extensions to the Hemis High Altitude National Park, Ladakh. Report to the Department of Wildlife Prptection, Jammu & Kashmir Government, Srinagar. Unpublished. 19 pp. (Unseen)

Mallon, D.P. (1987a). An ecological survey of the Hemis High Altitude National Park, proposed extension and Shun-shadi Sanctuary Report to the Department of Wildlifem Protection, Jammu & Kashmir Government, Srinagar. Unpublished. 16 pp.

Mallon, D.P. (1987b). An ecological study of the snow leopard in Ladakh. M.Sc.Thesis, University of Manchester, Manchester, UK. 107 pp.

Mallon, D.P. (1991). Status and conservation of large mammals in Ladakh. *Biological Conservation* 56: 101–19.

Mallon, D.P. and Bacha, M.S. (1989). Ecology and management of the Hemis National Park, proposed extensions and Shun-Shadi Sanctuary. Report to the Department of Wildlife Protection, Jammu & Kashmir Government, Srinagar. Unpublished. 42 pp.

MEF (1988). *The snow leopard conservation scheme*. Ministry of Environment and Forests, Government of India, New Delhi. 27 pp.

HIRAPORA SANCTUARY

IUCN Management Category   IV   (Managed Nature Reserve).

Biogeographical Province   2.13.12   (Himalayan Highlands)

Geographical Location Lies in the Pir Panjal Range, some 70 km south of Srinagar. Bounded to the north by Lake Gumsar, to the north-east by Hirapora Village, to the east by Rupri Forest, to the south by Lake Saransar and to the west by Pir Panjal Pass. 33°35′–33°40′N, 74°35′E

Date and History of Establishment Notified a sanctuary in 1987, having been a reserved forest within Shopian Forest Division.

Area 11,000 ha

Land Tenure Provincial government

Altitude Ranges from 2,557 m to 4,745 m.

Physical Features The slopes are gentle to moderately steep on the eastern side of the Pir Panjal divide and precipitous, with many cliffs, to the west and south. River beds consist of gravel, sand, and clay. Recent deposits form a great thickness of interstratified soft sand, stones, and partially hardened clay. Hilly tracts consist of schists, slates, limestone, and shales, together with Panjal trap which is of volcanic origins (Department of Wildlife Protection, 1987).

Climate The area is subject to the influence of the summer monsoon. Most precipitation falls as snow during winter (Department of Wildlife Protection, 1987).

Vegetation Six main vegetation types can be distinguished, namely: blue pine *Pinus griffithii* forests in dry and exposed aspects, with silver fir *Abies pindrow* and spruce *Picea smithiana*; silver fir forests, with blue pine and spruce, which forms the largest component of the vegetation and is confined to cooler, moister aspects; evergreen (e.g. *Juniperus* spp.), or deciduous (e.g. *Rosa* spp.) scrub in the middle and lower zones, respectively; birch *Betula utilis* forest, with an understorey of *Juniperus* spp. and *Rhododendron campanulatum*; alpine pastures; and, at highest altitudes, rock plants (Department of Wildlife Protection, 1987).

Fauna The fauna is impoverished due to habitat destruction, extensive grazing and heavy poaching. The sanctuary supports the largest population of markhor *Capra falconeri* (V) remaining in the State, the other smaller populations being restricted to the catchments of the Limber and Lachipora in Jhelum Valley Forest Division. Other animals recorded during recent surveys include rhesus macaque *Macaca mulatta*, fox *Vulpes vulpes*, common otter *Lutra lutra*, yellow-throated marten *Martes flavigula* and Royle's pika *Ochotona roylei*. Some 39 common species of birds have also been recorded (Department of Wildlife Protection, 1987).

Cultural Heritage No information

Local Human Population Graziers from Rajouri and Poonch bring their livestock to graze in the area (Department of Wildlife Protection, 1987).

Visitors and Visitor Facilities No information

Scientific Research and Facilities   No scientific research has been undertaken, other than a preliminary inventory of the fauna (Department of Wildlife Protection, 1987). There are no scientific facilities.

Conservation Value   The area is important primarily for its markhor population (Department of Wildlife Protection, 1987).

Conservation Management   No information

Management Constraints   The area is heavily disturbed and poaching is a problem (Department of Wildlife Protection, 1987).

Staff   No information

Budget   No information

Local Addresses   No information

References
Department of Wildlife Protection (1987). Status survey report of the proposed Hirapora Wildlife Sanctuary. Department of Wildlife Protection, Srinagar. Unpublished. 6 pp.

HOKARSAR SANCTUARY

IUCN Management Category   IV (Managed Nature Reserve)

Biogeographical Province   2.38.12 (Himalayan Highlands)

Geographical Location   Lies in the Vale of Kashmir, 10 km west of Srinagar, Badgam District. Approximately 34°05′N, 74°43′E

Date and History of Establishment   Originally established as a game reserve but recently upgraded to sanctuary status.

Area   1,000 ha

Land Tenure   The lake is state owned, but surrounding agricultural land is owned by local villagers.

Altitude   1,584 m.

Physical Features   Comprises a permanent eutrophic lake, once an ox-bow, surrounded by freshwater marshes on the floodplain of the Jhelum River. The lake is drained by a channel to the Jhelum River at Sozeth Narbal Village and is fed by two perennial streams (Doodhganga and Sukhnag) and flood waters. It reaches a maximum depth of 2.5 m in spring with snow-melt water, and a minimum of 0.7 m in autumn. The water is very turbid with little light penetration.

Underlying soils are of a silty-clayey loam type. The phH is greatly affected by the high summer temperatures which accelerate the process of decay of organic matter (Scott, 1989).

Climate   Conditions are sub-mediterranean with very warm, relatively dry summers (May to August) and cold, wet winters (October to March) with some precipitation falling as snow. Mean annual precipitation is 550 mm, most of which falls between January and March. Mean temperatures range from 7.5 °C in winter to 19.8 °C in summer (Scott, 1989).

Vegetation   The marsh vegetation is dominated by *Typha angustata, T. laximanii, Phragmites communis, Eleocharis palustris*, and *Butomus umbellatus. Trapa natans* occurs in open water areas. At least 156 species of phytoplankton have been recorded, with Chlorophyceae predominating. There are many floating gardens in the lake, plantations of *Salix alba* along the shoreline and rice paddies in surrounding areas (Scott, 1989).

Fauna   Otter *Lutra lutra* is still fairly common in the lake, and other mammals known to occur in the sanctuary include fox *Vulpes vulpes* and jackal *Canis aureus* (Scott, 1989).

The lake is particularly important as a wintering area for migratory ducks and as a breeding area for herons, egrets and rails. Up to 25,000 wintering ducks have been recorded at one time; the common species are wigeon *Anas penelope* (maximum 7,000), gadwall *A. strepera* (5,000), common teal *A. crecca* (10,000), mallard *A. platyrhynchos* (15,000), pintail *A. acuta* (15,000), shoveler *A. clypeata* (5,000), red-crested pochard *Netta rufina* (2,000), pochard *Aythya ferina* (10,000) and ferrugineous duck *A. nyroca* (1,000). Up to 10,000 greylag goose *Anser anser*, 100 ruddy shelduck *Tadorna ferruginea*, 10 crane *Grus grus*, and 5,000 common coot *Fulica atra* have also been reported in winter, and up to 3,000 garganey *Anas querquedula* occur on migration. Breeding species include little grebe *Tachybaptus ruficollis* (up to 1,000) little bittern *Ixobrychus minutus*, black-crowned night heron *Nycticorax nycticorax* (100), little egret *Egretta garzetta* (400), grey heron *Ardea cinerea* (500), water rail *Rallus aquaticus*, moorhen *Gallinula chloropus* (500), and pheasant-tailed jacana *Hydrophasanius chirurgus* (100). Pallas's fish-eagle *Haliaeetus leucoryphus* is resident in the area and kingfishers *Alcedo atthis, Halcyon smyrnensis*, and *Ceryle rudis* are common (Scott, 1989). Holmes et al. (1983) recorded a remarkably high number (130) of greenshank *Tringa nebularia* in 1983.

The lake supports a rich fish fauna, including *Cyprinus carpio, Crosso cheilus, Barbus conchonius*, and *Gambusia affinis*. The zooplankton includes at least 44 species of protozoans, 19 rotiferans and 38 crustaceans (mainly Cladocera and Rhizopoda) (Scott, 1989).

Cultural Heritage   No information

Local Human Population   The lake supports a small fishery and reed-cutting industry, and provides a source of water for irrigation. The harvesting of waterfowl populations used to provide a source of protein for local consumers (Scott, 1989).

Visitors and Visitor Facilities   The lake provides opportunities for nature-oriented outdoor recreation such as bird-watching.

Scientific Research and Facilities   Biologists from the Department of Botany, University of Kashmir, have conducted a considerable amount of limnological and ecological research at Hokarsar, including studies of mineral composition, biogeochemical cycling, plankton, biomass, productivity, trophic structure, ecology of macrophytes, and feeding ecology of breeding birds (Scott, 1989), including mallard (Shah and Qadri, 1988). The Department of Wildlife Protection has conducted waterfowl counts.

Conservation Value   The sanctuary is an important wetland for both resident and migratory waterfowl, and is of considerable scientific interest. It is also of socio-economic importance to the local people (Scott, 1989).

Conservation Management   Waterfowl hunting was allowed on a controlled basis in winter, and the harvesting of reeds permitted in summer, prior to **Hokarsar's** upgrading to sanctuary status. Management to date has included the construction of bunds and installation of a sluice gate to control water levels. Various proposals have been made for management of the lake, including the cutting of weeds, dredging, raising of bunds, diversion of the Doodhganga Flood Channel to reduce siltation, and erection of a perimeter fence (Scott, 1989).

Management Constraints   The main threats are increased siltation, eutrophication and the encroachment of agricultural land into the peripheral marshes. Some 400 ha of the lake have already been reclaimed for agricultural purposes, and the paucity of cultivable land in the region is likely to lead to further reclamation as population pressure mounts. Fertilisers used on nearby agricultural land enter the lake in run-off and accelerate the rate of eutrophication. The lake receives a heavy load of silt from the Dudhganga catchment area, and the expanses of open water are decreasing in size as reed-beds colonise the silt. Cattle grazing occurs in and around the marshes and rice is grown in the surrounding areas (Scott, 1989).

Staff   No information.

Budget   No information

Local Addresses   No information

References
Holmes, P.R., Holmes, H.J. and Parr, A.J. (Eds.) (1983). Report of the Oxford University Expedition to Kashmir, 1983. Liverpool School of Tropical Medicine, Liverpool. Unpublished. 126 pp.
Scott, D.A. (Ed.) (1989), *A directory of Asian wetlands*. IUCN, Gland, Switzerland and Cambridge, UK. Pp. 390–2.
Shah, G.M. and Qadri, M.Y. (1988). Food of mallard, *Anas platyrhynchos* at Hokarsar wetland, Kashmir. *Journal of the Bombay Natural History Society* 85: 325-31.

HYGAM GAME RESERVE

IUCN Management Category   Unassigned

Biogeographical Province   2.38.12 (Himalayan Highlands)

Geographical Location   Lies at the southern end of Lake Wular in the Vale of Kashmir, some 50 km west of Srinagar. The reserve is surrounded by a protective bank. Approximately 34°15′N, 74°30′E

Date and History of Establishment   No information.

Area   1,400 ha

Land Tenure   Provincial government.

Altitude   Approximately 1,580 m.

Physical Features   Hygam is the largest of the few remaining reed beds in the Vale of Kashmir. The reed bed is partitioned by a series of boat channels varying in width from 1 m to 4 m. Water in the *rakh* (marsh) varies in depth from 0.5 m to 1.0 m (Holmes et al., 1983).

Climate   Conditions in the Vale of Kashmir are temperate, often with heavy snowfalls in winter. The Vale is largely shielded from the influence of the south-west monsoon in summer by the Pir Panjal Range. Mean annual precipitation is 900 mm (Scott, 1989). Mean maximum temperatures range from 4.4 °C to 30.8 °C and mean minimum temperatures from −2.3 °C to 18.4 °C in January and July, respectively (Directorate of Tourism, 1986).

Vegetation   The *rakh* is covered largely by a dense growth of reeds and other emergent species. Common species are sedges *Carex* spp., common reed *Phragmites communis*, bulrush *Typha angustata*, bur-reed *Sparganium erectum*, club rushes *Scirpus lacustris* and *S. palustris*, and spike rush *Eleocharis palustris*. In open areas there are water lilies *Nymphaea stellata* and *N. alba*, fringed water lily *Nymphoides pellata*, and water chestnut *Trapa natans*. Inside the emban kment a strip of willows *Salix* sp. has been planted, while outside it (and in some places inside) most of the land is devoted to rice paddy (Holmes et al., 1983; Holmes and Parr, 1988).

Fauna   The *rakh* is noted for its variety of wetland birds. A total of 92 species of birds were recorded in 1978, 1983 and 1984, 45% of which are passage migrants and/or winter visitors (Holmes et al., 1983; Holmes and Parr, 1988). Noteworthy species include little bittern *Ixobrychus minutus*, Baillon's crake *Porzana pusilla*, whiskered tern *Chlidonias hybrida*, brown-fronted pied woodpecker *Dendrocopos auriceps*, and blunt-winged warbler *Acrocephalus concinens*, all of which breed or are suspected to breed in the *rakh*. Densities of little bittern, water rail *Rallus aquaticus*, common kingfisher *Alcedo atthis*, and clamorous reed warbler *Acrocephalus stentoreus* are particularly high. Details of the waterfowl are given by Scott (1989).

Cultural Heritage   No information

Local Human Population   The *rakh* is surrounded by villages, including Hanjypura near to its edge. Local people use the *rakh* for many purposes, some legitimate and others illegal. Activities include fishing, grazing cattle, cutting reeds for fodder and thatch, and cultivating rice. Reed cutting is carried out on a much larger scale by contractors (Holmes et al., 1983).

Visitors and Visitor Facilities   Hygam is visited by sportsmen in the open season. There is a Government rest house, known as Tippenshed, near Hanjypura.

Scientific Research and Facilities   Since Hygam is a shooting reserve, numbers of winter birds (especially ducks) are probably well documented. The first comprehensive survey of summer bird populations was conducted by Holmes (1979). This was followed up by a study of breeding birds including a detailed investigation of the breeding ecology of the little bittern (Holmes et al., 1983; Holmes and Hatchwell, 1991; Holmes and Parr, 1988). Other research includes studies of trophic structure (Pandit and Kaul, 1981), production (Kaul, 1982), freshwater snail ecology (Kaul et al., 1980) and feeding ecology of breeding birds (Pandit, 1982). There are no scientific facilities.

Conservation Value   Hygam is a site of outstanding importance for breeding marshland birds and as a staging ground for large numbers of migrant birds in autumn. Its renewable resources provide a living to many local people and, as a well-managed shooting reserve, it provides an income to the Department of Wildlife Protection. With strict management, there need be no conflict between these three functions (Holmes et al., 1983; Holmes and Parr, 1988; Scott, 1989).

Conservation Management   Measures taken by the Department of Wildlife Protection to control silt input to the system include construction of silt traps in several of the smaller inflow streams, construction of dykes to divert silt-laden water and planting willows to trap silt. Some clearing of reed beds and dredging of boat channels is also recommended (Holmes et al., 1983; Holmes and Parr, 1988). There is no management plan.

Management Constraints   The major long-term threat is siltation, high silt loads reflecting widespread deforestation in the surrounding hills. Human exploitation needs to be controlled. Local harvesting of reeds is not considered to be a threat, but large-scale harvesting by contractors results in areas being cleared and nests destroyed. Grazing of cattle causes some damage to reed beds. Perhaps the most insidious problem is the encroachment of rice paddy (Holmes et al., 1983; Holmes and Parr, 1988).

Staff   No information

Budget   No information

Local Addresses   Hygam Game Reserve Office, Hanjypura, Jammu and Kashmir

References

Directorate of Tourism (1986). *Tourism directory*. Department of Tourism, Srinagar. 131 pp.

Holmes, P. (Ed.) (1979). Report of the Oxford ornithological expedition to Kashmir, 1978. Unpublished. 63 pp.

Holmes, P.R. and Hatchwell, B.J. (1991). Notes on the ecology of the little bittern *Ixobrychus minutus* at Haigam Rakh, Kashmir, India. *Forktail* 6: 25–33.

Holmes, P.R. and Parr, A.J. (1988). A checklist of the birds of Haigam Rakh, Kashmir. *Journal of the Bombay Natural History Society* 85: 465–73.

Holmes, P.R., Holmes, H.J. and Parr, A.J. (Eds.) (1983). Report of the Oxford University Expedition to Kashmir, 1983. Liverpool School of Tropical Medicine, Liverpool. Unpublished. 126 pp.

Kaul, S. (1982). Community architecture, biomass and production in some typical wetlands of Kashmir. *Indian Journal of Ecology* 9: 320–9. (Unseen)

Kaul, V., Pandit, A.K. and Fotedar, D.N. (1980). Ecology of freshwater snails (gastropod molluscs) in Haigam—a typical wetland of Kashmir. *Tropical Ecology* 21: 32–46. (Unseen)

Pandit, A. (1982). Feeding ecology of breeding birds in five wetlands of Kashmir. *Indian Journal of Ecology* 9: 181–90. (Unseen)

Pandit, A.K. and Kaul, V. (1981). Trophic structure of some typical wetlands. *International Journal of Ecology and Environmental Science* 7: 55–82. (Unseen)

Scott, D.A. (Ed.) (1989). *A directory of Asian wetlands*. IUCN, Gland, Switzerland and Cambridge, UK. 1,181 pp.

JALDAPARA SANCTUARY

IUCN Management Category IV (Managed Nature Reserve).

Biogeographical Province 4.03.01 (Bengalian Rainforest).

Geographical Location Lies in the terai region of Jalpaiguri District, about 45 km north-west of Cooch Behar. Approximately 26°40'N, 89°20'E.

Date and History of Establishment Designated a sanctuary on 13 March 1941 under Government Order no. 10549, which was later amended by Notification no. 5238 on 3 April 1943.

Area 11,553 ha, having been enlarged from its original size of 10,454 ha.

Land Tenure State.

Altitude Ranges from 60 m to 140 m (Naranyan et al., 1989).

Physical Features The entire sanctuary lies in a level flood plain. The sanctuary is shaped like a pair of trousers. The western leg used to be drained by the Torsa River, which rises in Tibet and then flows across Bhutan before entering the Brahmaputra near Cooch Behar, and the eastern leg by the Malangi River which became the Siltorsa in the southern part of the sanctuary (Spillett, 1967). The Torsa continues to flow through the western leg but the Melangi has now merged into it (Narayan, 1989). There is a network of interconnecting water channels which are constantly changing, new channels being cut during the annual flood season. Floods can be serious, with entire forests washed downstream and vast amounts of silt deposited in their wake. Soils consist mainly of a deep bed of sand, superimposed by a thin layer of light, friable loam, all of which has been washed down from the Himalaya (Spillett, 1967).

Climate Jaldapara is situated in a moist tropical zone, with much of the annual precipitation of 4,191 mm falling during the monsoon (May–September). Mean daily temperatures range from 15 °C to 21 °C in winter (November–February), from 26 °C to 32 °C in the monsoon, and from 24 °C to 27 °C during the rest of the year. Severe winter storms are common between April and May and occasional in September and October (Spillett, 1967).

Vegetation Consists mainly of riverine forests, with grasslands or savanna, maintained by burning and flooding. 20–30% of the sanctuary is grassland (Narayan, 1989). A narrow fringe of deciduous forests, composed of more or less pure stands of khair *Acacia catechu* or sissu *Dalbergia sissoo* occurs along many rivers. In slightly more stable areas, khair and sissu are succeeded by pure or mixed stands of such species as silk cotton or simul *Bombax ceiba* and siris *Albizzia* spp., usually accompanied by numerous other species, such as sidha

Lagerstroemia parviflora, tun *Cedrela toona*, gamar *Gmelina arborea*, pitali *Trewia nudiflora*, kainjal *Bischofia javanica*, and kadam *Anthocephalus cadamba*. Where the water table is not low, almost pure stands of pitali and kainjal occur, with the occasional chalta *Dillenia indica* and other species. Along river beds, adjoining dry mixed forests or plateau-like areas where the permanent water table is fairly low, tanki *Bauhinia purpurea* is often predominant. Mixed forests occur in more stable areas and are dominated by trees such as harra *Grewia laevigata* and barkaule *Casearia graveolens*. Sal *Shorea robusta* is confined to the east bank of the Malangi in the northern and extreme southern portions of the sanctuary. The most common shrub is boroi or kool *Zizyphus mauritana* var. *fruticosa*. With fire protection, *Macaranga denticulata*, *Alphia alughas*, *Trema orientalis* and other species spread rapidly, particularly in damp areas. Assamlota *Eupatorium* spp., the most common weeds, are associated both with trees and other vegetation. Kowcha *Mucuna prurita*, a herbaceous climber which often kills trees, is quite common. Mikania *Mikania cordata* is becoming a problem in some areas and charchare *Vitis* spp., or *Cissus adnata*, is also present. Cassia or khasila *Saccharum spontaneum* is one of the primary colonisers of new riverine accretions. This grass is commonly found on sandy soils, but may also be encountered in clay pockets, as are dachla or khagri *Phragmites karka* and *Saccharum procerum*. Other grasses include *Erianthus elephantinus*, *Anthistiria gigantea*, *Andropogon nardus*, *Arundinella brasiliensis*, *Arundo donax*, *Paspalidium punctatum*, and *Sacciolepis myosuroides* (Spillett, 1967).

Fauna   Jaldapara is an important refuge of the Indian rhinoceros *Rhinoceros unicornis* (E), numbers of which appear to have dwindled from an estimated 72 in 1964 (Spillett, 1967) to 22 in 1980 (Chowdhuary and Ghosh, 1984). It also contains small populations of tiger *Panthera tigris* (E), sloth bear *Melursus ursinus* (I), swamp deer *Cervus duvauceli* (E), and gaur *Bos gaurus* (V), and good numbers of wild boar *Sus scrofa*, Indian muntjac *Muntiacus muntjak*, hog deer *Cervus porcinus*, spotted deer *Cervus axis*, and sambar *C. unicolor*. Leopard *Panthera pardus* (T) and elephant *Elephas maximus* (E) are occasional. Spillett (1967) gives details of other mammals present.

Reptiles include Indian python *Python molurus* (V), common cobra *Naja naja*, and water monitor *Varanus salvator* (Spillett, 1967).

There is a good variety of birds. Jaldapara was the last known locality for the Bengal florican *Houbaropsis bengalensis* (E) in West Bengal (Ali et al., 1985). The status of this species within the sanctuary was uncertain until recently when a few birds were seen. The population is estimated at up to 10 individuals (Narayan et al., 1989).

Cultural Heritage   Tribal people live in the surrounding area.

Local Human Population   The sanctuary is uninhabited but adjacent land is densely populated (Seshadri, 1986).

Visitors and Visitor Facilities   A range of accommodation is available: the Madarihat tourist lodge, Hollong and Borodbari forest bungalows and a youth hostel. There are no motorable roads within the sanctuary; visitors travel on elephant back.

Scientific Research and Facilities   Wildlife censuses were carried out in 1964, 1965 and 1966 (Spillett, 1967). The rhinoceros population was last censused in 1980 (Chowdhuary and Ghosh, 1984). Jaldapara was included in a status survey of the Bengal florican in 1985 (Ali et al., 1985) and subsequently in 1988 and 1989 (Narayan et al., 1989).

Upper alpine zone habitat, looking towards the 7,245m peak of Langtang Lirung from Ya La, Langtang National Park, Nepal. (*M. J. B. Green*)

The rugged terrain which forms the typical summer habitat of the Ibex *Capra ibex*, Baufo, Gilgit District, Pakistan. (*R. Hess*)

Limnological research vessel, Lake Issyk-Kul', Issyk-Kul'skiy Zapovednik (State Nature Reserve), Kirghizia, USSR. (*Russian Science & Culture Centre, New Delhi*)

Subtropical forest cover, Margalla Hills National Park, Pakistan.   (*IUCN, Islamabad*)

Alpine meadows, looking towards the Zailiisky Alatau mountain range, Alma-Atinskiy Zapovednik (State Nature Reserve), Kazakhstan, USSR.   (*Russian Science & Culture Centre, New Delhi*)

Conservation Value   Jaldapura, together with the nearby Buxa Sanctuary, is one of the most important areas in northern India, providing a refuge for potentially viable populations of several threatened species (tiger, elephant, rhinoceros, swamp deer, gaur, and wild buffalo, as well as certain lesser cats, hispid hare and Bengal florican) and critical as a corridor for wildlife moving between Bhutan and Assam (Rodgers and Panwar, 1988).

Conservation Management   The sanctuary was established primarily for the protection of the rhinoceros. All exploitation of natural resources is prohibited although, in practice, there have always been shortcomings. Past management practices included controlled burning, the **maintenance of firelines, and of glades for viewing wildlife** (Spillett, 1967). It is proposed that the sanctuary be extended to 37,300 ha and a core area of 10,000 ha be upgraded to national park status (Rodgers and Panwar, 1988).

Management Constraints   The sanctuary has always been under threat from the high densities of tribal and rural populations in the surrounding area, most of which is cultivated. Illegal grazing by domestic livestock continues to be the major problem, but also rhinos are poached and forest and grassland products are illegally collected for fuelwood, house construction and thatching, such resources having been largely depleted from the surrounding area (Spillett, 1967; Chowdhuary and Ghosh, 1984; Seshadri, 1986). During the 1962 Emergency, when the Chinese invaded Indian territory, the military established a camp at Boradabri along the north-eastern boundary. This has been a source of disturbance (Spillett, 1967). Human disturbance and grazing by cattle threaten the already sparse florican habitat (Narayan et al., 1989).

Staff   Headed by a divisional forest officer.

Budget   No information

Local Addresses   Divisional Forest Officer, Wildlife Division II, PO Jalpaiguri, West Bengal

References

Ali, S., Daniel, J.C., and Rahmani, A.R. (1985). Study of the ecology of certain endangered species of wildlife and their habitats. *The floricans. Annual Report 1, 1984–1985*. Bombay Natural History Society, Bombay. Pp. 79–84.

Chowdhuary, M.K. and Ghosh, S. (1984). Operation rhino—Jaldapara Sanctuary. *Indian Forester* 110: 1098–108.

Narayan, G., Sankaran, R., Rosalind, L., and Rahmani, A.R. (1989). The Floricans *Houbaropsis bengalensis* and *Sypheotides indica. Annual Report 1988–89*. Bombay Natural History Society. Pp. 22–3.

Rodgers, W.A. and Panwar, H.S. (1988). *Planning a wildlife protected area network in India*. 2 vols. Project FO: IND/82/003. FAO, Dehra Dun.

Seshadri, B. (1986). *India's wildlife and wildlife reserves*. Sterling, New Delhi. Pp. 106–9.

Spillett, J.J. (1967). A report on wild life surveys in North India and southern Nepal: the Jaldapara Wild Life Sancutary, West Bengal. *Journal of the Bombay Natural History Society* 63: 534–56.

KAIS SANCTUARY

IUCN Management Category   IV (Managed Nature Reserve).

Biogeographical Province   2.38.12 (Himalayan Highlands)

Geographical Location   Lies between Kulu and Manali townships in Kulu District, on the eastern side of the Beas River, and comprises Matikochar Forest. The eastern boundary runs approximately parallel to the Beas River but does not extend as far as it. 32°00'–32°03N', 77°09'–77°13'E

Date and History of Establishment   Notified as a sanctuary on 26 February 1954 under the Punjab Wild Birds and Wild Animals Protection Act 1933, but not renotified under the subsequent Wildlife (Protection) Act 1972.

Area   Notified as 1,419 ha, but re-estimated by IIPA/Environmental Studies Division (pers. comm.) as 1,220 ha using digitised maps.

Land Tenure   Provincial government. Local people exercise traditional rights.

Altitude   Ranges from 2,800 m to 3,680 m (Ramtu Peak).

Physical Features   Comprises the catchment area of Kais Nala which flows south-west until its confluence with Beas River. A check-dam has been built inside the sanctuary by the Forest · Department and a pipeline laid by the Irrigation Department.

Climate   The Manali area experiences a temperate climate characterised by cool summers and heavy snowfall in winter, regularly in excess of 1 m at 2,000 m. Snow remains from December to March and in January and February cold northerly winds keep temperatures low (Gaston et al., 1981). Mean annual precipitation is 1,071 mm. Temperature ranges from –5 °C to 30 °C (Singh et al., 1990).

Vegetation   An estimated 1,174 ha of the sanctuary is forested. Fir *Abies pindrow* and spruce *Picea smithiana*, with some oak *Quercus semecarpifolia* and cedar *Cedrus deodara*, predominate at lower altitudes, above which is birch *Betula utilis*–rhododendron *Rhododendron campanulatum* scrub forest (M.P. Sharma, pers. comm., 1987). A preliminary list of the flora is given by Singh et al. (1990).

Fauna   Large mammals reportedly include common langur *Presbytis entellus* (in troops of up to several hundreds), Himalayan black bear *Selenarctos thibetanus* (V), brown bear *Ursus arctos*, and leopard *Panthera pardus* (T) (M.P. Sharma, pers. comm., 1987). Other species listed by Singh et al. (1990) include Himalayan musk deer *Moschus chrysogaster* and Himalayan tahr *Hemitragus jemlahicus*. Indian muntjac *Muntiacus muntjak* and goral *Nemorhaedus goral* used to be present, but their current status is uncertain (W.A. Rodgers, pers. comm., 1987).

The avifauna is diverse. Pheasants include Himalayan monal *Lophophorus impejanus*, kalij *Lophura leucomelana*, and koklass *Pucrasia macrolopha*. Chukar partridge *Alectoris chukar* is also present (M.P. Sharma, pers. comm., 1987). Cheer pheasant *Catreus wallichii* (E) and western tragopan *Tragopan melanocephalus* (V) are listed by Singh et al. (1990).

Cultural Heritage   Pilgrims pass through the sanctuary annually in August to reach the shrine of Bijli Mahadev, situated just outside its southern border (Singh et al., 1990).

Local Human Population   There are no villages within the sanctuary but a number occur on the periphery. Three families of Gujjars graze their water buffalo in the sanctuary from May to September, one family owning 25 water buffalo and one cow. Villagers in adjacent areas also have grazing rights inside the sanctuary. Timber, fuelwood, medicinal plants and bark are collected by local people for domestic and commercial purposes (Hedau, n.d.).

Visitors and Visitor Facilities   There is a jeepable road from Naggar to Bijleemahadev, which is used by tourists, and a forest rest house at Matikochar. Three other rest houses are located outside the sanctuary.

Scientific Research and Facilities   None.

Conservation Value   Kais is a small, heavily disturbed sanctuary, but it reportedly holds populations of several species of pheasant including cheer and western tragopan (Singh et al., 1990).

Conservation Management   Traditional forms of land-use are practised under permits issued by Kulu Forest (Wildlife) Division. The entire sanctuary is open to grazing, apart from some plantations which have been fenced. There is no management plan (Singh et al., 1990).

Management Constraints   Considerable disturbance has been caused by clear-felling in many areas. Despite fencing, plantations have subsequently failed to become established due to inadequate protection. Forest fires are uncommon but much damage was caused by the last one in 1976. Bears and langurs regularly damage crops in areas peripheral to the sanctuary. Incidents of livestock-lifting by leopard are common and occasionally humans are mauled by bears (Hedau, 1987).

Staff   One guard is stationed at Matikochar Forest Rest House, but only in summer. The range officer at Manali takes overall responsibility for both Kais and Manali sanctuaries.

Budget   None allocated in 1987.

Local Addresses   Range Officer (Wildlife), PO Manali 175131, District Kulu, Himachal Pradesh

References
Gaston, A.J., Hunter, M.L. Jr., and Garson, P.J. (1981). The wildlife of Himachal Pradesh, Western Himalayas. *University of Maine School of Forest Resources Technical Notes* no. 82. 159 pp.
Hedau, S. (1987). Kais sanctuary. Indian Institute of Public Administration, State of National Parks and Sanctuaries in India Project. Unpublished. 2 pp.

Singh, S., Kothari, A. and Pande, P. (Eds.) (1990). *Directory of National Parks and sanctuaries in Himachal Pradesh*. Indian Institute of Public Administration, New Delhi. Pp. 36–8.

KALATOP-KHAJJIAR SANCTUARY

IUCN Management Category   IV (Managed Nature Reserve)

Biogeographical Province   2.38.12 (Himalayan Highlands)

Geographical Location   Lies between Dalhousie and Chamba townships at the north-western extremity of Daula Dhar in Chamba District. The Dalhousie–Chamba road runs through the sanctuary. 32°02′–32°04′N, 76°01′–76°06′E

Date and History of Establishment   Originally notified as a game sanctuary on 1 July 1949, and renotified on 29 August 1958 under the Indian Forest Act 1927 and Punjab Wild Birds and Wild Animals Protection Act 1933. Renotified again on 14 December 1982 (Singh et al., 1990).

Area   Notified as 2,027 ha, but re-estimated by the IIPA/Environmental Studies Division (pers. comm.) as 3,069 ha using digitised maps.

Land Tenure   Provincial government. Local people exercise traditional rights.

Altitude   Ranges from 1,185 m to 2,768 m.

Physical Features   The terrain is steep and typical of the Outer Himalaya. The sanctuary is drained by several tributaries of the Ravi River, which lies just to the north. There is a lake at Khajjiar.

Climate   Conditions are monsoonal. Mean annual precipitation is 2,648 mm, of which about 40% falls during the main monsoon period of July–August and 25% falls as snow. Temperatures range from − 10°C to 35 °C (Gaston et al., 1984; DFFC, 1984).

Vegetation   Most of the sanctuary is forested, the main types being ban oak *Quercus incana*, moist cedar *Cedrus deodara*, and western mixed coniferous interspersed with alpine pasture (DFFC, 1984). Cedar and blue pine *Pinus wallichiana* are predominant in lower altitude coniferous forest, and mixed with some moru oak *Quercus dilatata* and rhododendron *Rhododendron arboreum* (Gaston et al., 1979). A list of plants is given by Singh et al. (1990).

Fauna   Information about the fauna is scant. Common langur *Presbytis entellus*, leopard *Panthera pardus* (T), giant Indian flying squirrel *Petaurista petaurista*, and Indian porcupine *Hystrix indica* are present, as well as good numbers of Indian muntjac *Muntiacus muntjak* and goral *Nemorhaedus goral*. Himalayan black bear *Selenarctos thibetanus* (V) is also reported to be present (Gaston et al., 1981a, 1983). Goral is abundant (Cavallini, 1990). Other mammals listed by Singh et al. (1990) include leopard cat *Felis bengalensis*, jackal *Canis aureus*, Himalayan musk deer *Moschus chrysogaster*, and serow *Capricornis sumatraensis*.

Some 117 species of birds were recorded by Gaston et al. (1981a) in the Ravi Valley, including the Dalhousie–Chamba area. Published information specific to Kalatop-Khajjiar is limited to pheasants. Koklass pheasant *Pucrasia macrolopha* (with up to 14 males recorded at dawn counts nearby the Khajjiar Tourist Bungalow) and kalij pheasant *Lophura leucomelana* are both numerous. A single cheer pheasant *Catreus wallichii* (E) was recorded in the lowest part of the sanctuary and Himalayan monal *Lophophorus impejanus* reportedly visits in winter (Gaston et al., 1981a, 1981b).

Cultural Heritage There is a 'golden' domed temple of Naga Raja on the Khajjiar meadow, where an annual fair is attended by several hundred people (Singh et al., 1990).

Local Human Population There are 15 villages inside the sanctuary, having a total population of 1,766 people. The adjacent area has 35 villages with a population of 5,760. Some 135 ha are settled and cultivated. In 1982–3, the sanctuary's livestock population totalled 1,331 of which 223 belonged to residents, 430 to non-residents and 678 to Gujjars (Singh et al., 1990).

Visitors and Visitor Facilities In 1983–4, the sanctuary received 3,626 visitors. There is a tourist bungalow and rest house at Khajjiar and three other rest houses inside the sanctuary. There is a visitor centre outside the sanctuary at Banikher. One watchtower exists for wildlife viewing and more are under construction (Singh et al., 1990).

Scientific Research and Facilities Preliminary surveys of the wildlife were carried out in November 1978 and January 1979 (Gaston et al., 1979, 1981a). There are no scientific facilities.

Conservation Value The sanctuary holds patches of good coniferous and oak forest (Singh et al., 1990), and appears promising for wildlife compared to elsewhere in the Ravi Valley (Gaston et al., 1981a). The lake and meadows at Khajjiar are a popular tourist spot, and the nearby temple dedicated to Kajinag (from where the area derives its name) is of cultural importance (Singh et al., 1990).

Conservation Management Residents may collect timber, fodder, fuelwood and minor forest products. Residents and non-residents enjoy grazing rights within the sanctuary. Plantations have been established over an area of 637 ha from 1979 to 1984, primarily for commerical timber and fuelwood (Singh et al., 1990). There is a management plan for the period 1984–5 to 1988–9 (DFFC, 1984). It has been recommended that the sanctuary be extended by incorporating adjacent forest eastwards in the Sholadkar Range (Rodgers and Panwar, 1988). There is no zoning, although in the 1958 notification 63.2 ha were declared as *Sanctum sanctorum* and 3,108.8 ha as a surrounding buffer for a period of 20 years. No such demarcation is mentioned in the subsequent renotification (Singh et al., 1990).

Management Constraints Some of the habitat is heavily disturbed. (W.A. Rodgers, pers. comm., 1987), and there are reports of illegal hunting, grazing and habitat destruction (Singh et al., 1990).

Staff One range officer, three deputy range officers and ten forest guards (1987–8).

Budget Rs 537,500 (1987–8)

Local Addresses
Range Officer, Kalatop-Khajjiar Sanctuary, PO Banikhet 176 303, District Chamba, Himachal
Pradesh

References
Cavallini, P. (1990). Status of the goral (*Nemorhaedus goral*) in Himachal Pradesh, India.
Caprinae News 5(1) 4–6.
DFFC (1984). Scheme for intensive management of Kalatop-Khajjiar Wildlife Sanctuary
1984–5 to 1988–9. Department of Forest Farming and Conservation, Government of
Himachal Pradesh. (Unseen)
Gaston, A.J. (1979). Pheasant surveys in the Ravi Valley, 18–25 November 1978, 11–24 January
and 9–19 May 1979. Report to World Pheasant Association and Himachal Pradesh Forest
Department. Unpublished. (Unseen)
Gaston, A.J., Hunter, M.L. Jr., and Garson, P.J. (1981a). The wildlife of Himachal Pradesh,
Western Himalayas. *University of Maine School of Forest Resources Technical Notes* no.
82. 159 pp.
Gaston, A.J., Garson, P.J., and Hunter, M.L. Jr. (1981b). Present distribution and status of
pheasants in Himachal Pradesh, Western Himalayas. *World Pheasant Association Journal*
6: 10–30.
Gaston, A.J., Garson, P.J., and Hunter, M.L. Jr. (1983). The status and conservation of forest
wildlife in Himachal Pradesh, Western Himalayas. *Biological Conservation* 27: 291–314.
Rodgers, W.A. and Panwar, H.S. (1988). *Planning a wildlife protected area network in India*. 2
vols. Project FO: IND/82/003. FAO, Dehra Dun.
Singh, S., Kothari, A., and Pande, P. (Eds.) (1990). *Directory of National Parks and sanctuaries
in Himachal Pradesh*. Indian Institute of Public Administration, New Delhi. Pp. 39–41.

KANAWAR SANCTUARY

IUCN Management Category   IV (Managed Nature Reserve).

Biogeographical Province   2.38.12 (Himalayan Highlands)

Geographical Location   Lies in Kulu district, 2 km from Manikaran, the nearest village.
Access is via Kulu to Kasol, and onward by foot. 31°55′–32°01′N, 77°17′–77°23′E

Date and History of Establishment   Notified as a sanctuary on 26 February 1954.

Area   Notified as 6,070 ha, but re-estimated by IIPA/Environmental Studies Division (pers.
comm.) as 6,157 ha using digitised maps. To the south-east, the area is connected by a forest
corridor to Great Himalayan National Park.

Land Tenure   Provincial government. Local people enjoy certain rights.

Altitude   Ranges from 1,800 m to 4,833 m.

Physical Features   Kanawar is a high-altitude sanctuary, the terrain being mostly precipitous,
with rocky cliffs and narrow valleys.

Climate Temperatures range from −10 °C to 25 °C. Mean annual rainfall is 1,000 mm and mean annual snowfall 321 mm (Singh et al., 1990).

Vegetation Forest types include ban oak, moist deodar, western mixed coniferous, moist temperate deciduous, kharsu oak, West Himalayan subalpine fir and alpine pastures. The moist temperature deciduous forest is one of the last few undisturbed pockets left in Himachal Pradesh. *Cypressus* spp. have been introduced. The forest flora is diverse: a preliminary list of flora is given in Singh et al. (1990).

Fauna Mammals include common langur *Presbytis entellus*, rhesus macaque *Macaca mulatta*, Himalayan black bear *Selenarctos thibetanus* (V), brown bear *Ursus arctos*, jungle cat *Felis chaus*, leopard cat *Felis bengalensis*, leopard *Panthera pardus* (T), jackal *Canis aureus*, wolf *C. lupus* (V), yellow-throated marten *Martes flavigula*, Himalayan palm civet *Paguma larvata*, Himalayan weasel *Mustela sibirica*, fox *Vulpes vulpes*, snow leopard *Felis lynx* (E), goral *Nemorhaedus goral*, ibex *Capra ibex*, Indian muntjac *Muntiacus muntjak*, musk deer *Moschus chrysogaster*, serow *Capricornis sumatraensis*, blue sheep *Pseudois nayaur*, Himalayan tahr *Hemitragus jemlahicus*, Royle's pika *Ochotona roylei*, Indian porcupine *Hystrix indica*, and common giant flying squirrel *Petaurista petaurista* (Singh et al., 1990). In December 1989, 18 goral and 130 tahr were seen within an area of 2 sq. km (Pandey, 1991). Singh et al. (1990) provide a preliminary list of 80 bird species recorded in the sanctuary.

Cultural Heritage There are lakes and natural springs of religious and historical importance at Khirganga and Mantalai on the outskirts of the sanctuary. There is also a temple and a gurudwara at Manikaran, adjacent to the sanctuary (Singh et al., 1990).

Local Human Population Two villages are located within the sanctuary (with an estimated population of 460 people), four temporary settlements, and 14 villages are located in the adjacent area. During 1980–3, 468 tonnes of herbs were extracted from the sanctuary and adjoining area. Bamboo is extracted to make baskets and roofs for huts. Livestock belonging to the villages in and around the sanctuary total 7,615, while those brought in by nomads total 15,897 (Singh et al., 1990).

Visitors and Visitor Facilities In 1983-4, a total of 1,200 visitors (mostly trekkers) visited the sanctuary. Many visitors come to climb the peaks in and around the sanctuary. Four rest houses are situated on the outskirts of the sanctuary. Accommodation is also available at some *dharamshalas* in Manikaran. There are plans to extend tourist facilities and to construct five watchtowers (Singh et al., 1990).

Scientific Research and Facilities No information

Conservation Value The sanctuary contains a diverse forest flora, including a remnant patch of moist temperate deciduous forest. It is also important for its large population of Himalayan tahr.

Conservation Management Apart from habitation and grazing rights, local people have rights in relation to extraction of timber, quarrying, agriculture (200 ha), religious monuments and extraction of minor forest products. A management plan valid from 1984–5 to 1989–90 was drawn up in December 1983 (Anon., 1983). A proposal exists to extend the eastern boundary by an unspecified amount, as this land is good for wildlife populations and is devoid of permanent habitation. It is also planned to demarcate a tourist zone of 162 ha within the sanctuary.

Management Constraints   There are reports of illegal hunting of musk deer, Himalayan tahr, black bear and monal pheasant, but no offences have been reported as yet. Leopard and black bear are reported to take livestock. The wildlife authorities have protested against the construction of a tunnel through the sanctuary under the proposed Parvati Hydel Scheme II. Forest fires are known to occur (Singh et al., 1990).

Staff   One range officer, one deputy range officer and four forest guards.

Budget   No separate budget. Rs 50,000 were allocated in 1987–8 for the construction of guard huts.

Local Addresses   Range Officer (Wildlife), Kasol, District Kulu, Himachal Pradesh

References
Anon. (1983). Scheme of Kanawar Sanctuary. Department of Forest Farming and Conservation, Government of Himachal Pradesh, Simla. (Unseen)
Pandey, S. (1991). Species accounts. Unpublished report to the Wildlife Institute of India, Dehra Dun. 4 pp.
Singh, S., Kothari, A. and Pande, P. (Eds.) (1990). *Directory of national parks and sanctuaries in Himachal Pradesh: management status and profiles*. Indian Institute of Public Administration, New Delhi. Pp. 42–4.

KANJI SANCTUARY

IUCN Management Category   IV (Managed Nature Reserve)

Biogeographical Province   2.38.12 (Himalayan Highlands)

Geographical Location   Lies some 80 km south-east of Kargil in the Zanskar region of Ladakh. Bounded to the north by Dondaduk Village, south-west by Kanji La and east by Yogma La. The Srinagar–Leh road passes the mouth of the Kanji Valley at Heniskot. 34°05′–34°17′N, 76°30′–76°49′E

Date and History of Establishment   Notified a sanctuary in 1988 or 1989 (Mallon, 1987, 1989), having originally been established as a game reserve in 1981.

Area   According to departmental records the area is 10,000 ha, but it has been re-estimated as 25,000 ha using maps based on satellite imagery (Mallon, 1989). Lies adjacent to Boodkharbu Game Reserve (1,200 ha) to the north-west and abuts onto the proposed Rangdum Sanctuary to the south.

Land Tenure   Provincial government.

Altitude   Ranges up to 5,761 m.

Physical Features   Comprises the entire catchment area of Kanji Nala. The valley comprises a steep gorge opening out into more open, alpine slopes. There are passes from the valley west to Boodkharbu, east to Shilla Valley, and south to Rangdum.

Climate   No information

Vegetation   Valley bottoms support thickets of willow *Salix* spp., buckthorn *Hippophae* spp., and *Myricaria* spp., with the occasional birch *Betula utilis* tree. Patches of honeysuckle *Lonicera* spp., roses *Rosa* spp., and *Ephedra gerardiana* are also present. On the mountains slopes, *Caragana* spp., mixed with *Rosa* spp., and *E. gerardiana* (at lower altitudes) is abundant along with stands of birch (Department of Wildlife Protection, n.d.).

Fauna   The reserve contains a large population of ibex *Capra ibex*. Some 222 ibex were counted in January 1980 (Department of Wildlife Protection, n.d.). Other recorded species include wolf *Canis lupus* (V), fox *Vulpes vulpes*, lynx *Felis lynx*, snow leopard *Panthera uncia* (E), Himalayan marmot *Marmota bobak*, and cape hare *Lepus capensis*. Bharal *Pseudois nayaur* occurs in one side-valley, the westernmost extent of its distribution (Department of Wildlife Protection, n.d.; Mallon, 1989).

Little is documented about the avifauna. Some 19 species are listed by Department of Wildlife Protection (n.d.). The game birds present are Himalayan snowcock *Tetraogallus himalayensis* and chukar partridge *Alectoris chukar*.

Cultural Heritage   No information

Local Human Population   Kanji is the only village within the reserve. Here 20–25 families live with 900 head of livestock. Resources within the reserve are used for fuel and for grazing livestock (Department of Wildlife Protection, n.d.).

Visitors and Visitor Facilities   The route from Rangdum through Kanji Valley, via the Kanji La, is popular among trekkers. There are no visitor facilities.

Scientific Research and Facilities   Other than a census of the ibex population (Department of Wildlife Protection, n.d.), no research has been undertaken. There are no scientific facilities.

Conservation Value   Kanji forms part of a much larger protected areas complex. It is an important site for ibex (Mallon, 1989).

Conservation Management   There is no management plan.

Management Constraints   There is some use of natural resources by the resident human population (Department of Wildlife Protection, n.d.), but the level of this exploitation has not been assessed.

Staff   No information

Budget   No information

Local Addresses   No information

References

Department of Wildlife Protection (n.d.). *Status survey report of notified and proposed national parks, sanctuaries and reserves in Ladakh region.* Department of Wildlife Protection, Srinagar. 29 pp.

Mallon, D.P. (1989). An ecological survey of the protected area network in Ladakh. Report to the Department of Wildlife Protection, Jammu and Kashmir Government, Srinagar. Unpublished. 13 pp.

KEDARNATH SANCTUARY

IUCN Management Category   IV (Managed Nature Reserve)

Biogeographical Province   2.38.12 (Himalayan Highlands)

Geographical Location   Situated in the Garhwal region of the Great Himalaya, about 300 km north-east of Delhi. The sanctuary is bounded to the north by a range of peaks, mostly over 6,000 m, and in the south by the Mandal~Okhimath road. 30°26'–30°45'N, 78°54'–79°36'E

Date and History of Establishment   Notified a sanctuary on 21 January 1972. Its forests were originally notified as reserved forests between 1916 and 1920.

Area   97,524 ha (based on data given in the 1982–3 to 1991–2 Working Plan for Kedarnath Forest Division). The area given in the original notification is 96,725.61 ha.

Land Tenure   Provincial government, but local people continue to exercise traditional rights. All of the sanctuary falls within the jurisdiction of the Forest Department apart from 4,253 ha (4.4.%) of reserved forest belonging to panchayats (village councils) and administered by the Revenue Department.

Altitude   Ranges from 1,160 m (near Phata) to the peak of Chaukhamba at 7,068 m.

Physical Features   The entire sanctuary lies in the northern catchment of the Alaknanda River, the major tributary of the upper reaches of the Ganges River, and comprises a series of mostly north–south oriented river valleys. The main ones are the Mandakini, Kali, Biera, Balasuti, and Menan, all of which flow into the Alaknanda. Much of the sanctuary lies within the Central Crystallines that form the main axis of the Great Himalaya. This belt of metamorphic rocks consists of gneisses, granites and schists.

Climate   The main valleys are fully exposed to the summer monsoon, as there is very little rain-shadow effect from the 3,000 m high hill ranges to the south. Of the mean annual precipitation of 3,093 mm recorded at 3,050 m near Tungnath in 1979–81 (Green, 1985), 81% fell in the monsoon (June–September) and 11% fell as snow in winter (December–March). Temperatures were highest in May or June (25 °C) and lowest in the first half of January (−10 °C). The sanctuary is snow-bound for about three months, following heavy snowfalls in December.

Vegetation   The great variety of vegetation types reflects the complex and diverse nature of the climate, geology and topography in the region. From 44.4% to 48.8% of the sanctuary is forested, 7.7% comprises alpine meadows and scrub, 42.1% is rocky or under permanent snow and 1.5% represents formerly forested areas that have been degraded. The tropical zone, which does not occur above 1,200 m, is absent. The subtropical zone is represented mainly by chir pine *Pinus roxburghii* up to 2,000 m. *Euphorbia royleana* occasionally occurs on dry, southern aspects up to 1,500 m. Within the temperate zone occur ban *Quercus incana* (1,500–2,100 m), moru *Q. dilatata* (2,130–2,750 m) and karsu *Q. semecarpifolia* (2,500–3,300 m) oak forests. *Rhododendron arboreum* often constitutes a second storey. Oak may be mixed with fir *Abies pindrow* at higher elevations (2,600–3,400 m). The subalpine zone consists of birch *Betula utilis* (3,100–3,350 m) with an understorey of *Rhododendron campanulatum*. Rhododendron extends into the alpine zone, from above the forest limit to 3,500 m. The herb community of the subalpine and alpine meadows may be dominated by *Danthonia cu mminsii*, which forms tussocks of grass over extensive areas. The flowering plants of Tungnath and Kedarnath are enumerated by Semwal and Gaur (1981) and Semwal (1984), respectively. Two sedges, *Carex lacta* and *C. munda*, previously known to occur only as far west as Nepal have been recorded from near Tungnath (Green, 1985).

Fauna   Some 30 mammalian species, excluding bats, have been recorded (Green, 1985). The only primates are rhesus macaque *Macaca mulatta* and common langur *Presbytis entellus*. Carnivores include jackal *Canis aureus*, fox *Vulpes vulpes*, Himalayan black bear *Selenarctos thibetanus* (V), yellow-throated marten *Martes flavigula*, leopard cat *Felis bengalensis*, common leopard *Panthera pardus* (T), and snow leopard *P. uncia* (E). Noteworthy is the record of a snow leopard seen in March 1979 (Green, 1982). Ungulates are wild boar *Sus scrofa*, Himalayan musk deer *Moschus chrysogaster*, Indian muntjac *Muntiacus muntjak*, sambar *Cervus unicolor*, goral *Nemorhaedus goral*, serow *Capricornis sumatraensis*, Himalayan tahr *Hemitragus jemlahicus*, and bharal *Pseudois nayaur*. Densities of musk deer, sambar, serow and goral within a small part of the sanctuary were 3.2, 1.1, 1.6 and 2.6 animals per sq. km, respectively (Green, 1987a). Among the smaller mammals are brown-toothed shrews *Soriculus* spp., red giant flying squirrel *Petaurista petaurista*, Royle's mountain vole *Alticola roylei*, crested porcupine *Hystrix indica*, and Royle's pika *Ochotona roylei*.

Of the 146 species of bird so far recorded in the sanctuary, little pied flycatcher *Musicappa westermanni*, grey-cheeked warbler *Seicercus poliogenys*, and Nepal tree creeper *Certhia nipalensis* have not previously been reported west of Nepal. Himalayan monal pheasant *Lophophorus impejanus*, kalij pheasant *Lophura leucomelana,* and koklass pheasant *Pucrasia macrolopha* (5 pairs per sq. km) occur in good numbers (Green, 1986).

Notable species of reptile include Himalayan pit viper *Ancistrodon himalayensis* (common) and Boulenger's keelback *Amphiesma parallela*, previously known to occur only as far west as Sikkim and Assam (Green, 1985). Some 36 species of fishes have been recorded from the Mandakini River, including *Schizothorax* spp., mahseer *Tor tor*, *Labeo* spp., *Gara* spp., *Barilius* spp., *Neomacheilus* spp., *Glyptothorax* spp., and *Balitora brucei*, which is considered to be rare (Singh et al., 1987).

Cultural Heritage   There are a number of Hindu shrines in and around the sanctuary, the most renowned of which is Kedarnath whose history dates back to the 8th century. Less well-known shrines are those at Mandani, Madhyamaheshwar, Tungnath, Ansuya Devi and Rudranath. The Bhotiyas form an integral part of the local Hindu culture, possibly with some Tibetan influence, and pastoralism is an important part of their economy (Bhandari, 1981).

Local Human Population   There are 20–30 permanent settlements in the sanctuary, mostly in the west, and about 150 in its immediate vicinity. Both residents and non-residents, from villages to the south, depend largely on pastoralism and trade in minor forest products.

Visitors and Visitor Facilities   There are very few foreign tourists; most visitors are Indian nationals on pilgrimages. Kedarnath Temple, although just outside the northern border, can be reached only by passing through the sanctuary. It received over 97,000 visitors in 1981, almost double the number of visitors recorded in 1974 (Kaur, 1985). Food and accommodation are available in tea-houses along the more popular routes, and there are dharmashalas at Kedarnath, Madhyamaheshwar and Tungnath, and rest houses at Dougalbitta, Mandal and Kedarnath.

Scientific Research and Facilities   Floral surveys include those of Rau (1961), Mehrotra (1979) (medicinal plants), Semwal (1984) for Kedarnath in the Mandakini Valley, and Semwal (1981) for Tungnath. The Botany Department of Garhwal University has a high-altitude field station at Tungnath (3,500 m), where studies in plant physiology have been carried out for a number of years. An ecological study of the Himalayan musk deer and other ungulates (WWF Project 1328) was undertaken near Tungnath in 1979–81 (Green, 1985, 1987a, 1987b, 1987c, 1987d), together with surveys of the mammalian fauna (Singh, 1982) and avifauna (Green, 1986). The ungulates are currently the subject of further ecological studies by Sathyakumar (1990). The fish fauna in the Mandakini River has been surveyed by Singh et al. (1987). A breeding centre for musk deer was established at Khanchula Kharak on the periphery of the sanctuary in 1982. The centre achieved its first breeding success in 1984 and by November 1987 had nine musk deer, all but one of which were born in captivity.

Conservation Value   The sanctuary, which takes its name from the famous Hindu shrine of Kedarnath just outside its northern border, is the largest protected area in the western Himalaya. It is internationally important for the diversity of its flora and fauna, and its many Hindu temples are of great cultural value. Notable is its assemblage of ungulate species, unique to the Garhwal Himalaya (Green, 1985; Rodgers and Panwar, 1988).

Conservation Management   The sanctuary was established mainly to protect the musk deer (Agrawala, 1973). Under the current working plan (1982–3 to 1991–2), only 746 ha (0.8%) of the sanctuary's area is available for commercial exploitation, all of which is chir pine. There is no management plan at present. It has been recommended that a core area of 30,000 ha be upgraded to national park status (Rodgers and Panwar, 1988).

Management Constraints   Poaching, particularly of musk deer and pheasants, continues in less accessible areas. Grazing by domestic livestock (goats, sheep and water buffalo), burning of pastures and collection of forest products and medicinal herbs are not controlled. The forest understorey is heavily disturbed in places. Excessive pressure from tourism is evident in the Mandakini Valley, notably in the vicinity of Kedarnath Temple from where a large amount of minor forest and scrub has been removed (WWF/IUCN Project 1328). In 1988–9, 37 people were injured and six killed by leopard, bear and wild boar, and 164 livestock were killed by leopard (Sathya Kumar, 1991).

Staff   One wildlife warden, five assistant wildlife wardens, 23 wildlife guards, one junior clerk, one driver and one orderly. The musk deer breeding centre is staffed by one assistant wildlife warden, two wildlife guards and two *chaukidars* (1987).

Budget Approximately Rs 15 lakhs were allocated to the sanctuary in 1987–8 and Rs 3 lakhs to the musk deer breeding centre.

Local Addresses Wildlife Warden, Kedarnath Sanctuary, Gopeshwar 246401, Chamoli District, Uttar Pradesh

References
Agrawala, N.K. (1973). Working plan for the Kedarnath Forest Division 1972–3 to 1981–2. Parts 1 and 2. Working Plans Circle, Nainital, Uttar Pradesh. 417 pp.

Bhandari, J.S. (1981). Structure and change among the borderland communities of the Kumaon Himalaya. In: Hall, J.S. (Ed.), *The Himalaya: aspects of change*. Oxford University Press, Delhi. Pp. 204–16.

Green, M.J.B. (1982). Status, distribution and conservation of the snow leopard in North India. *International Pedigree Book of Snow Leopards* 3: 6–10.

Green, M.J.B. (1985). Aspects of the ecology of the Himalayan musk deer. Ph.D. thesis, University of Cambridge, Cambridge. 280 pp.

Green, M.J.B. (1986). The birds of the Kedarnath Sanctuary, Chamoli District, Uttar Pradesh: status and distribution. *Journal of the Bombay Natural History Society* 83: 603–17.

Green, M.J.B. (1987a). Ecological separation in Himalayan ungulates. *Journal of Zoology, London* (B) 1: 693–719.

Green, M.J.B. (1987b). Scent-marking in the Himalayan musk deer (*Moschus chrysogaster*). *Journal of Zoology, London* (B) 1: 721–37.

Green, M.J.B. (1987c). Diet composition and quality in Himalayan musk deer based on fecal analysis. *Journal of Wildlife Management* 51: 880–92.

Green, M.J.B. (1987d). Some ecological aspects of a Himalayan population of musk deer. In: Wemmer, C.M. (Ed.), *Biology and management of the Cervidae*. Smithsonian Institution, Washington DC. Pp. 307–19.

Kaur, J. (1985). *Himalayan pilgrimages and the new tourism*. Himalayan Books, New Delhi. 219 pp.

Mehrotra, B.N. (1979). A survey of medicinal plants around Kedarnath Shrine of Garhwal Himalayas. *Indian Forester* 105: 788–801.

Rau, M.A. (1961). Flowering plants and ferns of North Garhwal, Uttar Pradesh, India. *Bulletin of the Botanical Survey of India* 3: 215–51.

Rodgers, W.A. and Panwar, H.S. (1988). *Planning a wildlife protected area network in India*. 2 vols. Project FO: IND/82/003. FAO, Dehra Dun.

Sathyakumar, S. (1989). Human–animal conflicts at Kedarnath Wildlife Sanctuary. *Wildlife Institute of India News letter* 4 (6): 25–6.

Sathyakumar, S. (1990). Habitat ecology of major ungulates in Kedarnath Sanctuary, Western Himalaya. Report (March 1989–June 1990). Wildlife Institute of India, Dehra Dun. Unpublished. 20 pp.

Semwal, J.K. and Gaur, R.D. (1981). Alpine flora of Tungnath in Garhwal Himalaya. *Journal of the Bombay Natural History Society* 78: 498–512.

Singh, A.N. (1982). A survey of the mammalian fauna of the Kedarnath Sanctuary, Uttar Pradesh (India). *Tiger Paper* 9: 8–10.

Singh, H.R., Badola, S.P. and Dobriyal, A.K. (1987). Geographical distributional list of ichthyofauna of the Garhwal Himalaya with some new records. *Journal of the Bombay Natural History Society* 84: 126–32.

WWF/IUCN. Project no. 1328. Himalayan musk deer. India: ecological study to identify conservation needs.

KEIBUL LAMJAO NATIONAL PARK

IUCN Management Category   II (National Park).

Biogeographical Province   4.09.04 (Burma Monsoon Forest).

Geographical Location   Situated in the south-eastern part of Logtak Lake in Bishanpur District, some 32 km south of Imphal. 24°30′N, 93°46′E

Date and History of Establishment   Notified a national park on 5 April 1977, having been legally gazetted a sanctuary in 1966 (Ranjitsinh, 1978). The whole of Logtak Lake was closed to shooting and declared a 'sanctuary' in October 1953. Subsequently, in July 1954, Logtak was reopened for shooting except for the southern portion inhabited by the sangai, which continued to be protected as a 'sanctuary' (Gee, 1960, 1961). The area remained as unclassed forest until 1974 when it was notified as a reserved forest (Singh, 1980). Logtak Lake was designated a Ramsar site on 23 March 1990.

Area   4,010 ha. The original size of the 'sanctuary' created in 1954 was about 20 sq. miles (5,180 ha), but this was reduced to 10.75 sq. miles (2,784 ha) in 1959. Following notification of the sanctuary in 1966, a further 3 sq. miles were added in 1968 making a total area of 3,561 ha. It would appear that boundaries were realigned and extended in the north at the time that the sanctuary was upgraded to national park status.

Land Tenure   Provincial government. Private land inside the park is in the process of being acquired.

Altitude   Ranges from about 767 m, being the lowest level of the lake, to 813 m at the top of Chingjao Hill.

Physical Features   Manipur Valley, about 124,250 ha in extent, is broad, open, and characterised by numerous small hillocks dotted over the entire area. Six large streams and numerous smaller ones drain from the surrounding hills into the central plain and combine to flow southwards through a narrow gorge into the Chindwin River in Burma, a tributary of the Irrawaddy. Consequently, the southern portion of the valley contains a number of lakes and marshes, of which Logtak Lake (6,475 ha) is not only the largest, but also one of the largest freshwater lakes in India (Gee, 1960, 1961).

Keibul Lamjao is a large expanse of swamp with floating mats of vegetation, locally known as *phumdi*, covering much of its surface. *Phumdi* is composed of decaying vegetation, up to 1.6 m thick and 80% submerged, and can support the weight of large mammals. This habitat, considered 'too deep to be a marsh, and too shallow to be a lake', is unique in India. There are three small hillocks within Keibul Lamjao, namely Chingjao, Pabotching and Toyaching, which are reputed to provide a refuge for large mammals during wetter periods (Yadava and Varshey, 1982; Scott, 1989). The water level used to vary from 1.0 m to 1.5 m. At low water levels in February–March, peripheral areas of *phumdi* used to come to rest on the ground, rising to the surface again following the onset of the monsoon. Large amounts of *phumdi* used to be washed away during severe flooding (Yadava and Varshey, 1982; Scott, 1982). Such seasonal fluctuations no longer occur as the lake is maintained at a constant level (770 m) following the commissioning of the Ithai Barrage in 1984 (Green, 1990).

Climate   Meteorological data are available only for Imphal. Here, mean annual rainfall is 1,220 mm. Mean daily humidity is highest (81%) in August and lowest (49%) in March. Maximum and minimum temperatures are 34.4 °C and 1.7 °C, respectively. Frost is common in December and January (Deb, 1960).

Vegetation   The composition of *phumdi* is estimated as follows: ising kambong *Zizania latifolia* 24.5%, hoop *Leersia hexandra* 24.0%, tou *Phragmites karka* 13.9%, wana manbi *Cepithipedium* spp. 13.3%, hunding *Carex* spp. 6.5%, khoimom *Saccharum munja* 5.6%, yawachaning *Coix lecryma-jobi* 4.4%, singut *Narenga porphyrochroma* 3.6%., and lilhar *Polygonum perfoliatum* 3.3% (Singh, 1983). There have been some remarkable changes in the vegetation, as it used to consist predominantly of tou (45%), singut (25%) and khoimom (15%) (Gee, 1960, 1961). Ising kambong is much sought after by local people because its vegetative portion is rich in protein (Singh, 1980). A number of endemic plants are present, as well as wild varieties of cultivated plants such as rice.

Fauna   Keibul Lamjao is the last refuge of the Manipur subspecies of brow-antlered deer *Cervus eldi eldi* (E), known in the local Meitei language as 'sangai'. The subspecies was reported to be extinct in the wild in 1951 but was 're-discovered' in 1952–3, since when numbers decreased from an estimated 100 in 1960 (Gee, 1960, 1961) to what was probably an all time low of 14 in 1975 (Ranjitsinh, 1978). The population has since shown some signs of recovery, from 18 recorded in 1977 (Ranjitsinh, 1978) to over 50 by the mid-1980s (Singh 1988; Chakrabarty, 1989). There is a general consensus between the Forest Department and university scientists that the sangai population presently exceeds 50 but is less than 100 animals (Green, 1990). Other large mammals recorded in this habitat are large Indian civet *Viverra zibetha*, small Indian civet *Viverricula indica*, common otter *Lutra lutra*, wild boar *Sus scrofa,* and hog deer *Cervus porcinus* (Gee, 1960, 1961; Singh, 1980). In the past, leopard *Panthera pardus* (T) has occasionally been observed (Gee, 1960, 1961). Though formerly present (Higgins, 1934), wild dog *Cuon alpinus* (V) no longer occurs in the area (Gee, 1960).

The avifauna consists primarily of the smaller reed-dwelling species. Waterfowl are non-existent in the sanctuary due to the absence of open patches of water (Gee, 1960, 1961).

Several indigenous species of fish inhabited the lake, but the larger of these migratory species were inadvertently exterminated when the Logtak Hydroelectric Project curtailed access to the Chindwin River. The fish fauna includes *Channa strictus*, *C. punctatus*, *Cyprinus carpio*, *Wallago attu*, and *Puntius sophus* (Scott, 1989).

Cultural Heritage   The sangai features prominently in local mythology. A dance-drama 'Keibul Lamjao', choreographed by Chaotombi Singh, was produced by the Jawaharlal Nehru Manipur Dance Academy, and this formed the basis of the subsequent film 'Sangai: The Dancing Deer of Manipur'.

Local Human Population   There are four villages on the periphery of the park, Kumlakhon, Tera, Ithai, Vapuphi and Keibul (Rastogi, 1990), and 18 within a 10 km radius having a total population of 35,300 (IIPA/Environmental Studies Divsion, pers. comm., 1990). On all but the lakeside, the national park is surrounded by paddy fields belonging to the inhabitants of eleven nearby villages (Singh, 1980). Thanga, Keibul, Kumbi, and several other villages to the north-west, west, and south are inhabited by Manipuris, who are not hunters by virtue of being vegetarian. By contrast, the Muslim villagers from Uchiwa, Mayang Imphal, Turen Ahaubi and Samusang to the north-east are traditionally hunters (Gee, 1960, 1961). Two thirds of Manipur's 1.4 million people live in the Manipur Valley, one of the most densely populated areas in India (415 persons per sq. km), and rely on Logtak Lake as a fishery (Green, 1991).

Visitors and Visitor Facilities   A total of 3,942 visitors were recorded in 1983–4, with up to 300 visitors on a peak day (IIPA/Environmental Studies Division, pers. comm.). Foreigners require a special permit to visit Manipur. There are rest houses at Phubala and Sendra, and an observation tower on the top of Chingjao Hill.

Scientific Research and Facilities   The status of the sangai was first examined by Gee (1960, 1961) and later by Ranjitsinh (1976, 1978). Censuses have been carried out in most years from 1975, onwards (Ranjitsinh, 1976, 1978; Singh, 1980, 1988). More recently, studies on the behaviour and ecology of the sangai have been carried out by H. Tombi Singh, Kh. Shamungou Singh (1983) and Sanayaima Devi. Details of these and other ecological research in the Logtak area are su mmarised elsewhere (Green, 1990). WWF-India is due to embark on a wetland conservation programme for the Manipur Valley, beginning in 1991. There are no scientific facilities.

Conservation Value   Keibul Lamjao is unique for its floating mats of vegetation (*phumdi*), which support a variety of endemic plants and provide the last refuge in the wild for the endemic sangai. The park occupies a corner of Logtak Lake, recently designated a Wetland of International Importance under the Ramsar Convention. The lake and its associated swamps are all that remain of a vast 2,000 sq. km wetland that covered the entire Manipur Valley, before most of it was drained during the last century. Logtak is extremely important as a wintering area for migratory birds: 24% of the 51 species recorded from the area are migratory (Scott, 1989; Green, 1991).

Conservation Management   There is no management plan. Under the Central Assistance Scheme for the Development of National Parks, considerable financial assistance has been provided by the Government of India to compensate farmers for the acquisition of their land within the park, construct office and residential accommodation for staff, to erect 2,218 m of fencing along the most vulnerable section of the boundary, dig 870 m of cattle-proof trench, build an enclosure for breeding sangai in captivity and to purchase canoes for patrolling. Traditional practices of reed-cutting (for thatching and fuelwood), grazing (mainly by water buffalo) and fishing are now prohibited (Ranjitsinh, 1978). At the time of the park's establishment, compensation was paid for 'patta' land (private land for which the owner possesses a certificate of ownership) which accounted for 10% of total land area. No compensation was paid for 'kutcha patta' (traditionally owned land lacking any certificate for ownership) which covered 40% of the park. The government agreed to find alternative land to replace 'kutcha pattas' but apparently no action has been taken to date. Some Rs 10 lakhs (US $ 57,000) was to have been paid as compensation for 'pattas' in 1990, and a further Rs 8 lakhs was being requested from the Government of India (Green, 1990).

Management Constraints   Keibul Lamjao has a long history of management problems (Gee, 1960, 1961; Ranjitsinh, 1976, 1978). It has been included in IUCN's Register of Threatened Protected Areas of the World since 1985 due to problems of siltation and encroachment. Siltation is caused by deforestation and shifting cultivation in the surrounding hills (Yadava and Varshney, 1981). Agricultural encroachment is concentrated along a narrow wedge of 24 ha of cultivated land, which is known as Thang-Brel-Maril and almost divides the park into northern and southern parts, and along the park's western perimeter (Gee, 1960, 1961; Ranjitsinh, 1976, 1978). Conflict between the park authorities and local people reached a peak in February 1979, when villagers entered the park and set fire to the vegetation and guard posts. Following this uprising, a meeting was convened by the then Prime Minister, Mrs Indira Gandhi, at which local representatives pressed for a reduction of the park to some 1,100 ha of core sangai habitat. This was based on the premise that delimitation of the park boundary was in places *ad hoc*, incorporating large expanses of water not used by sangai but valuable as local fishing grounds. The Government of India responded by commissioning a study which concluded that conditions at Keibul Lamjao were symptomatic of a more widsespread and serious deterioration of the entire Logtak ecosystem (Panwar, 1979). A strategy of wise resource use was prescribed, with the park as a *sanctum sanctorum*, but little action has subsequently been taken to resolve the many human issues. Deterioration of the ecosystem has been accelerated by the Logtak Hydroelectric Project, designed to dam the lake to provide water for hydropower and irrigation. Silt, chemical fertilisers and insecticides from the catchment area are no longer flushed from the ecosystem following the completion of the Ithai Barrage in 1984. Their accumulation has lead to silation, eutrophication and pollution of the lake. Inundation of former cultivated land has added to human pressures on remaining land, while some land owners are still being taxed for land under water. Local people are no longer able to use shallow-fishing techniques, and have even resorted to poisoning fish to maintain catch levels. Aware of the economic implications of such problems, the Government of Manipur set up the Logtak Development Authority to be responsible for planning the future development of the lake on a sound ecological base. Despite a multi-disciplinary approach, conservation interests have largely been overlooked to date. The recent designation of Logtak as a Ramsar site and the implementation of a wetland conservation strategy for the Manipur Valley by WWF-India should help to address such issues and ultimately reverse the current deterioration of the Logtak ecosystem (Green, 1991).

Staff One range officer, five foresters, nine forest guards, six boatmen, three other staff (1984).

Budget No recent information

Local Addresses Range Officer, Keibul Lamjao National Park, BPO Kha-Thinungei, Manipur

References

Chakrabarty, K. (1989). Manipur–the world's lone abode of the rarest deer tribe—brow-antlered deer. *Tiger Paper* 16(1): 8–10.

Deb, D.B. (1960). Forest type studies in Manipur. *Indian Forester* 86: 94–111.

Gee, E.P. (1960). Report on the status of the brow-antlered deer of Manipur (India): October–November 1959 and March 1960. *Journal of the Bombay Natural History Society* 57: 597–617.

Gee, E.P. (1961). The brow-antlered deer of Manipur. October and November 1959 and March 1960. *Oryx* 6: 103–15. (Shortened version of Gee, 1960).

Green, M.J.B. (1990). Report on a preliminary visit to Manipur. WWF Project 4001.17/India. WWF, Gland, Switzerland. Unpublished. 14 pp.

Green, M.J.B. (1991). Conserving the 'jewel' of India. *WWF News* 69: 2.

Higgins, J.C. (1934). The game birds and animals of the Manipur State with notes on their numbers, migration and habits. *Journal of the Bombay Natural History Society* 37: 307.

Panwar, H.S. (1979). Are only the Sangai and Keibul Lamjao threatened? Are the people of Manipur themselves not? An Assessment of the environmental crisis in the State of Manipur. Ministry of Agriculture, Government of India, New Delhi. Unpublished. 34 pp.

Ranjitsinh, M.K. (1976) Keibul Lamjao Sanctuary and the brow-antlered deer—1972, with notes on a visit in 1975. *Journal of the Bombay Natural History Society* 72: 243–55.

Ranjitsinh, M.K. (1978) The Manipur brow-antlered deer (*Cervus eldi eldi*)—a case history. In: *Threatened deer*. IUCN, Morges, Switzerland, Pp. 26–32.

Scott, D.A. (Ed.) (1989). *A directory of Asian wetlands*. IUCN, Gland, Switzerland and Cambridge, UK, 1,181 pp.

Singh, Ashbindu (1980). World's most endangered mammal—Manipur brow-antlered deer (*Cervus eldi eldi*). Tiger Paper 7(2) 26–7. (Reproduced in *WWF-India Newsletter* 34: 7–8).

Singh, K.S. (1983). The biology of brow-antlered deer, *Cervus eldi eldi*, Meclellend, 1842, at Keibul Lamjao National Park, Manipur. Paper presented at Bombay Natural History Society Centenary Symposium, Powai, Bombay.

Singh, T. (1988). Report on aerial census of brow-antlered deer, locally known as sangai conducted on 29 February 1988. Government of Manipur, Imphal. Unpublished. 3 pp.

Yadava, P.S. and Varshey, C.K. (1981). Notes on the ecology and socio-economic importance of wetlands of Manipur, N.E. India. *International Journal of Ecology and Environmental Sciences* 7: 149–50.

KHANGCHENDZONGA NATIONAL PARK

IUCN Management Category II (National Park)

Biogeographical Province 2.38.12 (Himalayan Highlands)

Geographical Location Situated in North Sikkim District adjacent to the Nepal border and about 103 km from Gangtok. The nearest town is Chungthang, some 20 km away. 27°30′–27°50′N, 88°05′–88°40′E

Date and History of Establishment Notified a national park on 26 August 1977, having originally been established as reserved forest. Details of former individual reserved forests are given in the management plan (Anon., 1977). It is proposed to extend the park to the north and establish two sanctuaries in adjacent areas (Rodgers and Panwar, 1988).

Area 84,950 ha (Anon., 1977). Notified as 'about 850 sq. km'.

Land Tenure Provincial government. There are no local rights because of the area's former reserved forest status.

Altitude Ranges from about 1,830 m to 8,586 m.

Physical Features The national park is enclosed by some impressive mountain peaks and glaciers on all but its eastern side. A series of peaks above 7,000 m flank its western border, namely Khangchenjunga (third highest mountain in the world and India's highest), Nepal Peak, Talung and Tent Peak. Mount Narsing (5,825 m) and Pandim on the southern boundary, and Mount Siniolchu (6,888 m) in the north of the park add further to the dramatic scenery. Khangchenjunga and its satellite peaks form a huge mountain massif pushed southwards from the main Himalayan Range. The area is divided into northern and southern portions by an east–west ridge of high peaks. The northern portion features Tent Peak, Nepal Gap, Zemu and Simyo glaciers, which are drained by the eastward-flowing Zemu Chhu. Rukel Chhu, Uma Ram Chhu and Zumthulphuk and their associated network of deep ravines and side-valleys drain the southern portion and flow south-east to join the Teesta River at Mangan. Muletingtso, a large lake, lies at the head of the Ringi Chhu.

Climate Snowfall is heavy during winter. Showers in May and June herald the arrival of the monsoon, which continues until mid-October. Mean annual precipitation is about 3,800 mm and 2,540 mm below and above 2,440 m, respectively (Anon., 1977). Khangchenjunga is massive enough not only to generate its own climate but to attract the full force of the monsoon, with warm moist air from the Bay of Bengal travelling unimpeded up the Teesta Valley. Consequently, humidity is very high and annual snowfall on Khangchenjunga itself is probably higher than for any other peak in the Himalaya (Smythe, 1930; Lavkumar, 1980).

Vegetation Comprises temperate forest and alpine scrub. Temperate broadleaved forests are dominated by oaks *Quercus lineata, Q. lamellosa, Q. pachyphylla*. Mixed coniferous forests occur at higher altitudes, with fir *Abies densa*, birch *Betula* spp., maple *Acer* spp., and willow *Salix* spp. up to 3,660 m. Patches of eastern Himalayan larch *Larix griffithiana,* spruce *Picea spinulosa* and junipers *Juniperus* spp. occur at 2,740 m. There is a belt of juniper *Juniperus* spp. with *Rhododendron* spp. associates from 3,660 m to 4,270 m, above which are alpine scrub and meadows (Anon., 1977).

Fauna The area supports a diverse fauna, including a number of threatened species such as wild dog *Cuon alpinus* (V), red panda *Ailurus fulgens* (K), snow leopard *Panthera uncia* (E), clouded leopard *Neofelis nebulosa* (V), marbled cat *Felis marmorata* (I), Tibetan wild ass *Equus hemionus* (V), Himalayan musk deer *Moschus chrysogaster*, and Tibetan argali *Ovis ammon hodgsoni* (I). Other large mammals are common langur *Presbytis entellus*, red fox *Vulpes vulpes*, large Indian civet *Viverra zibetha*, binturong *Arctictis binturong* and an interesting variety of ungulates, namely: Indian muntjac *Muntiacus muntjak*, goral *Nemorhaedus goral*, serow *Capricornis sumatraensis*, Himalayan tahr *Hemitragus jemlahicus*, bharal *Pseudois nayaur*, and takin *Budorcas taxicolor* (Anon., 1977).

Of the avifauna, noteworthy species include ibisbill *Ibidorhyncha struthersii,* blood pheasant *Ithaginis cruentus,* satyr tragopan *Tragopan satyra,* Asian emerald cuckoo *Chrysococcyx maculatus*, red-headed trogon *Harpactes erythrocephalus*, great slaty woodpecker *Mulleripicus pulverulentus*, rufous piculet *Sasia abnormis*, and long-tailed broadbill *Psarisomus dalhousiae* (Anon., 1977).

Reptiles found at lower altitudes include rat snake *Ptyas mucosus* and Russell's viper *Viper russelli* (Anon., 1977).

Cultural Heritage The centuries old Tolung Gompa is just south of the national park. To the local people the five summits of Khangchenjunga are the 'five treasures of the snow' on which rests the throne of their God. There are even tales of human sacrifices having been made to this deity in the distant past (Smythe, 1930).

Local Human Population There are a few Lepcha settlements within the national park (Lavkumar, 1980).

Visitors and Visitor Facilities There are four resthouses.

Scientific Research and Facilities The first European to undertake serious exploration in the area was the botanist Sir Joseph Hooker in 1848–9 (Smythe, 1930). The vegetation of most (70%) of the park has yet to be mapped.

Conservation Value The area is a spectacular wilderness, with one of the world's highest peaks towering above some fine forests that remain virtually undisturbed (Lavkumar, 1980). The park must rank as one of the most important protected aras in the entire Himalayan (Rodgers and Panwar, 1988). Khangchenjunga is considered to be the finest example of an independent mountain having its own glacial system radiating from its several summits. It also boasts some of the most magnificent snow and ice scenery in the world (Smythe, 1930)

Conservation Management Following the park's establishment, a large-scale operation was mounted by the wildlife authorities in co-operation with the Sikkim Armed Police to demolish some 5,000 km of traplines, constructed for capturing musk deer and pheasants. Such operations have been repeated annually. Wildlife conservation films are screened in peripheral villages. Efforts to remove a herd of 70 yak from the park have failed, and it is proposed to use them for transport purposes (IIPA/Environmental Studies Division, pers. comm., 1990). The first management plan covered the period 1977–8 to 1978–9 (Anon., 1977). A new management plan was drafted by the Chief Wildlife Warden for 1980–5 (Anon., 1984). A small extension of 9,700 ha to the north of the park has been proposed to increase representation of Tibetan faunal elements (Anon., 1988; Rodgers and Panwar, 1988). It has also been proposed that two sanctuaries, Tolung (23,000 ha) and Dzongri (46,800 ha) be established as buffers to provide low altitude winter refuges for animals from the park (Rodgers and Panwar, 1988).

Management Constraints There was some poaching and encroachment by graziers (Anon., 1977) but, in general, the level of disturbance was minimal (Lavkumar, 1980). Pastoralists from across the border with Nepal continue to enter the park to hunt musk deer, often with sophisticated weapons. The location of the Assam Rifles Firing Range within the park is a source of disturbance (IIPA/Environmental Studies Division, pers. comm., 1990).

Staff Two wildlife wardens, three assistant wildlife wardens, fifteen wildlife guards (1984).

Budget Rs 886,500 (1983–4)

Local Addresses
Wildlife Warden, Khangchendzonga National Park, Forest Department, Deorali 737102, Sikkim

References
Anon. (1977). Management plan of Khangchendzonga National Park. Government of Sikkim , Gangtok. Unpublished. 13 pp.
Anon. (1984). Draft management plan of Khangchendzonga National Park. Government of Sikkim, Gangtok. Unpublished. (Unseen)

Anon. (1988). *The snow leopard conservation scheme*. Ministry of Environment and Forests, Government of India, New Delhi. (Unseen)

Lavkumar, Khacher (1980). Khangchendzonga. *WWF-India Newsletter* 33: 8–10.

Rodgers, W.A. and Panwar, H.S. (1988). *Planning a wildlife protected area network in India*. 2 vols. Project FO: IND/82/003. FAO, Dehra Dun.

Smythe, F.S. (1930). *The Kangchenjunga adventure*. Victor Gollanz, London. Pp. 18–23.

KISHTWAR NATIONAL PARK

IUCN Management Category   II (National Park)

Biogeographical Province   2.38.12 (Himalayan Highlands)

Geographical Location   Lies in Doda District, some 40 km north-east of Kishtwar Town. It is bounded to the north by the Rinnay River, south by Kibar Nala catchment, east by the main divide of the Great Himalaya and to the west by Marau River. 33°20′–34°00′N, 75°40′–76°10′E

Date and History of Establishment   The intention to declare Kishtwar a national park was notified on 4 February 1981 (Notification no. 21/FST of 1980–1), but final notification is outstanding.

Area   The area is 42,500 ha according to the management plans (Khan, n.d; Bacha, 1986) and Wildlife Institute of India (Rodgers and Panwar, 1988), but according to IIPA/Environmental Studies Division records it is 31,000 ha (a figure which may take into account the realignment of the park's boundaries).

Land Tenure   Provincial government

Altitude   Ranges from 1,700 m to the peak of Nun at 7,135 m

Physical Features   Kishtwar encompasses the catchments of the Kiar, Nanth and Kibar nalas, all·of which drain south-west into Marau River which joins the Chenab River just above Kishtwar Town. The Marau drains the western slopes of the Bramah and Nun Kun ranges. The terrain is generally rugged and steep, with narrow valleys bounded by high ridges opening out in their upper glacial parts. The area lies in the Central Crystalline belt of the Great Himalaya. Rocks are strongly folded in places and composed mainly of granite, gneiss and schist, with the occasional bed of marble. The shallow, slightly alkaline soils are mostly alluvial with gravel deposits (Kurt, 1976; Bacha, 1986).

Climate   The influence of the monsoon is weak. Mean annual rainfall at Palmar and Sirshi (1,761 m), located near the periphery of the national park, is 827 mm and 741 mm, respectively. Precipitation is maximal (and in excess of 100 mm per month) in March and April, and again in July and August. Most snow falls in December and January, when the whole area becomes snowbound. Mean maximum and minimum temperatures recorded at Sirshi are 13 °C and –7 °C in January and 35 °C and 11 °C in July, respectively (Kurt, 1976: Bacha, 1986).

Vegetation Based on the revised classification of Champion and Seth (1968), some 13 vegetation types are represented (Bacha, 1986). In general, silver fir *Abies pindrow* and spruce *Picea wallichiana*, mixed with cedar *Cedrus deodara* and blue pine *Pinus griffithii*, are predominant from 2,400 m to 3,000 m. Notable is the small expanse of chail pine *P. gerardiana* in the Dachan Range. At lower altitudes (1,700–2,400 m) occur nearly pure stands of cedar and blue pine, and moist temperate deciduous forest, represented by Indian chestnut *Aesculus indica*, walnut *Juglans regia*, maple *Acer* spp., poplar *Populus ciliata*, hazel *Corylus cornuta*, bird cherry *Padus cornuta*, ash *Fraxinus cornuta*, and yew *Taxus wallichiana*. The subalpine zone, from 3,000 m to the tree line at 3,700 m, supports mostly silver fir and birch *Betula utilis* forest. This merges with birch-rhododendron *Rhododendron campanulatum* scrub, above which is alpine pasture. Further details of the vegetation and a comprehensive list of trees and shrubs found in the park are given by Scott et al. (1988).

Fauna Bacha (1986) lists 14 species of large mammals that are reportedly present. Notable species include brown bear *Ursus arctos*, leopard *Panthera pardus* (T), snow leopard *P. uncia* (E), Himalayan musk deer *Moschus chrysogaster*, hangul *Cervus elaphus hanglu* (E), and ibex *Capra ibex sibirica*. In addition to those listed, wild boar *Sus scrofa*, Indian muntjac *Muntiacus muntjak*, serow *Capricornis sumatraensis*, bharal *Pseudois nayaur*, and possibly markhor *Capra falconeri* are present (Kurt, 1976, 1978; Ranjitsinh, 1979; Rodgers and Panwar, 1988), as well as Himalayan black bear *Selenarctos thibetanus* (V), common langur *Presbytis entellus*, and rhesus macaque *Maccaca mulatta* (Scott et al., 1988). The most important areas for wildlife are considered to be the Kiar and Kiber valleys. Hangul is reported to occur in Kiar, but only in the severest of winters when animals are thought to migrate from the Dachigam population 100–150 km to the north-west. Goral is reported to occur around Sondar and Sirshi, ibex in the Bramah area and snow leopard in Upper Kiar (Scott et al., 1988).

Some 78 species of birds have been recorded in the park (Scott et al., 1988). Among the pheasants, Himalayan monal *Lophophorus impejanus* and koklass *Pucrasia macrolopha* are present at low densities, but the status of western tragopan *Tragopan melanocephalus* (V) remains uncertain. The most recent evidence of the species is a specimen collected from the park in 1984.

Cultural Heritage Racial groups include Thakurs, Kashmiris, Gujjars, Rajputs and Brahmans (Bacha, 1986).

Local Human Population The park has a large human population, with an estimated 12,000 people in the six main villages and several smaller settlements of Marau Valley. In addition, there are large numbers of Gujjars, each family owning 200–300 sheep and goats, 3–4 horses and up to 5 buffalo and cattle (Scott et al., 1988). According to Khan (n.d.) there are some 115 families of nomadic graziers with 40,000 head of livestock, and an unspecified number of families from nearby villages with 20,000 head have grazing rights in the park. Some agriculture is practised in peripheral areas.

Visitors and Visitor Facilities The park is inaccessible by road but there are plans to link Inshan (to the north of the park) and Palmar (just beyond its south-western border) by a jeepable road (Scott et al., 1988). Kishtwar is a potential tourist attraction but there are almost no facilities at present. Forest rest houses exist at Ekhala and Sirshi. An additional two, with catering facilities for tourists, are planned for the tract between Sirshi and Yurdu (Bacha, 1986).

Scientific Research and Facilities Gaston (1982) made some preliminary observations of the wildlife in 1982. A survey of the wildlife and resident human population was conducted in 1988 by a team of students from Newcastle University (Scott et al., 1988).

Conservation Value Kishtwar is arguably the most important cis-Himalayan area in the state on account of its fairly large size and diverse mammalian fauna, including a number of rare and threatened species (Bacha, 1986).

Conservation Management Forests were exploited to their severe detriment up until 1948, since when logging has been scientifically managed and finally ceased with the establishment of the park (Bacha, 1986). A management plan has been prepared for the period 1985–90 (Khan, n.d.), according to which the park will be zoned into core and buffer areas of 27,500 ha and 15,000 ha, respectively. No grazing will be allowed in the core zone, existing grazing rights being compensated through payment and provision of alternative grazing grounds. The park has recently been earmarked as one of seven snow leopard reserves under a scheme launched by Central Government and aimed at conserving the species, its prey populations and its fragile mountain habitat (Freeman, 1987).

Management Constraints The level of disturbance from graziers and their livestock is high but the need to control this is recognised. Encroachment and poaching are persistent problems. Himalayan black bear and rhesus macaque cause damage to crops and leopard and brown bear take livestock (Kurt, 1976; Bacha, 1986, Scott et al., 1988). There are plans for a hydro-electric dam at Hunzal, on the Marau River, which would not only drown large areas of forest but pose a considerable threat to wildlife from the inevitable road construction and import of thousands of labourers (Gaston, 1982).

Staff One range officer, three foresters, fifteen wildlife guards, and nine clerical and other staff. A director and an additional fifteen wildlife guards are proposed under the snow leopard recovery plan (Bacha, 1986).

Budget An annual expenditure increasing from Rs 8.6 lakh (of which Rs 3.9 lakh is recurrent) in 1986–7 to Rs 11.20 lakh (of which Rs 6.8 lakh is recurrent) in 1989–90 has been proposed, on the basis of 50% of the costs being met by Central Government (Bacha, 1986).

Local Addresses
Range Officer, Marau Forest Division, Sirshi, Doda District, Jammu & Kashmir

References
Bacha, M.S. (1986). *Snow leopard recovery plan for Kishtwar High Altitude National Park, Jammu and Kashmir State, 1986–87 to 1989–90*. Department of Wildlife Protection, Srinagar. 51 pp.
Champion, H.G. and Seth, S.K. (1968). *Revised survey of the forest types of India*. Government of India, Delhi.
Freeman, H. (1987). India initiates snow leopard projects. *Snowline* 13: 2.
Gaston, A.J. (1982). A national park for Kishtwar. *Hornbill* (4): 10–14.
Khan, M.S. (n.d.). Ecological-cum management plan for Kishtwar High Altitude National Park, Jammu & Kashmir State (1985–1990). Department of Wildlife Protection, Srinagar. (Unseen)
Kurt, F. (1976). Study plan for IUCN/WWF Project no. 1103 (22–4): Hangul, India—ecological study to identify conservation needs. Unpublished. 20 pp.

Kurt, F. (1978). IUCN/WWF Project no. 1103 (22–4): Hangul, India—ecological study to identify conservation needs. Final report. Unpublished. 23 pp.

Ranjitsinh, M.K. (1979). Conservation in Kashmir. A brief note with some recommendations. UNEP, Bangkok. Unpublished. 17 pp.

Rodgers, W.A. and Panwar, H.S. (1988). *Planning a wildlife protected area network in India*. 2 vols. Project FO: IND/82/003. FAO, Dehra Dun.

Scott, G., Rowcliffe, M., Stoneman, J. and Watts, S. (1988). University of Newcastle Kashmir Expedition 1988. Final report. Unpublished. 40 pp.

KUGTI SANCTUARY

IUCN Management Category   IV (Managed Nature Reserve)

Biogeographical Province   2.38.12 (Himalayan Highlands)

Geographical Location   Lies in Chamba District some 87 km east of Chamba township. 32°25′–32°35′N, 76°44′76°53′E

Date and History of Establishment   First notified a sanctuary in 1962 and renotified on 27 March 1974, having been renowned as a good hunting area in the past.

Area   Notified as 37,887 ha, but re-estimated by IIPA/Environmental Studies Division (pers. comm.) as 33,000 ha using digitised maps. It is linked by a forest corridor to Tundah Sanctuary (41,948 ha) in the west.

Land Tenure   Provincial government. Local people exercise traditional rights.

Altitude   Ranges from 2,250 m to 6,044 m.

Physical Features   Kugti encompasses the catchment of the upper Budhil Nala, a tributary of the Ravi River. It is surrounded by high mountain ranges on all but its western side. The topography is diverse and features several peaks above 5,000 m and numerous glaciers.

Climate   Lying in an inner Himalayan valley, conditions are drier than on the southernmost slopes. Mean annual precipitation is 445 mm. Temperature ranges from −10 °C to 25° C (Singh et al., 1990).

Vegetation   Consists mainly of higher altitude conifers, predominantly fir *Abies pindrow*, with some mixed deciduous woodland, particularly along the valley-bottom. There are also extensive areas of subalpine forest and alpine scrub (Gaston et al., 1981a). Moist cedar forest *Cedrus deodara* extends over 5,800 ha and western mixed coniferous forest over 6,028 ha (Singh et al., 1990). A preliminary list of the flora is given by Singh et al. (1990).

Fauna   Information about the fauna is scanty. The locality is reputed to be particularly good for brown bear *Ursus arctos*, which traditionally was hunted in this area by the Rajas of Kulu. The species is still present, together with goral *Nemorhaedus goral* and Himalayan tahr *Hemitragus jemlahicus*. Serow *Capricornis sumatraensis* and ibex *Capra ibex* are also reputed to be present (Gaston et al., 1981a, 1983). Other mammals listed by Singh et al. (1990) include Himalayan black bear *Selenarctos thibetanus* (V), leopard cat *Felis bengalensis*, leopard *Panthera pardus* (T), common langur *Presbytis entellus* and yellow-throated marten *Martes flavigula*.

Some 117 species of birds were recorded by Gaston et al. (1981a) in the Ravi Valley, from Dalhousie and Chamba upwards. Published information specific to Kugti Sanctuary is limited to pheasants. Koklass pheasant *Pucrasia macrolopha* is numerous and Himalayan monal *Lophophorus impejanus* occurs in small numbers. Cheer pheasant *Catreus wallichii* (E) has been recorded on the north side of Budhil Nala, but not within the sanctuary itself (Gaston et al., 1981a, 1981b). Western tragopan *Tragopan melanocephalus* (V) is reported by local people to be present and Gaston (1979) obtained inconclusive evidence, but no sign of the species was found during a recent survey by the Zoological Survey of India (Narang et al., 1987, cited in Singh et al., 1990).

Cultural Heritage The annual pilgrimage to Mani Mahesh Temple is attended by thousands of people (Singh et al., 1990).

Local Human Population There are two villages (Kugti and Upril Kugti) inside the sanctuary with a total population of 651, and a further nine villages with 1,255 people in adjoining areas. Some 7,384 livestock from inside and surrounding villages graze within the sanctuary, together with an additional 25,000 brought in by Gaddis (Singh et al., 1990).

Visitors and Visitor Facilities The sanctuary is remotely located, being two days walk from the roadhead at Brahmaur. It is a thoroughfare for trekkers travelling to Lahul and Spiti via Kugti Galu (pass). There is a forest rest house at Kugti and another on the outskirts of the sanctuary at Sandi (Singh et al., 1990).

Scientific Research and Facilities A preliminary survey of the wildlife was carried out in May 1979 (Gaston et al., 1979, 1981a). Subsequently, the Zoological Survey of India included Kugti in its survey of western tragopan (Singh et al., 1990). There are no scientific facilities.

Conservation Value Kugti has a diverse topography, appearing promising for wildlife compared to elsewhere in the Ravi Valley (Gaston et al., 1981a). Its Mani Mahesh Temple is an important pilgrimage site (Singh et al., 1990).

Conservation Management Residents have rights or leases in relation to grazing, cultivation and collection of fuelwood, timber, fodder and minor forest products. Plantations were established over 133 ha from 1979 to 1984. There is no management plan (Singh et al., 1990). It has been recommended that the sanctuary be extended to include a forest buffer to increase its long-term viability (Rodgers and Panwar, 1988).

Management Constraints Some hunting occurs, notably of Himalayan tahr for meat (Gaston et al., 1981a). In 1984, there was a major forest fire and avalanches carried away thousands of trees (Singh et al., 1990).

Staff One range officer (also responsible for Tundah and Gamgul Siahbehi sanctuaries), one deputy range officer, five forest guards, and one part-time *chowkidar*.

Budget No information

Local Addresses

Range Officer, Kugti Sanctuary, Kugti Village, Tehsil Brahmaur, District Chamba, Himachal
    Pradesh

References

Gaston, A.J. (1979). Pheasant surveys in the Ravi Valley, 18–25 November 1978, 11–24 January,
    and 9–19 May 1979. Report to World Pheasant Association and Himachal Pradesh Forest
    Department. Unpublished.
Gaston, A.J., Hunter, M.L. Jr., and Garson, P.J. (1981a). The wildlife of Himachal Pradesh,
    Western Himalayas. *University of Maine School of Forest Resources Technical Notes* no.
    82. 159 pp.
Gaston, A.J., Garson, P.J., and Hunter, M.L. Jr. (1981b). Present distribution and status of
    pheasants in Himachal Pradesh, Western Himalayas. *WPA Journal* 6: 10–30.
Gaston, A.J., Garson, P.J., and Hunter, M.L. Jr. (1983). The status and conservation of forest
    wildlife in Himachal Pradesh, Western Himalayas. *Biological Conservation* 27: 291-314.
Rodgers, W.A. and Panwar, H.S. (1988). *Planning a wildlife protected area network in India.* 2
    vols. Project FO: IND/82/003. FAO, Dehra Dun.
Singh, S., Kothari, A., and Pande, P. (Eds.) (1990). *Directory of national parks and sanctuaries
    in Himachal Pradesh.* Indian Institute of Public Administration, New Delhi. Pp. 48–50.

LACHIPORA SANCTUARY

IUCN Management Category IV (Managed Nature Reserve)

Biogeographical Province 2.38.12 (Himalayan Highlands)

Geographical Location Lies 83 km west of Srinagar and occupies the north bank of the
River Jhelum. It is bounded to the north by Kakau Forest in Langet Forest Division, to the
south by Maidan Forest, to the south-east by the River Jhelum, to the west by the cease-fire
line and to the east by Bagna and Limber forests (Department of Wildlife Protection, 1987).
Approximately 34°13′N, 74°08′E

Date and History of Establishment Notified a sanctuary in 1987.

Area 8,000 ha. Nearby, to the east, is Limber Sanctuary (2,600 ha).

Land Tenure Provincial government. Local people enjoy certain rights.

Altitude Ranges from 1,630 m to over 3,300 m.

Physical Features Encompasses the catchment of Katha Nilnag, which flows into the River
Jhelum. The terrain is mountainous, with high cliffs and narrow gullies arising from heavy
folding (Department of Wildlife Protection, 1987).

Climate This section of the Jhelum Valley is exposed to the influence of the south-west
monsoon, with much precipitation occurring in summer (Department of Wildlife Protection,
1987).

Vegetation   Forests are predominantly coniferous, with cedar *Cedrus deodara*, blue pine *Pinus griffithii*, silver fir *Abies pindrow*, and a little spruce *Picea smithiana*. Blue pine forest occurs at lowest altitudes (1,630–2,500 m), sometimes in pure stands but usually mixed with cedar, silver fir, and spruce. Broadleaved associates include maple *Acer* spp., Indian chestnut *Aesculus indica*, walnut *Juglans regia*, and ash *Fraxinus* spp. The understorey is dominated by *Indigofera heterantha* and *Viburnum* spp. There is an almost pure stand of cedar in Compartment 9. Silver fir forest, with spruce and blue pine as associates at higher altitudes, occurs on steeper slopes up to 3,350 m, above which is birch *Betula utilis* forest, and higher up alpine pasture (Department of Wildlife Protection, 1987).

Fauna   The area is one of the few remaining refuges of the markhor *Capra falconeri* (V) in Jammu & Kashmir. Twelve other mammals are reportedly present, including rhesus macaque *Macaca mulatta*, common langur *Presbytis entellus*, Himalayan black bear *Selenarctos thibetanus* (V), brown bear *Ursus arctos*, leopard *Panthera pardus* (T), and Himalayan musk deer *Moschus chrysogaster* (Department of Wildlife Protection, 1987).

A considerable variety of birds has been reported (Department of Wildlife Protection, 1987). Most noteworthy is the reported presence of western tragopan *Tragopan melanocephalus* (V).

Cultural Heritage   No information

Local Human Population   There are eleven villages within the catchment area of Katha Nilnag, of which Lachipora is the largest. Villagers have their own fields and orchards, and they have rights of grazing in the sanctuary. In addition, graziers from Rajouri and Poonch bring their livestock to graze in the upper reaches. According to the Revenue Department's 1980–1 census figures, the Katha Nilnag catchment supports 6,905 residents and several thousand livestock (Department of Wildlife Protection, 1987).

Visitors and Visitor Facilities   No information

Scientific Research and Facilities   Apart from a preliminary survey of the wildlife (Department of Wildlife Protection, 1987), no research has been undertaken. There are no scientific facilities.

Conservation Value   The area is particularly important for markhor and western tragopan (Department of Wildlife Protection, 1987).

Conservation Management   Lachipora was established as a sanctuary primarily to protect the markhor (Department of Wildlife Protection, 1987).

Management Constraints   Natural resources within the sanctuary are used by the local people, but there is no information about the level of this exploitation.

Staff   No information

Budget   No information

Local Addresses   No information

References
Department of Wildlife Protection (1987). Status survey report of proposed Lachipora Wildlife
   Sanctuary. Department of Wildlife Protection, Srinagar. Unpublished. 6pp.

LIMBER SANCTUARY

IUCN Management Category   IV (Managed Nature Reserve)

Biogeographical Province   2.38.12 (Himalayan Highlands)

Geographical Location   Lies about 74 km west of Srinagar and occupies the north bank
of the River Jhelum. It is bounded to the north by Bhurji Forest in Langet Forest Division,
south by the River Jhelum, east by Katha Forest and to the west by Islamabad Forest.
Approximately 34°09'N, 74°09'E

Date and History of Establishment   Notified a sanctuary in 1987, the core of 1,200 ha
having originally been a game reserve.

Area   2,600 ha. Lachipora Sanctuary (8,000 ha) is very near to the west.

Land Tenure   Provincial government.

Altitude   No information

Physical Features   Comprises the entire catchment of Limber Nala, which flows into the
Jhelum River near Pringal Village. The topography consists of steep slopes, broken by
precipitous cliffs in the upper reaches of the catchment. Extensive avalanches and occasional
landslips are characteristic of the upper valley (Department of Wildlife Protection, 1987).

Climate   Conditions are similar to those prevailing in the Vale of Kashmir (Department of
Wildlife Protection, 1987).

Vegetation   Forests are predominantly coniferous, with cedar *Cedrus deodara*, blue pine
Pinus griffithii, silver fir *Abies pindrow*, and a little spruce *Picea smithiana*. Blue pine, often
accompanied by scattered stands of cedar, occurs on exposed southern slopes at lower altitudes.
Broad-leaved associates include maple *Acer* spp., Indian chestnut *Aesculus indica*, and walnut
Juglans regia. The understorey is dominated by *Indigofera heterantha* and *Viburnum* spp. or,
in the case of cedar forests, by *Parrotiopsis jacquemontiana*. Silver fir predominates at higher
altitudes, above which occurs birch *Betula utilis* forest and, higher up, alpine pastures
(Department of Wildlife Protection, 1987).

Fauna   The area is one of the few remaining refuges of the markhor *Capra falconeri* (V)
in Jammu & Kashmir. Eleven other mammal species are present, including rhesus macaque
Macaca mulatta, common langur *Presbytis entellus*, Himalayan black bear *Selenarctos
thibetanus* (V), brown bear *Ursus arctos*, leopard *Panthera pardus* (T), and Himalayan musk
deer *Moschus chrysogaster* (Department of Wildlife Protection, 1987).

A considerable variety of birds has been reported (Department of Wildlife Protection, 1987).

Cultural Heritage   No information

Local Human Population   There are five villages with a total human population of 2,312 persons in the catchment of Limber Nala, but none occurs inside the core areas as demarcated by the boundaries of the former game reserve. They have their own fields and orchards. Concessions include collection of fuelwood and fodder from the catchment area, as well as grazing livestock (1,848 head) in the alpine pastures during summer. These pastures are also used by graziers from the Rajouri and Poonch areas (Department of Wildlife Protection, 1987).

Visitors and Visitor Facilities   No information

Scientific Research and Facilities   Apart from a preliminary survey of the wildlife (Department of Wildlife Protection, 1987), no research has been undertaken. There are no scientific facilities.

Conservation Value   The core of the sanctuary is uninhabited and is an important refuge for markhor (Department of Wildlife Protection, 1987).

Conservation Management   Limber was established as a sanctuary primarily to protect the markhor. It is proposed that the sanctuary be zoned, with the upper uninhabited section of Limber Valley, formerly a game reserve, forming a core area of about 1,200 ha which will be kept free from disturbance (including graziers). The core is surrounded by a buffer comprising compartments 10 to 19 (Department of Wildlife Protection, 1987).

Management Constraints   Natural resources within the sanctuary are used by the local people, but there is no information about the level of this exploitation.

Staff   No information

Budget   No information

Local Addresses   No information

References
Department of Wildlife Protection (1987). Status survey report of the proposed Limber Wildlife Sanctuary. Department of Wildlife Protection, Srinagar. Unpublished. 5 pp.

LIPPA ASRANG SANCTUARY

IUCN Management Category   IV (Managed Nature Reserve)

Biogeographical Province   2.38.12 (Himalayan Highlands)

Geographical Location   Lies in Kinnaur District, 28 km from Morang, the nearest town. Access is via Kalpa to Jangi, and onward by foot (26 km). 31°40′–31°44′N, 78°08′–78°17′E.

Date and History of Establishment   First notified as a sanctuary in 1962 and renotified on 27 March 1974.

Area   Notified as 3,090 ha, but re-estimated by IIPA/Environmental Studies Division (pers. comm.) as 2,953 ha using digitised maps.

Land Tenure   Provincial government. Villagers from outside the sanctuary enjoy certain rights.

Altitude   Ranges from 4,000 m to 5,022 m.

Physical Features   Much of this high-altitude sanctuary is a plateau of barren cold desert.

Climate   Temperatures range from −10 °C to 15 °C. Mean annual rainfall is 226 mm (Singh et al., 1990).

Vegetation   Forest types include lower Western Himalayan temperate, upper West Himalayan temperate, kharsu oak, dry broad-leaved and coniferous, dry temperate coniferous, dry alpine scrub, and dwarf junifer scrub. A preliminary list of the flora is given in Singh et al. (1990).

Fauna   Mammals reportedly include leopard *Panthera pardus* (T), Himalayan black bear *Selenarctos thibetanus* (V), brown bear *Ursus arctos*, musk deer *Moschus chrysogaster*, goral *Nemorhaedus goral*, ibex *Capra ibex*, blue sheep *Pseudois nayaur*, and yak *Bos grunniens* (E) (Singh et al., 1990). In April 1989, 26 bharal and 11 ibex were seen on the same hillside by Pandey (1990). Singh et al. (1990) provide a preliminary list of eight bird species recorded in the sanctuary.

Cultural Heritage   No information

Local Human Population   One farmstead and seven summer settlements are located inside the sanctuary. One village, nine summer settlements and a few farmsteads are located in adjacent areas, with a total population of 500 people. The total number of livestock grazing inside the sanctuary is 23,429 (Singh et al., 1990).

Visitors and Visitor Facilities   The area is not yet open for tourism. Inner Line permits are required to visit the area, and foreign nationals are not ordinarily allowed entry. Three rest houses are located outside the sanctuary.

Scientific Research and Facilities   Pandey (1991) surveyed the ungulate populations in April 1989.

Conservation Value   The sanctuary is one of the few in India in which yak is reportedly present, although it may well be feral (Singh et al., 1990).

Conservation Management   Villagers from adjoining areas have rights in relation to grazing, collection of timber, fuelwood and minor forest produce and extraction of fodder.

There is no management plan. A 9 km unmetalled road that passes through the sanctuary is under the control of the Public Works Department.

Management Constraints   No information

Staff   One range officer and one forest guard. The range officer, located at Nugulsari, is additionally in charge of Rakchham Chitkul Sanctuary.

Budget   None

Local Addresses
Range Officer (Wildlife), Nugulsar, District Kinnaur, Himachal Pradesh

References
Pandey, S. (1991). Species accounts. Report to the Wildlife Institute of India, Dehra Dun. Unpublished. 4 pp.
Singh, S., Kothari, A., and Pande, P. (Eds.) (1990). *Directory of national parks and sanctuaries in Himachal Pradesh: management status and profiles.* Indian Institute of Public Administration, New Delhi. Pp. 51–3.

LUNG NAG SANCTUARY

IUCN Management Category   Proposed

Biogeographical Province   2.38.12 (Himalayan Highlands)

Geographical Location   Lies about 8 km south-east of Padum, in the southern Zanskar region of Ladakh. Occupies sections of the Tsarap and Kargiakh valleys, collectively referred to as Lung Nag. Approximately 32°57′–33°22′N, 76°53′–77°18′E

Date and History of Establishment   Proposed as a sanctuary by the Department of Wildlife Protection.

Area   According to the Department of Wildlife Protection, the area is 40,000 ha, but the actual extent of the sanctuary is unclear. It is shown in a map as extending to Kargiakh but described in the same document as extending well beyond this village, as far as Shingo La (Department of Wildlife Protection, n.d.). In the case of the latter, the area would be nearer 75,000 ha (Mallon, 1987, 1989).

Land Tenure   No information

Altitude   Ranges from 3,600 m to 6,100 m (Mallon, 1989).

Physical Features   Lung Nag, meaning 'dark valley' in Ladakhi, occupies the catchment of Lung Nag River (also known as Tsarap Chu), the eastern arm of the Zanskar River. Below Tangtse the valley changes from being wide and glacial, with river terraces, to having a narrow V-shaped profile. Between Purne and Mune, it continues to be narrow and steep, thereafter opening out.

Climate   Proximity to the main Himalayan range ensures a greater amount of precipitation than elsewhere in Ladakh but data are not available. Winter snowfall is usually heavy (Mallon, 1989).

Vegetation   Lung Nag is a dry, temperate, and predominantly alpine valley, with well-developed grasslands and herbaceous cover in some areas and dense scrub along some valley bottoms (Dhar and Kachroo, 1983). There is virtually no forest cover, but the most common shrubs are willow *Salix* spp. and cultivated poplar *Populus* spp. (Department of Wildlife Protection, n.d.). Rose *Rosa webbiana* is particularly widespread, and junipers *Juniperus* spp. are occasional.

Fauna   Some seven species of mammals are known to occur in the area, including wolf *Canis lupus* (V), snow leopard *Panthera uncia* (E), ibex *Capra ibex*, and bharal *Pseudois nayaur* (Department of Wildlife Protection, n.d.). Fox et al. (1986) found considerable evidence of snow leopard activity and recorded 225 ibex and 10 bharal in 1986. The area falls within a zone of overlap marking the eastern limit of the ibex and the western limit of bharal in Ladakh (Osborne et al., 1983).

Published information about the avifauna is not available.

Cultural Heritage   The local Zanskari people are Buddhists of Indo-Tibetan descent. There are monasteries at Bardan, Mune and Phuktal, the last-mentioned being one of two rare cave monasteries in Zanskar.

Local Human Population   A number of villages occur within the area. There are 200–250 resident families, with some 5,200 head of livestock. In addition, Gaddis from Himachal Pradesh bring their livestock to graze in the area in summer (Department of Wildlife Protection, n.d.).

Visitors and Visitor Facilities   Lung Nag lies along a popular trekking route between Darcha in Lahul and Padum. The route is accessible only in summer when the road from Kargil to Padum is open. Phuktal receives many visitors, where limited food and accommodation is available.

Scientific Research and Facilities   A preliminary survey of the snow leopard and its prey species was carried out in June 1986 (Fox et al., 1986). There are no scientific facilities.

Conservation Value   No information

Conservation Management   The area affords good habitat for snow leopard and ibex, in particular. With its many villages and several monasteries, it is also of considerable cultural importance, especially Phuktal Gompa.

Management Constraints   Resources are used by the local people and pastoralists from Himachal Pradesh, but the level of this exploitation has not been assessed.

Staff   None

Budget None

Local Addresses None

References

Dhar, U. and Kachroo, P. (1983). *Alpine flora of Kashmir Himalaya.* Scientific Publisher, Jodhpur.

Department of Wildlife Protection (n.d.). *Status survey report of notified and proposed national parks, sanctuaries and reserves in Ladakh region.* Department of Wildlife Protection, Srinagar. 29 pp.

Fox, J.L., Sinha, S.P., Chundawat, R.S., and Das, P.K. (1986). A survey of snow leopard and associated species in the Himalaya of north-western India. Project Completion Report. Wildlife Institute of India, Dehra Dun. 51 pp.

Mallon, D.P. (1987). An ecological survey of the protected area network in Ladakh. Report to the Department of Wildlife Protection, Srinagar. Unpublished. 15 pp.

Mallon, D.P. (1989). An ecological survey of the protected area network in Ladakh. Report to the Department of Wildlife Protection, Jammu and Kashmir Government, Srinagar. Unpublished. 13 pp.

Osborne, B.C., Mallon, D.P., and Fraser S.J.R. (1983). Ladakh, threatened stronghold of rare Himalayan mammals. *Oryx* 17: 182–9.

MAJATHAL SANCTUARY

IUCN Management Category IV (Managed Nature Reserve)

Biogeographical Province 2.38.12 (Himalayan Highlands)

Geographical Location Lies in Simla District, some 76 km by road from Simla to the south-east. Bounded to the north by the Sutlej River and to the south by a mountain ridge. 31°15′–31°18′N, 76°56′–77°02′E

Date and History of Establishment First notified a sanctuary in 1962 and renotified on 27 March 1974.

Area Notified as 3,939 ha, but re-estimated by IIPA/Environmental Studies Division (pers. comm.) as 3,164 ha using digitised maps. Darlaghat Sanctuary lies to the south-west on the other side of the mountain ridge.

Land Tenure Provincial government. Local people enjoy certain rights.

Altitude Ranges from 900 m to 1,966 m.

Physical Features Comprises a short section of the southern side of the Sutlej Valley. The terrain is steep.

Climate Mean annual precipitation is 1,040 mm. Temperature ranges from −1 °C to 29 °C (Singh et al., 1990).

Vegetation   Slopes are sparsely forested with chir pine *Pinus roxburghii* and ban oak *Quercus incana*, and mostly dominated by grassy tracts, often extending continuously from the ridge-tops down to about 1,000 m (Garson, 1983). A preliminary list of the flora is given by Singh et al. (1990).

Fauna   Mammals reportedly include common langur *Presbytis entellus*, rhesus macaque *Maccaca mulatta*, Himalayan black bear *Selenarctos thibetanus* (V), jackal *Canis aureus*, yellow-throated marten *Martes flavigula*, common palm civet *Paradoxurus hermaphroditus*, Himalayan palm civet *Paguma larvata*, jungle cat *Felis chaus*, leopard *Panthera pardus* (T), sambar *Cervus unicolor*, Indian muntjac *Muntiacus muntjak*, goral *Nemorhaedus goral*, and wild boar *Sus scrofa* (Singh et al., 1990). Muntjac is common (Garson, 1983) and goral is extremely common within a 25 sq. km area of grassy slopes at Majathal Harsingh (Cavallini, 1990).

Cheer pheasant *Catreus wallichii* (E) has been recorded at a density approaching 24 pairs per sq. km (Garson, 1983), higher than for anywhere else surveyed in Himachal Pradesh (Gaston et al., 1983). Kalij pheasant *Lophura leucomelana* is also common (A.J. Gaston, pers. comm.).

Cultural Heritage   Places of religious interest include Harsingh Temple (Singh et al., 1990).

Local Human Population   There are 17 villages, with a total population exceeding 700 people, inside the sanctuary. Some 1,277 ha of the sanctuary are cultivated. The livestock population totals 2,615 of which 915 belong to residents and 1,700 to non-residents (Singh et al., 1990).

Visitors and Visitor Facilities   There is one rest house in the sanctuary.

Scientific Research and Facilities   A preliminary survey of the cheer pheasant population was carried out in March–April 1983 (Garson, 1983), and the goral population surveyed in late-1989 (Cavallini, 1990).

Conservation Value   The flora and fauna of Majathal is representative of the lower altitudes of the Western Himalaya (Singh et al., 1990). The sanctuary may be one of the most important sites in Himachal Pradesh for cheer pheasant and the only contemporary site known within the Sutlej catchment (Garson, 1983).

Conservation Management   There is no management plan. Residents have rights in relation to cultivation, grazing, collection of timber, fuelwood, fodder and minor forest products. Rights also exist in relation to religious pilgrimages, monuments and burial grounds (Singh et al., 1990). In 1983, the grasslands did not appear to have been grazed, cut nor burned for several seasons. The reasons for such apparent neglect need to be identified in order to safeguard the future of the cheer population (Garson, 1983).

Management Constraints   There is heavy pressure on the sanctuary's natural resources from surrounding villages (W.A. Rodgers, pers. comm., 1987). Forest fires are common (Singh et al., 1990).

Staff   One range officer, one deputy range officer and three forest guards.

Budget   No information

Local Addresses   Range Officer (Wildlife), Piplughat, District Solan, Himachal Pradesh

References

Cavallini, P. (1990). Status of the goral (*Nemorhaedus goral*) in Himachal Pradesh, India. *Caprinae News* 5(1): 4–6.

Garson, P.J. (1983). The cheer pheasant *Catreus wallichii* in Himachal Pradesh, Western Himalayas: an update. *World Pheasant Association Journal* 8: 29–39.

Gaston, A.J., Hunter, M.L. Jr., and Garson, P.J. (1981). The wildlife of Himachal Pradesh, Western Himalayas. *University of Maine School of Forest Resources Technical Notes* no. 82. 159 pp.

Singh, S., Kothari, A. and Pande, P. (Eds.) (1990). *Directory of national parks and sanctuaries in Himachal Pradesh.* Indian Institute of Public Administration, New Delhi. Pp. 54–6.

MANALI SANCTUARY

IUCN Management Category   IV (Managed Nature Reserve)

Biogeographical Province   2.38.12 (Himalayan Highlands)

Geographical Location   Lies immediately west of Manali township in Kulu District and comprises the catchment area of the Manalsu Nala. 32°13'–32°15'N, 77°05'–77°10'E

Date and History of Establishment   Notified a sanctuary on 26 February 1954 under the Punjab Birds and Wild Animals Protection Act 1933, but not subsequently renotified under the Wildlife (Protection) Act, 1972.

Area   Notified as 3,180 ha, but re-estimated by IIPA/Environmental Studies Division (pers. comm.) as 3,127 ha using digitised maps.

Land Tenure   Provincial government. Local people enjoy certain rights.

Altitude   Ranges from 2,273 m to 5,173 m.

Physical Features   Manalsu Nala is a minor tributary of the Beas River. It flows south from its headwaters, comprising Neliall Lake, and then east until its confluence with the Beas River. Only the upper section of the valley shows signs of recent glaciation.

Climate   The Manali area experiences a temperate climate characterised by cool summers and heavy snowfall in winter, regularly in excess of 1 m at 2,000 m. Snow remains from December to March, and in January and February cold northerly winds keep temperatures low (Gaston et al., 1981). Mean annual precipitation is 1,080 mm. Temperature ranges from –4 °C to 30 °C (Singh et al., 1990).

Vegetation   The main forest types distinguished by Gaston et al. (1981) are: lower altitude coniferous forest (up to 2,500 m), dominated by cedar *Cedrus deodara* and blue pine *Pinus wallichiana*, in the lower Manalsu Valley; higher altitude oak forest (2,300–3,200 m), dominated by *Quercus semecarpifolia*, and higher altitude fir forest, dominated by fir *Abies* *pindrow* and spruce *Picea smithiana* on the north and south sides of the valley, respectively; and a substantial area of mixed deciduous forest (1,800 –3,000 m), where the dominant species are horse chestnut *Aesculus indica*, walnut *Juglans regia*, bird cherry *Prunus padus*, elm *Ulmus wallichiana*, and birch *Betula alnoides*. Disturbed areas below 3,000 m often support *Indigofera heterantha* scrub. *Rhus javanica* is also a common component of the forest understorey. Above the tree-line there are patches of juniper *Juniperus communis* and rhododendron *Rhododendron campanulatum* scrub. The herb communities of the alpine pastures are often dominated by nitrophilous species, such as *Bistorta* spp. and *Rumex nepalensis* (Gaston et al., 1981; Green, 1987). A preliminary list of the flora is given by Singh et al. (1990).

Fauna   Some 18 species of larger mammals have been recorded in the Manali area (Gaston et al., 1981, 1983), some of which occur in Manalsu Valley. These include rhesus macaque *Macaca mulatta*, common langur *Presbytis entellus*, Himalayan black bear *Selenarctos thibetanus* (V), leopard *Panthera pardus* (T), Himalayan musk deer *Moschus chrysogaster*, and a population of some 40–50 ibex *Capra ibex* (M.P. Sharma, pers. comm., 1987). The absence of lower altitude refuge areas to which to retreat during periods of deep snow may influence the distribution of goral *Nemorhaedus goral* (present until recently) and Himalayan tahr *Hemitragus jemlahicus* (apparently never present above Manali), neither of which occurs in Manalsu Valley (Gaston et al., 1981, 1983). Snow leopard *Panthera uncia* (E) may have become locally extinct, having been seen last in the Manali area in 1965 (Harnam Singh, cited in Gaston et al., 1983). Other mammals listed by Singh et al. (1990) include brown bear *Ursus arctos*, jungle cat *Felis chaus*, Himalayan palm civet *Paguma larvata*, yellow-throated marten *Martes flavigula*, Indian muntjac *Muntiacus muntjak*, and serow *Capricornis sumatraensis*.

The species diversity for pheasants is high, with western tragopan *Tragopan melanocephalus* (E), Himalayan monal *Lophophorus impejanus*, and koklass pheasant *Pucrasia macrolopha* present in low numbers (Gaston et al., 1981). Some 149 species of birds have been recorded from the Manali area (Gaston et al., 1981). Compared with other areas surveyed in Himachal Pradesh, this area is relatively rich in raptors, both in terms of species abundance and population sizes. The resident passerine avifauna, which is quite distinct in terms of species composition, is less diverse than that of other areas, probably due largely to climatic differences.

Cultural Heritage   No information

Local Human Population   There are no villages within the sanctuary. During the summer six settlements are temporarily occupied by pastoralists, having a total of 50–60 water buffalo and 500–700 sheep and goats (M.P. Sharma, pers. comm., 1987). According to Singh et al. (1990), some 10,000 livestock graze within the sanctuary.

Visitors and Visitor Facilities   Manali Town is a popular summer resort with thousands of visitors arriving annually in April and May, and again in September and October, but relatively few tourists visit the sanctuary which is accessible by foot. There are no visitor facilities in the sanctuary, but various accommodation is available in town.

Scientific Research and Facilities   Manalsu Nala was included in a survey of the wildlife of Himachal Pradesh conducted in 1979–80 (Gaston et al., 1981, 1983). There are no scientific facilities.

Conservation Value   The sanctuary forms part of the catchment of Manalsu Nala, an important tributary of the Beas River. It is particularly important as a refuge for western tragopan (Gaston et al., 1981).

Conservation Management   People from nearby villages have rights to graze livestock, extract fodder, fuelwood, timber and minor forest products and to quarry. Semi-nomadic Gujjars and Gaddis also have grazing rights. A management plan was due to be prepared in 1987. It has been recommended that the sanctuary be enlarged to 25,000 ha to include the Solang Nala watershed to the north (Rodgers and Panwar, 1988).

Management Constraints   Resource use by the local people is not controlled and results in considerable disturbance to the wildlife (Green, 1987). There is some poaching of Himalayan black bear for bile and ibex for meat (M.P. Sharma, pers. comm., 1987).

Staff   One range officer (with additional responsibility for Kais Sanctuary) and four forest guards.

Budget   None allocated in 1987

Local Addresses
Range Officer (Wildlife), PO Manali 175131, Kulu District, Himachal Pradesh

References
Gaston, A.J., Hunter, M.L. Jr., and Garson, P.J. (1981). The wildlife of Himachal Pradesh, Western Himalayas. *University of Maine School of Forest Resources Technical Notes* no. 82. 159 pp.
Gaston, A.J., Garson, P.J., and Hunter, M.L. Jr., (1983). The status and conservation of forest wildlife in Himachal Pradesh, Western Himalayas. *Biological Conservation* 27: 291–314.
Green, M.J.B. (1987). India—trip report. IUCN Conservation Monitoring Centre, Cambridge. Unpublished. 4 pp.
Rodgers, W.A. and Panwar, H.S. (1988). *Planning a wildlife protected area network in India.* 2 vols. Project FO: IND/82/003. FAO, Dehra Dun.
Singh, S., Kothari, A. and Pande, P. (Eds.) (1990). *Directory of national parks and sanctuaries in Himachal Pradesh.* Indian Institute of Public Administration, New Delhi. Pp. 57–9.

NAMDAPHA NATIONAL PARK

IUCN Management Category   II (National Park)

Biogeographical Province   2.38.12 (Himalayan Highlands)

Geographical Location   Lies in Tirap District of eastern Arunachal Pradesh, some 62 km from the town of Marghritta. Bounded to the north by Lohit District boundary, to the east and south by the international border with Burma, to the south-east by unclassified state forest of the Vijoynagar Circle, and to the west by Lohit District boundary and Diyun Reserved Forest of Tirap District. 27°23′–27°39′N, 96°15′–96°58′E

Date and History of Establishment   Notified a national park on 9 June 1983, having originally been designated a reserve forest in 1970 and then a sanctuary in 1972. Declared a tiger reserve in March 1983. Proposed as a biosphere reserve (Ministry of Environment and Forests, 1987).

Area   198,524 ha. Enlarged by 17,741.5 ha on 2 February 1985. Area of proposed biosphere reserve is 450,000 ha, of which 250,000 ha is proposed as a core (Department of Environment, 1983).

Land Tenure   Provincial government

Altitude   Ranges from 200 m to 4,578 m at the top of Daphabum (meaning 'peak of the hills').

Physical Features   The entire area is mountainous and comprises the catchment of the Noa-Dehing River, a tributary of the Brahmaputra River. The Noa-Dehing flows westwards through the middle of the park. Lakes, locally known as *beels*, are scattered throughout the area and attract migratory waterfowl. Also in abundance are salt licks, or *poongs*, of which Bulbulia is famous for its congregations of elephants and other large mammals. Geologically, rocks and soils are of recent origin and include shales, sandstone, conglomerate, clay and coalseams (Chatterjee and Chandiramani, 1986). Further details of the geology and topography are given by Ghosh (1987).

Climate   Conditions are subtropical, with a distinct cold season from December to February. Temperature varies from 5 ° C to 35 ° C at lower altitudes and drops to below freezing point at higher altitudes. July and August are the warmest months. Annual precipitation varies from 2,500 mm to 3,500 mm, 75% of which falls between April and October during the south monsoon. The rest is under the influence of the north-east monsoon from December to March (Chatterjee and Chandiramani, 1986). According to Forest Department sources, total annual precipitation is 6,300 mm (Ghosh, 1987).

Vegetation   The vegetation is luxuriant. Species diversity is high, a reflection of the high annual precipitation, altitudinal range and biogeographic location, being adjacent to the Burma Monsoon Forest Province. Tropical, temperate, and alpine formations are present, with tropical and subtropical evergreen forests predominant. Tropical wet evergreen forests occur in the lower reaches and alpine vegetation higher up near Daphabum. The lowland tropical evergreen forest is perhaps the largest *Dipterocarpus* forest remaining in India. Valley forests can be classified into the following types: Assam Valley tropical evergreen forests, which are typically three-storeyed and dominated by hollong *Dipterocarpus macrocarpus* in well-drained areas and by mekai *Shorea assamica* on drier, gravelly soils; North Indian tropical moist deciduous forests of alluvial flats; and miscellaneous types. Further descriptions of the vegetation are given by Department of Environment (1983), Jain and Sastry (1983), and Ghosh (1987). Some 150 timber species occur in the area. Lists of common species of trees, shrubs, bamboos, climbers, and grasses are given by Chatterjee and Chandiramani (1986).

Fauna   Faunal diversity is high. Chatterjee and Chandiramani (1986) list 61 species of mammals and Ghosh (1987) lists 96 species. The park is an important refuge for hoolock gibbon *Hylobates hoolock* (V) (Choudhury, 1987). Among carnivores present are leopard *Panthera pardus* (T), tiger *P. tigris* (E), snow leopard *P. uncia* (E), and clouded leopard *Neofelis nebulosa* (V), an assemblage that is globally unique to Namdapha. Leopard and tiger populations were estimated to total 40 and 43, respectively, in 1984 (Anon., 1986) but actual numbers are expected to be higher as only accessible areas were censused. A variety of other threatened mammals is present including wild dog *Cuon alpinus* (V), red panda *Ailurus fulgens* (K), Asian golden cat *Felis temmincki* (I), Asian elephant *Elephas maximus* (E), Himalayan musk deer *Moschus chrysogaster*, gaur *Bos gaurus* (V), and wild Asiatic water buffalo *Bubalus bubalis* (E). There were an estimated 150 elephants in 1979 (Forest Department, n.d.). Takin *Budorcas taxicolor* is present, at the southernmost extremity of its distribution in Arunachal Pradesh (Katti et al., 1990).

Of the avifauna, notable species include lesser fishing eagle *Icthyophaga humilis*, mountain hawk-eagle *Spizaetus nipalensis*, grey peacock-pheasant *Polyplectron bicalcaratum*, imperial pigeon *Ducula senex*, mountain imperial pigeon *D. badia*, pin-tailed green pigeon *Treron apicauda*, Oriental bay owl *Phodilus badius*, rufous-necked hornbill *Aceros nipalensis* (R), great (pied) hornbill *Buceros bicornis*, red-headed trogon *Harpactes erythrocephalus*, Hodgson's frogmouth *Batrachostomus hodgsoni*, lesser shortwing *Brachypteryx leucophrys*, scarlet-backed flowerpecker *Dicaeum cruentatum*, Wynaad laughing-thrush *Garrulax delesserti*, rufous-necked laughing-thrush *G. ruficollis*, crimson-winged laughing-thrush *G. proeniceus*, white-hooded shrike babbler *Gampsorhynchus rufulus*, and sultan tit *Melanochlora sultanea* (Chatterjee and Chandirami, 1986). Also present are white-winged wood duck *Cairina scutulata* (V) and tragopan *Tragopan* sp. (Forest Department, n.d.). A flock of seven white-winged wood duck was observed in February 1988 (Singh, 1989). Chatterjee and Chandirami (1986) list 105 species of birds and Ghosh (1987) 233 species.

A total of 76 species of fishes belonging to 35 genera have been recorded from the drainage system, of which five are new to science (*Danio horae, Barilius jayarami, Garra tirapensis, Aborichthys tikadari* and *Kryptoterus indicus*), and three are new to India (*Semiplotus modestus, Garra graveli* and *Noemacheilus rudippinis*). Amphibians total 25 species and include 24 out of 150 species of Anuran known from India. Species new to science are *Rhacophorus namdaphaensis, Philautus namdaphaensis*, and *P. shyamprupus*. At least 11 other species, including *Rhacophorus maximus* (rediscovered after 75 years), are considered to be rare in India. Reptiles total 28 species, of which *Lycodon laoensis* and *Natrix punctutata* are new records for India, and *Cyclemys mouhati, Elaphe mandarina*, and *Trimeresurus macrosquamatus* are considered rare. Invertebrates include 188 species of beetles, of which 14 are new to science, 102 of butterflies, 35 of moths, 24 of Hemiptera, and 15 of Mantodea (Ghosh, 1987).

Cultural Heritage   Many different tribal communities live in the vicinity of the park. They include Chakmas, Lisus, Mizos, and local tribal groups (Ghosh, 1987).

Local Human Population   In 1984 there were 28 villages, with a total population of 5,850 people, in the park (IIPA/Environmental Studies Division, pers. comm.). Miao, just west of the park, has a population in excess of 3,000 people. It has grown since 1974 and is the administration's subdivisional headquarters. Nearby at Choephelling there is a large Tibetan refugee settlement, as well as resettlements of Tikhak Tangsa, Mogba (Naga), and Cha kma tribals. Opposite the Deban Tourist Lodge, on the north bank of the Noa-Dehing River and just outside the western boundary of the national park, is a settlement of about 300 refugee Lamas from Bhutan. There is an old Lisu settlement, known as Siddi and comprising 800 Burmese tribals, on the south-eastern edge of the national park. Details of other settlements in the proposed biosphere reserve are given by Khoshoo (1984).

Visitors and Visitor Facilities   There are rest houses at Miao, Namchik, and Deban. An Inner-Line permit is required for entry into Arunachal Pradesh.

Scientific Research and Facilities   A preliminary survey of the vegetation was conducted by the Botanical Survey of India, revealing species hitherto known only from other parts of the Himalaya, China, Mainland South-east Asia and S. India (Jain and Sastry, 1983). The Zoological Survey of India conducted five faunal surveys between 1981 and 1987. A series of 30 scientific papers, each dealing with a specific animal group, was published in the *Records of the Zoological Society of India* 82: 1–330 (1984) based on collections of 1981–3. A second series of papers is due to be published (Ghosh, 1987). Censuses of tiger and leopard are carried out under Project Tiger. Chandramani (1989) has studied the hoolock gibbon. There is a captive breeding centre with 24 white-winged wood duck at Miao (Singh, 1989).

Conservation Value   Namdapha is 'an area which should pre-eminently be left alone, for future study as an index of a vanishing environment' (Ali and Ripley, 1979). It is a centre of plant and animal diversity, supporting a rich and extremely interesting large number of endemic species, many wild relatives of cultivated plants, and a variety of rare and threatened species. The *Dipterocarpus* forest is considered to be the most extensive tract remaining in India. While the core, constituted by the national park, is reportedly pristine, the surrounding area of the proposed biosphere reserve supports a diversity of tribal communities which is reflected in a wide spectrum of land-use practices (Khoshoo, 1984; Ghosh, 1987). Also, Namdapha's wetlands are of international importance (Scott, 1989).

Conservation Management   A management plan, valid up to 1990, was drafted in March 1983. Recommendations on the demarcation of boundaries and managing the proposed biosphere reserve have been documented (Ministry of Environment and Forests, 1987). It has been recommended that the park be extended to 250,000 ha to incorporate rich temperate forest to the north, and buffered by a 20,000 ha sanctuary to contain threats on lower altitude forests (Rodgers and Panwar, 1988).

Management Constraints   Lower altitude forests are under potential threat from human demand for resources (Rodgers and Panwar, 1988). Within the proposed biosphere reserve, the vast tract of forest on the north bank of the Noa-Dehing River, stretching from the Assam Valley to the Champhaibum foothills, remained uninhabited until the 1960s when it was settled by Hazangs. The area was later resettled by about 15,000 Chakma refugees from the Chittagong Hill Tracts. This rapidly increasing population of primarily slash-and-burn agriculturalists has encroached into reserve forests and unclassified state forests (Department of Environment, 1983).

Staff   Total staff of 86, headed by a divisional forest officer (1989).

Budget   No information

Local Addresses
Divisional Forest Officer, Namdapha National Park, PO Box Miao 792122, District Tirap, Arunachal Pradesh

References
Ali, S. and Ripley, S.D. (1979). Namdapha Wildlife Sanctuary—an appeal for its preservation. *Hornbill* 11: 5–6.

Anon. (1986). Indian tiger census. *Cat News* 4: 4.

Chandramani, S. (1989). Study of hoolock gibbon ecology in Namdapha National Park. Namdapha National Park, Miao. Unpublished. (Unseen)

Chatterjee, A.K. and Chandramani, S.S. (1986). An introduction to Namdapha Tiger Reserve, Arunachal Pradesh, India. *Tiger Paper* 13(3): 22–7.

Choudhury, A. (1987). Notes on the distribution and conservation of Phayre's leaf monkey and hoolock gibbon in India. *Tiger Paper* 14(2): 2–6.

Forest Department (n.d.). Namdapha tiger reserve. Pamphlet produced by VIKSAT, Ahmedabad.

Ghosh, A.K. (1987). *Qualitative analysis of faunal resources. Proposed Namdapha Biosphere Reserve, Arunachal Pradesh*. Zoological Survey of India, Calcutta. 129 pp.

Jain, S.K. and Sastry, A.R.K. (1983). *Botany of some tiger habitats in India*. Botanical Survey of India, Howrah. Pp. 26–9.

Katti, M.V., Manjrekar, N., Mukherjee, S., and Sharma, D. (1990). A report on wildlife survey in Arunachal Pradesh with special reference to takin. Wildlife Institute of India, Dehra Dun. Unpublished. 104 pp.

Khoshoo, T.N. (1984). Biosphere reserves: an Indian approach. In: *Conservation, science and society*. Contributions to the First International Biosphere Reserve Congress, Minsk, USSR, 26 September 1983–2 October 1983. Pp. 185–9.

Ministry of Environment and Forests (1987). *Biosphere reserves*. Government of India, New Delhi. 250 pp.

Rodgers, W.A. and Panwar, H.S. (1988). *Planning a wildlife protected area network in India*. 2 vols. Project FO: IND/82/003. FAO, Dehra Dun.

Scott, D.A. (Ed.) (1989). *A directory of Asian wetlands*. IUCN, Gland, Switzerland and Cambridge, UK. 1,181 pp.

Singh, R.L. (1989). Letter to the editor, dated 3 October 1989. *Zoo's Print* 4(12): 11.

NANDA DEVI NATIONAL PARK

IUCN Management Category   I (Strict Nature Reserve)
X (World Heritage Site—Criteria: iii, iv)

Biogeographical Province   2.38.12 (Himalayan Highlands)

Geographical Location   Lies in Chamoli District, within the Garhwal Himalaya. The main entry point to the park is via Lata Village, some 25 km from Joshimath township. The park is bounded by high mountain ridges and peaks on all sides except its western side, which features a deep and virtually inaccessible gorge. 30 °16′–30 °32′N, 79°44′–80°02′E

Date and History of Establishment   Established as a national park with effect from 6 November 1982 as per Notification no. 3912/14-3-35-80 of 6 September 1982, the intention having been declared under Notification no. 2130/14-3-35-80 of 18 August 1980. Dang (1961) provides an historical account of the exploration of the Nanda Devi basin. The first recorded attempt to enter the sacred basin was by W. W. Graham in 1883, but he was unable to proceed beyond the gorge of the lower Rishi Ganga. Subsequent attempts by Dr T. G. Longstaff in 1870 and Hugh Ruttledge in 1926, 1927, and 1932 also met with failure. Finally, in 1934, Eric Shipton and H. W. Tilman pioneered a route to the 'Inner Sanctuary' by forcing a passage up the gorge of the upper Rishi Ganga. Later, in 1936, Tilman and N. E. Odell made the first ascent of Nanda Devi, reputedly the most outstanding mountaineering success of the pre-Second World War era. It was their accounts of this natural sanctuary that first drew attention to the spectacular mountain wilderness (Tilman, 1935; Shipton, 1936), following which the area was established as a game sanctuary on 7 January 1939 (Government Order no. 1493/XIV-28). Commonly referred to as the 'Nanda Devi Sanctuary', the name was changed to Sanjay Gandhi National Park at the time of notification. This met with local opposition and the site was gazetted as Nanda Devi National Park. The park was inscribed on the World Heritage List in December 1988. The park constitutes the core zone of a much larger area (200,000 ha), extending as far north as the Dhauli Ganga, that has been proposed as a biosphere reserve (Indian National MAB Committee, n.d.).

Area   63,033 ha. This is the official and correct size. Lavkumar (1979) gives the area of the Nanda Devi Basin as 79,900 ha, while Hajra (1983a), Tak and Lamba (1984, 1985) and Lamba (1987) cite a similar figure of c. 80,000 ha for the park but their demarcation of the boundary is inaccurate.

Land Tenure   Provincial government

Altitude   The entire basin is above 3,500 m, apart from the lower Rishi Gorge which descends to 2,100 m. Nanda Devi West at 7,817 m is the highest peak.

Physical Features   The national park comprises the catchment area of the Rishi Ganga, an eastern tributary of Dhauli Ganga which flows into the Alaknanda River at Joshimath. The area is a vast glacial basin, divided by a series of parallel, north-south oriented ridges. These rise up to the encircling mountain rim along which are about a dozen peaks above 6,400 m (21,000 ft), the better known including Dunagiri (7,066 m), Changbang (6,864 m) and Nanda Devi East (7,434 m). Nanda Devi West, India's second highest mountain, lies on a short ridge projecting into the basin and rises up from Nanda Devi East on the eastern rim. Trisul (7,120 m), in the south-west, also lies inside the basin. The upper Rishi Valley, often referred to as the 'Inner Sanctuary', is fed by Changbang, North Rishi and North Nanda Devi glaciers to the north, and by South Nanda Devi and South Rishi glaciers to the south of the Nanda Devi massif. There is an impressive gorge cutting through the Devistan-Rishikot ridge below the confluence of the North and South Rishi rivers. The Trisuli and Ramani glaciers are features of the lower Rishi Valley or 'Outer Sanctuary', below which the Rishi Ganga enters the narrow, steep-sided lower gorge (Lavkumar, 1979b). The basin presents a diverse array of glacial and periglacial forms. The glaciers cover a wide spectrum of growth phases. The combinations of normal and perched glaciers on different rock types add interest to the basin (T.M. Reed, pers. comm., 1988). The greater part of the park falls within the Central Crystallines, a zone of young granites and metamorphic rocks. Along the northern edge is exposed the Tibetan-Tethys, consisting of sediments of sandstones, micaceous quartzite, limestones and shales (Kumar and Sah, 1986). The Tethys sediments form Nanda Devi itself and many of the surrounding peaks, and display spectacular folding and thrusting, while mountains like Changbang are granite (M. P. Searle, pers. comm., 1988). The crystalline rocks of the Vaikrita Group and lower part of the Tethys sediments have been tentatively subdivided into four formations, namely: Lata, Ramani, Kharapatal and Martoli (Maruo, 1979). Further geological details are given by Lamba (1987).

Climate   Being an inner Himalayan valley, Nanda Devi Basin enjoys a distinctive microclimate. Conditions are generally dry with low annual precipitation, but there is heavy rainfall during the monsoon, from late June to August. Prevailing mist and low cloud during the monsoon keeps the soil moist, hence the lusher vegetation than is usually characteristic of drier inner Himalayan valleys. The basin is snow-bound for about six months of the year, snow being deeper and at lower altitudes on the southern side than the northern (Lavkumar, 1979b; Lamba, 1987). Meteorological data is not available.

Vegetation Forests are restricted largely to the Rishi Gorge and are dominated by fir *Abies pindrow*, rhododendron *Rhododendron campanulatum* and birch *Betula utilis* up to about 3,350 m. Forming a broad belt between these and the alpine meadows is birch forest, with an understorey of rhododendron. Conditions are drier within the 'Inner Sanctuary', becoming almost xeric up the main Nanda Devi glaciers. Beyond Ramani, the r egetation switches from forest to dry alpine communities, with scrub juniper *Juniperus pseudosabina* becoming the dominant cover within the 'Inner Sanctuary'. Juniper gives way altitudinally to grasses, prone mosses and lichens, and on riverine soils to annual herbs and dwarf willow *Salix* spp. Woody vegetation extends along the sides of the main glaciers before changing gradually to squat alpines and lichens (Lavkumar, 1979; Reed, 1979; Hajra, 1983a). A total of 312 species, distributed over 199 genera, and 81 families, has been recorded and preserved in the herbarium of the Northern Circle, Botanical Survey of India. At least 17 of these are considered rare (Hajra, 1983a). Not included in this list is *Saussurea sudhanshui*, newly described from the area (Hajra, 1983b). A total of 773 plants has been reported from the proposed biosphere reserve (Indian National MAB Committee, n.d.), but this list is unreliable.

Fauna An account of the 14 known species of mammals is given by Tak and Lamba (1985) and Lamba (1987). The basin is renowned for the abundance of its ungulate populations, notably bharal *Pseudois nayaur* (Tilman, 1937) estimated to number 820 in 1977 (Lavkumar, 1979) and 440 in 1981–4 (Tak and Lamba, 1985; Lamba, 1987). Preliminary observations suggest that Himalayan musk deer *Moschus chrysogaster*, serow *Capricornis sumatraensis*, and Himalayan tahr *Hemitragus jemlahicus* are also fairly common (Lavkumar, 1979; Tak and Lamba, 1985; Lamba, 1987), but probably not as plentiful as previously due to hunting (Dang, 1961). The distribution of goral *Nemorhaedus goral* does not appear to extend to within the basin, although the species does occur in the vicinity of the national park (Tak and Lamba, 1985; Lamba, 1987). Snow leopard *Panthera uncia* (E) is reported to have been 'extraordinarily common' (Dang, 1961).

This may reflect the relative ease with which the species is observed here and in the vicinity (Green, 1982), it being unlikely that the park supports a large snow leopard population because of its comparatively small size and the deep snow in winter (Green, 1988). Other large carnivores are leopard *P. pardus* (T), Himalayan black bear *Selenarctos thibetanus* (V), and brown bear *Ursus arctos*, which is rarely seen. The only primate present is common langur *Presbytis entellus* (Tak and Lamba, 1985; Lamba, 1987). Some 83 species are reported from the proposed biosphere reserve (Indian National MAB Committee, n.d.), but this list is unreliable.

Little has been documented about the avifauna. Reed (1979) recorded 43 species in the North Rishi Gorge. Here the major stronghold was the scrub juniper in which were warblers *Phylloscopus* spp., rubythroat *Erithacus pectoralis*, grosbeaks *Mycerobas* spp., redstarts *Phoenicurus* spp., and rose finches *Carpodacus* spp. A total of approximately 57 species was recorded within the park. Lamba (1987) lists 80 species for the area but the distribution of some of these is restricted to lower altitudes in adjacent areas. Some 546 species are reported from the proposed biosphere reserve (Indian National MAB Committee, n.d.), but this list is unreliable.

Cultural Heritage   Nanda Devi, after Devi (meaning goddess), consort of Shiva, is a manifestation of Parvati and has been revered as a natural monument since ancient times (Reinhard, 1987). Hindus have deified the entire basin and every twelfth year devotees have approached the foot of Trisul to worship Nanda Devi, the 'Blessed Goddess' (Kaur, 1982). The local people are Bhotias, those of Lata Village being Tolchas (Kandari, 1982).

Local Human Population   The park is uninhabited but there are two small villages (Reni and Lata) on the north-western side. Local people used to bring more than 4,000 goats and sheep to Dharansi and Dibrugheta for grazing (Lavkumar, 1979) and derive an income from employment as porters and guides before the area was closed in 1983.

Visitors and Visitor Facilities   The trek to Nanda Devi basecamp is considered to be one of the toughest in the world and has attracted large numbers of mountaineers and trekkers from all over the world (Lamba, 1987). There were an estimated 4,000 visitors (mostly expedition members and porters) in 1982 (Aitken, 1981–2), but the park has since been closed. There are no facilities.

Scientific Research and Facilities   A geological survey was conducted by Maruo (1979). Among the first published observations on the wildlife of Nanda Devi are those of Dang (1961), Lavkumar (1977, 1979) and, in the case of birds, Reed (1979). More recently, surveys of the flora and mammalian fauna have been carried out by the Botanical Survey of India (Hajra, 1983a) and Zoological Survey of India (Tak and Lamba, 1984, 1985; Lamba, 1987), respectively.

Conservation Value   The area is reputedly one of the most spectacular wildernesses in the Himalaya. The basin is dominated by Nanda Devi, a natural monument and India's second highest peak, and drained by the Rishi Ganga which has cut for itself one of the.finest gorges in the world (Shipton, 1936; Kaur, 1982). It supports a diverse flora, largely on account of the wide altitudinal range, and an interesting variety of large mammals, including a number of rare or threatened species. Unlike many other Himalayan areas, it is free from human settlement and has remained largely unspoilt due to its inaccessibility, particularly the forests of the lower Rishi Valley. Nanda Devi National Park meets criteria (iii) and (iv) of the World Heritage Convention based on its exceptional natural beauty and populations of rare and threatened mammals (IUCN Technical Evaluation).

Conservation Management   Traditionally, the alpine pastures around Dharansi and Dibrugheta were grazed by livestock from Lata Village (and latterly from villages as far away as Malari) until the establishment of the park in 1982. The 'Inner Sanctuary' remained unexplored until 1934, when it was opened up to mountaineering. As a result, hunting, collection of medicinal plants and other forms of exploitation ensued. This part of the Himalaya was subsequently closed to foreign visitors from 1945 to 1974 (Lavkumar, 1979; Kaur, 1983). There followed a spate of mountaineering and trekking but, because of the considerable disturbance being caused to the environment (see Aitken, 1981, 1983), tourism was banned following a meeting held on 18 February 1983 under the chairmanship of the Chief Secretary of Uttar Pradesh.

A preliminary management plan has been prepared (Semwal and Asthana, 1986) but by 1988 this had not been sanctioned by the Chief Wildlife Warden. Included in the plan are recommendations concerning the present ban on tourism and ways in which to provide employment for local people. Nandi Devi was earmarked as one of several protected areas for inclusion under the Government of India's Project Snow Leopard (Ministry of Environment and Forests, 1987), but this project has not materialised to date. It has been recommended that the Pindari and Sundadhunga valleys at the southern edge of the Nanda Devi massif be designated a sanctuary to protect their reportedly large and viable ungulate and pheasant populations (Rodgers and Panwar, 1988).

Management Constraints   Litter, felling of trees, and even cultural vandalism caused by expeditions, along with the introduction of sheep and goats to the 'Inner Sanctuary', reached serious proportions prior to the closure of the park (Clarke, 1979; Aitken, 1981, 1983). Virtually nothing is known about the present status of the wildlife within the park, although local people report that poachers from Pithoragarh District are operating in the 'Inner Sanctuary'. The two routes of access into the 'Inner Basin' used to be kept open by expeditions but have not been maintained by the park authorities since the ban on tourism. A few of the wildlife staff have been trained at the Nehru Institute of Mountaineering, Uttarkashi, but they lack the necessary mountaineering equipment to keep routes open.

Staff   There is a total of 31 personnel, including four assistant wildlife wardens, and 22 wildlife guards, headed by a divisional forest officer (1987).

Budget   Approximately Rs 10 lakhs in 1987–8.

Local Addresses
Divisional Forest Officer, Nanda Devi National Park, Joshimath, Chamoli District, Uttar
     Pradesh

References
Aitken, W.M. (1981). The sad saga of Nanda Devi. *Indian Wildlifer, New Delhi* 1(4): 37–41.
Aitken, W.M. (1981-2). Nanda Devi Sanctuary revisited, 1982. *The Himalayan Journal* 39:
     44–50.
Aitken, W.M. (1983). Nanda Devi revisited—1982. *Sanctuary, Asia* 3(1): 44–8.
Clarke, M.D. (1979). Ecological impact on the Nanda Devi area. *The American Alpine Journal*
     53: 281.
Dang, H. (1961). A natural sanctuary in the Himalaya: Nanda Devi and the Rishiganga basin.
     Journal of the Bombay Natural History Society 58: 707–14.
Dang, H. (1967). The snow leopard and its prey. *Cheetal, Journal of the Wildlife Preservation
     Society of India, Dehra Dun* 10: 72–84.
Green, M.J.B. (1982). Status, distribution and conservation of the snow leopard in North India.
     International Pedigree Book of Snow Leopards 3: 6–10.
Green, M.J.B. (1988). Protected areas and snow leopards: their distribution and status. In:
     Freeman, H. (Ed.), *Proceedings of the Fifth International Snow Leopard Symposium.*
     International Snow Leopard Trust, Seattle and Wildlife Institute of India, Dehra Dun. Pp.
     3–20.
Hajra, P.K. (1983a). *A contribution to the botany of Nanda Devi National Park in Uttar Pradesh,
     India.* Botanical Survey of India, Howrah. 38 pp.
Hajra, J. (1983b). A new species of *Saussurea* (Asteraceae) from Nandadevi National Park,
     Chamoli District, Uttar Pradesh. *Indian Forester* 109: 77–9.
Indian National MAB Committee (n.d.). The Nanda Devi Biosphere Reserve Project
     Document 3. Department of Environment, New Delhi. 128 pp.

Kandari, O.P. (1982). Nanda Devi—India's highest Himalayan national park: the problem of resource use and conservation. *Cheetal, Journal of the Wildlife Preservation Society of India, Dehra Dun* 24: 29–36.

Kaur, J. (1982). Nanda Devi, Himalaya's superlative nature phenomenon. In: Singh, T.V., Kaur, J., and Singh, D.P. (Eds.), *Studies in tourism, wildlife parks, tourism.* Metropolitan, New Delhi. Pp. 79–87.

Kumar, G. and Sah, S.C.D. (1986). Effects of changing environment on fauna and flora of Himalayan national parks—case studies of Corbett and Nanda Devi national parks. In: *Corbett National Park Golden Jubilee Souvenir.* Pp. 62–71.

Lamba, B.S. (1987). Status survey report of fauna: Nanda Devi National Park. *Records of the Zoological Survey of India Occasional Paper* no. 103. 50 pp.

Lavkumar, K. (1977). Report on the preliminary survey of the Nanda Devi Basin. WWF-India, Bombay. Unpublished. 27 pp.

Lavkumar, K. (1979). Nanda Devi Sanctuary—1977. *Journal of the Bombay Natural History Society* 75: 868–87.

Lavkumar, K. (1979). Nanda Devi Sanctuary—a naturalist's report. *The Himalayan Journal* 35: 191–209.

Maruo, Y. (1979). Geology and metamorphism of the Nanda Devi region Kumaon Higher Himalaya, India. *Himalayan Geology, Wadia Institute of Himalayan Geology, Dehra Dun* 9: 3–17.

Ministry of Environment and Forests (1987). *Annual report 1986–87.* Government of India, New Delhi. 73 pp.

Reed, T.M. (1979). A contribution to the ornithology of the Rishi Ganga Valley and the Nanda Devi Sanctuary. *Journal of the Bombay Natural History Society* 76: 275–82.

Reinhard, J. (1987). The sacred Himalaya. *The American Alpine Journal* 29: 123–32.

Semwal, D.N. and Asthana, J.S. (1986). Preliminary management plan report of Nanda Devi National Park. Nanda Devi National Park, Joshimath. Mimeo.

Shipton, E.E. (1936). *Nanda Devi.* Hodder and Stoughton, London. 310 pp.

Tak, P.C. and Lamba, B.S. (1984). Field observations on abundance of some smaller mammals at Nanda Devi National Park. *Indian Journal of Forestry.* 7: 242–4.

Tak, P.C. and Lamba, B.S. (1985). Nanda Devi National Park: a contribution to its mammalogy. *Indian Journal of Forestry* 8: 219–30.

Tilman, H. (1935). Nanda Devi and the sources of the Ganges. *Himalayan Journal* 7: 1–25.

Tilman, H.W. (1937). *The ascent of Nanda Devi.* Cambridge University Press, Cambridge. 235 pp.

NOKREK NATIONAL PARK

IUCN Management Category   II (National Park)

Biogeographical Province   4.09.04 (Burma Monsoon Forest)

Geographical Location   Occupies the Tura Range which lies east of Tura Town in the district of Garo Hills West. Approximately 25°23′–25°32′N, 90°19′–90°41′E

Date and History of Establishment   Declared a national park on October 1985. The Tura Range has been recognised and protected as an important watershed by its indigenous people since the beginning of this century. The national park represents the core of the proposed Nokrek (Tura Ridge) Biosphere Reserve (Gogoi, 1981; Ministry of Environment and Forests, 1987), recently designated at the national level by the Government of India (Anon., 1988) but not yet recognised by Unesco.

Area   6,801 ha

Land Tenure   The state government is in the process of acquiring 28 Nokma-owned *Akhing* lands, amounting to a total of 6,650 ha (Gogoi, 1981).

Altitude   Ranges from 600 m to 1,412 m (Nokrek Peak).

Physical Features   The Tura Range constitutes the backbone of the Garo Hills which lie at the western end of the Patkai Range in Assam. This central ridge is oriented along a north-west to south-east axis and lies at about 1,200 m. Numerous rivers and streams originate from these hills and flow over narrow, rocky beds to join the Brahmaputra or Meghna rivers. Southern slopes are very much steeper than northern ones. The terrain is rocky and in many places the ridge is devoid of top soil.

Climate   Conditions in the Garo Hills are tropical, characterised by high rainfall and humidity in the summer monsoon (April–October) and a moderately cold winter. Mean maximum temperature ranges from 25 °C in winter to 30.4 °C in summer. Mean annual rainfall is 3,112 mm spread over 113 days, with June and July as the wettest months (Gogoi, 1981).

Vegetation   The area supports broad-leaved evergreen and semi-evergreen forest, with brakes of bamboo at lower altitudes. Vegetation on southern slopes is limited to occasional patches of moist deciduous forest, dominated by birch *Betula* sp. at higher altitudes, and secondary scrub and forest at lower altitudes. Very little vegetation remains on the gentler northern slopes and it is restricted to a narrow fringe of evergreen and semi-evergreen forest along the ridge. Varieties of mamang narang *Citrus indica*, a wild and primitive relative of cultivated citrus plants, are present in large numbers (Gogoi, 1981).

Fauna   The area forms an important part of the ranges of herds of Indian elephant *Elephas maximus* (E). Other mammals include jackal *Canis aureus*, wild dog *Cuon alpinus* (V), sloth bear *Melursus ursinus* (I), Asiatic black bear *Selenarctos thibetanus* (V), large Indian civet *Viverra zibetha*, small Indian civet *Viverricula indica*, palm civet *Paguma larvata*, binturong *Arctictis binturong*, leopard cat *Felis bengalensis*, jungle cat *F. chaus*, Asiatic golden cat *F. temmincki* (I), tiger *Panthera tigris* (E), leopard *P. pardus* (T), clouded leopard *Neofelis nebulosa* (V), various cervids, and gaur *Bos gaurus* (V) (Gogoi, 1981).

The avifauna includes a variety of pheasants such as hill partridge *Arborophila* sp., kalij pheasant *Lophura leucomelana*, common pheasant *Phasianus colchicus*, and grey peacock-pheasant *Polyplectron bicalcaratum* (Gogoi, 1981).

Cultural Heritage   Over 80% of the population in the district consists of Scheduled Tribes, predominated by Garos. Other tribes are Hajongs, Koches, Ranhas, Salus and Nanais (Gogoi, 1981).

Local Human Population   The centre of the national park is uninhabited. Peripheral areas are settled by 28 Nokmas dependent on forest resources for their livelihood. They practise *jhum* (shifting) cultivation and keep livestock (cattle, water buffalo, pigs, and poultry) (Gogoi, 1981).

Visitors and Visitor Facilities   There are no proper approach roads, but it is proposed to connect the national park by a motorable road. There is a tourist lodge at Tura Peak (Gogoi, 1981). Foreigners require a special permit to visit Meghalaya.

Scientific Research and Facilities   A preliminary survey of Akhing lands was carried out in 1979–80 (Gogoi, 1981). The Botanical and Zoological Surveys of India are making an inventory of the flora and fauna, and detailed studies are being carried out by the Institute of Rain and Moist Deciduous Forests Research (Jorhat), North Eastern Hill University and Guwahati University (Anon., 1988).

Conservation Value   The area is the principal watershed for the district. Its forests are largely undisturbed and contain pockets of *Citrus indica*, which is known from only a few other locations in the north-eastern region of India. The area is also an important refuge for a variety of threatened mammals, including migratory herds of elephants (Gogoi, 1981).

Conservation Management   The state government is in the process of acquiring *Akhing* lands. Social forestry schemes are being developed (Gogoi, 1981).

Management Constraints   Vegetation on the lower slopes of the Tura Range has been heavily disturbed from shifting cultivation. Considerable damage is caused by elephants marauding crops (Gogoi, 1981).

Staff   No information

Budget   No information

Local Addresses   No information

References
Anon. (1988). A biosphere reserved in Meghalaya. *Himal* 1 (2): 33.
Gogoi, P.C. (1981). *Tura Ridge Biosphere Reserve (Citrus Gene Sanctuary)*. Department of Forests, Government of Meghalaya, Shillong. 99 pp.
Ministry of Environment and Forests (1987). *Biosphere reserves*. Government of India, New Delhi. 250 pp.

OVERA-ARU SANCTUARY INCLUDING OVERA SANCTUARY

IUCN Management Category   Overa-Aru Sanctuary: IV (Managed Nature Reserve)
Overa Sanctuary: IV (Managed Nature Reserve)

Biogeographical Province   2.38.12 (Himalayan Highlands)

Geographical Location   Overa-Aru, which encompasses Overa Sanctuary, lies in Lidder Forest Division about 76 km by road east of Srinagar. It is bounded to the north by Sindh Forest Division, south by Lidder Forest Division, east by Pahalgam and west by Dachigam National Park. 33°55′–34°15′N, 75°05′–75°22′E

Date and History of Establishment   Overa was first established as a game reserve by the Mahajara of Jammu & Kashmir and then upgraded to a sanctuary in 1981. Overa-Aru was notified a sanctuary in 1981. It was designated a biosphere reserve under state legislation, as of 4 February 1981, but this is not nationally or internationally recognised.

Area   Overa Sanctuary: 3,237 ha. Overa-Aru Sanctuary: 42,500 ha.

Land Tenure   Provincial government

Altitude   Ranges from 2,100 m to 5,425 m (Kolahoi Peak).

Physical Features   Overa-Aru lies in the catchment of the West Lidder River which flows south into Lidder River. It is surrounded by high mountain ridges, which form a natural boundary. Rocks are predominantly shales and slates, with Panjal Trap exposed in the higher reaches, and limestone outcropping in the inner valleys (Department of Wildlife Protection, n.d.).

Climate   Conditions are temperate and not subject to the influence of the monsoon. Snowfall is heavy in winter, accounting for most of the annual precipitation (Department of Wildlife Protection, n.d.).

Vegetation   The following types can be distinguished: deciduous forest below 2,600 m, with *Aesculus indica*, *Juglans regia*, and other riparian associates, such as *Fraxinus* spp., *Padus cornuta*, *Rhus succedanea*, and *Pyrus lanata*; coniferous forest from 2,600 m to 3,000 m, dominated by silver fir *Abies pindrow* on moist aspects and blue pine *Pinus griffithii* on dry aspects; birch forest from 3,000 m to 3,500 m, dominated by *Betula utilis*; and alpine scrub from 3,500 m to 3,800 m, with *Juniperus* spp. (Green, 1979; Department of Wildlife Protection, n.d.).

Fauna   Large mammal populations in Overa are considered to be depleted, based on preliminary surveys carried out by Green in 1979. Species recorded were fox *Vulpes vulpes*, Himalayan black bear *Selenarctos thibetanus* (V), leopard *Panthera* sp., hangul *Cervus elaphus hanglu* (E), and marmot *Marmota* sp. No evidence of Himalayan musk deer *Moschus chrysogaster* was found, although both this species and brown bear *Ursus arctos* are present. In 1978, the hangul population was estimated to total about seven animals (Kurt, 1978). Other mammals thought to be present are listed by the Department of Wildlife Protection (n.d.).

The avifauna of Overa is diverse. Of 117 species recorded in or near Overa Sanctuary, 89 breed within its boundaries. These are listed by Price and Jamdar (1990) and include several species previously not known to occur in the area. Both Himalayan monal pheasant *Lophophurus impejanus* and koklass pheasant *Pucrasia macrolopha* are present but not western tragopan *Tragopan melanocephalus* (V), despite the sanctuary falling within this species' range (Rodgers and Panwar, 1988).

Cultural Heritage   No information

Local Human Population   There are no permanent settlements within Overa Sanctuary. An area of 2,500 ha was first occupied by Gujjars in the 1950s (Kurt, 1978a). They used to bring their livestock into the sanctuary during the summer, but this was stopped in 1979 (Green, 1979).

Visitors and Visitor Facilities   Overa Sanctuary receives few visitors, although the nearby beauty spot at Pahalgam is a very popular tourist resort. There is a rest house in the sanctuary; other accommodation is available at Pahalgam.

Scientific Research and Facilities   The impact of human activities, including wood cutting and grazing, was examined in 60 different plots (Kurt et al., 1978). Other research includes preliminary surveys of the wildlife (Kurt, 1978a; Green, 1979) and a study of the breeding birds (Price and Jamdar, 1990). There are no scientific facilities.

Conservation Value   Scenically very attractive, Overa Sanctuary is particularly important as a refuge for its remnant population of hangul (Kurt, 1978a, 1978b). It supports a wide variety of birds, and may prove to be a vital refuge for threatened or endemic taxa (Price and Jamdar, 1990).

Conservation Management   Measures have been taken to restrict graziers from entering Overa Sanctuary but elsewhere in the area human disturbance is considerable (Green, 1979). There is no management plan. It is recommended that Overa-Aru be enlarged to 52,500 ha through extensions to the north and east (Rodgers and Panwar, 1988).

Management Constraints   There has been deforestation and extensive removal of the forest understorey in Overa Sanctuary, particularly in the montane and subalpine zones (Green, 1979). Overgrazing has lead to the almost complete disappearance of food plants palatable to wild ungulates; moreover, it has resulted in extreme fluctuations in the hydrological regimes (Kurt et al., 1978). The vegetation should regenerate and animal populations be restored to former levels with effective protection measures (Green, 1979).

Staff   One forest ranger and five guards (1978)

Budget   No information

Local Addresses   No information

References
Department of Wildlife Protection (n.d.). Status survey of the proposed Overa-Aru Wildlife Sanctuary. Department of Wildlife Protection, Srinagar. 3 pp.
Green, M.J.B. (1979). Himalayan musk deer, India. Progress Report no. 3. WWF, Gland, Switzerland. Pp. 6–9.
Kurt, F. (1978a). IUCN/WWF Project no. 1103 (22–4): Hangul, India—ecological study to identify conservation needs. Final report. Unpublished. 23 pp.
Kurt, F. (1978b). Kashmir deer (*Cervus elaphus hanglu*) in Dachigam. In *Threatened deer*. IUCN, Morges. Pp. 87–108.
Kurt, F. et al. (1978). *Bericht einer Beobachtungsreise nach Kashmir*. WWF Switzerland. 149 pp.
Price, T, and Jamdar, N. (1990). The breeding birds of Overa Wildlife Sanctuary, Kashmir. *Journal of the Bombay Natural History Society* 87: 1–15.

Rodgers, W.A. and Panwar, H.S. (1988). *Planning a wildlife protected area network in India.* 2 vols. Project FO: IND/82/003. FAO, Dehra Dun.

PIN VALLEY NATIONAL PARK

IUCN Management Category   II (National Park)

Biogeographical Province   2.38.12 (Himalayan Highlands)

Geographical Location   Lies in Lahul and Spiti districts, 48 km west of Tabe. 31°45′–32°11′N, 77°45′–78°06′E

Date and History of Establishment   The intention to constitute Pin Valley as a national park was declared on 9 January 1987.

Area   Notified as 67,500 ha, but re-estimated by IIPA/Environment Studies Division (pers. comm.) as 80,736 ha using digitised maps. The park forms part of a much larger protected areas complex: it abuts onto Rupi Bhabha Sanctuary to the south and onto the buffer zone of Great Himalayan National Park to the south-west.

Land Tenure   Provincial government. Local people from adjoining areas enjoy certain rights.

Altitude   Ranges from 3,300 m to 6,632 m.

Physical Features   The park encompasses the headwaters of the Parahio River, a tributary of the Spiti. The entire area is a cold desert (Singh et al., 1990).

Climate Conditions are generally cold and dry, with heavy snowfalls in winter. Mean annual precipitation is 170 mm (Singh et al., 1990).

Vegetation   Forest types include dry alpine and dwarf junifer scrub. Preliminary details of the flora are given by Singh et al. (1990).

Fauna   Mammals reportedly include fox *Vulpes vulpes*, wolf *Canis lupus* (V), snow leopard *Panthera uncia* (E), ibex *Capra ibex*, bharal *Pseudois nayaur*, Tibetan gazelle *Procapra picticaudata*, Himalayan marmot *Marmota bobak*, woolly hare *Lepus oiostolus*, and Royle's pika *Ochotona royeli* (Singh et al. 1990). The northern part of the park is a stronghold for ibex, with 174 animals recorded in 76 sq. km in 1989, but only limited numbers of bharal have been observed (Pandey, 1991).

Cultural Heritage   No information.

Local Human Population   The park is uninhabited but there are 17 villages, with a total population of 1,258 people, in the adjacent buffer zone. Some 2,800 livestock from these villages graze inside the park, together with additional numbers of sheep and goats from Kinnaur (Singh et al., 1990).

Visitors and Visitor Facilities   An Inner-Line permit is required by all nationals wishing to visit the park; foreign nationals are normally not allowed into the area. There are three rest houses in the vicinity of the park.

Scientific Research and Facilities   Pandey (1991) carried out preliminary surveys of Caprinae.

Conservation Value   Pin Valley is a high-altitude Himalayan park typical of Tibetan cold desert and supports a variety of rare and threatened mammals. It is largely unstudied owing to its remote location within a politically sensitive area (Singh et al., 1990).

Conservation Management   Local people are allowed to graze their livestock inside the park, and enjoy herb collection rights. A management plan is under preparation (Singh et al., 1990).

Management Constraints   No information

Staff   One deputy range officer and two forest guards. Overall responsibility for the park lies with the Divisional Forest Officer, Kaza.

Budget   Rs 610,000 (1987-8)

Local Addresses
Divisional Forest Officer (Wildlife), Sarah Division, Sarahan Bushehar 172102, District Simla, Himachal Pradesh

References
Pandey, S. (1991). Species accounts. Report to the Wildlife Institute of India, Dehra Dun. Unpublished. 4 pp.
Singh, S., Kothari, A., and Pande, P. (1990). *Directory of national parks and sanctuaries in Himachal Pradesh: management status and profiles*. Indian Institute of Public Administration, New Delhi. Pp. 9–11.

PONG DAM SANCTUARY

IUCN Management Category   IV (Managed Nature Reserve)

Biogeographical Province   2.38.12 (Himalayan Highlands)

Geographical Location   The lake, created by damming the Beas River in 1976, lies in Kangra District on the border with Punjab State. 31°50′–32°07′N, 75°58′–76°25′E

Date and History of Establishment   Notified a sanctuary on 1 June 1983.

Area   Notified as 30,729 ha, but re-estimated by IIPA/Environmental Studies Division (pers. comm.) as 32,270 ha using digitised maps. All land above 440 m within a 5 km radius of the lake (an area of about 20,000 ha) is notified as a buffer zone (Singh et al., 1990).

Land Tenure   Provincial government: the Beas Bhakhara Management Board controls the reservoir, and the State Forest Department the catchment areas. Local people have rights to fish in the lake.

Altitude   The lake level fluctuates between 335 m and 436 m (Singh et al., 1990).

Physical Features   Lying between the outer Siwaliks and Daula Dhar, Pong Dam is the largest standing water body in Himachal Pradesh and covers about 7,000 ha at its maximum extent. It includes one permanent island (Ransar) and several others that are periodically connected to the shore (Gaston, 1985, 1986). Five perennial streams flow south-west into the reservoir, namely Bul Khad, Dehr Kad, Dehri Kad, Gaj Khad, and Baner Kad (Singh et al., 1990).

Climate   Conditions are monsoonal, with hot humid summers and cool, dry winters. Mean annual rainfall is 1,780 mm. Temperatures range from 5.6 °C to 44.3 °C (Singh et al., 1990).

Vegetation   There is a little submerged aquatic vegetation, but the shoreline does not support much emergent vegetation due to the pronounced seasonal changes in water level. There is an extensive swamp with reedbeds and grasslands in the seepage area below the dam (Gaston, 1985, 1986). The surrounding hillsides still support some mixed deciduous and chir pine *Pinus roxburghii* forest. A preliminary list of the flora is given in Singh et al. (1990).

Fauna   The lake is an important wintering ground for waterfowl. Some 10,000 ducks were recorded in December 1985, with mallard *Anas platyrhynchos* predominant and smaller numbers of northern pintail *Anas acuta*, common teal *Anas crecca*, and common pochard *Aythya ferina* present (Gaston, 1985; Gaston and Pandey, 1987). Two red-necked grebes *Podiceps grisegena*, previously not recorded in India, and several great black-headed gulls *Larus ichthyaetus*, a species that is fairly uncommon in India away from the coast, were also observed. Waders, such as greenshank *Tringa nebularia*, green sandpiper *T. ochropus*, common sandpiper *T. hypoleucos*, and Temmink's stint *Calidris temminkii*, occurred in considerable numbers. A wide variety of raptors was also recorded including osprey *Pandion haliaetus*, Pallas's sea eagle *Haliaeetus leucoryphus*, marsh harrier *Circus aeruginosus*, and tawny eagle *Aquila rapax*. Gaston (1985) observed a total of 103 species in the area, but more than 220 species have since been recorded (Pandey, 1989).

Singh et al. (1990) provides a preliminary list of the mammals, but the presence of several species is uncertain. Reptiles include common cobra *Naja naja*, python *Python molurus* (V), and common monitor *Varanus bengalensis*. Fishes are mahseer *Tor tor*, mallip *Wallago attu*, and soal *Ophiocaphalus marulius*.

Cultural Heritage   Bathu da Mandir, an old temple, was inundated when the valley was flooded.

Local Human Population   The sanctuary is uninhabited, but there are 128 villages in the intensively cultivated buffer zone, with a total population of 50,000 people. Here, residents enjoy rights to cultivate, collect fallen wood and fodder, and graze livestock (Singh et al., 1990).

Visitors and Visitor Facilities   There are five rest houses in the buffer zone. These are located at Dehra Gopipur, Jawali, Nagrota Surain, Dhameta, and Haripur. The main island of Ransar is being developed for visitors. Watchtowers are being built at Bari and Dhameta. The wildlife wing has two small motor launches.

Scientific Research and Facilities　The avifauna has been extensively surveyed (Gaston, 1985; Gaston and Pandey, 1987; Pandey, 1989). There are no scientific facilities.

Conservation Value　Apart from its importance as a source of water for irrigation and domestic use, Pong Dam attracts a large number of migratory waterfowl which to some extent compensates for drainage of wetland habitat elsewhere in northern India over the last 50 years (Gaston, 1986; Gaston and Pandey, 1987; Scott, 1989).

Conservation Management　A management plan for the period 1983–4 to 1988–9 was prepared in November 1982 and approved in December 1984. The protection of the sanctuary presents little difficulty given the vast size of the lake, provided that adequate manpower is made available. A number of recommendations to enhance the attractiveness of the area for waterbirds, and to facilitate access and provide interpretive services for the public have been made (Gaston, 1985). The management of the buffer zone is not yet under the control of the sanctuary authorities due to the large number of residents (Singh et al., 1990).

Management Constraints　The boundary of the sanctuary has not been demarcated: this is holding up settlement procedures (H.P. Forest Department, pers. comm., 1988). Illegal fishing and cultivation of the reservoir bed are reported (Singh et al., 1990).

Staff　One assistant conservator of forests, two range officers, three deputy range officers, and ten forest guards (1990).

Budget　No information

Local Addresses
Assistant Conservator of Forests, Pong Dam Sanctuary, Nagrota Surian 176027, Tehsil Jwali, District Kangra, Himachal Pradesh.

References
Gaston, A.J. (1985). Report on a visit to Pong Dam Lake, 2–3 December. Canadian Wildlife Service, Ottawa. Unpublished. 8 pp.

Gaston, A.J. (1986). West Himalayan wildlife survey. Report on activities in 1985. Unpublished. 18 pp.

Gaston, A.J. and Pandey, S. (1987). Sighting of red-necked grebes on Pong Dam Lake, Himachal Pradesh. *Journal of the Bombay Natural History Society* 84: 676–7.

Pandey, S. (1989). The birds of Pong Dam Lake Sanctuary. *Tiger Paper* 16(2): 20–6.

Scott, D.A. (Ed.) (1989). *A directory of Asian wetlands*. IUCN, Gland, Switzerland and Cambridge, UK. 1,181 pp.

Singh, S., Kothari, A. and Pande, P. (Eds.) (1990). *Directory of national parks and sanctuaries in Himachal Pradesh*. Indian Institute of Public Administration, New Delhi. Pp. 67–9.

RAJAJI NATIONAL PARK

IUCN Management Category II (National Park)

Biogeographical Province 4.08.04 (Indus–Ganges Monsoon Forest)

Geographical Location Lies in the Siwalik Hills of the Himalayan foothills in the districts
of Pauri Garhwal, Dehra Dun, and Saharanpur. It is 13 km south-east of Dehra Dun, 9 km
from Hardwar and Rishikesh, and 200 km north of Delhi. 29°52′–30°15′N, 77°55′–78°19′E.

Date and History of Establishment The intention to declare Rajaji as a national park was
notified on 12 August 1983, but final notification is outstanding. The national park includes
three erstwhile sanctuaries: Rajaji, Motichur, and Chilla which were originally established
on 8 October 1948, 1935 and 25 January 1977, respectively.

Area 83,153 ha (Government of India records). According to the Wildlife Institute of India,
the total area is 82,042 ha and divided into two sections by the Ganges River: the larger
western portion (Rajaji and Motichur) occupies about 57,100 ha and the smaller eastern
portion (Chilla) 24,900 ha. The former Motichur and Rajaji sanctuaries are contiguous with
each other, but separated from the erstwhile Chilla Sanctuary to the south-east by the Ganges
River, Chilla River and agricultural and settled land, which are included within the park.

Land Tenure Provincial government. Local people continue to exercise traditional rights.

Altitude Ranges from approximately 450 m to 1,000 m.

Physical Features The main feature is the north-west to south-east oriented Siwalik Ridge,
which runs through the middle of the park and is cut by deep gorges and gullies. Numerous
streams originate from the ridge and form an intensive network throughout the park. Most
are seasonal and dry up from March to June, resulting in a shortage of water during this
period. The water table is very low. The Siwaliks belong to a Tertiary formation consisting
of conglomerates interbedded with clays and sandstones. Soils are generally poor and infertile,
with accumulation of humus in only a few places (Burton, 1950; Rodgers et al., 1991).

Climate There are three seasons in the Himalayan foothills: cool, hot and rainy. During the
cool season (November to February), days are warm (20–25 °C), nights are cold and humidity
is low. Precipitation in December to February totals 50–150 mm. Temperature rises rapidly
to 40–48 °C in the hot season (March to June) and rainfall increases with the occasional
thunderstorm. Humidity is high in the rainy season (July to October), with over 750 mm of
precipitation in July to August, and there is little temperature variation (Singh, 1956). Annual
rainfall ranges from 1,200–1,500 mm, and mean monthly temperature from 13.1 °C in January
to 38.9 °C in May (Tiwari, 1986).

Vegetation Based on Landsat imagery for 1986, approximately 84% of the park is forested
(Tiwari, 1986). Moist deciduous forest, characterised by sal *Shorea robusta*, covers about
75% of the park. The remaining area is under mixed forest along streams and on the hills.

Riparian forests occur along the Ganges. Sal forests occur mainly in plains, the understorey being dominated by species such as *Mallotus philipinensis* and *Ehretia laevis*. Mixed forests in the plains comprise a canopy layer of *Wrightia tomentosa*, *Grewia* spp, *Holarrhena antidysentrica*, and *Holoptelea integrifolia*. The understorey is dominated by *Adhatoda vasica* and *Lantana camara*. *Zizyphus mauritiana*, *Acacia catechu* and *Dalbergia sissoo* are important species along stream banks. Sal forests on the lower slopes of hills are replaced by open mixed forests of *Anogeisus latifolia*, *Ougenia oogenensis*, *Bauhinia variegata*, *B. malabaria*, and *Nyctanthes* sp. on higher slopes. Ridge topes are usually sparsely forested by chir pine *Pinus roxburghii*, with extensive grasslands (Rodgers et al., 1991).

Fauna An historic account of the fauna is given by Burton (1950), but a number of species listed have since become locally extinct, notably mugger *Crocodylus palustris* (V) and gharial *Gavialis gangeticus* (E). The area is important as the north-western limit of the Asian elephant *Elephas maximus* (E). Other large mammals include rhesus macaque *Macaca mulatta*, common langur *Presbytis entellus*, wild dog *Cuon alpinus* (V), jackal *Canis aureus*, sloth bear *Melursus ursinus* (V), striped hyaena *Hyaena hyaena*, leopard *Panthera pardus* (T), tiger *P. tigris* (E), wild boar *Sus scrofa*, Indian muntjac *Muntiacus muntjak*, spotted deer *Cervus axis*, sambar *C. unicolor*, goral *Nemorhaedus goral*, and nilgai *Boselaphus tragocamelus* (Rodgers et al., 1991). The common otter *Lutra lutra* population is estimated at 250 individuals (Sharma and Ashok, 1988). Some 240 species of birds have been recorded (Rodgers et al., 1991).

Cultural Heritage The area has been inhabited by Gujjars (transhumant pastoralists) for the last 100–200 years (Tiwari, 1986). They herd primarily water buffalo between high Himalayan pastures in the hot season and lower Himalayan foothills, notably the Siwaliks, in the cool season (Clark et al., 1986).

Local Human Population Some 512 families of Gujjars, with a total population of over 10,000 individuals, officially reside within the park. Their population of over 30,000 livestock rely on the park's resources for pasture and leaf fodder. In addition, a large number of livestock from outside villages graze inside the park. There are 57 villages within the park's 'zone of influence', with a total population of about 65,000 inhabitants. In addition, there are nearly 200,000 residents in the adjacent townships of Clement town, Bhel Ranipur, and Hardwar (Rodgers et al., 1991). The dependency and impact of the local people on the park's resources is assessed by Berkmüller et al. (1987).

Visitors and Visitor Facilities No recent information. The former Chilla Sanctuary received 1,527 visitors in 1983–4. There are five rest houses in Chilla, three in Motichur, and four in Rajaji (Variava and Singh, 1985).

Scientific Research and Facilities A team from Wye College, University of London, undertook a study of pastoral ecology, habitat utilisation and wildlife interaction in the former Rajaji Sanctuary in January–April 1985 (Clark et al., 1986). This was followed in 1986 by an assessment of grazing and fuelwood collection pressure on park resources, but the study was never completed due to withdrawal of permission (Berkmüller et al., 1987). The vegetation cover and biomass of the park has been assessed by remote sensing in an attempt to estimate net primary production of palatable species available for elephant (Tiwari, 1986). Corridors for elephants to migrate between Rajaji and Corbett national parks have been identified (Saxena, 1986) and, more recently, the status of the Chilla–Motichur corridor assessed

(Johnsingh et al., 1990). Other studies include the effect of wildfire on sal forest (Rodgers et al., 1986), and protein availability for wild grazing herbivores (Rodgers et al., 1991).

Conservation Value Rajaji is an important refuge for wildlife in the Siwaliks. In particular, it harbours about a third of the Uttar Pradesh elephant population.

Conservation Management As yet, there is no management plan for the park. Management efforts are concentrated on resettling the resident Gujjar population, in accordance with national park policy, and provision of waterholes for wildlife. Encroachment is largely under control (W.A. Rodgers, pers. comm., 1991). Recommendations for absorbing the pressure of local people on the park's resources include provision of extension services, ecodevelopment, and establishment of buffer zones both within and outside the park (Berkmüller et al., 1987). Maintaining corridors between the eastern and western portions of the park is an urgent priority, particularly improvement of the Chilla–Motichur corridor for elephant monuments (Johnsingh et al., 1990). The proposal to link Rajaji with Corbett National Park will necessitate adequate protection of suitable intervening forest habitat (Gupta, 1986). It has also been recommended that the park should be extended to include Golatappar Swamp, a small outlier some 5 km to the north which features a distinctive swamp forest association with a number of rare plant species (Rodgers and Panwar, 1988).

Management Constraints Resettlement in a caring way with adequate help and compensation is the major human relations task facing the park authorities. Dissatisfied with the land offered as compensation, Gujjars and taungya cultivators have obtained a stay order from the Supreme Court and the issue is likely to take a long time to resolve (Berkmüller et al., 1987). The results of a study by Wye College suggest that the impact of the Gujjars on the park's resources has not been as detrimental as is commonly believed. The need to develop a compromise of joint land-use for the benefit of the land, local people and wildlife, rather than managing the area exclusively for conservation purposes, is emphasised (Clark et al., 1986). Buffering the park from surrounding human pressures and maintaining corridors for elephant migration in the north-western part of the species' distribution are the other major constraints impinging on the long-term intregrity of the park (W.A. Rodgers, pers. comm., 1991).

Staff No information

Budget No information

Local Addresses
Director, Rajai National Park, Dehra Dun

References
Berkmüller, K.L. Mukherjee, S.K., and Mishra, B. (1987). Environmental impact of tourism to Hemkund Lake and Valley of Flowers. Wildlife Institute of India, Dehra Dun. Unpublished. 12 pp.
Burton, Lt.-Col. R.W. (1950). Wild life reserves in India: Uttar Pradesh. *Journal of the Bombay Natural History Society* 49: 749–54.
Clark, A., Sewill, H., and Watts, R. (1986). Pastoralists in an Indian wildlife sanctuary. *Occasional Paper* no. 17. Department of Environmental Studies and Countryside Planning, Wye College, Ashford. 62 pp.
Gupta, R.D. (1986). Elephants in northern India. *WWF Monthly Report* January 1986: 1–6.

Johnsingh, A.J.T., Narendra Prasad, S. and Goyal, S.P. (1990). Conservation status of the Chila–Motichur corridor for elephant movement in Rajaji–Corbett National Parks area, India. *Biological Conservation* 87: 125–38.

Rodgers, W.A. (1991). Grassland production and nutritional implications for wild grazing herbivores in Rajaji National Park, India. *Tropical Ecology* (in press).

Rodgers, W.A., Bennett, S.S.R. and Sawarkar, V.B. (1986). Fire and vegetation structure in sal forests, Dehra Dun, India. *Tropical Ecology* 27: 49–61.

Rodgers, W.A., Rao, K., Negi, V.S., Yadav, R., and Bashir, S. (1991). An introduction to the workshop. WII–Unesco Regional Training Workshop on Protected Area Buffer Zone Management, 18–23 February. Wildlife Institute of India, Dehra Dun. Unpublished. Pp. 25–6.

Saxena, K.G. (1986). Forest cover changes between proposed Rajaji National Park and Corbett National Park during the period 1972–1983 for identifying elephant corridors. In: D.S. Kamet and H.S. Panwar (Eds.), *Wildlife Habitat evaluation using remote sensing techniques*. Indian Institute of Remote Sensing and Wildlife Institute of India, Dehra Dun. Pp. 229–37.

Sharma, R.P. and Ashok (1988). Status report on the otters in Uttar Pradesh. *Asian Otter Specialist Group Newsletter* 1: 18.

Singh, S. (1956). Forest working plan—Saharanpur Working Circle. Uttar Pradesh. Forest Department, Lucknow. (Unseen)

Tiwari, A.K. (1986). Vegetation cover and biomass assessment in proposed Rajaji National Park through remote sensing and field sampling. In: D.S. Kamet and H.S. Panwar (Eds.), *Wildlife Habitat evaluation using remote sensing techniques*. Indian Institute of Remote Sensing and Wildlife Institute of India, Dehra Dun. Pp. 213–28.

Variava, D. and Singh, S. (Eds.) (1985). Directory of national parks and sanctuaries in India.

Verma, V.K. (1982). Motichur and Rajaji sanctuaries. *Cheetal, Journal of the Indian Wildlife Association, Dehra Dun* 24(4).

RANGDUM SANCTUARY

IUCN Management Category   Proposed

Biogeographical. Province   2.38.12   (Himalayan Highlands)

Geographical Location   Situated some 100 km south of Kargil and occupies that section of the Suru Valley lying between the villages of Parkachik in the west and Tashidongze in the east. The proposed area is bounded by high mountain ranges to the north and south, and bisected by the Kargil–Padum road which provides access to the Upper Suru Valley. 33°55′–34°08′N, 76°00′–76°30′E

Date and History of Establishment   Proposed as a sanctuary by the Department of Wildlife Protection.

Area   20,000 ha. Contiguous with Kanji Sanctuary (25,000 ha) in the north-east, and abuts onto Kishtwar National Park (42,500 ha) at Nun Kun.

Land Tenure   No information

Altitude   Ranges from 3,430 m at Parkachik to the twin peaks of Nun and Kun at 7,135 m and 7,134 m, respectively.

Physical Features   The Suru River is formed from the confluence of several streams in the vicinity of Rangdum Gompa, from where it flows west for about 40 km across the plain, then turns sharply north through a narrow gorge near Parkachik and runs for a final 70 km to its confluence with the Dras River near Kargil.   Between Parkachik and Gulma Tongas, the valley sides are steep.   Higher up, the valley opens out into a wide, marshy area, known by early travellers as the Great Rangdum Swamp, which gives way to a flat, stony desert towards Rangdum Gompa.   Here, five valleys meet to form a huge and almost circular amphitheatre, 1–2 km in diameter.   The Suru River meanders across the extensive gravel flow, bifurcating repeatedly to form a fine example of braided drainage with gravel bars separating the numerous channels.   The valley is bordered by high peaks on both sides, the highest being the Nun Kun massif opposite Parkachik.   Soils tend to be silty loams on the valley bottoms and lower slopes, becoming dry and sandy in rocky areas (University of Southampton, 1982; Holmes et al., 1983).

Climate   The influence of the monsoon is minimal, due to the shielding effect of the Great Himalayan Range, but Suru Valley receives a small amount of rainfall resulting in a greater diversity of habitats than is found further east in Ladakh (University of Southampton, 1982). Deep snow covers the valley from about December to April (Fox et al., 1986).

Vegetation   There is no forest this high up the Suru Valley, although patches of birch *Betula utilis* apparently were present (probably up to 3,800 m) in the past.   Willows *Salix* spp. are the most common shrubs and form two distinct vegetation types, namely: 1 m tall thickets, sometimes with a dense understorey of sedges and grasses, on northerly aspects, moist slopes, gullies and valley bottom wetlands; and 2–3 m tall open shrubland, with virtually no understorey, restricted to an area of several hectares in the vicinity of Rangdum Gompa (where they are protected) and a few other locations. *Myricaria* spp. are sparsely distributed on the river washes, sometimes associated with willow thickets.   Scattered on hillsides up to 4,300 m occur rose *Rosa webbiana*, *Ephedra gerardiana* and honeysuckles *Lonicera* spp. *Juniperus* spp. appear to be very rare.   Upper valleys are dominated by grasslands and herbaceous meadows, covering about 60% of the land area up to 5,000 m.   Grasslands are dominated by *Carex* spp. and *Kobresia* sp. on moist slopes, especially on northern aspects, and valley bottoms, and by *Agrostis canina*, *Agropyron repens*, *Elymus nutans* and *Poa* sp. on southerly slopes of 15–20 °C.   Herbaceous meadows dominated by *Artemisia* sp., with *Anemone rupicola*, chick-pea *Cicer microphyllum*, *Astragalus zanskaransis*, and *Araizanthu* sp., occur in patches on drier slopes of 30–40 ° (Fox et al., 1986).   Rocky outcrops and scree slopes support a sparse cover (less than 25%) of herbaceous vegetation.   A large proportion of the south-facing slopes above the marsh is covered by *C. microphyllum* and *Acantholimon lycopodioides*, both economically useful plants.   Further details of the flora are available elsewhere (University of Southampton, 1982).

Fauna   Some nine species of mammals have been recorded in the area, notably brown bear *Ursus arctos* and stoat *Mustela erminea*, as well as wolf *Canis lupus* (V), snow leopard *Panthera uncia* (E), bharal *Pseudois nayaur*, and ibex *Capra ibex* (Department of Wildlife Protection, n.d; Mallon, 1989).   Compared with Central Ladakh, relatively few signs of snow leopard were found during surveys in 1985–6.   The density of the ibex population is approximately 0.3 animals per sq. km, based on a total of 250 observed during the same surveys.   Long-tailed marmot *Marmota caudata* is also common.   The brown bear population represents the only occurrence of the species on the north side of the Great Himalayan Range in the region (Fox et al., 1986).

A total of 128 species of birds has been recorded from the Suru Valley (Holmes, 1986), of which 87 (70%) occur within the proposed area. Notable records include Arctic tern *Sterna paradisaea* (Whistler, 1936), the only record for the Indian subcontinent, and barred warbler *Sylvia nisoria* (Holmes et al., 1983), only the fifth record for India but the fourth for Ladakh. Breeding species found in the Rangdum marsh include ruddy shelduck *Tadorna ferruginea*, common merganser *Mergus merganser*, common redshank *Tringa totanus,* and Mongolian plover *Charadrius mongolus* (University of Southampton, 1982). In addition to local birds, a variety of species are migrants. These include various ducks, raptors, waders and passerines, such as barred warbler and Blyth's reed warbler *Acrocephalus dumetorum* (Holmes et al., 1983).

Cultural Heritage Inhabitants of Suru Valley are generally Muslims of Tibeto-Dard descent who were converted from the Buddhist faith around the 16th century, but those of the upper valley have remained Buddhists. Rangdum Gompa dates back to the 17th century (ITDC, n.d.).

Local Human Population There are two villages, Parkachik and Rangdum Juldo, and a small monastery, Rangdum Gompa, with a total human population of about 200, in the proposed area. Human settlements, together with cultivated land, occupy about 350 ha of the valley bottom. Livestock includes sheep, goats, yaks, yak-hybrids and horses. In addition, livestock from villages and government sheep-breeding faims in the lower Suru Valley graze the pastures in summer, together with several thousand sheep and goats brought in by Bakarwal pastoralists from the south side of the Great Himalayan divide, Other resources used include willow scrub for fuelwood and construction material, grass and forbs for winter livestock fodder and *Artemisia* sp. for fuei in summer grazing grounds (Fox et al., 1986).

Visitors and Visitor Facilities The Kargil–Padum road is serviced by bus only in summer when the Pensi La is open. Recent completion of this road has resulted in a large influx of tourists. Several popular trekking routes pass through the area. There is a small hotel in Rangdum Juldo and, nearby, a PWD resthouse.

Scientific Research and Facilities Little botanical work has been carried out in the Suru Valley prior to a survey by the University of Southampton Ladakh Expedition in 1980 (University of Southampton, 1982). A total of 270 species of plants was recorded. Specimens collected are housed in herbaria at Kew, University of Southampton, and University of Kashmir. The survey also included an altitudinal transect of the vegetation at Gulmalungo, half way between Parkachik and Rangdum Juldo.

The proposed area was surveyed for snow leopard and associated prey species in November–December 1985 and June–July 1986 (Fox et al., 1986). Holmes (1986) provides an historical account of ornithological exploration in the Suru Valley. Following the early expeditions of Ludlow (1920), Osmaston (1926, 1930) and Koelz (1939), when specimens were collected from as high up the valley as Rangdum, interest in the region waned until after the opening of the road in the late 1970s. There followed a series of surveys, in some cases including studies of migration, by university expeditions (Holmes, 1978; University of Southampton, 1980, 1982, Holmes et al., 1983; Williams and Delaney, 1985, 1986). There are no scientific facilities.

Conservation Value   Rangdum is an important area for wildlife, particularly on account of the presence of snow leopard and brown bear, and the large ibex population (Fox et al., 1986). Although Great Rangdum Swamp does not attract large numbers of waterfowl (Holmes, 1986), it is an uncommon feature of high Himalayan valleys.

Conservation Management   With the recently completed Kargil–Padum road bisecting the proposed area and increasing grazing pressure from Bakarwals and Government sheep farms, immediate steps need to be taken to develop a conservation plan (Fox et al., 1986).

Management Constraints   The Bakarwal transhumance, which began only 10–15 years ago, conflicts with the traditional grazing rights of the local people. Grazing pressure is exacerbated by sheep brought up from Government farms. There is some hunting, particularly of brown bear and ibex, by Bakarwals and road workers, as well as by persons with vehicles (Fox et al., 1986).

Staff   None

Budget   None

Local Addresses   None

References
Chadwell, C., Delaney, S., Denby, C., Norton, J., Sulston, C., and White, A. (1982). University of Southampton Ladakh Expedition 1980. Unpublished. 204 pp.
Department of Wildlife Protection (n.d.). *Status survey report of notified and proposed national parks, sanctuaries and reserves in Ladakh region*. Department of Wildlife Protection, Srinagar. 29 pp.
Fox, J.L., Sinha, S.P., Chundawat, R.S., and Das, P.K. (1986). A survey of snow leopard and associated species in the Himalaya of northwestern India. Project Completion Report. Wildlife Institute of India, Dehra Dun. 51 pp.
Holmes, P. (Ed.) (1978). Report of the Oxford Ornithological Expedition to Kashmir, 1978. Unpublished.
Holmes, P.R. (1986). The avifauna of the Suru River Valley, Ladakh. *Forktail* 2: 21–41.
Holmes, P.R., Holmes, H.J. and Parr, A.J. (Eds.) (1983). Oxford University Expedition to Kashmir, 1983. Unpublished. 126 pp.
ITDC (n.d.). Ladakh-Kargil and Zanskar. India Tourist Development Corporation, New Delhi.
Koelz, W. (1939). Notes on the birds of Zanskar and Purig, with appendices givine new records for Ladakh, Rupshu and Kulu. *Papers of the Michigan Academy of Science, Arts and Letters* 25: 297–322. (Unseen)
Ludlow, F. (1920). Notes on the nidification of certain birds in Ladakh. *Journal of the Bombay Natural History Society* 27: 141–6. (Unseen)
Mallon, D.P. (1989). An ecological survey of the protected area network in Ladakh. Report to the Department of Wildlife Protection, Jammu and Kashmir Government, Srinagar. Unpublished. 13 pp.
Osmaston, B.B. (1926). Birds nesting in the Dras and Suru Valleys. *Journal of the Bombay Natural History Society* 31: 186–96. (Unseen)
Osmaston, B.B. (1930). A tour in further Kashmir. *Journal of the Bombay Natural History Society* 36: 108–34. (Unseen)
University of Southampton (1980). University of Southampton Ladakh Expedition 1977. Unpublished.

Whistler, H. (1936). Arctic tern in Kashmir. *Ibis* 13: 600–1. (Unseen)

Williams, C. and Delaney, S. (1985). Migration through the north-west Himalaya—some results of the Southampton University Ladakh expeditions. Part 1. *Bulletin of the Oriental Bird Club* 2: 10–14.

Williams, C. and Delaney, S. (1986). Migration through the north-west Himalaya—some results of the Southampton University Ladakh expeditions. Part 2. *Bulletin of the Oriental Bird Club* 3: 11–16.

RIZONG SANCTUARY

IUCN Management Category   Proposed

Biogeographical Province   2.38.12 (Himalayan Highlands)

Geographical Location   Lies in Ladakh, about 52 km west of Leh on the north bank of the Indus River. It is bounded to the north by Lago La and Likir La, south by the Ley–Srinagar national highway, east by Ny and Bazgoo villages and to the west by Temisgam Village. 34°16′–34°28′N, 76°59′–77°47′E

Date and History of Establishment   Proposed as a sanctuary by the Department of Wildlife Protection.

Area   10,000 ha

Land Tenure   No information

Altitude   Ranges from 3,020 m to 5,800 m.

Physical Features   Comprises the catchments of Hemis Shukpachen, Wulch, Saspotche, and Likir nalas, all of which run south, parallel with each other, into the Indus River. The terrain is rugged and precipitous. Rocks consist of slates, phyllites, schists, quartzites, crystalline limestones, and dolomites (Department of Wildlife Protection, 1984). Two geological zones can be distinguished. The first extends northwards from the Indus for 7–8 km and consists of old sandstones and shales that have weathered into open, rounded slopes. To the north is the second zone, with granite forming steep, rocky mountains and cliffs (Mallon. 1989).

Climate   The climate of Ladakh is one of extremes, with considerable daily and seasonal fluctuations. Precipitation is scanty, with only 76 mm per year. During winter, when night temperatures fall to −30 °C and below, the rivers have a thick cap of ice. As the valleys are oriented north–south, snow melts quickly during the spring thaw (Osborne et al., 1983; Department of Wildlife Protection, 1984).

Vegetation   The mountain slopes are largely devoid of scrub and support mainly alpine meadows. The main valley bottoms support riverine scrub, characterised by *Caragana pymaea*, *Myricaria germanica*, *Hippophae rhamnoides*, and *Salix* spp. There are also plantations of walnut *Juglans regia*, *Prunus armanica*, *Populus* spp. and *Salix* spp. up to

3,500 m (Department of Wildlife Protection, 1984). Further details are given by Mallon (1989).

Fauna The area contains good numbers of ibex *Capra ibex* and Ladakh urial *Ovis orientalis vignei*, with 174 and 145 recorded for respective populations in November–December 1984 (Department of Wildlife Protection, 1984). Evidence of two snow leopards *Panthera uncia* (E) was found during this census. Other mammals present are Pallas's cat *Felis manul* (an extremely rare species in Ladakh), wolf *Canis lupus* (V), fox *Vulpes vulpes*, Royle's pika *Ochotona roylei*, and possibly cape hare *Lepus capensis* (Department of Wildlife Protection, 1984; Mallon, 1989).

Less is known about the avifauna, but some 51 species have been recorded by Mallon (1989). Included are jackdaw *Corvus monedula*, and Evermann's redstart *Phoenicurus erythronotus* (Mallon, 1989).

Cultural Heritage There is a monastery at Rizong.

Local Human Population The proposed sanctuary is located in one of the most densely populated parts of Ladakh. There are villages in all the main valleys, with over 100 families in the larger ones. Domestic livestock are grazed throughout the proposed area, and shrubs (mainly *Artemisia* and *Acantholimon*) are gathered for fuel (Mallon, 1989).

Visitors and Visitor Facilities No information

Scientific Research and Facilities Surveys of the wildlife, notably urial, were first carried out by Mallon (1984) during three visits in 1981–2. Subsequently, the ibex and urial populations were censused by the Department of Wildlife Protection (Department of Wildlife Protection, 1984).

Conservation Value The proposed sanctuary is one of the last strongholds of the remaining population of Ladakh urial. It also supports a large ibex population.

Conservation Management None

Management Constraints Natural resources within the proposed area are used by the local people, but there is no information about the level of this exploitation. A new road is being constructed between Likir and Temisgam. This will divide the proposed sanctuary in two and provide easy access to the urial population, which is already under pressure from grazing competition and hunting (Mallon, 1989).

Staff No information

Budget No information

Local Addresses No information

References
Department of Wildlife Protection (1984). Survey and census report of the proposed Rizong Closed Area, Ley (Ladakh). Department of Wildlife Protection, Srinagar. Unpublished. 5 pp.

Mallon, D. (1983). The status of Ladakh urial *Ovis orientalis vignei* in Ladakh, India. *Biological Conservation* 27: 373–81.

Mallon, D.P. (1989). An ecological survey of the protected area network in Ladakh. Report to the Department of Wildlife Protection, Jammu and Kashmir Government, Srinagar. Unpublished. 13 pp.

Osborne, B.C., Mallon, D.P. and Fraser, S.J.R. (1983). Ladakh, threatened stronghold of rare Himalayan mammals. *Oryx* 17: 182–9.

RUPI BHABHA SANCTUARY

IUCN Management Category   IV (Managed Nature Reserve)

Biogeographical Province   2.38.12 (Himalayan Highlands)

Geographical Location   Lies in Kinnaur District, 40 km from Rampur Bushahr, the nearest town. Access is via Chauhra and onward by foot (3 km), or by road to Kathgaon which is inside the sanctuary. 31°30′–31°47′N, 77°45′–78°09′E

Date and History of Establishment   First notified as a sanctuary on 28 March 1982 and renotified on 30 June 1982.

Area   Notified as 26,915 ha, but re-estimated by IIPA/Environmental Studies Division (pers. comm.) as 85,414 ha using digitised maps. Rupi Bhabha is part of a much larger protected areas complex, with Great Himalayan and Pin Valley national parks located on its western and northern boundaries, respectively.

Land Tenure   Provincial government. Residents enjoy certain rights.

Altitude   Ranges from 909 m to 5,650 m.

Physical Features   The north of the sanctuary is covered by glaciers. Drainage is southwards via three main streams, Sorang Gad, Salaring Khad, and Wangar Gad.

Climate   Temperatures range from 10 °C to 20 °C. Mean annual rainfall is 45 mm and mean annual snowfall 300 mm (Singh et al. (1990).

Vegetation   Forest types include lower Western Himalayan temperate, kharsu oak, dry broad-leaved and coniferous, dry temperate coniferous and alpine pastures. The total area under forest cover is 7,492 ha. Kail and deodar were planted in 1982–4 to improve wildlife habitat. Conifers such as cedar *Cedrus deodara*, kail *Pinus wallichiana*, spruce *Picea spinulosa*, and fir, and broad-leaved species such as Indian chestnut *Aesculus indica*, robinia *Robinia pseudoacacia*, poplar *Salix* sp., *Prunus* sp., and walnut *Juglans regia* are planted to meet the growing fuel, fodder, and timber requirements of the local people. A preliminary list of the flora is given in Singh et al. (1990).

Fauna   Mammals reportedly include fox *Vulpes vulpes*, leopard *Panthera pardus* (T), snow leopard *P. uncia* (E), brown bear *Ursus arctos*, Himalayan black bear *Selenarctos thibetanus*

(V), Indian muntjac *Muntiacus muntjak*, musk deer *Moschus chrysogaster*, goral *Nemorhaedus goral*, ibex *Capra ibex*, serow *Capricornis sumatraensis*, blue sheep *Pseudois nayaur*, and Himalayan tahr *Hemitragus jemlahicus* (Singh et al., 1990). Goral has been recorded at a density of 1.5 animals per sq. km, serow and bharal are common, and tahr is less common, being near the northern limit of its distribution (Pandey, 1991). Singh et al. (1990) provide a preliminary list of 27 bird species recorded in the sanctuary.

Cultural Heritage No information.

Local Human Population Fifteen villages are located within the sanctuary, with a total population of 2,420 people. There are also three farmsteads and three summer settlements. Gaddis and Gujjars graze their cattle (numbering 19,694) inside the sanctuary,. In addition, there are 7,500 sheep from the breeding centre at Jeori graze.

Visitors and Visitor Facilities An Inner-Line permit is required to enter the sanctuary. Foreign nationals are not ordinarily permitted to visit.

Scientific Research and Facilities Pandey (1991) carried out a survey of ungulate populations between March 1989 and January 1990.

Conservation Value The remarkably wide range in altitude is reflected by the high diversity of habitats and associated wildlife populations in this catchment area of the Sutlej River (Singh et al., 1990).

Conservation Management Residents have rights of grazing, collection of timber, fuelwood, and minor forest produce, habitation, agriculture and quarrying. A management plan covering the period 1986–7 to 1990–1 has been approved.

Management Constraints The integrity of the sanctuary is severely threatened by the forthcoming Sanjay Vidyut Hydel Project, located within its boundaries. Apart from use of the area for hydroelectric purposes, other activities include the construction of roads, industry, transmission lines and housing. When completed, the installation will submerge 10 ha of the sanctuary, and encroach on another 40 ha for tunnels, dams, and other constructions. Heavy vehicular traffic carrying construction materials passes through the sanctuary. In addition, the proposed Nathpa–Jhakri Project across the Sutlej River will submerge another portion of the sanctuary. Other problems include tree felling and use of explosives for poaching. About 50 ha of forest were affected by fire in 1983–4 (Singh et al., 1990).

Staff Two range officers at Rupi and Kathgaon, two deputy range officers, and nine forest guards.

Budget None

Local Addresses
Range Officer (Wildlife) Bhaba, Kathgaon, Tehsil Nichar, District Kinnaur, Himachal Pradesh
Range Officer (Wildlife) Rupi, Nigulsari, Tehsil Nichar, District Kinnaur, Himachal Pradesh

References
Pandey, S. (1991). Species accounts. Report to the Wildlife Institute of India, Dehra Dun. Unpublished. 4 pp.

Singh, S., Kothari, A., and Pande, P. (Eds.) (1990). *Directory of national parks and sanctuaries in Himachal Pradesh: management status and profiles.* Indian Institute of Public Administration, New Delhi. Pp. 75–9.

SECHU TUAN NALA SANCTUARY

IUCN Management Category   IV (Managed Nature Reserve)

Biogeographical Province   2.38.12 (Himalayan Highlands)

Geographical Location   Lies in Chamba District, 113 km from Chamba, the nearest town. Access is from Kilar by foot to Sechu (15 km) or, alternatively, via Kishtwar in Jammu & Kashmir to Sarsu and onwards by foot to Sechu (85 km). 30°15′–32°00′N, 76°20′–77°00′E

Date and History of Establishment   First notified as a sanctuary in 1962 and renotified on 27 March 1974.

Area   Notified as 10,295 ha, but re-estimated by IIPA/Environmental Studies Division (pers. comm.) as 65,532 ha using digitised maps. A surrounding area of 4,570 ha is regarded as a buffer zone.

Land Tenure   Provincial government. Local people enjoy certain rights.

Altitude   Ranges from 2,550 m to 6,072 m.

Physical Features   There are several glaciers.

Climate   Temperatures range from −20 °C to 27 °C. Mean annual rainfall is 500 mm (Singh et al., 1990).

Vegetation   Forest types include lower Western Himalayan temperate, moist alpine scrub, and dry alpine scrub. Species of medicinal importance include *Aconitum heterophyllum*, *Jurinea macrocephala*, and *Ephedra gerardiana*. Plantations exceeding 113 ha have been established between 1979 and 1987 for fuelwood and other commercial purposes. Species planted include cedar *Cedrus deodara*, poplar *Salix* sp., kail *Pinus wallichiana*, willow *Alnus* sp., robinia *Robinia pseudoacacia*, and walnut *Juglans regia*. A preliminary list of flora is given in Singh et al. (1990).

Fauna   Mammals reportedly include common langur *Presbytis entellus*, Himalayan black bear *Selenarctos thibetanus* (V), brown bear *Ursus arctos*, jungle cat *Felis chaus*, snow leopard *Panthera uncia* (E), musk deer *Moschus chrysogaster*, goral *Nemorhaedus goral*, ibex *Capra ibex*, markhor *Capra falconeri*, serow *Capricornis sumatraensis*, blue sheep *Pseudois nayaur*, Himalayan tahr *Hemitragus jemlahicus*, and Royle's pika *Ochotona roylei*. Singh et al. (1990) provide a preliminary list of 16 bird species recorded in the sanctuary.

Cultural Heritage   Hindu and Buddhist temples are located at Bhat, Tuan, Hilu, Chrroti, and Kalichor.

Local Human Population   There are 11 villages inside the sanctuary with a total population of 1,049 people. Fourteen villages with a population of 2,853 are located in the surrounding area. The number of livestock grazing inside the sanctuary is 3,188 (Singh et al., 1990).

Visitors and Visitor Facilities   No record is kept of the number of tourists visiting the sanctuary. There are three rest houses inside the sanctuary and a forest range rest room is under construction at Tuan.

Scientific Research and Facilities   None

Conservation Value   Sechu Tuan is a high-altitude sanctuary with significant populations of ibex, musk deer and pheasants. Snow leopard has also been reported (Singh et al., 1990).

Conservation Management   Rights or leases exist in relation to collection of timber and fuelwood, agriculture, settlement, burial grounds, and religious practices. There is no management plan. There are 23 km of Public Works Department roads and Irrigation Department pipelines and canals within the sanctuary. In addition, about 3 ha is used for schools by the Education Department, and some area for dispensaries at Chasog. The Forest Department fells trees, extracts timber and maintains three nurseries. In 1987 felling was undertaken by the Forest Development Corporation (Singh et al., 1990).

Management Constraints   Minor clashes between the local people and forest and police officials occurred in 1985 and 1986. Injuries or death to livestock caused by brown bear, Himalayan black bear, and snow leopard are reported. In 1986, 240 ha were affected by fire. Landslides are reported to be common (Singh et al., 1990).

Staff   One range officer and one forest guard.

Budget   Rs 90,000 (1987–8)

Local Addresses
Divisional Forest Officer (Wildlife), Chamba Division, Chamba 176 310, Himachal Pradesh

References
Singh, S., Kothari, A., and Pande, P. (Eds.) (1990). *Directory of national parks and sanctuaries in Himachal Pradesh: management status and profiles*. Indian Institute of Public Administration, New Delhi. Pp. 80-2.

SIMLA WATER CATCHMENT SANCTUARY

IUCN Management Category   I (Strict Nature Reserve)

Biogeographical Province   2.38.12 (Himalayan Highlands)

Geographical Location   Situated adjacent to National Highway 22 and immediately north of Kufri, which lies some 12 km by road east of Simla. 31°05′–31°07′N, 77°13′–77°16′E

Date and History of Establishment   First notified a sanctuary on 29 July 1958 for a period of 20 years and renotified on 14 December 1982. It was originally the property of the Rana of Koti and came under state control in 1947-8. In 1952 it was notified a protected forest (Singh et al., 1990).

Area   Notified as 1,025 ha, but re-estimated by IIPA/Environmental Studies Divsion (pers. comm.) as 951 ha using digitised maps. The sanctuary is connected by a forest corridor to Chail Sanctuary in the south.

Land Tenure   Provincial government. No rights exist in the area which is under the control of Simla Municipal Corporation (Singh et al., 1990).

Altitude   Ranges from 1,900 m to 2,620 m.

Physical Features   Comprises a moderately steep catchment which is the main water supply for Simla. Nine perennial streams flow from this area, the main ones being Churat Nala and God Ki Nala.

Climate   According to the management plan, mean annual rainfall is 1600 mm and temperatures range from −5.4 °C to 32 °C (Singh et al., 1990). Meteorological data are also available from nearby at Simla at 2,200 m. Here, annual precipitation is in excess of 1500 mm, over half of which falls during the summer monsoon. Mean monthly maximum and minimum temperatures range from 8.6 °C in January to 24.1 °C in July and from 1.9 °C to 15.7 °C, respectively (Gaston et al., 1981).

Vegetation   The entire sanctuary is forested, mostly of temperate coniferous forest. Cedar *Cedrus deodara* is predominant (69%) and mixed with ban oak *Quercus incana* (11% for *Quercus* spp.) and chir pine *Pinus roxburghii* (2%) at lower altitudes, and fir *Abies pindrow* (13%), blue pine *Pinus wallichiana* (4%), moru oak *Q. dilatata*, and spruce *Picea smithiana* at higher altitudes. Shrub and ground layers are generally well-developed, with shrubs forming 50% cover on average. Ground vegetation is mainly grasses, but includes a variety of ferns and forbs (Gaston, 1979; S. Pandey, pers. comm., 1990). A list of the flora is given by Singh et al. (1990).

Fauna   Large mammals include rhesus macaque *Macaca mulatta*, common langur *Presbytis entellus*, yellow-throated marten *Martes flavigula*, leopard *Panthera pardus* (T), Indian muntjac *Muntiacus muntjak*, goral *Nemorhaedus goral*, and porcupine *Hystrix indica* (Gaston et al., 1981, 1983). Goral is fairly common (Cavallini, 1990). Flying squirrel *Petaurista petaurista* is also present but Himalayan musk deer *Moschus chrysogaster*, reported by local people to have existed in the past, may now be locally extinct (Green, 1981). A.J. Gaston (pers. comm.) found signs of musk deer in 1979.

Documentation on the avifauna is limited to pheasants. The density of koklass pheasant *Pucrasia macrolopha*, estimated at 17-25 pairs per sq. km in April 1979, is probably close to the maximum reached under natural conditions (Gaston et al., 1981). Similar densities were recorded by P.J. Garson (pers. comm.) in 1988. The population of Kalij pheasant *Lophura leucomelana* also appears to be large (Gaston et al., 1981).

Cultural Heritage   No information

VALLEY OF FLOWERS NATIONAL PARK

IUCN Management Category II (National Park)

Biogeographical Province 2.38.12 (Himalayan Highlands).

Geographical Location Situated above Ghangaria in the upper reaches of the Bhyundar Ganga in the Zaskar Range of the Garhwal Himalaya, Chamoli District. It is bounded by high mountain ridges and peaks on all sides. Approximately 30°44′N, 79°36′E

Date and History of Establishment Created a national park as per Notification no. 4278/XIV-3-66-80 with effect from 6 September 1982, the intention having been declared under Notification no. 5795/XIV-3-66-80 of 1 January 1981.

Area 8,950 ha

Land Tenure Provincial government.

Altitude Ranges from 3,350 m to the peak of Gauri Parbat at 6,719 m.

Physical Features The Valley of Flowers is essentially the catchment area of the Pushpawati River, which forms the Bhyundar Ganga downstream of Ghangaria. It consists of a east-north-east to west-south-west-oriented glacial corridor, 7 km long and 2 km wide, and has its source in the Tipra Glacier which descends from Gauri Parbat. A wall of steep cliffs rises 2,000 m from the valley floor on the north side, while the terrain slopes less precipitously to the south.

Climate The valley enjoys a microclimate of its own, being protected from the cold, dry winds from Tibet to the north and partly shielded from the full effects of the monsoon to the south. In the monsoon, mornings often begin clear but conditions progressively deteriorate with the accumulation of cloud. The valley is snowbound from late-December until the end of April. Meteorological data are not available.

Vegetation The northern slopes are thickly forested with birch *Betula utilis*, rowan *Sorbus* sp. and rhododendron *Rhododendron campanulatum* up to an elevation of 3,800 m. The fine birch forest and profusion of lichens on the ground is indicative of the pristine conditions. The southern slopes at the base of the rock wall consist largely of meadows, where occur a great variety of alpine flowers for which the valley is famous. These include anemones, fritillarias, gentians, geraniums, larkspurs, lilies, orchids, poppies, potentillas, and primulas. Medicinal herbs, such as rhubarb and aconite, are also found in the valley and Brahma Kamal *Saussurea obvallata*, the celestial flower which is offered to the gods, grows on the higher reaches. Smythe (1938) lists 262 species collected by himself and a further 29 species by R.L. Holdsworth from the Bhyundar Valley and neighbourhood. In a more recent enumeration, Ghildyal (1957) describes 283 species but only a proportion of these were collected from within the Bhyundar Valley and its immediate vicinity.

Local Human Population None.

Visitors and Visitor Facilities The sanctuary is closed to visitors. There is one rest house inside, and three outside the sanctuary.

Scientific Research and Facilities Preliminary wildlife surveys have been carried out with respect to pheasants (Gaston et al., 1981), musk deer (Green, 1981) and goral (Cavallini, 1990).

Conservation Value Simla Water Catchment Area is one of very few sanctuaries in Himachal Pradesh which is uninhabited and has been totally protected ever since its reservation. It may represent the only remaining example of undisturbed middle-altitude forest in the front ranges of the Western Himalaya and is the main catchment area upon which Simla depends for its water supply (Gaston et al., 1981, Singh et al., 1990).

Conservation Management Apart from a little felling during World War II, the area has been totally protected since settlements were relocated in the early part of this century (Gaston et al., 1981). Public access is prohibited, but permits are issued for extraction of fodder. The last working plan for the period 1963–4 to 1982–3 has not been updated (Singh et al., 1990).

Management Constraints A few cattle, sheep and goats from adjacent villages graze illegally inside the sanctuary, and some poaching is reported (Singh et al., 1990).

Staff One range officer, one deputy range officer, and four forest guards (1990).

Budget No information

Local Addresses
Forest Officer, Municipal Forest Office, Cart Road, Simla 171001, Himachal Pradesh

References
Cavallini, P. (1990). Status of the goral (*Nemorhaedus goral*) in Himachal Pradesh, India. *Caprinae News* 5(1): 4–6.
Gaston, A.J. (1979). Preliminary reports on the results of the course on 'Techniques for Censusing Pheasants, held from 1–28 April 1979 at Simla Water Catchment Area and Chail Reserve, Himachal Pradesh. Report to World Pheasant Association and Himachal Pradesh Forest Department. Unpublished. (Unseen)
Gaston, A.J., Hunter, M.L. Jr., and Garson, P.J. (1981). The wildlife of Himachal Pradesh, Western Himalayas. *University of Maine School of Forest Resources Technical Notes* no. 82. 159 pp.
Gaston, A.J., Garson, P.J., and Hunter, M.L. Jr. (1983). The status and conservation of forest wildlife in Himachal Pradesh, Western Himalayas. *Biological Conservation* 27: 291–314.
Green, M.J.B. (1981). Himalayan musk deer, India. Progress Report no. 7. WWF Project no. 1328. P. 14.
Singh, S., Kothari, A., and Pande, P. (Eds.) (1990). *Directory of national parks and sanctuaries in Himachal Pradesh*. Indian Institute of Public Administration, New Delhi. Pp. 89–91.

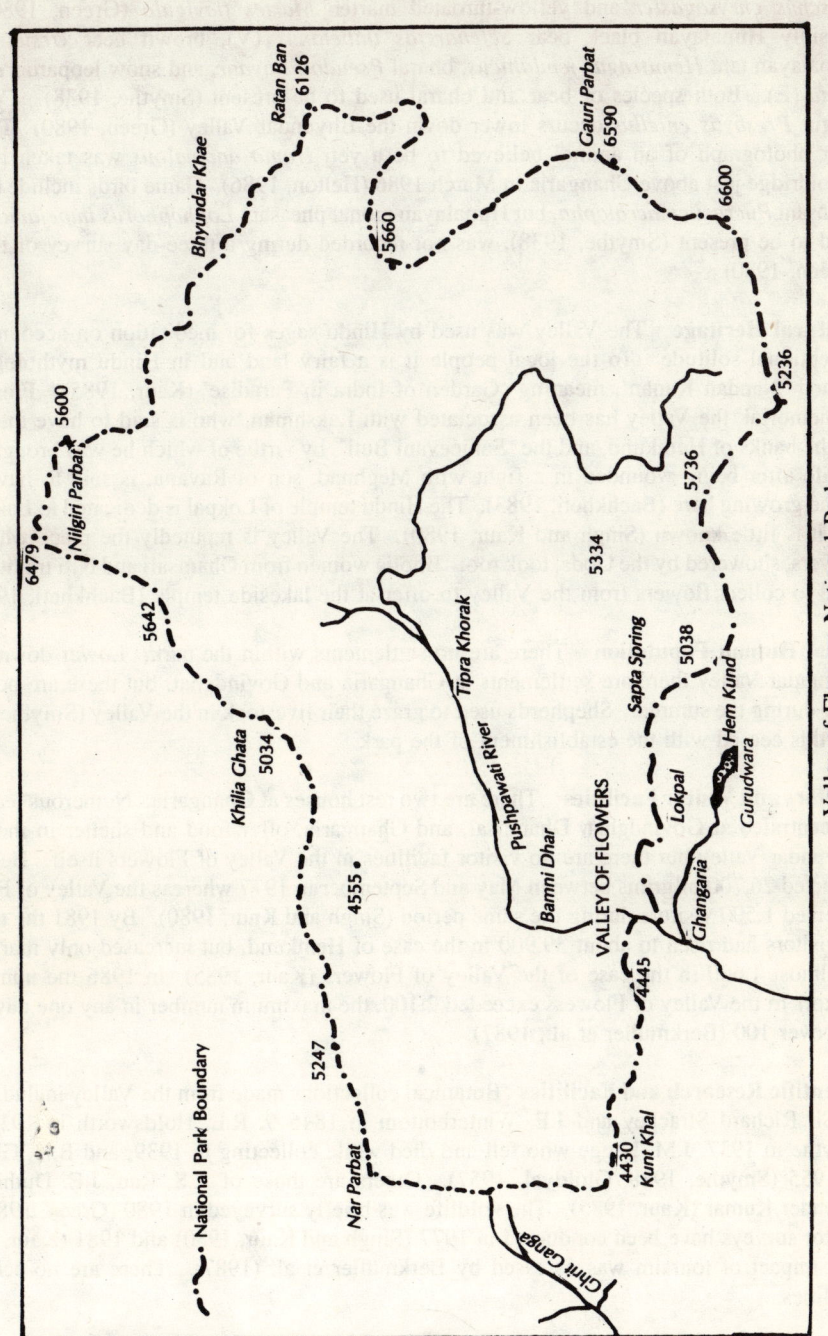

Valley of Flowers National Park

Fauna   The large mammalian fauna appears to be sparse but includes Himalayan musk deer *Moschus chrysogaster* and yellow-throated marten *Martes flavigula* (Green, 1980), and possibly Himalayan black bear *Selenarctos thibetanus* (V), brown bear *Ursus arctos*, Himalayan tahr *Hemitragus jemlahicus*, bharal *Pseudois nayaur*, and snow leopard *Panthera uncia* (E).   Both species of bear and bharal used to be present (Smythe, 1938).   Common langur *Presbytis entellus* occurs lower down the Bhyundar Valley (Green, 1980)   The first ever photograph of an animal believed to be a yeti *Homo anomalous* was taken by A.B. Wooldridge just above Ghangaria in March 1986 (Helton, 1986).   Game birds include koklass pheasant *Pucrasia macrolopha*, but Himalayan monal pheasant *Lophophorus impejanus* which used to be present (Smythe, 1938), was not recorded during a three-day survey of the area (Green, 1980).

Cultural Heritage   The Valley was used by Hindu sages for meditation on account of its exceptional solitude.   To the local people it is a fairy land and in Hindu mythology it is named 'Nandan Kanan', meaning 'Garden of Indra in Paradise' (Kaur, 1985).   From time immemorial, the Valley has been associated with Lakshman, who is said to have meditated on the banks of Hemkund, and the 'Sanjeevani Buti', by virtue of which he was brought back to life after being wounded in a fight with Meghnad, son of Ravana, is said to have been found growing here (Bachkheti, 1983).   The Hindu temple of Lokpal is dedicated to Lakshman but it is little known (Singh and Kaur, 1980).   The Valley is reputedly the place where the flowers, showered by the Gods, took root.   Bhotia women from Ghamsali and Niti traditionally used to collect flowers from the Valley to offer at the lakeside temple (Bachkheti, 1986).

Local Human Population   There are no settlements within the park.   Lower down in the Bhyundar Valley there are settlements at Ghangaria and Govindghat, but these are occupied only during the summer.   Shepherds used to graze their livestock in the Valley (Smythe, 1938) but this ceased with the establishment of the park.

Visitors and Visitor Facilities   There are two rest houses at Ghangaria.   Numerous teashops, concentrated at Govindghat, Dhandisal, and Ghangaria, offer food and shelter in the lower Bhyundar Valley but there are no visitor facilities in the Valley of Flowers itself.   Hemkund attracted 26,700 pilgrims between May and September in 1977 whereas the Valley of Flowers received 1,500 visitors during the same period (Singh and Kaur, 1980).   By 1981 the number of visitors had risen to about 39,900 in the case of Hemkund, but increased only marginally to almost 1,600 in the case of the Valley of Flowers (Kaur, 1985)   In 1986 the number of visitors to the Valley of Flowers exceeded 2,100, the maximum number in any one day being just over 100 (Berkmüller et al., 1987).

Scientific Research and Facilities   Botanical collections made from the Valley include those of Sir Richard Strachey and J.E. Winterbottom in 1846–9, R.L. Holdsworth in 1931, F.S. Smythe in 1937, J.M. Legge who fell and died while collecting in 1939, and B.N. Ghildyal in 1955 (Smythe, 1938; Ghildyal, 1957).   Others are those of A.S. Rau, J.E. Duthie, and Virender Kumar (Kaur, 1985).   The wildlife was briefly surveyed in 1980 (Green, 1980) and visitor surveys have been conducted in 1977 (Singh and Kaur, 1980) and 1981 (Kaur, 1985).   The impact of toursim was assessed by Berkmüller et al. (1987).   There are no scientific facilities.

Conservation Value   The upper Bhyundar Valley became internationally renowned following its exploration by Frank Smythe, first as a member of the successful Kamet Expedition in 1931 (Smythe, 1932) and later in 1937 when he made an extensive herbarium collection

(Smythe, 1938). Overawed by the profusion of wild flowers he named the place 'Valley of Flowers'. At that time, the flora was considered to be as rich as and probably richer than any valley in Sikkim, with many plants having a restricted distribution (Smythe, 1938).

Conservation Management Following the establishment of the park, access is controlled at the entrance to the gorge just above Ghangaria. Access is prohibited to livestock, and visitors pay a nominal entry fee. A preliminary management plan has been prepared (Semwal and Asthana, 1986) but awaits sanctioning It has been recommended that a local committee be set up to initiate the necessary measures to control the impact of tourism on the Valley of Flowers and along its approach route (Berkmüller et al., 1987).

Management Constraints The Byundar Valley has been promoted by The Garhwal Mandal Vikas Nigam, in association with Uttar Pradesh Tourism, Air India and India Tourism, but visitors are becoming increasingly dissatisfied and disillusioned due to the lack of planned development and interpretative facilities (Kaur, 1985). The major impacts of tourism are litter, poor sanitation, and fuelwood collection by hotel and tea stall owners at Govindghat and Ghangaria; but visitor impact within the Valley of Flowers itself is slight and mostly confined to an area of 2.5 ha or 0.5% of the Valley (Berkmüller et al., 1987). Weeds, particularly *Polygonum* spp. and ferns (bracken), are a more serious threat to the flora and now cover a significant part of the Valley. Some 10 ha were treated in 1984 by pulling out the roots and this bore immediate dividends (Bachkheti, 1986).

Potentially, a much more serious threat is the planned Vishnuprayag Dam in the upper Alaknauda Valley (CSE, 1985). In order to boost its generating capacity, it is proposed to divert water from the Pushpavati River via a 7.5 km long tunnel. The construction of the tunnel as well as 10 km of motorable road would not only have an immediate impact on the Bhyundar Valley, but also change its character forever.

Staff One assistant wildlife warden, five wildlife guards (1987).

Budget Approximately Rs 5 lakhs were allocated in 1987–8.

Local Addresses
Deputy Conservator of Forest, Nanda Devi National Park, Joshimath, Chamoli District, Uttar Pradesh

References
Bachkheti, N.D. (1986). The Valley of Flowers. *Indian Forester* 112: 583–7.
Berkmüller, K.L., Mukherjee, S.K., and Mishra, B.K. (1987). Environmental impact of tourism to Hemkund Lake and Valley of Flowers. Wildlife Institute of India, Dehra Dun. Unpublished. 12 pp.
CSE (1985). *The state of India's environment 1984–85. The Second Citizen's Report.* Centre for Science and Environment, New Delhi. Pp. 107–8.
Ghildyal, B.N. (1957). A botanical trip to the Valley of Flowers. *Journal of the Bombay Natural History Society* 54: 365–86.
Green, M.J.B. (1980). WWF Project no 1328—Himalyan musk deer, India. Progress Report no. 6. Pp. 7–9.
Helton, D. (1986). The creature from the avalanche. *BBC Wildlife Magazine* 4: 422–5.
Kaur, J. (1985). *Himalayan pilgrimages and the new tourism.* Himalayan Books, New Delhi. Pp. 158–65.

Semwal, D.N. and Asthana, J.S. (1986). Preliminary management plan report of Valley of Flowers National Park. Wildlife Preservation Organisation, Lucknow. (Unseen)
Singh, T. and Kaur, J. (1980). The Valley of Flowers in Garhwal: an ecological preview. In: Singh, T. (Ed.) assisted by Kaur, J., *Studies in Himalayan ecology and development strategies*. The English Book Store, New Delhi. Pp. 117–22.
Smythe, F.S. (1932). *Kamet conquered*. Hodder & Stoughton, London. 420 pp.
Smythe, F.S. (1938). *The Valley of Flowers*. Hodder & Stoughton, London. 322 pp.

MYANMAR

Area 676,550 sq. km

Population 41,300,000 (1990) Natural increase 2.05%

GNP US $ 203 per capita (1988)

Policy and Legislation The 1947 Burmese Constitution, implemented after independence in 1949, defined the State as the 'ultimate owner of all lands'. Consequently, the State has the right to regulate, alter or abolish land tenures or resume possession of any land for redistribution as it sees fit (Maung, 1961).

Forest policy recognises the basic tenets of conservation, and has three salient principles: the maintenance of environmental stability for the preservation of permanent forest estates; preservation of natural heritage by conserving species and ecosytem diversity and the establishment of a system of protected areas; and ensuring sustainable utilisation of forest resources for the direct benefit of the present and future generations (Forest Department, 1991).

Legal protection of natural resources currently rests on two acts, both dating from the pre-World War II colonial period. The 1902 Burma Forest Act repealed all earlier forest acts. This Act allows the Ministry of Agriculture and Forests to establish game sanctuaries and reserved forests on any land at the disposal of the government, and places responsibility for their management and protection on the Forest Department (see Annex). Game sanctuaries were primarily intended to protect hunting stock; the first was established in 1911. The procedure for establishing reserved forests, as laid down in the Act, entails the appointment of a settlement officer to adjudicate in disputes over extant rights and forest use, and makes provision for certain activities, such as agriculture, to continue after designation. Under the Act, wildlife is defined as 'forest produce', and local governments are able to issue Game Rules. However, these were not comprehensively formulated until 1927 (Weatherbe, 1940). The application of the Act was complex, and some areas, occupied by hill tribes, were exempt.

The 1902 Forest Act was enhanced by the 1936 Burma Wild Life Protection Act, a consolidation of the earlier Wild Birds and Animal Protection Act 1912 which was repealed in 1936. Under sections 26 and 28 of the 1936 Act, the Burma Wildlife Protection Rules were published in the Department of Agriculture and Forests Notification no. 2, dated 2 January 1941 and effective from 11 January 1941. Similar to the 1902 Forest Act, the 1936 Act was not applicable nationwide and certain tribal areas were exempt under the Scheduled

Areas Wildlife Protection Regulation no. 1 of 1941, published by the Defence Department, Political Branch, on 10 Febuary 1941. Tun Yin (1954) details the application of the regulations to specific areas. The 1936 Act makes provision for the establishment of wildlife sanctuaries on any government-owned land or on private land where the owner's consent has been obtained. The Act prohibits all hunting, fishing and wilful disturbance to any animal in sanctuaries and similar activities in reserved forests have to be licensed (see Annex). In addition, nationwide closed hunting seasons were established and a limited number of species received year-round protection. Although the 1902 Forest Act and the 1936 Wildlife Protection Act theoretically provide protection for wildlife in both reserved forests and in wildlife sanctuaries, neither act includes measures specifically to protect habitat. In 1985, new legislation was proposed which would not only strengthen conservation efforts but also for the first time make provision for the establishment of national parks and nature reserves (FAO, 1985b).

International Activities   Myanmar is not yet party to any of the three major international conventions concerned with nature conservation, namely the Unesco Man and Biosphere Programme, the Convention on Wetlands of International Importance especially as Waterfowl Habitat (Ramsar Convention), and the Convention concerning the Protection of the World Cultural and Natural Heritage (World Heritage Convention).

Administration and Management   Responsibility for managing protected areas remains with the Forest Department, which is one of the oldest in Asia. Myanmar is divided into some 40 forest divisions, each of which is supervised by a Divisional Forest Officer; final responsibility rests with the Director-General of Forestry. The Forest Department is responsible for a network of 722 forest reserves, although these are managed primarily for production (FD, 1991). It also manages an Elephant Control Scheme whereby extensive, temporary sanctuaries are established, and elephant capture by the State Timber Corporation is suspended. However, these sanctuaries have no legal status (FAO, 1983). The Forest Department is overshadowed by the politically more influential State Timber Corporation which generates about 25% of the nation's foreign exchange through its monopoly on timber exploitation in reserved forests (Blower, 1985; FAO, 1985a). The Wildlife Conservation and Sanctuaries Division recently established within the Department, is mainly responsible for the management of 'national parks' and other protected areas. It has a mandated staff of 2,251, with 498 appointed by 1987; the number of staff currently employed is not available. In addition to responsibilities for protected areas, the Division is concerned with species conservation activities. A National Commission for Environmental Affairs, comprising committees on pollution, conservation, research, and international co-operation, was established in 1990 to co-ordinate a number of ministries (Uga, 1992).

Management of wildlife sanctuaries tends to be on an *ad hoc* basis, usually limited to infrequent patrols, and is hampered by inadequate staff, resources, support and relevant infrastructure in the Forest Department. Priorities within the Forest Department have tended to be production oriented, with only modest support for conservation activities. Consequently, there has been a failure to stem both poaching and illegal felling in sanctuaries and reserved forests, some of which have lost their original conservation value (FAO, 1985a; Than, 1989).

Systems Reviews   Situated between the Indian subcontinent and the South-east Asian peninsula, Myanmar extends some 2,093 km from north to south. Between these extremes there exists an ecological spectrum of almost unique variety, ranging from tropical rain forests and coral reefs in the south to temperate forests of conifers, oaks and rhododendrons in the far north, where snow-capped mountains up to 5,729 m high mark the eastern extremity of the Himalaya. High mountain ranges form a continuous barrier along the western border with India and Bangladesh, extending southward parallel with the coast to the Ayeyarwady (Irrawaddy) Delta. In the north-east, the border with China follows the high crest of the Irrawaddy-Salween divide, then bulges out eastward to enclose the ruggedly mountainous Shan Plateau forming the border with Laos and Thailand. Between these mountain barriers to the east and west lies the fertile, heavily-populated basin of the Ayeyarwady, with its largest tributary, the Chindwin, joining from the north-west. Myanmar's other great river, the Salween, flows south through neighbouring Yunnan and then cuts through the Shan Plateau in deep, heavily forested gorges before finally reaching the sea in the Gulf of Martaban. Further south, Tenasserim extends in a long, mountainous arm bordering Thailand down to the Kra Isthmus (Blower, 1982).

The climax vegetation in coastal areas is lowland rain forest, with mangroves and freshwater swamp forest in the Ayeyarwady Delta and flood plain. The Ayeyarwady Basin includes a central dry zone of open, stunted dry deciduous woodland, known as *indaing*. Peripheral to this dry zone are extensive mixed deciduous forests which are of great economic importance as the source of Myanmar's teak and other commercial hardwoods. These are in turn surrounded by a fringe of moist, semi-evergreen and evergreen forest on the semi-circle of higher hills to the west, north, and east, merging in the far north with temperate oak and conifer forests and ultimately fir, birch, rhododendron and other sub-alpine vegetation (Blower, 1989). The Forest Department recognises 11 Burma Standard Forest Types, as follows: closed broad-leaf forests, comprising tidal mangroves, beach and dune, swamp, evergreen, mixed deciduous, deciduous dipterocarp, and hill formations; closed coniferous pine forest; bamboo forest, and scrub formations comprising dry scrub and *indaing* scrub (FAO, 1985a).

Results from the UNDP/FAO National Forest Survey and Inventory Project, based on Landsat MSS and RBV imagery for the period 1979–81, indicate that the total area of closed and degraded forest was 42.3% of total land area. According to an appraisal using 1989 Landsat imagery, closed forest covered 252,000 sq. km (37.2%) and degraded forest 41,000 sq. km (6.1%). The 1975–89 annual rate of forest depletion is estimated at 2,200 sq. km (Uga, 1992). However, the extent of closed forest may be less than 20% (J. Sayer, pers. comm., 1989). Much of the closed canopy forests are temperate formations in the north, dominated by oak *Quercus* spp., *Castanopsis* spp. and a variety of Ericaceae. Effectively, all forest in the Shan states has been affected by shifting cultivation and is consequently degraded or cleared. There is little intact forest in the Arakan Yoma in the west, with forest on the coastal side degraded to bamboo and only some managed mixed deciduous formations on the eastern side. Conditions in the southern and northern Chin Hills are extremely degraded with only very small islands of natural forest remaining (J. Sayer, pers. comm., 1989). The status and distribution of forests in Myanmar is discussed further in Collins et al. (1991).

A current summary of wetlands in Myanmar is given in Scott (1989). With a coastline of 2,278 km, several very large estuarine and delta systems and numerous offshore islands, Myanmar possesses a considerable diversity of coastal wetland habitats, including coral reefs, sandy beaches, and mudflats. The most extensive wetlands in the interior of the country are the seasonally inundated floodplains of the three main river systems: Ayeyarwady–Chindwin, Sittaung (Sittang), and Salween. These plains have a surface area of some six million hectares during the monsoon season, providing feeding grounds for waterfowl and spawning grounds for fish, notably carp, catfish, and perch. The practice of constructing embankments and cultivating floodplains restricts major areas of natural floodplain to the north. Permanent freshwater bodies, including the two main lakes, Inle and Indawngy, cover about 1,300,000 ha (Scott, 1989). At least 17 important wetland sites have been identified in Myanmar (Scott, 1989).

The main coral reefs lie in the Mergui Archipelago (Duncan, 1889; Harrison and Poole, 1909). There are no data on the ecology of these reefs but 65 species in 31 genera have been described in a more recent study (Kyi, 1985), suggesting a moderate diversity. It may be assumed from the brief early descriptions and by inference from the better-known islands of adjacent Thailand, that coral reef development in Mergui is appreciable. Rosen (1971) predicts that perhaps 43 or 44 coral genera may be found. There are no known major coral reefs along the mainland coast, although corals have been reported near the mouth of the Bassein River and around Thamihla Kyun (UNEP/IUCN, 1988).

In 1980 the government requested the Food and Agricultural Organisation of the United Nations and the United Nations Development Programme to assist in a joint Nature Conservation and National Parks Project with the Working Peoples Settlement Board. The 1981–4 FAO/UNDP Nature Conservation and National Parks Project was formulated to conserve natural ecosystems, protect endangered species and develop a system of national parks and nature reserves. Immediate objectives included the development of institutions for conservation, assistance in surveys and feasibility studies for the establishment of national parks and nature reserves, and preparation of management plans and their implementation. A comprehensive set of recommendations was made, covering the following: policy, legislation and organisation; recruitment and training; conservation education; co-ordination of surveys and planning; establishment, development and management of protected areas; establishing species conservation priorities, law enforcement; control of hunting and capture; control of trade in wildlife and wildlife products; completing natural resource inventories; and obtaining external assistance for a second-phase project (FAO, 1983).

The principal measures required for the planning and implementation of an effective nature conservation programme, and the establishment of a protected areas system, is discussed in some detail in FAO (1985b), drawing on the experience of FAO/UNDP Nature Conservation and National Parks project. The recommendations cover a broad range of topics, namely: policy; legislation and organisation; staff recruitment and training; conservation education; co-ordination of surveys and planning; establishment, development and management of protected areas; and the establishment of species conservation priorities. Implementation of these recommendations has been slow, with some development of Alaungdaw Kathapa, Hlawga Wildlife Park, Popa Mountain Park, and Kyatthin and Shwesettaw game sanctuaries. A further FAO/UNDP project to implement the recommendations was proposed for implementation during 1987–90, but this was not finalised. Entitled 'Support to nature conservation programme' the project was intended to build on the earlier work with the following objectives in view: development and management of protected areas, especially for the benefit of local communities; protection of watersheds, landscapes, representative ecosystems and threatened species; and the strengthening of institutions and administrative capabilities (UNDP, 1985). This has been superceded by a similar FAO/UNDP National Park and Protected Area Management Project due to be implemented in 1992–5 (Uga, 1992).

At the 25th Working Session of IUCN's Commission on National Parks and Protected Areas regional field managers developed an action plan for protected areas in the Indomalayan realm (IUCN, 1985). The plan identifies a number of goals for the region, and makes the following specific recommendations for Myanmar: upgrading of Kyatthin Game Sanctuary to a nature reserve and establishment of Thamihla Kyun, South Moscos and Kadonlay Kyun as marine reserves; accession to, and implementation of the World Heritage Convention; exchange of expert staff with national management agencies in Thailand, India, Sri Lanka, and Indonesia to address control and management problems; and promotion of intergovernmental co-operation to implement the bilateral management of species (for example, the elephant and tiger, which cross the borders with Bangladesh, Bhutan, and India) and riverine ecosystems (for example, the Naaf, Mekong, and Salween rivers).

Sanctuaries cover only 0.7% of the total land area which is considered to be an inadaquate sample of the nation's natural resources (FAO, 1985a). In contrast, reserved forests, which for conservation purposes are in many respects comparable to wildlife sanctuaries, cover some 100,222 sq. km or 14% of the total land area. Coastal protected areas are limited to Thamihla Kyun and Moscos Islands wildlife sanctuaries but there is no current legislation for establishing marine protected areas. The most serious omissions from the current protected areas system are lowland evergreen, hill evergreen and semi-evergreen forest (FAO, 1985a; MacKinnon and MacKinnon, 1986) and tidal forest (R.E. Salter, pers. comm., 1987). The proposed Pakchan Nature Reserve, and Natma Taung and Pegu Yomas national parks are intended to rectify much of this (FAO, 1985a; Mackinnon and Mackinnon, 1986). However, MacKinnon and MacKinnon (1986) suggest that even with the designation of the proposed protected areas all vegetation types, with the exception of subalpine, will remain threatened. Wetlands are unprotected, even in Wethtigan Wildlife Sanctuary which provides protection for wildlife but not habitat. The proposed Inle Lake and Mong Pai Lake wildlife sanctuaries, and Moyingyi Game Sanctuary are intended to address this omission.

Protected areas are directly threatened by their inadequate size, both individually and in aggregate, by failure to provide representative coverage of several important biota, and by weak and poorly-enforced legislation (Blower, 1982). Effective law enforcement and the prevention of poaching in reserved forests and game sanctuaries is difficult due to the shortage of Forest Department field staff and to the large numbers of firearms in the hands of military personnel, para-military People's Militia and, in some areas, insurgents (Whitmore and Grimwood, 1976). There is also extensive encroachment in many of the existing forest reserves (J. Blower, pers. comm., 1989). Game sanctuaries only legally protect fauna and not habitat. Many have been seriously damaged and some of the smaller areas, for example Maymyo Game Sanctuary, have little justification for being retained as protected areas (FAO, 1985a). Continuing civil unrest, particularly in more remote regions, largely precludes development of the protected areas system.

Addresses

Wildlife Conservation and Sanctuaries Division (Director), Forest Department, Yangon Forest Department (Director General), Yangon

References

Anon. (1937). Note on the Burma Wild Life Protection Act. *Journal of the Bombay Natural History Society* 39(3): 606–8.

Blower, J. (1982). Species conservation priorities in Burma. In: Mittermeier, R.A. and Konstant, W.R. (Eds.), Species conservation priorities in the tropical forests of South-east Asia. *IUCN SSC Occasional Paper* no. 1: 53–8.

Blower, J. (1985). Conservation priorities in Burma. *Oryx* 19: 79–85.

Blower, J. (1989). Burma: conservation of biological diversity. Draft. World Conservation Monitoring Centre, Cambridge, UK. 13 pp.

Collins, N.M., Sayer, J.A., and Whitmore, T.C. (Eds.)(1991). *The Conservation Atlas of Tropical Forests: Asia and the Pacific*. Macmillan Press Limited, London. 266 pp.

Duncan, P.M. (1889). On the Madreporaria of the Mergui Archipelago, collected for the trustees of the Indian Museum by Dr John Anderson, F.R.S., superintendent of the Museum. *Journal of the Linnean Society (Zoology)* 21: 1–25. (Unseen)

FAO (1983). *Summary of currently available information on internationally threatened species in Burma*. Nature Conservation and National Parks Project FO:BUR/80/006. Field Document 7/83. FAO, Rangoon. 76 pp.

FAO (1985a). *Burma: survey data and conservation priorities*. Nature Conservation and National Parks Project FO:BUR/80/006. Technical Report no. 1. FAO, Rome. 102 pp.

FAO (1985b). *Burma: project findings and recommendations*. Nature Conservation and National Parks Project FO:DP/BUR/80/006. Terminal Report. FAO, Rome. 69 pp.

FAO/UNEP (1981). *Tropical forest resources assessment project: forest resources of tropical Asia*. FAO, Rome. 475 pp.

Forest Department (1991). *Forest resources of Myanmar: conservation and management*. Forest Department, Yangon. 13 pp.

Harrison, R.M. and Poole, M. (1909). Marine fauna from Mergui Archipelago, collected by Jas. J. Simpson M.A., B.Sc. and R.N. Redmose Brown B.Sc., University of Aberdeen. Madreporaria. *Proceedings of the Zoological Society of London* 1909: 897–912.

IUCN (1985). *The Corbett Action Plan for protected areas of the Indomalayan Realm*. IUCN, Gland, Switzerland and Cambridge, U.K. 23 pp.

Kyi, A. (1983). Systematic study of some Scleratinian Corals from Mergui Archipelago of Burma. M.Sc. thesis, Moulmeim Degree College, Moulmeim, Burma. (Unseen)

MacKinnon, J. and MacKinnon, K. (1986). *Review of the protected areas system in the Indo-malayan Realm*. IUCN, Gland, Switzerland and Cambridge, UK/UNEP, Nairobi, Kenya. 284 pp.

Maung, K. (1961). *Burma's Constitution*. Martinus Nijhoff, The Hague. 340 pp. (Unseen)

Rosen, B.R. (1971). The distribution of reef coral genera in the Indian Ocean. In: Stoddart, D.R. and Yonge, C.M. (Eds.), Region Variation in Indian Ocean Coral Reefs. *Symposium of the Zoological Society of London* 28: 263–99.

Scott, D.A. (Ed.) (1989). *A directory of Asian wetlands*. IUCN, Gland, Switzerland and Cambridge, UK. 1,181 pp.

Tun Yin, U. (1954). Wildlife preservation and sanctuaries in the Union of Burma. *Journal of the Bombay Natural History Society* 52: 264–84.

Than, A. (1989). A proposal for ecological study and conservation of brow-antlered deer (*Cervus eldi thamin*) in Myanmar (Burma). Unpublished. 19 pp.

Uga. (1992). Situation of wildlife and protected areas in Myanmar. Forest Department, Yangon. Unpublished. 7 pp

UNDP (1985). Support to nature conservation programme: project of The Socialist Republic of the Union of Burma. Revised Draft. 16 pp.

UNEP/IUCN (1988). *Coral reefs of the world*. Vol. 1. *Indian Ocean, Red Sea and Gulf*. UNEP Regional Seas Directories and Bibliographies. IUCN, Gland, Switzerland and Cambridge, UK/UNEP, Nairobi, Kenya. 389 pp.

Weatherbe, D.A. (1940). Burma's decreasing wild life. *Journal of the Bombay Natural History Society* 42: 150–60.

Whitmore, T.C. and Grimwood, I.R. (1976). The conservation of forests, plants and animals in South-east Asia. Vol. 2. Part 1. Continental South East Asia. IUCN, Gland, Switzerland. Unpublished. 82 pp.

ANNEX Definitions of protected area designations, as legisted, together with authorities responsible for their administration.

Title (English title): The Burma Forest Act.

Date: 27 March 1902 (amended 1906, 1912, 1926, 1938 and 1941)

Brief description:
An Act to consolidate and amend the law relating to forests, forest produce and the duty leviable on timber. After independence in 1948, the Act was reinstated with only the titles of government and authorities changed (Adaptation of Laws, Order 1948, dated 4 January 1948).

Administrative authority: Forest Department

Designations:
  Reserved forest [1]
  — A forest and every part of a forest a) declared to be a reserved forest under the provisions of Section 18 of this Act or the corresponding section of any enactment previously in force in Burma; or b) declared to be a reserved forest under the provisions of any rules in force in Lower Burma previous to 1st July 1882, and brought within the provisions of the Burma Forest Act 1881 by Section 30 of that Act, which shall not, at the time being, have ceased to be a reserved forest under Section 29 of this Act or the corresponding provision of any such enactment or rules.
  — Prohibited activities include trespass, pasturing, damaging trees, setting fires, quarrying, cultivation, poisoning or dynamiting, hunting, shooting, fishing or setting traps or snares.

Source: Original legislation.

Title (English title): Burma Wild Life Protection Act

Date: 1936 (amended 1954)

Brief description:
Makes provision for the establishment of sanctuaries (game sanctuaries) on any land at the disposal of the government or, subject to the consent of the owner, any land which is private property. Also provides for the protection of a number of named species outside sanctuaries and reserved forests.

Administrative authority:
Wildlife Conservation and Sanctuaries Division, Forest Department.

Designations:

Game Sanctuaries

— No person is permitted to hunt without the special permission of the Local Government (which is only granted for scientific purposes or to preserve the balance of animals) or, drive, stam pedeor wilfully disturb any animal.

Reserved forest

— No person shall hunt, drive, stampede or wilfully disturb any animal or remove any animal or part of product thereof except under a licence.

Source: Anon (1937)

---

[1] Forest is classified as follows: commercial reserves, managed for the production of hardwoods for domestic consumption and export ;and local supply reserves in close proximity to villages and managed for supply of minor forest products for domestic consumption. Land at the disposal the state, other than reseed forest, may be tuted public forest land to meet local requirements for forest products and to discourage encroachment into reserved forest. Timber may also be extracted for commercial purposes from public forest land (Forest Department, 1991).

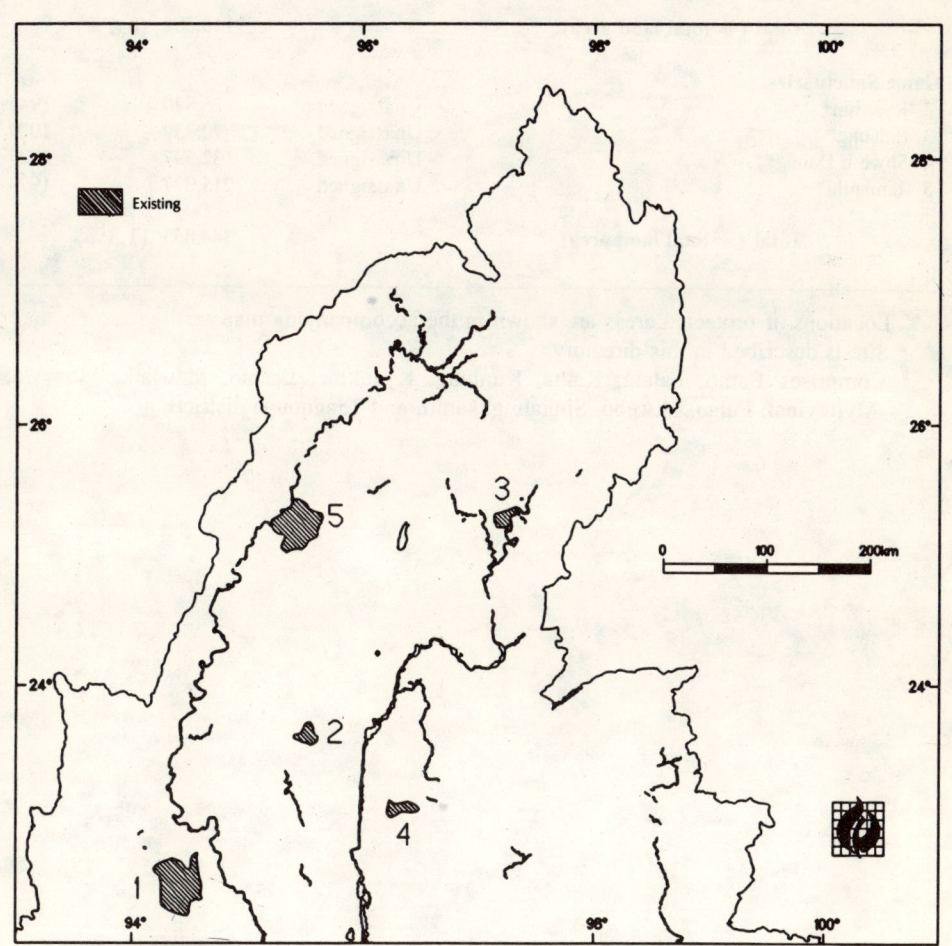

Northern Myanmar

Summary of Protected Areas of Myanmar

National designation Name of area and map reference[+]	IUCN Management category	Area (ha)	Year notified
MYANMAR (northern)[#]		**27,257,000**	
National Parks			
1 Alaungdaw Kathapa*	II	160,580	1984
Total (% total land area)		**160,580 (0.6%)**	
Game Sanctuaries			
2 Kyatthin*	Unassigned	26,820	1941
3 Pidaung*	Unassigned	70,359	1927
4 Shwe u Daung*	Unassigned	32,597	1927
5 Tamanthi*	Unassigned	215,077	1974
Total (% total land area)		**344,853 (1.3%)**	

[+] Locations of protected areas are shown in the accompanying map.

* Site is described in this directory.

[#] Comprises Bamo, Falam, Katha, Kunlung, Kyaukme, Lashio, Mawlaik, Monywa, Myitkyinai, Putao, Shwebo, Sinkalinghkamti, and Tengnoupa districts.

ALAUNGDAW KATHAPA NATIONAL PARK

IUCN Management Category   II (National Park)

Biogeographical Province   4.09.04   (Burma Monsoon Forest)

Geographical Location Situated in the Sagaing Division between the Chindwin and Myittha rivers, about 160 km west of Mandalay. The boundaries of Taungdwin and Patolon reserved forests, formerly in the Upper Chindwin and Lower Chindwin forest divisions, respectively, delimit the national park. Local towns include Kani 25 km to the east, and Gangaw about 15 km to the south-west. 22°08′–22°42′N, 94°15′–94°37′E

Date and History of Establishment Notified as a national park under Ministry of Agriculture and Forests Working People's Settlement Board Notification no. 57/84-85, dated 25 April 1984 (U Saw Han, pers. comm., 1988). Patolon Reserved Forest was originally established on 21 July 1893 under the Revenue Department Notification no. 264 (Forests). It was reconstituted in its present form on 5 July 1917 under Revenue/Forest Notification no. 112. Taungdwin Reserved Forest was established on 1 December 1893 under the Revenue/Forest Department Notification no. 365 dated 21 September 1893.

Area Approximately 160,580 ha. Comprises Patolon Reserved Forest (111,189 ha) and Taungdwin Reserved Forest (70,640 ha, of which 21,250 ha in the northernmost compartments are excluded due to the presence of two villages). Apart from an enclave of unclassified forest around Kuzeik Village in the lower Patolon Valley, the area is entirely surrounded by Thingadon, Pindaung, Sindon, Kunze, To, and Nwa reserved forests (FAO, 1982).

Land Tenure Government

Altitude 204 m to 1,299 m.

Physical Features The national park comprises the upper catchments of the Patolon and Taungdwin rivers, which flow north into the Chindwin River. The main features are three north–south oriented ridges, with fairly steep escarpments to the east and more gentle backslopes to the west. The Ponyadaung ridge is adjacent to the western boundary and separates the park from the heavily settled Myittha Valley. The Letpanpandaung–Modaung ridge, rising to over 1,200 m, divides the Patolon and Taungdwin rivers. The Mahudaung ridge in the eastern part of the area separates the Patolon drainage from the broad valley of the Chindwin. Although the Patolon and Taungdwin rivers are perennial, many of their tributaries are seasonal. Water supply, however, remains adequate throughout the year due to deep rock pools in the drainage courses and a number of perennial springs in the south of the area. In the extreme west, limestones and shales of Tertiary origin are exposed, although the Ponyadaung ridge also has some outcrops of granite and quartz. To the east, the uppermost strata are more recent Miocene clays and sandstones. The eastern Mahudaung ridge consists largely of sandstone, with some calcareous rock, gravelly conglomerates, and onyx. Seepages of petroleum and outcrops of very soft and commercially worthless coal occur in a few places.

301

Soils throughout the area are variable sandy-loams, with nearly pure sand on some hilltops (FAO, 1982).

Climate   The climate is monsoonal, although the area lies in the rain shadow of the Chin Hills, which rise to about 2,000 m and lie between the national park and the Bay of Bengal. Mean annual rainfall at Gangaw was 1495 mm between 1971 and 1981 but only half this amount may fall in some years. Rainfall occurs mainly from May to October, the wettest period being from August to September (FAO, 1982). Although monsoonal rainfall ceases in October, wet weather continues until November (U Saw Han, pers. comm., 1988). Temperatures range from a mean minimum of 10.7 °C in January to a mean maximum of 41.5 °C in April. Prevailing winds are from the south-west during the monsoon period and from the north-east in the cold season (FAO, 1982).

Vegetation   The whole area is well forested, with only minimal disturbance resulting from previous selective logging of teak *Tectona grandis*. A number of distinct communities are present, reflecting the variable topography of the area. Moist upper mixed deciduous forest covers the greatest area and is characterised by teak, pyinkado *Xylia dolabriformis*, taukkyan *Terminalia tomentosa*, zinbyun *Dillenia pentagyna*, myaukchaw *Homalium tomentosum*, padauk *Pterocarpus macrocarpus*, nabe *Lannea grandis*, and bamboo species such as tinwa *Cephalostachyum pergracile* and wabo *Dendrocalamus brandisii*. This merges into dry upper mixed deciduous forest at higher altitude, where pyinkado and padauk are the most common species and teak is reduced in both occurrence and quality. Other species include hnaw *Adina cordifolia*, myaukchaw, thinwin *Milletia pendula*, gyo *Schleichera toleosa*, and thitmagyi *Albizia odoratissima*. Semi-indaing forest grows on higher ridges, and includes ingyin *Pentacme siamensis*, in *Dipterocarpus tuberculatus*, thitya *Shorea oblongifolia* and taukkyan. At the highest levels, above 750 m, pine *Pinus kesiya* is dominant. There is also a limited occurrence of evergreen forest near the crest of Mahudaung ridge and along certain rocky streams where gallery forest prevails.   The understorey of bamboos, such as wabo *Dendrocalamus hamiltonii*, thaik *Bambusa tulda*, and tin *Cephalostachyum pergracile*, in association with grass *Imperata* sp., provides big game habitat (FAO, 1982).

Fauna   The lack of disturbance and the largely intact habitat is reflected in an abundant fauna. Common mammals include gaur *Bos gaurus* (V), sambar *Cervus unicolor*, and Indian muntjac *Muntiacus muntjak*. Elephant *Elephas maximus* (E) is found in the west, but is not very numerous, possibly due to poaching (FAO, 1983). The area is notable for the widespread occurrence of tiger *Panthera tigris* (E), but its abundance may be responsible for the relative dearth of leopard *Panthera pardus* (T). Other mammals include Himalyan black bear *Selenarctos thibetanus* (V), wild dog *Cuon alpinus* (V), jungle cat *Felis chaus*, Asiatic golden cat *F. temmincki* (I), fishing cat *F. viverrina*, wild boar *Sus scrofa*, serow *Capricornis sumatraenis*, Assam macaque *Macaca assamenis*, and capped langur *Presbytis pileata*. Birds commonly seen include white-capped redstart *Chaimarrornis leucocephala*, red-wattled lapwing *Hoplopterus indicus*, wagtails, sandpipers, and forktails *Enicurus* spp. Forest birds include great hornbill *Buceros bicornis* and occasional hill myna *Gracula religiosa*. The use of pesticides in the area may be responsible for the scarcity of raptors and the marked lack of water birds and other aquatic fauna, such as fish, crustacea, and otters *Lutra* sp. (FAO, 1982).

Cultural Heritage   Aluangdaw Kathapa Pagoda in the south-east is a religious shrine of national significance, annually attracting up to about 40,000 pilgrims. It commemorates the cave where Maha Kassapa, the *arahat* who died in the 13th century, was laid to rest (FAO, 1982).

Local Human Population   There are population centres to the north, west and east of the area.   The only settlements in the national park are two village enclaves in the north of Taungdwin Reserved Forest: Zanabok and Pya.   Both enclaves are legally excluded from the reserved forest.   About 1,000 people live in a number of villages in the lower Patolon Valley.   A similar number of people live in and around Tongyi, situated about 6 km beyond the boundary in the north.   Both the Chindwin and Myittha va'lèys to the east and west, repectively, are heavily settled.   The rugged terrain, however, has largely precluded incursions into the park.   Apart from some employment with the State Timber Corporation, the main livelihood of the local population is agriculture. Rice, groundnuts, maize, chilis and tomatoes are the principal crops, supplemented by hunting and fishing.   Both reserved and unclassified forests were exploited for timber and forest products, although this has now been stopped (U Saw Han, pers. comm).   The lack of wildlife around the villages suggests that game is hunted illegally in the reserved forests (FAO, 1982).   Four Buddhist monks live permanently at the shrine (U Saw Han, pers comm., 1988).

Visitors and Visitor Facilities   At present, the only visitors are pilgrims to Alaungdaw Kathapa Pagoda.   There are no all-weather roads and, during the wet season, travel is possible only on foot or by elephant.   Accommodation is extremely limited: there are six small rest houses near the pagoda and one at Magyibin Sakan on the main pilgrim route (FAO, 1982).   Two bungalows are being constructed at Thabeiksay chaung, mainly for the use of official visitors.   During the peak season pilgrims either stay in the rest houses or camp out under makeshift shelters.   Very few people go to the shrine during the rainy season (U Saw Han, pers. comm., 1988).

Scientific Research and Facilities   The area was surveyed during December 1981 to March 1982 and again in March 1983 (FAO, 1982; R.E. Salter, pers. comm., 1988).   There are no scientific facilities.

Conservation Value   The park is considered the foremost in Myanmar, because of its outstanding natural beauty, its historical, religious and scientific interest; the lack of disturbance; the protection of catchment areas of both the Chindwin and Myitha rivers; the protection of habitat for wildlife, especially the economically important elephant; and relatively easy access (Thein Lwin et al., 1990).   Moreover, with a low human population restricted to two enclaves, the risk of land-use conflicts is low (FAO, 1982).

Conservation Management   Although the site is termed a national park there is no legal provision for it being gazetted as such.   The park is administered by a park warden whose headquarters is located at Yinmabin.   Patolon Reserved Forest is administered by the District Forest Officer, Lower Chindwin Forest Division, Monywa, and Taungdwin Reserved Forest by the District Forest Officer, Upper Chindwin Forest Division, Mawlaik (FAO, 1982).   The reserved forests have been managed for teak production under the Burma selection system since 1887 (FAO, 1982).   This entailed the removal of less commercially valuable trees, climber cutting and felling of *Ficus*-bound trees (U Saw Han, pers. comm., 1988).   However, these management activities have declined in recent years (FAO, 1982).   The park has been zoned into a wilderness area, an intensively used visitor zone, and other zones.   Field staff are posted at outstations in Gonnyinmyaung, Wetkya, Kabaing, Payawa, Kunze, Gangaw, and elsewhere.   Guard posts are located along the park boundary (U Saw Han, pers. comm., 1988).

Objectives outlined in the preliminary master plan for the area are: to protect as much of the natural habitat as possible; preserve viable populations of flora and fauna; protect watersheds; facilitate public access to the pagoda; encourage tourism, recreation, education, and research; and to benefit the local human population as much as possible through employment and the sale of local produce (FAO, 1982). Of the five national parks proposed by the FAO/UNDP Nature Conservation and National Parks project, Alaungdaw Kathapa is the only one that has been designated.

Management Constraints   Apart from an indeterminate amount of poaching and the use of pesticides, the area is relatively undisturbed and in good condition. The large number of pilgrims passing through the park, although probably the major human activity, does not appear to threaten the site, (FAO, 1982). There has been a degree of conflict between the management objectives of the park and the management of the constituent reserved forest which had not been settled by 1988. However, as timber extraction has ceased there has been no practical problem (U Saw Han, pers. comm., 1988).

Staff   A staff of 215, comprising three officers and 212 other ranks, has been sanctioned to run the park. However, only about one-third of this number had been appointed by 1988 (U Saw Han, pers. comm., 1988).

Budget   No information

Local Addresses   No information

References

Anon. (1937). Note on the Burma Wild Life Protection Act. *Journal of the Bombay Natural History Society* 39: 606–7.

Blower, J. (1985). Conservation priorities in Burma. *Oryx* 19: 79–85.

FAO (1982). *Proposed Aluangdaw Kathapa national park: preliminary master plan.* Nature Conservation and National Parks Project FO/BUR/80/006. Field Document no. 2. FAO, Rangoon. 35 pp.

FAO (1983). *Summary of currently available information on internationally threatened wildlife species in Burma.* Nature Conservation and National Parks Project FO:BUR/80/006. Field Document 7/83. FAO, Rangoon. 76 pp.

FAO (1985). *Burma: survey data and   conservation priorities.* Nature Conservation and National Parks Project FO:DP/BUR/80/006. Technical Report no. 1. FAO, Rome. 102 pp.

Thein Lwin, Uga and Saw Tun Khaing (1990). Wildlife conservation in Myanmar. Ministry of Agriculture and Forests, Deaprtment of Forests. Unpublished. 16 pp.

KYATTHIN GAME SANCTUARY

IUCN Management Category   Unassigned

Biogeographical Province   4.09.04 (Burma Monsoon Forest)

Geographical Location   Situated approximately 160 km north-north-west of Mandalay in Kanbalu township, in the upper Sagaing Division. The sanctuary lies between the Mu and

Irrawaddy rivers and west of the Myitkyina–Sagaing railway, which passes through Kyatthin village, five kilometres to the east (FAO, 1983a). Access is via Kyatthin railway station which has a daily service, or by the fair-weather road from Shwebo (FAO, 1983a). The boundary is marked by pillars, blazed trees and notice boards (Hundley, 1981). 23°30′–23°42′N, 95°24′–95°40′E

Date and History of Establishment   Established under Department of Agriculture and Forests Notification no. 117 dated 19 June 1941 with effect from 1 September 1941. Under this notification, Kyatthin Fuel Reserve and Kyatthin Extension Reserve became incorporated into the newly constituted game sanctuary (FAO, 1983a; Tun Yin, 1954).

Area   26,820 ha. The sanctuary comprises Kyatthin Fuel Reserve (12,129 ha), Kyatthin Extension Reserve Forest (4,924 ha), and adjacent unclassed forest (9,787 ha) (FAO, 1982).

Land Tenure   Government, with the exception of the unclassed forest.

Altitude   Averages 200 m, with a minimum of 170 m to a maximum of 250 m (Hundley, 1981; FAO, 1982).

Physical Features   The topography is flat to undulating, with a limited area of gullies and ridges in the south-west. Relatively straight and narrow streams drain the sanctuary and flow into the Mu River, a tributary of the Irrawaddy. Isolated pools remain in the drainage courses throughout the dry season, and a number of large, permanent ponds in the centre of the sanctuary, linked with seasonally flooded grassy depressions, known as *lwins*, ensure a year-round water supply. There is an artesian well near the western boundary, but it does not produce potable water. The streams in the sanctuary have cut through a layer of alluvium to the underlying Tertiary sandstone, conglomerates and shales (FAO, 1983a, 1985).

Climate   Lying on the northern edge of Burma's dry zone, the estimated annual rainfall of 1,100 mm to 1,500 mm is low, with some 50–60 wet days, mainly between June and October (FAO, 1983a, 1985). The heaviest rainfall occurs during August and September. Kyunhla in the west has a notably higher mean annual rainfall (1,232 mm) than Kanbulu in the east (1,001 mm) (Hundley, 1981). The monsoon season is characterised by erratic showers, light southerly winds, moderate temperatures and overcast conditions (FAO, 1983a). Maximum and minimum temperatures in the sanctuary range between 40 °C and 3 °C, with an mean annual temperature of 29.4 °C (Hundley, 1981).

Vegetation   The vegetation has been modified as a result of fuelwood extraction and annual grass burning (FAO, 1985), and primary forest covers only 20% of the sanctuary (Hundley, 1981). Deciduous dipterocarp forest, or indaing, covers most of the sanctuary and is dominated by *Dipterocarpus tuberculatus*, *Shorea oblongifolia* and *Pentacme siamensis* (FAO, 1982). On more shallow, eroded soils, and in areas of abandoned cultivation, semi-indaing or scrub-indaing predominates, with some bamboo, particularly near the north-eastern boundary. *Lwins* suppport a variety of tall grasses and there are areas of aquatic vegetation, as well as illegal taunggya cutting and paddy cultivation. A 6.4 km wide strip of natural indaing forest, centered on an abandoned railway line, was heavily exploited until the railway fell into disuse in the 1960s. A small (*c*.1 ha) eucalyptus plantation was established near Kinsan Sakan for fuelwood production (R.E. Salter, pers. comm.).

305

Fauna Kyatthin supports the largest thamin *Cervus eldi thamin* (V) population in a protected area in Burma, and the species is considered virtually extinct outside the country (FAO, 1983b). Reçent population censuses indicate that some 2,200 animals live in the sanctuary (FAO, 1983a; Salter and Sayer, 1986), in contrast to earlier estimates of between 50 and 500 individuals (FAO, 1983a), although this recent estimate is considered to be optimistic (Than, 1989). The only other thamin in a protected area are an estimated 400 or more animals in Shwesettaw Game Sanctuary, some 450 km to the south-west. Other noteworthy mammals include leopard *Panthera pardus* (T), wild dog *Cuon alpinus* (V), reportedly common, a small number of banteng *Bos javanicus* (V), and hog deer *Cervus porcinus*, which is not well represented in other Burmese protected areas. Sambar *Cervus unicolor*, Indian muntjac *Muntiacus muntjak*, wild boar *Sus scrofa*, macaque *Macaca* sp., hare *Lepus* sp., small cats and mustelids are also found (FAO, 1983a). The avifauna is listed in FAO (1982) and includes a number of species restricted within Burma to the dry zone. White-winged wood duck *Cairina scutulata* (V), formerly reported present (Tun Yin, 1954), is possibly still found in the sanctuary. Reptiles include Burmese python *Python molurus bivittatus* (V) (FAO, 1983a).

Local Human Population The sanctuary embraces three villages with a combined population approaching 1,000 people (FAO, 1983a). In addition, seventeen villages are located on its periphery (FAO, 1982). Agriculture is the only occupation, with rice and other crops being grown; both paddy and taunggya cultivation is practised in the sanctuary. Some 688 households have legal rights to collect timber house-posts, fuelwood, bamboo, thatching and other forest products, in addition to holding grazing rights for 3,464 cattle. Much of the sanctuary is burnt annually to promote grass growth, and the resumption of fuelwood extraction from the plantations straddling the railway is being considered (FAO, 1983a).

Visitors and Visitor Facilities The sanctuary is not considered to be of sufficient general interest to become a major tourist attraction. A rest house at Kinsan Sakan, in the centre of the sanctuary, was destroyed by fire in 1982. Its replacement with simple accommodation would allow thamin to be observed.

Scientific Research and Facilities The area was surveyed in April 1982 (FAO, 1982) and during March to April (FAO, 1983a). The rest house was originally intended to facilitate observations of thamin and efforts to capture live specimens (FAO, 1982). A proposal for an ecological study of thamin, with a view to its conservation, has been proposed (Than, 1989).

Conservation Value The sanctuary was established to protect thamin, which receives nationwide nominal protection from hunting under the 1936 Burma Wild Life Protection Act. This species continues to be the outstanding feature of the site (Thein Lwin et al., 1990).

Conservation Management In 1983 a series of recommendations aimed at safeguarding the thamin population was made: the appointment of a sanctuary superintendent and ten guards; construction of an office in the sanctuary; control over ox-cart traffic: regulation of forest produce extraction; initiation of research into thamin ecology and methodical surveys of the population; the survey and relocation of the boundary to exclude two villages from the sanctuary; and the possible expansion of the sanctuary to the south (FAO, 1983a). The Wildlife and Sanctuaries Division has introduced systematic wildlife management since 1986 with a staff complement that is described as adequate (Thein Lwin et al., 1990).

Management Constraints   The sanctuary is partially settled and is heavily used for agriculture, grazing, and the extraction of fuelwood and other forest products. The legal protection of thamin is ineffective (R.E. Salter, pers. comm). The species is easy to hunt and firearms are readily available. In the early 1970s a number of ponds were auctioned annually as fisheries, although this practice has since ceased. Nevertheless, fish are still caught illegally by netting or the use of fish poisons and the insecticide endrin (Hundley, 1981). Bullock-cart traffic has lead to the disturbance of wildlife and also facilitates poaching, although the latter appears to be limited at present (FAO, 1983a). Although annual fires appear to encourage regeneration of the vegetation, the number of waterholes available during the dry season is declining. Adjacent unclassed forest is under threat from local human populations, although extraction of forest produce from these has deflected some demand away from the sanctuary (Hundley, 1981).

Staff   A deputy range officer and a game forester are based near Kyatthin and there are two daily-paid, untrained workers. A range officer based at Kawlin, about 40 km to the north-east, has overall responsibility (FAO, 1983a).

Budget   The recurrent 1979–80 budget was K 4,560 (approximately US $ 500) and K 3,660 (approximately US $ 400) during 1980–1 (Hundley, 1981). More recent information is not available.

Local Addresses   Deputy Director, Shwebo Forest Division, Shwebo

References
FAO (1982). *Kyatthin Wildlife Sanctuary: report on a survey of the area and a preliminary census of the thamin*. Nature Conservation and National Parks Project FO/BUR/80/006. Field Report 7/82. FAO, Rangoon. 21 pp.
FAO (1983a). *Kyatthin Wildlife Sanctuary. Draft management plan*. Nature Conservation and National Parks Project FO/BUR/80/006. Field Document 6/83. FAO, Rangoon. (Unseen)
FAO (1983b). *Summary of currently available information on internationally threatened species in Burma*. Nature Conservation and National Parks Project FO/BUR/80/006. Field document 7/83. FAO, Rangoon. 76 pp.
FAO (1985). *Burma: survey data and conservation priorities*. Nature Conservation and National Parks Project FO/BUR/80/006. Technical Report no. 1. FAO, Rome. 102 pp.
Hundley, H. G. (1981). Kyatthin Wildlife Sanctuary. Unpublished. 6 pp.
Salter, R.E. and Sayer, J.A. (1986). The brow-antlered deer in Burma—its distribution and status. *Oryx* 20: 241–5.
Than, A (1989). A proposal for ecological study and conservation of brow-antlered deer (*Cervus eldi thamin*) in Myanmar (Burma). Unpublished. 19 pp.
Thein Lwin, Uga and Saw Tun Khaing (1990). Wildlife conservation in Myanmar. Ministry of Agriculture and Forests, Department of Forests. Unpublished. 16 pp.
Tun Yin, U. (1954). Wildlife preservation and sanctuaries in the Union of Burma. *Journal of the Bombay Natural History Society* 52: 264–84

PIDAUNG GAME SANCTUARY

IUCN Management Category   Unassigned

Biogeographical Province   4.09.04   (Burma Monsoon Forest)

Geographical Location   Lies approximately 20 km west of Myitkyina, which is on the west bank of the Irrawaddy River, in Myitkyina Forest Division.   25°15′–25°35′N, 97°04′E–97°20′

Date and History of Establishment   Originally declared a game reserve in October 1917 under the Burma Game Rules 1917. A southern extension was notified in 1921. Both reserves were notified as a game sanctuary in September 1927, with a total area of 71,928 ha, although some sources indicate the date of notification was in 1928. The first proposal to protect the area was made by the Commissioner of the Mandalay Division in 1908 and the southern extension was added on the orders of the Lieutenant-Governor, Sir Harcourt Butler. Pidaung East Extension Reserve (1,300 ha) and Kamaing Kachin Hill Tract (191 ha) were gazetted as Pidaung West Extension Reserve in 1938 and added to the sanctuary. During World War Two parts were converted to paddy cultivation: these areas have been excised from the sanctuary (Tun Yin, 1954).

Area   70,359 ha

Land Tenure   Government

Altitude   148 m to 1,362 m.

Physical Features   The sanctuary comprises rolling downs, hills and valleys (Burton, 1950) and constitutes part of the relatively flat riverine plains along the Irrawaddy to the east. Both Myitkyina Town and the sanctuary are situated in an amphitheatre of hills rising to some 2,400 m, 50 km away. The underlying strata are probably Irrawaddy alluvial deposits (FAO, 1985).

Climate   The mean annual rainfall in South Kachin varies between 1,800 mm and 2,500 mm (FAO, 1985).

Vegetation   The original vegetation cover included extensive areas of short grass, known as *lwins*. These areas were divided by hills with dense tropical broad-leaved evergreen forest dominated by *Terminalia* spp. and *Shorea* spp. This forest type was also widespread in the south of the sanctuary. Dense thickets are found in hollows and luxuriant grass in valleys (Burton, 1950). The present condition of the vegetation is not known.

Fauna   The following species were observed in the sanctuary in 1953–4: tiger *Panthera tigris* (E), leopard *P. pardus* (T), bear (possibly Himalayan black bear *Selenarctos thibetanus* (V)), elephant *Elephas maximus* (E), gaur *Bos gaurus* (V), banteng *B. javanicus* (V), hog deer *Cervus procinus*, sambar *C. unicolor*, Indian muntjac *Muntiacus muntjak*, wild dog *Cuon* *alpinus* (V), and wild boar *Sus scrofa* (Tun Yin, 1954). Leopard, tiger, and green peafowl *Pavo muticus* (V) are still present (FAO, 1983). Rhinoceros, probably Sumatran *Dicerorhinus sumatraensis* (E), was reported in the 1950s but was not considered to be resident. Elephant is relatively abundant to the west of the sanctuary (FAO, 1983), although neither it nor banteng is currently present within the sanctuary itself.

Cultural Heritage   No information

Local Human Population   The nearest major local population centres are Myitkyina, Mogaung, Namti, and Mayan, located between 1 km and 12 km to the west. There are a number of villages just outside the sanctuary (Tun Yin, 1954). Although no details are known, the immediate vicinity of the sanctuary, in common with much of the Irrawaddy Valley, is probably heavily settled.

Visitors and Visitor Facilities   No information

Scientific Research and Facilities   No information

Conservation Value   No information

Conservation Management   No information

Management Constraints   Security problems in northern Myanmar have led to a ready supply of firearms. This, and the 164 km of roads and paths within the sanctuary noted by Tun Yin (1954), probably leads to widespread poaching. In addition, three tea plantations in the southern part, and six villages, have rights over parts of the protected area.

Staff   A special game staff of a head keeper and five assisstant keepers were maintained in the sanctuary (Tun Yin, 1954). The current staffing is not known.

Budget   No information

Local Addresses
Divisional Forest Officer, Myitkyina Forest. Division, Northern Circle, Myitkyina

References
Anon. (1937). Note on the Burma Wildlife Protection Act. *Journal of the Bombay Natural History Society* 39: 606–8.
Burton, R.W. (1950). Game sanctuaries in Burma (pre-1942) with present status of rhinoceros and thamin. *Journal of the Bombay Natural History Society* 49: 729–37.
FAO (1983). *Summary of currently available information on internationally threatened wildlife species in Burma*. Nature Conservation and National Parks Project FO:BUR/80/006. Field Document 7/83. FAO, Rangoon. 76 pp.
FAO (1985). *Burma: survey data and conservation priorities*. Nature Conservation and National Parks Project FO:DP/BUR/80/006. Technical Report no. 1. FAO, Rome. 102 pp.
Tun Yin, U. (1954). Wildlife preservation and sanctuaries in the Union of Burma. *Journal of the Bombay Natural History Society* 52: 254–84.
Tun Yin, U. (1955). Wildlife preservation in Burma. *Oryx* 3: 89–98.

SHWE-U-DAUNG GAME SANCTUARY

IUCN Management Category   Unassigned

Biogeographical Province   4.09.04 (Burma Monsoon Forest)

Geographical Location   Situated on the edge of the Shan Plateau in Shan State, 20 km east of the Irrawaddy River and about 120 km north of Mandalay. The nearest major town is Mogok, which is some 26 km south-east of the main peak in the sanctuary. 22°49′–23°05′N, 96°12′–96°21′E

Date and History of Establishment   The area, lying in the Mogok and Thabeikkyin subdivisions of the Katha District, was notified as a 20,995 ha game sanctuary in Forest Department (Ministry of Forests) Notification no. 243, dated 29 September 1927. That part (11,664 ha) lying in the Mongmit Forest Division was notified under Forest Department Notification no. 138, dated 22 July 1929, effective from 1 August 1929 (Tun Yin, 1954).

Area   32,597 ha

Land Tenure   Government

Altitude   The main ridge in the sanctuary ranges between 1,200 m and 1,897 m (Peacock, 1931).

Physical Features   The sanctuary comprises a relatively isolated massif forming a high watershed which extends for some 16 km. The three main peaks are Nanmadawgyi, Nanmadawgalay and Shwe-u-daung, which is the highest (Peacock, 1931). To the east of the sanctuary is the undulating Shan Plateau and to the west the Irrawaddy flood plain. The area is considered to be scenically almost unequalled in Myanmar.

Climate   The climate of the Shan Plateau is monsoonal, in common with all but the most northern part of the country. Mean annual rainfall on the plateau varies from 1,300 mm to 3,800 mm, increasing from north to south (FAO, 1985).

Vegetation   The lower slopes of the sanctuary support evergreen forest featuring numerous orchids. On the peaks, main ridge and most of the high spurs, trees are largely absent and coarse grass, 30 cm to 90 cm high, is dominant. Much taller kaing grass *Saccharum* sp. occupies hollows and the upper margins of the forest.

Fauna   A population survey estimated that 12 to 15 Sumatran rhinoceros *Dicerorhinus sumatraensis* (E) occupied the sanctuary in 1939 (Tun Yin, 1954). More recent population estimates of 2–4 animals in 1980 are attributed to Tun Yin (FAO, 1983). Other important species which may still be present include tiger *Panthera tigris* (E), leopard *P. pardus* (T), Asian elephant *Elephas maximus* (E), gaur *Bos gaurus* (V), and serow *Capricornis sumatraensis*. The avifauna reportedly includes green peafowl *Pavo muticus* (V) (FAO, 1983).

Cultural Heritage   The three main peaks in the sanctuary were formerly believed by local villagers to be inhabited by *nats*, or spirits, hostile to poachers. As a consequence, wildlife in the sanctuary was largely undisturbed (Peacock, 1931). In more recent years this belief has declined (Tun Yin, 1955).

Local Human Population   The nearest major centres are Mogok, and the smaller settlement of Thabeikkyin about 28 km to the west. Details concerning human population in the more immediate vicinity of the sanctuary are not available.

Visitors and Visitor Facilities   No information

Scientific Research and Facilities   With the exception of infrequent surveys of the rhinoceros populatation in the sanctuary, there does not appear to have been any research undertaken.

Conservation Value   The sanctuary was constituted primarily for the protection of Sumatran rhinoceros.

Conservation Management   Details of any management measures are not known. Teak *Tectona* sp. logging was permitted in the sanctuary until 1967.

Management Constraints   Tun Yin (1955) reports that both poachers and insurgents are present in the sanctuary and evidence suggests that since about 1940 at least 17 rhinoceros have been killed (FAO, 1983). All parts of the rhinoceros body are valued in Chinese and Burmese traditional medicine and horn was allegedly on sale in Mandalay in 1980 for US $ 20,200 per kg. Although genuine rhinoceros products are now very rare, the high market value continues to threaten those individuals remaining in the wild (Bradley Martin, 1983).

Staff   One deputy ranger and three foresters.

Budget   No information

Local Addresses   District Forest Officer, East Katha Forest Division, Thabeikkyin

References
Bradley Martin, E. (1983). *Rhino exploitation: the trade in rhino products in India, Indonesia, Malaysia, Burma, Japan and South Korea*. World Wildlife Fund, Hong Kong. 122 pp.
Peacock, E.H. (1931) Shwe-U-Daung Game Sanctuary. *Journal of the Bombay Natural History Society* 35: 446–8.
FAO (1983). *Summary of currently available information on internationally threatened wildlife species in Burma*. Nature Conservation and National Parks Project FO:BUR/80/006. Field Document 7/83. FAO, Rangoon. 76 pp.
Tun, Yin U. (1954). Wildlife preservation and sanctuaries in the Union of Burma. *Journal of the Bombay Natural History Society* 52: 264–84.

TAMANTHI GAME SANCTUARY

IUCN Management Category Unassigned.

Biogeographical Province 4.09.04 (Burma Monsoon Forest)

Geographical Location Located close to the east bank of the Chindwin River, in the Upper Chindwin/Myittha forest divisions, and approximately 1,000 km (by air) north of Rangoon. The nearest major town is Tamanthi, situated about 6 km west of the sanctuary and on the opposite bank of the Chindwin. The site is accessible by boat, up the Chindwin, or by air to Hkanti, some 30 km north of the boundary, and thence by road. The boundary partly comprises the Temein Hill range and one river course, and is identified by blazed trees and pillars for compass bearings (FAO, 1982; H.G. Hundley, pers. comm.). 25°05′–25°48′N, 95°18′–95°56′E

Date and History of Establishment 1974

Area 215,077 ha

Land Tenure Government

Altitude 141 m to 631 m.

Physical Features The sanctuary slopes down from the Temein Range in the east to the Chindwin Valley in the west. The Pilin, Nat-E-Su, Pagan, Yanyin, and Kwedaing rivers drain the sanctuary and flow westward into the Chindwin. Little information about the geology of the area is available, although it is likely to be similar to the Miocene shale and sandstone to the found east of the river. Saramanti (3,826 m), one of Burma's highest mountains, lies about 40 km to the west of the sanctuary (H.G. Hundley, pers. comm.).

Climate Homalin, about 50 km south of the sanctuary, receives a mean annual rainfall of 2,250 mm, but this is greatly exceeded in the sanctuary. Heavy fog is usual in the cold season and may occur as late as April. The area does not experience extremes of temperature (H.G. Hundley, pers. comm.).

Vegetation The area has not been heavily exploited and largely intact evergreen and semi-evergreen forest covers most of the sanctuary. Oak *Quercus* spp. and *Castanopsis* spp. occur along the higher hill ranges. Characteristic trees include kanyin *Dipterocarpus turbinatus*, *D. macrocarpus*, aukchinsa *Dysoxylum binectariferum*, yetama *Acrocarpus fraxinifolium*, taungtama *Cedrela* sp., thabye *Syzygium spp.*, yinma *Chukrasia tabularis*, and *C. velutina*. Bamboo species include tinwa *Cephalostachyum* spp., wabomyetsangye *Dendrocalamus hamiltonii*, and wa-kha *Pseudostachyum polymorphum*. There is an abundance of evergreen climbers and canes (H.G. Hundley, pers. comm.). As there is no teak *Tectona* sp., the State Timber Corporation is not active in either the sanctuary or its environs (FAO, 1982).

312

Fauna During the last twenty years Sumatran rhinoceros *Dicerorhinus sumatraensis* (E) has been reported only in Tamanthi Wildlife Sanctuary and Shwe-U-Daung Wildlife Sanctuary (Blower, 1982), although it may also be present in the Arakan Yoma hills to the south (FAO, 1983). Other mammals include leopard *Panthera pardus* (T), tiger *Panthera tigris* (E), wild dog *Cuon alpinus* (V), gaur *Bos gaurus* (V), sambar *Cervus unicolor,* Indian muntjac *Muntiacus muntjak*, and wild boar *Sus scrofa.* Troops of monkeys are often seen on the river banks and Hoolock gibbon *Hylobates hoolock* occurs in the forest. Green peafowl *Pavo muticus* (V) and jungle fowl are fairly plentiful. Porpoise, teal, and duck are to be seen in the Chindwin, although the river is not included in the sanctuary (H.G. Hundley, pers. comm.).

Local Human Population There are no settlements within the sanctuary. Tamanthi is the largest of a number of population centres in the Chindwin Valley and Maungkan, Hkanti, and Mansein are all located within about 30 km of the boundary (FAO, 1982).

Visitors and Visitor Facilities The site is not developed for tourism, in part due to its remoteness and security considerations.

Scientific Research and Facilities The most recent survey of rhinoceros in the sanctuary was carried out in 1978 (H.G. Hundley, pers. comm.).

Conservation Value The sanctuary was constituted specifically for the protection of Sumatran rhinoceros *Dicerorhinus sumatrensis* (E), numbered at seven individuals in 1981 (U Tun Yin, pers. comm.). Rhinoceros receives nationwide protection under the 1936 Burma Wildlife Protection Act as well as protection under the Burma Game Rules 1917 (FAO, 1983). Whilst the primary interest of the sanctuary lies in the possible presence of the rhinoceros, the site is also valued for its large size, intact vegetation and protection of the Chindwin River watershed (FAO, 1982; H.G. Hundley, pers. comm., 1987).

Conservation Management The site is believed to have high potential as a national park and should be investigated as soon as circumstances permit (FAO, 1985).

Management Constraints The area lies in a military zone and the status of the sanctuary is difficult to assess (H.G. Hundley pers. comm., 1987). Rhinoceros horn, blood, urine, and other parts of the body have long been considered by the Chinese and the Burmese hill tribes to have medicinal qualities. This has lead to widespread poaching of the species and its subsequent decline in numbers. A proposal exists to dam the Chindwin River at Minsin, close to the sanctuary, for hydroelectricity and to extend navigation.

Staff The District Forest Officer, Mawlaik, has executive responsibilty and one range officer, with a game ranger and two forest guards as field staff are assigned to the sanctuary (H.G. Hundley, pers. comm., 1987).

Budget No information.

Local Addresses
District Forest Officer, Mawlaik.

References

Blower, J. (1982). Species conservation priorities in Burma. In: Mittermeier, R.A. and Konstant, W.R. (Eds.), Species conservation priorities in the tropical forests of South-East Asia. *IUCN SSC Occasional Paper* no. 1: 53–8.

FAO (1982). *Preliminary survey of a part of the Mu-Chindwin watershed together with a note on conservation problems in the Sagaing Hills.* Nature Conservation and National Parks Project FO:BUR/80/006. Field Report 13/82. FAO, Rangoon. 22 pp.

FAO (1983). *Summary of currently available information on internationally threatened species in Burma.* Nature conservation and National Parks Project FO:BUR/80/006. Field Document 7/83. FAO, Rangoon. 76 pp.

FAO (1985b). *Burma: project findings and recommendations.* Nature Conservation and National Parks Project FO:DP/BUR/80/006. Terminal Report. FAO, Rome. 69 pp.

NEPAL

Area   141,415 sq. km

Population   19,100,000 (1990)   Natural increase 2.5% per annum

GNP   US $ 170 per capita (1988)

Policy and Legislation   The new Constitution of the Kingdom of Nepal 2047 (1991) formally recognises the need to preserve the environment and use natural resources wisely. In Chapter 4 it is stated that, 'The Kingdom of Nepal will give priority to raising public awareness on environmental issues, to mitigating the adverse effects development works have on the environment, and to the conservation of rare fauna and flora.' The Constitution makes provision for the formation of committees on Natural Resources and Environmental Conservation by the House of Representatives (Chapter 8).

A National Conservation Strategy for Nepal was completed in 1987 and endorsed as policy in 1988 (HMG Nepal/IUCN, 1983, 1988). Policy resolutions cover the basic requirements of the people, as well as the need to safeguard natural and aesthetic values and to maintain the country's cultural heritage. It was also resolved that a separate body, the National Council for the Conservation of Natural and Cultural Resources, was to replace the National Commission for the Conservation of Natural Resources to be responsible for implementing the National Conservation Strategy and formulating policy guidelines concerning resource conservation matters. This council has since been formed and represents the most important step to date towards establishing an institutional framework for co-operative environmental management and protection in the country.

Conservation awareness dates back many centuries in Nepalese society. The tradition of preserving large expanses of forest adjacent to places of worship or important sources of water is deep-rooted. In Kathmandu Valley, for example, there are 45 sacred forests ranging in size from one to several thousand hectares which have been preserved by countless generations in accordance with ancient religious traditions (Mansberger, 1990). Various traditional systems of resource administration have also evolved: for example, the *shingo nawa* (forest caretakers) in Sherpa society; the *kipat* system of exclusive and unalienable communal rights over large areas in the eastern Hills; and the *chitaidar*, (local non-official functionaries) responsible for the use of village forests in the 19th century (HMG Nepal/IUCN, 1988). In the first half of this century there was a National Code under which forests in the hills were controlled by village heads and private forests by forest watchers, with the district administrator holding superior authority. Forest clearance was prohibited unless authorised by the Government. Traditional forms of resource conservation, such as *shingo nawa*, *chitaidari* and *kipat*, disappeared with the handing over of private forests to the state in 1957 under the Forest Nationalisation Act. This Act was introduced to bring forests under management and also to prevent land being converted to agriculture. Increasing pressures on land in the *terai* led to the passing of the Forest Act in 1961 to protect forests by restricting access to them and to regulate forest utilisation. State, panchayat, panchayat protected, religious, and contract forests are defined under this Act (see Annex). Following recent changes to Nepal's political system, these terms are due to be replaced by national, community plantation, community protected, religious, and leased forests, respectively, under new forest legislation which awaits approval by the newly elected government. The Forest Protection Special Act 1968 provides forest officials with policing and judicial powers. Such measures, introduced to help counter encroachment and wanton destruction of forests, became less applicable with the change in policy towards community forestry and decentralisation. For example, various rules such as the Panchayat Forest Rules 1978 and Panchayat Forest Protection Rules 1978 were framed under the Forest Act to give local communities access to or ownership of forest lands to encourage sustained use of such resources. Other forestry-related legislation includes the Soil and Watershed Conservation Act 1982 which enables the Department of Soil Conservation and Watershed Management to declare, develop and conserve critical watersheds. Under this Act, any area may be designated as a protected watershed area (see Annex). The Act has not yet been applied but two nationally important watersheds are under consideration for designation as protected watershed areas (MFSC, 1988).

Nepal has a well-developed mechanism for formulating and declaring policy through its national five-year plans. Stated policies that affect the forestry sector are more or less adequate, the main problem being translating policy to legislation, and in its effective implementation. Moreover, existing laws are not always consistent with current policy. Present forest policy is based on the 1976 National Forestry Plan. Its main objectives are to meet the people's needs for forest products, to maintain and restore the ecological balance through programmes of reforestation and watershed management, and to derive maximum economic gains from forest products. Policies are incorporated within the most recent (seventh) five-year plan. A new forestry sector policy (1989) was formulated under the Master Plan for the Forestry Sector. It was proposed that: forest resources be managed with priority given to products that best contribute to the needs of the people; forest resources be managed according to their ecological capability so as to conserve the forests, soil, water, flora, fauna, and scenic beauty, with representative examples of ecosystems unique to Nepal protected, and tourism regulated according to local carrying capacities; and that community forestry and the establishment of private forests on leased and private lands be promoted in accordance with the principles of the decentralisation policy. Official endorsement and implementation of this new policy was considered to be a priority, requiring extensive reform of existing forest legislation (MFSC, 1988). A revised forestry sector policy (1991) has since been prepared under the Master Plan.

A national conservation programme was initiated by HMG Nepal in 1971. This was given a legal basis following the passing of the National Parks and Wildlife Conservation Act 2029 in March 1973 which provides for the establishment and administration of protected areas and 'the conservation of animals and birds and their habitats'. This act supersedes the Wildlife Conservation Act 2015 (1958) and the Hunting Rules of 1967, under which six royal hunting reserves were established in July 1969. The 1973 Act enables the Government to establish any area as a national park, reserve (i.e. controlled natural reserve, wildlife reserve, and hunting reserve) and, following an amendment in 1989, conservation area (see Annex). A controlled natural reserve (more commonly referred to as a strict nature reserve) is at the protection end of the spectrum, with entry permitted only for scientific study (none has been created to date); a hunting reserve is at the utilisation end and is managed for recreational hunting on a sustained yield basis. National parks and wildlife reserves both provide for the conservation of fauna and their habitats, but national parks have a broader emphasis encompassing landscape values. A conservation area provides for a flexible system of resource management through people's participation. It may be managed by the relevant government agency or entrusted to a non-governmental organisation. The Government may alienate, transfer ownership, or alter the boundaries of national parks, reserves or conservation areas by notification in the *Nepal Gazette*. The various regulations introduced under the Act are the National Parks and Wildlife Protection Regulations 2030 (1974), Royal Chitwan National Park Regulations 2030 (1974), Wildlife Reserve Regulations 2034 (1977), Himalayan National Park Regulations 2036 (1979), and Khaptad National Park Regulations (1987). Provisions under the Himalayan National Park Regulations include the disposal of rubbish in designated places, prohibition of the use of forest products or their purchase from local residents by visitors, self-sufficiency in fuel for visitors, exemption of park entry fees for pilgrims, and collection of forest products and grazing of livestock by residents in places designated by the warden. Conservation Area Regulations are under preparation. While the Act and accompanying regulations provide considerable discretionary powers to authorised officers, the lack of policy guidelines is a major constraint to achieving effective management of protected areas. A working policy has recently been drafted as part of the Master Plan for the Forestry Sector and represents a guide to the application of the National Parks and Wildlife Conservation Act. In addition to the adoption of a working policy, the Act needs to be amended to strengthen protected areas management by providing for zonation (including the creation of buffer zones), the addition of a new category (biological reserve) of protected area for biologically important areas and wetlands that do not meet national park or wildlife reserve criteria nor need the restrictions on entry of the controlled natural reserve, and income for community development. It is also proposed that the long-term security of protected areas be strengthened by requiring that their alienation or transfer be made subject to special legislation passed through the national parliament (MFSC, 1988).

Certain other legislation relates to tourism in protected areas. Under the Tourism Act 2035 (1979), mountaineering expeditions must obtain a permit from the Ministry of Tourism in order to climb listed Himalayan peaks, some of which are in national parks. Similarly, tourists wishing to trek anywhere in Nepal must obtain permission from the Central Immigration Office, Home Ministry, in accordance with the Trekking and River Rafting Regulations 2041 (1985). Many of the popular trekking routes are in national parks.

International Activities Nepal has entered a number of obligations and co-operative agreements related to conservation. It is a signatory to the Convention concerning the Protection of the World Cultural and Natural Heritage (World Heritage Convention) which it accepted in 20 June 1978. Two natural sites, Sagarmatha and Royal Chitwan national parks, have been inscribed on the World Heritage List.

Nepal acceded to the Convention on Wetlands of International Importance especially as Waterfowl Habitat (Ramsar Convention) on 17 December 1987, at which time Koshi Tappu was added to the List of Wetlands of International Importance established under the terms of the Convention.

Nepal participates in the Unesco Man and Biosphere Programme. A National Committee for MAB was established in 1974 under the framework of the Nepal National Committee for Unesco formed in 1971. No biosphere reserves have been established to date. Following initiatives by MAB/Unesco and MAB/Nepal in 1975, the International Centre for Integrated Mountain Development was established in Kathmandu in 1983 following an agreement between HMG Nepal and Unesco signed in 1981. Its primary objectives are 'to help promote the development of an economically and environmentally sound mountain ecosystem ...', thereby complementing regional efforts towards conservation. The participating nations are Afghanistan, Bangladesh, Bhutan, Burma, China, India, Nepal, and Pakistan (Glaser, 1984; ICIMOD, 1989).

Other regional initiatives concerned with resource conservation in which Nepal participates are the South Asian Co-operative Environmental Programme and the South Asian Association for Regional Co-operation. Further details are given elsewhere (HMG Nepal, IUCN, 1988).

Nepal and China have both established protected areas on their respective sides of Mount Everest (Sagarmatha/Chomolangma). Management plans are being formulated by both countries under co-operative agreements with the Woodlands Mountain Institute.

Administration and Management A new institutional structure for the Ministry of Forests and Soil Conservation was developed during the formulation of the Master Plan for the Forestry Sector and this is being implemented ahead of legislative reforms under directives issued by His Majesty the King on 1 May 1988 (MFSC, 1988). The focus of the organisational changes is to strengthen the field units in the Department of Forest in order to develop community and private forests based on people's participation and to develop national forests based on management by government agencies. The Department of Forest, one of four departments within the Ministry, and now headed by a Director General, is responsible for protection and utilisation of forest resources. It is split into four divisions responsible for administration, planning, management, and community forests, respectively. There are 5 regional directorates of forests, each headed by a Regional Director, 75 district forest offices, each under a District Forest Officer, and 222 range offices, each under a range officer. In addition, 453 forest service centres are proposed to assist with community forestry. Protection responsibilities are assigned to the armed forest guards in the case of national forests, but in community forests they are the responsibility of the user groups. The total number of approved posts in 1988 was 8,855, of which 1,329 were for armed forest guards.

Wildlife conservation, prior to the National Parks and Wildlife Conservation Act was the responsibility of the Forest Department, which established wildlife and hunting reserves, issued hunting licences and controlled hunting within forest reserves. A National Parks and Wildlife Conservation Office was set up in July 1972 as a semi-autonomous branch of the Forest Department (FAO, 1980). In 1982, it was upgraded to departmental status within the Ministry of Forests, now the Ministry of Forests and Soil Conservation. The Department is the primary agency for *in situ* conservation of ecosystems and genetic resources. It is headed by a Director General and comprises two divisions (National Parks and Reserves, Planning and Research), three sections (Administration, Financial Administration, Hatisar/Elephant Camps) and a Central Zoo. Law enforcement within parks and reserves has been the responsibility of the Royal Nepal Army since 1974 (MFSC, 1988). The total number of approved posts for 1990–1 is 998, of which 595 are field units (but not protection units) responsible for administering parks and reserves. The Department's financial allocation for 1990–1 is NRs 124.3 million, of which 84% is for protection units (Royal Nepal Army).

Revenue totalled NRs 0.6 million from headquarters and NRs 22.2 million from parks and reserves (B.N. Upreti, pers. comm). In recent years, income generated from tourism, concessions, permits, and other sources has consistently exceeded expenditure if the costs of the protection units are excluded. The Smithsonian-Nepal Tiger Ecology Project was launched in 1973 as a joint programme supported by HMG Nepal and the US Government. The project was based in Royal Chitwan National Park and in 1984 was succeeded by the Smithsonian-Nepal Terai Ecology Project. Recently, in 1988, the Department of National Parks and Wildlife Conservation signed a 12-year co-operative agreement with the Woodlands Mountain Institute to support the Makalu-Barun Conservation Project (Shrestha et al., 1990).

The Department of Soil Conservation and Watershed Management was established in 1974 in response to a growing awareness of soil conservation and watershed degradation problems. Its objectives are to maintain ecological equilibrium by conserving important watershed areas and by reducing the incidence of natural disasters such as soil erosion, landslides, and floods. The Department is a project-based territorial organisation. It is split into Environment and Management and Technology Development divisions, and three sections, with a total complement of 594 staff in 1988, of which 274 were permanent and the rest temporarily assigned to projects (MFSC, 1988).

The Shivapuri Watershed and Wildlife Reserve Board was established in 1975 with the aim of improving the quality and quantity of drinking water in Kathmandu Valley, conserving the natural environment, and developing it for tourism. A watershed area of 144 sq. km has been demarcated by a boundary wall and declared a wildlife reserve. The reserve is managed by a committee, members of which include the Director-General of the departments of Forests, National Parks and Wildlife Conservation, and Soil Conservation and Watershed Management. It is planned that management of the reserve should eventually be handed over to the Department of National Parks and Wildlife Conservation (MFSC, 1988).

The shortcomings of the Ministry of Forests and Soil Conservation were assessed as part of the Master Plan process (MFSC, 1988). It is widely accepted that: protective forestry as a general strategy for forest conservation has failed; the management of forests located close to farmland should be handed over to the local people; and that only areas which can be legitimately defined and demarcated can be managed successfully by a professional body such as the Department of Forest. Constraints within this Department include a distorted staffing distribution, due primarily to the large number of vacancies still to be filled in the remote areas. The Department of Soil Conservation and Watershed Management is relatively new and lacks the resources to fulfil its mandate. In the long term, the Department should become economically sustainable. Criteria need to be formulated to identify priority areas and authorities, with a view to optimising the allocation of scarce resources. The Department of National Parks and Wildlife Conservation has been inadequately staffed for the size of its task, a problem exacerbated by secondments, research assignments, and overseas fellowships. Many of these constraints have been addressed in the recent organisational reform of the Ministry. Within the Department of National Parks and Wildlife Conservation, however, the assignment of protection responsiblities to the military continues to be a considerable drain on the Department's financial resources. Moreover, this sharing of responsibilities is a constraint to the effective management of protected areas (Upreti, 1990).

The King Mahendra Trust for Nature Conservation is an autonomous non-profit organisation established in October 1983 under the King Mahendra Trust for Nature Conservation Act 2039. The King Mahendra Trust for Nature Conservation Regulations 2041 were published on 15 October 1984. The Trust aims to conserve and manage natural resources in order to improve the quality of life of the human population, complementing the efforts of HMG and foreign agencies. The Trust has been instrumental in the establishment of the Annapurna Conservation Area (pending legal notification) and is entrusted with its management. Support for protected areas has also been extended to preliminary surveys of the Barun Valley in co-operation with the Woodlands Mountain Institute, USA (Rana et al., 1986). Major objectives planned for 1988–9 to 1991–2 include the implementation of the conservation area concept in the Annapurna basin and the establishment of the Nepal Conservation Research and Training Centre at Sauraha in Royal Chitwan National Park (KMTNC, 1988).

The Nepal Nature Conservation Society, founded in 1971, encourages local interest in natural history and conservation, but is seriously handicapped by lack of financial resources (FAO, 1980). Other non-governmental organisations with a conservation outlook include the Nepal Forum of Environmental Journalists, and the Nepal Forestry Association. A small-scale but effective initiative is the Jara Juri programme whereby each year leading efforts to promote resource conservation by an individual or community are formally recognised (HMG Nepal, IUCN, 1988; Pandey, 1988). IUCN–The World Conservation Union has a project office in Nepal to assist with implementing the Nepal Conservation Strategy.

Systems Reviews Nepal, with its rich biological diversity and spectacular landscape, extends for 800 km along the southern slopes of the Himalaya, separating the arid Tibetan Plateau to the north from the fertile Gangetic Plain to the south. More than 80% of the total area is covered by rugged hills and mountains, including Sagarmatha (Mount Everest) and another seven of the world's ten highest peaks. Five physiographic zones can be distinguished: High Himal (23% of the total area) comprising alpine meadows, rock, and ice, between the tree line and Great Himalayan divide; High Mountains (20%), extending from the heavily populated hills of the Middle Mountains to the tree line; Middle Mountains or Middle Hills (30%) of central Nepal; Siwaliks (13%), representing the first and lowest ridges of the Himalayan system and extending from the Gangetic Plain to the Mahabharat Lekh at the southern edge of the Middle Mountains; and the *terai* (14%), a northern extension of the Gangetic Plain (Kenting, 1986; MFSC, 1988). There are four main ecological zones: transhimalaya (a small, semi-arid zone north of the main Himalayan axis in Western Nepal), highlands, subtropical/temperate midlands, and tropical lowlands or *terai* (HMG Nepal/IUCN, 1988). The main river systems from west to east are the Mahakali, Karnali, Narayani, and Kosi, all of which originate from the Himalaya. Together with other smaller rivers rising in the Mahabharat Lekh and Siwaliks, they contribute up to 40% of the annual flow of the Ganges River and 71% of its dry season flow. Other wetlands include numerous small lakes, reservoirs, and village tanks, and a number of large reservoirs under construction in the Gandaki, Bagmati, and Karnali river basins (Scott, 1989).

Based on aerial surveys in 1978–9, it has been estimated that forest (i.e. land with at least 10% tree crown cover) covers 56 million hectares or 38% of the country (most of which is found in the Siwaliks, Middle Mountains, and High Mountains). Scrubland accounts for a further 4.7%, cultivation and non-cultivated inclusions 26.8%, grasslands 11.9%, and other lands 18.5%. Much of this forest is in poor conditions with only a scattering of trees: forest cover at 40% tree crown cover is only 28.1%. Furthermore, it is estimated that there has been a 5.7% of loss of forest land during the preceding 14 years, most of which occurred in the *terai* and Siwaliks. Such losses are due to uncontrolled exploitation for fodder, fuelwood, timber, and grazing, and to their conversion for agriculture, which has been exacerbated by the mass migration of people from the Middle Mountains following the eradication of malaria in the lowlands. Although forest cover may not have changed significantly in the Middle

Mountains from 1964–5 to 1978–9, its quality deteriorated more than anywhere else in the country. Moreover, deforestation has been more extensive in the Middle Mountains (with 41% forest cover) and *terai* (23%) during recent historical times, than in the Siwaliks (76%) and High Mountains (55%) (Kenting, 1986).

Following initiatives in the late-1950s to protect the Indian rhinoceros and its habitat, the need to establish protected areas elsewhere in Nepal was highlighted under the HMG/UNDP/FAO Trisuli Watershed Project (Caughley, 1969). Subsequently, in 1973, HMG embarked on a National Parks and Wildlife Conservation Project with assistance from UNDP and FAO. Its objective was to ensure the more effective conservation and management of Nepal's valuable yet diminishing wildlife resources and associated habitats by establishing a system of national parks and reserves which, in addition to their conservation role, would contribute to the development of the country's economically important tourist industry. Many of Nepal's protected areas were established under this project, which ended in 1979. A conservation education programme was included in the project and wildlife staff were trained overseas under this project and a New Zealand Co-operation Project (FAO, 1980). In 1974, the Royal Chitwan National Park, the Royal Karnali Wildlife Reserve (renamed the Royal Bardia Wildlife Reserve) and the Royal Sukla Phanta Wildlife Reserve were identified by HMG as important areas for tiger conservation and received substantial support for their development from WWF under the aegis of Operation Tiger. The New Zealand Government was instrumental in the establishment of Sagarmatha National Park, providing funds for its development over a six-year period beginning 1975 (Lucas, 1977). A third two-year HMG/UNDP/FAO National Parks and Protected Areas Management Project was launched in 1986 to strengthen the capability of the Department of National Parks and Wildlife Conservation and to effectively manage its protected areas by preparing and implementing management plans and integrating local people into the planning and management process (Heinen et al., 1988). Initiatives are now underway to extend the protected areas network to the Annapura and Makalu–Barun regions, with particular emphasis on promoting the 'conservation area' concept to facilitate people's participation in conserving natural resources (Upreti, 1990).

Nepal has a fairly extensive protected areas network covering 7.7% of total land area. It is in the process of being expanded by a further 2.9%, with the establishment of conservation areas in the Annapurna and Makalu–Barun regions (Sherpa et al., 1986; Shrestha et al., 1990), and a number of earlier proposals for setting up hunting reserves remain outstanding (Wegge, 1976a, 1976b). General recommendations to develop the protected areas network are made in the *IUCN Systems Review of the Indomalayan Realm* (MacKinnon and MacKinnon, 1986) and in the *Corbett Action Plan* (IUCN, 1985). A more recent assessment shows that of Nepal's five physiographic zones, the Middle Mountians are poorly represented, with only 1.4% protected areas coverage as compared with at least 4% for all other zones and 17.1% in the case of the High Himal. The limited coverage of the Middle Mountains is improved somewhat by the royal forests of Nagarjun (1,600 ha) and Gokarna (250 ha), and there are two protected watersheds due to be established in this zone (MFSC, 1988). A more refined review of protected areas coverage of Nepal's forests with respect to breeding birds (Inskipp, 1989) shows that all upper temperate, subalpine and alpine and most tropical forest types are well represented. Tropical evergreen forests, subtropical and lower temperate broad-leaved forests in the far east, and subtropical broad-leaved forests further west are unrepresented or very poorly represented. A high priority for bird conservation is that of the protection of the species-rich forests of Phulchowki Mountain in Kathmandu Valley, which is severely threatened by quarrying and the removal of fuelwood (Inskipp and Inskipp, 1989), and the

Mai Valley in the far east. A comprehensive systems review covering the full range of habitat types and floral and faunal assemblages is needed to assess the adequacy of the protected areas system (MFSC, 1988). The policy regarding the selection of additional lands for protection is outlined in the National Conservation Strategy (HMG Nepal/IUCN, 1988).

Nepal's natural resources are being exploited above their sustainable capacity to meet the increasing needs of a rising human population that is predominantly agrarian and subsistence in nature. The pressure on land and forest resources to meet daily food, fuelwood, and fodder requirements inevitably leads to conflicts at the boundaries of protected areas (Upreti, 1985). Major development projects also threaten the integrity of protected areas, as in the case of the proposed irrigation and hydropower projects planned near the Royal Chitwan National Park (now listed as a threatened protected area by the IUCN Commission for National Parks and Protected Areas) and the Royal Bardia National Park. The need to integrate conservation and development needs is widely recognised and is gradually being addressed through, for example, the national planning process and implementation of the National Conservation Strategy.

Other Relevant Information Protected areas play a very important role in the tourism industry, being a popular destination for mountaineers, trekkers, and those interested in Nepal's wildlife or cultural diversity. The number of visitors to Nepal increased from 45,000 in 1970 to 223,000 by 1986. During this period, the number of tourists who came for trekking and mountaineering rose from 12,600 to 33,600. In 1985, tourism accounted for 48.5% of gross foreign exchange earnings (HMG Nepal, IUCN, 1988). In 1989, protected areas received a total of 84,840, visitors; Annapurna Conservation Area and Royal Chitwan National Park being the most popular destinations.

Addresses
Department of National Parks and Wildlife Conservation (Director General), PO Box 860, Babar Mahal, Kathmandu (Tel. 1 229012/220850/227926; FAX: 1 227675; Tlx: 2567 kmtnc np)
Department of Forest (Director General), Babar Mahal, Kathmandu (Tel. 1 220303/221231)
IUCN–The World Conservation Union (Senior Advisor), PO Box 3923, Kathmandu (Tel. 1 229012/220850/227926; Fax: 1 227675; Tlx: 2566 hohil np)
King Mahendra Trust for Nature Conservation (Secretary), PO Box 3712, Kathmandu (Tel. 1 223229/220109; FAX: 1 226602; Tlx: 2567 kmtnc np; Cable NATRUST)
Nepal Nature Conservation Society (General Secretary), Kathmandu

References

Caughley, G. (1969). *Wildlife and recreation in the Trisuli Watershed and other areas in Nepal.* Report no. 6 HMG/FAO/UNDP Trisuli Watershed Development Project, Kathmandu. 44 pp.

FAO (1980). *National parks and wildlife conservation, Nepal: project findings and recommendations.* UNDP/FAO Terminal Report, Rome. 63 pp.

Glaser, G. (1984). The role of ICIMOD: a presentation of the Centre. In: *Mountain Development: challenges and opportunities.* International Centre for Integrated Mountain Development, Kathmandu. Pp. 59–63.

Heinen, J.T., Kattel, B., and Mehta, J.N. (1988). National park administration and wildlife conservation in Nepal. Draft. Department of National Parks and Wildlife Conservation, Kathmandu. 72 pp.

HMG Nepal/IUCN (1983). *National conservation strategy for Nepal: a prospectus.* IUCN, Gland, Switzerland. 36 pp.

HMG Nepal/IUCN (1988). *Building on success. The National Conservation Strategy for Nepal.* HMG National Planning Commission/NCS for Nepal Secretariat, Kathmandu. 179 pp.

ICIMOD (1989). *The first five years—a summary presentation*. International Centre for Integrated Mountain Development, Kathmandu. 25 pp.

Inskipp, C. (1989). Nepal's forest birds: their status and conservation. *International Council for Bird Preservation Monograph* no. 4. 160 pp.

Inskipp, C. and Inskipp, T. (1989). Pulchowki—hill of flowers. *Oryx* 23: 135–7.

IUCN (1985). *The Corbett Action plan for protected areas of the Indomalayan Realm*. IUCN, Gland, Switzerland and Cambridge, UK. 23 pp.

Kenting (1986). *HMG Nepal/Government of Canada Land Resource Mapping Project*. Kenting Earth Sciences Limited, Kathmandu.

KMTNC (1988). *Strategy for environmental conservation in Nepal*. The initial five-year (1988–9 to 1992–3) Action Plan of The King Mahendra Trust for Nature Conservation (KMTNC). KMTNC, Kathmandu. 70 pp.

Lucas, P.H.C. (1977). Nepal's park for the highest mountain. *Parks* 2(3): 1–4.

MacKinnon, J. and MacKinnon, K. (1986). *Review of the protected area system in the Indomalayan Realm*. IUCN, Gland, Switzerland and Cambridge, UK/UNEP, Nairobi, Kenya. 284 pp.

Mansberger, J. (1990). Keeping the covenant: sacred forests of Nepal. *The New Road* 12: 2.

MFSC (1988). Master Plan—Forestry Sector Nepal. 13 reports. HMG Nepal/ADB/FINNIDA with Jaakho Poyry/Madecor Consultancy, Kathmandu.

Pandey, S. (1988). Jarajuri—A Nepal NGO with a difference. *Tiger Paper* (*Forest News*) 15(1): 11–13.

Rana, P.S.J.B., Pandey, N.R., and Mishra, H.R. (1986). An introduction to the King Mahendra Trust for Nature Conservation. *King Mahendra Trust for Nature Conservation Publication Series* no. 1. 35 pp.

Scott, D.A. (Ed.) (1989). *A directory of Asian wetlands*. IUCN, Gland, Switzerland and Cambridge, UK. 1,181 pp.

Sherpa, M.N., Coburn, B. and Gurung, C.P. (1986). *Annapurna Conservation Area, Nepal Operation Plan*. King Mahendra Trust for Nature Conservation, Kathmandu. 74 pp.

Shrestha, T.B., Sherpa, L.N., Banskota, K., and Nepali R.K. (1990). *The Makalu–Barun National Park and Conservation Area management plan*. Department of National Parks and Wildlife Conservation, Kathmandu/Woodlands Mountain Institute, West Virginia, USA. 85 pp.

Upreti, B.N. (1985). The park–people interface in Nepal: problems and new directions. In: McNeely, J.A., Thorsell, J.W., and Chalise, S.R., *People and protected areas in the Hindu Kush—Himalaya*. King Mahendra Trust for Nature Conservation/International Centre for Integrated Mountain Development, Kathmandu. Pp. 19–24.

Upreti, B.N. (1990). Status of national parks and protected areas in Nepal. *Tiger Paper* 18 (2): 27–32.

Wegge, P. (1976a). *Terai shikar reserves: surveys and management proposals*. Field Document no. 4. FAO/NEP/72/002 Project, Kathmandu. 78 pp.

Wegge, P. (1976b). *Himalayan shikar reserves: surveys and management proposals*. Field Document no. 5. FAO/NEP/72/002 Project, Kathmandu. 96 pp.

ANNEX   Definitions of protected area designations, as legisted, together with authorities responsible for their administration.

Title (English title):
Forest Act 2018

Date: 27 December 1961; amended 1963, 1977, 1978

Brief description:
To provide for the demarcation and administration of state forests.

Administrative authority:
Department of Forest, Ministry of Forests and Soil Conservation (Director-General)

Designations:[1]
State forest [1]
— All forest, inclusive of waste land, streams and ponds, or paths, other than a forest parkand Panchayat forest as mentioned in this Act. Designated by the Government by notification in the *Nepal Gazette*. No person has any rights within state forests unless provided through contract or permit by the Government.
— Prohibited activites include deforestation, cultivation, setting fires, grazing, damaging trees, removing stone, manufacturing charcoal or lime etc, and removing forest products.
— Any state forest may be declared a forest park.
— Panchayat forest.
— State forest, or part thereof, which has been rendered waste or contains only stumps, entrusted to any village Panchayat for reforestation in the interest of the village community.

---

[1] Designations have recently been revised under the Master Plan for the Forestry Sector and are due to be incorporated within new forest legislation. Definitions, as provided by the Department of Forest, are as follows:

NATIONAL FOREST
— All forests except those designated otherwise
COMMUNITY FOREST
— Government forest land entrusted to user groups to encourage sustained use of such resources. It is further subdivided according to the management criteria.
  COMMUNITY PLANTATION FOREST
— Any government forest land, devoid of trees or in which only scattered trees or shrubby vegetation is left, which has been notified for forest development through reforestation by the active participation of user groups.
  COMMUNITY FOREST
— Any government forest which has been notified for management and conservation by the active involvement of user groups.
  LEASED FOREST
— Forest on land that has been leased by central or local agencies of the government, village development committees or private owners to individuals, co-operatives, institutions or commercial firms for forest production purposes.
  RELIGIOUS FOREST
— Forest belonging to religious institutions under the Guthi Act.

— Under the Panchayat Forest Rules 1978, ordinarily up to 200 bighas in the *terai* or 2,500 ropanies (125 ha) elsewhere shall be maintained as Panchayat forest in each Village Panchayat. The Panchayat is obliged to plant and maintain the forest, and act in accordance with the operational plan of the relevant Forest Division. It is forbidden to sell, mortgage, alienate, reclaim, cultivate or use the land in any manner other than prescribed in the approved plan.

Panchayat protected forest
— State forest, or part thereof, entrusted to a local Panchayat for its protection and proper management.
— Under the Panchayat Protected Forest Rules 1978 (amended 1980), ordinarily 400 bighas in the *terai* or 10,000 ropanis (500 ha) elsewhere shall be designated as Panchayat protected forest in each Village Panchayat. The Panchayat is obliged to: maintain and protect the forest; prevent poaching of forest produce, fires, destruction and damage to trees, and quarrying; and to act in accordance with a specified working plan. It is forbidden to damage, mortgage, sell or alienate, reclaim, or cultivate the forest, or deviate from the agreed working plan.

Religious forest
— State forest, or part thereof, located at a place of religious importance entrusted to a religious institution for its protection and proper management.

Contract forest
— State forest, or part thereof, devoid of trees, or has only stray trees, entrusted to any individual or agency for production and consumption of forest products.

Private forest reserve
— Any person may plant a forest on his land. Such forested land must be registered with the State. Activities may be controlled or prohibited within a private forest reserve by order published in the *Nepal Gazette*. If any order is contravened, management may be transferred to the local forest officer for up to a maximum period of 30 years.
— All provisions of this Act relating to state forests are applicable to private forests.

Source: Translation of original legislation

Title (English title):
The National Parks and Wildlife Conservation Act 2029

Date: March 1973; amended 1975 and 1983

Brief description:
To provide for national parks and the conservation of wildlife.

Administrative authority:
Department of National Parks and Wildlife Conservation (Director General)

Designations:
National Park
— Area set aside for conservation, management and utilisation of animals, birds, vegetation, and landscape together with the natural environment.
— Entry is restricted to persons possessing an entry permit or written permission from an authorised officer, except in the case of Government officials or persons travelling on an existing right-of-way.

— Prohibited activities include: hunting or damaging any animal; building or occupying any form of shelter or house; occupying, clearing or cultivating land; pasturing or watering any domesticated animal; damaging, felling or removing any tree or other plant; mining, quarrying or removing stone, minerals, or earth; carrying or using any weapon, ammunition or poison; carrying any domestic or other animal or trophy, except by a Government official on duty or by a person travelling along an existing right-of-way; blocking or diverting any river, stream or other source of water flowing into a national park, or introducing any harmful or poisonous substance therein; and damaging or removing any boundary marks, signposts or notices.

— Services or amenities may be provided by HMG or under contract to the Government.

Reserve

— Means controlled natural reserve, wildlife reserve or hunting reserve.

— None of the activities prohibited within a national park is permitted without written permission from an authorised officer.

Controlled Nature Reserve (Strict Nature Reserve).

— Area of ecological or other significance set aside for the purpose of scientific study.

— Entry is restricted to persons having written permission from an authorised officer.

Wildlife reserve

— Area set aside for the conservation and management of animals, birds and other resources and their habitats.

Hunting reserve

— Area set aside for the management of animals, birds, and other resources to provide for hunting.

Conservation area (1989 amendment)

— Area managed in accordance with an integrated plan for the conservation of the natural environment and the sustainable use of natural resources.

Source: Original legislation

Title (English title):
Soil and Watershed Conservation Act 2039

Date: 1982

Administrative authority:
Department of Soil Conservation and Watershed Management

Brief description:
Not available

Designations:
Protected watershed area

— Area protected to conserve soil and watersheds, and in which measures for afforestation may be taken.

— Official permission is required for cutting trees and other plants or forest products. Land use, including cultivation and planting of trees, may be subject to official controls.

Source: MFSC, 1988

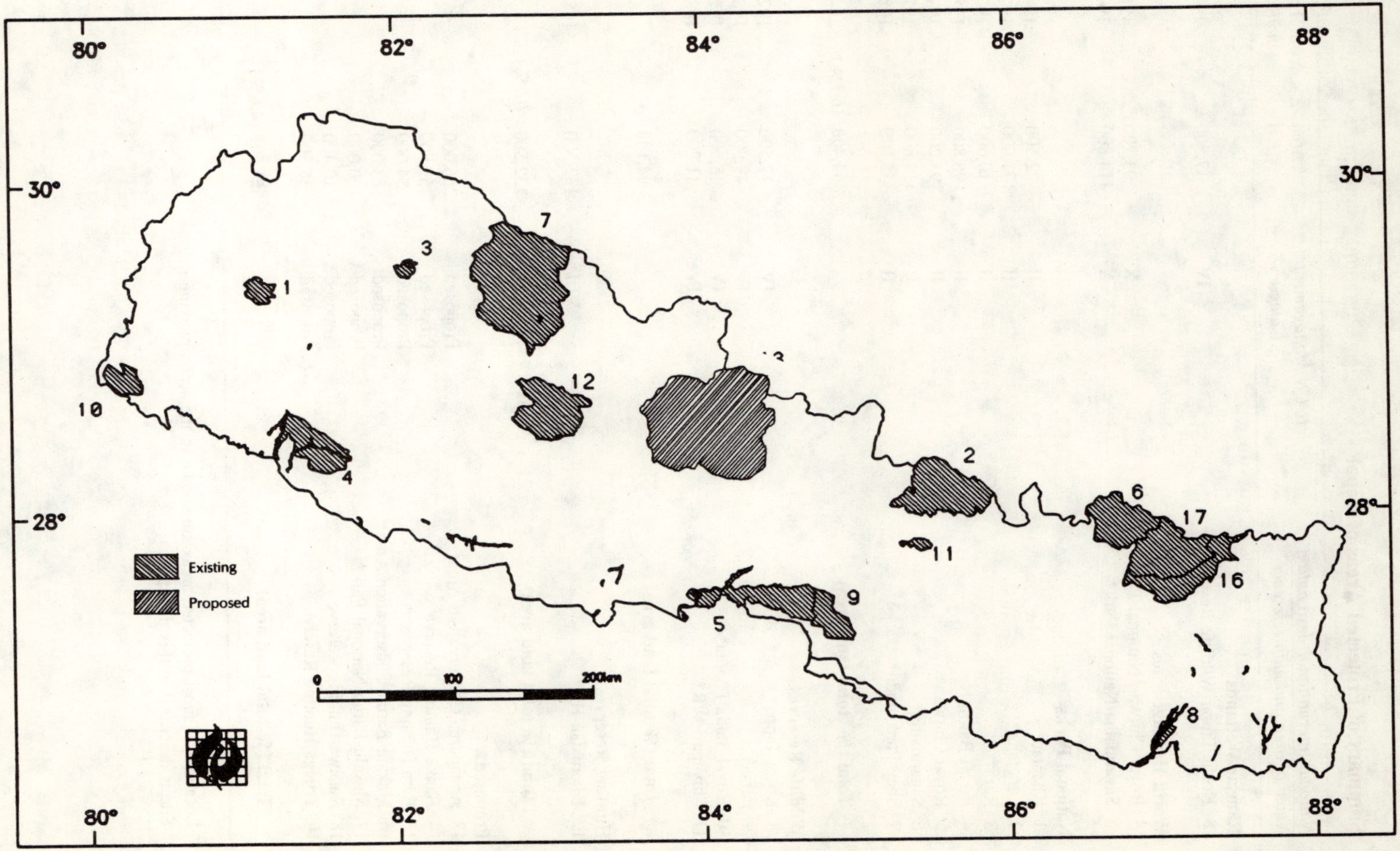

Nepal

Summary of Protected Areas of Nepal

National/International designation Name of area and map reference[+]	IUCN Management Category	Area (ha)	Year notified
Ramsar Wetlands			
8 Koshi Tappu Wildlife Reserve*	IV	17,500	1987
World Heritage Sites			
5 Royal Chitwan National Park*	X	93,200	1984
6 Sagarmatha National Park*	X	114,800	1979
National Parks			
1 Khaptad*	II	22,500	1986
2 Langtang*	II	171,000	1976
3 Rara*	II	10,600	1977
4 Royal Bardia*	II	96,800	1988
5 Royal Chitwan*	II	`93,200	1973
6 Sagarmatha*	II	114,800	1976
7 Shey-Phoksundo*	II	355,500	1984
Total (% total land area)		**864,400 (6.1%)**	
Wildlife Reserves			
8 Koshi Tappu*	IV	17,500	1976
9 Parsa*	IV	49,900	1984
10 Royal Sukla Phanta*	IV	15,500	1976
11 Shivapuri WR*	IV	11,200	1985
Total (% total land area)		**94,100**	
Hunting Reserves			
12 Dhorpatan HR*	VIII	132,500	1987
Total (% total land area)		**132,500 (0.9%)**	
Proposed			
13 Annapurna Conservation Area*	Proposed	266,000	
14 Banke Hunting Reserve	Proposed	51,800	
15 Bara Hunting Reserve	Proposed	54,000	
16. Makalu-Barun Conservation Area*	Proposed	83,000	
17 Makalu-Barun National Park*	Proposed	150,000	
18 Rasuwa Hunting Reserve	Proposed	10,400	
19 Trijuga Hunting Reserve	Proposed	36,300	
Total (% total land area)		**651,500 (4.6%)**	

[+] Locations of most protected areas are shown in the accompanying map.
* Site is described in this directory.

ANNAPURNA CONSERVATION AREA

IUCN Management Category   Proposed

Biogeographical Province   2.38.12 (Himalayan Highlands)

Geographical Location   The proposed conservation area encompasses the Annapurna range in Western Nepal. It is bounded to the north by the dry alpine deserts of Mustang and Tibet (China), to the west by the Kali Gandaki River, to the east by Marsyandi Valley and to the south by valleys and foothills north of Pokhara (Sherpa et al., 1986). The nearest town is Pokhara, some 30 km to the south. Access is by road from Pokhara to Nandanda, and from then onwards by foot. 28°15′–28°50′N, 83°35′–84°25′E.

Date and History of Establishment   Protection of this area as a national park was first proposed by Choate (1971) and subsequently incorporated in the Nepal Tourism Master Plan of 1972. Blower (1974) also supported the recommendations for a national park. Subsequently, the World Pheasant Association recommended that a wildlife reserve be established at Pipar for pheasants (Forster and Lelliott, 1982). The idea of a multiple-use area originated from a recommendation that environmental protection be carefully integrated with rural development and tourism (Sakya, 1982). Following a visit to the Western Development Region in 1985, His Majesty King Birendra Bir Bikram Shah Dev issued directives for the integration of conservation with tourism development in the Annapurna region. A plan for the area to be privately managed by the King Mahendra Trust for Nature Conservation (KMTNC) was presented to participants of the International Workshop on the Management of National Parks and Protected Areas in the Hindu Kush-Himalaya held in Kathmandu in May 1985 (Bunting and Wright, 1985) and subsequently endorsed by His Majesty's Government on 6 July 1986 (Sherpa, 1986). Legal designation of the property as a conservation area under a recent amendment of the National Parks and Wildlife Act is anticipated.

Area   266,000 ha. It is proposed to develop 80,000 ha on the southern slopes of Annapurna Himal initially as a conservation area (Stage I) and, subsequently, extend management over the entire Annapurna range (Stage II). The recommended Pipar Wildlife Reserve on the southern flanks of Machhapuchhare is included in Stage I (Sherpa et al., 1986).

Land Tenure   State. Traditional rights of occupancy and use are enjoyed by the local people.

Altitude   Ranges from 1,151 m on the Mardi Khola to 8,091 m at the top of Annapurna I.

Physical Features   The 'Annapurna Sanctuary', one of the most impressive mountain cirques in the world, is surrounded by seven Himalayan peaks over 7,000 m: Fang (7,647 m), Roc Noir, renamed Khangsar Kang in 1984 (7,485 m), Gangapurna (7,455 m), Annapurna I (8,091 m), Annapurna II (7,551 m) and Annapurna South, renamed Annapurna Daksnin in 1984 (7,219 m); and four other high peaks, including Machhapuchhare (6,933 m). Entry to this natural amphitheatre, via the narrow Modi Valley between Hiunchuli and

Machhapuchhare, is marked by Hinko Cave. Lying between the Annapurna and Dhaulagiri ranges inside the western border of the proposed conservation area is one of the world's deepest gorges, the Kali Gandaki. Its bed is 6,780 m below Annapurna I and features fossil ammonites dating back to when it flowed into the Tethys Sea, some 60 million years ago. Titi Tal, a 6 ha lake lying at 2,620 m just east of the Kali Gandaki River, and its associated marshes, are likely to be a wetland of international importance, but little is known about them (Scott, 1989).

Climate   The southern slopes of Annapurna experience some of the highest rainfall in Nepal (approximately 5,000 mm), mainly due to the low (2,500 m) ranges to the south. Pipar (3,325 m), in the upper Seti Valley, receives at least 4,520 mm of precipitation per year (Lelliott, 1981). There are nine meteorological stations located within the park but records from these are not cited in the available literature (Sherpa et al., 1986).

Vegetation   The forests south of Annapurna Himal range from sal *Shorea robusta* at 1,000 m, through oak *Quercus lamellosa* (2,000–2,400 m), upper temperate mixed broadleaved (2,400–3,200 m) or *Rhododendron arboreum* (2,600–3,700 m), to birch *Betula utilis* forest (3,200–4,000 m). Moist alpine scrub and meadows occur above the tree-line at 4,000 m. Bamboo, *Arundinaria* and *Bambusa* spp., is the most important component of the forest understorey between 2,000 m and the tree-line. Some eight species of bamboo occur in the Pipar area which is more than at any other known locality in Nepal. The abundance of bamboo and the extensive rhododendron forest on the southern slopes of the Annapurna range may be due to the very high rainfall (Lelliott, 1981). The area to the north of the Annapurna range is dry subalpine steppe (Sherpa et al., 1986).

Fauna   Mammal species include common langur *Presbytis entellus*, yellow-throated marten *Martes flavigula*, jungle cat *Felis chaus*, leopard *Panthera pardus* (T), snow leopard *P. uncia* (E), Himalayan black bear *Selenarctos thibetanus* (V), red panda *Ailurus fulgens* (K), Indian muntjac *Muntiacus muntjak*, goral *Nemorhaedus goral*, serow *Capricornis sumatraensis*, Himalayan tahr *Hemitragus jemlahicus*, bharal *Pseudois nayaur* and Royle's pika *Ochotona roylei* (Forster and Lelliott, 1982; Sherpa et al., 1986). Bharal occur at the highest densities yet recorded in Nepal (10 per sq. km) between Manang and the Thorong La (Wegge and Oli, 1988). Some 30 species have been recorded as present or probably present (Inskipp, 1989a).

The avifauna is the most diverse of all Himalayan protected areas in Nepal, with a total of 441 species recorded (Inskipp, 1989a; 1989b). This is attributed to the great variety of habitat types and to the Kali Gandaki which is a major biogeographical divide for bird distribution, as well as an important migration flyway. Of the 329 breeding species, 38 are considered to be at risk in Nepal and 100 may have internationally significant populations in the country. The property will be the only protected area where the rare rufous-throated partridge *Arborophila rufogularis*, chestnut-crowned bush warbler *Cettia major*, grey-cheeked warbler *Seicercus poliogenys*, pygmy blue flycatcher *Muscicapella hodgsoni*, brown parrotbill *Paradoxornis unicolor*, cutia *Cutia nipalensis*, golden-breasted fulvetta *Alcippe chrysotis*, and red-browed finch *Callacanthis burtoni* have been recorded in the breeding season. It is also the only place with all six species of pheasants found in Nepal. Five of these occur at Pipar, namely: blood pheasant *Ithaginis cruentus*, satyr tragopan *Tragopan satyra*, Kalij pheasant *Lophura leucomelana*, Koklass pheasant *Pucrasia macrolopha*, and Himalayan monal *Lophophorus impejanus* (Forster and Lelliott, 1982). All six species, including cheer pheasant *Cartreus wallichii* (E), can be seen from Ghasa in the Kali Gandaki Valley (Roberts, 1987).

Little is known about the invertebrate fauna (Shrestha, 1984).

Cultural Herjtage Gurungs have inhabited the Modi Valley for many centuries. Originating from Tibet, they have combined their Buddhist beliefs with Hinduism. They and their Magar neighbours to the west have developed elaborate social and religious customs. For instance, Machhapuchhare is sacred to Gurungs and consequently is closed to mountaineering. The powerful spirit of Pujinim Barahar guards the approach to 'Annapurna Sanctuary' and customarily only males of certain castes could pass beyond the gorge of the Modi Khola (Roberts, 1958; Stevens, 1988). The Phu Valley, north of the Annapurna range, used to belong to Tibet. Here, the Bhotias of Naur and Phu villages continue to practise orthodox Tibetan Buddhism. Remnants of the Pre-Buddhist Bönpo religion persist in Naur (Fürer-Haimendorf, 1985).

Local Human Population Some 40,000 people reside in the proposed conservation area, including several thousand Gurungs in the upper Modi Valley, Magars to the west and south-west, and small numbers of various Hindu castes, such as Brahmin and Chhetri (farmers), Damai (tailors), Sarki (cobblers) and Kami (blacksmiths) (Messerschmidt, 1984). Traditionally agro-pastoralists, the Gurungs and Magars are also well known as Gurkha soldiers and have become increasingly involved in other economic pursuits such as migrant labour and tourism. Sheep and goat populations totalled 9,169 and 6,173, respectively, for Kaski, Lamjung, and Manang districts in 1982 (Karki, 1985).

Visitors and Visitor Facilities The Annapurna region received some 36,800 foreign visitors in 1989, and slightly fewer (34,000) in 1990 due to the India–Nepal trade dispute and civil disturbances (Annapurna Conservation Area Project records). Food and accommodation are available in local hotels and houses along the more popular trekking routes. The Annapurna Regional Museum in Pokhara has been developed as an information centre for visitors to Annapurna Conservation Area. There is a popular guide to the birds and mammals (Inskipp, 1989a).

Scientific Research and Facilities The vegetation of this region has been surveyed by Dobremez and Jest (1971) and Stainton (1972). Wegge and Oli (1988) surveyed the bharal population in Manang District in 1987. The World Pheasant Association has supported research at Pipar since 1979 (Lelliott, 1981; Forster and Lelliott, 1982; Picozzi, 1984; Bhandary et al., 1986; Yonzon, 1987). A study of snow leopard is currently being carried out in Manang Valley (Oli, 1991). There is no research centre in the Annapurna region but there are plans to rehabilitate facilities at Kuldi Ghar (Bunting and Wright, 1985).

Conservation Value The Annapurna region contains an unique mix of natural and cultural values. The mountain scenery is spectacular, notable features being the Kali Gandaki gorge and 'Annapurna Sanctuary'. A wide range of habitats and associated vegetation types is present, ranging from subtropical forest to alpine scrub and, north of the Annapurna range, alpine steppe. Floral diversity is extremely high on the southern slopes of Annapurna Himal due to the high rainfall. In addition to being important for large mammals, notably snow leopard, musk deer and bharal, the conservation area is one of the three most internationally valuable protected areas for birds in Nepal. Thirteen of the 33 bird species for which Nepal may hold significant breeding populations are recorded from the southern slopes of Annapurna Himal (Inskipp and Inskipp, 1986).

Conservation Management   Following the proposal that management be the responsibility of the KMTNC in order to demonstrate how a nationally established but privately managed park can catalyse socio-economic development while increasing environmental awareness at both local and national levels, a feasibility study was carried out in 1985 and an operational plan forumlated (Sherpa et al., 1986). The Annapurna Conservation Area Project (ACAP) was officially launched by HRH Prince Gyanendra Bir Bikram Shah in 1987. In accordance with the operation plan, which was approved by the Cabinet in July 1987, the conservation area is divided into the following five zones: special management (outstandingly beautiful or pristine areas which are being degraded as a result of high visitor use and where special management is required to reverse present trends), wilderness (fully protected areas above the upper altitudinal limits of seasonal grazing where development is prohibited), protected forest/seasonal grazing (areas lying between the extensive use and wilderness zones in which swidden agriculture is prohibited, hunting, and collection of fuelwood, timber, leaf litter, bamboo, and fodder are restricted, and where medicinal plant collection is restricted to residents for domestic consumption only), intensive use (settled areas in which traditional forestry and pastoral management practices are encouraged, and where forest resources may be used without authorisation of the Conservation Officer, but hunting is strictly controlled), and biotic/anthropological (natural areas to which visitors are restricted entry to minimise the influence of modern man on the traditional lifestyles of the inhabitants). Management objectives provide for the conservation of viable communities of flora and fauna, as well as watersheds and catchments, and the cultural haritage of the various ethnic groups within a framework of environmentally-sound development for the benefit of the local people. Execution and enforcement of management policies will be the responsibility of the local management committees, of which the first 13-member forest management committee was set up in 1985 for Ghandruk Panchayat. Other initiatives taken to date include the installation of a micro-hydroelectric plant at Ghandruk, introduction of back-boilers, electric slow-cookers and a kerosene depot at Chhomrong (to reduce fuelwood requirements), and the distribution of about 78,000 seedlings in 1986–9 (M. Rowntree, pers. comm., 1991).

An area of approximately 4,600 ha has been proposed for Pipar Wildlife Reserve to support a minimum breeding population of at least 50 individuals for each of the reserve's pheasant species. As a total ban on pheasant hunting would be difficult to enforce, it has been recommended that no hunting of any species of pheasant should be permitted during the breeding season from March to September. It has since been recommended that this proposal should be adopted as part of ACAP (Sherpa et al., 1986).

Management Constraints   Environmental and cultural deterioration has been severe in 'Annapurna Sanctuary' due to: pressure on marginal land for cultivation by the increasing local population; persistent hunting of declining populations of mammals and birds; over-use of existing forest and grassland resources, leading to deforestation and erosion; and the impact of uncontrolled tourism. Rapidly changing economic and social conditions have eroded the unique Gurung culture, partly due to their involvement in tourism (Messerschmidt, 1984). Similar pressures of a less intensive nature exist in parts of Manang. These problems are being addressed by ACAP but implementation of Stage II has been delayed due to a lack of local support, a reflection of the local perception of the project (M. Rowntree, pers. comm., 1991).

Staff   ACAP is staffed by one project director, four conservation officers and 20 support staff (1991), and aided by local management committees. Three wildlife guards (Gurungs) have been posted at Pipar since 1981, with funds from the World Pheasant Association (Roberts, 1982).

Budget   US $ 118,950 was provided to KMTNC by WWF for the first of a five-year implementation of the Operational Plan (Stage I). The total budget for '–90 was US $ 347,380, or about US $ 70,000 per year (Sherpa et al., 1986). At the end of Stage I, it is anticipated that operating costs will be covered by visitor entry fees, concessions and permits. HMG has approved the collection of a levy of US $ 8 per tourist (1989) by the KMTNC.

Local Addresses
Director, Annapurna Conservation Area Project Headquarters, Ghandruk Village,
Ghandruk Village Panchayat, Kaski District. Four other regional headquarters are planned for
    Sikles, Bhujung, Manang, and Jomson (KMTNC, 1989)

References

Bhandary, H.R., Schemnitz, S.D., and Picozzi, N. (1986). Autumn foods of forest pheasants of Pipar, central Nepal. *The World Pheasant Association Journal* 11: 29–31.

Blower, J.H. (1974). Notes on the establishment of a national park in the Annapurna region. HMG/UNDP/FAO Project NEP/72/002. Kathmandu. Unpublished. 7 pp.

Bunting, B.W. and Wright, R.M. (1985). Annapurna National Park: the Nepal Plan for joining human values and conservation of a mountain ecosystem. In: McNeely, J.A., Thorsell, J.W., and Chalise, S.R. (Eds.), *People and protected areas in the Hindukush-Himalaya*. King Mahendra Trust for Nature Conservation and International Centre for Integrated Mountain Development, Kathmandu. Pp. 63–70.

Choate, T.S. (1971). Report on a preliminary reconnaissance of the western Annapurna Range with special reference to the wildlife and national park potential. Unpublished.

Dobremez, J.F. and Jest, C. (1971). Carte écologique du Nepal. Région Annapurna–Dhaulagiri 1/250,000. *Documents Carte Vegetation Alpes* 9: 147-90.

Forster, J.A. and Lelliott, A.D. (1982). Pipar Wildlife Reserve, Nepal: management proposals. Unpublished. 34 pp.

Fürer-Haimendorf, von C. (1985). Good and evil in Nepal. *The Geographical Magazine* 57: 660–5.

Inskipp, C. (1989a). *A popular guide to the birds and mammals of the Annapurna Conservation Area.* King Mahendra Trust for Nature Conservation, Kathmandu. 54 pp.

Inskipp, C. (1989b). Nepal's forest birds: their status and conservation. *International Council for Bird Preservation Monograph* no. 4. 184 pp.

Inskipp, C. and Inskipp, T.P. (1986). Some important birds and forests in Nepal. *Forktail* 1: 53–64.

Karki, N.P.S. (1985). Report on the evaluation of foot-rot disease at Lumle Agriculture Centre. Lumle Agriculture Centre, Kaski. Unpublished. 13 pp. (Unseen)

KMTNC (1989). *Annapurna Conservation Area Project.* King Mahendra Trust for Nature Conservation, Kathmandu..

Lelliott, A.D. (1981). Studies of Himalayan pheasants in Nepal with reference to their conservation. M.Sc. thesis, University of Durham, UK. 232 pp.

Messerschmidt, D.A. (1984). The Annapurna Project: a proposal for research and development planning for the proposed Annapurna National Park, Nepal Himalaya. Anthropology Department, Washington State University, Washington. 41 pp.

Oli, M. (1991). Snow leopard studies in Nepal Himalayas. *Cat News* 14: 17–18.

Picozzi, N. (1984). Pipar Project—Nepal: an ecological survey of a proposed reserve for Himalayan pheasants at Pipar, Nepal. *World Pheasant Association News* 5: 9–11.

Roberts, J.O.M. (1958). Background and reconnaissance. In: W. Noyce, *Climbing to the Fish's Tail*. Heineman, London. Pp. 3–17.

Roberts, J.O.M. (1982). The Machapuchare wildlife conservation project in Nepal. *Tiger Paper* 9(4): 18-20.

Roberts, J. (1987). The Mahhapuchare Wildlife Conservation Project in Nepal. In: Savage, C.D.W. and Ridley, M.W., *Pheasants in Asia 1982*. World Pheasant Association, Lower Basildon, UK. Pp. 15–17.

Sakya, K. (1982). Annapurna National Recreation Area, or Rashtriya Prakritik Manoranjan Sthal: a proposal. Kathmandu. Unpublished.

Scott, D.A. (Ed.) (1989). *A directory of Asian wetlands*. IUCN, Gland, Switzerland and Cambridge, UK. 1,181 pp.

Sherpa, M.N. (1986). Brief on Annapurna Conservation Area. King Mahendra Trust for Nature Conservation, Kathmandu. Unpublished. 5 pp.

Sherpa, M.N., Coburn, B. and Gurung, C.P. (1986). *Annapurna Conservation Area, Nepal Operation Plan*. King Mahendra Trust for Nature Conservation, Kathmandu. 74 pp.

Shrestha, P.K. (1984). Some insects of Pipar. *Journal of the Natural History Museum, Kathmandu* 8: 67–78. (Unseen)

Stevens, S. (1988). Sacred and profane Himalayas. *Natural History* 97(1): 27–34.

Stainton, J.D.A. (1972). *Forests of Nepal*. John Murray, London. 181 pp.

Wegge, P. and Oli, M. (1988). Survey of naur (blue sheep, *Pseudois nayaur*) in Manang District. Report to King Mahendra Trust for Nature Conservation and Department of National Parks and Wildlife Conservation, Kathmandu. 9 pp.

Yonzon, P.B. (1987). Nepal-Himalaya pheasant surveys at Pipar, Machhapuchare. *Pheasants in Asia 1982*. World Pheasant Association, Lower Basildon, UK. Pp. 55–7.

DHORPATAN HUNTING RESERVE

IUCN Management Category   VIII (Multiple Use Management Area)

Biogeographical Province   2.38.12 (Himalayan Highlands)

Geographical Location   Lies in Baglung District in the Dhaulagiri Himalaya of Western Nepal, some 260 km north-west of Kathmandu. Dhorpatan Village is just inside the southern boundary. The northern boundary of the reserve is formed by the Dhaulagiri Range; eastern and southern borders are defined by the Barse Range and Uttar Ganga, respectively. 23°30′N–28°50′N, 82°50′E–83°15′E

Date and History of Establishment   Dhorpatan is the first and only hunting reserve to have been officially established in Nepal. It was gazetted in April 1987, having previously been used for hunting purposes for a number of years.

Area   132,500 ha

Land Tenure   State

Altitude   Ranges from 2,850 m to 5,500 m.

Physical Features Dhorpatan lies on the southern flanks of the Dhaulagiri Range and is surrounded by mountain ranges on all sides, except in the west. Phagune Dhuri, which is north-west to south-east oriented, divides the reserve into northern and southern sectors. The northern catchment is drained by the Gustang, Dogadi, Seng, and Saunre rivers which flow west into the Bheri. The southern catchment is drained by the Uttar Ganga, also a tributary of the Bheri. Valleys are often steep-sided in their lower sections, opening out into broad basins in their upper reaches (Wegge, 1976).

Climate Located in front of an only moderately high saddle connecting the high Dhaulagiri and Hiunchuli, and shielded by several ranges south of Uttar Ganga, the area receives less precipitation than other areas in the Nepal midlands. Wegge (1976) estimated total annual precipitation to be less than 1,000 mm, of which roughly half falls as rain in the summer monsoon and the rest as snow, mostly in January and February. In view of variable winter snow accumulation and severity of the monsoon, total annual precipitation can be expected to range from 600–700 mm upwards to 1,300–1,400 mm (Wilson, 1981). Temperatures are lowest in January (–20 °C at 2,835 m) and highest (18.9 °C) prior to the monsoon (Wilson, 1981).

Vegetation The area is characterised by many plant species of the drier climatic belt to the north, but remnants of the more humid zone are also present, giving the area a mixed vegetation cover. Falling in a transition zone, the dry northern elements are more pronounced at higher altitudes and on south-easterly aspects. In more moist and shaded habitats mixed hardwoods form well-developed strands at lower elevation, yielding first to fir *Abies spectabilis* and then to birch/rhododendron at higher altitudes. In the upper Gustung drainage the climatic effects of aspect are well illustrated. The upper northern slopes are densely covered with birch *Betula utilis* and rhododendron *Rhododendron campanulatum* to the tree line, between 3,050 m and 3,660 m; below is a belt of fir and hemlock *Tsuga dumosa*, which gives way to a rich mixed-hardwood forest next to the river. The southern slopes, on the contrary, in a wide belt from approximately 3,500 m to 2,440 m, consist of a very sparse scrub forest of oak *Quercus semecarpifolia*, interspersed with isolated blue pine *Pinus excelsa* trees and occasionally rhododendron *Rhododendron arboreum*. The understorey is virtually absent. On dry sites, oak and blue pine are often the major forest types, sometimes dominated by juniper *Juniperus indica*. Typical of a transitional climatic zone is also the replacement of *J. recurva* by the xeric *J. squamata* at higher elevations. Above the tree-line at 3,660 m to 3,960 m on north slopes and about 300 m lower on south slopes, the area is mostly covered by various grass/sedge communities. On rich soil at elevations up to 4,420 m, a mixed forb type has been identified, which apparently is an important winter/spring food for blue sheep. Little vegetation is found above 4,720 m to 4,800 m (Wegge, 1976).

Fauna Dhorpatan is noted for its blue sheep *Pseudois nayaur* population, estimated to be 700–740 animals within a 96,000 ha survey area (Wilson, 1981). Other ungulates include goral *Nemorhaedus goral*, Himalayan tahr *Hemitragus jemlahicus*, and wild boar *Sus scrofa* (particularly common in the upper coniferous zone, especially in the Gurbad and Uttar Ganga catchments), Himalayan musk deer *Moschus chrysogaster* (widely distributed), serow *Capricornis sumatraensis*, and Indian muntjac *Muntiacus muntjak*. Leopard *Panthera pardus* (T) is common and widely distributed up to altitudes of 4,420 m. Other predators include lynx *Felis lynx* (known to occur in the Upper Seng Valley). Wild dog *Cuon alpinus* (V), red fox *Vulpes vulpes*, wolf *Canis lupus* (V), and snow leopard *Panthera uncia* (E) are occasional visitors to the area. Himalayan black bear *Selenarctos thibetanus* is common in forested areas. Red panda *Ailurus fulgens* is reported to be fairly common in the upper forests of the Lower Seng and Upper Bakre valleys (Wegge, 1976; Fox, 1985).

The avifauna comprises 136 species, of which 124 are breeding species. Western specialities include cheer pheasant Catreus wallichi (V), for which Dhorpatan is the best locality known in Nepal, and Himalayan pied woodpecker *Dendrocopos himalayensis*. A total of 41 breeding species for which Nepal may hold internationally significant populations has been recorded, including satyr tragopan *Tragopan satyra* (Inskipp, 1989).

Cultural Heritage   Dhorpatan lies on an important trading route for Bhotias from Tarakot and Dolpo to the north. Buddhist prayer flags and prayer stones are scattered throughout the area. Hindu pilgrims visit the reserve during August (Wegge, 1976).

Local Human Population   Nepalese villagers graze their livestock (mainly sheep and goats) on the alpine pastures in summer, and cultivate potatoes in the fertile valley of the Uttar Ganga. Approximately 1,300 families (Wegge, 1976), with some 80,000 head of livestock (Heinen, 1988), move into the area from neighbouring regions each year, notably Mayars, Kamis and Nauthors, from their winter villages south of Surtibang and the lower Uttar Ganga. Tibetan refugees were settled in Dhorpatan in 1960; there are currently 200–250 refugees (Wilson, 1981).

Visitors and Visitor Facilities   The reserve receives few visitors, most are licensed hunters. In 1989 there were 149 visitors. There are STOL airstrips at Dhorpatan, Taka, and Belera. The Department of Trade plans to develop a camping ground in the vicinity of the reserve headquarters (Jaakko Poyry Oy and Madecor, 1987).

Scientific Research and Facilities   The area was surveyed by Wegge (1976) in November 1974 and from March to June 1975. Research included investigations into the population ecology of blue sheep (Wegge, 1979). Subsequently, Wilson (1981) studied blue sheep habitat use and population dynamics.

Conservation Value   Dhorpatan is the only hunting reserve in Nepal and is particularly important for its blue sheep population. It is regularly used by hunters from overseas (Wegge, 1976; FAO, 1980).

Conservation Management   National Parks and Wildlife Conservation Regulation 2030 provides for the designation of hunting reserves and regulation of hunting. Wegge (1976) has proposed that hunting of all harvestable species be encouraged while, at the same time, the quality of the game populations be maintained and priority be given to managing the blue sheep population. The reserve is split into several 'blocks' for hunting purposes (Wegge, 1976). In 1988 two professional 'shikaris' operated in the reserve (P. Wegge, pers. comm.).

Management Constraints   The biggest management problems in the reserve are grass-burning, firewood cutting, deforestation and uncontrolled grazing by domestic livestock (Wegge, 1976; Heinen et al., 1988). There is some poaching, although the extent is not known. Local people frequently cut vertical sections out of the trunks of conifer trees to make torches, resulting in the deaths of many trees. Some 25%–30% of all grassy slopes between the tree-line and approximately 4,620 m are burned in spring and autumn to improve pastures (Wegge, 1976).

Staff One warden, one assistant warden, five rangers, five senior game scouts, twenty game scouts, and thirteen office staff (1991)

Budget In 1989–90 expenditure was NRs 1,137,588 (US $ 37,920) and income NRs 47,195 (US $ 1,573). The budget for 1990–1 was NRs 1,400,000 (US $ 46,667).

Local Addresses
Warden, Dhorpatan Hunting Reserve Headquarters, Dhorpatan Village, Baglung District

References
FAO (1980). *National parks and wildlife conservation. Nepal. Project findings and recommendations.* FAO, Rome. 63 pp.
Fox, J.L. (1985). An observation of lynx in Nepal. *Journal of the Bombay Natural History Society* 82: 394.
Heinen, J.T., Kattel, B., and Mehta, J.N. (1988). National park administration and wildlife conservation in Nepal. Draft. 93 pp.
Jaakko Poyry Oy and Madecor (1987). Master plan for forestry sector, Nepal. National parks and wildlife development plan. Draft for comments. Ministry of Forests and Soil Conservation, Kathmandu. 103 pp.
Inskipp, C. (1989). Nepal's forest birds: their status and conservation. *International Council for Bird Preservation Monograph* no. 4. 184 pp.
Wegge, P. (1976). *Himalayan shikar reserves; surveys and management proposals.* Field Document no. 5. FAO/NEP/72/002 Project, Kathmandu. 96 pp.
Wegge, P. (1979). Aspects of the population ecology of blue sheep in Nepal. *Journal of Asian Ecology* 1: 10–20.
Wilson, P. (1981). Ecology and habitat utilization of blue sheep *Pseudois nayaur* in Nepal. *Biological Conservation* 21: 55–74.

KHAPTAD NATIONAL PARK

IUCN Management Category II (National Park)

Biogeographical Province 2.38.12 (Himalayan Highlands)

Geographical Location Lies south of the main Himalayan range in far western Nepal, some 446 km by air from Kathmandu. It encompasses part of four districts, Doti, Bajura, Bajhang and Achham, in the Seti Zone. 29°17′–29°27′N, 81°00′–81°13′E

Date and History of Establishment Gazetted as a national park in 1986, partly as a result of representations made to the King of Nepal by the Swami of Khaptad (Inskipp, 1988).

Area 22,500 ha

Land Tenure Land is mostly state owned, but some small pockets are under private ownership (Jefferies, 1988).

Altitude Ranges from 2,800 m to 3,300 m.

Physical Features   Khaptad is an isolated massif, whose slopes are steep and thickly vegetated. The top comprises a rolling plateau of extensive grasslands interspersed with forest, scrub, and marsh. Khaptad Daha, a small shallow lake of 1.5 ha, lies on the top of the plateau. The main drainages are Phulaut Gad to the south, Samajiraho Gad to the east, tributaries of the Seti River to the north, and Sail Gad to the west (Kattel, 1981; Inskipp, 1988).

Climate   Conditions are monsoonal. Mean annual precipitation is about 1,550 mm, based on records from Tribeni (3,050 m) for 1978-81. Most precipitation falls between May and September. About 1 m of snow accumulates on the plateau during winter. Mean monthly maximum and minimum temperatures range from about 16 °C and 8 °C, respectively, in January to 31 °C and 21 °C in June at Silgari Doti, which is 1,630 m lower than Tribeni (Kattel, 1981).

Vegetation   The main vegetation types are described by Inskipp (1988, 1989a), based on the classification system of Dobremez and Joshi (1984). The subtropical zone (1,250–1,600 m) covers only a small portion of the park, as land between 1,250 m and 1,450 m is mostly cultivated. Broad-leaved forest and chir pine *Pinus roxburghii* are predominant. The lower temperate zone (1,500–2,500 m) comprises broad-leaved, mixed oak, and chir pine forests. Noteworthy are the extensive stands of the oaks *Quercus leucotrichophora* and *Q. floribunda* not found in other protected areas in Nepal. The upper temperate zone (2,400–2,900 m) supports mixed hygrophytic forests of oak *Quercus semecarpifolia-Q. floribunda*, hemlock *Tsuga dumosa*, fir *Abies pindrow* and maple *Acer pictum*, and montane forests of oak *Q. semecarpifolia*, and rhododendron *Rhododendron arboreum*.   Dense stands of bamboo *Thamnocalamus* sp. occur on the southern slopes around Choya Gadne. The subalpine zone (2,900–3,300 m) features forest comprising fir *A. spectabilis*, hemlock *T. dumosa*, oak *Q. semecarpifolia*, rhododendron *Rhododendron barbatum*, and shrubberies of rhododendron *R. barbatum*, as well as grasslands and swamp. The local people maintain that the distribution of forest and grassland on the plateau has remained the same over the last 100 years. As the soil is very shallow and lies on impermeable rock, some of the grasslands are very wet and it is unlikely that they can support forests. Khaptad is nationally renowned for its medicinal plants and, until recently, there was a medicinal plant farm on the plateau. A preliminary list of plant species recorded by T. Inskipp and Kattel (1981) has been compiled by Inskipp (1988).

Fauna   Large mammals include rhesus macaque *Macaca mulatta*, common langur *Presbytis entellus*, jackal *Canis aureus*, fox *Vulpes vulpes*, Himalayan black bear *Selenarctos thibetanus*, yellow-throated marten *Martes flavigula*, masked palm civet *Paguma larvata*, Indian grey mongoose *Herpestes edwardsi*, leopard cat *Felis bengalensis*, jungle cat *F. chaus*, leopard *Panthera pardus* (T), wild boar *Sus scrofa*, Himalayan musk deer *Moschus chrysogaster*, and Indian muntjak *Muntiacus muntjak*. Common langur, jackal, fox, yellow-throated marten, and Indian muntjac are quite common (Inskipp, 1988).

The avifauna comprises 223 species, of which 176 breed in the park. Of the 36 breeding species for which Nepal is especially important, 5 breed at Khaptad, namely: pied thrush *Zoothera wardii*, great parrot bill *Conostoma aemodium*, hoary-throated barwing *Actinodura nipalensis*, rusty-flanked treecreeper *Certhia nipalensis*, and spot-winged rosefinch *Carpodacus rhodopeplus*. Also present are satyr tragopan *Tragopan satyra* for which Nepal's population is of world importance, and black-chinned yuhina *Yuhina nigrimenta*, which has not been recorded in any other protected area in Nepal (Inskipp, 1989a, 1989b).

Some fifteen species of butterflies have been recorded (Inskipp, 1988).

Cultural Heritage Khaptad is of religious importance. It is the home of the Swami, usually known as the Baba, who lives in an ashram at lower Tribeni and has a strong influence over the local people. A meditation zone of 5 sq. km has been delimited in the core area of the park which includes the temples of lower Tribeni. Grazing, firewood-cutting, and certain other activities considered inappropriate by the Baba (e.g. drinking alcohol and smoking) are prohibited within this zone. Other places of religious significance include Khaptad Daha, a shrine at upper Tribeni, and the temples of Khaptad Mai. A festival, called Mella, is held near the Tribeni temples at the end of May and another smaller one at Khaptad Daha at the end of the summer grazing season (Kattel, 1981; Inskipp, 1988).

Local Human Population There are no permanent settlements within the park, other than the small isolated pockets of private land on the lower slopes. The grasslands, locally known as patans, are grazed by livestock during the summer months (April/May to August/September) (Kattel, 1981; Inskipp, 1988).

Visitors and Visitor Facilities Khaptad receives few visitors. According to records held by the Department of National Parks and Wildlife Conservation, there were eight tourists in 1989. There are no visitor facilities.

Scientific Research and Facilities A preliminary ecological survey of Khaptad was conducted by Kattel (1981). Dr Robert Fleming Sr. was the first ornithologist to visit the area but his trip in October 1959 was hampered by heavy rain (Fleming and Traylor, 1961, 1964). Subsequently, A. van Riessen (cited in Inskipp, 1989a) and Inskipp (1988, 1989a) made major contributions to the ornithological knowledge of Khaptad.

Conservation Value Khaptad is the only protected area representative of Nepal's western mid-mountain region. Its importance is due mostly to the variety and quality of its forests which, for example, support a large number of breeding species of birds. A wealth of plant species, including many medicinal herbs, grow in the park. The high-altitude bog system on the plateau is a rare habitat in Nepal (Inskipp, 1989a).

Conservation Management Use of the park's natural resources by local people is controlled on a permit basis. Daphne, bamboo, grass, and firewood may be collected for a total of ten days in May, September, October and April, respectively. Grazing is permitted from May to September (Jefferies, 1988). There are plans to compensate and resettle those persons owning land inside the park (Inskipp, 1988). There is no management plan but the park is zoned, with a 5 sq. km meditation zone delimiting the area occupied by the temples of lower Tribeni.

Management Constraints Kattel (1981) and Jefferies (1988) make a number of recommendations for improved management. Forests are exploited far less in Khaptad than in many other forests in Nepal, a reflection of the low human population density and availability of forest outside the park. The grasslands, however, are overgrazed and pools are filled in by the local people to prevent their cattle from drowning. Fires are deliberately lit annually in the chir pine forests to encourage the growth of grasses for livestock to graze. There is widespread ignorance among the local people of the park's value (Inskipp, 1988, 1989a).

Staff One senior warden, one assistant warden, four rangers, four senior game scouts, sixteen game scouts, eight others. One company of the Royal Nepal Army is stationed in the park.

Budget In 1989–90 expenditure was NRs 968,739 (US $ 32,290) and revenue NRs 36,210 (US $ 1,207). The budget for 1990–1 is NRs 1,163,000 (US $ 38,770).

Local Addresses Senior Warden, Khaptad National Park, P O Doti, Scti Zone

References

Dobremez, J.F. and Joshi, D.P. (1984). Carte écologique du Nepal. Région Dhangarhi-Api. 1:250,000. Documents de Cartographie Ecologique, Grenoble. (Unseen)

Fleming, R.L. and Traylor, M.A. (1961). Notes on Nepal birds. *Fieldiana Zoology* 35: 447–87.

Fleming, R.L. and Traylor, M.A. (1964). Further notes on Nepal birds. *Fieldiana Zoology* 35: 495–558.

Inskipp, C. (1988). Khaptad National Park. An account of current knowledge and conservation value. Report to the Department of National Parks and Wildlife Conservation, Kathmandu. Unpublished. 57 pp.

Inskipp, C. (1989a). The ornithological importance of Khaptad National Park, Nepal. *Forktail* 5: 49-60.

Inskipp, C. (1989b). Nepal's forest birds: their status and conservation. *International Council for Bird Preservation Monograph* no. 4. 184 pp.

Jefferies, B. (1988). Khaptad National Park duty travel report 9–16 February 1988. Report to the Department of National Parks and Wildlife Conservation, Kathmandu. Unpublished. 7 pp.

Kattel, B. (1981). A cursory ecological survey of Khaptad area. *Journal of Natural History Museum, Kathmandu* 5(2): 57–73.

KOSHI TAPPU WILDLIFE RESERVE

IUCN Management Category IV (Managed Nature Reserve)

Biogeographical Province 4.03.01 (Bengalian Rainforest)

Geographical Location Lies in the flood plain of the Sapta Kosi River at the most north-easterly extension of the Gangetic Plain, close to Nepal's southern border with Bihar State in India. 26°35'–26°40'N, 86°56'–87°04'E

Date and History of Establishment Gazetted as a wildlife reserve in July 1976. New boundary descriptions were published in the *Nepal Gazette* in 1980. Designated a Ramsar site on 17 December 1987 at the time of Nepal's accession to the Convention.

Area 17,500 ha. There were plans to extend the reserve as far south as the Kosi Barrage on the international border with India, an extension of about 13,000 ha, but this is complicated because the barrage is leased to the State Government of Bihar in India for 199 years. It is also planned to include the proposed Trijuga Hunting Reserve (36,300 ha) in the west.

Land Tenure State

Altitude Ranges from 75 m to 81 m.

Physical Features The reserve, running along the Sapta Kosi River for some 24 km, consists of extensive mudflats and fringing marshes. The discharge varies from a minimum of 287 cu. m per second in March to a maximum of 15,940 cu. m per second in August. Just south of the reserve is a large expanse of open water, marshes, and reed-beds, created by the construction of a barrage between 1958 and 1964. Embankments to the east and west contain the river during flooding, while borrow pits situated alongside retain water for most of the year (Scott, 1989).

Climate Conditions are tropical monsoonal, with a mean annual rainfall of 2,110 mm, mean maximum temperature of 37 °C, and mean minimum temperature of 8 °C (Scott, 1989).

Vegetation Originally comprised khair-sissoo forest, dominated by *Acacia catechu* and *Dalbergia sissoo*, mixed deciduous forest and grassland, but much of it has been degraded due to siltation and over-exploitation (Poppleton and Shah, 1977). Extensive reed-beds and other fresh water marshes occur along the banks of the Sapta Kosi and around parts of the reservoir (Scott, 1989).

Fauna Contains Nepal's last surviving population of wild water buffalo *Bubalus bubalis* (E), which appears to have increased from an estimated 60 in 1977 (Poppleton and Shah, 1977) to 91 in 1988 (Inskipp, 1988). It is reported, however, that the entire population has hybridised with feral water buffalo. Other mammals include leopard *Panthera pardus* (T), fishing cat *Felis viverrinus*, jungle cat *F. chaus*, gangetic dolphin *Platanista gangetica* (V) (occasionally seen), smooth-coated otter *Lutra perspicillata* (K), spotted deer *Cervus axis*, hog deer *Cervus porcinus*, nilgai *Boselaphus tragocamelus*, and wild boar *Sus scrofa*. Tiger *Panthera tigris* (E) is no longer present (Poppleton and Shah, 1977).

A total of 256 species of birds has been recorded, of which 176 breed in the reserve. Winter visitors and passage migrants recorded so far total 125 species, and more are likely to be found. There are 18 breeding species which are at risk in Nepal, although the changeable hawk-eagle *Spizaetus cirrhatus* and dusky eagle owl *Bubo coromandus* (E) have not been recorded since 1976. Other notable species are swamp francolin *Francolinus gularis* (V), red-necked falcon *Falco chicquera*, Bengal florican *Houbaropsis bengalensis* (E), brown fish owl *Ketupa zeylonensis*, and striated marsh warbler *Megalurus palustris*. Koshi Tappu is the only protected area in Nepal where watercock *Gallicrex cinerea* and Abbott's babbler *Trichastoma abbotti* are known to occur (Inskipp, 1989). Koshi Barrage is of international importance and by far Nepal's most important wetland for waterfowl, particularly as a staging and wintering area for a variety of transhimalaya migrants, notably ducks and shorebirds. Further details are given by Scott (1989).

Gharial *Gavialis gangeticus* (E) from the Chitwan rearing project were released upstream from the reserve in 1981 and 1984; a recent survey indicates that very few of these crocodiles have stayed in the area (Heinen et al., 1988). Fifty-two species of fish have been reported from the Nepalese side of the Kosi drainage (Khan and Yusuf-Kamal, 1979).

Cultural Heritage Jhangads, tribals originating from the forests of Bihar in India, inhabit areas adjacent to the reserve, but their culture and traditions have been influenced by development (B. Kattel, pers. comm., 1986).

341

Local Human Population   Subsistence fishing and agriculture are the main forms of livelihood for people living in the surrounding areas (Scott, 1989).

Visitors and Visitor Facilities   The reserve receives few visitors: in 1989, 12 were recorded by the Department of National Parks and Wildlife Conservation. A visitor lodge has been built at Kusaha and basic accommodation is also available at Koshi Village.

Scientific Research and Facilities   A fish survey was conducted in the Kosi drainage in 1949 (Khan and Yusuf-Kamal, 1979). The avifauna has been well-documented (Inskipp, 1989; Scott, 1989). The status of Bengal florican in the reserve was investigated in 1982 and the species was found to be absent (Inskipp and Inskipp, 1983). There are no research facilities.

Conservation Value   The reserve is an important breeding area for birds, as well as a valuable wintering area and staging point for migratory species (Inskipp, 1989; Scott, 1989). It is also important as the last refuge of wild water buffalo in Nepal.

Conservation Management   A primary reason for the reserve's establishment was to build up a healthy breeding population of wild water buffalo, from which other areas can be restocked, and this remains a long-term objective. Considerable progress has been made, including the establishment of a headquarters at Kusaha and three guard posts elsewhere, and the provision of the necessary staff. The reserve was brought under reasonable control in 1978, and by 1979 12,000 villagers had been moved and resettled elsewhere. The Churia or Siwalik Range to the west provides refuge for some Terai fauna, including gaur *Bos gaurus* (V), hence the plan to incorporate the proposed Trijuga Hunting Reserve within the reserve (FAO, 1980). The reserve is scheduled to be extended to the north; landowners will be financially compensated with revenues generated from the sale of sissoo trees killed by changing water tables. Grass is cut annually by the local people for thatching purposes. An estimated US $ 250,000 worth of thatch grass was legally removed during the 1987 thatch-cutting season. Reserve staff also supply permits for the collection of fish, edible fruits and ferns, and cotton. A fence was erected in 1982 to try to prevent the reserve's water buffalo from wandering into adjacent cultivations and to keep local people and their livestock out of the protected area. The feral cattle population is being reduced by allowing them to be caught by local residents, to whom ownership is conferred. Eight domesticated female elephants *Elephas maximus* (E) are kept at reserve headquarters, Koshi Tappu being the only protected area in Nepal where domesticated elephants have been successfully and repeatedly bred (Heinen et al., 1988).

Management Constraints   The construction of the Kosi Barrage on the Nepal–India border for irrigation and hydroelectric power has had a devastating effect on the reserve, although it has created an area of extensive wetland to the south which is used by migrating waterfowl (up to 50,000 ducks have been recorded in February). Habitat destruction, overstocking by domestic animals, disease introduced by domestic livestock and flooding have undoubtedly limited the increase in populations of water buffalo and other wild ungulates (Poppleton and Shah, 1977). The grazing problem is especially acute as there are several thousand head of feral cattle and over 100 domestic water buffalo in the reserve (Heinen et al., 1988). Another factor is the negative visual impact of high-tension electrical lines passing through the reserve and supported by huge towers (Jaakko Poyry Oy and Madecor, 1987).

Staff One warden, one assistant warden, three rangers, three senior game scouts, twelve game scouts and fourteen office staff (1991). One company of the Royal Nepal Army is deployed in the reserve for protection duties and there is a veterinarian (Heinen et al., 1988).

Budget In 1989–90 expenditure was NRs 890,216 (US $ 29,670) and revenue NRs 100,552 (US $ 3,350). The budget proposed for 1990–1 is NRs 1,074,000 (US $ 35,800).

Local Addresses Warden, Koshi Tappu Wildlife Reserve Headquarters, Kusaha, Sunsari District

References
FAO (1980). National parks and wildlife conservation, Nepal: project findings and recommendations. UNDP/FAO Terminal Report, Rome. 63 pp.
Heinen, J.T., Kattel, B. and Metha, J.N. (1988). National Park administration and wildlife conservation in Nepal. Draft. 93 pp.
Inskipp, C. (1989). Nepal's forest birds: their status and conservation. *International Council for Bird Preservation Monograph* no. 4. 184 pp.
Inskipp, C. and Inskipp, T. (1983). Results of a preliminary survey of Bengal floricans *Houbaropsis bengalensis* in Nepal and India, 1982. *International Council for Bird Preservation Study Report* no. 2. 54 pp.
Jaakko Poyry Oy and Madecor (1987). Master plan for forestry sector, Nepal: national parks and wildlife development plan. Draft for review. Ministry of Forests and Soil Conservation, Kathmandu. 103 pp.
Khan, H.A. and Yusuf-Kamal, M. (1979). On a collection of fish from River Kosi (Bihar). *Journal of the Bombay Natural History Society* 76: 530–4.
Poppleton, F. and Shah, B.B. (1977). WWF/IUCN Project 1605. Nepal–Koshi Tappu Buffalo Sanctuary.
Scott, D.A. (Ed.) (1989). *A directory of Asian wetlands*. IUCN, Gland, Switzerland and Cambridge, UK. 1,181 pp.
Wegge, P. (1976). *Terai shikar reserves: surveys and management proposals*. Document no. 4. HMG/UNDP/FAO National Parks and Wildlife Conservation Project, Kathmandu. 78 pp.

LANGTANG NATIONAL PARK

IUCN Management Category II (National Park)

Biogeographical Province 2.38.12 (Himalayan Highlands)

Geographical Location Lies in the central Himalayan region of Nepal. The southern boundary is some 32 km north of Kathmandu. To the west the boundary follows the rivers Bhote Kosi and Trisuli Ganga, to the north and east it is defined by the international border with the Tibetan Autonomous Region of China. 28°00′–28°20′N, 85°15′–86°00′E

Date and History of Establishment Established as a national park in March 1976, having been first proposed in 1969 under the HMG/FAP/UNDP Trisuli Watershed Development Project (Caughley, 1969). The boundaries were demarcated in 1979 prior to final notification.

Area   171,000 ha

Land Tenure   State. Residents enjoy traditional rights.

Altitude   Ranges from 792 m on the Bhote Kosi to the peak of Langtang Lirung at 7,245 m.

Physical Features   Natural morpho-tectonic divisions represented in the park are the Fore Himalaya (Helambu), Great Himalaya Range (Langtang and Jugal himals), Inner Himalaya valleys (Langtang and Lende) and, bordering the park to the east, the Tibetan Marginal Range (Shisha Pangma).   The park is bisected east–west by the Gosainkund Lekh–Dorje Lhapka range.   In the north, the rivers flow westwards into the Bhote Kosi–Trisuli Ganga, which cuts southwards through the Great Himalaya and ultimately flows into the Narayani.   The north-east of the park is dominated by the 20 km-long Langtang Glacier, encompassed by Langtang and Jugal himals.   From the glacier's snout to 3,800 m, Langtang Valley is steep-sided with a U-shaped profile.   Extensive alluvial plains, which are the flattest portions of the park, have developed as a result of blocking by terminal moraines of glaciers converging from the north.   The glaciated profile of the valley descends in a series of outwash terraces of recent origin to 3,000 m near Ghora Tabela, after which the profile is steep, water-worn and V-shaped.   Lende Valley probably has a similar morphology.   South of the Gosainkund Lekh–Dorje Lhapka range, most rivers run southwards and then into the Sun Kosi.   The pattern of deep valleys and intervening ridges, aligned north–south, contrasts with the east–west axis of those to the north but physiographically they are similar.   The valleys' upper reaches are glaciated and plains of similar topography to that of Langtang are present in the upper Melamchi and Yangri valleys.   Movement between north and south sectors of the park is restricted to a number of high passes, such as Gangja La (5,122 m) and Laurebina (4,609 m).   A number of lakes occur in the upper Trisuli Valley (e.g. Gosainkund) and elsewhere (e.g. Panch Pokhari).   These are described in Scott (1989).

Climate   Conditions are characterised by warm, moist summers, coinciding with the monsoon season (June–September); relatively warm and sunny autumn and spring seasons; and cold winters with clear skies and occasional snowfalls (the coldest months being January and February).   Altitudinal and topographic variation, however, produces considerable localised differences in conditions.   Thus, the Helambu area is exposed to the full force of the monsoon and has the highest precipitation (mean annual precipitation at Sarmathang, 2,625 m, just outside the park's southern boundary, is 3,363 mm), whereas Langtang Valley is shielded by the Gosainkund ridge and receives much less (annual precipitation at Langtang Village at 3,429 m was 1,027 mm in 1976–7) (Borradaile et al., 1977).

Vegetation   The great variety of vegetation types is one of the park's most striking features. Eight vegetation zones, based on the classification by Dobremez et al. (1975) are represented. The tropical zone (0.2%) comprises a small amount of sal *Shorea robusta* forest below 1,000 m in the lower Bhote Kosi.   The subtropical zone (2.0%), 1,000–2,000 m, is represented by *Schima wallichii* and *Castanopsis indica* forest in the damper areas of many lower valleys, chir pine *Pinus roxburghii* forest on drier slopes and *Euphorbia royleana* heath in the driest, rocky habitats along the Bhote Kosi and lower Langtang Valley.   The hill zone (4.8%), 2,000–2,600 m, comprises *Quercus lamellosa* forest mainly in the damper, southern sector of the park, *Q. lanata* forest with *Rhododendron arboreum* and *Lyonia ovalifolia* on southern slopes and blue pine *Pinus wallichiana* and *R. arboreum* forest with spruce *Picea smithiana* in the drier regions of the upper Bhote Kosi and lower Langtang and Lende valleys.   The occurrence of *P. smithiana* marks the eastern limits of its recorded distribution in the Himalaya.

The forests of the montane zone (9.9%) at 2,600–3,000 m vary from the damp, shaded *Quercus semecarpifolia* and hemlock *Tsuga dumosa* type to the mesohydrophyllic stands of almost pure *Q. semecarpifolia*. The lower subalpine zone (3,000–3,600 m), which together with the upper subalpine zone comprises 21.5% of the park, is characterised by the predominance of conifers, *T. dumosa*, fir *Abies spectabilis*, larch *Larix nepalensis* and, in drier habitats, *Juniperus* spp. Pure stands of *Rhododendron barbatum* often occur on damper, northern slopes. The presence of *L. nepalensis* in areas of lower rainfall, to the north of the Gosainkund Lekh–Dorje Lhapka range, is of special interest due to the species' peculiarly localised distribution in the Eastern Himalaya. Heaths and pastures occur in more exposed areas, with *Rhododendron lepidotum* amidst scattered *A. spectabilis*, and a plagioclimax community of *Caragana sukiensis* and other shrubs has developed on the southern slopes of the Langtang Valley, following removal of the forest and overgrazing by livestock. Birch *Betula utilis* forest, in association with *Rhododendron campanulatum*, is characteristic of the upper subalpine zone (3,600–4,000 m), although it may be replaced by *Juniperus* spp. in drier localities. Lying above the tree-line, the lower alpine zone (4,000–4,500 m) is rich in shrubs with heaths dominated by *Rhododendron* spp. (damp) or *Juniperus* spp. (dry). *R. anthopogon* is characteristic of the dampest habitats while *Ephedra gerardiana* and *Spiraea arcuata* occur in the sheltered, semi-arid environment of the upper Langtang Valley. *Salix* spp. occur in Langtang Valley but seldom in the south of the park, *Myricaria rosea* is present on riverside gravels and flats, and *Hippophae tibetana* is found on old moraines. The upper alpine zone (4,500–5,500 m), which together with the lower alpine zone comprises 21.5% of the park, consists of pastures whose species composition is extremely varied, depending on the soil and microclimate. Snow and ice above the lower limit of permanent snow at 5,500 m constitute 31.9% of the park. The remaining 3.6% includes areas of cleared forest, burnt vegetation and cultivations. Over 1,000 plant species have been recorded (Borradaile et al., 1977).

Fauna   The mammalian fauna has been documented by Green (1981). The only primates are rhesus macaque *Macaca mulatta* and common langur *Presbytis entellus*. The locality (near Routang) of the highest recorded sighting (4,270 m) of the latter species is in the park (Bishop, 1977). Carnivores include fox *Vulpes vulpes*, wild dog *Cuon alpinus* (V), Himalayan black bear *Selenarctos thibetanus* (V), red panda *Ailurus fulgens* (K) estimated at less than 40 individuals for the entire park (Yonzon and Hunter, 1991a), Himalayan weasel *Mustela sibirica subhemachalana*, pale-footed weasel *M. altaica temon*, beech marten *Martes foina*, yellow-throated marten *M. flavigula*, leopard cat *Felis bengalensis*, clouded leopard *Neofelis nebulosa* (V), and leopard *Panthera pardus* (T). Snow leopard *Panthera uncia* (E) may also be present. Ungulates include wild boar *Sus scrofa*, Himalayan musk deer *Moschus chrysogaster*, Indian muntjac *Muntiacus muntjak*, goral *Nemorhaedus goral*, serow *Capricornis sumatraensis*, and Himalayan tahr *Hemitragus jemlahicus*. There were about 220 tahr in the upper Langtang Valley in 1976–7 (Green, 1979). Small mammals include shrews, *Soriculus* spp. and *Suncus murinus*, Royle's pika *Ochotona roylei*, orange-bellied Himalayan squirrel *Dremomys lokriah*, rats *Rattus* spp., house mouse *Mus musculus*, Sikkim vole *Pitymys sikimensis*, and Indian porcupine *Hystrix indica*.

The avifauna comprises 283 species, more than recorded for any protected area in the Nepal Himalaya other than the proposed Annapurna Conservation Area (Inskipp, 1989). Breeding species total 246, of which 84 are species for which Nepal may hold internationally significant populations. The park is the only place in Nepal where dark-rumped rosefinch *Carpodacus edwardsii* has been recorded in the breeding season. Other notable breeding species include satyr tragopan *Tragopan satyra*, ibisbill *Ibidorhyncha struthersii*, orange-rumped honeyguide

Indicator xanthonotus, bay woodpecker *Blythipicus pyrrhotis*, Gould's shortwing *Brachypteryx stellata*, rufous-breasted bush-robin *Tarsiger hyperythrus*, long-billed thrush *Zoothera monticola*, smoky warbler *Phylloscopus fuligiventer*, large niltava *Niltava grandis*, fulvous parrotbill *Paradoxornis fulvifrons*, scaly laughing-thrush *Garrulax subunicolor*, fire-tailed Myzornis *Myzornis pyrrhoura*, yellow-bellied flowerpecker *Dicaeum melanoxanthum*, vinaceous rosefinch *Carpodacus vinaceus*, crimson-browed finch *Propyrrhula subhimachala*, scarlet finch *Haematospiza sipahi* and spot-winged grosbeak *Mycerobas melanozanthos* (Inskipp, 1989). Further details of the avifauna are given by Borradaile et al. (1977), Green (1980) and, in the case of waterbirds, by Scott (1989).

Notable reptiles include Himalayan rock lizard *Agama tuberculata* and a number of snakes. A toad *Bufo himalayanus* is common at lower altitudes and a frog *Rana polunii* occurs around Langtang Village. Fish are restricted to the periphery of the park. Blunt snow trout *Schizothorax plagiostomus* occurs in the lowest reaches of Langtang Khola and a large sporting fish, most likely mahseer *Tor tor*, is found in the Trisuli Ganga (Borradaile et al., 1977).

Cultural Heritage There is a variety of cultural groups, which to some extent have become intermingled. The Langtang people and others in the north of the park are believed to be Bhotias, probably originating from the Kyirong area in Tibet two or three centuries ago. People living in the south-west of the park, from Ramche to the upper Tadi Khola, are predominantly Tamangs with some Brahmans/Chhetris. Those from Helambu, in the south, call themselves Sherpas but there is historical evidence that they also originated from the Kyirong area and were subsequently influenced by Tamangs. Sherpas are present, however, in the eastern part of the park, along with Tamangs, Brahmans/Chhetris and Gurungs. The holy lake of Gosainkund, which commemorates the Hindu god Siva, attracts some 8,000 Hindu and Buddhist pilgrims each summer from all over the Indian subcontinent. The lakes at Panch Pokhari are also an important pilgrimage site and elsewhere in the park there are a number of Buddhist monasteries (Borradaile et al., 1977).

Local Human Population Of an estimated 111 villages (16,250 people) that depend on the park's resources, 45% (4,315 people) occur within its boundaries. Most of these villages are situated in the vicinity of the western and southern borders of the park. The Tibetan Khampas, who were allowed to settle at Ghora Tabela in Langtang Valley, have since been resettled elsewhere. Resident and peripheral human populations have traditionally depended on the park's resources for their agricultural, pastoral, fuel, timber and other requirements. Populations are increasing at an estimated 2% per annum. Associated with all permanent settlements are small areas of arable land on which are cultivated barley, wheat, maize, finger millet, soyabean and potato or at higher altitudes, barley, wheat, buckwheat and potato. Yields from cultivations have fallen due to decreasing soil fertility and the expansion of arable areas onto poorer, marginal land. All accessible areas of grassland up to the snow-line are grazed during summer by yak, yak/cattle hybrids, sheep and goats. This is the major form of land-use in the park (Borradaile et al., 1977).

Visitors and Visitor Facilities Visitor numbers have increased fourfold in the last ten yars. In 1975–9, the annual total was about 2,000 (Borradaile et al., 1977), compared with 8,145 visitors recorded in 1989. There is a landing strip above Kyangjin. Lodges and tea houses, providing food and accommodation, are located along the more popular trekking routes and elsewhere villagers may take in guests. The Department of National Parks and Wildlife Conservation has built lodges in traditional styles at Ghora Tabela and Kyangjin in Langtang Valley (Gut, 1981).

Scientific Research and Facilities   Langtang was included in Hagen's (1969) geological survey of Nepal. A botanical survey of Langtang Valley was carried out by His Majesty's Government in 1966 and vegetation surveys have been undertaken by Stainton (1972), Dobremez et al. (1972, 1975) and Tokyo University Museum in conjunction with the Department of Medicinal Plants. The flora and fauna (mammals and birds) are well documented (Green, 1981; Department of Medicinal Plants, 1986; Inskipp, 1989). Multidisciplinary studies were conducted in the park and adjacent areas under the Trisuli Watershed Development Project and by the Centre National de la Recherche Scientifique, Paris. A survey of the area was carried out in 1970–1 by the FAO Wildlife Management Advisor and Forest Department officers. Subsequently, Fox (1974) completed a six-month ecological survey of the park under the National Parks and Wildlife Conservation Project. This was followed by the Durham University Himalayan Expedition's eighteen month socio-ecological study (Borradaile et al., 1977). In 1986, over 16,000 plant specimens were collected from the Langtang-Helambu region (Ohba and Malla, 1988). Large mammal research includes ecological studies of red panda (Yonzon and Hunter, 1991a, 1991b) and Himalayan tahr (Green, 1979), and preliminary behavioural studies of muntjac (Oli, 1986). The use of forest resources by villagers of Syabru and the effects of tourism on their livelihood has been examined by Joshi (1987). There are no research facilities.

Conservation Value   The area is representative of the Central Nepal Himalaya, which supports a high diversity of flora and fauna because it lies at the junction of eastern and western extremities of species' distributions. A great variety of vegetation types is present, ranging from tropical forest to alpine meadows (Borradaile et al., 1977). The park is one of the three most internationally important protected areas in Nepal for birds (Inskipp, 1989), and is also significant for the diversity of its mammalian fauna (Green, 1981). In addition to its scenic and amenity values, the park features many cultural attributes (Borradaile et al., 1977).

Conservation Management   Following a preliminary development plan for the park (Blower, 1974), an outline management plan was produced by Bolton (1976) in anticipation of a five-year management plan. This was prepared by the Durham University Himalayan Expedition, based on its eighteen month multidisciplinary study of the park (Borradaile et al., 1977). The plan provides an overall framework for the park's management and proposes a system of zonation to reconcile conservation requirements with the needs of the local people, with 'protected natural areas' (39% of the park's area) to preserve a representative sample of the area's wildlife and 'cultivated landscapes' (48% of the park's area) designated for use only by residents to meet local timber, fuelwood, agricultural, and pastoral requirements. Five strict nature zones have been designated to protect sal and larch forests, and red panda habitat (T. Maskey, pers. comm., 1991). Restrictions on grazing and the collection of fuelwood and timber have been introduced. Livestock from outside the park are no longer allowed to be grazed inside its boundaries. Live wood may not be cut except sometimes for timber on a permit basis. There are no plans to direct much management effort to the south-eastern region of the park because human pressures on natural resources are minimal and tourism is negligible (Saryo Pandey, pers. comm., 1986). A conservation committee, with local representatives, has been set up to address conservation and management issues.

Management Constraints   Pressures on the park's natural resources are becoming increasingly severe. The fairly widespread deforestation that has occurred in response to the local demand for pasture, arable land, timber, and fuelwood has been accelerated by the needs of visitors and the cheese factories at Kyangjin (Langtang Valley) and Phalung Ghyang (Trisuli

Valley) for fuelwood (Borradaile et al., 1977). It has been estimated that 317,000 kg of fuelwood are harvested annually from the Kyangjin area, of which one-third is consumed by the cheese factory and the rest by the lodge and porters. This is well above the 216,419 kg produced annually by the forests (Department of National Parks and Wildlife Conservation, 1988). The other big management problem arises from the villages in Nuwakot District to the south, most of which rely heavily on the park's resources (Saryo Pandey, pers. comm., 1986). There is considerable scarring of the landscape along the park's western border due to the construction of the new road from Betrawati to beyond Dunche to service mining operations in the Ganesh region. At 4,460 m, this is one of the highest mines in the world. Production of lead and zinc ore is scheduled to begin in 1992. The main environmental impact will be from debris displaced by the mines damaging farmlands, choking river beds, and disrupting the hydrological system (Bhattarai, 1989). Such improved access is having important repercussions on the development of the park and its residents, contributing to the increasing pressure from tourism which, in turn, could alter the local culture and economy in undesirable ways. Other constraints include competition between wild ungulates such as Himalayan tahr and goral with livestock (Green, 1979), and poaching of Himalayan musk deer (Green, 1978, 1980). Black bear, wild boar, and muntjac, in particular, regularly raid and damage crops, while wild dog and leopard occasionally prey on livestock (Borradaile et al., 1977). The presence of large herds of chauris (female yak/cattle hybrids), maintained for cheese production, and accompanying herders and dogs has led to he death of many red pandas, a species which is thought to be on the verge of extinction in Langtang. One solution might be to reduce cheese production and restrict the number of chauris, while increasing the price of cheese to maintain income levels (Yonzon and Hunter, 1991b).

Staff One chief warden, one warden, two assistant wardens, ten rangers, ten senior game scouts, forty game scouts, and fifteen office staff (1991). One battalion of the Royal Nepal Army is deployed for protection purposes.

Budget In 1989–90 expenditure was NRs 2,109,482 (US $ 70,316) and income from park entrance fees was NRs 1,579,500 (US $ 52,650). The budget for 1990–1 is NRs 2,239,000 (US $ 74,633).

Local Addresses
Chief Warden, Langtang National Park Headquarters, Dhunche, Rasuwa District, Bagmati Zone

References

Bhattarai, B. (1989). Mining the mountain. *Himal* 2(3): 16–18.

Bishop, N.H. (1977). Langurs living at high altitudes. *Journal of the Bombay Natural History Society* 74: 518–20.

Blower, J. (1974). Langtang National Park: preliminary development plan. Working Document no. 1. HMG/UNDP/FAO Project NEP/72/002, Kathmandu. Unpublished.

Bolton, M. (1976). *Langtang National Park Management Plan: an outline.* Field Document no. 1a. HMG/UNDP/FAO Project FO NEP/72/002, Kathmandu.

Borradaile, L.J., Green, M.J.B., Moon L.C., Robinson, P.J., and Tait, A. (1977). *Langtang National Park Management Plan 1977-1982.* Field Document no. 7. HMG/UNDP/FAO Project NEP/72/002, Kathmandu. 273 pp.

Caughley, G. (1969). *Wildlife and recreation in the Trisuli Watershed and other areas in Nepal.* Report no .6. HMG/UNDP/FAO Trisuli Watershed Development Project, Kathmandu. 54 pp.

Department of Medicinal Plants (1976). *Flora of Langtang and cross section vegetation survey (Central Zone)*. HMG Ministry of Forests, Kathmandu.

Department of National Parks and Wildlife Conservation (1988). Cheese and national park. *Wildlife Nepal* April: 2.

Dobremez, J.F., Jest, C., Toffin, G., Vartanian, M.C., and Vigny, F. (1974). Carte écologique du Nepal. Région Kathmandu-Everest 1/250,000. *Documents de Cartographie Ecologique, Grenoble*.

Dobremez, J.F., Maire, A. and Yon, B. (1975). Carte écologique du Nepal V. Région Ankhu Khola-Trisuli 1/50,000. *Documents de Cartographie Ecologique, Grenoble* 15: 1–20.

Fox, J.L. (1974). An ecological survey of the proposed Langtang National Park. HMG/UNDP/FAO National Parks and Wildlife Conservation Project, Kathmandu. Unpublished. 40 pp.

Green, M.J.B. (1978). Himalayan musk deer (*Moschus moschiferus moschiferus*). In: *Threatened deer*. IUCN, Morges. Pp. 56–64.

Green, M.J.B. (1979). Tahr in a Nepal National Park. *Oryx* 15: 140–4.

Green, M.J.B. (1980). A report on conservation and management issues within the Langtang National Park, Nepal. Unpublished. 9 pp.

Green, M.J.B. (1981). A checklist and some notes concerning the mammals of the Langtang National Park, Nepal. *Journal of the Bombay Natural History Society* 78: 77–87.

Gut, P. (1981). Tourist lodges in Nepal's Langtang National Park. *Parks* 6(3): 16–19.

Hagen, T. (1969). *Reports on the geology of Nepal*. Vol. 1. *Reconnaissance Survey*. Denkschriften der Schweiz. Naturforsch. Gesellschaft, Basel. (Unseen)

Inskipp, C. (1989). Nepal's forest birds: their status and conservation. *International Council for Bird Preservation Monograph* no. 4. 184 pp.

Inskipp, C. and Inskipp, T. (1985). *A guide to the birds of Nepal*. Croom Helm, Beckenham, UK. 392 pp.

Joshi, A.R. (1987). A study of the environment relationships of certain village communities in the Central Development Region of Nepal. Ph.D. thesis, University College, Cardiff. 189 pp.

Ohba, H. and Malla, S.B. (1988). *Newsletter of Himalayan Botany* 4. (Unseen)

Oli, M.K. (1986). Studies on stereotyped behavior of barking deer (*Muntiacus muntjak*). Report to King Mahendra Trust for Nature Conservation, Kathmandu. Unpublished. 68 pp.

Polunin, O. (1950). An expedition to Nepal. *Journal of the Royal Horticultural Society* 75: 302–15.

Sayers, J. and Schilling, A.D. (1969). The Langtang Valley of Nepal. *Journal of the Royal Horticultural Society* 94: 222–32.

Scott, D.A. (Ed.) (1989). *A directory of Asian wetlands*. IUCN, Gland, Switzerland and Cambridge, UK. 1,181 pp.

Stainton, J.D.A. (1972). *Forests of Nepal*. John Murray, London. 181 pp.

Yonzon, P.B. and Hunter, M.L. Jr. (1991a). Conservation of the red panda, *Ailurus fulgens*. *Biological Conservation* 57: 1–11.

Yonzon, P.B. and Hunter, M.L. Jr. (1991b). Cheese, tourists, and red pandas in the Nepal Himalayas. *Conservation Biology* 5: 196–202.

MAKALU-BARUN NATIONAL PARK AND CONSERVATION AREA

IUCN Management Category   II (National Park)
VIII (Multiple Use Management Area)

Biogeographical Province   2.38.12 (Himalayan Highlands)

Geographical Location   Lies in the Solukhumba and Sankhuwasabha districts of eastern Nepal and represents an extension of Sagarmatha National Park which stretches eastwards as far as the Arun River. The southern boundary follows the Saune Danda (ridge) and the northern boundary is defined by the international border with the Tibetan Autonomous Region of China. The conservation area forms a peripheral zone to the national park along its southern and eastern sides, distinguishing between the northern wilderness and southern inhabited zones.

Date and History of Establishment   Following a series of high-level seminars and visits to the Makalu-Barun region, organised mainly by the King Mahendra Trust for Nature Conservation and Woodlands Mountain Institute, USA (e.g. Taylor-Ide, 1984; Shrestha et al., 1985), a twelve-year co-operative agreement (1988–2000) to support the Makalu-Barun Conservation Project was signed on 29 August 1988 between the Department of National Parks and Wildlife Conservation and the Woodlands Mountain Institute. Under this agreement, and in response to a Royal directive issued in 1988, a task force was appointed for a two-year period to produce a conservation plan for the region (Shrestha, 1989) In its plan, the task force recommended the immediate establishment of a Makalu-Barun National Park and Conservation Area, which were subsequently notified on 22 November 1991.

Area   The total area is 233,000 ha, of which 150,000 ha is a national park and 83,000 ha a conservation area. Makalu-Barun is contiguous with Sagarmatha National Park (114,000 ha) in the west and, across the international border to the north, with Qomolangma Nature Reserve (3,500,000 ha) in Tibet.

Land Tenure   State

Altitude   Ranges from 435 m at the confluence of the Arun River and Sankhuwa Khola to 8,463 m at the summit of Mt. Makalu.

Physical Features   The region comprises seven largely uninhabited watersheds (Barun, Kasuwa, Isuwa, Apsuwa, Sankhuwa, Hongu, and Inkhu), most of which are drained by the Arun River to the south-east. Notable features include the world's fifth highest mountain (Makalu), one of the world's deepest river gorges (Arun) and the wild valley of the Barun. Geologically, there are two major lithotectonic units, the norther Khumbu nappe being tectonically superimposed over the Khumbu nappe. The southward movement of these rock masses occurred 26 million years ago during the early Miocene. The axis of the Arun anticline, a pre-Himalayan geological structure reactivated during the Himalayan orogenic movement, runs north–south through the Arun Valley. The downcutting of the antecedent Arun River has usually kept pace with the rising Himalaya, eroding a rock sequence of at least 8,000 m thick (Shrestha et al., 1990). The 22 km-long Barun Valley is an unique and relatively pristine ecosystem, enjoying a microclimate of extreme precipitation. The valley is particularly impenetrable by virtue of its exceptionally severe angle of repose, with even the steepest of slopes forested (Taylor-Ide, 1984). The Arun River basin is described by Dunsmore (1988).

Climate Conditions are monsoonal, with more than 70% of the annual precipitation received between June and September (Dunsmore, 1988). Annual precipitation ranges from more than 4,000 mm at lower elevations to less than 1,000 mm in the subalpine and alpine zones (Shrestha et al., 1990).

Vegetation A series of distinct vegetation zones can be distinguished ranging from tropical sal *Shorea robusta* forest below 1,000 m, through subtropical *Schima-Castanopsis* forest (1,000–2,000 m), temperate evergreen oak and deciduous broad-leaved forests (2,000–3,000 m), subalpine fir *Abies spectabilis* and birch *Betula utilis* forests (3,000–4,000 m), to alpine *Juniperus-Rhododendron* scrub and pastures (4,000–5,000 m). Over 3,000 species of flowering plants have been recorded, including 25 of Nepal's 30 varieties of rhododendron, 48 primrose species, 47 orchid species, 19 bamboo species, 15 oak species, 86 species of fodder trees, and 67 species of economically valuable medicinal and aromatic plants. Unrecorded elsewhere in Nepal is the oak *Lithocarpus fenestratus* (Shrestha et al., 1990).

Fauna Mammals, reptiles and amphibians known or suspected to occur in the Makalu-Barun are listed by Jackson et al. (1990), as are birds observed in Makalu-Barun and adjacent Sagarmatha National Park. Large mammals include leopard *Panthera pardus* (T), possibly snow leopard *P. uncia* (E), red panda *Ailurus fulgens* (K), musk deer *Moschus chrysogaster*, goral, *Nemorhaedus goral* and Himalayan tahr *Hemitragus jemlahicus*, as well as more substantial populations of Himalayan black bear *Selenarctos thibetanus*, Indian muntjac *Muntiacus muntjak*, serow *Capricornis sumatraensis*, and wild boar *Sus scrofa* (Shrestha et al., 1990). Some 25 species of mammals have been recorded from the Barun Valley (Taylor-Ide, 1984). No sign of snow leopard, or potential large prey species, was found in the Hongu Valley in 1986 (Hillard, 1987).

Forests in the Barun Valley are among the most important for birds in Nepal. Of the 169 species recorded to date, 159 are breeding species of which 66 may have internationally significant breeding populations in Nepal. The valley is the only known breeding season locality in the country for dark-sided thrush *Zoothera marginata*, slaty-bellied tesia *Tesia olivea*, broad-billed warbler *Abroscopus hodgsoni*, spotted wren-babbler *Spelaeornis formosus*, and coral-billed scimitar-babbler *Pomatorhinus ferruginosus* (Inskipp, 1989).

Little is known about the invertebrate fauna, but the blue duke butterfly, a new record for Nepal, has been collected from the region (Shrestha, 1989).

Cultural Heritage The main ethnic groups classified on the basis of their first languages are Rai (64%), Shingsawa (Bhote) (18%), and Sherpa (8%). Speakers of Tibeto-Burman languages other than Rai and Tibetan are represented in smaller numbers and include Gurung, Tamang, Magar, and Newar. The Makalu-Barun is the heartland of the Rai, of which the main subtribes represented are the Kulung, Mewahang, and Yamphu. Tibetan speakers include the Sherpa, originally from Solukhumbu to the west, Khumbo (Nava) descended from intermarriage between Sherpas and other Tibetan groups, and the culturally distinct Shingsawa. All three groups are adherents to the Nyingmapa sect of Tibetan Buddhism. There are a small number of *gompas* (monasteries) which provide the focus of religious practice.

351

Considerable religious significance is attached to sacred sites, especially the legendary Khembalung caves of mythological importance (Shrestha et al., 1990).

Local Human Population   The Makalu-Barun is populated by approximately 32,000 people, but permanent settlements are confined to the lower reaches of the main watersheds which fall within the proposed conservation area (mean population density is twenty-three persons per sq. km). There are no permanent settlements within the proposed national park although livestock are traditionally taken to alpine pastures during the summer months. Subsistence agriculture, supplemented by pastoralism, is the principal form of livelihood. Nearly all households (98%) own land which is used for cultivating crops, growing trees, and as pasture. Slash-and-burn agroforestry is practised between 1,500 m and 2,300 m on a 5–15 year rotational basis that is largely sustainable (Shrestha et al., 1990).

Visitors and Visitor Facilities   The region is little visited (about 200 visitors per year) because of its ruggedness and poor transportation networks. It has very high potential for trekking, mountaineering and ecotourism, which is likely to be realised with the completion of the access road for the Arun III Hydroelectric Project in the late 1990s. There are no visitor facilities but a visitor centre is planned for Khandbari (Shrestha et al., 1990).

Scientific Research and Facilities   A number of ecological, socio-economic and tourism surveys, and impact assessments were carried out during 1988–90, and form the basis of the management plan. Details of these are given elsewhere (Shrestha et al., 1990). There are no scientific facilities.

Conservation Value   The Makalu-Barun is one of the last pristine and varied ecosystems of the Nepal Himalaya, with nearly all ecological zones from tropical forests to arctic snows of the High Himalaya represented. Its notable features include Mt. Makalu, the Arun gorge, and the wild and undisturbed Barun Valley whose forests are of outstanding importance for Nepal's birds. Floral and faunal diversity is high and includes a number of species not recorded elsewhere in Nepal. The region is also culturally rich, with seven different languages spoken (Inskipp, 1989; Shrestha et al., 1990). The region constitutes about half of the Arun River drainage basin within Nepal that is upstream of the projected Arun III Hydroelectric Project site at Num (Shrestha et al., 1990).

Conservation Management   A plan to manage the Makalu-Barun National Park and Conservation Area was formulated in 1990 and comprises four components covering scientific research, and park, tourism and community resource management (Shrestha et al., 1990). The strategy is to establish a national park and conservation area that serves to provide an ecological extension to the adjacent Sagarmatha National Park while promoting the economic development of the local people, based on recognition of the crucial role which local people play in all aspects of natural resource management. The concept of buffering the core national park area with a conservation area attains additional importance in view of the forthcoming construction activities of the Arun III Hydroelectric Project. Three management zones are proposed for the national park: strict nature reserves encompassing the Barun Valley, in which all but traditional pilgrimage rights will be prohibited; protected areas, being mixed cultural/natural landscapes of high scenic value where traditional land use practices are carefully controlled and recreation is permitted; and special sites and trails, being areas currently used by visitors and pilgrims and developed appropriately to guard against landscape degradation. The conservation area will be classified into land use categories for biodiversity protection, community forest and pasture, slash-and-burn/agroforestry, and agriculture and settlement, but these have yet to be identified. Policies and programmes with regard to the management of the national park and conservation area are set out in the management plan. It is proposed that management be the responsibility of the Department of National Parks and Wildlife Conservation, with technical and administrative support provided by the Woodlands Mountain Institute. A temporary headquarters will be established in Khandbari.

Management Constraints   Most of the rivers drain into the upper reaches of the Arun which originates from the adjoining Qomolangma Nature Reserve in Tibet. This river is the site of Nepal's largest development project to date: the 402 megawatt Arun III Hydroelectric Project and 192 km access road financed by a consortium of international donors co-ordinated by the World Bank. Besides the ecological and scenic disturbances caused by this project, the impact of the labour force on the forest and wildlife will be negative unless properly managed. The identification and implementation of opportunities for combining conservation with development are essential to mitigate the potentially negative impacts of the Arun project on the environment. Conversely, the negative impacts of poor watershed management practices upon the project must be acknowledged and addressed. Additional feasibility studies for a proposed 302 megawatt Upper Arun Project located upstream of the Arun/Barun confluence are underway. This project would require an extension of the Arun III road to the vicinity of the pristine Barun catchment. Other constraints include deteriorating rangeland conditions in certain valleys, such as the Hongu (Hillard, 1987), and hunting of commercially valuable species such as Himalayan black bear, red panda, and musk deer (Shrestha et al., 1990).

Staff   Proposed staffing levels: three wardens, four assistant wardens, eight rangers, and a number of scouts (Shrestha et al., 1990).

Budget   The budget for 1991–5 is estimated to be US $ 6,219,000, with a further US $ 1,608,000 to cover support from the Woodlands Mountain Institute (Shrestha et al., 1990).

Local Addresses   None

References
A list of reports and other documents prepared under the Makalu Barun Conservation Project is given in the management plan (Shrestha et al., 1990).

Dunsmoore, J.R. (1988). Mountain environmental management in the Arun River Basin of Nepal. *ICIMOD Occasional Paper* no. 9. International Centre for Integrated Mountain Development, Kathmandu. 65 pp.
Hilliard D. (1987). Field report from the Himalayan snow leopard project. *Snowline* 12: 7–9.
Inskipp, C. (1989). Nepal's forest birds: their status and conservation. *International Council for Bird Preservation Monograph* no. 4. 184 pp.
Jackson, R., Nepali, H.S., and Sherpa, A.R. (1990). Aspects of wildlife protection and utilization in the Makalu-Barun Conservation Area. *The Makalu-Barun Conservation Project Working Paper Publications Series* Report 11. Department of National Parks and Wildlife Conservation, Kathmandu/Woodlands Mountain Institute, West Virginia, USA. 76 pp.
Shrestha, T.B. (1989). Summary report on Sagarmatha National Park extension project, Makalu-Barun area. Unpublished. 10 pp.
Shrestha, T.B., Dhungel, S., and Davis R. (1985). *Makalu-Barun Nature Conservation Seminar.* 16–21 November, Saldima and Kathmandu. Sahayogi Press, Tripureshwar, Kathmandu. 25 pp.

Shrestha, T.B., Sherpa, L.N., Banskota, K., and Nepali R.K. (1990). *The Makalu-Barun National Park and Conservation Area management plan*. Department of National Parks and Wildlife Conservation, Kathmandu/Woodlands Mountain Institute, West Virginia, USA. 85 pp.

Taylor-Ide, E. (1984). *The Barun Valley Report*. King Mahendra Trust for Nature Conservation, Kathmandu/Woodlands Mountain Institute, Cherry Grove, West Virginia. 11 pp.

RARA NATIONAL PARK

IUCN Management Category   II   (National Park)

Biogeographical Province   2.38.12   (Himalayan Highlands)

Geographical Location   Lies in Mugu and Jumla districts in the mid-western Himalaya, about 371 km by air west-north-west of Kathmandu. The southern border is about 24 km north of Jumla. Approximately 29°34′N, 82°05′E

Date and History of Establishment   First proposed as a national park following a visit by the FAO Wildlife Management Advisor and his Nepali colleague in 1972 (Bolton, 1976), Lake Rara and its surrounding area was gazetted as a national park in 1977, following the establishment of an office in July 1976.

Area   10,600 ha

Land Tenure   State

Altitude   Ranges from 2,800 m to 4,048 m.

Physical Features   Lake Rara, locally known as Mahendra Tal, lies at 2,983 m. Rara (1,036 ha) is the largest and most scenically beautiful lake in Nepal. The basin of the lake occupies the northern half of the park and Chuchamara Dara, which rises to the highest point in the park, forms a horseshoe in the south. The main watershed is Chuchamara, around which drainage is fairly symmetrical. Some streams on the northern slopes flow into the lake, which is drained by the Khatyar Khola on its west side. The lake lies in the first and oldest of the Kathmandu nappes and is thought to have formed as the result of river capture (Hagen, 1969). It is very deep (167 m), the margin generally shelving steeply below water level, and does not freeze over in winter, unlike lakeside streams which are frozen for at least four months of the year.

Climate   Conditions are temperate monsoonal. Jumla, the nearest station for which meteorological data is available, receives 462 mm of precipitation during the summer monsoon (June–September). Mean maximum and minimum temperatures are 27 °C (June) and –4 °C (December), respectively. The park is likely to be drier because of the intervening Dori and Churchi ranges. Winters are colder and there is more snow than at Jumla. Fox (1975) recorded 1,560 mm of snow falling between December and 5 February 1975. Other observations indicate that the area is snow-bound to a depth of at least 600 mm from December until March or April (Bolton, 1976).

354

Vegetation   Blue pine *Pinus wallichiana* is predominant below 3,150 m, particularly around the lake where it may be mixed with oak *Quercus semecarpifolia*, rhododendron *Rhododendron arboreum*, juniper *Juniperus indica*, and spruce *Picea smithiana*.   Pine forest becomes increasingly mixed with spruce and fir *Abies spectabilis* at higher altitudes on the northern slopes of Chuchamara.   Above 3,350 m fir is the dominant conifer, while oak and birch *Betula utilis* are relatively more plentiful and juniper persists as a shrub.   Above 3,660 m fir gives way to birch-rhododendron scrub and a narrow belt of dwarf rhododendron, which fringes the alpine grassland.   The lake is oligotropic, its clear blue water obviously containing little plankton.   Patches of marsh with reeds (probably *Phragmites*) and rushes (*Juncus* sp. and *Fimbristylis* sp.) occur around the lake's margin, and there is a rich growth of *Myriophyllum* sp. in shallow water.   A large open area of marshy meadows and abandoned fields lies south of the lake, with species such as *Polygonum* sp., *Oxygraphis polypetala*, and *Ranunculus* sp. (Bolton, 1976).   Further details and a map of the vegetation are given by Barber (1990).

Fauna   Mammals include rhesus macaque *Macaca mulatta*, common langur *Presbytis entellus*, jackal *Canis aureus*, wild dog *Cuon alpinus* (V), Himalayan black bear *Selenarctos thibetanus* (V), red panda *Ailurus fulgens* (K), yellow-throated marten *Martes flavigula*, Himalayan weasel *Mustela sibirica*, leopard *Panthera pardus* (T), wild boar *Sus scrofa*, Himalayan musk deer *Moschus chrysogaster*, serow *Capricornis sumatraensis*, goral *Nemorhaedus goral*, flying squirrel *Petaurista* sp., and vole *Microtus (sikimensis?)* (Bolton, 1976).   More recently, the presence of fox *Vulpes vulpes* and jungle cat *Felis chaus* has been confirmed (Brearey and Pritchard, 1985).

The avifauna comprises 187 species, of which 39 are breeding species for which Nepal may hold internationally significant populations.   These include the western specialities: cheer pheasant *Catreus wallichi* (V), Himalayan pied woodpecker *Dendrocopos himalayensis*, white-throated tit *Aegithalos niveogularis*, spot-winged black tit *Parus melanolophus*, white-cheeked nuthatch *Sitta leucopsis*, and Kashmir nuthatch *S. cashmirensis* (Inskipp, 1989; Barber, 1990).   The lake is an important stopover for waterfowl migrating across the Himalaya (35 species recorded so far), and small numbers of mallard *Anas platyrhynchos*, common teal *A. crecca*, red-crested pochard *Netta rufina*, tufted duck *Aythya fuligula*, great crested grebe *Podiceps cristatus*, black-necked grebe *P. nigricollis*, and common coot *Fulica atra* overwinter here (Bolton, 1976).   Further details of the waterfowl are given by Scott (1989).

The lake has a rich invertebrate fauna.   Mayflies (Ephemeroptera), *Gammarus lacustris*, and lumbriculid worms are abundant.   Aquatic beetles, hemipterans, molluscs *Radis auricularia*, and leeches *Helobdella stagnalis* are present (Bolton, 1976; Byrne, 1982).   Snow trout *Schizothorax hodgsoni* and *S. progastus* occur in the lake (Byrne, 1982).

Cultural Heritage   The Thakuris, who live by subsistence agriculture, have been resident in the area for many years.   They are descended from the royal court at Jumla which fled to Rara with the advances of the Gorkha king into Jumla over 200 years ago (Bolton, 1976; Heinen et al., 1988).

Local Human Population   Prior to their resettlement, some 600 people lived in the villages of Chapra and Rara by the lake.   Many more villages, supporting thousands of people, occur within several kilometres of the park's boundary, particularly to the east.   Subsistence agriculture and pastoralism are practised in areas surrounding the park (Bolton, 1976).

Visitors and Visitor Facilities   The park receives relatively few visitors because of its remoteness; in 1989 there were 157. Tourist accommodation has been built near the park headquarters on the north shore of the lake. There is a STOL airstrip at Mili Chaur on the southern shore of the lake, but it is no longer in operation. Another for Twin-Otters was under construction at Talcha in 1989.

Scientific Research and Facilities   Preliminary ecological surveys were undertaken by Fox (1975) and Bolton (1976) for purposes of a management plan. Limnological studies of Lake Rara were conducted by Ferro (1978–9). Brearey and Pritchard (1985) visited the park in summer (June 1979), autumn (October 1982) and winter (February 1983) to survey the birds and other wildlife. Further ornithological surveys were undertaken in 1989 (Bàrber, 1990). Upreti (1989) reports that an ecological survey of the park was carried out by a Japanese team from Kyoto University. Botanical surveys have been carried out by the Department of Medicinal Plants. There are no research facilities.

Conservation Value   The park's vegetation is representative of the Humla–Jumla division of Stainton (1972), which is very different to that of the West Midlands to the south. As a large, deep body of standing water, there is nothing comparable to Lake Rara elsewhere in Nepal. Moreover, the lake is noted for its scenic beauty and is important as a staging and winter area for waterfowl (Bolton, 1976; Scott, 1989).

Conservation Management   A management plan was prepared in 1976. The park is considered too small to accommodate a system of zonation to provide for use of natural resources by local people in certain areas (Bolton, 1976). The recommendation in the management plan to resettle the inhabitants of Chapra and Rara had been implemented by 1980. Abandoned fields are gradually reverting to forest; blue pine is regenerating particularly well. Persuaded by the improved economic standards of those resettled, the inhabitants of Jhari and Murma on the periphery of the park are also seeking resettlement. It is recommended that these people should either be resettled in the Terai or their villages included within the park as enclaves. Residents of Tum Village, however, will need to be resettled to protect the eastern rim of the lake. A proposal has been prepared to extend the park to include surrounding forests. Concessions to local villagers include collection of leaf litter for fifteen days in March and cutting of grass in October (Upreti, 1989).

Management Constraints   Pressures on the park's natural resources have been alleviated following the resettlement of former inhabitants. The main management problem is the reversion of formerly grazed pastures to forest. The meadows to the south of the lake arwe floristically rich and important for birds and other wildlife, as well as being of scenic value. Their maintenance will require active management (Brearey, 1985; Upreti, 1989).

Staff   One warden, one assistant warden, three rangers, three senior game scouts, twelve game scouts and nine office staff (1991). A company of the Royal Nepal Army is stationed at Hutu, with outposts at Jhari and Gorusinga.

Budget   In 1989–90 expenditure was NRs 914,706 (US $ 30,490) and NRs 72,960 (US $ 2,430). The budget for 1990–1 is NRs 1,035,000 (US $ 34,500).

Local Addresses
Warden, Lake Rara National Park Headquarters, Rara, Nr. Jumla, Mugu District, Karnali Zone.

References

Barber, I. (1990). Lake Rara National Park bird survey. Report to Department of National Parks and Wildlife Conservation, Kathmandu. Unpublished. 40 pp.

Bolton, M. (1976). *Lake Rara National Park Management Plan 1976–81*. Project Working Document no. 3. HMG/UNDP/FAO Project FO NEP/72/002, Kathmandu. 70 pp.

Brearey, D.M. and Pritchard, D.E. (1985). *Birds and other wildlife at Lake Rara National Park, northwest Nepal*. Castro Valley, California. 25 pp.

Byrne, P. (1982). The Rara expedition. *Explorers Journal* 60: 114–21.

FAO (1980). *National parks and wildlife conservation: project findings and recommendations*. UNDP/FAO Terminal Report, Rome. 63 pp.

Ferro, W. (1978–9). Some limnological and biological data from Rara, a deep Himalayan lake in Nepal. *Journal of the Nepal Research Centre* 2/3: 241–61.

Fox, J. (1975). A short survey of Lake Rara and Sinja Khola areas. HMG/UNDP/FAO National Parks and Wildlife Conservation Project, Kathmandu. Unpublished.

Hagen, T. (1969). *Report on a geological survey of Nepal*. Vol 1. Orell Fussli, Arts Graphiques SA, Zurich. (Unseen)

Inskipp, C. (1989). Nepal's forest birds: their status and conservation. *International Council for Bird Preservation Monograph* no. 4. 184 pp.

Upreti, B.N. (1989). Rara National Park. Department of National Parks and Wildlife Conservation, Kathmandu. Unpublished. 7 pp.

ROYAL BARDIA NATIONAL PARK

IUCN Management Category   II   (National Park)

Biogeographical Province   4.08.04   (Indus-Ganges Monsoon Forest)

Geographical Location   Situated in south-west Nepal, 396 km west of Kathmandu in the Bardia District of Bheri Zone. Girwa River, a branch of the Karnali, forms the western boundary, the Churia or Siwalik Range delimits the park to the north, and the Nepalgunj–Surkhet road marks the eastern boundary. The southern boundary has been determined by the local limit of cultivation and human settlement and is delimited by a forest road. A number of islands in the Karnali are included in the park. 28°15'–28°40'N, 81°15'–81°40'E

Date and History of Establishment   Upgraded to national park status in December 1988, having originally been gazetted as the Royal Karnali Wildlife Reserve (36,800 ha) on 8 March 1976. The reserve was renamed the Royal Bardia Wildlife Reserve in 1982, and enlarged almost threefold to its present size in 1984 to include the Babai Valley, which was originally proposed as a hunting reserve (Wegge, 1976). The former reserve area was originally declared as a Royal Shikar (hunting) reserve in 1969 (Bolton, 1976; Upreti, 1989).

Area   96,800 ha

Land Tenure   State

Altitude   Ranges from 152 m to 1,441 m at Sukarmala on the crest of the Churia Range.

Physical Features   Much of the park is known as *bhaber* and consists of a broad alluvial plain that slopes gently away from the foothills of the Himalaya (Churia Range) in the north-east to India in the south-west. A number of rivers rise in the Churia Range and flow south-west into the Karnali, the largest being the Babai River which flows through the eastern half of the park. The only standing body of water is Khodha Tal. This pond is said to dry up in the dry season. The Churia Range is composed of late Tertiary material, containing fine-grained sandstone with deposits of clay, shale, freshwater limestone, and conglomerate. Southern slopes of the Churia have shallow, easily eroded soils and are subject to landslides. Bhaber deposits consist of boulders, cobbles and layers of coarse sand amidst silt and clay Underlying the bhaber are older deposits of silt, clay, sand and pebble gravel which constitute the northernmost extension of the Gangetic alluvium of India. Slightly alkaline, calcareous sandy loams predominate in the bhaber (HMG Nepal, 1971; Bolton, 1976; Dinerstein, 1979a).

Climate   Conditions are monsoonal, with most of the annual precipitation falling between June and September. Mean annual rainfall at Chisapani at the foot of the Churias is 2,230 mm, and at Gularia in an agricultural area to the south of the park, 1,560 mm. Following the monsoon is a cool season (November to mid-February) when temperatures fall to 10 °C. Temperatures rise steadily during the hot season (mid-February to June) up to a maximum of 41 °C in May (Bolton, 1976).

Vegetation   About 70% of the park is covered by sal *Shorea robusta* forest, the rest being grassland, savannah and riverine forest. Dinerstein (1979b) identified six major vegetation associations: sal forest, with a discontinuous upper canopy dominated by sal and *Terminalia alata* and a lower canopy composed of *Buchanania latifolia* and other smaller tree species; early riverine forest, with khair *Acacia catechu* and sissoo *Dalbergia sissoo* forming the first seral stand of trees along the major river courses because they are able to withstand flooding; moist mixed riverine forest, dominated by *Ficus racemosa* and *Eugenia jambolana* in the upper canopy, and *Mallotus philippinensis* and young *Eugenia* trees in the lower canopy; savanna/grassland, with silk cotton *Bombax ceiba* as the dominant tree species and tall coarse grasses such as *Imperata cylindrica*, *Erianthus ravennae*, and *Vetiveria zizanioides* comprising much of the understorey; ecotonal secondary open mixed hardwood forest, similar in tree species composition to savanna but having a conspicuous shrub layer dominated by *Colebrookea oppositifolia*, *Pogostemon benghalensis*, *Clerodendrum viscosum*, and *Murraya koenigii*; and tall grass flood-plain, dominated by the grass *Saccharum spontaneum* and the shrub *Tamarix dioica*. Various sequences of succession from tall grass, which first colonises silt exposed after periods of inundation, through to the climax vegetation (sal forest) have been proposed by Dinerstein (1979a). In general, biotic factors, such as grazing by livestock, burning, clearing for cultivation, selective felling of trees, logging and cutting grass for thatch, tend to result in the vegetation reverting to an earlier succession.

Fauna   Some 32 species of mammal occur in the park (Dinerstein 1979b). Threatened species include tiger *Panthera tigris* (E), leopard *P. pardus* (T), sloth bear *Melursus ursinus* (I), Ganges river dolphin *Platanista gangetica* (V) in the Karnali River (Bolton, 1976), a small relict population of swamp deer *Cervus duvauceli* (E) which appeared to decline from 15 individuals in 1976 to only 6 in 1977 (Dinerstein, 1979b), and hispid hare *Caprolagus hispidus* (E) (Oliver, 1985). The 5–6 elephant *Elaphas maximus* (E) are not resident (Dinerstein, 1979b). More common large mammals include rhesus macaque *Macaca mulatta*, common langur *Presbytis entellus*, jackal *Canis aureus*, Bengal fox *Vulpes bengalensis*, wild dog *Cuon alpinus* (V), smooth-coated otter *Lutra perspicillata*, large Indian civet *Viverra zibetha*, small Indian civet *Viverricula indica*, Indian grey mongoose *Herpestes edwardsi*, striped hyaena *Hyaena hyaena*, jungle cat *Felis chaus*, wild boar *Sus scrofa*, Indian muntjac *Muntiacus muntjak*, spotted deer *Cervus axis*, hog deer *C. porcinus*, sambar *C. unicolor*, and nilgai *Boselaphus tragocamelus*. Small mammals include short-nosed fruit bat *Cynopterus sphinx*, Indian pipistrelle *Pipistrellus coromandra*, greater yellow bat *Scotophilus heathi*, five-striped palm squirrel *Funambulus pennanti*, red giant flying squirrel *Petaurista petaurista*, house rat *Rattus rattus*, Indian porcupine *Hystrix indica*, and Indian hare *Lepus nigricollis*. Nine blackbuck *Antilope cervicapra* were introduced to the Baghora area in 1980, and a further three animals were subsequently added to the original stock (Upreti, 1989), but none has survived (Anon., 1991). The only remaining population of blackbuck in Nepal occurs outside the park at Panditpur, Bardia District and totals about 200 within an area of 84 ha (Anon., 1991). Indian rhinoceros *Rhinoceros unicornis* (E) has been successfully reintroduced, using a total of 25 animals translocated from the Royal Chitwan National park in several phases, beginning 1986. Breeding commenced in 1988 (Bauer, 1988; Anon., 1991).

The avifauna comprises 256 species. Of the 193 breeding species, 22 are threatened in Nepal including rufous-bellied eagle *Hieraaetus kienerii*, changeable hawk-eagle *Spizaetus cirrhatus*, pin-tailed green pigeon *Treron apicauda*, forest eagle owl *Bubo nipalensis*, brown fish owl *Ketupa zeylonensis*, Oriental pied hornbill *Anthracoceros coronatus*, great pied hornbill *Buceros bicornis*, great slaty woodpecker *Mulleripicus pulverulentus*, silver-eared mesia *Leiothrix argentauris*, and crow-billed drongo *Dicrurus annectans*. The grasslands support a small population of the Bengal florican *Houbaropsis bengalensis* (E). Lesser florican *Sypheotides indica* (E) has been recorded and possibly breeds. Western specialities include grey francolin *Francolinus pondicerianus*, Sarus crane *Grus antigone*, brown-headed barbet *Megalaima zeylanica*, white-naped woodpecker *Chrysocolaptes festivus*, and Tickell's blue flycatcher *Cyornis tickelliae*. The Karnali Valley is a migration pathway for wildfowl, notably for bar-headed goose *Anser indicus*. The reserve is also important for winter visitors; although only 63 species have been recorded, many more are likely to occur (Inskipp, 1989).

In 1981, the Karnali supported one of the largest populations of gharial *Gavialis gangeticus* (E), with a minimum of 10–15 adults (Groombridge, 1982). A project to rear gharial in captivity for reintroduction to the Karnali River system has been abandoned because of the high juvenile mortality (Anon., 1988). The Karnali River is noted for its mahseer *Tor tor*, a premier sporting fish. Other fish species include barbels *Barbus* spp., large silurid catfish, and *Ompac bimaculatus* (Bolton, 1976).

Cultural Heritage The indigenous Tharu people have been present for centuries. They live by subsistence agriculture.

Local Human Population Chisapani was the only village within the original wildlife reserve (Bolton, 1976) but its 110 inhabitants have been resettled. Approximately 1,500 families from Sano Shree Panchayat in the eastern extension of the park have been resettled to Taratal in Bardia District (Upreti, 1989). Numerous settlements lie immediately to the south of the park.

Visitors and Visitor Facilities The park received few visitors in the past because of its relative inaccessibility, but numbers are expected to increase with the completion of the western section of the east–west highway. However, extensive development for tourism is not envisaged. The number of visitors fell from 250 in 1988 to 42 in 1989 due to Nepal's internal political problems. Facilities are limited to a tented camp (for 25 persons) at Karnali Chisapani and a lodge (for 24 persons) at Chitkaiya, both run by West Nepal Adventure

Company. Elephant rides, rafting trips and mahseer fishing are organised by the company. A NRs 10 million accommodation complex for engineers is proposed under the Mahendra Raj Marg Project. It has been agreed to hand over this complex to the Department of National Parks and Wildlife Conservation after completion of the Karnali Bridge Project (Upreti, 1989). An airstrip has been built close to park headquarters at Thakurdwara, where there is a guest house. Advice for birdwatchers and other visitors is given by Cox (1987) and Israel and Sinclair (1987), respectively.

Scientific Research and Facilities An ecological survey was undertaken between June 1975 and June 1977, with emphasis on habitat utilisation by the larger herbivores (Dinerstein, 1979a, 1979b, 1980). The status of the Bengal florican was examined in 1982 (Inskipp and Collar, 1984). Other research includes status surveys of the Ganges river dolphin by T.K. Shrestha and of the Sarus crane by Mahendra Shrestha and Rajendra Suwal (Upreti, 1989). There are no research facilities.

Conservation Value Bardia is the largest protected area and least disturbed wildland in the Terai (Upreti, 1989). It contains a rich variety of wildlife in an attractive stretch of relatively unspoilt country. Its forests, grasslands, and wetlands provide important habitat for a variety of threatened mammals, notably tiger, gharial, and now rhinoceros (reintroduced), as well as birds (Bolton, 1976; Inskipp, 1989; Scott, 1989).

Conservation Management First proposed as a wildlife reserve by the FAO Wildlife Management Adviser in 1971, this recommendation was subsequently endorsed (Poppleton and Mishra, 1974), and a reserve was established in order to conserve a representative example of the flora and fauna of the western Terai, in particular the tiger along with its habitat and prey (Bolton, 1976). The reserve was considered to be a model of control, all hunting, agricultural practices and stock grazing having been stopped (FAO, 1980). Following the exclusion of livestock from the reserve in 1975, controlled burns have dramatically improved forage conditions in savanna, grasslands and riverine forests at critical times of the year for wild ruminants (Dinerstein, 1979b).

There is an outdated management plan for the former reserve in which it is proposed that Keraha Island be managed as a sanctuary zone, free from disturbance in view of its fragile, species-rich environment (Bolton, 1976). Currently, the main thrust of management is to protect the natural resources from illegal exploitation, notably hunting, grazing, fuelwood collection, and grass cutting. Natural succession has started in many formerly disturbed sites as a result of protection measures. Since the availability of water limits the movements of ungulates in the dry season, the existing waterhole at Khodha Tal has been deepened and another constructed at Lamkauli Phanta to encourage ungulates to use other parts of the park. Grass at Baghora Phanta is kept short by regular cutting to provide optimum habitat for blackbuck. Concessions to the local people include annual collection of thatch grass (*Imperata cylindrica* is preferred) for fifteen days in December/January (30,000 permits were issued in 1988), and construction of canals and other water diversion schemes inside the park to irrigate cultivations outside the boundaries. Conservation education activities include annual park orientation meetings with local leaders, and organising tours and lectures for school children. A district-level co-ordination committee has been formed to provide a forum for addressing management issues (Upreti, 1989).

Ramuwapur Village, with about eight houses, and Dudwa-Thanfena (8 ha) are enclaves just inside the southern boundary which should be acquired by the government. It is also proposed that about 10,000 ha of land adjacent to the southern boundary be acquired as a buffer zone, subject to amendment of the National Parks and Wildlife Conservation Act to provide for the designation of buffer zones. There are six villages and 350 ha of cultivated land within this area (Upreti, 1989).

Management Constraints   Nepal's east–west highway is due to pass through the park in order to cross the Karnali at the gorge near Chisapani, since the river cannot be bridged further south. Feasibility studies regarding the construction of one of the world's largest hydropower plants on the Karnali at Chisapani have been in progress since the early 1960s. This would generate 10,800 megawatts of electricity, 67 times more than Nepal's present output. Most of this would be for sale to India. Such major development projects are likely to have significant impacts on the park's integrity. The migratory or dispersal movements of large aquatic animals such as Ganges river dolphin, gharial, and mahseer, for example, have already been restricted by the damming of the Karnali downstream in India. Further obstruction to their movements could jeopardise their future survival (Bolton, 1976; Bhattarai, 1989; Upreti, 1989). Encroachment is a source of conflict: in February 1989, two game scouts were killed following an encounter with local people who had illegally entered the park (Anon., 1989).

Staff   One chief warden (vacant), one warden, two assistant wardens, nine rangers, nine senior game scouts, thirty-six game scouts, and twenty-two office staff (1991). Two companies of the Royal Nepal Army are based at Thakurdwara and East Chisapani for enforcement duties (Upreti, 1989).

Budget   In 1989, the expenditure was NRs 1,805,911 (US $ 60,197) and income NRs 2,746,037 (US $ 91,534). The budget for 1990-1 is NRs 1,943,000 (US $ 64,767).

Local Addresses
Warden, Royal Bardia National Park Headquarters, Thakurdwara, Bardia District, Bheri Zone

References
Anon. (1988). Rearing business. *Wildlife Nepal* May: 1.
Anon. (1989). Two game scouts killed in encounter with local people. *Wildlife Nepal* April 1.
Anon. (1991). Rhino translocation. *Wildlife Nepal* March–April: 1.
Bauer, J.J. (1988). Preliminary assessment of the reintroduction success of the Asian one-horned rhinoceros (*Rhinocenos unicornis*) in Bardia Wildlife Reserve, Nepal. *Tiger Paper* 15(4): 26–32.
Bhattarai, B. (1989). Karnali update: to build or not to build. *Himal* 2(4): 17.
Bolton, M. (1976). *Royal Karnali Wildlife Reserve Management Plan 1976–1981*. Project Working Document no. 4. HMG/UNDP/FAO National Parks and Wildlife Conservation Project, Kathmandu. 70 pp.
Cox, J. (1987). Trekking in Nepal. *Oriental Bird Club Bulletin* 6: 12–17.
Dinerstein, E. (1979a). An ecological survey of the Royal Karnali-Bardia Wildlife Reserve, Nepal. Part I: vegetation, modifying factors, and successional relationships. *Biological Conservation* 15: 127–50.
Dinerstein, E. (1979b). An ecological survey of the Royal Karnali-Bardia Wildlife Reserve, Nepal. Part II: habitat/animal interactions. *Biological Conservation* 16: 265–300.
Dinerstein, E. (1980). An ecological survey of the Royal Karnali-Bardia Wildlife Reserve, Nepal. Part III: ungulate populations. *Biological Conservation* 18: 5–38.

FAO (1980). *National parks and wildlife conservation, Nepal: project findings and recommendations.* UNDP/FAO Terminal Report, Rome. 63 pp.

Groombridge, B. (1982). *The IUCN Amphibia–Reptilia Red Data Book.* Part I. *Testudines, Crocodylia, and Rhynchocephalia.* IUCN, Gland, Switzerland. Pp. 405–13.

HMG Nepal (1971). Soil survey of Bardia Division, Ministry of Forests. *Forest Resources Survey Publications* no. 17. (Unseen)

Inskipp, C. and Collar, N.J. (1984). The Bengal florican: its conservation in Nepal. *Oryx* 18: 30–5.

Israel, S. and Sinclair, T. (1987). *Indian wildlife: Sri Lanka, Nepal.* APA Productions, Hong Kong. 363 pp.

Oliver, W.L.R. (1985). *The distribution and status of the hispid hare Caprolagus hispidus—with some additional notes on the pigmy hog Sus salvanius.* Jersey Wildlife Preservation Trust, Jersey. 94 pp.

Poppleton, F. and Mishra, H.R. (1974). A preliminary project proposal for the conservation of wildlife in Nepal's Terai, with particular reference to the Royal Karnali Wildlife Reserve, Royal Sukla Phanta Wildlife Reserve and the Royal Chitwan National Park. HMG/UNDP/FAO National Parks and Wildlife Conservation Project, Kathmandu. Unpublished.

Scott, D.A. (Ed.) (1989). *A directory of Asian wetlands.* IUCN, Gland, Switzerland and Cambridge, UK. 1,181 pp.

Upreti, B.N. (1989). *Royal Bardia National Park.* Department of National Parks and Wildlife Conservation. Unpublished. 13 pp.

Wegge, P. (1976). *Terai shikar reserves: surveys and management proposals.* Field Document no. 4. FAO/FO/NEP/72/002 Project, Kathmandu. 78 pp.

ROYAL CHITWAN NATIONAL PARK
INCLUDING PARSA WILDLIFE RESERVE

IUCN Management Category   II (National Park)
                               X (World Heritage Site: Criteria: ii, iii. iv)

Biographical Province   4.08.04   (Indus-Ganges Monsoon Forest)

Geographical Location   Chitwan lies in the lowlands or Inner Terai of southern central Nepal on the international border with India. The park's boundaries extend from the Dauney Hills on the west bank of the Narayani River eastward 78 km to Hasta and Dhoram rivers. The park is bounded to the north by the Narayani and Rapti rivers and to the south by the Panchnad and Reu rivers and a forest road. 27°20'–27°40'N, 83°52'–84°45'E

Parsa is contiguous with the eastern boundary of the park and extends as far eastwards as the Bheraha and Bagali rivers. 27°15'–27°35'N, 84°45'–84°58'E

Date and History of Establishment   Chitwan was declared a national park in 1973, following approval by the late King Mahendra in December 1970. The by-laws (Royal Chitwan National Park Regulations) were introduced on 4 March 1974. Substantial additions were made to the park in 1977 and the adjacent Parsa Wildlife Reserve was established in

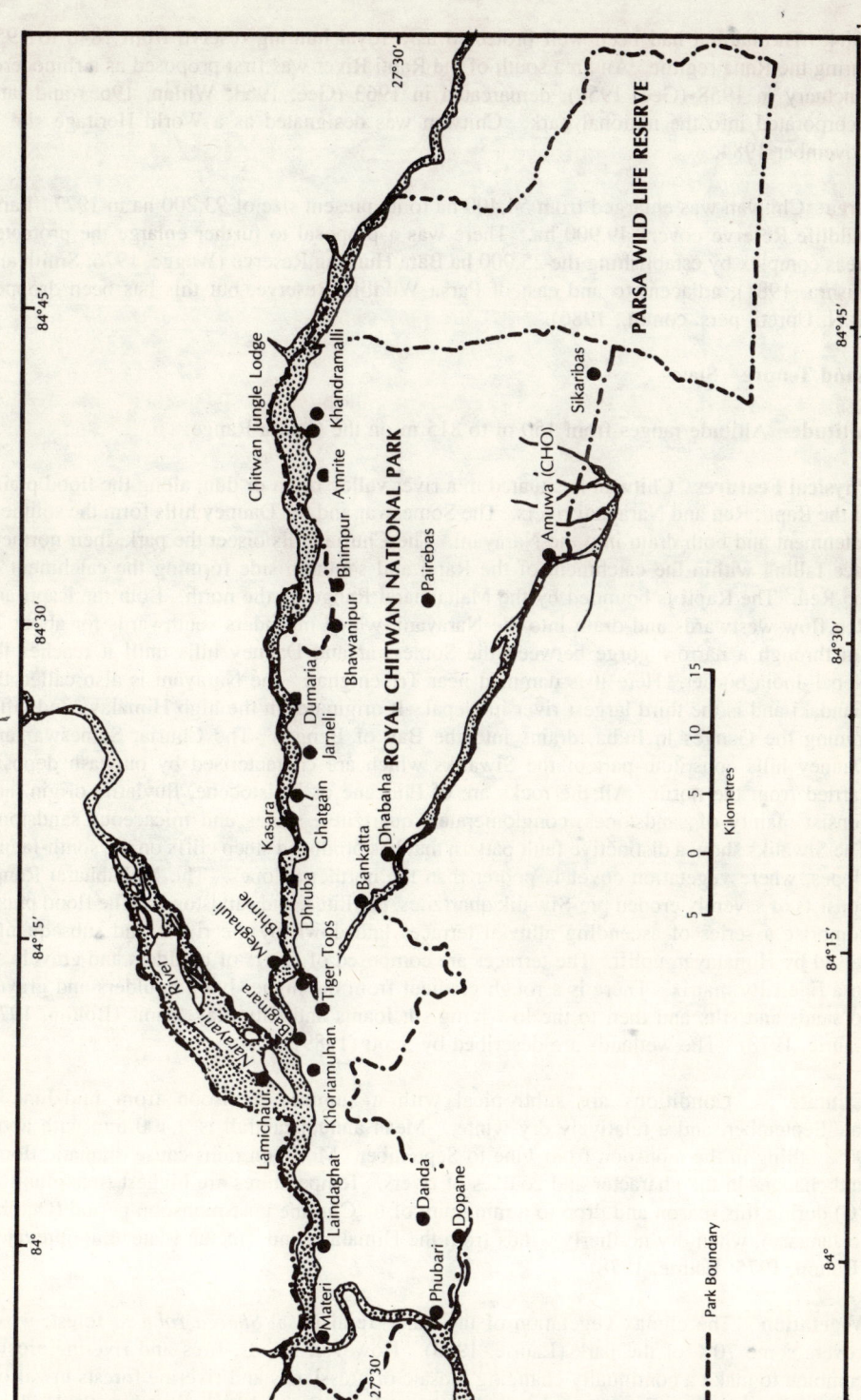

Royal Chitwan National Park

1984. The habitat had been well protected as a royal hunting reserve from 1846 to 1951 during the Rana regime. An area south of the Rapti River was first proposed as a rhinoceros sanctuary in 1958 (Gee, 1959), demarcated in 1963 (Gee, 1963; Willan, 1965) and later incorporated into the national park. Chitwan was designated as a World Heritage site in November 1984.

Area Chitwan was enlarged from 54,400 ha to its present size of 93,200 ha in 1977. Parsa Wildlife Reserve covers 49,900 ha. There was a proposal to further enlarge the protected areas complex by establishing the 25,900 ha Bara Hunting Reserve (Wegge, 1976; Smith and Mishra, 1981), adjacent to and east of Parsa Wildlife Reserve, but this has been dropped (B.N. Upreti, pers. comm., 1986).

Land Tenure State

Altitude Altitude ranges from 150 m to 815 m on the Churia Range.

Physical Features Chitwan is situated in a river valley basin or dun, along the flood plains of the Rapti, Reu and Narayani rivers. The Someswar and the Dauney hills form the southern catchment and both drain into the Narayani. The Churia Hills bisect the park, their northern face falling within the catchment of the Rapti and southern side forming the catchment of the Reu. The Rapti is bounded by the Mahabharat Range on the north. Both the Rapti and Reu flow westwards and drain into the Narayani, which meanders southwards for about 25 km through a narrow gorge between the Someswar and Dauney hills until it reaches the Nepal–India border. Here it is dammed near Tribenighat. The Narayani is also called the Gandaki and is the third largest river in Nepal. It originates in the high Himalaya and, after joining the Ganges in India, drains into the Bay of Bengal. The Churia, Someswar and Dauney hills constitute part of the Siwaliks which are characterised by outwash deposits carried from the north. All the rocks are of Pliocene or Pleistocene, fluviatile origin, and consist mainly of sandstones, conglomerates, quartzites, shales and micaceous sandstone. The Siwaliks show a distinctive fault pattern that has produced steep cliffs on the south-facing slopes, where vegetation cover is poorer than the northern slopes. The Mahabharat Range consists of severely eroded pre-Siwalik quartzites, phyllites, and sandstones. The flood plains comprise a series of ascending alluvial terraces laid down by the rivers and subsequently raised by Himalayan uplift. The terraces are composed of layers of boulders and gravels set in a fine silty matrix. There is a rough gradient from the higher-lying boulders and gravels to sands and silts and then to the low-lying silt loams and silty clay loams (Bolton, 1975; Laurie, 1978). The wetlands are described by Scott (1989).

Climate Conditions are subtropical with a summer monsoon from mid-June to late-September, and a relatively dry winter. Mean annual rainfall is 2,400 mm with about 90% falling in the monsoon from June to September. Monsoon rains cause dramatic floods and changes in the character and courses of rivers. Temperatures are highest (maximum 38 °C) during this season and drop to a minimum of 6 °C in the post-monsoon period (October to January), when dry northerly winds from the Himalaya and Tibetan Plateau are prevalent (Bolton, 1975; Laurie, 1978).

Vegetation The climax vegetation of the Inner Terai is sal *Shorea robusta* forest, which covers some 70% of the park (Laurie, 1978). However, floods, fires and riverine erosion combine to make a continually changing mosaic of grasslands and riverine forests in various stages of succession. Purest stands of sal occur on better drained ground such as the lowlands around Kasra in the centre of the park. Elsewhere, sal is intermingled with chir pine *Pinus roxburghii* along the southern face of the Churia Hills and with tree species such as *Terminalia bellerica, Dalbergia latifolia, Anogeisus latifolia, Dillenia indica,* and *Garuga pinnata* on northern slopes. Creepers, such as *Bauhinia vahlii* and *Spatholobus parviflorus* are common. The understorey is scant with the exception of grasses such as *Themeda villosa*. Riverine forest and grasslands, which form a mosaic along the river banks, are maintained by seasonal flooding. Khair-sissoo *Acacia catechu-Dalbergia sissoo* associations predominate on recent alluvium deposited during floods and in lowland areas that escape the most serious flooding. Semal-bhellar *Bombax ceiba-Trewia nudiflora,* with understorey shrubs *Callicarpa macrophylla, Clerodendrum viscosum,* and *Phyllanthus emblica,* represent a later stage in succession. Two other types of riverine forest (*Eugenia* woodland and tropical evergreen forest) occur in areas outside the present boundary of the park. Laurie (1978) identified seven major grassland types, which consitute about 20% of the park's area: *Themeda villosa* forms a tall grass cover in clearings in the sal forest; *Saccharum-Narenga* associations grow as mixed and pure stands of tall grass (*Saccharum spontaneum* is one of the first species to colonise newly created sandbanks); *Arundo-Phragmites* associations form dense tall stands along stream beds on the flood plain and around lakes; *Imperata cylindrica* grows prolifically in areas within the park which were occupied by villages prior to their evacuation in 1964; various short grasses and herbs grown on exposed sandbanks during the dry months and become much more prolific with the outset of rain in May (e.g. *Polygonum plebeium, Persicaria* spp. and sedges such as *Cyperus, Kyllinga,* and *Mariscus* spp.); *Cynodon dactylon* and *Chrysopogon aciculatus* and other short grasses grow in highest areas near riverine forest all the year round; and low-lying stands of *Saccharum spontaneum,* which are destroyed by repeated flooding early in the monsoon. A list of plant species is given by Laurie (1978).

Fauna A detailed account of the park's fauna is given by Gurung (1983). Over 40 species of mammals have been recorded. Prior to its reintroduction to Royal Bardia National Park in 1986, the park contained the last Nepalese population of the Indian rhinoceros *Rhinoceros unicornis* (E). This had increased from about 300 in 1975 (Laurie, 1978, 1982) to about 350 in 1986 (Anon., 1986). It is currently estimated at 375–400 (Dinerstein, 1989). Tiger *Panthera tigris* (E) is present and has been the subject of a long-term study begun in 1974. The population increased from an estimated 25 in 1974 to 70–110 in 1980, of which 24–30 are resident breeders at any one time (Smith et al., 1983), but has recently crashed. Half of the resident tigers in the western portion of the park disappeared during the 1990 monsoon and two-thirds of dependent young were also missing (McDougal, 1991). Leopard *Panthera pardus* (T) is widespread and other threatened mammal species include wild dog *Cuon alpinus* (V), sloth bear *Melursus ursinus* (I), Ganges river dolphin *Platanista gangetica* (V), and gaur *Bos gaurus* (V). Hispid hare *Caprolagus hispidus* (E) is also present (Oliver, 1985). The sloth bear population totalled 50–60 in 1979 (Laurie and Seidensticker, 1977). The river dolphin population may have declined following the construction of a dam towards the Indian border. Seven were recorded in 1980 but none in 1990 (T.M. Maskey, pers. comm.). Wild elephant *Elephas maximus* (E) occasionally pass through the Churia Hills. Other mammals include rhesus macaque *Macaca mulatta* and common langur *Presbytis entellus,* smooth-coated otter *Lutra perspicillata,* yellow-throated marten *Martes flavigula,* ratel *Mellivora capensis,* spotted linsang *Prionodon pardicolor,* large Indian civet *Viverra zibetha,* small Indian civet *Viverricula indica,* common palm civet *Paradoxurus hermaphroditus,* Himalayan palm civet *Paguma larvata,* mongoose *Herpestes* spp., fishing cat *Felis viverrina,* leopard cat *F. bengalensis,* jungle cat *F. chaus,* jackal *Canis aureus,* striped hyena *Hyaena hyaena,* Indian fox *Vulpes bengalensis,* sambar *Cervus unicolor,* hog deer *C. porcinus,* spotted deer *C. axis,* Indian muntjac *Muntiacus muntjak,* wild boar *Sus scrofa,* Chinese pangolin

Manis pentadactyla, five-striped palm squirrel *Funambulus pennanti*, Indian porcupine *Hystrix indica*, and Indian hare *Lepus nigricollis*. The wild ungulate biomass within riverine/tall grass habitats has been estimated at 18,590 kg/sq. km. (Seidensticker, 1976), far exceeding that reported anywhere else in the Indian subcontinent. Most mammals found in the park also occur in the Parsa Wildlife Reserve with the exception of hog deer. Four-horned antelope *Tetracerus quadricornis* occur in Parsa, on the southern slopes of the Churia Hills, and the reserve contains Nepal's only reproducing herd of about 21 elephants (Smith et al.; 1983).

A larger number of bird species has been recorded in Chitwan (489 in total) than in any other protected area in Nepal. This is attributed to the park's wide range of habitat types and location within the tropical lowlands of Central Nepal where eastern and western species overlap in their distributions. There are ten breeding species for which Nepal may hold internationally significant populations including Bengal florican *Houbaropsis bengalensis* (E) and rufous-necked laughing-thrush *Garrulax ruficollis*. It is the only locality in the country for striped buttonquail *Turnix sylvatica*, bristled grass warbler *Chaetornis striatus* and slender-billed babbler *Turdoides longirostris*. In addition, Chitwan is the only protected area where the following species considered to be at risk in Nepal have been found: yellow bittern *Ixobrychus sinensis*, black baza *Aviceda leuphotes*, laggar falcon *Falco jugger*, blue-breasted quail *Coturnix chinensis*, thick-billed green pigeon *Treron curvirostra*, mountain imperial pigeon *Ducula badia*, vernal hanging parrot *Loriculus vernalis*, red-winged crested cuckoo *Clamator coromandus*, banded bay cuckoo *Cacomantis sonneratii*, tawny fish owl *Ketupa flavipes*, white-vented needletail *Hirundapus cochinchinensis*, deep blue kingfisher *Alcedo meninting*, white-browed piculet *Sasia ochracea*, long-tailed broadbill *Psarisomus dalhousiae*, hooded pitta *Pitta sordida*, white-throated bulbul *Criniger flaveolus*, lesser necklaced laughing-thrush *Garrulax monileger*, greater necklaced laughing-thrush *G. pectoralis*, ruby-cheeked sunbird *Anthreptes singalensis*, and little spiderhunter *Arachnothera longirostra*. Chitwan is very important for wintering birds (about 160 in total)—both for winter visitors from outside Nepal and for the many altitudinal migrants which descend to the lowlands outside the breeding season—as well as being a valuable staging point for numerous passage migrant species (Inskipp, 1989). Details of the waterfowl are given by Scott (1989).

Some 19 species of snake occur in the park including king cobra *Ophiophagus hannah*, green pit viper *Trimeresurus albolabris*, common krait *Bungarus caeruleus*, and Indian python *Python molurus* (V). Other notable reptiles are mugger *Crocodylus palustris* (V) (having declined from at least 200 in 1978 to 70 in 1986–8), gharial *Gavialis gangeticus* (E), Indian starred tortoise *Geochelone elongata*, and monitor lizards *Varanus* spp.

Some 113 species of fish have been recorded, including *Barilius* spp., *Tor tor*, *T. putitora*, and *Puntius* spp. (Edds, 1986).

Cultural Heritage The indigenous Tharus have lived in the Chitwan area for centuries, but they are out-numbered by settlers from the hills who poured into the Inner Terai following the eradication of malaria in the 1950s. There are two Hindu religious sites, Bikram Baba at Kasara and Balmiki Ashram at Tribeni, which are very significant to both the local people living around the park and visitors from India (B.N. Upreti, pers. comm., 1989).

Local Human Population Padampur Panchayat, located immediately to the south of the Rapti River, is a heavily populated area as well as providing some of the last remaining habitat for tiger, rhinoceros, and gharial. With the fall of the Rana regime and the eradication of malaria from the area, the human population of Chitwan rose dramatically from 36,000 to 100,000 between 1950 and 1960. By 1980 there were 261,300 people in 320 settlements around the park (Milton and Binney, 1980; Mishra, 1982a).

Visitors and Visitor Facilities   Chitwan is one of the most popular tourist destinations outside Kathmandu and Pokhara. Visitor numbers have risen from less than 1,000 in 1974 to 31,446 in 1989. Tiger Tops operates a Jungle Lodge and Tented Camp in the west of the park, and Tharu Village Resort peripheral to the park. Its Jungle Lodge pre-dates the park, having been set up by John Coapman in the mid-1960s (Willan, 1965). Other concession lodges inside the park are Chitwan Jungle Lodge and Machan Wildlife Resort in the east, and Tiger Temple in the west. Similar luxury lodges on the edge of the park are Gaida Wildlife Camp and Elephant Camp at Sauraha, and Island Resort and Narayani Safari. There are over 30 low-budget lodges and guest houses outside the park. Sauraha has a good visitor information centre (Berkmüller, 1979). There are no provisions for visitors in Parsa Wildlife Reserve, and no visitors were recorded in 1989.

Scientific Research and Facilities   Chitwan is one of the best studied protected areas in the subcontinent. A programme of research concerning the ecology of the tiger and its prey species was initiated in 1973 by His Majesty's Government, the Smithsonian Institution and WWF (Sunquist, 1981; Wemmer et al., 1983). This was superseded in 1984 by the Smithsonian-Nepal Terai Ecology Project, the scope of which encompasses broader aspects of ecology, including the relationship between habitats, invertebrate, vertebrate, and human populations. Further details of its research activities can be found in the project's newsletter. McDougal (1977) also studied the tiger in the west of the park. The ecology of the Indian rhinoceros has been studied by Laurie (1978, 1982) and more recently by Dinerstein (1989). Other mammals studied include chital (Mishra, 1982b), hog deer (Dhungel, 1985) and muntjac (Oli, 1986). The avifauna is well documented (Gurung, 1983; Inskipp, 1989), with research including surveys of wetland species (Halliday, 1983). A gharial breeding centre, funded by the Frankfurt Zoological Society, was established at Kasara Durbar in 1977. More than 200 young have been reared and reintroduced to the wild (Dhungel, 1987). T.M. Maskey has studied the survival and dispersal of gharial released in the Narayani River. Aberdeen University Expedition to Nepal (1980) surveyed fish resources in the Narayani River system with respect to the endangered gharial population. Studies on grassland ecology have been carried out by Lemkuhl et al. (1988). A proposal to establish the Nepal Conservation Training and Wildlife Institute has been made by the King Mahendra Trust for Nature Conservation, the Department of National Parks and Wildlife Conservation, Tribhuvan University and the Institute of Forestry (B.N. Upreti, pers. comm., 1989). The Smithsonian–Nepal Terai Ecology Project has its field station at Sauraha, where accommodation and facilities for scientists are available.

Conservation Value   Chitwan National Park and the adjacent Parsa Wildlife Reserve constitute the largest and least disturbed example of sal forest and associated communities of the Terai, with a long history of protection dating back to the early 1800s in the case of Chitwan. Species diversity is high, notably for mammals and birds which are well documented. Chitwan supports the world's second largest population of Indian rhinoceros and is also an important refuge for tiger and gharial. Its tall grasslands and riverine forest support a very high wild ungulate biomass which greatly exceeds that reported elsewhere in the Indian subcontinent. Large numbers of visitors are attracted to the area because of its exceptional natural beauty, with the distant Himalaya providing a spectacular backdrop to views of forested hills, grasslands, and great rivers. Research on the natural history of the area has been an important contribution to understanding ecological systems in the Terai (IUCN Technical Evaluation of World Heritage Nomination, 1984).

Conservation Management   Chitwan was identified as the priority area in the Terai for conservation due to its important faunal elements, particularly Indian rhinoceros which had been extirpated from its former range elsewhere in Nepal (Bolton, 1975). Development of the then proposed national park began in 1971 with a modest budget provided by the Forest Department and supplemented by a grant from WWF. Conservation measures have been an outstanding success, as indicated by the substantial increase in wildlife populations and regeneration of vegetation along the Rapti River over subsequent years (Mishra, 1982). Much of this success can be attributed to several resettlement schemes. Some 22,000 people were resettled from the Rapti area, including 4,000 from the former rhinoceros sanctuary, following the creation of a Land Settlement Commission in 1964. Subsequently, 7,000 people from 10 of the 16 villages in Padampur Panchayat on the eastern side of the park were resettled to more fertile lands devoid of wild herbivores, based on recommendations from a study by the International Centre for Environmental Renewal (Milton and Binney, 1980). The scheme met with local support but further relocation of any of the other 310 villages that surround the park is not politically or economically feasible (Mishra, 1982a).

There is a park management plan for the period 1975-9 (Bolton, 1975) but it needs to be completely revised. The establishment of Parsa Wildlife Reserve as an eastern extension to the park has increased the area under protection by about 60%. This extension was also intended to prevent possible isolation of the proposed Bara Hunting Reserve from the park (Smith and Mishra, 1981).

The main concession to local people is the annual harvesting of tall grasses, a valuable building material which is not readily available elsewhere (Mishra, 1982). In 1987, an estimated 11,132 tonnes of grass were removed by 60,000 people during the fifteen-day grass-cutting period, valued at approximately NRs 9.9 million (US $ 450,000). The net contribution to the local economy, after subtraction of labour and permit costs, is NRs 5.5 million (US $ 250,000) (Lehmkuhl et al., 1988). The opening of the Bhrikuti Paper Mill at nearby Gaidakot is introducing a new dimension to local requirements for grass. In view of Chitwan's importance as a tourist attraction, the park authorities, in collaboration with Peace Corps/Nepal, run a two-week training programme annually for tour guides. In future, it is planned to permit only licensed guides who have attended and passed the course to operate in the park (Heinen, 1990).

Management Constraints   The park was listed as a Threatened Protected Area of the World by the IUCN Commission on National Parks and Protected Areas in 1990 in view of the proposed establishment of a hydroelectric barrage on the Narayani River upstream of the park and the East Rapti Irrigation Project, which would reduce the base flow by 75%. Both projects would result in changes to the riverine ecosystems, and could seriously affect aquatic and terrestrial faunal populations (Sharma, 1990; Anon., 1991). In a recent assessment of the East Rapti Irrigation Project for the Asian Development Bank, Talbot (1991) concludes that environmental risks from the project are unacceptably high and recommends that it be reformulated or replaced by one or more lower-cost projects.

Considerable antagonism has long existed between the park and local people, particularly residents of Padampur Panchayat. The main areas of conflict are loss of life (three to five people are killed each year by rhinoceros and tiger), loss of livestock (domestic cattle may consititute up to 30% of tiger kills in settled areas peripheral to the park), damage to crops (estimated to range from 10% to 100%) and restrictions concerning the use of the park's resources (hunting, fishing, grazing, and collection of timber, fuelwood, and other forest products for food and medicine are prohibited within the park) (Milton and Binney, 1980; Mishra, 1982). Sixteen people were killed by tigers in and around the park between October 1980 and early 1989 (McDougal, 1989). Such conflicts will escalate as the local human population continues to increase and remnant forest and grassland areas outside the protected areas complex decline, but they are being addressed by the park authorities and local people are beginning to appreciate the value of the park for managed natural resources (Lehmkuhl et al., 1988). Illegal collection of fuelwood during the grass-cutting season is a hindrance to the proper management of the programme and, in the long-term, will need to be resolved by establishing community fuelwood plantations around the park (Lehmkuhl et al., 1988). Collection of tall grasses is well controlled but has inevitably led to changes in the floral composition of the grassland communities. Annual burning seems to maintain the grasslands but semal *Bombax ceiba*, the only fire resistant tree, is encroaching this habitat (Troth, 1976). Overgrazing along Padampur Panchayat's riverine boundary is seriously accelerating the already extensive erosion of the river bank. Consequently, valuable crop lands are being lost. The development of tourist facilities (hotels and teashops) on the eastern side of the park has not been controlled. In general, the rapid increase in the number of foreigners visiting Chitwan has led to locally inflated prices for basic foods and household products. This problem is compounded by the fact that few local people are employed in the park so that the local population is poorer as a result of the park's presence (Mishra, 1982). Poaching has increased recently. At least eight rhinos were killed between August 1990 and March 1991 and three tigers poisoned since November 1990 (M. Rowntree, pers. comm.).

Staff A chief warden, 1 warden, 2 assistant wardens, 11 rangers, 11 senior game scouts, 44 game scouts, and 29 office staff. One battalian of the Royal Nepal Army is stationed in the park for enforcement duties. Elephant staff total 67 at Chitwan and 34 at Birganj.

Budget Expenditure was NRs 2,447,353 (US $ 81,578) and income NRs 13,449,910 (US $ 448,330) in 1989–90. Income was derived from entrance and camping fees (65.4%), elephant rides (14.4%), hotel concessions (12.2%), grass-cutting permits (2.3%) and various other sources (5.6%). The budget for 1990-1 is NRs 2,970,000 (US $ 99,000).

Local Addresses
Chief Warden, Chitwan National Park Headquarters, Kasra Durbar, Narayani Zone

References
Aberdeen University Expedition to Nepal (1980). Expedition report. Unpublished. 120 pp.
Anon. (1986). The 1986 Rhino Census for Chitwan National Park. *Smithsonian–Nepal Terai Ecology Project Newsletter* 4: 3–5.
Anon. (1991). World Heritage site in danger. *Wildlife Nepal* January/ February: 1.
Berkmüller, K. (1979). Visitor information center at Nepal's Royal Chitwan National Park. *Parks* 4(2): 17–19.
Bolton, M. (1975). *Royal Chitwan National Park Management Plan 1975–79*. Project Working Document no. 2. HMG/UNDP/FAO National Parks and Wildlife Conservation Project, Kathmandu. 105 pp.
Dhungel, S.K. (1985). Ecology of the hog deer in Royal Chitwan National Park, Nepal. Ph.D. thesis. University of Montana, USA. Unpublished.

Dhungel, S.K. (1987). Reintroduction of gharial (*Gavialis gangeticus*) in Nepal. *Tiger Paper* 14(4): 11–15.

Dinerstein, E. (1989). King of the marsh. *International Wildlife* 19(2): 5–8.

Edds, D. (1986). The fishes of Royal Chitwan National Park. Department of Zoology, Oklahoma State University, Stillwater. 14 pp. (Unseen)

Gee, E.P. (1959). Report on a survey of the rhinoceros area of Nepal. *Oryx* 5: 59–85.

Gee, E.P. (1963). Report on a brief survey of the wildlife resources of Nepal, including the rhinoceros. *Oryx* 7: 67–76.

Gurung, K.K. (1983). *Heart of the jungle: the wildlife of Chitwan, Nepal.* Andre Deutsch, London. 197 pp.

Halliday, J.B. (1983). A study of the ecological distribution of resident and migratory birds along the Rapti and Narayani rivers in the Royal Chitwan National Park. November/December 1982. A report to the Department of National Parks and Wildlife Conservation, Nepal. 35 pp.

Heinen, J.T. (1990). The design and implementation of a training program for tour guides in Royal Chitwan National Park, Nepal. *Tiger Paper* 17(2): 11–15.

Inskipp, C. (1989). Nepal's forest birds: their status and conservation. *International Council for Bird Preservation Monograph* no. 4. 184 pp.

Laurie, W.A. (1978). The ecology and behaviour of the greater one-horned rhinoceros. Ph.D. thesis, University of Cambridge, Cambridge. 450 pp.

Laurie, W.A. (1982) Behavioural ecology of the greater one-horned rhinoceros (*Rhinoceros unicornis*). *Journal of Zoology, London* 196: 307–41.

Laurie, A. and Seidensticker, J. (1977). Behavioural ecology of the sloth bear (*Melursus ursinus*). *Journal of Zoology, London* 182: 187–204.

Lehmkuhl, J.F., Upreti, R.K., and Sharma U.R. (1988). National parks and local development: grasses and people in Royal Chitwan National Park, Nepal. *Environmental Conservation* 15: 143–8.

McDougal, C. (1977). *The face of the tiger.* Rivington-Deutsch, London. 180 pp.

McDougal, C. (1989). Tiger attacks around Chitwan National Park. *Cat News* 11: 13.

McDougal, C. (1991). Chitwan tiger numbers crash. *Cat News* 14: 8–9.

Milton, J.P. and Binney, G.A. (1980). *Ecological planning in the Nepalese Terai.* Threshold, International Centre for Environmental Renewal, Washington, DC. 35 pp.

Mishra, H.R. (1982a). Balancing human needs and conservation in Nepal's Royal Chitwan National Park. *Ambio* 11: 246–51.

Mishra, H.R. (1982b). The ecology and behaviour of chital (*Axis axis*) in the Royal Chitwan National Park, Nepal. Ph.D. thesis, University of Edinburgh, Edinburgh. 233 pp.

Oli, M.K. (1986). Studies on stereotyped behavior of barking deer (*Muntiacus muntjak*). Report submitted to the King Mahendra Trust for Nature Conservation, Kathmandu. 67 pp.

Oliver, W.L.R. (1985). *The distribution and status of the hispid hare Caprolagus hispidus—with some additional notes on the pigmy hog Sus salvinius.* Jersey Wildlife Preservation Trust, Jersey. 94 pp.

Scott, D.A. (Ed.) (1989). *A directory of Asian wetlands.* IUCN, Gland, Switzerland and Cambridge, UK. 1,181 pp.

Seidensticker, J. (1976). Ungulate populations in Chitwan Valley, Nepal. *Biological Conservation* 10: 183–210.

Sharma, U.R. (1990). The disaster that is ERIP. *Himal* November/December: 32–3.

Smith, J.L.D. and Mishra, H.R. (1981). Management recommendations for the Chitwan tiger population: the Parsa Extension and Bara Hunting Reserve. Smithsonian Institution/WWF Project 1051. 28 pp.

Smith, J.L.D., Mishra, H.R., and Jordan, P.A. (1983). Population level management: a step in developing a tiger conservation strategy. Paper presented at Bombay Natural History Society Centenary Seminar on Conservation in Developing Countries. Indian Institute of Technology, Powai, Bombay. 6–10 December 1983. 13 pp.

Sunquist, M.E. (1981). The social organisation of tigers (*Panthera tigris*) in Royal Chitwan National Park. *Smithsonian Contributions in Zoology* 336: 1–98.

Talbot, L.M. (1991). Nepal: East Rapti Irrigation Project (ERIP) (Loan no. 867): environmental impact asssessment for the project reformulation. Final Report. Asian Development Bank, Manila. Unpublished. 12 pp.

Troth, R.G. (1976). Successional role of *Bombax ceiba* in savannas in Nepal. Smithsonian Institution/WWF Tiger Ecology Project, Nepal. Unpublished.

Wegge, P. (1976). *Himalayan shikar reserves; surveys and management proposals*. Field Document no. 5. FAO/NEP/72/002 Project, Kathmandu. 96 pp.

Wemmer, C., Simons, R., and Mishra, H.R. (1983). Case history of the co-operative conservation program: the Nepal Tiger Ecology Project. Paper presented at Bombay Natural History Society Centenary Seminar on Conservation in Developing Countries. Indian Institute of Technology, Powai, Bombay. 6–10 December.

Willan, R.S.M. (1965). Rhinos increase in Nepal. *Oryx* 8: 156–60.

ROYAL SUKLA PHANTA WILDLIFE RESERVE

IUCN Management Category   IV (Managed Nature Reserve)

Biogeographical Province   4.08.04 (Indus-Ganges Monsoon Forest)

Geographical Location   Lies in the extreme south-western section of Nepal's Terai in Kanchanpur District. The reserve shares a common boundary with the Indian state of Uttar Pradesh in the south and west which is formed by the Mahakali (Sarda) River, a major tributary of the Ganges. It is bordered on the eastern side by the Chaudhar River and to the north by a forest belt and cultivations. 28°49′–28°57′N, 80°07′–80°15′E

Date and History of Establishment   Gazetted as a wildlife reserve in July 1976, having formerly been decreed a royal shikar (hunting) reserve in 1965.

Area   15,500 ha. There are plans to extend the reserve by about 15,500 ha as far eastwards as Sayali River to include Dhaka Block, a former hunting reserve of approximately 3,700 ha. Plans are being delayed owing to problems of resettlement (M. Weaver, pers. comm., 1990).

Land Tenure   State

Altitude Ranges from 90 m to 270 m.

Physical Features   The area is generally flat, with occasional gently rolling hills. Rani Tal, a small lake, is situated inside the eastern border. The reserve lies south of the *bhaber* zone, a broad alluvial flood plain that slopes gently away from the foothills (Churia Range) of the Himalaya. *Bhaber* deposits are a conglomerate of boulders, gravel and sand washed down from the foothills.

Climate   Conditions are monsoonal, with over 90% of the annual precipitation (1000–2000 mm) falling between June and September. Mean maximum temperatures are 40 °C–42 °C in summer (April–May), when hot westerly winds of up to 160 km per hour have been recorded, and 10 °C–12 °C in winter (Balson, 1976).

Vegetation   Some 54.7% of the reserve is covered by mixed deciduous forest, grassland and marsh in the south-west where soils are of recent alluvium. The rest is moist deciduous forest and savanna, supported by the better drained soils on higher terrain in the north-east (Balson, 1976). The main vegetation types distinguished by Schaaf (1978a, 1978b) are: sal *Shorea robusta* forest; sal savanna, which is part of a continuum between climax forest and grassland that is maintained by fire or floods; mixed deciduous forest, which is patchily distributed among the more extensive grasslands in the south-west (sal is absent); grasslands, which may be dry (locally known as *phantas*) or wet in the case of areas inundated during the monsoon; lowland savanna, which occurs on the fringes of all main grasslands and covers most of Karaiya Phanta; khair-sissoo forest, dominated by *Acacia catechu* and *Dalbergia sissoo*, and forming an early succession in riverine areas; and marsh, in which tall dense grasses are predominant (e.g. *Phragmites karka, Saccharum spontaneum,* and *Sclerostachya fusca*). Fifty-four species of grass and sedge were collected by Schaaf (1978b).

Fauna   A total of 24 mammal species was recorded by Schaaf (1978b), to which can be added hispid hare *Caprolagus hispidus* (E) (Oliver, 1985; Bell, 1987) and Kashmir flying squirrel *Hylopetes fimbriatus* (Bell, 1987). An unconfirmed report of pygmy hog *Sus salvanius* (E) (Oliver, 1985) has not been substantiated (Bell, 1987). The reserve harbours Nepal's largest remaining population of swamp deer *Cervus duvauceli* (E), estimated at a minimum size of 908 in 1976 (Schaaf, 1978a) and currently in excess of 3,000 (T.M. Maskey, pers. comm., 1990). Other ungulate species are spotted deer *Cervus axis* (numerous), sambar *C. unicolor* (scarce), hog deer *C. porcinus* (common), Indian muntjac *Muntiacus muntjak* (few), and nilgai *Boselaphus tragocamelus* (50–60) (D.J. Bell, pers. comm., 1988). Other mammals include rhesus macaque *Macaca mulatta*, common langur *Presbytis entellus*, tiger *Panthera tigris* (E), leopard *P. pardus* (T), jungle cat *Felis chaus*, small Indian civet *Viverricula indica*, Indian grey mongoose *Herpestes edwardsi*, jackal *Canis aureus*, Indian fox *Vulpes bengalensis*, sloth bear *Melursus ursinus* (I), smooth-coated otter *Lutra perspicillata*, porcupine *Hystrix indica*, rufous-tailed hare *Lepus nigricollis caudatus*, and Indian elephant *Elephas maximus* (E).

The avifauna comprises 268 species of which 180 are breeding species (Inskipp, 1989). Sukla Phanta is important for grassland birds, particularly swamp francolin *Francolinus gularis* (V), Bengal florican *Houbaropsis bengalensis* (E), grass owl *Tyto capensis*, large grass warbler *Graminicola bengalensis*, and striated marsh warbler *Megalurus palustris*. The reserve supports the largest population of Bengal florican in Nepal (17 were recorded by D. Weaver in 1990) and it is the only locality where black bittern *Dupetor flavicollis* regularly occurs. There are 22 breeding species at risk in Nepal, including Pallas's fish eagle *Haliaeetus leucoryphus*, lesser fishing eagle *Ichthyophaga nana*, grey-headed fishing eagle *I. ichthyaetus*, changeable hawk-eagle *Spizaetus cirrhatus*, brown fish owl *Ketupa zeylonensis*, oriental pied hornbill *Anthracoceros coronatus*, and great slaty woodpecker *Mulleripicus pulverulentus*. Several specialities of the western lowlands occur such as sarus crane *Grus antigone*, brown-headed barbet *Megalaima zeylanica*, white-naped woodpecker *Chrysocolaptes festivus*, and Tickell's blue flycatcher *Cyornis tickelliae*. Rani Tal is visited by large numbers of wintering and migratory wildfowl and waders (Scott, 1989).

Reptiles include Indian python *Python molurus* (V) and mugger *Crocodylus palustris* (V), which occurs in Rani Tal as well as in Bawani River.

Bhatt and Shrestha (1977) provide an annotated list of 14 species of fish, including mahseer *Tor tor*, snake heads *Ghanna* spp., and catfish *Mystus* spp.

Schaaf (1978b) recorded 10 species of ectoparasites and biting flies, including a new species of Haematopinidae (*Solenopotes* sp.) and Tabanidae (*Haematopota* sp.).

Cultural Heritage The aboriginal Tharus, agro-pastoralists, were until recently almost the only inhabitants of the remote western Terai, including what is now the reserve (Schaaf, 1978b). Singa Pal is an important religious site.

Local Human Population Less than three decades ago the area was mostly pristine wilderness interspersed with occasional meadows and Tharu villages. Following the control of malaria in the 1950s, with help from World Health Organisation, settlers moved down from the nearby Mahabharat Lekh in large numbers during the early 1960s.

Visitors and Visitor Facilities The reserve was first opened up to tourists in 1985. In 1989 there were 42 visitors. There is an airport near Mahendranagar which has weekly scheduled flights to Kathmandu, but these are irregular during the monsoon season. The reserve is also accessible by road from Kathmandu, or road and rail from India. Elephants can be hired for viewing wildlife.

Scientific Research and Facilities An ecological study of swamp deer was undertaken in 1974–6 (Schaaf, 1978b). The status of Bengal florican in the reserve was investigated in 1982 (Inskipp and Collar, 1984). A comparative ecological study of hispid hare and rufous-tailed hare was carried out in 1986 (Bell, 1987). There are no research facilities.

Conservation Value Sukla Phanta contains a rich mosaic of habitats and is particularly important for its *phantas* or open grasslands which support several threatened species of mammals and birds, notably swamp deer and Bengal florican (Schaaf, 1978a; Inskipp, 1989).

Conservation Management The reserve was established largely on account of its *phantas*, refuge for the endangered swamp deer, and also because of its healthy resident population of tiger. Excellent progress has been made since 1976. The reserve is adequately staffed and the necessary infrastructure has been provided. Poaching has been reduced to a minimum, other illegal activities are being brought under control and two villages have been removed (FAO, 1980). Sukla Phanta itself, covering about 400 ha, and other areas of short grassland are maintained by regular controlled burning in January and repeated in April or May. Other grasslands in the reserve are cut for thatch and subsequently burnt. Grass cutting is restricted to a period of 21 days between mid-December and mid-January. Approximately 23,000 permits are issued annually, each permit being valid for one person for one week (Oliver, 1985; D.J. Bell, pers. comm., 1988).

Management Constraints There are problems associated with the resettlement of eight villages from the proposed Dhaka extension to the reserve (Oliver, 1985). Illegal cattle grazing and burning are major problems. Over 1,000 cattle graze in the reserve each day. The clearance of a 3–4 km belt of forest buffering the reserve's northern boundary, under the World Bank funded Mahakali Irrigation Project, will add to existing pressures on the reserve.

A further 150 ha of forest within the reserve may be lost to this project. The project could also interfere with hispid hare habitat. The present management policy of harvesting tall grasslands for thatch during the dry season also threatens the survival of the hispid hare, which is restricted to the tall riverine grasslands during this season. A strategy of controlled rotational burning may help to alleviate the immediate risk to this species (Bell, 1987).

Staff   One warden, one assistant warden, six rangers, six senior game scouts, twenty-four game scouts, and, eighteen office staff (1991). One company of the Royal Nepal Army is posted in the reserve for enforcement duties.

Budget   In 1989–90, expenditure was NRs 1,466,273 (US $ 48,876) and revenue NRs 1,747,659 (US $ 58,255), of which 13% originated from tourist concessions and fees and 87% from other sources. The budget for 1990–1 is NRs 1,666,000 (US $ 55,533).

Local Addresses
Warden, Royal Sukla Phanta Wildlife Reserve Headquarters, Majhagaon, Kanchanpur District, Mahakali Zone

References

Bhatt, D.D. and Shrestha, T.K. (1977). The environment of Suklaphanta. National Parks and Wildlife Conservation Project, Tribhuvan University, Kathmandu. Unpublished.

Balson, E.W. (1976).   General report on the Royal Suklaphanta Wildlife Reserve. HMG/UNDP/FAO National Parks and Wildlife Conservation Project, Kathmandu. Unpublished. 46 pp.

Bell, D.J. (1987). A study of the biology and conservation problems of the hispid hare. School of Biological Sciences, University of East Anglia, Norwich. Unpublished. 38 pp.

FAO (1980). *National parks and wildlife conservation, Nepal: project findings and recommendations.* UNDP/FAO Terminal Report, Rome. 63 pp.

Inskipp, C. and Collar, N.J. (1984). The Bengal florican: its conservation in Nepal. *Oryx* 18: 30–5.

Inskipp, C. (1989). Nepal's forest birds: their status and conservation. *International Council for Bird Preservation Monograph* no. 4. 184 pp.

Oliver, W.L.R. (1985). *The distribution and status of the hispid hare Caprolagus hispidus—with some additional notes on the pigmy hog Sus salvanius.* Jersey Wildlife Preservation Trust, Jersey. 94 pp.

Schaaf, C.D. (1978a). Some aspects of the ecology of the swamp deer or barasingha (*Cervus d. duvauceli*) in Nepal. In: *Threatened Deer.* IUCN, Morges, Switzerland. Pp. 65–86.

Schaaf, C.D. (1978b). Population size and structure and habitat relations of the barasingha deer (*Cervus d. duvauceli*) in Sukla Phanta Wildlife Reserve. Ph.D. thesis, Michigan State University, Michigan. 111 pp.

Schaaf, C.D. (1981). Royal refuge. *Animal Kingdom* 84(4): 29–33.

Scott, D.A. (Ed.) (1989). *A directory of Asian wetlands.* IUCN, Gland, Switzerland and Cambridge, UK. 1,181 pp.

SAGARMATHA NATIONAL PARK

IUCN Management Category   II (National Park)
X (World Heritage Site; Criteria: i, ii, iii, plus cultural)

Biogeographical Province   2.38.12   (Himalayan Highlands)

Geographical Location   Lies in the Solu-Khumbu District of the north-eastern region of Nepal. The park encompasses the upper catchment of the Dudh Kosi River system, which is fan-shaped and forms a distinct geographical unit enclosed on all sides by high mountain ranges. The northern boundary is defined by the main divide of the Great Himalayan Range, which follows the international border with the Tibetan Autonomous Region of China. In the south, the boundary extends almost as far as Monjo on the Dudh Kosi. The 63 settlements within the park are technically excluded as enclaves. 27°45'–28°07'N, 86°28'–87°07'E

Date and History of Establishment   Created a national park on 19 July 1976 and inscribed on the World Heritage List in 1979.

Area   114,800 ha. The park lies adjacent to the Makalu-Barun National Park and Conservation Area (233,000 ha).

Land Tenure   State. Many of the resident Sherpas have legal title to houses, agricultural land and summer grazing lands (Jefferies, 1984).

Altitude   Ranges in altitude from 2,845 m at Jorsalle to 8,848 m at the top of Mt. Everest (Sagarmatha), the world's highest mountain.

Physical Features   This is a dramatic area of high, geologically young mountains and glaciers. The deeply-incised valleys cut through sedimentary rocks and underlying granites to drain southwards into the Dudh Kosi and its tributaries, which form part of the Ganges River system. The upper catchments of these rivers are fed by glaciers at the head of four main valleys, Chhukhung, Khumbu, Gokyo and Nangpa La. Lakes occur in the upper reaches, notably in the Gokyo Valley, where a number are impounded by the lateral moraine of the Ngozumpa Glacier (at 20 km the longest glacier in the park). There are seven peaks over 7,000 m. The mountains have a granite core flanked by metamorphosed sediments and owe their dominating height to two consecutive phases of upthrust. The main uplift occurred during human history, some 500,000–800,000 years ago. Evidence indicates that the uplift is still continuing at a slower rate, but natural erosion processes counteract this to an unknown degree (Garratt, 1981).

Climate   On average, 80% of the annual precipitation occurs in the monsoon season from June to September and the remainder of the year is fairly dry. Precipitation is low as the park is in the rain shadow of the Karyalung-Kangtega range to the south. Annual precipitation is 984 mm in Namche Bazar, 733 mm in Khumjung and 1,043 mm in Tengboche (Garratt, 1981). The climate of Namche Bazar can be classified as humid and tropical, based on the seasonal occurrence of rains, range in annual precipitation, number of rainy days per year and the length of the dry season (Joshi, 1982). The mean temperature of the coldest month, January, is –0.4 °C. Some 56% of years experience a tropical regime (summer rain), 35% are bixeric (two dry periods), and 1% are trixeric (three dry periods) or irregular.

Vegetation Most of the park (69%) comprises barren land above 5,000 m, 28% is grazing land, and nearly 3% is forested (Sherpa, 1985). Six of the eleven vegetation zones described by Dobremez (1975) for the Nepal Himalaya are represented in the park: lower subalpine, above 3,000 m, with forests of blue pine *Pinus wallichiana*, fir *Abies spectabilis*, and fir–juniper *Juniperus recurva*; upper subalpine, above 3,600 m, with birch–rhododendron forest (*Betula utilis*, *Rhododendron campanulatum*, and *R. campylocarpum*); lower alpine, above the tree-line at 3,800–4,000 m, with scrub (*Juniperus* spp., *Rhododendron anthopogon*, and *R. lepidotum*); upper alpine, above 4,500 m, with grassland and dwarf shrubs; and sub-nival zone with cushion plants from 5,500 m to 6,000 m. Oak *Quercus semecarpifolia* used to be the dominant species in the upper montane zone but former stands of this species and *Abies spectabilis* have been colonised by *Pinus* sp. *Rhododendron arboreum*, *R. triflorum*, and yew *Taxus baccata wallichiana* are associated with pine at lower altitudes and shrubs include *Pieris formosa*, *Cotoneaster microphyllus*, and *R. lepidotum*. Vine *Parthenocissus himalayana* and clematis *Clematis montana* are also common, and other low altitude trees include maple *Acer campbellii* and whitebeam *Sorbus cuspidata*. *Abies spectabilis* occupies medium to good sites above 3,000 m and forms stands with *Rhododendron campanulatum* or *Betula utilis*. Towards the tree-line, *R. campanulatum* is generally dominant. *Juniperus indica* occurs above 4,000 m, where conditions are drier, along with dwarf rhododendrons and cotoneasters, shrubby cinquefoil *Potentilla fruticosa* var. *rigida*, willow *Salix sikkimensis*, and *Cassiope fastigiata*. In association with the shrub complex are a variety of herbs such as *Gentiana prolata*, *G. stellata*, edelweiss *Leontopodium stracheyi*, *Codonopsis thalictrifolia*, *Thalictrum chelidonii*, lilies *Lilium nepalense* and *Notholirion macrophyllum*, *Fritillaria cirrhosa*, and primroses, *Primula denticulata*, *P. atrodentata*, *P. wollastonii*, and *P. sikkimensis*. The shrub layer diminishes as conditions become cooler, and above 5,000 m *Rhododendron nivale* is the sole representative of its genus. Other dwarf shrubs in the dry valley uplands include buckthorn *Hippophae tibetana*, horsetail *Ephedra gerardiana*, juniper *J. indica*, and cinquefoil *Potentilla fruticosa*. Associated herbs are gentians, *Gentiana ornata* and *G. algida* var. *przewalskii*, edelweiss *Leontopodium jacotianum*, and Himalayan blue poppy *Meconopsis horridula*. Above this and up to the permanent snow line at about 5,750 m, plant life is restricted to lichens, mosses, dwarf grasses, and sedges and alpines, such as *Arenaria polytrichoides* and *Tanacetum gossypinum* (Garratt, 1981).

Fauna In common with the rest of the Nepal Himalaya, the park has a comparatively low number (28) of mammalian species, apparently due to the geologically recent origin of the Himalaya and other evolutionary factors. The low density of mammal populations is almost certainly the result of human activities. Larger mammals include common langur *Presbytis entellus*, jackal *Canis aureus*, a small number of wolf *Canis lupus* (V), Himalayan black bear *Selenarctos thibetanus* (V), red panda *Ailurus fulgens* (K), yellow-throated marten *Martes flavigula*, Himalayan weasel *Mustela sibirica*, masked palm civet *Paguma larvata*, snow leopard *Panthera uncia* (E), Himalayan musk deer *Moschus chrysogaster*, Indian muntjac *Muntiacus muntjak*, serow *Capricornis sumatraensis*, Himalayan tahr *Hemitragus jemlahicus*, and goral *Nemorhaedus goral* (Garratt, 1981; Jefferies and Clarbrough, 1986). Sambar *Cervus unicolor* has also been recorded. The tahr population is estimated to total at least 300 individuals. Both goral and serow appear to be uncommon (Lovari, 1990). Results from recent surveys suggest that populations of both tahr and musk deer have increased substantially since the park was gazetted and could lead to a recovery in the snow leopard population, probable signs of which were seen in the Gokyo Valley by Jackson (1987). Smaller mammals include short-tailed mole *Talpa micrura*, Tibetan water shrew *Nectogale elegans*, Himalayan water shrew *Chimarrogale himalayica*, bobak marmot *Marmota bobak*, Royle's pika *Ochotona roylei*, woolly hare *Lepus oiostolus*, rat *Rattus* sp., and house mouse *Mus musculus* (Garratt, 1981).

Inskipp (1989) lists 152 species of birds, 36 of which are breeding species for which Nepal may hold internationally significant populations. The park is important for a number of species breeding at high altitudes, such as blood pheasant *Ithaginis cruentus*, robin accentor *Prunella rubeculoides*, white-throated redstart *Phoenicurus schisticeps*, grandala *Grandala coelicolor*, and several rosefinches. The park's small lakes, especially those at Gokyo, are used as staging points for migrants and at least 19 water bird species have been recorded (Inskipp, 1989; Scott, 1989).

A total of six amphibians and seven reptiles occur or probably occur in the park. Documentation of the invertebrate fauna is limited to common species of butterfly. Of the 30 species recorded, orange and silver mountain hopper *Carterocephalus avanti* has not been recorded elsewhere in Nepal, and the common red apollo *Parnassius epaphus* is rare (Jefferies and Clarbrough, 1986).

Cultural Heritage The Sherpas are of great cultural interest, having originated from Salmo Gang in the eastern Tibetan province of Kham, some 2,000 km from their present homeland. They probably left their original home in the late 1400s or early 1500s, to escape political and military pressures, and later crossed the Nangpa La into Nepal in the early 1530s. They separated into two groups, some settling in Khumbu and others proceeding to Solu. The two clans (Minyagpa and Thimmi) remaining in Khumbu are divided into twelve subclans. The introduction of the potato to Khumbu in about 1850 revolutionised the economic life of the Sherpas. Until then, the high-altitude Sherpas had lived mainly on barley. Both the population and the growth of the monasteries took a dramatic upturn soon after that time. Another significant influence on Sherpa life has been mountaineering expeditions, which have been a feature of life in the Khumbu since the area was first opened to westerners in 1950. The Sherpas belong to the Nyingmapa sect of Tibetan Buddhism, which was founded by the revered Guru Rimpoche who was legendarily born of a lotus in the middle of a lake. It is to him that the ever-present prayers and *mani* wall inscriptions are addressed: *'Om mani padme hum'*—'hail to the jewel of the lotus', (Garratt, 1981). There are several monasteries in the park, the most important being Tengpoche. However, on 19 January 1989 the main building and courtyard of Tengpoche was burned to the ground (Sassoon, 1989). A Reconstruction Committee has been formed and it was planned to commence reconstruction work in 1990 (B.N. Upreti, pers. comm., 1989). Further details about the Sherpa culture are given by Fürer-Haimendorf (1975, 1985), and Jefferies and Clarbrough (1986).

Local Human Population There were approximately 3,000 Sherpas residing in the park in 1987, mainly in the south and distributed among 63 settlements. However, there has not been an accurate census since the park was established. The traditional economy is subsistence agro-pastoralism, supplemented by barter trading with Tibet and the middle hills of Nepal. The main activities include potato and buckwheat cultivation, and raising yaks for wool, meat, manure, and transport. Cattle and yaks are also hybridised locally for trading purposes. Cattle numbers remained constant at about 2,900 between 1957 and 1978 but the numbers of sheep and goats increased from very few to 641 (Bjoness, 1979). Goats have since been removed from the park. More recently tourism has become an integral part of the local economy, including activities such as the provision of guides, porters, lodges, and trekking services (Garratt, 1981; Jefferies, 1982, 1984; Sherpa, 1985, 1987).

Visitors and Visitor Facilities   The number of visitors has increased from about 1,400 in 1972–3 (Jefferies, 1984) to 7,492 in 1989.   There is an airstrip at Lukla, south of the park boundary, which has a regular air service from Kathmandu, and is the most popular means of access to the park. Everest View Hotel and associated Shyangboche airstrip above Namche Bazar are the most sophisticated tourist facilities developed in the park but they do not account for a high proportion of visitor use.   A national park lodge has been built at Tengpoche providing sleeping accommodation, with detached cooking and toilet facilities, as well as basic food and drinks. Other accommodation is available in 'Sherpa hotels' and some villagers take in guests. An imposing visitor centre, providing information and interpretative services, has been constructed on the hill adjoining Namche Bazar. Further facilities, by way of park accommodation and campsites, are planned.   A handbook has been produced for the park (Jefferies and Clarbrough, 1986).

Scientific Research and Facilities   Considerable research in various fields has been undertaken over many years.   The Sherpa culture and changes that have taken place over the last decade or more have been extensively documented (Fürer-Haimendorf, 1964, 1975, 1985). Under the HMG/Government of New Zealand Co-operation Project, the impact of pastoralism and tourism on the natural resource base has been assessed (Bjonness, 1979, 1980a, 1980b, 1983).   Research into alternative sources of energy has focused on hydropower, solar heating, and developing more efficient methods of cooking (Coburn, 1982).   A WWF-funded study of the ecology of Himalayan musk deer has been carried out in the park (Kattel, 1987).   A proposal has been made for forest research and management, focused primarily on the protection of representative samples of ecosystems, reaf forestation, and the introduction of alternative energy sources to minimise human impact on natural forests (Sherpa, 1987).

Conservation Value   Sagarmatha ('Mother of the Universe') and its surroundings, as the highest point of the Earth's surface, are of international importance, representing a major stage of the Earth's evolutionary history and one of the most geologically interesting regions in the world.   Its scenic and wilderness values are outstanding.   As an ecological unit, the Dudh Kosi catchment is of biological and socio-economic importance, as well as being of major cultural and religious significance (Blower, 1972).

Conservation Management   The creation of a national park in the Sagarmatha area was proposed by the FAO Wildlife Management Adviser in March 1971 and approved in principle by His Majesty's Government in January 1972.   Funds for its development were made available by the Government of New Zealand over a five year period, commencing May 1975 (Lucas, 1977; FAO, 1980; Jefferies, 1984).   Normally accepted criteria for the management of national parks have been substantially modified in the case of Sagarmatha in order to reconcile the requirements of the resident Sherpa population with those of conservation objectives and to accommodate special demands made on the area by tourism and mountaineering. The objectives outlined in the management plan (Garratt, 1981) seek to ensure the protection of wildlife, water and soil resources, not only because of the park's national and international significance but also to safeguard the interests of the resident Sherpa population, as well as the many other people in Nepal and India whose welfare is affected by the condition of the Dudh Kosi catchment.   At the same time, every effort is required to enable the Sherpas to determine their own lifestyle and progress, while insulating their cultural

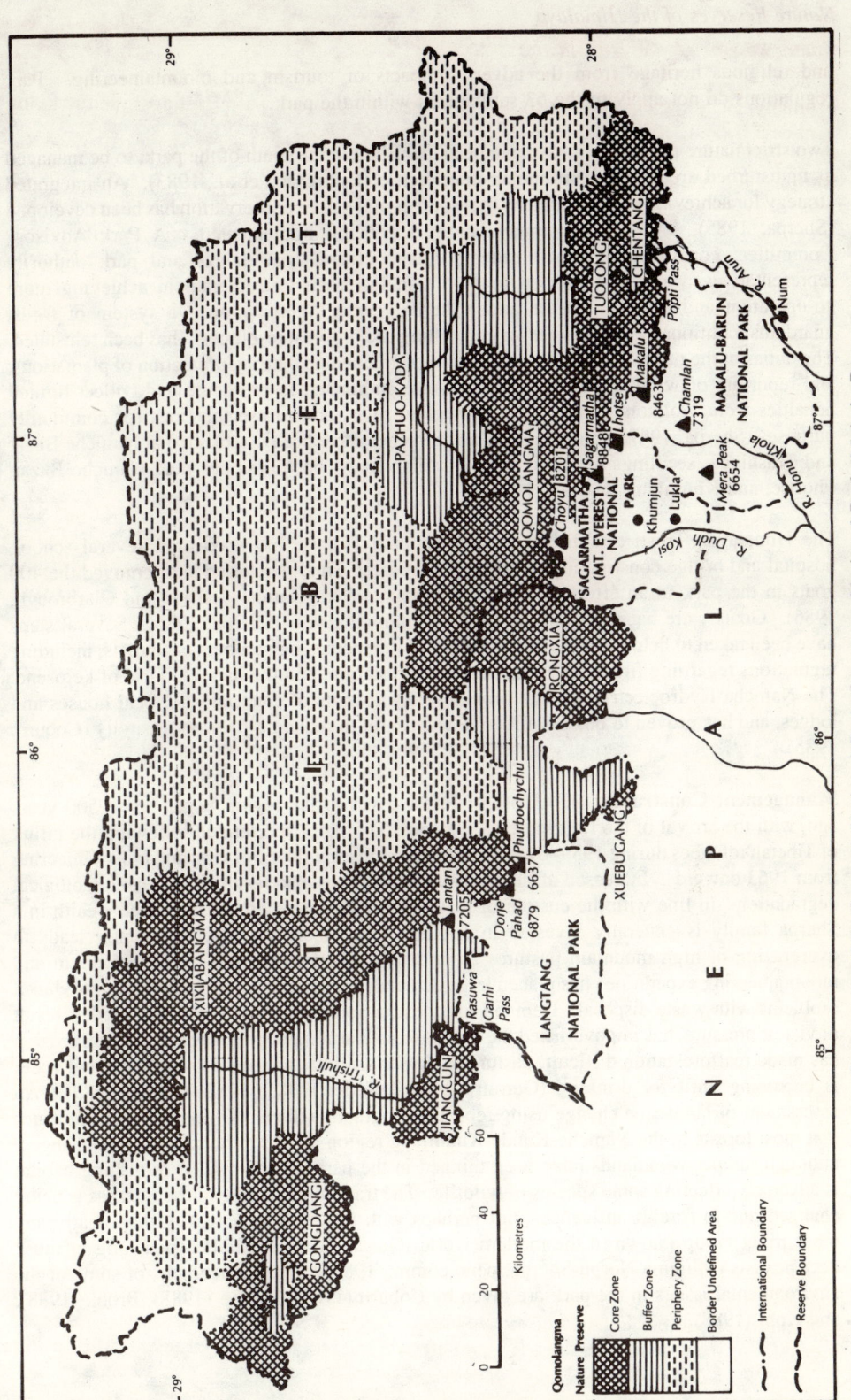

Sagarmatha (Mt. Everest) National Park, Langtang National Park, Makalu-Barun
National Park, and Qomolangma Nature Reserve, Tibet

and religious heritage from the adverse impacts of tourism and mountaineering. Park regulations do not apply to the 63 settlements within the park.

Two strict nature protection areas have been identified in the south of the park, to be managed as undisturbed areas free from human interference (Hinrichsen et al., 1983). An integrated strategy for achieving self-sufficiency in resources and nature conservation has been developed (Sherpa, 1985). Various recommendations are being implemented. A Park Advisory Committee, consisting of local leaders, village elders, head lamas and park authority representatives, was re-established in 1987 and has been instrumental in achieving more co-operation and support for the park (Sherpa, 1985). *Shinga nawa*—a system of forest guardians traditionally responsible for controlling use of forest resources—has been reinstated. The duties of the nawas include the prevention of greenwood cutting, protection of plantations, and reporting of wildlife poaching. Nawas are authorised to prosecute and collect limited penalties from violators of the forest protection rules, and to use the fines for community purposes (Sherpa, 1987). Indigenous plant nurseries have been established at Namche Bazar and Trashinga; seedlings are used to re-establish forest on hill slopes near Namche Bazar, Phortse, and Khumjung (Garratt, 1981).

The Himalayan Trust, established by Sir Edmund Hillary, has sponsored several school, hospital and bridge construction projects. In 1982 the Trust purchased and removed the 400 goats in the park in an effort to protect the mountain vegetation (Jeffries and Clarbrough, 1986). Goats were banned from the park the following year (Sherpa, 1985). Several steps have been taken to help meet the energy needs of the increasing numbers of tourists, including regulations regarding firewood collection, reafforestation, and the increased use of kerosene. The Namche Hydroelectric scheme provides 27 kilowatts of electricity to local houses and lodges, and has proven to be cost effective and useful in reducing firewood scarcity (Coburn, 1985).

Management Constraints The loss of forest cover in the region began some 500 years ago, with the arrival of the first settlers. Destruction rapidly accelerated following the influx of Tibetan refugees during 1959–61 and the large-scale growth of trekking and mountaineering from 1963 onwards. Increased affluence from tourism has also resulted in greater ecological degradation. In line with the custom of many ethnic Nepalese groups, acquired wealth in a Sherpa family is generally invested in additional livestock, which consequently leads to overgrazing of high mountain pastures around villages. Heavy pressure from tourism and mountaineering expeditions has placed large demands on natural resources and has introduced problems with waste disposal. Demand for construction timber and firewood, another result of visitor pressure, has impoverished the forests to an alarming degree; consequent soil erosion has made reafforestation difficult, pastures at lower altitudes are being overgrazed and water is becoming unfit for drinking (Garratt, 1981; Jefferies, 1981, 1982; Luhan, 1989). An assessment of landscape change using repeat photography (Byers, 1987), however, indicates that most forests in the Namche-Kunde-Khumjung region appear to be relatively unchanged, although juniper woodlands have been thinned in the period 1962–84. Diminishing habitat is adversely affecting some species of wildlife. The traditional culture of the Sherpas is being changed due to foreign influences, but perhaps with better social integrity than nearly any other tribal group known to the modern world (Garratt, 1981). Limited poaching of musk deer persists (Mingma Norbu Sherpa, pers. comm., 1987). Popular accounts of some of the environmental issues in the park are given by Coburn (1983), Bishop (1988), Brook (1988), and Kohl (1988).

Staff   One chief warden, two assistant wardens, one veterinary surgeon, seven rangers, seven senior game scouts, twenty-five game scouts, and fourteen office staff (1989).   One company of the Royal.Nepal Army is deployed for protection purposes.

Budget   In 1989–90 expenditure was NRs 2,003,800 (US $ 66,793) and income NRs 2,262,050 (US $ 75,402).   The budget for 1990–1 is NRs 1,982,000 (US $ 66,067).

Local Addresses
Warden, Sagarmatha National Park Headquarters, Namche Bazar, Solu-Khumbu District, Sagarmatha Zone

References
The World Heritage nomination includes an extensive bibliography.

Bishop, B.C. (1988).   A fragile heritage: the mighty Himalaya.   *National Geographic* 174: 624–31.

Blower, J.H. (1972).   Establishment of Khumbu National Park: outline project proposal. HMG/UNDP/FAO Project NEP/72/002, Kathmandu. Unpublished.

Bjonness, I.M. (1979).   Impacts on a high mountain ecosystem: recommendations for action in Sagarmatha (Mount Everest) National Park. Unpublished. 38 pp.

Bjonness, I.M. (1980a).   Animal husbandry and grazing, a conservation and management problem in Sagarmatha National Park. *Norsk Geogr. Tidskr.* 33: 59–76.

Bjonness, I.M. (1980b).   Ecological conflicts and economic dependency on tourist trekking in Sagarmatha National Park, Nepal. An alternative approach to park planning. *Norsk Geogr. Tidskr.* 34: 119–38.

Bjonness, I.M. (1983).   External economic dependency and changing human adjustment to marginal environment in the high Himalaya, Nepal. *Mountain Research and Development* 3: 263–72.

Brook, E. (1988).   Through Sherpa eyes. *Geographical Magazine* 60(8): 28–34.

Byers, A. (1987).   An assessment of landscape change in the Khumbu region of Nepal using repeat photography. *Mountain Research and Develoment* 7: 77–81.

Coburn, B. (1982).   Alternate energy sources for Sagarmatha National Park. Park techniques. *Parks* 7(1): 16–18.

Coburn, B.A. (1983).   Managing a Himalayan world heritage site. *Nature and Resources* 19(3): 20–5.

Coburn, B.A. (1985).   Energy alternatives for Sagarmatha National Park.   In: *People and protected areas in the Hindu Kush-Himalaya*. King Mahendra Trust for Nature Conservation/International Centre for Integrated Mountain Development, Kathmandu. Pp. 71–2.

Dobremez, J.F. (1975).   *Le Nepal, écologique et phytogéomorphique*.   Centre National de la Recherche Scientifique, Paris.

Dobremez, J.F. and Jest, C. (1972).   Carte écologique du Nepal. Région Kathmandu-Everest 1/250,000. *Documents de Cartographie Ecologique, Grenoble*.

FAO (1980).   *National parks and wildlife conservation, Nepal: project findings and recommendations*. UNDP/FAO Terminal Report, Rome. 63 pp.

Fürer-Haimendorf, C. von (1964). *The Sherpas of Nepal*. John Murray, London. 298 pp.

Fürer-Haimendorf, C. von (1975). *Himalayan traders*. John Murray, London. 316 pp.

Fürer-Haimendorf, C. von (1985). *The Sherpas transformed*. Sterling, New Delhi. 197 pp. (Unseen)

Garratt, K.J. (1981). *Sagarmatha National Park management plan*. HMG/New Zealand Co-operation Project. Department of Lands and Survey, New Zealand.

Hinrichsen, D., Lucas, P.H.C., Coburn, B., and Upreti, B.N. (1983). Saving Sagarmatha. *Ambio* 12: 203–5.

Inskipp, C. (1989). Nepal's forest birds: their status and conservation. *International Council for Bird Preservation Monograph* no. 4. 160 pp.

Jackson, R. and Ahlborn, G. (1987). Snow Leopard surveys in Nepal. Sagarmatha (Everest) National Park. *Cat News* 7: 24-5.

Jefferies, B.E. (1982). Sagarmatha National Park: the impact of tourism in the Himalayas. *Ambio* 11: 274–81.

Jefferies, B.E. (1984). The Sherpas of Sagarmatha. In: McNeely, J.A. and Miller, K., *National Parks, conservation and development*. Smithsonian Institution Press, Washington DC. Pp. 473–8.

Jefferies, M. and Clarbrough, M. (1986). *Sagarmatha: mother of the universe. The story of Mount E verest National Park*. Cobb/Horward Publications, Auckland, New Zealand. 192 pp.

Joshi, D.P. (1982). The climate of Namche Bazar: a bioclimatic analysis. *Mountain Research and Development* 2: 399–403.

Kattel, B. (1987). Himalayan musk deer ecology project, Nepal. Annual Report. King Mahendra Trust for Nature Conservation/WWF-US Project no. 6076. 10 pp.

Kohl, L. (1988). Heavy hands on the land. *National Geographic* 174: 633–51.

Lovari, S. (1990). Some notes on the wild ungulates of the Sagarmatha National Park, Khumbu Himal (Nepal). *Caprinae News* 5(1): 2–4.

Lucas, P.H.C. (1977). Nepal's park for the highest mountain. *Parks* 2(3): 1–4.

Luhan, M. (1989). Following the toilet paper trail. *Himal* 2(2): 18–19.

Sassoon, D. (1989). The Tengboche fire: what went up in flames. *Himalayan Research Bulletin* 8(3): 8–14.

Sherpa, M.N. (1985). Conservation for survival: a conservation strategy for resource self-sufficiency in the Khumbu region of Nepal. M.Sc. dissertation, Natural Resources Institute, University of Manitoba, Canada. 175 pp.

Sherpa, L.N. (1987). A proposal for forest research and management in Sagarmatha (Mt. Everest) National Park, Nepal. *Working Paper* no. 8. East–West Center, Hawaii. 47 pp.

Smith, C. (in press). Commoner butterflies of Sagarmatha National Park. In: *National Park Handbook*.

MAPS

1:100,000 *Mount Everest Region*. Royal Geographical Society, London, 1975.
1:50,000 *Mount Everest*. National Geographic Society, Washington DC, 1988.

SHEY-PHOKSUNDO NATIONAL PARK

IUCN Management Category II (National Park)

Biogeographical Province 2.38.12 (Himalayan Highlands)

Geographical Location Situated in the Dolpo and Mugu districts of north-west Nepal. The northern boundary, stretching from the mountain pass of Namja in the west to that of Marim in the east, borders on the Tibetan Autonomous Region of China. 29°08'–29°45'N, 82°33'–83°20'E

Date and History of Establishment   Gazetted as a national park on 6 August 1984.

Area   355,500 ha

Land Tenure   State

Altitude   Ranges from 2,000 m to 6,883 m at the peak of Kanjiroba South.

Physical Features   Much of the park lies north of the Great Himalayan Range, locally represented by Kanjiroba Himal, at the southern edge of the transhimalayan region of the Tibetan Plateau. Here the landscape is near-desert. The heavily folded strata consist primarily of gneisses belonging to Tibetan Tethys sediments of Jurassic and Protoerozoic ages, with intrusive Tertiary tourmaline granites. Soils are poorly developed, with substantial expanses of bedrock. The high Dolpo Plateau in the north-east of the park is drained by the Langu (Namlang) River, which flows westwards until its confluence with the Mugu Karnali. South of Kanjiroba Himalaya, conditions remain fairly dry as much of the area is in the rain-shadow of Hiunchuli Patan (5,916 m) to the south. The southern catchment of the park is drained by the Jagdula and Suli rivers, which flow south and eventually drain into the Beri River. Phoksundo, Nepal's second largest lake, lies at 3,660 m in the upper reaches of the Suli Gad, which falls from a height of 150 m, the highest waterfall in Nepal (Jackson, 1986; Upreti, 1989).

Climate   Conditions are extremely variable as the park encompasses both north and south sides of the main Himalayan divide. Annual precipitation is about 500 mm in the north and 1,500 mm in the south (Sherpa, 1990). Jackson and Ahlborn (1986) recorded a mean annual precipitation of 542 mm at Eding Base Camp (2,875 m) in 1982–5 (n.b. no data for November in any year). Mean daily temperatures ranged from 1 °C in January to 17.5 °C in June. Diurnal temperature ranges of more than 25 °C were not uncommon, especially in winter. Snow rarely remained more than a few days on southern slopes, in contrast to northern slopes which retained their winter snow cover for up to several months. The nearest weather station is at Mugu, about 18 km north-east of Eding.

Vegetation   Probably less than 5% of the park is forested, the rest comprising steppe communities and barren lands (R. Jackson, pers. comm., 1986). A diverse range of vegetation types is present, representative of the South Himalaya, Inner Himalaya, and transhimalaya. The South Himalaya is characterised by temperate and subalpine forests with oaks *Quercus semecarpifolia* and *Q. incana*, blue pine *Pinus wallichiana*, spruce *Picea smithiana*, birch *Betula utilis*, juniper *Juniperus recurva*, rhododendron *Rhododendron arboreum*, fir *Abies spectabilis*, and bamboo *Thamnocalamus* sp. The Inner Himalaya may have floral affinities to the South Himalayan region, but birch is predominant on the lower northern flanks of Kanjiroba Himal. Fir, prostrate juniper *J. squamata*, and *Sorbus cuspidata* are occasional. Upper reaches are predominantly meadows up to 4,800 m. The transhimalaya is devoid of forest. Sparse scrub covers the hillsides, the main species being rhododendrons *R. nivale* and *R. lepidotum*, *Caragana* sp., and honeysuckle *Lonicera* sp. (Yonzon, 1990). The vegetation of the Southern Himalaya and Inner Himalaya (Langu Valley) is described in more detail by Sherpa (1990) and Jackson and Ahlborn (1986), respectively. A map of the potential vegetation has been prepared by Shrestha (1982).

Fauna   Includes many Tibetan species. Yonzon (1990) provides an annotated list of 20 mammal species known or reported to occur in the park. Threatened species are wild dog *Cuon alpinus* (V) (unconfirmed), wolf *Canis lupus* (V), leopard *Panthera pardus* (T), and snow leopard *P. uncia* (E). The density of snow leopards in Langu Valley is 5–10 animals per 100 sq. km (Jackson and Ahlborn, 1986), and that around Shey and Phoksundo Lake is 1.2 per 100 sq. km (Schaller, 1977). Other mammals include rhesus macaque *Macaca mulatta*, langur *Presbytis entellus*, fox *Vulpes vulpes*, Himalayan black bear *Selenarctos thibetanus*, yellow-throated marten *Martes flavigula*, Himalayan musk deer *Moschus chrysogaster*, goral *Nemorhaedus goral*, serow *Capricornis sumatraensis*, Himalayan tahr *Hemitragus jemlahicus*, bharal *Pseudois nayaur*, Himalayan marmot *Marmota bobak*, Royle's pika *Ochotona roylei*, and Tibetan hare *Lepus oiostolus*. Jackal *Canis aureus*, red panda *Ailurus fulgens* (K), Himalayan weasel *Mustela sibirica*, and beech marten *Martes foina* are also reported to be present. Nayaur *Ovis ammon hodgsoni* occasionally cross from China over Ladakh Himal and into the park according to local reports (Jackson, 1978).

Shey-Phoksundo is important for avifaunal species typical of transhimalayan Nepal, such as Tibetan partridge *Perdix hodgsoniae*, brown accentor *Prunella fulvescens*, Hume's ground jay *Pseudopodoces humilis*, and crimson-eared rosefinch *Carpodacus rubicilloides*. Western specialities include white-throated tit *Aegithalos niveogularis*, spot-winged black tit *Parus melanolophus*, white-cheeked nuthatch *Sitta leucopsis*, and Kashmir nuthatch *S. cashmirensis*. Out of a total of 105 species recorded in the park, 18 are breeding species for which Nepal may hold internationally significant populations (Inskipp, 1989). The avifauna is under-recorded, as demonstrated by a recent survey of that portion of the park lying in Mugu District, as a result of which the total number now stands at 121 species (Yonzon, 1990).

The butterfly fauna, although not diverse, includes a large proportion of rare species not commonly found elsewhere in Nepal. A total of 28 species has been recorded, including the rare *Parnassius acdestic* (Yonzon, 1990).

Cultural Heritage   Shey, at 4,480 m, is one of the highest inhabited areas on earth. Its people are of pure Tibetan stock, with a way of life that cannot differ much from that of the Ch'ang Tartars out of Central Asia who are thought to have been the original Tibetans. Shey Gompa is a monastery of the Kagyu Sect, which was established in the 11th century as a departure of the Kalachakra Tantrism of the Old Sect or Nyingma. The monastery lies at the foot of Crystal Mountain, a shrine for pilgrims from all over Dolpo and beyond who come to attend a holy festival at Shey in July (Snellgrove, 1961; Matthiessen, 1978). A detailed account of the people is given by Jest (1975).

Local Human Population   There are 19 villages with a total population of 1,483 people within the park (R. Jackson, pers. comm., 1986). Dolphu, at the entrance to the Namlang Valley and with 208 residents, is the only village in Mugu District that is in the park, the rest are in Dolpo District. Residents are entirely dependent on the park's natural resources for their livelihood. Further details are given by Sherpa (1990).

Visitors and Visitor Facilities   The park is very inaccessible, but the southern portion was first opened to tourists in May 1989. Only organised trekking groups sufficiently equipped with food, tents and fuel are allowed to visit the park (Basnet, 1989; Sherpa, 1990). The number of visitors totalled 275 in 1989. The nearest airstrip is at Jufal in Dolpo.

Scientific Research and Facilities   The Shey-Phoksundo area was surveyed in 1973 to assess its suitability as a wildlife reserve and to study the behaviour of the blue sheep (Schaller, 1974). Namlang Valley was surveyed in 1976–7 (Jackson, 1978) and subsequently its snow leopard population was the subject of a three-year investigation (Jackson and Ahlborn, 1984, 1986, 1988). There are several popular accounts of this study (Jackson and Hillard, 1986; Jackson, 1987; Jackson and Ahlborn, 1987). The main prey species (blue sheep and Himalayan tahr) of the snow leopard have been studied by K.B. Shah. Floral surveys were carried out by the Department of Forest and Plant Research in 1966 and 1986. In 1990, a wildlife survey of that portion of the park falling within Dolpo District was carried out by Yonzon (1990), and a socio-ecological survey of Phoksundo, Saldang and Vijer panchayats was conducted by Sherpa (1990).

Conservation Value   Shey-Phoksundo is the largest of Nepal's protected areas and contains many unparalleled features, of which the most important is its representation of the transhimalaya, including floral, faunal, and cultural elements. Inner Himalayan and South Himalayan zones are also represented, providing a wide range of vegetation types (Upreti, 1989; Yonzon, 1990). The park is particularly important for snow leopard and its prey populations (Jackson and Ahlborn, 1986). The Langu Valley, described as among the most forbidding and rugged areas in the Himalaya (Tyson, 1969), is atypical for the Himalaya because it is essentially unpopulated by humans and ungrazed by livestock (Jackson and Ahlborn, 1986).

Conservation Management   The area around Shey and Phoksundo Lake was first proposed as a wildlife reserve in 1974 (Schaller, 1974). No further action was taken until 1984, when a very much larger area was established as a national park. A park headquarters has since been established at Sumduwa. As yet, there is no management plan but a number of recommendations have been made by Upreti (1989). These include: demarcation of all villages and cultivations; a ban on stone quarrying, cutting of trees and bushes, and cultivation around Phoksundo Lake where the natural environment has been disturbed by the expansion of agricultural activities; opening up of trekking corridors to Lake Phoksundo; and the protection of Shey Gompa and surroundings as a strict nature reserve in view of its cultural importance and blue sheep population.

Management Constraints   The main problems are over-grazing by domestic livestock (leading to erosion, a lowered carrying capacity, and adverse competition with bharal), pervasive hunting of wildlife (except in a few areas such as Shey Gompa) and clearing of forests (Phokundo Lake area). Hunting still occurs in the Langu Valley, and especially to the south in the Sisne/Jagdula/Kagmara area. Musk deer are still heavily hunted in the Karnali Zone (R. Jackson, pers. comm., 1986). Further details are given by Sherpa (1990) and Yonzon (1990). Measures are being introduced to address these issues (Upreti, 1990).

Staff   One warden, one assistant warden, five rangers, five senior game scouts, twenty game scouts, ten office staff (1991). One company (234 soldiers) of the Royal Nepal Army is deployed for protection purposes.

Budget   Expenditure was NRs 1,257,608 (US $ 41,920) and income NRs 69,993 (US $ 2,333) in 1989–90. The for 1990–1 is NRs 1,395,000 (US $ 46,500).

Local Addresses
Warden, Shey-Phoksundo National Park Headquarters, Sumduwa, Dolpo District

References

Basnet, D. (1989). Opening up Dolpo. *Himal* 2(3): 9.

Jackson, R. (1978). A report on wildlife and hunting in the Namlang (Langu) Valley of West Nepal. National Parks and Wildlife Conservation Office, Kathmandu. Unpublished. 20 pp.

Jackson, R. (1979). Aboriginal hunting in West Nepal with reference to musk deer *Moschus moschiferus moschiferus* and snow leopard *Panthera uncia*. *Biological Conservation* 16: 63–72.

Jackson, R. (1987). Snow cats of Langu Gorge. Snow leopard research: a project of Wildlife Conservation International. *Animal Kingdom* 90 (4): 44–53.

Jackson, R. and Ahlborn, G. (1984). A preliminary habitat suitability model for the snow leopard, *Panthera uncia*, in West Nepal. *International Pedigree Book of Snow Leopards* 4: 43–52.

Jackson, R. and Ahlborn, G. (1986). Himalayan snow leopard project. *Final progress report: Phase 1*. California Institute of Environmental Studies. 17 pp.

Jackson, R. and Ahlborn, G. (1987). Snow leopards of Langu Gorge. *Sanctuary, Asia* 7: 114–25.

Jackson, R. and Ahlborn, G. (1988). A radio-telemetry study of the snow leopard *Panther uncia* in West Nepal. *Tiger Paper* 15(2): 1–14.

Jackson, R. and Hillard, D. (1986). Tracking the elusive snow leopard. *National Geographic* 169: 792–809.

Jest, C. (1975). *Dolpo: communautés de langue Tibetaine du Nepal*. Editions du Centre National de la Recherche Scientifique, Paris. 481 pp.

Matthiessen, P. (1978). *The snow leopard*. Chatto and Windus, London. 312 pp.

Sakya, K. (1978). *Dolpo: the world behind the Himalayas*. Sharda Prakashan Griha, Kathmandu. 198 pp.

Schaller, G.B. (1974). A wildlife survey of the Shey Gompa area in Dolpo District, Nepal. New York Zoological Society, New York. Unpublished. 5 pp.

Schaller, G.B. (1977). *Mountain monarchs: wild sheep and goats of the Himalaya*. Chicago University Press, Chicago. 425 pp.

Sherpa, N.W. (1990). Natural features and vegetation of Shey-Phoksundo National Park, Dolpo. Progress report. Department of National Parks and Wildlife Conservation, Kathmandu. Unpublished. 9 pp.

Shrestha, T.B. (1982). Ecology and vegetation of north-west Nepal (Karnali Zone). *Silver Jubilee Publication Series* no. 23. Royal Nepal Academy, Kathmandu. 121 pp. (Unseen)

Snellgrove, D. (1961). *Himalayan pilgrimage*. Cassirer, Oxford.

Stainton, J.D.A. (1972). *Forests of Nepal*. John Murray, London. 181 pp.

Tyson, J. (1969). Return to the Kanjiroba. *Himalayan Journal* 29: 96–104.

Upreti, B.N. (1989). Shey-Phoksundo National Park. Summary report. Department of National Parks and Wildlife Conservation. Unpublished. 15 pp.

Yonzon, P.B. (1990). The 1990 Wildlife Survey of Shey-Phuksundo National Park, Dolpo, West Nepal. Nepal Conservation Research and Training Centre, The King Mahendra Trust for Nature Conservation, Kathmandu. Unpublished. 15 pp.

SHIVAPURI WATERSHED AND WILDLIFE RESERVE

IUCN Management Category   IV (Managed Nature Reserve)

Biogeographical Province   2.38.12 (Himalayan Highlands)

Geographical Location   Lies on the north side of Kathmandu Valley about 12 km from Kathmandu City.

Date and History of Establishment   Established as a wildlife reserve in 1985 under the Shivapuri Watershed Management and Fuelwood Plantation Project. Measures to protect the watershed began in 1975 under the Shivapuri Watershed Development Board.

Area   The watershed extends over 14,487 ha, of which 11,200 ha falls within the wildlife reserve and is demarcated by a 114 km-long boundary wall.

Land Tenure   State

Altitude   Ranges from 1,366 m to 2,732 m at Shivapuri Dada.

Physical Features   Shivapuri, the second highest hill surrounding Kathmandu Valley, is the main source of water for domestic consumption in Kathmandu. Streams on the north of the watershed drain into the Likhu Khola, and those on the south into the Bagmati River which flows through Kathmandu Valley. The summit is a large flat area commanding excellent views of the Himalaya. Rocks are mostly gneisses. Southern slopes, with their sandy soils, are unstable and prone to erosion (Anon., 1986; Joshi, 1986).

Climate   Mean annual precipitation ranges from less than 1,800 mm to more than 3,200 mm, about 90% of which falls during the monsoon between May and October. Temperatures are highest, up to 23 °C, in August (Joshi, 1986).

Vegetation   About 50% of the watershed is still forested (Joshi, 1986). Subtropical pine *Pinus roxburghii* forests are predominant on southern slopes below 1,600 m, while *Schima wallichii*, *Castonopsis indica*, *Alnus nepalensis*, and *Prunus ceresoides* occur on northern aspects. Mixed temperate forests of oak (*Quercus lanata*, *Q. semecarpifolia*) and rhododendron *Rhododendron arboreum* predominate at higher elevations (Anon., 1986). Important medicinal plants include patpate or dhasingar *Gaultheria fragrantissima*, bajradanti *Potentilla fulgens*, aryili *Edgeworthia gardneri*, kurkure ghans or ankhali ghans *Equisetum dubile* and bokri lahara or dhude lahara *Hedyotis scandens* (Joshi, 1986).

Fauna   Mammals include common langur *Presbytis entellus*, leopard *Panthera pardus* (T), sloth bear *Melursus ursinus* (V), yellow-throated marten *Martes flavigula*, wild boar *Sus scrofa*, Indian muntjac *Muntiacus muntjak*, and orange-bellied Himalayan squirrel *Dremomys lokriah* (Anon., 1986; Joshi, 1986).

The avifauna comprises 149 species, of which 100 are breeding species. Shivapuri supports 26 breeding species for which Nepal may hold internationally significant populations, and is important for birds of *Quercus semecarpifolia* forest, notably yellow-bellied bush warbler *Cettia acanthizoides* and grey-sided laughing-thrush *Garrulax caerulatus*. The reserve is also important for wintering birds, of which 36 species have been recorded (Inskipp, 1989).

Most noteworthy is the relict Himalayan dragonfly *Epiophlebia laidlawi* (V), whose distribution is restricted to the eastern Himalaya, from Kathmandu Valley to Darjeeling in Sikkim (Wells et al., 1983). Healthy populations of the dragonfly were found between 1,860 m and 2,380 m during a recent status survey (Saville et al., 1990).

Cultural Heritage   Places of religious significance to Hindus and Buddhists include Baghdwar, Tareswar Mahadev, Manichur, Naghi Monastery, Vishnudwar, and Shivapuri Mahadev. On the Nepalese New Year's Day, pilgrims flock to Baghdwar and Vishnudwar, sources of the sacred Bhagmati and Vishnumati rivers, respectively (Anon., 1986).

Local Human Population   An estimated 5,000 people reside in the reserve and there are a further 15,000 nearby. They live by subsistence agriculture (Joshi, 1986).

Visitors and Visitor Facilities   The summit is popular with tourists, many of whom camp overnight in order to see the Himalaya at sunrise. No records are kept of visitor numbers.

Scientific Research and Facilities   A land use map (1:50,000) has been prepared under the Shivapuri Watershed Management and Fuelwood Plantation Project (Anon., n.d.). The dependence of villagers from Chaubas on the reserve's natural resources has been assessed, in conjunction with the effect of tourism on the local economy (Joshi, 1987). Socio-economic studies have also been conducted by Dahal and Sutihar (1986). The status of the relict Himalayan dragonfly was surveyed in 1988 (Saville et al., 1990).

Conservation Value   Shivapuri is an important watershed, providing Kathmandu with its main supply of water. Its avifauna is diverse and it is a vital refuge for the relict Himalayan dragonfly (Anon., 1986; Inskipp, 1989; Saville et al., 1990).

Conservation Management   The reserve is managed by an eleven-member board under the Shivapuri Watershed Management and Fuelwood Plantation Project. The main conservation objectives of the project are to protect the natural environment, ensure a reliable and high-quality supply of drinking water for Kathmandu and local people, minimise degradation of land by applying appropriate corrective measures, improve the standard of living of the resident and adjacent rural populations, and establish fuelwood and fodder plantations. Disturbance to the vegetation or wildlife and grazing by livestock are prohibited within the reserve. Activities undertaken or underway include the construction of a 114 km-long boundary wall and a 95 km-long motorable road, the construction and improvement of 82 km of footpaths, the reafforestation of 2,684 ha of land, the construction of 106 check-dams as well as gully control and landslide protection measures at twelve localities, and provision of guard posts (Anon., 1986). Utis *Alnus nepalensis*, used as timber and fodder, and the exotic Napier grass *Panisetum purpureum*, also valuable as fodder, are widely used for reafforestation and control of gully erosion (H. Stennet, pers. comm., 1986). On completion of the project, it is planned to hand over management of the reserve to the Department of National Parks and Wildlife Conservation.

Management Constraints Deforestation, reclamation, grazing by livestock, and tourism have proved deleterious to natural communities in the area. Forest resources, mostly in the form of fuelwood, have been overexploited to meet local, tourist, and urban needs (Joshi, 1986). In a recent study of Chaubas Village, it has been demonstrated that forest resources are adequate to meet local fuelwood requirements but insufficient for export to Kathmandu (Joshi, 1987). Problems of overexploitation are being addressed by the Shivapuri Watershed Management and Fuelwood Plantation Project, and the improvement in forest condition and water quality are already apparent to the local people. The benefit of the new road in providing better communications between Kathmandu and the villages in the west of the reserve is questionable since it is little used by local people. Moreover, the road, as well as the boundary wall, are constantly in need of repairs (M. Rowntree, pers. comm., 1991). Concern has been expressed about the potential impact of the road on relict Himalayan dragonfly populations (Asahina, 1982). In the event, the road is almost entirely below 2,000 m and will have minimal impact on the species which occurs mainly in mature forests at higher altitudes (Saville et al., 1990).

Staff Seventy staff under the Shivapuri Watershed Management and Fuelwood Plantation Project. A battalion (742 soldiers) of the Royal Nepal Army is stationed in the reserve for protection duties.

Budget Rs 11,014,000 (US $ 367,133) in 1990–1.

Local Addresses
National Project Chief, Shivapuri Watershed Management and Fuelwood Plantation Project, Department of Soils and Water Conservation, Ministry of Forests and Soil Conservation, Kathmandu

References
Anon. (n.d.). Watershed development plan of the Shivapuri Watershed Management and Fuelwood Plantation Project. Unpublished. 3 pp.
Anon. (1986). *Shivapuri Watershed and Wildlife Reserve Project.*
Asahina, S. (1982). Survey of the relict dragonfly *Epiophlebia laidlawi* Tillyard in Nepal, May 1981. *Reports of the Odonata Specialist Group* no. 1. IUCN, Gland, Switzerland. 6 pp.
Dahal, K.K. and Sutihar, D.N. (1986). The study of Shivapuri watershed environment: an evaluation of socio-economic impact. *The Economic Journal of Nepal* 9(2): 35–44.
Joshi, A.R. (1986). Shivapuri watershed and wildlife reserve. Unpublished. 2 pp.
Joshi, A.R. (1987). A study of the environment relationships of certain village communities in the Central Development Region of Nepal. Ph.D. thesis, University College, Cardiff. 189 pp.
Saville, N., Northcott, P., Tufton, T., and Jones, N. (1990). *Report of the Cambridge Entomological Expedition to Nepal 1988.* University of Cambridge, Cambridge. 47 pp.
Wells, S.M., Pyle R.M., and Collins, M.N. (1983). *The IUCN invertebrate red data book.* IUCN, Gland, Switzerland. Pp. 339–40.

PAKISTAN

Area   803,940 sq. km

Population   114,600,000 (1990)   Natural increase   3.0% per annum

GNP   US $ 350 per capita (1988)

Policy and Legislation   Environmental protection and ecology are included in the concurrent legislative list of Pakistan's 1973 constitution. This initiative, together with the formation of an Environment and Urban Affairs Division in 1973, was largely responsible for enactment of the Environment Protection Ordinance 1983. The Ordinance is a landmark in Pakistan's legislation and represents official recognition of a holistic approach to environmental issues. It provides for the control of pollution and preservation of a comprehensive national environmental policy, and filing of detailed environmental impact statements by proponents of projects likely to adversely affect the environment. The main drawback of the Ordinance, however, is its much narrower scope—focusing on anti-industrial pollution—than was envisaged in the original draft, which included legal provisions for the protection of Pakistan's natural resource base (Mumtaz, 1989).

A significant step towards meeting the environmental challenge was taken in 1988, with the support of IUCN, in initiating the National Conservation Strategy development process. A secretariat has been set up in the Environment and Urban Affairs Division (Ministry of Housing and Works), which reports to a high-level steering committee comprising representatives of eight ministries directly concerned with natural resources, and five representatives from the private sector. The NCS development process represents an unique policy review of economic issues and their collective impact on the environment. Public consultations are an integral part of this review and planning exercise (Kabraji, 1986; Mumtaz, 1989). As part of the review process, a national workshop was held in 1986 (IUCN/GOP, 1987). The first phase of the development process, namely the formulation of Pakistan's NCS, was completed in 1990 (JRC, n.d.).

Early Hindu and Muslim rulers, recognising the inadvisability of uncontrolled hunting, were the first to set aside game reserves wherein hunting was restricted during breeding seasons. By the late 16th century, the Mughals had codified regulations pertaining to hunting and these policies were adopted by succeeding Sikh and British administrations (ALIC, 1981). Indiscriminate exploitation of forest resources during the 19th century led to the realisation of the need for a forest policy. Although not of direct relevance to Pakistan, the first forest policy directive issued by the Government of India was in the form of a Memorandum

(3 August 1855) for the protection and extraction of teak. It restricted the rights of forest dwellers to conserve the forests. Government of India Circular no. 22-F (19 October 1894) represented a more comprehensive forest policy statement, which emphasised management of forests for timber production, watershed protection and maintenance of productive capacity. It also provided guidelines on basic principles associated with rights of people living adjacent to forest lands (Mumtaz, 1989).

Among the first pieces of legislation that directly benefited wildlife were the rules and regulations formulated in Sind under the Indian Forest Act in 1887 and later incorporated in the Bombay Forest Manual. Under this legislation, forests were protected from grazing by livestock but hunting was not legally controlled. Hunting and other forms of resource exploitation were subsequently controlled within areas declared as reserved or protected forests under the Indian Forest Act 1927, the title of which was changed to Pakistan Forest Act 1927 following Pakistan's adoption of the Act after partition in 1947 (Ferguson, 1978; Rao, 1984). The 1927 Act sought to 'consolidate the law relating to forests, the transit of forest produce and the duty leviable on timber and other forest produce.' It further 'empowers the government to set aside forest reserves, appoint officers charged with the management of those territories, enforce rules governing the use of forests, determine the degree to which timber and other products may be exploited, and regulate the movement of cattle upon these lands. Moreover, the Act authorises the Government to punish violators of the stipulations contained in it.' The 1927 Act has since been amended by the West Pakistan Goats (Restriction) Ordinance of 1959 and the West Pakistan Goats Restriction Rules of 1961, which enable the government to protect rangelands from grazing damage by goats through limiting their numbers and movements.

The 1927 Act is not conservation oriented, commercial forestry interests being foremost. Subsequent forest policy, under the directives of 1955, 1962, and 1980, has attempted to bring forests under sound scientific management and included provisions for the creation of national parks to conserve major ecosystems, but it has not been successful (Mumtaz, 1989). The need to reassess and redefine policy is being addressed by the Forest Department, following on from a recent evaluation of Pakistan's forest policy at an international seminar organised by the Ministry of Food, Agriculture and Co-operatives in 1989. Existing forest legislation is regulatory in nature. It needs to be revised to meet the requirements of development and extension forestry, with more persuasive rather than punitive provisions (Shekh and Jan, n.d.).

Wildlife conservation legislation inherited from British India was superseded by the now obsolete West Pakistan Wildlife Protection Ordinance 1959 and the West Pakistan Wildlife Protection Rules 1960 issued under that ordinance. Apart from prohibiting the killing of certain species of fauna, this legislation made provision for the declaration of game sanctuaries in which hunting was prohibited, and game reserves in which hunting was controlled under license, but did not protect the habitat against settlement, cultivation, grazing, and other forms of exploitation. Furthermore, both the West Pakistan Wildlife Protection Ordinance and the Pakistan Forest Act applied only to the settled areas of Pakistan (i.e. the flood plains of the Kabul and Indus rivers and all the land to the east of them); neither were applicable to the Special/Tribal Areas, which constituted most of the mountainous half of the country to the west of the Indus and where much of Pakistan's remaining wildlife was to be found (Grimwood, 1969).

A Wildlife Enquiry Committee was set up in 1968 to review *inter alia* the existing conservation legislation, based on recommendations by the World Wildlife Fund (Mountfort and Poore, 1967, 1968). Legislation was drafted by this committee (Government of Pakistan, 1971) and, with minor modifications, was subsequently adopted at provincial level through the provision of various acts and an ordinance, namely: Sind Wildlife Protection Ordinance 1972, Punjab Wildlife (Protection, Preservation, Conservation and Management) Act 1974, Baluchistan Wildlife Protection Act 1974, and North-West Frontier Province Wildlife (Protection, Preservation, Conservation and Management) Act 1975. Separate laws were passed for the Northern Areas, Azad State of Jammu & Kashmir, and Federal Capital Territory of Islamabad. These are the Northern Areas Wildife Preservation Act 1975, Azad Jammu and Kashmir Wildlife Act 1975, and the Islamabad Wildlife (Protection, Preservation, Conservation and Management) Ordinance 1979 (Rau, 1984). This is the first time in the history of Pakistan's wildlife legislation that an attempt has been made to provide for the conservation of habitat (although limited to protected areas) and species other than game species.

All of these statutes provide for the creation and management of national parks, wildlife sanctuaries (synonymous with wildlife reserves in the Northern Areas Act), game reserves (synonymous with controlled hunting areas in the Northern Areas Act) and, in the case of the Punjab, North-West Frontier Province and Islamabad legislation, private game reserves. A national park is a comparatively large area of outstanding scenic merit and natural interest, wherein the primary objective is to protect the landscape, flora, and fauna in its natural state and to which the public are allowed access for purposes of recreation, education and research. No hunting or trapping of animals or birds is permitted. Harvesting of forest produce on a sustained basis is allowed, provided national park values are not jeopardised. Construction of access roads, accommodation facilities, and public amenities should be carefully planned so as not to impair the primary objective of a park's establishment. A wildlife sanctuary is an area set aside as an undisturbed breeding ground, primarily for the protection of all natural resources, to which public access is prohibited or regulated. Whereas settlement and grazing by domestic livestock is allowed in national parks (see Grimwood, 1972, for a discussion of the implications arising from this aspect of the legislation), such activities are prohibited within wildlife sanctuaries. A game reserve is an area wherein controlled hunting and shooting is allowed on a permit basis. A private game reserve is an area of private land set aside by its owner for the same purpose as a game reserve. Parts of areas protected under some statutes may be denotified under pressure for agricultural extension or land development (Ullah, 1970; Government of Pakistan, 1971; Rao, 1984; Khan and Hussain, 1985). To date, there are no notified private game reserves, but a number exist in Baluchistan (e.g. Goth Raisani, Serajabad, Nasirabad area) and Sind (e.g. Khairpur), where there is no legal provision for their establishment, and in Punjab (e.g. Kalabagh). Existing wildlife legislation is reviewed by Rao (1984). Model legislation (Pakistan Wildlife Protection Act) is currently being prepared by the National Council for Conservation of Wildlife (Rao, 1987).

International Activities Pakistan ratified both the Convention concerning the Protection of the World Cultural and Natural Heritage (World Heritage Convention) and the Convention on Wetlands of International Importance especially as Waterfowl Habitat (Ramsar Convention) on 23 July 1976. No natural sites have been inscribed to date under the World Heritage Convention. Nine wetlands were designated at the time of Pakistan's ratification of the Ramsar Convention, of which two (Kandar Dam and Kheshki Reservoir) are no longer considered to be of international importance (Scott, 1989). Pakistan participates in the Unesco Man and Biosphere Programme, but there does not appear to have been any significant development in recent years. Pakistan also participates in the South Asian Co-operative Environmental Programme.

Administration and Management   Originally, the Game Department was responsible for administering the West Pakistan Wildlife Protection Ordinance up until 1967, when it was absorbed into the Forest Department (Grimwood, 1969). Following the recommendations of the Wildlife Enquiry Committee (Government of Pakistan, 1971), a National Council for Conservation of Wildlife was established on 7 July 1974 within the then Federal Ministry of Food and Agriculture. It has an advisory board, and is responsible for co-ordinating central and provincial government effort in the formulation and implementation of wildlife policies. The Inspector General of Forests is assisted by a Conservator of Wildlife, who acts as an adviser on wildlife, but the actual management of wildlife is handled by the provincial forest (wildlife) departments. Punjab and Sind have separate wildlife administrations, but in the Azad State of Jammu & Kashmir, Baluchistan, Northern Areas and North-West Frontier Province, wildlife is administered by branches of the respective forest departments. In practice, forest staff look after wildlife in reserved or protected forests, and wildlife staff are responsible for protecting wildlife in other protected areas and elsewhere. In North-West Frontier Province, wildlife staff are solely responsible for wildlife. Within the Federal Capital Territory of Islamabad, the Directorate of Environment is responsible for the administration of protected areas. Legal provision has been made for the creation of wildlife management boards to approve wildlife policies and monitor development activities in Punjab, Sind, North-West Frontier Province, and Islamabad. Sind has an effective wildlife management board, while those of North-West Frontier Province and Punjab are progressing. Boards exist in Azad State of Jammu & Kashmir, Baluchistan, and Northern Areas, but only in an advisory capacity. That for Islamabad is not yet active. Provision has also been made for the appointment of honorary officers to help implement wildlife legislation in all political units except Baluchistan and Islamabad. The idea was first introduced in Sind in the 1970s and proved to be very successful in Kirthar National Park, resulting in the recovery of markhor and other large mammal populations. It has since been adopted in Azad State of Jammu & Kashmir and Punjab with the appointment of local dignitaries as honorary game wardens invested with considerable legal power to help enforce the law within protected areas (Ferguson, 1978; NCCW, 1978; Roberts, 1983; Rao, 1984; Mumtaz, 1990, 1991).

The allocation of funds to the forestry subsector has increased from 10.2% in the Sixth Five-Year Plan (1983–8) to 12.5% in the Seventh Five-Year Plan (1988–93). Of the Rs 2 billion allocated to the subsector under the Seventh Plan, Rs 332 million (16.6%) is earmarked for wildlife conservation (Sheikh and Jan, n.d.). Within the wildlife sector, the total budget allocated to the federal units in 1990–1 is Rs 93.4 million (US $ 4.3 million), of which 52.5% represents recurrent expenditure and 47.5% capital development costs. The total number of staff within the wildlife sector is 3,206: 121 are administrative and executive, 2,375 are protection and operational, and 710 are supporting staff (Malik, 1990).

The Environmental Protection Ordinance is enforced by the Pakistan Environment Protection Council, but this has not yet been formed. The Council is also responsible for establishing a national environmental policy, providing direction to conserve renewable and expendable resources and ensuring that environmental considerations are incorporated within national development plans and policies. Administration of the Ordinance is the responsibility of the Pakistan Environment Protection Agency. Provincial Environment Protection Agencies have been set up, but other implementation procedures have yet to be streamlined (Mumtaz, 1989).

Among the non-governmental organisations involved with conservation is the Pakistan Wildlife Conservation Foundation, a registered charity established in 1979. Its president is appointed by a resolution of the National Council for Conservation of Wildlife. A main objective is to promote wildlife conservation activities through provision of funds in accordance with the policies of the National Council for Conservation of Wildlife. The International Union for Conservation of Nature and Natural Resources–The World Conservation Union has a regional office in Karachi. Field programmes concerned with protected areas management issues are focused on Korangi/Phitti Creek in the Indus Delta, juniper forests in Baluchistan, and Khunjerab National Park in the Northern Areas. World Wide Fund for Nature-Pakistan (formerly World Wildlife Fund-Pakistan) has offices in Lahore and Karachi. Two bodies are concerned specifically with promoting the conservation of pheasants, namely the World Pheasant Association (Pakistan) and the Pheasant Conservation Forum.

The management of national parks has given emphasis to the development of recreation facilities for tourists rather than nature conservation, as in Lal Suhanra and Margalla Hills national parks. Management categories need to be modified (Grimwood, 1972; Rao, 1984), perhaps by the introduction of nature reserves and country parks to replace wildlife sanctuaries. Protected and reserved forests continue to be managed under forest working plans after being designated national parks or wildlife sanctuaries, thereby undermining the purpose of their renotification. Hunting in game reserves is not controlled on a sustained yield basis, permits being issued arbitrarily and subject to political influence (Rao, 1984). The Government of Punjab, however, has restricted the number of shoots under an amendment to the Punjab Wildlife Act (Khan and Hussain, 1985). Weak enforcement of the law is an overall constraint, but safeguards against habitat degradation within protected areas are also inadequate (Rao, 1984). This is largely a reflection of the inadequate financial and technical resources. In addition, except in Punjab, the present administrative arrangements handicap wildlife and protected areas management due to the lack of independence of the wildlife adminstrations within the federal units (Mumtaz, 1990, 1991).

Systems Reviews Predominantly arid and semi-arid, Pakistan is a land of great contrasts. Nearly 60% of the country consists of mountainous terrain and elevated plateaux; the rest is lowland, generally below 300 m. The highlands comprise: the Himalaya and adjacent mountain ranges to the north, rising to 8,611 m at the top of K2, the world's second highest peak; the central Sulaiman Range and its southern extensions (Ras Koh, Siahan and Kirthar ranges); and the western Baluchistan Plateau. The lowlands comprise the Indus River plain and a narrow stretch of coastline bordering the Arabian Sea. A profile of the environment has been prepared by the Government of Pakistan (1989).

Pakistan did not inherit a very rich forest resource base, a reflection of its arid climate and the incessant cutting of trees throughout much of the country over the last few centuries. Under extensive reafforestation schemes and extension programmes, forest coverage has increased from 1.4 million ha at the time of independence to 4.6 million ha (5.2% of total land area) by 1984. One million ha of forest, for example, was planted in North-West Frontier Province with the co-operation of the people. Forest cover is most extensive in Azad State of Jammu & Kashmir (27.7%), North-West Frontier Province (13.9%), and Northern Areas (13.4%); in the other three states it is below five per cent. There are two types of forest in Pakistan: production forest managed for commercial extraction of timber; and protection forest which has no commercial value and is primarily for soil protection. Only 27.6% of forest is commercially used, the bulk (72.4%) of this resource being under protection (Sheikh and Jan, n.d.; JRC, 1989).

Most of Pakistan's remaining wildlife is to be found in the mountainous country west of the Indus, where human pressures have not been as great as in the plains. The two regions of outstanding importance are the Himalayan and Karakoram massifs in the extreme north and the desert in the south-west of the country (Grimwood, 1969). To the east of the Indus, Hazara Division in North-West Frontier Province and several areas in Punjab have a considerable amount of wildlife (M.M. Malik, pers. comm., 1987), as does the Neelum Valley in Azad State of Jammu & Kashmir (G. Duke, pers. comm., 1990). Wildlife resources and their exploitation have been reviewed for Baluchistan (Roberts, 1973; Mian and O'Gara, 1987; Groombridge, 1988) and Sind (Roberts, 1972). Major irrigation systems, built to tap the water resources of the Indus and its tributaries to meet the demands of an increasing human population, have resulted in the disappearance of extensive tracts of the original tropical thorn scrub, riverine swamp, and forest in the plains (Roberts, 1977). In a recent review of critical ecosystems in Pakistan, Roberts (1986) identifies the Indus riverine zone, and the Chaghai Desert and juniper forests of Baluchistan as being of unique ecological interest and international conservation importance.

Pakistan possesses a great variety of wetlands distributed throughout much of the country. Inland waters cover 7.8 million ha, over half of which comprises waterlogged areas, seasonally flooded plains and saline wastes. Coastal mangrove swamps cover at least 260,000 ha. Pakistan's wetlands are important for waterfowl, particularly those of the Indus Valley—a major wintering ground for a wide variety of central and northern Asian species, as well as being of socio-economic value (Scott, 1989).

Prior to 1966, Pakistan had taken no significant steps towards establishing a protected areas network. That year, at the invitation of the Government of Pakistan, the World Wildlife Fund carried out a survey of the country's wildlife resources and recommended measures to arrest their deterioration (Mountfort and Poore, 1967, 1968). These included the establishment of two large national parks and eight wildlife sanctuaries. This initiative was followed by the constitution of a Wildlife Enquiry Committee in 1968, which made further recommendations for the establishment of 4 national parks, 18 wildlife sanctuaries and 52 game reserves (Government of Pakistan, 1971). These recommendations have been substantially exceeded: 4 national parks, 44 wildlife sanctuaries and 65 game reserves had been declared by 1978 (ALIC, 1981). During the period 1968–71, various techinal assistance was received from the Food and Agricultural Organisation of the United Nations, which latterly included the appointment of an adviser to the Wildlife Enquiry Committee (Grimwood, 1969, 1972). The network currently comprises 10 national parks, over 80 wildlife sanctuaries and over 80 game reserves, covering 7.2 million ha (9% of the total land area). Although extensive, given Pakistan's human population, only a fraction of the network is protected. Game reserves, in particular, which are often on private land, receive minimal protection due to the lack of legal provisions to control land use. Wildlife sanctuaries enjoy better protection but, in practice, legal restrictions are seldom enforced other than in preventing hunting. Most sanctuaries have been designated in reserved forests of commercial value, where timber and minor forest products are harvested. Enforcement is better in national parks but only Kirthar currently has a management plan. Plans for some of the other national parks are due to be prepared, although that for Khunjerab has met with difficulty due to land ownership disputes between the Government and local people (Malik, 1990, 1991).

Protected areas have been created haphazardly, often in the absence of any criteria for their selection, and boundaries drawn with little or no ecological basis. Priorities to develop the existing network of protected areas are identified in the IUCN systems review of the Indomalayan Realm (MacKinnon and MacKinnon, 1986) and further recommendations are made in the Corbett Action Plan (IUCN, 1985). Malik (1990, 1991) recommends a doubling of protected areas coverage. While most major habitats are represented within the existing protected areas system (MacKinnon and MacKinnon, 1986), a comprehensive systems review has never been carried out at the national level. Clearly, this is a priority in order to plan the further development of Pakistan's protected areas network.

Other Relevant Information

Federal Capital Territory The Directorate of Environment, within the Capital Development Authority, is responsible for protected areas management. It is headed by a Director, who is supported by a Deputy Director, two Assistant Directors, a field staff of sixty-eight and thirty other staff. The Directorate is well organised and enjoys good support from other government agencies by virtue of being in the capital (Malik; 1990).

Northern Areas The Northern Areas Forest Department manages the protected areas in its jurisdiction. Apart from Khunjerab National Park, which is independently managed under a Park Director, wildlife staff are attached to the territorial forest divisions under Divisional Forest Officers. The total number of wildlife staff is 87, of which 60 are operational/protection personnel. The budget allocated for 1990–1 is Rs 1.8 million, of which 83.3% is recurrent expenditure, the rest (16.6%) being for development costs (Malik, 1990).

North-West Frontier Province Protected areas management has been assigned to an independent Wildlife Wing within the Forest Department, headed by a Conservator of Wildlife. The province is divided into six wildlife divisions, each headed by a Divisional Forest Officer, Wildlife. A wildlife ranger is allocated to each of the fourteen districts, as well as to each of the two national parks. The total number of wildlife staff is 502, of whom 357 are operational/protection personnel. Although the Wildlife Wing enjoys considerable independence in its operations, policy and financial constraints are a source of conflict. The budget allocated for 1990–1 Rs 9.9 million, of which 67.7% is recurrent expenditure, the rest (32.3%) being for development costs (Malik, 1990).

Addresses
National Council for Conservation of Wildlife (Conservator, Wildlife), Ministry of Food, Agriculture and Co-operatives, 485 Street 84, G-6/4 Islamabad (Tel. 829756; Tlx 5844 MINFA PK; Cable AGRIDIV)
Ministry of Food, Agriculture and Co-operatives (Inspector-General of Forests), Room 323, Block B, Pakistan Secretariat, Islamabad (Tel. 825289; Tlx 5844 MINFA PK; Cable AGRIDIV)
Forest Department—Wildlife Wing (Wildlife Warden), Azad State of Jammu & Kashmir, Muzaffarabad (Tel. 18)
Forestry & Wildlife Department, (Divisional Forest Officer, Wildlife), Government of Baluchistan, Spinny Road, Quetta (Tel. 71298)
Environment Directorate (Director), Capital Development Authority, Sitara Market, Islamabad (Tel. 826397)
Forest Department (Conservator of Forests), Northern Areas, PO Box 501, Gilgit (Tel. 360)

Forest Department—Wildlife Wing (Conservator, Wildlife), Government of North-West Frontier Province, Shami Road, Peshawar (Tel. 73184)

Wildlife Department, (Conservator of Forests, Parks & Wildlife), Government of Punjab, 2 Sanda Road, Lahore (Tel. 61798, 63947)

Sind Wildlife Management Board, (Conservator of Forests, Wildlife), Aiwan-e-Saddar Road, PO Box 3722, Karachi 1 (Tel. 523176)

IUCN–The World Conservation Union (Country Representative), 1 Bath Island Road, Karachi 75530 (Tel. 573046/79/82; Tlx 24154 MARK PK)

Pakistan Wildlife Conservation Foundation, 485 Street 84, G-6/4 Islamabad (Tel. 829756; Tlx 5844 MINFA PK; Cable AGRIDIV)

Pheasant Conservation Forum (Secretary), c/o National Council for Conservation of Wildlife, Ministry of Food, Agriculture and Co-operatives, 485 Street 84, G-6/4 Islamabad (Tel. 829756; Tlx 5844 MINFA PK; Cable AGRIDIV)

World Pheasant Association-Pakistan (Chairman), 7 Aziz-Bhatti Road, The Mall, Lahore

WWF-Pakistan, 1 Bath Island Road, Karachi 75530 (Tel. 573046/79/82; Tlx 24154 MARK PK)

WWF-Pakistan (Director), P.O. Box 5180, Lahore (Tel. 851174, 856177; Fax 370429; Tlx 44866 PKGS PK).

References

ALIC (1981). Draft environmental profile: the Islamic Republic of Pakistan. US Agency for International Development/US National Park Service/US Man and the Biosphere Secretariat. Arid Lands Information Centre, Office of Arid Lands Studies, University of Arizona, Tucson, USA. 227 pp.

Ferguson, D.A. (1978). Protection, conservation, and management of threatened and endangered species in Pakistan. US Fish and Wildlife Service, Washington DC. Unpublished. 62 pp.

Government of Pakistan (1971). *Summary of Wildlife Enquiry Committee Report.* Printing Corporation of Pakistan Press, Islamabad. 44 pp.

Government of Pakistan (1989). *Environmental profile of Pakistan.* Environment and Urban Affairs Division, Government of Pakistan, Islamabad. 248 pp.

Grimwood, I.R. (1969). Wildlife conservation in Pakistan. *Pakistan National Forestry Research and Training Project Report* no. 17. UNDP/FAO, Rome. 31 pp.

Grimwood, I.R. (1972). *Wildlife conservation and management.* Report no. TA 3077. FAO, Rome. 58 pp.

Groombridge, B. (1988). Baluchistan Province, Pakistan: a preliminary environmental profile. IUCN Conservation Monitoring Centre, Cambridge, UK. Unpublished. 104 pp.

IUCN (1985). *The Corbett Action Plan for protected areas of the Indomalayan Realm.* IUCN, Gland, Switzerland and Cambridge, UK. 23 pp.

IUCN/GOP (1987). *Towards a national conservation stategy for Pakistan.* Proceedings of the Pakistan Workshop 1986. Asian Art Press, Lahore. 367 pp.

JRC (n.d.) *Towards sustainable development: the Pakistan National Conservation Strategy.* Journalists' Resource Centre for the Environment, IUCN Pakistan, Karachi.

Kabraji, A.M. (1986). A national conservation strategy for Pakistan. In: Carwardine, M. (Ed.), *The nature of Pakistan.* IUCN, Gland, Switzerland. Pp. 69–71.

Khan, A. and Hussain, M. (1985). Development of protected area system in Pakistan in terms of representative coverage of ecotypes. In: Thorsell, J.W. (Ed.), *Conserving Asia's natural heritage.* IUCN, Gland, Switzerland. Pp. 60–8.

MacKinnon, J. and MacKinnon, K. (1986). Review of the protected areas systems in the Indo-Malayan realm. IUCN, Gland, Switzerland and Cambridge, UK. 284 pp.

Malik, M.M. (1990). Management status of protected areas in Pakistan. Paper presented at Regional Expert Consultation on Management of protected areas in the Asia–Pacific Region. FAO Regional Office for Asia and the Pacific, Bangkok, 10–14 December 1990. 40 pp.

Malik, M.M. (1991). Management status of protected areas in Pakistan. Tiger Paper 18 (1): 21–8.

Mian, A. and O'Gara, B.W. (1987). Baluchistan and wildlife potentials. University of Baluchistan, Quetta, Pakistan and University of Montana, Missoula, USA. Unpublished. 32 pp.

Mountfort, G. and Poore, D. (1967). The conservation of wildlife in Pakistan. World Wildlife Fund, Morges, Switzerland. Unpublished. 27 pp.

Mountfort, G. and Poore, D. (1968). Report on the Second World Wildlife Fund Expedition to Pakistan. World Wildlife Fund, Morges, Switzerland. Unpublished. 25 pp.

Mumtaz, K. (1989). Pakistan's environment: a historical perspective. In: Shirkat Gah–Women's Resource Centre, Pakistan's environment: a historical perspective and selected bibliography with annotations. Journalists' Resource Centre for the Environment–IUCN Pakistan, Karachi. Pp. 7–38.

National Council for Conservation of Wildlife (1978). Wildlife conservation strategy: Pakistan. National Council for Conservation of Wildlife, Islamabad, Pakistan. Unpublished. 73 pp.

Rao, A.L. (1984). A review of wildlife legislation in Pakistan. MSc. thesis, University of Edinburgh, Edinburgh, UK. 66 pp.

Rao, A.L. (1987). Nature conservation in Pakistan. In: Towards a national conservation strategy. Pp. 223–50.

Roberts T.J. (1972). A brief examination of ecological changes in the province of Sind and their consequences on the wildlife resources of the region. Pakistan Journal of Forestry 22: 89–96.

Roberts, T.J. (1973). Conservation problems in Baluchistan with particular reference to wildlife preservation. Pakistan Journal of Forestry 23: 117–27.

Roberts, T.J. (1977). The mammals of Pakistan. Ernest Benn, London. 361 pp.

Roberts, T.J. (1983). Problems in developing a national wildlife policy and in creating effective natural parks and sanctuaries in Pakistan. Paper presented at Bombay Natural History Society Centenary Seminar. Powai, Bombay, December 1983. 9 pp.

Scott, D.A. (Ed.) (1989). A directory of Asian wetlands. IUCN, Gland, Switzerland and Cambridge, UK. 1,181 pp.

Sheikh, M.I. and Jan, A. (n.d.). Role of forests and forestry in national conservation strategy of Pakistan. Draft for comment. National Conservation Strategy Secretariat, Islamabad. Unpublished. 86 pp.

Ullah, Ch. I. (1970). National parks, past, present and future. Pakistan Journal of Forestry 20: 361–8.

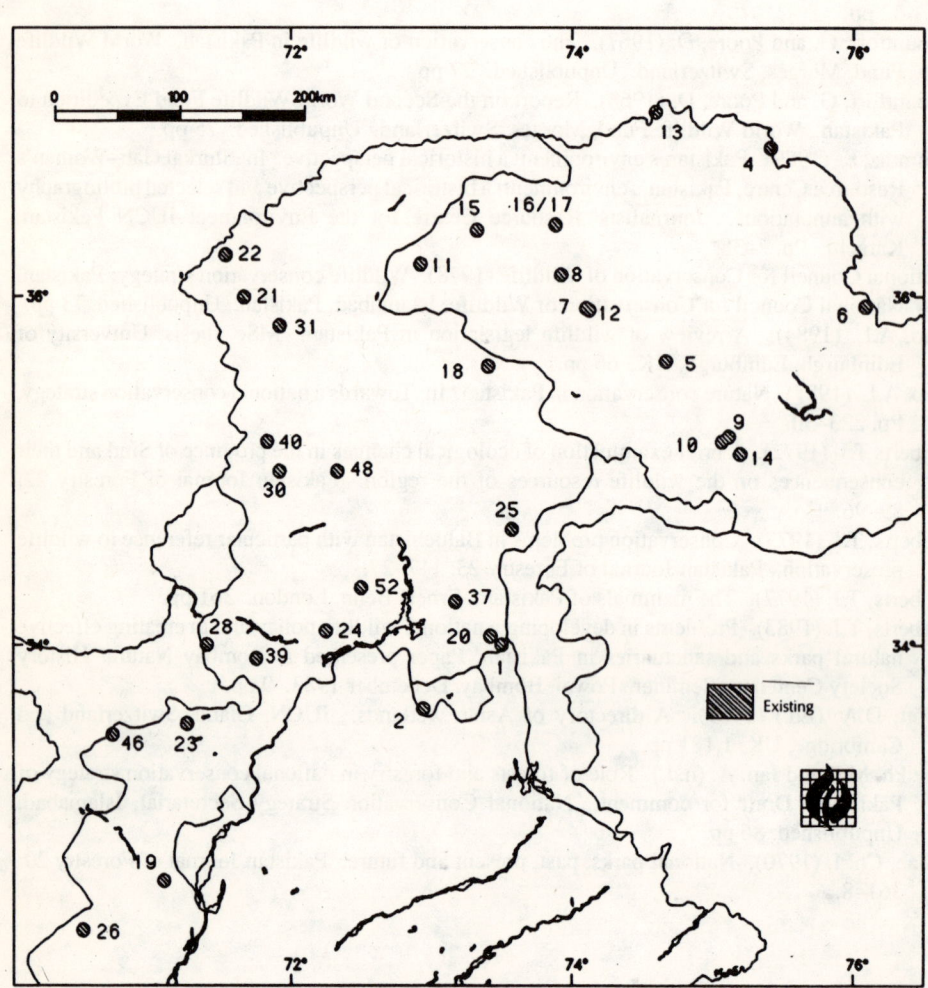

Northern Pakistan

Summary of Protected Areas of Pakistan

National/International designation Name of area and map reference+	IUCN Management Category	Area (ha)	Year notified
Federal Capital Territory		**90,700**	
National Park			
1 Margalla Hills*	V	17,386	1980
Subtotal (% total land area)		**17,386 (19.2%)**	
Wildlife Sanctuary			
2 Islamabad	IV	7,000	1980
Subtotal (% total land area)		**7,000 (7.7%)**	
Game Reserve			
3 Islamabad	Unassigned	69,800	1980
Subtotal (% total land area)		**69,800 (77.7%)**	
Northern Areas		**7,033,600**	
National Park			
4 Khunjerab*	II	226,913	1975
Subtotal (% total land area)		**226,913 (3.2%)**	
Wildlife Sanctuaries			
5 Astore*	IV	41,472	1975
6 Baltistan*	IV	41,457	1975
7 Kargah*	IV	44,308	1975
8 Naltar*	IV	27,206	1975
9 Satpara*	IV	31,093	1975
Subtotal (% total land area)		**185,536 (2.6%)**	
Game Reserves			
10 Askor Nallah*	Unassigned	12,955	1975
11 Chassi/Baushdar*	Unassigned	37,053	1975
12 Danyor Nallah*	Unassigned	44,308	1975
13 Kilik/Mintaka*	Unassigned	65,036	1975
14 Nar/Ghoro Nallah*	Unassigned	7,255	1975
15 Nazbar Nallah*	Unassigned	33,425	1975
16 Pakora*	Unassigned	7,515	1975
17 Sher Qillah*	Unassigned	16,842	1975
18 Tangir*	Unassigned	14,251	1975
Subtotal (% total land area)		**238,640 (3.4%)**	
North-West Frontier Province		**7,452,100**	
Ramsar Wetlands			
19 Thanadarwala Game Reserve*	Unassigned	4,047	1976

National/International designation Name of area and map reference+	IUCN Management Category	Area (ha)	Year notified
National Parks			
20 Ayubia	V	1,684	1984
21 Chitral Gol*	II	7,750	1984
Subtotal (% total land area)		**9,434 (0.1%)**	
Wildlife Sanctuaries			
22 Agram Basti	IV	29,866	1983
23 Borraka	IV	2,025	1976
24 Manglot	IV	715	1976
25 Manshi*	IV	2,321	1977
26 Sheikh Buddin	IV	15,540	1977
Subtotal (% total land area)		**50,467 (0.7%)**	
Game Reserves			
27 Bagra	Unassigned	2,560	1987
28 Bilyamin	Unassigned	4,047	1974
29 Darmalak	Unassigned	9,788	1987
30 Drosh Gol	Unassigned	2,061	1979
31 Gehrait Gol	Unassigned	4,800	1979
32 Ghorazandi	Unassigned	6,649	1987
33 Goleen Gol	Unassigned	49,750	1982
34 Indus River	Unassigned	44,200	1974
35 Jabbar	Unassigned	13,288	1987
36 Kacha Marai	Unassigned	5,300	1984
37 Makhnial	Unassigned	4,148	1977
38 Maraiwam	Unassigned	5,300	1984
39 Nizampur	Unassigned	780	1976
40 Purit Gol/Chitral Chinar Gol	Unassigned	6,446	1979
41 Qalandar Abad	Unassigned	8,490	1980
42 Rakh Sardaran	Unassigned	4,200	1986
43 Rakh Topi	Unassigned	17,600	1984
44 Resi	Unassigned	5,050	1976
45 Shewaki-Chukhtoo	Unassigned	11,379	1987
46 Shina-Wari Chapri	Unassigned	1,000	1974
47 Sudham	Unassigned	11,500	1984
48 Swegali	Unassigned	1,820	1984
49 Teri/Isak Khumari	Unassigned	19,966	1987
50 Thanadarwala*	Unassigned	4,047	1976
51 Tooshi	Unassigned	1,545	1979
52 Totalai	Unassigned	17,000	1984
53 Zarkani	Unassigned	12,800	1984
Subtotal (% of total land area)		**275,514 (3.7%)**	
TOTALS			
National parks (% total land area)		**253,733 (1.7%)**	
Wildlife sanctuaries (% total land area)		**243,003 (1.7%)**	
Games reserves (% total land area)		**583,954 (4.0%)**	

+ Locations of most protected areas are shown in the accompanying map.

* Site is described in this directory.

ASKOR NALLAH GAME RESERVE

IUCN Management Category   Unassigned

Biogeographical Province   2.38.12 (Himalayan Highlands)

Geographical Location   Situated in Baltistan District, 105 km and 137 km by road from the towns of Skardu and Gilgit, respectively. Approximately 35°10′N, 75°04′E

Date and History of Establishment   Declared a game reserve in on 22 November 1975.

Area   12,955 ha

Land Tenure   State (Administration of Northern Areas)

Altitude   Ranges from 1,424 m to 4,242 m.

Physical Features   Occupies the entire Askor Nallah and contains rugged and precipitous slopes. The area is composed of meta-sedimentary, sedimentary and various types of igneous rocks. Schistose, quartzite and other Quaternary lake deposits, alluvium, and stream gravels are present (Rasul, 1985).

Climate   Mean annual precipitation ranges from 76 mm to 102 mm, mostly in the form of snow. Winters are dry and severe, while summers are mild (Rasul, 1985).

Vegetation   Includes species of juniper *Juniperus*, birch *Betula*, and willow *Salix*. Ground flora comprises *Artemisia* and a variety of grasses (Rasul, 1985).

Fauna   Large mammals include markhor *Capra falconeri* (V), ibex, *C. ibex*, and snow leopard *Panthera uncia* (E). Avifauna includes chukar partridge *Alectoris chukar*, snow partridge *Lerwa lerwa*, and snowcock *Tetraogallus* sp. (Rasul, 1985).

Cultural Heritage   No information

Local Human Population   No information

Visitors and Visitor Facilities   No information

Scientific Research and Facilities   None

Conservation Value   No information

Conservation Management   Wildlife is afforded full protection. Local inhabitants enjoy concessions to collect fallen dead wood, to cut grass, and to graze livestock (Rasul, 1985).

Management Constraints   Poaching is a problem due to the shortage of manpower (Rasul, 1985).

Staff   One game watcher (1985)

Budget   Rs 10,000 p.a. (1985)

Local Addresses   No information

References
Rasul, G. (1985). *National parks and equivalent reserves in northern areas of Pakistan.* Wildlife Division, Northern Areas, Forest Department, Gilgit. 36 pp.

ASTORE WILDLIFE SANCTUARY

IUCN Management Category   IV (Managed Nature Reserve)

Biogeographical Province   2.38.12 (Himalayan Highlands)

Geographical Location   Lies in the catchment area of Astore Nallah, between Nanga Parbat (8,126 m) to the west and the Plains of Deosai to the east, and about 11 km from the town of Bunji. Approximately 35°38′N, 74°40′E

Date and History of Establishment   Declared a wildlife sanctuary on 22 November 1975.

Area   41,472 ha. The sanctuary is contiguous to Baltistan Wildlife Sanctuary (41,457 ha) to the north-west.

Land Tenure   State (Administration of Northern Areas)

Altitude   Ranges from 1,212 m to 6,060 m

Physical Features   Comprises rugged and precipitous terrain, mostly composed of meta-sedimentary rocks, schistose gneiss, and quartzite intruded by some basic dykes. The area contains a sequence of sedimentary and meta-sedimentary, and several types of igneous rocks. Late cretaceous sediments overlay the green stone complex, while quaternary deposits, lake deposits, stream gravel, and alluvium cover the bed rock in valleys (Rasul, 1985).

Climate   Mean annual precipitation is 254–381 mm, most of which falls as snow from November to January. Rain falls during the months of March, April, and May, whilst August, September, and October are the driest months. July and August are the hottest months (Rasul, 1985).

Vegetation   Trees and shrubs include *Fraxinus*, *Olea*, *Juniperus*, kail, *Picea*, *Julgoza*, *Lonicera*, and *Rosa*. *Artemisia* is prominent among the herbs, along with a variety of grasses.

Fauna   Large mammals include markhor *Capra falconeri* (V), ibex *C. ibex*, musk deer *Moschus chrysogaster* (V), snow leopard *Panthera uncia* (E), brown bear *Ursus arctos*, lynx *Felis lynx*, wolf *Canis lupus* (V), and fox *Vulpes vulpes*. Avifauna includes a variety of game birds, such as chukar *Alectoris chukar*, snow partridge *Lerwa lerwa*, snowcock *Tetraogallus* sp., monal pheasant *Lophophorus impejanus*, raptors, and vultures (Rasul, 1985).

Cultural Heritage   No information

Local Human Population   No information

Visitors and Visitor Facilities   No information

Scientific Research and Facilities   None

Conservation Value   The site was originally proposed as part of a much larger national park on account of the spectacular scenery and large mammal populations (Mountfort and Poore, 1968).

Conservation Management   There is no management plan. Local people enjoy concessions to extract timber and firewood, to graze livestock, and to cut grass (Rasul, 1985).

Management Constraints   Include shortage of manpower, poaching and encroachment (Rasul, 1985).

Staff   One range forest officer, one game inspector and one game watcher (1985).

Budget   Rs 66,000 p.a. (1985)

Local Addresses   No information

References
Mountfort, G. and Poore, D. (1968). Report on the Second World Wildlife Fund Expedition to Pakistan. WWF, Switzerland. Unpublished. 25 pp.
Rasul, G. (1985). *National parks and equivalent reserves in northern areas of Pakistan*. Wildlife Division, Northern Areas, Forest Department, Gilgit. 36 pp.

BALTISTAN WILDLIFE SANCTUARY

IUCN Management Category   IV (Managed Nature Reserve)

Biogeographical Province   2.38.12 (Himalayan Highlands)

Geographical Location   Lies in Baltistan District, 193 km and 48 km from the towns of Skardu and Gilgit, respectively. Approximately 35°36'N, 75°08'E

Date and History of Establishment   Declared a wildlife sanctuary on 22 November 1975.

Area 41,457 ha. The sanctuary is contiguous with Astore Wildlife Sanctuary (41,472 ha) to the south-east.

Land Tenure State (Administration of Northern Areas).

Altitude Ranges from 1,515 m to 5,527 m.

Physical Features The sanctuary lies in Rondu Valley where the terrain is rugged, with precipitous mountain slopes. Rocks are meta-sedimentary, schistose, and quartzite, and also include a sequence of sedimentary, meta-sedimentary, and igneous types. Quaternary lake deposits, stream gravel, and alluvium are present in valleys. The major source of water is glacial meltwater, springs, and snow (Rasul, 1985).

Climate Conditions are dry temperate. Annual precipitation is 76–102 mm, most of which falls as snow during the months of November, December, and January. Winters are severe (Rasul, 1985).

Vegetation Trees and shrubs include kail, *Picea*, *Juniperus*, *Olea*, *Fraxinus*, *Lonicera*, and *Artemisia* (Rasul, 1985).

Fauna Large mammals include markhor *Capra falconeri* (V), ibex *C. ibex*, musk deer *Moschus chrysogaster* (V), urial *Ovis vignei*, snow leopard *Panthera uncia* (E), brown bear *Ursus arctos*, wolf *Canis lupus* (V), and fox *Vulpes vulpes*. Avifauna includes a variety of game birds, such as chukar *Alectoris chukar*, snow partridge *Lerwa lerwa*, snowcock *Tetraogallus* sp., raptors, and vultures (Rasul, 1985).

Cultural Heritage No information

Local Human Population No information

Visitors and Visitor Facilities No information

Scientific Research and Facilities None

Conservation Value The sanctuary supports populations of a variety of threatened animal species.

Conservation Management Wildlife is afforded full protection. No management plan exists for the area. People living within an 8 km radius of the sanctuary enjoy concessions to extract timber and firewood, to graze livestock, and to cut grass (Rasul, 1985).

Management Constraints Include shortage of manpower, poaching, and encroachment.

Staff One range forest officer, one game inspector and one game watcher (1985).

Budget Rs 66,000 p.a. (1985)

Local Addresses No information

References
Rasul, G. (1985). *National parks and equivalent reserves in northern areas of Pakistan.* Wildlife Division, Northern Areas, Forest Department, Gilgit. 36 pp.

CHASSI/BAUSHDAR GAME RESERVE

IUCN Management Category   Unassigned

Biogeographical Province   2.38.12   (Himalayan Highlands)

Geographical Location   Lies in Gilgit District, 160 km by road from the town of Gilgit. Approximately 36°11′N, 72°55′E

Date and History of Establishment   Declared a game sanctuary on 22 November 1975.

Area   37,053 ha. Contiguous to Nazbar Nallah Game Reserve (33,177 ha).

Land Tenure   State (Administration of Northern Areas)

Altitude   Ranges from 2,878 m to 5,151 m.

Physical Features   The terrain is generally flat, with barren cliffs and scree slopes. Sedimentary and meta-sedimentary rocks, and a sequence of quartzite, schistose, and limestone are present. Baushter Nallah is perennial.

Climate   Conditions are dry temperate. Annual precipitation ranges from 127 mm to 254 mm, most of which falls as snow. Winters are severe and long, while summers are short and mild.

Vegetation   Trees and shrubs include stunted *Juniperus*, *Fraxinus*, *Betula*, *Salix*, and *Rosa*. Herbs include *Artemisia*, *Stipa*, and other grasses.

Fauna   Large mammals include ibex *Capra ibex*, snow leopard *Panthera uncia* (E), brown bear *Ursus arctos*, and fox *Vulpes vulpes*. Of the avifauna, there are a variety of game birds, such as chukar *Alectoris chukar*, snow partridge *Lerwa lerwa*, and snowcock *Tetraogallus* sp. (Rasul, 1985).

Cultural Heritage   No information

Local Human Population   No information

Visitors and Visitor Facilities   No information

Scientific Research and Facilities   None

Conservation Value   No information

Conservation Management Wildlife is afforded full protection and the reserve is completely closed to hunting and shooting. No management plan exists at present. Local inhabitants enjoy concessions to extract firewood, to graze livestock, and to cut grass (Rasul, 1985).

Management Constraints Include shortage of manpower and poaching.

Staff One game watcher (1985)

Budget Rs 10,000 p.a. (1985)

Local Addresses No information

References
Rasul, G. (1985). *National parks and equivalent reserves in northern areas of Pakistan.* Wildlife Division, Northern Areas, Forest Department, Gilgit. 36 pp.

CHITRAL GOL NATIONAL PARK

IUCN Management Category II (National Park)

Biogeographical Province 2.38.12 (Himalayan Highlands)

Geographical Location Lies in Chitral, the northernmost district of North-West Frontier Province, about 3 km west of Chitral Town. Approximately 35°50′N, 71°47′E

Date and History of Establishment Declared a national park in 1984. Originally established as a private hunting reserve in 1880 by the Mehtars, the ruling family of the former State of Chitral. Subsequently declared a wildlife sanctuary on 23 December 1971 (Akbar, 1974).

Area 7,750 ha

Land Tenure The entire Chitral Gol became state property in 1975, except for 8 ha of cultivated land and several houses which still belong to the ex-Mehtar (Malik, 1985).

Altitude Ranges from about 1,500 m at Hyrankot to 4,979 m above Dunduni Gol. Twenty-four peaks exceed 3,000 m.

Physical Features Chitral Gol is a narrow valley, its gorge running for some 18 km before broadening out into a basin surrounded by high peaks. Numerous tributaries drain into the Chitral Gol, which flows southwards into the Kunar River. Parent rock comprises shale and limestone from which are derived fairly fertile soils of up to a metre in depth on gentle slopes. The soil is porous and fragile, easily eroded by rainwater.

Climate Conditions are dry temperate and not influenced by the monsoon. Climatic data is available from Chitral Town (1,436 m) where mean annual rainfall is 462 mm, with a range of between 218 mm (1905) and 675 mm (1931). Mean annual temperature is 16.8 °C, ranging from a maximum of 43.3 °C to a minimum of 12.2 °C. Most of the park is under snow from December until March (Akbar, 1974; Malik, 1985).

Vegetation The dry temperate oak *Quercus ilex* forest of lower altitudes merges into temperate coniferous forest above 2,400 m, with the addition of *Cedrus deodara* and *Pinus gerardiana*. At higher altitudes, pine is replaced by *Juniperus macropoda* scrub. Above the tree-line at 3,350 m occur *Salix* spp., *Viburnum cotinifolium*, and *Juniperus communis*, along with numerous herbs (Akbar, 1974; Aleem, 1977a).

Fauna Chitral is famous for its markhor *Capra falconeri* (V). Schaller and Mirza (1971) estimated 100-125 in 1970, and Aleem (1976) 225 in 1975. A more recent estimate indicates a population size of 650 (Malik, 1985). Other ungulates, such as ibex *Capra ibex* and urial *Ovis vignei*, occur in very small numbers, as do black bear *Selenarctos thibetanus* (Aleem, 1977a; Malik, 1985). The status of snow leopard *Panthera uncia* (E) changed from tenuous security in 1970 to seriously threatened by 1974 (Schaller, 1976). The species does not appear to be resident, visiting the park occasionally (Malik, 1985). Wolves *Canis lupus* (V) are seen less frequently following restrictions on grazing by livestock (Malik, 1985).

Game birds include Himalayan snowcock *Tetraogallus himalayensis*, a small remnant population of Himalayan monal pheasant *Lophophorus impejanus*, snow partridge *Lerwa lerwa*, and rock partridge *Alectoris graeca* (Akbar, 1974; Khan, 1976; Malik, 1985).

Cultural Heritage No information

Local Human Population None—the five families remaining in the park with their 40 cattle and 500 goats were evicted in December 1984. Seven villages with 300 families occur on the periphery of the park but their associated 100–150 cattle and 3,000–4,000 sheep and goats are no longer allowed to seasonally graze inside the park (Malik, 1985).

Visitors and Visitor Facilities Include two hunting lodges, originally built by the Mehtars.

Scientific Research and Facilities Large mammal populations were surveyed in the 1970s (Schaller and Mirza, 1971; Aleem, 1976; Schaller, 1976). The impact of grazing by domestic livestock on the vegetation, soil, and wildlife has been examined (Aleem, 1977a). There are no research facilities.

Conservation Value The park is representative of an ecosystem that is unique in Pakistan.

Conservation Management Originally declared a wildlife sanctuary in order to protect the markhor. Objectives are to: preserve the landscape in its natural state, along with indigenous flora and fauna; manage wildlife populations, particularly the markhor, to maximise their production; and to develop facilities for research and tourism. Top priority has been given to controlling poaching and the government has decided to acquire all private lands and houses within the park. Concessions for firewood have been withdrawn in the case of inhabitants of villages peripheral to the park. Persons affected by these measures are receiving financial and other compensation to help offset losses, and former residents are being given preference for employment opportunities in the park. A special project to develop the park is planned to last until June 1988 at a cost of 4.8 million rupees. Apart from improving facilities (roads, footpaths, and visitor accommodation), game reserves will be established in areas adjacent to the park to act as buffer zones (Malik, 1985).

Management Constraints   Former management problems associated with land tenure, livestock grazing, firewood collection, and poaching have largely been alleviated (Malik, 1985). There is some concern about the markhor population, which is presently managed for trophy hunting. In the 1985–6 winter, four permits (at US $ 10,000 each) were issued to Shikar Safari Club International by the Conservator of Wildlife (T.J. Roberts, pers. comm.).

Staff   One ranger, twelve wildlife guards (1990).

Budget   No information

Local Addresses
Divisional Forest Officer (Wildlife), Chitral Gol National Park, Chitral, North-West Frontier Province

References

Akbar, A. (1974). Chitral Gol Sanctuary for markhor. *Pakistan Journal of Forestry* 24: 209–12.

Aleem, A. (1976). Markhor in Chitral Gol. *Pakistan Journal of Forestry* 26: 117–28.

Aleem, A. (1977a). The ecological impact of domestic stock on Chitral Gol Game Sanctuary, Pakistan. *Tiger Paper* 4(3): 26–9.

Aleem, A. (1977b). Population dynamics of markhor in Chitral Gol. *Pakistan Journal of Forestry* 27: 86–92.

Beg, A.R. and Ilahi Bux (1974). Vegetation of scree slopes in Chitral Gol. *Pakistan Journal of Forestry* 24(4). (Unseen)

Khan, Y.M. (1976). A comprehensive report on wildlife resources (wildlife population census) of Chitral. Forest Department, Peshawar. Unpublished. 11 pp.

Malik, M.M. (1985). Management of Chitral Gol National Park, Pakistan. In: McNeely, J.A., Thorsell, J.W., and Chalise, S.R. (Eds.), *People and protected areas in the Hindu Kush-Himalaya*. King Mahendra Trust for Nature Conservation and International Centre for Integrated Mountain Development, Kathmandu. Pp. 103–6.

Schaller, G.B. (1976). Mountain mammals in Pakistan. *Oryx* 13: 351–6.

Schaller, G.B. and Mirza, Z.B. (1971). Observations on urial and markhor in West Pakistan. New York Zoological Society, New York. Unpublished. 4 pp.

WWF/IUCN. Project no. 562. Chitral Gol Reserve, Pakistan.

DANYOR NALLAH GAME RESERVE

IUCN Management Category   Unassigned

Biogeographical Province   2.38.12 (Himalayan Highlands)

Geographical Location   Lies in Gilgit District, 6 km from the town of Gilgit. It is accessible only by bridle path. Approximately 35°55′N, 74°07′E

Date and History of Establishment   Declared a game reserve on 22 November 1975.

Area   44,308 ha

Land Tenure   State (Administration of Northern Areas)

Altitude   Ranges from 1,454 m to 7,575 m.

Physical Features   The topography is undulating and rugged. In some places there are steep, precipitous slopes, becoming gentler at their upper limits. There are sedimentary, meta-sedimentary, and igneous rocks with schist, quartzite, and limestone. Alluvial deposits and stream gravels are also present in valleys (Rasul, 1985).

Climate   Conditions are dry temperate. Mean annual precipitation is 76–102 mm, most of which falls as snow during the months of November, December, and January.

Vegetation   Trees and shrubs include kail, *Picea*, *Salix*, *Juniperus*, *Olea*, *Pistacia*, *Hippophae*, *Fraxinus*, *Rosa*, and *Betula*. Ground flora comprises *Artemisia*, *Haloxylon*, *Stipa*, and other grasses (Rasul, 1985).

Fauna   Large mammals include markhor *Capra falconeri* (V), ibex *C. ibex*, urial *Ovis vignei*, snow leopard *Panthera uncia* (E), and fox *Vulpes vulpes*. Avifauna includes a variety of game birds, such as chukar *Alectoris chukar*, snow partridge *Lerwa lerwa*, snowcock *Tetraogallus* sp., and vultures (Rasul, 1985).

Cultural Heritage   No information

Local Human Population   No information

Visitors and Visitor Facilities   No information

Scientific Research and Facilities   None

Conservation Value   No information

Conservation Management   Wildlife is afforded full protection and hunting is banned. No management plan exists for the area. Local people have concessions to collect firewood and timber and to also graze livestock.

Management Constraints   Include shortage of manpower and poaching.

Staff   One game watcher (1985)

Budget   Rs 10,000 p.a. (1985)

Local Addresses   No information

References
Rasul, G. (1985). *National parks and equivalent reserves in northern areas of Pakistan.* Wildlife Division, Northern Areas, Forest Department, Gilgit. 36 pp.

KARGAH WILDLIFE SANCTUARY

IUCN Management Category   IV (Managed Nature Reserve)

Biogeographical Province   2.38.12 (Himalayan Highlands)

Geographical Location   Lies in the Northern Areas, 5 km from the town of Gilgit. Approximately 35°56'N, 74°06'E

Date and History of Establishment   Declared a wildlife sanctuary on 22 November 1975.

Area   44,308 ha

Land Tenure   State (Administration of Northern Areas)

Altitude   Ranges from 1,515 m at the mouth of Kargah Nullah to 4,242 m at Chilali.

Physical Features   The sanctuary comprises the catchment area of the Kargah Nullah. The meta-sedimentary and sedimentary sequence includes slates, quartzites, limestone, and gneiss of pre-Carboniferous age.   There are granodiorite and horn-blended granite intrusions. Igneous rocks are post Permo-Carboniferous in age (Rasul, 1985).

Climate   Annual precipitation in the valley is 152–203 mm, most of which falls as snow during the severe winter months of December and January.   June and July are the hottest months (Rasul, 1985).

Vegetation   Trees and shrubs include *Fraxinus*, *Salix*, *Olea*, *Pistacia*, *Juniperus*, kail, *Picea*, *Betula*, *Rosa*, and *Daphnes oleides*. Ground cover consists of *Artemisia*, *Stipa*, *Haloxylon*, and other grass species.

Fauna   Large mammals include markhor *Capra falconeri* (V), ibex *C. ibex*, musk deer *Moschus chrysogaster* (V), and snow leopard *Panthera uncia* (E). The avifauna includes chukar *Alectoris chukar*, snow partridge *Lerwa lerwa*, and snowcock *Tetraogallus* sp. Monal pheasant *Lophophorus impejanus* is seen occasionally (Rasul, 1985).

Cultural Heritage   No information

Local Human Population   No information

Visitors and Visitor Facilities   No information

Scientific Research and Facilities   None

Conservation Value   The sanctuary provides a refuge for a variety of threatened mammals.

Conservation Management   No management plan exists. Wildlife is afforded full protection. People living near the forest and in the town of Gilgit enjoy concessions to extract firewood and to graze livestock. Residents of Kargah benefit from timber for domestic use (Rasul, 1985).

Management Constraints   Include shortage of manpower, poaching, and agricultural encroachment.

Staff   One game watcher (1985)

Budget   Rs 10,000 p.a. (1985)

Local Addresses   No information

References
Rasul, G. (1985). *National parks and equivalent reserves in northern areas of Pakistan.* Wildlife Division, Northern Areas, Forest Department, Gilgit. 36 pp.

KHUNJERAB NATIONAL PARK

IUCN Management Category   II (National Park)

Biogeographical Province   2.38.12 (Himalayan Highlands)

Geographical Location   Situated 269 km north-east of Gilgit in the former Hunza State. The park lies in the upper Khunjerab and Shimshal valleys in the extreme north-east of the Northern Areas. Its northern and eastern boundaries follow the Pakistan–China border, its southern boundary is delineated by the divides between the upper Shimshal Valley and Hisper and other glaciers, while its western boundary is more irregular. Starting at the northern end, the western boundary includes the Dhi Valley and the mouth of the Ghujerab Valley, then runs eastwards along the divide between the Ghujerab and Shimshal drainages, finally dipping southwards to include the upper Shimshal Valley. 36°50′N, 75°35′E

Date and History of Establishment   Designated a national park on 29 April 1975.

Area   Officially cited as 226,913 ha but this figure is considered to be an underestimate (Wegge, 1988). It is recommended that the park be enlarged in the south-west to include the whole of the Shimshal Valley (Wegge, 1988). The park is adjacent to Taxkorgan Natural Reserve (1,400,000 ha) in China.

Land Tenure   State (Administration of Northern Areas). Local people enjoy traditional grazing rights.

Altitude   Ranges from about 3,200 m at the entrances to the park to over 6,000 m. Over half of the park is above 4,000 m (Wegge, 1988). Khunjerab Pass, the gateway to China via the Karakoram Highway, is at 4,934 m.

Physical Features   The physiography of the park can be divided into three main parts: in the north, the Khunjerab Valley with its narrow nullahs opens out into open, undulating meadows near the Pass; in the centre, the Ghujerab River drains the high mountain massifs and glaciers of the Chapchingal and Ghujerab; and in the south, the Shimshal Valley with its many impressive glaciers.   The main Khunjerab, Shimshal, and Ghujerab rivers flow westwards and drain into the Hunza River. All the waterways are perennial but the upper reaches freeze during the winter fall in temperature.   There is a variety of sedimentary, metamorphic, and igneous rocks.   Soils are generally shallow and immature, containing fragments of rocky material, drifted sand, and clay. They are formed mainly by the deposition of glacial material carried downstream in large quantities.   Soils are deeper in the upper Khunjerab Valley and support good meadows.   Cloudbursts and ice-falls from glaciers frequently wreak havoc in the area.   Rivers and streams become blocked by debris, and subsequent flooding occurs when the water breaks through these blockades.

Climate   The nearest meteorological station is at Misgar, which is about 32 km from the park entrance in a separate valley towards the south-west. Conditions vary considerably with altitude. Winter is long and severe and summer is cold and dry. The minimum temperature during winter (December and January) is −12 °C. July and August are the hottest months, with a mean temperature of 14 °C. Most precipitation falls during the winter.

Vegetation   Following the classification of Beg (1975) and Roberts (1977), four main vegetation types can be distinguished.   Permanent snowfields and cold desert cover an estimated 25%–30% of the park, mainly above 4,000 m. The latter is very sparsely vegetated by species such as *Salix* spp., *Potentilla desertorum*, *Mertensia tibetica*, and a few grasses and sedges. Alpine meadows (20% of total cover) are confined to level ground and depressions above 3,500 m and along glaciers. They are generally rich in plant biomass due to an adequate moisture regime and are therefore important food habitats for both domestic and wild herbivores. Sedges and grasses dominate, but forbs such as *Potentilla* spp., *Saxifraga sibirica*, *Primula macrophylla*, *Sedum* spp., and *Polygonum* spp. are also common.   Subalpine scrub and birch forest (20% of total cover) occur as narrow belts along stream bottoms and in ravines throughout most of the altitudinal range of the park. Characteristic species are birch *Betula utilis*, willow *Salix* spp., tamarisk *Myricaria germanica*, buckthorn *Hippophae rhamnoides*, and water-dependent forbs and graminoids.   Alpine dry steppe (15%–20% of total cover) is found at medium and low elevations on south-facing and dry slopes not covered by subalpine scrub and forest.   It is sparsely vegetated by junipers *Juniperus* spp. and *Artemisia* spp.

Fauna   A total of 15 mammal species is known to reside in the park and several others are likely to be present (Wegge, 1988). Marco Polo sheep *Ovis ammon polii* (I), now one of the rarest mammals in Pakistan, occurs in the vicinity of Khunjerab Pass. According to the Mir of Hunza, the population was around 400 but had dropped to below 180 by the time of the completion of the Karakoram Highway (T.J. Roberts, pers. comm., 1988). A herd of almost 75 Marco Polo sheep was recorded in the spring of 1984 (Islam and Islam, 1984) and park staff saw at least 50 crossing the Pass in May 1989 (P. Wegge, pers. comm.).   The species also occurs in the headwaters of Karchanai Nullah in the north-west corner of the park, where 28 females and young were sighted in June 1986 (Nissar Ullah Beg, cited in Wegge, 1988). Pakistan's only population of bharal *Pseudois nayaur* occurs at the western limit of its range in the upper Ghujerab and Shimshal valleys (Schaller, 1974). The Shimshal population had declined to an alarming extent because of hunting (Rasool, 1981), but it has responded to subsequent protection measures and a total of 170 was tallied in 1986 (Rasul, 1986).   Wegge

(1988) recorded 133 bharal within less than 40 sq. km of the Chatpert drainage, and estimates a total population of 1,500-2,000 animals for the upper Ghujerab, Pamir, and Chatpert. Kiang *Equus kiang* used occasionally to visit the Shimshal Pass area from China (Schaller, 1974). There are reliable reports of a small population of 20–25 animals between the lower Baraldo and Mustagh rivers on the Pakistan side of the border (Rasul, 1988; Wegge, 1988). Snow leopard *Panthera uncia* (E) is considered to be common. There is recent indirect evidence that the park supports one of the densest snow leopard populations in Asia (Wegge, 1988). Also present are fox *Vulpes vulpes*, wolf *Canis lupus* (V), which preys on Marco Polo sheep and domestic livestock, brown bear *Ursus arctos*, considered to be threatened with extinction in Pakistan (Schaller, 1974), alpine weasel *Mustela altaica*, over 2,000 ibex *Capra ibex*, widely distributed and abundant in the park but absent from neighbouring China, brown hare *Lepus capensis*, and a variety of rodents including long-tailed marmot *Marmota caudata* (Rasool, 1981; Mallon, 1987; Wegge, 1988). There are local reports indicating that wild dog *Cuon alpinus* (V) is present (P. Wegge, pers. comm., 1989).

Mallon (1987) recorded 66 bird species from the park and adjacent area. Additional records are given by Wegge (1988) and T.J. Roberts (pers. comm., 1988). Game birds such as Himalayan snowcock *Tetraogallus himalayensis* and chukar *Alectoris chukar* are common (Rasool, 1981; Wegge, 1988).

Cultural Heritage A useful account of Hunza culture and history is given by Bamber et al. (1984). The economy has always been primarily based on subsistence-level farming. With the completion of the Karakoram Highway the degree of acculturation has been considerable. Since 1970, many people have resettled in Gilgit and men have sought employment elsewhere, some 40% spending five years or more away from the Hunza Valley, often in the army. The Aga Khan Foundation, which aims to benefit the religious and secular life of Ishmaeli muslims and the wider community, is having an increasing role in the development of the region and has essentially replaced that of the Mir who traditionally played a central part in Hunza life.

Local Human Population There are no permanent settlements, although a few shepherds move between different localities inside the park throughout the year. The nearest village is Shimshal on the park boundary, with 120 households and 1,000–1,200 people. Road maintenance gangs live more or less permanently along the Karakoram Highway, inside the park. Some 8,000 domestic stock from seven villages south of the park graze its pastures during the summer. Grazing rights in the Dih and Barakhun valleys in the north are allocated by the former Mir. In the Shimshal catchment, there are an estimated 8,000 goats, 2,000 sheep, 1,500 cattle and 500 yaks at a density of 10 animals per sq. km during the three-month summer (Wegge, 1988).

Visitors and Visitor Facilities Khunjerab Valley, accessible from the Karakoram Highway, receives more and more visitors each year, but numbers are still low. Shimshal Valley remains relatively inaccessible and receives 30–50 tourists annually. There are three economy-style lodges/hotels at Passu on the Karakoram Highway. An access road to Shimshal is under construction; when finished, this attractive mountain valley is expected to become very popular among tourists (Wegge, 1988).

Scientific Research and Facilities The wildlife was surveyed in 1974 (Schaller, 1974, 1976). Censuses of large mammal populations have been conducted on a regular basis since 1978 (Rasool, 1981). In autumn 1987 the park was included in a preliminary survey of the large mammals of northern Hunza, as part of Operation Raleigh (Mallon, 1987). Recently, in October–November 1988, Wegge (1988) assessed the status of natural resources and land use practices with a view to identifying management priorities.

Conservation Value   The park was established primarily to protect Marco Polo sheep and snow leopard, besides preserving a high mountain environs in a near undisturbed condition. It is also the only known refuge for kiang in Pakistan. With the construction of the Karakoram Highway over the Khunjerab Pass and the establishment of Taxkorgan Natural Reserve across the border in 1984, the foundation for an international peace park was laid, giving Khunjerab added conservation significance.

Conservation Management   A 12 km zone in the vicinity of Khunjerab Pass was closed for domestic stock grazing in order to protect Marco Polo sheep (Rasool, 1981). Little or no development of park infrastructure or management took place until 1988 when a Directorate of Khunjerab National Park was formed as a semi-autonomous organisation within the Forest Department of the Administration of Northern Areas (Wegge, 1988). A workshop was held in the park in 1989 to draft a managment plan; this has yet to be finalised. There are plans to develop the park, including 162 ha of reafforestation (Rasul, 1985). Wegge (1988) suggests that the park be zoned into core, protected and hunting areas, with all activities prohibited in the core zone, grazing and fuelwood collection allowed in protected zones, and controlled hunting and other activities permitted in the hunting zone. The establishment of a hunting programme, including subsistence hunting, would help compensate for restrictions on previous grazing rights. High priority actions identified by Wegge are: co-operating with Chinese authorities for the joint protection of Marco Polo sheep and kiang, controlling hunting and grazing in the 12 km protection zone by the Pass, instigating a 'no-stop' regulation for motorists travelling between Kuksil and the Pass (to reduce disturbance to Marco Polo sheep), providing adequate transport and equipment for field staff, and undertaking thorough field studies of Marco Polo sheep and kiang to assess their status and habitat requirements.

IUCN is developing a sustainable forestry project in the upper Hunza Valley as part of the Aga Khan Rural Support Programme (IUCN, 1987). In the long term, this should help to reduce the depletion of forest resources in and around the park.

Management Constraints   Some 66 km of the Karakoram Highway runs through the park. This has contributed to the decline of Marco Polo sheep, largely as a result of hunting and general disturbance. Further disturbances are anticipated now that Pakistan and China have signed an agreement to establish a trade-free zone on the Chinese side of the Khunjerab Pass. Some pastures are overgrazed, including those within the 12 km protected zone where restrictions on livestock have been violated. Illegal hunting still takes place but at insignificant levels, that of Marco Polo sheep by Pakistanis having stopped. Over-collection of fuelwood has also contributed to degradation of vegetation cover in some areas. Snow leopard accounts for a significant offtake of livestock, thought to be about 10% annually. Relatively few snow leopards are killed in retaliation because to do so is difficult and time-consuming (Wegge, 1988). The construction of a motorable road up the Shimshal Valley will have an enormous impact on the bharal population unless protection measures are adequately enforced. The presence of a permanent police quarters within the park is a source of friction, particularly as police regularly hunt ibex (T.J. Roberts, pers. comm., 1988).

Staff   The total field staff is fourteen, comprising one park ranger, six game watchers and seven chowkidars (Wegge, 1988).

Budget   Rs 0.3 million (1985)

Local Addresses
Director, Directorate of Khunjerab National Park, Gilgit   (Field staff are stationed at Dih under the charge of a field ranger)

References

Bamber, J., Bishop, K., Holmes, R., Mayers, J., and Thomas, P. (1984).   The Cambridge Karakoram Expedition 1984.   Final report.   Scott Polar Research Institute, Cambridge. Unpublished. 92 pp.

Islam, S-U and Islam, Z. (1984).   Sighting of Marco Polo sheep in Khunjerab.   *WWF-Pakistan Newsletter* 3: 11–13.

IUCN (1987).   Sustainable forestry development in the Aga Khan Rural Support Programme, Northern Areas, Pakistan.   IUCN, Gland, Switzerland.   Unpublished.   85 pp.

Mallon, D. (1987).   A survey of the large mammals of northern Hunza.   Unpublished.   8 pp.

Rasool, G. (1981).   Khunjerab National Park.   Divisional Forest Office, Gilgit.   Unpublished. 5 pp.

Rasul, G. (1985).   *National parks and equivalent reserves in northern areas of Pakistan.* Wildlife Division, Northern Areas, Forest Department, Gilgit.   36 pp.

Rasul, G. (1986).   Population status of blue sheep in Shamshal Valley.   *WWF-Pakistan Newsletter* 5: 1–2.

Rasul, G. (1988).   Tibetan wild ass—verging on extinction.   Unpublished. 4 pp. (Unseen)

Schaller, G.B. (1974).   The Marco Polo sheep in Pakistan.   New York Zoological Society, New York.   Unpublished. 5 pp.

Schaller, G.B. (1976).   Mountain mammals in Pakistan.   *Oryx* 13: 351–6.

Schaller, G.B., Li Hong Talipu, Lu Hua, Ren Junrang, Qiu Mingjiang, and Wang Haibin (1987). Status of large mammals in the Taxkorgan Reserve, Xinjiang, China.   *Biological Conservation* 42: 53–71.

Wegge, P. (1988).   Assessment of Khunjerab National Park and environs, Pakistan.   IUCN, Gland, Switzerland.   Unpublished. 25 pp.

KILIK/MINTAKA GAME RESERVE

IUCN Management Category   Unassigned

Biogeographical Province   2.38.12 (Himalayan Highlands)

Geographical Location   Lies in Hunza, Gilgit District, on the Pakistan–China border, 225 km from the town of Gilgit.   The northern boundary runs along the international border between Kilik and Mintaka passes.   Access is from Misgar Village by bridlepath. Approximately 36°56′N, 75°04′E

Date and History of Establishment   Declared a game reserve on 22 November 1975.

Area   65,036 ha

Land Tenure   State (Administration of Northern Areas)

Altitude   Ranges from 4,545 m to 6,060 m.

Physical Features   The main north–south oriented valley is forked, with the Kilik and Mintaka passes lying at the head of each branch. The terrain is rugged and mountainous. There is a variety of sedimentary, metamorphic, and igneous rocks, and a mixture of rock and mineral deposits (Rasul, 1985).

Climate   Temperatures at higher elevations remain below freezing point for most of the year. Winters are severe, and summers cold and dry. Most precipitation is in the form of snow.

Vegetation   Higher altitudes are devoid of higher plants. Lower areas contain patches of *Juniperus, Artemisia, Haloxylon, Salix* and a variety of grasses (Rasul, 1985).

Fauna   Large mammals include Marco Polo sheep *Ovis ammon polii* (I), ibex *Capra ibex*, snow leopard *Panthera uncia* (E), brown bear *Ursus arctos*, wolf *Canis lupus* (V), and fox *Vulpes vulpes* (Rasul, 1985). In 1974, only a few Marco Polo sheep from neighbouring China were reported to frequent the vicinity of Kilik Pass. At that time, ibex were the most numerous ungulate, with 59 recorded between Murkshi and Kilik Pass (Schaller, 1974). The avifauna includes a variety of game birds, such as chukar *Alectoris chukar*, snow partridge *Lerwa lerwa*, and snowcock *Tetraogallus* sp., and raptors and vultures (Rasul, 1985).

Cultural Heritage   No information

Local Human Population   In 1974, the Kilik Pass area was frequented by some 3,000 head of livestock belonging to the Mir of Hunza and people of Misgar (Schaller, 1974).

Visitors and Visitor Facilities   No information

Scientific Research and Facilities   The Kilik Pass area was surveyed by Schaller (1974) in November 1974.

Conservation Value   The reserve is particularly important as a refuge for Marco Polo sheep, in view of which it has been recommended that the reserve be included within Khunjerab National Park (P. Wegge, pers. comm., 1989).

Conservation Management   The area was first proposed as a game reserve, with provision for licensed hunting of Marco Polo sheep and ibex, in an attempt to conserve these species (Schaller, 1974). Wildlife is now afforded full protection. Local people enjoy concessions to collect firewood and to graze livestock. There is no management plan, but limited manpower is available for protecting the area (Rasul, 1985).

Management Constraints   Marco Polo sheep, in particular, and also ibex populations had dwindled by the early 1970s due to severe hunting pressures. In addition, the habitat of the former species was heavily disturbed and overgrazed by domestic livestock (Schaller, 1974).

Staff   The staff of Khunjerab National Park are responsible for the game reserve.

Budget   Included in annual budget for Khunjerab National Park (Rs 0.3 million in 1985).

Local Addresses   No information

References
Rasul, G. (1985). *National parks and equivalent reserves in northern areas of Pakistan.*
    Wildlife Division, Northern Areas, Forest Department, Gilgit. 36 pp.
Schaller, G.B. (1974). The Marco Polo sheep in Pakistan. New York Zoological Society, New
    York. Unpublished. 5 pp.

MANSHI WILDLIFE SANCTUARY

IUCN Management Category   IV   (Managed Nature Reserve)

Biogeographical Province   2.38.12   (Himalayan Highlands)

Geographical Location   Lies in Kaghan Valley on the east bank of the Kunhar River, 12
km north of Paras Village in Hazara District, North-West Frontier Province. It is close to
the border with Azad State of Jammu & Kashmir. The sanctuary is accessible via Paras along
a very poor track, which is impassable during winter snow.   34°48′N, 73°34′E

Date and History of Establishment   Declared a wildlife sanctuary in 1977. Originally
designated a reserve for a five-year period ending 1973.

Area   2,321 ha. Forms part of Manshi Reserved Forest.

Land Tenure   State (Government of North-West Frontier Province)

Altitude   Exceeds 4,000 m.

Physical Features   The Kaghan Valley, through which flows the Kunhar River, is steep-sided
and aligned north–south. Surrounding ridges form a natural amphitheatre, opening to the
south and broken only in the north-west where a side valley leads up to Mt.
Musa-ka-Mussallah.

Climate   No information

Vegetation   Lower Kaghan Valley is characterised by Himalayan moist temperate forest,
with oak *Quercus dilatata*, sycamore *Acer caesium*, poplar *Populus ciliata*, yew *Taxus baccata*,
and walnut *Juglans nigra* predominant, and some scattered blue pine *Pinus wallichiana*, cedar
Cedrus deodara, spruce *Picea smithiana*, and silver fir *Abies alba*. This vegetation type is
replaced by dry temperate coniferous forest in the upper reaches, where blue pine forest is
interspersed with cedar, spruce, and silver fir. Above 2,500 m are alpine meadows, with a
rich herbaceous flora, including an abundance of peony *Paeonia* sp. (Wayre, 1971; Roberts,
1977).

Fauna   The mammals have not been surveyed, but are known to include common langur
Presbytis entellus and Royle's pika *Ochotona roylei* (Wayre, 1971). Himalayan black bear
Selenarctos thibetanus, Himalayan musk deer *Moschus chrysogaster* (V), and occasionally

leopard *Panthera pardus* (T) are also present (M.M. Malik, pers. comm., 1987). The avifauna is rich in species. There is prime habitat for koklass pheasant *Pucrasia macrolopha* and monal pheasant *Lophophorus impejanus*, both of which are numerous (Wayre, 1971; T.J. Roberts, pers. comm., 1986). The sanctuary is one of the few known breeding locations in Pakistan for white-bellied redstart *Hodgsonius phoenicuroides*. Long-legged buzzard *Buteo rufinus* and lammergeier *Gypaetus barbatus* also breed here (T.J. Roberts, pers. comm., 1986). Five species of fish occur in Kaghan Valley but their distribution within the sanctuary is not specified (Mirza and Hussain, 1985).

Cultural Heritage   No information

Local Human Population   There are no permanent settlements within the sanctuary but Gujars live lower down in the valley. These graziers spend the summer (June–July) in the sanctuary with their cattle, buffalo, goats, and sheep (Wayre, 1971).

Visitors and Visitor Facilities   There is a Forest Department rest house and youth hostel at Sharan.

Scientific Research and Facilities   Parts of Manshi Forest Reserve were surveyed for pheasants in 1971 (Wayre, 1971).

Conservation Value   This part of Manshi Forest Reserve was recommended as being the most suitable area in Kaghan Valley for protecting high-altitude pheasants. The relative inaccessibility of the valley, coupled with the presence of snow during winter facilitates protection of the sanctuary.

Conservation Management   No information

Management Constraints   The lower reaches of Kaghan Valley are the site of a West German-funded project to produce virus-free seed potatoes. A large area of forest has been cleared within the forest reserve and camps established for imported local labour, all of which are jeopardising the integrity of the sanctuary (T.J. Roberts, pers. comm., 1986). Grazing by domestic livestock is not controlled.

Staff   No information

Budget   No information

Local Addresses   Range Officer, Balakot Range, NWFP Forest Department

References
Mirza, M.R. and Hussain, S. (1985). A note on the fish fauna of Kaghan Valley, Pakistan, with the record of *Schistura nalbanti*. *Pakistan Journal of Zoology* 17: 101.
Roberts, T.J. (1977). *The Mammals of Pakistan*. Ernest Benn, London. Pp. 6–7.
Wayre, P. (1971). Pheasant conservation in Pakistan. WWF Project no. 1563. Pp. 17–21.

MARGALLA HILLS NATIONAL PARK

IUCN Management Category V (Protected Landscape)

Biogeographical Province 4.08.04 (Indus-Ganges Monsoon Forest)

Geographical Location Comprises the hill ranges immediately to the north of the Federal Capital of Islamabad. 33°48′N, 73°10′E

Date and History of Establishment Declared a national park on 27 April 1980 under Section 21(1) of the Islamabad Wildlife (Protection, Conservation and Management) Ordinance 1979. Prior to 1960 much of the area was reserved forest. Subsequently, it was declared a wildlife sanctuary under the West Pakistan Wildlife Protection Ordinance 1959.

Area 17,386 ha. The park comprises compartments 2–5, 7–23, 28, 30–8(i) and 41(ii) of Margalla Forest Reserve, compartments 1–25 of the Military Grass Farm and various other lands making a total area of 14,786 ha, together with Rawal Lake and a surrounding buffer area of 2 km from the high water mark. Rawal Lake is not contiguous with the rest of the park, the intervening area constituting part of Islamabad Game Reserve (69,800 ha).

Land Tenure State (Federal Government). The land transferred to the Capital Development Authority in 1961, when Islamabad was declared the capital of Pakistan, includes 4,794 ha of reserved forest, 3,315 ha managed by the Military Farm Authorities, and 3,636 ha under private ownership (Masud, 1979).

Altitude Ranges between 456 m and 1,580 m.

Physical Features The topography is rugged, with numerous valleys and many steep and even precipitous slopes. The area is drained by the River Kurang and its tributaries, which flow into the River Soan. Rocks are Jurassic and Triassic in age, limestone being characteristic of the Margalla Range (though shales, clays, and sandstones are also present). Soils are dark, with a high mineral content, and are capable of supporting good tree growth despite being shallow.

Climate Lying in the monsoon belt, the area experiences two rainy seasons. Winter rains last from January until March and summer rains from July until September. Based on climatic data from Rawalpindi for 1951 to 1965, mean annual rainfall is 951 mm and mean monthly maximum and minimum temperatures range from 16.9 °C to 40.1 °C and from 3.1 °C to 24.7 °C, respectively (Masud, 1979).

Vegetation The two distinct types of vegetation are subtropical dry semi-evergreen forest and subtropical pine forest. The former is dominated by phulai *Acacia modesta* and kao *Olea ferruginea*, associated with sanatha *Dodonaea viscosa*, granda *Carissa spinarum*, and ber *Zizyphus jujuba*, and having an undergrowth of bhekar *Justicia adhatoda*, gunger *Sageratia thea*, mullah *Zizyphus nummularia*, and khokhal *Myrsine africana*. About 50 species of grass are present, the most common being dhauloo *Chrysopogon serrulatus*, palwan *Bothrichloa* *pertusa*, survala *Heteropogon contortus*, maniara *Pennisetum orientale*, and loonder *Themeda anthera*. Introduced ornamental tree species include: silver oak *Grevillea robusta*, gulenishtar *Erythrina suberosa*, jacaranda *Jacaranda mimosoefolia*, bottle brush *Callistemon viminalis*, sakar *Ehretia laevis*, chir pine *Pinus roxburghii*, *Cassia glauca*, *Porgania glabra*, and *Eucalyptus* sp. Subtropical pine forest occurs above 1,000 m, chir pine *Pinus roxburghii* being the characteristic canopy species with an undergrowth of *Myrsine africana*, *Woodfordia fruticosa*, *Berberis lycium*, and granda *Carissa spinarum*. Forests are well-stocked on cooler aspects but those on the hotter southern slopes with poor soils are sparse and mixed with scrub.

Fauna Margalla Hills are unique in Pakistan, being rich in Sino-himalayan fauna, some species (especially birds) of which are at the western extremity of their distribution. Larger mammals are known to include rhesus macaque *Macaca mulatta*, leopard *Panthera pardus* (T), wild boar *Sus scrofa*, Indian muntjac *Muntiacus muntjak*, and goral *Nemorhaedus goral*. Noteworthy birds include white-eyed buzzard *Butastur teesa*, lannar falcon *Falco biarmicus*, black-shouldered kite *Elanus caeruleus*, kalij pheasant *Lophura leucomelana*, black partridge *Francolinus francolinus*, sirkeer cuckoo *Taccocua leschenaultii*, jungle nightjar *Caprimulgus indicus*, long-tailed nightjar *C. macrurus*, lesser golden-backed woodpecker *Dinopium benghalense*, and lanceolated jay *Garrulus lanceolatus*. A list of mammals and birds believed to be found in the park is given in the master plan (Masud, 1979). Further details of the avifauna can be found in Corfield (1983).

Cheer pheasant *Catreus wallichii* (E), reared at Dhok Jewan and Jabri, are being released into the park. The reintroduction programme is being carried out by the World Pheasant Association in collaboration with the Capital Development Authority (Howman, 1985; Anon., 1987).

Cultural Heritage There are a number of historical and religious sites but their importance needs to be evaluated. Shah Faisal Mosque lies outside the southern boundary of the park.

Local Human Population Shadarah is the only village remaining in the park; it is due to be relocated. Formerly, there were over a dozen villages inside the park, and the residents of Phulgran retained traditional rights to graze cattle in compartments 1 and 6 of Margalla Reserved Forest (Masud, 1979).

Visitors and Visitor Facilities Large numbers of residents from Islamabad and Rawalpindi, as well as foreigners, visit the park due to its proximity to the capital. There is a small zoo near the park entrance which will eventually be transferred to Islamabad Zoo and located in Islamabad Game Reserve. A visitor centre is planned for Daman-E-Koh, providing lounge accommodation and an information service. Lodges, camping grounds and picnic sites are also planned and the provision of a chair lift may be considered.

Scientific Research and Facilities The wildlife was surveyed in December 1977 by WWF in collaboration with the National Council for Conservation of Wildlife. The avifauna is well-documented (Corfield, 1983).

Conservation Value In its report of 1971, the Wildlife Enquiry Committee recommended that the park should be established in the interests of the people of Islamabad. It is also an extremely important watershed for the capital. With regard to its fauna, Margalla Hills is one of the richest areas for birds in Pakistan.

Conservation Management   Margalla Hills has been managed by the Capital Development Authority since 1961 when it was declared a 'green' area. Reserved forests, *rakhs* (military grass farms) and *chaks* (private holdings) have since been taken over by the Authority. Much of the original forest has been removed, even prior to the transferral of the forests to the Forest Department in the late 19th century (Elahi, 1970), but is gradually reverting to its original condition under the present management regime. The loss of grass habitat on southern slopes (former *rakhs*) is likely to be associated with the disappearance of cheer pheasant and the difficulties experienced in trying to reintroduce it (Young, 1986).

The objectives outlined in the master plan include restoring the vegetation and wildlife to its previous condition, stopping erosion, conserving the water supply and meeting the increased demand for outdoor recreation through the development of proper visitor facilities (Masud, 1979). A system of zonation, based on areas of varying intensities of visitor use, has been proposed to facilitate management. This includes a 3,100 ha enclosure for captive breeding and reintroduction purposes, and wilderness areas (comprising 70% of the park area) in which development is permitted. It is proposed that the park be surrounded by a buffer zone of 8 km, in which shooting is to be prohibited. An enclosure, with a 14 km perimeter, is due to be sited in Dhoke Jewari Valley, as part of a plan to reintroduce muntjac and goral to the park.

Management Constraints   Being adjacent to Islamabad, the park is subject to very high levels of use by visitors. Illegal grazing and collection of fuelwood are persistent problems. The large-scale planting of ornamental trees by the Horticultural Directorate detracts from the integrity of the area (Masud, 1979).

Staff   One deputy director, one assistant director, one veterinary officer, six range officers, eleven foresters, forty-three forest guards, approximately sixty permanent labourers, and an additional one hundred and twenty casual labourers in April–June for fire-control work (1986).

Budget   Recurrent expenditure (including upkeep of the zoo) of Rs 4.7 million is met by the Capital Development Authority; capital expenditure of Rs 2 million for the reintroduction of goral, chinkara, cheer pheasant, and development of public amenities is met by this Authority and the National Council for Conservation of Wildlife in equal proportions (1986).

Local Addresses
Deputy Director, Margalla Hills National Park, Capital Development Authority, Sitara Market, Islamabad

References
Anon. (1987). Summary of radio tracking of cheer pheasants in the Margalla Hills, Pakistan. *World Pheasant Association News* 15: 16–17, 20–1.

Corfield, D.M. (1983). *Birds of Islamabad, Pakistan and the Muree Hills*. Asian Study Group, Islamabad.

Elahi, M. (1970). *Working plan for the scrub forest of Rawalpindi District: 1966–67 to 1975–76*. Government Printing Press, Lahore. (Unseen)

Howman, K.C.R. (1985). Cheer pheasant release project Margallah Hills, Pakistan. Review of cheer pheasant reintroduction programme in Margallah Hills, Islamabad, Pakistan. *World Pheasant Association News* 7: 8–10.

Masud, R.M. (1979). Master plan for Margalla Hills National Park, Islamabad, Pakistan 1979 to 1984. National Council for Conservation of Wildlife, Islamabad. 48 pp.

Roberts, T. (1984). Pakistan's wildlife today. *World Wildlife Fund Monthly Report*. January.
Young, L. (1986). Forest history of the Margalla Hills. Draft. Unpublished. 3 pp.

NALTAR WILDLIFE SANCTUARY

IUCN Management Category IV (Managed Nature Reserve)

Biogeographical Province 2.38.12 (Himalayan Highlands)

Geographical Location Lies close to Hunza Valley in northern Pakistan, 45 km from the town of Gilgit. Approximately 36°07′N, 74°14′E

Date and History of Establishment Declared a wildlife sanctuary on 22 November 1975.

Area 27,206 ha. Contiguous to Sher Qillah Game Reserve (16,842 ha) and Pakora Game Reserve (7,515 ha).

Land Tenure State (Administration of Northern Areas)

Altitude Ranges from 1,972 m to 5,926 m at Shanni Glacier.

Physical Features Naltar Valley lies at about 3,000 m and is aligned in a north-west to south-east direction, with mountains on either side rising to about 5,800 m (Winser and Winser, 1985). This fluvio-glacial valley follows the southern limbs of the Kailas Range for about 24 km until its confluence with the Hunza River. The profile of the upper portion is glacial and typically U-shaped, while that of the lower portion is V-shaped due to river erosion. The meta-sedimentary and sedimentary sequence includes slates, quartzites, limestone, and gneiss of pre-Carboniferous age. There are green stone, granodiorite, and horn-blended granite intrusions. Igneous rocks are post Permo-Carboniferous in age. Late Cretaceous sediments overlay the green stone complex in Yasin Valley. The upper reaches of the Naltar River freeze during winter (Rasul, 1985).

Climate Annual rainfall ranges from 254 mm to 381mm. Winter is severe (Rasul, 1985).

Vegetation The area falls within the dry temperate zone, but because of high rainfall supports luxuriant forests and ground cover (Rasul, 1985). Trees and shrubs include species of *Pistacia*, *Olea*, *Fraxinus*, *Sageratia*, *Eurotia*, *Juniperus*, *Picea*, *Betula*, *Salix*, and *Populus*. Herbs include *Artemisia*, *Stipa* and *Haloxylon*.

Fauna Large mammals include markhor *Capra falconeri* (V), ibex *C. ibex*, snow leopard *Panthera uncia* (E), brown bear *Ursus arctos*, fox *Vulpes vulpes*, wolf *Canis lupus* (V), stone marten *Martes foina*, and leopard cat *Felis bengalensis* (Rasul, 1985). Some 35 species of birds have been recorded (N. MacCallum, pers. comm.).

Cultural Heritage No information

Local Human Population   There are a number of settlements in Naltar Valley, those higher up being used only in summer (Winser and Winser, 1985).

Visitors and Visitor Facilities   No information

Scientific Research and Facilities   An expedition from Aberdeen University carried out ecological studies on the pika *Ochotona roylei* and choughs *Pyrrhocorax* spp., and made collections of mosses, spiders, and pseudo-scorpions (Winser and Winser, 1985).

Conservation Value   Naltar is part of a protected areas complex which is important for a variety of threatened mammal species.

Conservation Management   Wildlife is given complete protection. People residing within an 8 km radius of the sanctuary enjoy concessions to extract timber and firewood, graze livestock and cut grass. A conservation management plan and plan for the establishment of a mini-zoo are being prepared (Rasul, 1985).

Management Constraints   Include shortage of manpower, poaching and agricultural encroachment (Rasul, 1985).

Staff   One game watcher (1985)

Budget   Rs 10,000 p.a. (1985)

Local Addresses   No information

References
Rasul, G. (1985). *National parks and equivalent reserves in northern areas of Pakistan*. Wildlife Division, Northern Areas, Forest Department, Gilgit. 36 pp.
Winser, N. and Winser, S. (Eds.) (1985). *Expedition Yearbook 1984*. Expedition Advisory Centre, London. Pp. 111–12.

NAR/GHORO NALLAH GAME RESERVE

IUCN Management Category   Unassigned

Biogeographical Province   2.38.12 (Himalayan Highlands)

Geographical Location   Lies in Baltistan District, about 26 km by road from the town of Skardu. Approximately 35°06′N, 75°12′E

Date and History of Establishment   Declared a game reserve on 22 November 1975.

Area   7,255 ha

Land Tenure   State (Administration of Northern Areas)

Altitude   Ranges from 2,424 m to 4,242 m.

Physical Features   The terrain is rugged and precipitous. Stream deposits of alluvium and gravel cover valley bottoms. Sedimentary, meta-sedimentary, and igneous rocks are present (Rasul, 1985).

Climate   Conditions are dry temperate. Annual precipitation is 76–102 mm, with most falling as snow. Winters are severe and summers mild (Rasul, 1985).

Vegetation   Trees and shrubs include *Juniperus*, *Betula*, *Salix*, and *Fraxinus*. Ground flora consists of *Artemisia* and various grass species (Rasul, 1985).

Fauna   Large mammals include ibex *Capra ibex*, musk deer *Moschus chrysogaster* (V), and snow leopard *Panthera uncia* (E). The larger birds include chukar *Alectoris chukar*, snow partridge *Lerwa lerwa*, snowcock *Tetraogallus* sp., and various raptor species (Rasul, 1985).

Cultural Heritage   No information

Local Human Population   No information

Visitors and Visitor Facilities   No information

Scientific Research and Facilities   None

Conservation Value   No information

Conservation Management   Wildlife is afforded full protection and the reserve is closed to hunting. Local people enjoy concessions to collect firewood, graze livestock, and cut grass.

Management Constraints   Include shortage of staff and poaching.

Staff   One game watcher (1985)

Budget   Rs 10,000 p.a. (1985)

Local Addresses   No information

References
Rasul, G. (1985). *National parks and equivalent reserves in northern areas of Pakistan.* Wildlife Division, Northern Areas, Forest Department, Gilgit. 36 pp.

NAZBAR NALLAH GAME RESERVE

IUCN Management Category   Unassigned

Biogeographical Province   2.38.12 (Himalayan Highlands)

Geographical Location   Lies in Yasin Tehsil of Gilgit District, 137 km by bridle path from Gilgit Town. Approximately 36°22′N, 73°19′E

Date and History of Establishment   Declared a game reserve on 22 November 1975.

Area   33,177 ha. The reserve is contiguous to Chassi/Baushdar Game Reserve (37,053 ha).

Land Tenure   State (Administration of Northern Areas)

Altitude   Ranges from 2,039 m to 5,212 m.

Physical Features   The Nazbar catchment area includes numerous side nullahs with rugged, undulating topography.

Climate   The climate is dry, with an annual precipitation of 127 –254 mm, most of which falls as snow. Winters are severe and summers mild (Rasul, 1985).

Vegetation   Trees include *Juniperus* (sporadic and stunted), *Salix*, *Rosa*, *Fraxinus*, and *Populus*. Ground flora includes *Artemisia*, *Stipa*, and other grasses.

Fauna   Large mammals include ibex *Capra ibex*, snow leopard *Panthera uncia* (E), lynx *Felis lynx*, and fox *Vulpes vulpes*. Larger birds include chukar *Alectoris chukar*, snow partridge *Lerwa lerwa*, snowcock *Tetraogallus* sp., and various raptors and vultures (Rasul, 1985).

Cultural Heritage   No information

Local Human Population   Local inhabitants cultivate in the lower part of the reserve and graze livestock in the upper part (Rasul, 1985).

Visitors and Visitor Facilities   No information

Scientific Research and Facilities   None

Conservation Value   No information

Conservation Management   Wildlife is afforded full protection. Local inhabitants enjoy concessions to extract firewood and timber for domestic use, to graze livestock, and to cut grass. There is no management plan (Rasul, 1985).

Management Constraints   Include shortage of staff and poaching.

Staff   One game watcher (1985)

Budget   Rs 10,000 p.a. (1985)

Local Addresses   No information

References
Rasul, G. (1985). *National parks and equivalent reserves in northern areas of Pakistan.* Wildlife Division, Northern Areas, Forest Department, Gilgit. 36 pp.

PAKORA GAME RESERVE

IUCN Management Category   Unassigned

Biogeographical Province   2.38.12   (Himalayan Highlands)

Geographical Location   Lies in Gilgit District, 97 km by road from the town of Gilgit. The reserve is located in Ishkuman, 47 km from Gakuch Punial. Approximately 36°24′N, 73°53′E

Date and History of Establishment   Declared a game reserve on 22 November 1975.

Area   7,515 ha. The reserve is contiguous to Naltar Wildlife Sanctuary (27,206 ha).

Land Tenure   State (Administration of Northern Areas)

Altitude   Ranges from 2,333 m to 4,848 m.

Physical Features   Pakora Nullah is very narrow at its mouth, which is flanked by steep slopes. Higher up it opens out, giving way to gentle slopes. Schist, quartzite, and limestone are present in sedimentary, meta-sedimentary, and igneous rocks (Rasul, 1985).

Climate   Conditions are dry temperate. Annual precipitation ranges from 127–254 mm, most of which is in the form of snow. Winters are severe and summers cool (Rasul, 1985).

Vegetation   Trees and shrubs include *Juniperus*, *Fraxinus*, *Olea*, and *Rosa*, *Artemisia*, *Stipa*, and other grasses are present (Rasul, 1985).

Fauna   Large mammals include ibex *Capra ibex*, snow leopard *Panthera uncia* (E), wolf *Canis lupus* (V), and fox *Vulpes vulpes*. Larger birds include chukar *Alectoris chukar*, snow partridge *Lerwa lerwa*, snowcock *Tetraogallus* sp., and various raptors and vultures (Rasul, 1985).

Cultural Heritage   No information

Local Human Population   No information

Visitors and Visitor Facilities   No information

Scientific Research and Facilities   None

Conservation Value   The reserve is part of a protected areas complex which is important for a variety of threatened mammal species.

428

Conservation Management   Wildlife is afforded full protection.   Local inhabitants enjoy concessions to extract firewood and timber and to graze livestock,.   The reserve is completely closed for hunting.   No management plan exists.

Management Constraints   Include shortage of manpower and poaching.

Staff   One game watcher (1985)

Budget   Rs 10,000 p.a. (1985)

Local Addresses   No information

References
Rasul, G. (1985). *National parks and equivalent reserves in northern areas of Pakistan.* Wildlife Division, Northern Areas, Forest Department, Gilgit. 36 pp.

SATPARA WILDLIFE SANCTUARY

IUCN Management Category   IV (Managed Nature Reserve)

Biogeographical Province   2.38.12 (Himalayan Highlands)

Geographical Location   Lies in Baltistan District, 3 km from the town of Skardu. Approximately 35°12'N, 75°07'E

Date and History of Establishment   Declared a wildlife sanctuary on 22 November 1975.

Area   31,093ha

Land Tenure   State (Administration of Northern Areas)

Altitude   Ranges from 2,691 m to 4,242 m.

Physical Features   The site consists of the catchment area of Satpara Nullah and lake, and borders on the Deosai Plains.   The terrain is rugged with scree slopes.   Sedimentary and meta-sedimentary rocks with schist and quartzite, as well as various types of igneous rocks, are found in the area.   Stream deposits of alluvium and gravel occur in valley bottoms (Rasul, 1985).

Climate   Conditions are dry temperate.   Annual precipitation is 76–102 mm, most of which falls as snow in December and January.   Winters are dry and severe, while summers are mild (Rasul, 1985).

Vegetation   Comprises stunted juniper *Juniperus*, birch *Betula* and *Rosa* (Rasul, 1985).

Fauna Large mammals include ibex *Capra ibex*, musk deer *Moschus chrysogaster* (V), and urial *Ovis vignei*. Larger birds include chukar *Alectoris chukar*, snowcock *Tetraogallus* sp., and a variety of raptors and vultures.

Cultural Heritage No information

Local Human Population No information

Visitors and Visitor Facilities No information

Scientific Research and Facilities None

Conservation Value The site was originally proposed as part of a much larger national park, on account of its spectacular scenery and large mammal populations (Mountfort and Poore, 1968).

Conservation Management Wildlife is afforded full protection. Local people enjoy concessions to collect fallen dead wood for fuel and graze livestock. No management plan exists for the area (Rasul, 1985).

Management Constraints Include a shortage of manpower.

Staff One game watcher under the control of a Forest Range Officer (1985).

Budget Rs 10,000 p.a. (1985)

Local Addresses Forest Range Officer, Wildlife Headquarters, Skardu

References
Rasul, G. (1985). *National parks and equivalent reserves in northern areas of Pakistan.* Wildlife Division, Northern Areas, Forest Department, Gilgit. 36 pp.
Mountfort, G. and Poore, D. (1968). Report on the Second World Wildlife Fund Expedition to Pakistan. World Wildlife Fund, Morges, Switzerland. Unpublished. 25 pp.

SHER QILLAH GAME RESERVE

IUCN Management Category Unassigned

Biogeographical Province 2.38.12 (Himalayan Highlands)

Geographical Location Lies in Ghizer Forest Division, about 48 km from the town of Gilgit. Approximately 36°24'N, 73°53'E

Date and History of Establishment Declared a game reserve on 22 November 1975.

Area 16,842 ha. The reserve is contiguous to Nalter Wildlife Sanctuary (27,206 ha).

Land Tenure   State (Administration of Northern Areas)

Altitude   Ranges from 1,983 m to 5,818 m.

Physical Features   The terrain is rugged and mountainous. Sedimentary, meta-sedimentary, and a sequence of quartzite, slate, and limestone rocks are present, all with intrusions of granodiorite and horn-blended granite of Tertiary age (Rasul, 1985).

Climate   Conditions are dry temperate. Annual precipitation varies from 254 mm to 381 mm, most of which falls as snow during the severe winter.

Vegetation   Trees and shrubs include kail, *Picea*, *Juniperus*, *Betula*, *Salix*, *Fraxinus*, and *Olea*. Herbs include *Haloxylon*, *Artemisia*, and *Stipa* (Rasul, 1985).

Fauna   Large mammals include markhor *Capra falconeri* (V), ibex *C. ibex*, snow leopard *Panthera uncia* (E), brown bear *Ursus arctos*, lynx *Felis lynx*, and fox *Vulpes vulpes*. Larger birds include chukar *Alectoris chukar*, snow partridge *Lerwa lerwa*, snowcock *Tetraogallus* sp., and a variety of raptors and vultures (Rasul, 1985).

Cultural Heritage   No information

Local Human Population   No information

Visitors and Visitor Facilities   No information

Scientific Research and Facilities   None

Conservation Value   The reserve falls within a protected areas complex which is important for a variety of threatened mammal species.

Conservation Management   Wildlife is afforded complete protection and the area is closed to hunting. Local people enjoy concessions to collect firewood and timber for domestic use and for livestock grazing. No management plan exists at present.

Management Constraints   Include shortage of manpower and poaching.

Staff   One game watcher (1985)

Budget   Rs 10,000 p.a. (1985)

Local Addresses   No information

References
Rasul, G. (1985). *National parks and equivalent reserves in northern areas of Pakistan.* Wildlife Division, Northern Areas, Forest Department, Gilgit. 36 pp.

TANGIR GAME RESERVE

IUCN Management Category   Unassigned

Biogeographical Province   2.38.12   (Himalayan Highlands)

Geographical Location   Lies in Diamer District on the boundary with Swat, some 113 km and 274 km from the towns of Chilas and Gilgit, respectively. It is accessible only by foot. Approximately 35°36′N, 73°24′E

Date and History of Establishment   Declared a game reserve on 22 November 1975.

Area   14,251 ha

Land Tenure   State (Administration of Northern Areas). Some land is privately owned.

Altitude   Ranges from 1,515 m to 4,545 m.

Physical Features   Terrain is mostly mountainous with rugged, steep slopes. Rocks are igneous, sedimentary and meta-sedimentary, with schist, quartzite, and limestone deposits.

Climate   Annual rainfall ranges from 254 mm to 381mm. Snow falls during the severe winter months of November and December, and light showers are characteristic of the summer monsoon season. Summers are mild (Rasul, 1985).

Vegetation   Trees and shrubs include *Olea*, *Quercus*, *Pistacia*, *Lonicera*, *Salix*, *Betula*, *Juniperus*, *Pinus gerardiana*, *Cedrus deodara*, and *Rosa*. Ground flora comprises *Ferula*, *Artemisia*, *Stipa*, and other herbs.

Fauna   Large mammals include markhor *Capra falconeri* (V), snow leopard *Panthera uncia* (E), Himalayan black bear *Selenarctos thibetanus*, fox *Vulpes vulpes*, wolf *Canis lupus* (V), and lynx *Felis lynx*. Of the avifauna, there are a variety of pheasants, including chukar *Alectoris chukar*, snow partridge *Lerwa lerwa*, snowcock *Tetraogallus* sp., and monal pheasant *Lophophorus impejanus* (Rasul, 1985).

Cultural Heritage   No information

Local Human Population   No information

Visitors and Visitor Facilities   No information

Scientific Research and Facilities   None

Conservation Value   The reserve supports a variety of threatened mammal species.

Conservation Management Wildlife is afforded full protection. Hunting is banned. Local inhabitants enjoy concessions to graze livestock, cut grass, and to collect firewood and timber for domestic use. There is no management plan (Rasul, 1985).

Management Constraints Include shortage of staff and poaching.

Staff One game watcher (1985)

Budget Rs 10,000 p.a. (1985)

Local Addresses No information

References
Rasul, G. (1985). *National parks and equivalent reserves in northern areas of Pakistan.* Wildlife Division, Northern Areas, Forest Department, Gilgit. 36 pp.

THANADARWALA GAME RESERVE

IUCN Management Category Unassigned

Biogeographical Province 4.08.04 (Indus-Ganges Monsoon Forest)

Geographical Location Lies at the junction of Gambilla and Kurram rivers, 15 km east of Lakki in Bannu District. 32°37′N, 71°05′E

Date and History of Establishment Thanadarwala was declared a game reserve in 1976, and subsequently designated a Wetland of International Importance at the time of Pakistan's ratification of the Ramsar Convention on 23 July 1976.

Area 4,047 ha

Land Tenure The wetland is under communal ownership; surrounding areas are owned by local villagers

Altitude 303 m

Physical Features Thanadarwala comprises a shallow, fresh to brackish seepage lagoon and an extensive marshy area. The depth of water fluctuates from 0.1 m to 1.5 m according to the supply of flood water from the two rivers, their levels rising in March and again in July–September. The pH value is 9.0. Surrounding areas are mostly saline.

Climate Conditions are dry subtropical, with a mean annual rainfall of 250 mm. Temperatures range from 4 °C to 18 °C in winter, and from 25 °C to 47 °C in summer.

Vegetation The marsh vegetation includes *Tamarix dioica*, *Typha angustata*, *Phragmites karka*, *Cyperus laevigatus*, *Kochia indica*, *Desmostachya bipinnata*, *Imperata cylindrica*, and species of *Chara*, *Launaea*, *Phoenix*, *Potamogeton*, *Ranunculus*, and *Saccharum*. Much of the surrounding area is cultivated for wheat and other crops. The natural vegetation of the region is tropical thorn forest, with dominant species including *Prosopis cineraria*, *Tamarix aphylla*, *Zizyphus nummularia*, *Calligonum polygonoides*, *Rhazya stricta*, *Aerua javanica*, *Chenopodium album*, *Cassia obovata*, *Heliotropium* sp., *Tribulus terrestris*, *Asphodelus tenuifolius*, *Cenchrus ciliaris*, and *Dactyloctaenium scindicum*.

Fauna The reserve is a wintering area for great egret *Egretta alba* and Anatidae, notably shelduck *Tadorna ferruginea*, teal *Anas crecca*, mallard *A. platyrhynchos*, shoveler *A. clypeata*, pochard *Aythya ferina*, and ferruginous duck *A. nyroca*. Waterfowl recorded during the mid-January censuses in 1987 and 1988 included up to 600 shorebirds of eight species and small numbers of three species of Ardeidae, white stork *Ciconia ciconia*, three species of Anatidae, and purple swamphen *Porphyrio porphyrio*. Other fauna includes agamid *Uromastix* sp. and common monitor *Varanus bengalensis*.

Cultural Heritage No information

Local Human Population Activities include the cutting of *Typha* and *Saccharum* for a local cottage industry, and the hunting (shooting and trapping) of waterfowl. Surrounding areas are cultivated and grazed by livestock.

Visitors and Visitor Facilities No information

Scientific Research and Facilities Mid-winter waterfowl counts were carried out by the Pakistan Forest Institute in 1979–81, and have been undertaken annually since then by the Zoological Survey Department.

Conservation Value Thanadarwala is important for waterfowl and under proper management could become important for fish conservation.

Conservation Management Information about the management of the property is not available. Proposals have been made for the reclamation of saline soils for agriculture, and for the afforestation of saline and water-logged areas. There are also plans for a watershed management project to control erosion and reduce siltation.

Management Constraints Include hunting, cutting of aquatic vegetation, and excessive grazing by domestic livestock (goats, sheep, cattle, and camels). Salinity levels are increasing, and there is a possibility that the wetland will be drained if public pressure for the reclamation of land continues to increase.

Staff No information

Budget No information

Local Addresses No information

References Information is taken directly from:
Scott, D.A. (Ed.) (1989). *A directory of Asian wetlands*. IUCN, Gland, Switzerland and Cambridge, UK. 1,181 pp.

UNION OF SOVIET SOCIALIST REPUBLICS

Area 22,402,200 sq. km

Population 288,595,000 (1990)   Natural increase 1.0% per annum

GNP US $ 8,375 per capita (1988)

Policy and Legislation Several articles in the 1977 Constitution of the USSR reflect the growing prominence given to environmental protéction. Under Article 18 it is a primary duty of the State to protect and make scientific use, of natural resources, and to ensure air and water quality, while under Article 67 all Soviet citizens are obliged to protect nature and to conserve its riches. This is augmented by the 1985 Decree on the enforcement of nature conservation laws and the rational use of natural resources. A draft law to update and encompass all forms of environmental protection was prepared and submitted to the Council of Ministers in 1989 (Anon., 1988). The draft Treaty on the Union of Soviet Sovereign Republics (USSR) is now under discussion and may have a bearing on the administration of environmental protection (Dobrynina, pers. comm., 1991).

Legislation relevant to the protection of areas appeared in Imperial Russia during the 1880s in the form of hunting, land use, and forestry regulations (Karpowicz, 1988), followed by the first conservation measures in 1909. The first legislation of an environmental nature, however, was adopted as early as the 11th–12th centuries: the core of the Beloveshskaya Pushia was set aside in the 13th century and forests along the southern boundaries of the Russian state were granted protection in the 14th–17th centuries (Dobrynina, pers. comm., 1991). Protected areas legislation appeared in 1921 in the form of a decree of the Council of People's Commissioners entitled 'Protection of Natural Monuments, Gardens and Parks' and signed by V.I. Lenin. In 1957 a series of acts addressing conservation was passed in the wake of the Conservation of Nature Act in Estonia. This was followed in 1968 by the Principles of Land Legislation of the USSR and Union Republics. In 1972 a decree was passed by the Central Committee of the Communist Party of the Soviet Union and the USSR Council of Ministers to strengthen nature conservation and improve the use of natural resources. This led to the current Law on Wildlife Protection and Use which is based on the State regulations of 25 June 1980 (coming into force on 1 January 1981). This law includes regulations on protected natural areas and measures to ensure wildlife protection (Articles 21–6) approved by the State Planning Committee and the State Science and Technological Committee of the USSR Council of Ministers (Kolbasov, 1981; Karpowicz, 1988). In 1985 the decree of the USSR Supreme Soviet covered nature conservation legislation and rational use of natural resources.

The legislative status of state nature reserves (*zapovednik*) is based on Article 21 (Section 6 on creating preserves and reserves) and Article 25 (on protection of animals in preserves, reserves, and other protected areas) of the 1981 Law on Wildlife Protection and Use, following the earlier two acts of the Supreme Soviet: Principles of Land Legislation of the USSR and Union Republics (adopted on 13 December 1968), and Principles of Water Legislation of the USSR and Union Republics (adopted on 10 December 1970). Under the Principles of Land Legislation, any activity disturbing natural ecosystems within state nature reserves, or threatening the conservation of natural objects of special scientific or cultural value is prohibited both within state nature reserves and their surrounding protected zones. The state regulations entitled The Status of State Nature Reserves enacted by the Council of Ministers of the USSR on 27 November 1951, together with the relevant regulations of the Republics, has been revised in the 1981 Act.

There are approximately 60 different categories of protected area which provide for nature conservation to varying extents. The six main categories of nature conservation areas, represented both at national and republic levels are: state nature reserve (*Zapovednik*), national park (*Natsional'nyi park*), nature sanctuary or partial reserve (*Zakaznik*), national hunting reserve (*Zapovedno-okhotnich'ye khozyastvo*) and nature reserve or natural monument (*Natsional'nyi pamyatnik*). The principal category, and the most rigorously protected, is the state nature reserve. In addition, there are protected seashore areas, sea islands, and sea shelves, set up to protect the environment, conserve gene pools, and to provide for the restoration of resources, recreation, and education. State forests and forest reserves protect watersheds, provide windbelts, and control erosion. There are also green zones and forest parks which tend to be protected green belts around cities and health resorts. They have limited nature conservation value, usually being managed landscapes with a high recreation priority (Borodin et al., 1984).

International Activities   In a *Pravda* article entitled 'The Reality and Guarantee of a Safe World', the President, Mikhail Gorbachov identified the need to develop a global strategy for environmental protection and rational use of natural resources. This highlights present policy within the Soviet Union towards international conservation (Anon., 1989). In 1988, the USSR participated in 55 international conventions and agreements concerning environmental protection, several of which related to protected areas (Anon., 1989).

A network of wetlands of international importance has been established under the Convention on Wetlands of International Importance especially as Waterfowl Habitat (Ramsar Convention), which was ratified by the USSR on 11 October 1976. In 1990 there were 12 sites. A further 16 are proposed adding 8,000,000 ha to the network. The USSR is also actively involved in developing a network of biosphere reserves under the Unesco MAB programme, 19 sites having been established by 1990. The USSR signed the Convention Concerning the Protection of the World Cultural and Natural Heritage (World Heritage Convention) on 12 October 1990. No natural sites are inscribed on the World Heritage List as yet. International co-operation between the USSR and the USA has extended to the twinning of biosphere reserves for comparative research and management purposes. Negotiations are underway with the USA and Finland to establish transfrontier parks on the shores of the Bering Straits and adjacent to Kostomukhskiy, respectively.

Multilateral co-operation between the members of the Warsaw Pact is implemented within the framework of a Permanent Commission on Co-operation in Environmental Protection. This ceased to exist after the Pact was disbanded in 1991. Co-operation with Sweden has been implemented within the framework of a Joint Working Group on Environmental Protection under the Soviet–Swedish Intergovernmental Commission on Economic and Scientific and Technical Co-operation. Among the primary areas of co-operation is the conservation of ecological systems and individual floral and faunal species (Anon., 1989).

Administration and Management Until 1988 the supreme authority for broad and comprehensive environmental issues (executive and management roles in nature conservation) was the central government's Council of Ministers, and its representatives within each republic. Administration was handled by national bodies such as: the State Committee for Hydrometeorology and Natural Environmental Control (concerned with nature conservation, forestry and game management), and the USSR Agro-Industrial Trust (formerly USSR Ministry of Agriculture) with committees at republic level.

In January 1988 the administrative bureaucracy was streamlined and simplified by the creation of the USSR State Committee for Nature Conservation (*Goskompriroda*), which was responsible for co-ordinating conservation activities throughout the entire USSR. *Goskompriroda* has offices at the Republic level, further divided into 200 oblast (district) offices each with some 200 staff. Its main tasks include: monitoring the use and conservation of natural resources (including hunting activities), management of nature reserves, registration of threatened fauna and production of the USSR red book, and dissemination of information about the environment. In 1991 the structure was revised with the creation of the USSR ministry of Nature Use and Environmental Protection (Dobrynina, pers. comm., 1991). The relationship between this ministry and the republican authorities will only be defined once the Treaty on the Union of Soviet Sovereign Republics (USSR) has been agreed.

As from 1 January 1975 state nature reserves were under the direct or indirect supervision of the Department of Nature Conservation, and Game Management of the USSR Ministry of Agriculture. The majority of state nature reserves were managed by the departments or committees of nature conservation in the republics, but some fell under the supervision of the USSR Academy of Sciences. Final approval for the establishment of state nature reserves was given by *Gosplan*, the State Planning Committee (Braden, 1986). By 1988 most state nature reserves had come under the administration of the Chief Administration for Nature Conservation, Nature Reserves, Forestry and Game Management (*Glavpriroda*). By 1990, 135 of 168 state nature reserves were under *Goskompriroda*, now the Ministry, and the rest under the USSR Academy of Sciences and the republics. National parks, however, remain under the USSR State Committee for Forestry. Most state nature reserves have 5 to 20 scientific staff, additional research being undertaken by the Academy of Sciences, universities and other institutions (Braden, 1986). In the RSFSR, national hunting reserves are administered by the Chief Administration for Hunting and Nature Reserves (*Glavokhota*). Rangers are responsible for controlling poaching, and hunting is limited to sustainable levels.

In 1985, 4.4 million roubles were spent on national parks and 27.8 million roubles on the state nature reserve system by 28 different administrative bodies employing over 1,000 specialists. In 1988 a budget of 10,000 million roubles was earmarked for use by the State for environmental protection, as compared with a total of 60,000 million roubles spent during the previous decade (Karpowicz, 1988). A long-term programme for environmental protection and rational utilisation of natural resources has been formulated for the Thirteenth Five-Year Plan (1991–5) and up to the year 2005 by the former USSR State Committee for Nature Protection and other key institutions. Total investment for the period 1991–2005 is estimated at 240–335 billion roubles, increasingly from 48–55 billion roubles for the Thirteenth Plan to 120–180 billion roubles for the Sixteenth Plan (IUCN, 1991).

The oldest and largest nature conservation organisation in the USSR is the All Russian Society for Nature Conservation. Founded in 1924, it is reputed to be the largest in the world, with 38 million members active in local groups, collectives and state farms, factories, offices, and schools. In all Soviet republics there are national nature conservation societies which work within the framework of the peace council of the USSR. Other societies include the USSR Geographical Society, USSR Theriological Society, and the USSR Ornithological Society. The basis of nature conservation is taught both in schools and in universities and other institutions of higher education (Kaystautas, 1987). A union of environmental protection societies was set up in early 1989.

Systems Reviews The USSR is the world's largest country covering one sixth of the globe's land surface. For the most part it is lowland, with only 5% lying above 1,500 m. There are four distinct vegetation zones: tundra, forest (broad-leaf woodland and coniferous taiga), steppe and desert. The deserts and semi-deserts (Central Asia) fringing the southern borders give way to steppe and temperate grasslands, which in turn are replaced by a great zone of broad-leaf woodland and conifer taiga forest stretching for more than 11,250 km east–west, and by treeless cold desert and tundra along the northern coasts. Forests now cover 7.47 million sq. km (33% of the USSR) with vast areas of forest remaining virgin in the far north, parts of Siberia, and in the high mountains. The main centres of plant diversity include the Carpathian mountains, southern shores of the Crimea, western and eastern Transcaucasus region, western Kopet, Tien-Shan, the Pamirs, and the Primorskiy region (Davis et al., 1986).

Protected areas play an important role in the conservation of rare faunal species, containing 39% of mammal species, 55% of bird species, 56% of fish species, 68% of reptile species, and 90% of amphibians listed in the *Red Book* of the USSR. Moreover, they have proved to be vital for the conservation of a number of species such as tiger and Bactrian deer (Anon., 1989). Strict protection is afforded to about 1.5% of total land area in the USSR under the existing network of national parks and state nature reserves. There are plans to establish 40 national parks over the next 10 years, mainly in the Far East (N. Zabalina, pers. comm., 1991). Overall, it is planned to extend the protected areas network to at least 2% of total land area by 1995, 4% by 2000, and to at least 6% by 2005 (IUCN, 1991).

In the past, even designated protected areas were not completely secure from short-term economic exploitation, with reserves temporarily removed from the system. A total of 88 state nature reserves were thus removed between 1940 and 1950. The protected areas system has been threatened over time by a number of activites such as oil prospecting, livestock grazing, over-fishing, uncontrolled tourism, illegal building schemes, and hunting by the privileged few (Braden, 1986; Karpowicz, 1988). The Dneprovsko-eterevskoe National Hunting Reserve lies partly within Zone A (total evacuation) of the Chernobyl reactor accident site.

Addresses
USSR Ministry of Nature Use and Environmental Protection, Nezhdanovoi St 11, Moscow 103
    009 (Tel. 95 229 5759; Tlx: 411258 zerno su)

References

Anon. (1988). Resolution on the formation of USSR State Committee for the Protection of Nature. *Pravda* 17 January.

Anon. (1989). *Report on the state of the environment in the USSR, 1988.* USSR State Committee for the Protection of Nature, Moscow. 151 pp.

Bannikov, A.G. (Ed.) (1969). *Zapovedniki Sovetskogo Soyuza.* Kolos, Moscow. 552 pp.

Borodin, A.M., Isakov, Y. and Krinitsky, V.V. (1984). The system of natural protected areas in the USSR: biosphere reserves as part of this system. In: *Conservation, Science and Society.* Unesco, Paris. Pp. 221–8.

Borodina, A.G. and Syroechkovskogo, I.Y.Y. (Ed.) (1983). *Zapovedniki SSSR.* Lesnaya Promyshlennost', Moscow. 248 pp.

Braden, K. (1986). Wildlife reserves in the USSR. *Oryx* 20: 165–9.

Cerovsky, J. (1988). *Nature conservation in the socialist countries of East Europe.* East-Europe Committee, IUCN Commission on Education/Ministry of Culture of the Czech Socialist Republic, Prague.

Davis, S. D., Droop, S. J. M., Gregerson, P., Henson, L., Leon, C. J., Lamlein Villa-Lobos, J., Synge, H., and Zantovska, J. (1986). *Plants in danger, what do we know?* Threatened Plants Unit. IUCN, Gland, Switzerland and Cambridge, UK. 461 pp.

Karpowicz, Z.J. (1988). Conservation and environment protection. In: M.J. Berry (Ed.), *Science and technology in the USSR.* Longmans, London. Pp. 361–79.

Kolbasov, O.S. (1981). Two new environmental laws. *Environmental Policy and Law* 7: 79–100.

Knystautas, A. (1987). *The natural history of the USSR.* Century, London. 224 pp.

Nikalaevskiy, A.G. (1985). *Natsional'nye parki.* Agropromizdat, Moscow. 189 pp.

Sokolov, V.Y. and Syroechkovskogo, Y.Y. (Eds.) (1985). *Zapovedniki SSSR.* 11 vols. Mysl, Moscow.

IUCN (1991). *Environmental status report 1991.* Vol. 3. USSR. IUCN-East European Programme, Gland, Switzerland and Cambridge, UK.

ANNEX Definitions of protected area designations, as legislated, together with authorities responsible for their administration

Title (English title): Law on Wildlife Protection and Use

Date: 25 June 1980 (entered into force 1 January 1981)

Brief description: No information

Administrative authority: *Goskompriroda* (USSR State Committee for Nature conservation

Designations:

Zapovednik (State nature reserve)

— Typical or unique plot of natural land used by 'scientific institutions . . . and studied for its natural complexes and established on land excluded from economic utilisation'. Both protect threatened flora and fauna, and serve as an outdoor laboratory for field study. As far as possible, maintained in its natural condition unchanged by man.

— Prohibited activities include building construction, any economic activities, such as agriculture or industry, and unrestricted entry.
— Main management objectives include: (1) protection of wildlife and its habitats, including maintenance of entire ecosystems; (2) scientific research; and (3) strictly limited recreational activities or, in some cases, controlled tourism.-
— Surrounded by an area of semi-protected land which provides a buffer to the adjacent countryside. Existing economic activities are allowed to continue, providing they are not harmful.

Natsional'nyi park (National park)
— Protected natural area established in natural wilderness or altered landscapes (including arable land), although mainly on state forest property. Designated for recreation as well as nature protection and, as in the case of a protected lakeshore, differs from a state nature reserve in that tourism is allowed.
— Legislation for national parks is complex. Parks are zoned into: areas in which economic activities are controlled; nature reserves, containing the finest examples of original natural habitat, where economic activities and public entry is forbidden; nature sanctuaries where tourists are allowed but economic activities are strictly prohibited; and peripheral buffer areas of economic activity, where habitation and sustainable levels of exploitation of natural resources (including fishing) are permitted.

Zakaznik (Nature sanctuary or partial reserve)
— Natural area partly withdrawn from economic utilisation because of its outstanding landscape, rare plants, or breeding colonies of threatened species. Controlled hunting is sometimes allowed.
— Established to enable certain floral and faunal populations to recover within a specified time period. Exploitation is prohibited during this period, unless it does not interfere with management objectives.
— May only be fully protected in certain seasons when all economic activities and entry is banned. Status and administration varies in the different republics of the USSR.

Zapovedno-okhotnich'ye khozyastvo (National hunting reserve or reserved hunting unit).
— Highly protected, and provides vital refuges for wildlife. Numbers of some game species is regulated by controlled hunting.

Natsional'nyi pamyatnik (Nature monument or national monument)
— Limited area surrounding isolated natural features such as geological sites or exceptionally old trees.

Sources: Braden (1986), Kynstautas (1987), Cerovsky (1988).

Southeast USSR

Existing

Summary of Protected Areas of USSR

National/International designation Name of area and map reference[+]	IUCN Management Category	Area (ha)	Year notified
Biosphere Reserve			
Chatkal Mountains Biosphere Reserve[=]	IX	71,400	1978
Kazakhstan SSR (southern[@])		**271,730,000**	
State Nature Reserves			
1 Aksu-Dzhabagly	I	75,094	1927
2 Alma-Atinskiy*	I	73,342	1961
Subtotal (% total land area)		**148,436 (0.1%)**	
Kirghizia SSR		**19,850,000**	
Ramsar Wetlands			
5 Issyk-Kul Lake*	Unassigned	629,800	1976
National Parks			
3 Ala-Archa*	II	19,400	1976
Subtotal (% total land area)		**19,400 (0.1%)**	
State Nature Reserves			
4 Besh-Aral'skiy	I	116,732	1979
5 Issyk-Kul'skiy*	I	18,999	1948
6 Narynskiy	I	18,260	1983
7 Sary-Chelekskiy*	I	23,868	1959
Subtotal (% total land area)		**177,859 (0.9%)**	
Tadzhikistan SSR		**14,310,000**	
State Nature Reserves			
8 Dashti-Dzhumskiy	I	19,700	1983
9 Ramit*	I	16,168	1959
10 Tigrovaya Balka*	I	49,700	1938
Subtotal (% total land area)		**85,568 (0.6%)**	
Turkmenistan SSR (south-eastern[#])		**48,810,000**	
State Nature Reserves			
11 Badkhyzskiy	I	87,680	1941
12 Repetekskiy	I	34,600	1928
Subtotal (% total land area)		**122,280 (0.3%)**	

National/International designation Name of area and map reference[+]	IUCN Management Category	Area (ha)	Year notified
Uzbekistan SSR (south-eastern[°])		**44,740,000**	
State Nature Reserves			
13 Chatkal'skiy*	I	35,686	1947
14 Gissarskiy (Kyzylsuyskiy & Mirakinskiy)	I	87,538	1983
15 Kitabskii	I	5,378	1979
16 Zaaminskiy	I	15,600	1959
17 Zeravshanskiy	I	2,352	1975
Subtotal (% total land area)		146,554 (0.3%)	
TOTALS			
State nature reserves (% total land area)		680,697 (0.2%)	
National parks (% total land area)		19,400 (0.0%)	

[+] Locations of most protected areas are shown in the accompanying map.

* Site is described in this directory.

= Consists of Sary-Chelekskiy and Chatkal'skiy state nature reserves in Kirghizia and Uzbekistan, respectively.

@ Comprises Taldy-Kurgan, Alma-Ata, Dzhambul, and Chimkent oblast'iy.

Comprises Chardzhou and Mary oblast'iy.

° Comprises Andizhán, Namangan, Tashkent, Syrdar'in, Dzhizak, Samarkand, Kashkadar'in and Surkhandar'in oblast'iy.

443

ALA-ARCHA NATIONAL PARK

IUCN Management Category II (National park)

Biogeographical Province 2.36.12 (Pamir-Tian Shan Highlands)

Geographical Location Situated on the northern slopes of the Kirghizian Range (Tian Shan) in the upper Ala-Archa Valley, approximately 30 km from Frunze. Approximately 43°10′N, 75°10′E

Date and History of Establishment Established in April 1976.

Area 19,400 ha

Land Tenure State

Altitude Ranges from 1,579 m to 4,855 m. Fifty peaks are above 4,000 m.

Physical Features The relief is typically mountainous with peaks, glaciers, canyons, gorges, cliffs, and rich vegetation in the valleys.

Climate No information.

Vegetation According to 1984 data, there are 967 species of plants of which three rare species are included in the *Red Data Book of the Soviet Union*. There are about 70 species of trees and shrubs. The land is covered by sparse growth of archa trees up to 3,000 m. In some places there are fir, birch and willow trees.

Fauna According to 1983 data, there are 16 species of mammals including snow leopard *Panthera uncia* (E), brown bear *Ursus arctos*, mountain goat *Capra* sp. (more than 300), porcupine *Hystrix* sp. marten *Martes* sp., and ermine *Mustela* sp. Wolf *Canis lupus* (V) and wild sheep occasionally visit the park. There are 120 species of birds, including golden eagle *Aquila chrysaetos* and bearded vulture *Gypaetus barbatus*, and two species of fish.

Cultural Heritage No information

Local Human Population The park has never been inhabited, but the valleys have been used for cattle grazing. There are no roads, and the nearest village is 8 km outside of the park.

Visitors and Visitor Facilities No information

Scientific Research and Facilities Limited to preliminary observations and censuses of mammal and bird populations.

Conservation Value   The landscape is impressive and provides important habitat for a number of rare species. It is also important for scientific research and recreation, including mountaineering.

Conservation Management   The park is divided into three zones: strict reserve (2,200 ha), breeding zone and zone of intensive recreation (5%). Unorganised tourism and driving cars in the park are both prohibited.

Management Constraints   No information.

Staff   Thirty-five and twenty-two forestry staff (1983).

Budget   Approximately 100,000 roubles is allocated by the state annually. Income is generated from tourism and mountaineering.

Local Addresses   No information

References
Nickolaevskiy, A.G. (1985). *Nazionalny parky*. Agropromizdat, Moscow. 96 pp.

ALMA-ATINSKIY ZAPOVEDNIK (STATE NATURE RESERVE)

IUCN Management Category   I (Strict Nature Reserve)

Biogeographical Province   2.36.12 (Pamir-Tian-Shan Highlands)

Geographical Location   Lies 25 km east of Alma-ata, capital of Kazakhstan, in the central part of the Zailiisky Alatau Range. Three-quarters of the territory consists of the northern Kailiisky alatan. Its boundary follows the River Leviy Jalgar in the west, the River Pravy Talgar in the north, and in the east, the ridge separating the valleys of the Issyk and Jurgen rivers. The distance from the west to the east is 32 km. The rest of the reserve is in southern Zailiisky alatan, where the southern border of the reserve extends from near the Toguzak mountain pass, down the Zugo-Vossochniy, Talgar and Chilik rivers, to the Koshulak and Jamchi rivers. Approximately 43°N, 78°E

Date and History of Establishment   First established in May 1931 and designated a state nature reserve in 1935, but ceased to exist in 1951. It was re-established as a state nature reserve in 1961. Between 1966 and 1983 the Kalkany mountain semi-desert zone (17,800 ha) was included in the reserve, together with an unique natural object, the 'Singing Sands'. In 1983 this site was transferred to Kapchagayskiy Hunting Reserve.

Area   73,342ha. The reserve was extended from 13,000 ha in 1931 to 600,000 ha in 1935 and reached 1,000,000 ha during the following five years, but after World War II it was reduced.

Land Tenure   State

Altitude   Ranges from 4,000 m to 4,973 m at the peak of Talgar mountain, the highest point.

Physical Features   Forms part of a northern ridge of the Tien-Shan Mountains and consists of the northern Zailiisky Alatau and the Illissky Depression. The former is characterised by a network of peaks culminating in Mt Talagar, and has strongly dissected relief resulting from intense erosion.   It includes stretches of the fast-flowing Talgar and Issyk rivers which ultimately drain into Lake Balkash.   Soils range from degraded chernozems to black earths. The latter is the desert and consists of a tectonic trough, through which the Ili River flows.

Climate   Conditions are continental. The mean annual temperature is 6.8 °C in the valleys and 0.8 °C on the mountains.   Temperatures in the valleys vary from –4.3 °C in January to 18.1 °C in July, and from –9.7 °C to 10. 6 °C on the mountains.   The annual number of frost-free days varies from 145 in the valleys to 90 on the mountains.   Mean annual precipitation is 830–870 mm.   Snow cover lasts for 160–190 days and is 600–800 mm deep.

Vegetation   The forest-meadow steppe (1,300–2,600 m) comprises conifers, mixed forest, grasslands, and forest grasslands with spruce *Picea schrenkiana* and feather grasses *Stipa capillata*, *Phleum phleoides*, and *Festuca ganeschinii*. The subalpine belt (2,600–3,000 m) supports evergreen scrub, *Juniperus turkestanica*, steppe, and mixed grasslands. In the alpine zone (3,000–3,600 m), meadows are interspersed with rock outcrops. Other species present include apple *Malus sieversii*, honeysuckle *Lonicera altmanii*, and representatives of the genera *Armeniaca*, *Crataegus*, *Rosa*, *Artemisia*, *Geranium*, *Myosotis*, *Gentiana*, and *Kobresia*. Some 950 species have been recorded, including 13 trees, and 63 shrubs.

Fauna   Mammals include red and large-eared pikas *Ochotona rutila* and *O. macrotis*, marmot *Marmota bobak*, vole *Clethrionomys frater*, birch mouse *Sicista concolor*, wolf *Canis lupus* (V), stoat *Mustela erminea*, stone marten *Martes foina*, lynx *Felis lynx*, red deer *Cervus elaphus*, roe deer *Capreolus capreolus*, and ibex *Capra ibex*. Snow leopard *Panthera uncia* (E) is a rare visitor to the high mountains. Birds include lammergeier *Gypaetus barbatus*, golden eagle *Aquila chrysaetos*, Himalayan snowcock *Tetraogallus himalayensis*, and chukar *Alectoris chukar*. Of the passerines, there are whistling thrush *Myiophonius caeruleus*, grosbeak *Mycerobas carnipes*, and Guldenstadt's, blue-headed and Eversmann's redstarts *Phoenicurus erythrogaster*, *P. caeruleocephalus* and *P. erythronotus*.

Cultural Heritage   No information

Local Human Population   No information

Visitors and Visitor Facilities   The system of reserve trails is used for specialist scientific and educational excursions, with guides drawn from local researchers.

Scientific Research and Facilities   Includes research on preservation of montane landscape and vegetation.

Conservation Value   No information

Conservation Management   The reserve is buffered by a 200 ha protected zone.

Management Constraints   The introduction of red squirrel is a problem.

Staff   No information

Budget   No information

Local Addresses

Kazakh Soviet Socialist Republic, Alma-Ata Region, Talgar, Lebedinka 48334

References

Anon. (1963). Works of the Alma-Atinskiy Reserve. In: *Reserves of Kazakhstan* (*Essays*), 2nd edition. Kazakh State Publishing House, Alma-Ata.

Bannikov, A.G. (Ed.) (1969).. *Nature Reserves (Zapovedniki) in the Soviet Union*. Publishing House, Kolos, Moscow. Pp. 459–63.

Bannikov, A.G. (1974). *Around the reserves of the USSR*. 2nd Edition. Publishing House, Mysl', Moscow. Pp. 234–5.

Borodin, A.M. and Syroechkovski, E.E. (1983). *Zapovedniki SSSR*. Lesnaya Promyshlennost', Moscow. Pp. 163–6.

Proskuryakov, M.A. (1967). The Alma-Atinsky Reserve. *Agriculture of the Kazakhstan*. P. 12.

CHATKAL'SKIY ZAPOVEDNIK (STATE NATURE RESERVE)

IUCN Management Category   I   (Strict Nature Reserve)
IX   (Biosphere Reserve)

Biogeographical Province   2.36.12 (Pamir-Tian-Shan. Highlands)

Geographical Location   Lies 70 km south-east of Tashkent in Tashkent oblast'. Occupies the south-western end of the Chatkal'skiy Range in the western Tien-Shan Mountains. The reserve is 183 km south-west of its twinned cluster reserve Sary–Chelek. Approximately 41°08′N, 69°59′E

Date and History of Establishment   Established in 1947 by Act of Council of Ministers of Uzbek SSR no. 2020. Twinned as a 'cluster reserve' with Sary–Chelek State Nature Reserve in Kirghizia, and designated as part of Chatkal Mountains Biosphere Reserve in April 1978.

Area   35,809 ha, having been enlarged from its original size of 22,000 ha. The biosphere reserve component covers 47,500 ha.

Land Tenure   State

Altitude   Ranges from 1,110 m to 4,000 m.

Physical Features   Encompasses the ridge and spurs of the Chatkal'skiy Range, with the smaller Bashkyzylsaya sector occupying the southern slopes and the larger Maydantalu sector the northern slopes. Rocky outcrops of Devonian and Carboniferous age are common, with thin deluvial and eluvial deposits lying on shallow bed rocks, and valleys are deeply entrenched. Soils are various brown earths.

Climate Conditions are sharply continental, with mean temperatures (at 1,200 m) of −16 °C during the coldest months of January and February, and of 20 °C–25 °C during the warmest month, July. At low altitude, mean annual temperature is 11.5 °C. Maximum and minimum temperatures are 37.9 °C and −21°C, respectively. Annual precipitation is 680–900 mm, with a mean of 656 mm at 1,200 m. The frost-free period is 190–200 days.

Vegetation The reserve consists of 6,833 ha of forest, 11,001 ha of rocks and scree, 6,126 ha of meadows, 1,938 ha of sandy areas, and 23 ha of water bodies. Three vegetation belts can be distinguished: mountain Turanian-type semi-savanna, forest/shrub (mostly juniper and hardwood with the notable presence of wild fruit tree species), and alpine steppe. River valleys are characterised by turgai-type landscapes. Forests of junipers (*Juniperus turkestanica*, *J. semiglobosa*, and *J. seraphsenanica*), and deciduous trees such as *Prunus sogdiana*, *Acer turkestanicum*, *Crataegus turkestanica*, and *Malus kirghisorum* are present. South- and west-facing slopes support mountain steppe and sclerophytic communities, including groves of *Pistacia vera*. Highland areas have meadows. There are records for 1,100 species of plants, including 40 species of trees and shrubs. Some 72 are rare and endemic.

Fauna A total of 32 mammal species, 146 species of birds and four species of fish has been recorded. Characteristic but rare species are: brown bear *Ursus arctos*, snow leopard *Panthera uncia* (E), roe deer *Capreolus capreolus*, ibex *Capra ibex*, and Menzbier's marmot *Marmota menzbieri* (E) (endemic to the western Tien Shan). Birds include: snowcock *Tetraogallus himalayensis* at higher altitudes and numerous chukar partridge *Alectoris chukar*, as well as golden eagle *Aquila chrysaetos*, booted eagle *Hieraaetus pennatus*, saker falcon *Falco cherrug*, lammergeier *Gypaetus barbatus*, and black stork *Ciconia nigra*.

Cultural Heritage In 1963, ancient drawings were discovered on the cliffs along the Tereksay River in Karasau, 2,000 m above sea level in the southern part of the Maydontalskiy plot. Ancient hunters recorded different events, mostly depicting animals, especially turs (goats), which still exist and deer which do not. It appears that they lived in the mountains of Chatkala. The earliest drawings are thought to date back to 2000–1000 BC. Later drawings of riders, houses and dogs also exist, indicating that people have inhabited the area since ancient times.

Local Human Population There are no settlements within the reserve.

Visitors and Visitor Facilities Visits can be made only by special arrangement and must be guided along specific predetermined routes.

Scientific Research and Facilities Research has been co-ordinated by the USSR Academy of Sciences since 1958 and includes the biology of wood-producing plants and of rare animal species, such as marmot and snow leopard. Research is focused on studying the complex structure and dynamics of the western Tien Shan, including an inventory of flora and fauna, and on developing techniques to reafforest the mountains, especially the nut-tree forest areas. There are equipped laboratories, experimental plots, and climatic stations. Accommodation is available for scientists.

Conservation Value The reserve is representative of the western Tien Shan and harbours a variety of rare and threatened species of plants and animals. It is also an important cultural site, with cliff drawings dating back to prehistoric times.

Conservation Management   Managed as a strict nature reserve, with a core zone of 35,200 ha split into two sections, Bashkyzylsayu (11,100 ha) and Maydantalu (24,200 ha). A surrounding buffer zone covers 12,200 ha. Within the core area, 2,339 ha are zoned for conservation and plant community restoration and another 34 ha for the administrative centre.

Management Constraints   Before its establishment, part of the reserve was used for hunting and grazing, and for mineral prospecting.

Staff   Seventy-two, of which twenty-five are in administration, protection and management, and twenty-six are researchers.

Budget   Total 271,200 roubles: operational expenses 162,200 roubles (including 90,700 roubles for wages), capital costs 58,000 roubles, capital repairs 28,000 roubles, and equipment purchase 23,000 roubles (1980).

Local Addresses
Uzbek SSR, Tashkent Region, Verkhnechirchiksky District, Parkent Village

References
Bannikov, A.G. (Ed.) (1969). *Nature Reserves (Zapovedniki) in the Soviet Union*. Publishing House, Kolos, Moscow. Pp. 486–94.
Bannikov, A.G. (1974). *Around the reserves of the USSR*. 2nd Edition. Publishing House Mysl', Moscow. 235 pp.
Borodin, A.M. and Syroechkovski, E.E. (1983). *Zapovedniki SSSR*. 'Lesnaya Promyshlennost', Moscow. Pp. 159–61.

ISSYK-KUL'SKIY ZAPOVEDNIK (STATE NATURE RESERVE)

IUCN Management Category   I   (Strict Nature Reserve)

Biogeographical Province   2.36.12   (Pamir-Tian-Shan Highlands)

Geographical Location   Situated on the shores of Lake Issyk-Kul' in the Issyk'Kul' oblast of Kirghizia SSR, some 75 km due south of Alma-Ata. The reserve lies in the eastern part of the Tian-Shan range within the territory of Issyk-Kul'sk, Tyupsk, Dzhety-Oguzsk and Tonsk rayons. 42°30'N, 77°00'E. The lake itself lies at 42°09'–42°45'N, 76°09'–78°23'

Date and History of Establishment   Issyk-Kul'skiy, meaning 'hot lake' in Kirgizky, was established as a state nature reserve in December 1975 within its present boundaries, but was first created in 1948. In 1959 the site was managed as two separate hunting sanctuaries, called Teploklyuchenski and Dzhety-Oguzskiy. In the late 1960s the reserve included the whole of the lake and covered 762,000 ha. Declared a Ramsar site on 11 October 1976.

Area   Enlarged from 17,310 ha to 18,999 ha beginning in 1986. The area of the Ramsar site is 629,800 ha.

Land Tenure   State

Altitude   The lake lies at 1,607 m.

Physical Features   Lake Issyk-kul' occupies a tectonic basin between the ranges of Kusgei Alatau to the north and Terskei Alatau to the south. The lake is 178 km long, 60 km wide and, on average, 270 m deep, but less so in the eastern part. It is a highland water body, fed by over 80 inlets but with no outlet. All of these are fed by snow melt, and many have reduced flows in the months of June and July. Only six rivers have an average flow greater than 5 cu. m per second. The lake is brackish and oligotrophic, and winter water temperatures never fall below 4.0 °C. It is the largest highland lake in the world and, besides Baykal and the Caspian, is the deepest in the world, 702 m at its extreme. The relief is folded, and consists of two main forms: the floodplain and the foothills. Soils vary throughout the valley. In the western floodplain they are grey-brown; in the centre light chestnut, whilst in the east they are predominantly dark-chestnut. Soils in the west are of low fertility, in the east they are fertile, while the foothills provide good agricultural land. The lake occupies a tectonic basin between the ranges of Kusgei Alatau to the north and Terskei Alatau to the south.

Climate   Conditions vary greatly from east to west and can differ from north to south. Mean monthly temperature in July is 18.6 °C, and in the northern floodplain, 17 °C; in January it is –3 °C and –2 °C, respectively. In the west mean temperature in January is –4 °C, whilst in the east it is –8 °C to –11° C. Major fluctuations in temperature are due to the presence of the large body of water. The lowest recorded temperatures of –23 °C to –26 °C occur in January, with –28 °C in the west and –33 °C to –38 °C in the east. The highest recorded temperature is 35 °C. There are between 226–250 days with temperatures suitable for plant growth. Mean annual precipitation is 100–120 mm in the west and 350–400 mm in the east, with most rain falling in May to August. In winter 2% of all precipitation occurs in the west, 8% in the centre, and 13% in the east. Winds called *ulan* or *boom* in the west are characteristically strong and reach 30–40 m per second.

Vegetation   There are 687 ha of forest and 1,329 ha of meadows. The vegetation is varied. In the western parts of the floodplain there is steppe, whilst along the lake shore and river valleys there are meadows. Towards the east the vegetation is more species-rich, acquiring the character of dry steppes, and in the easternmost parts of the valley are steppe meadows. Marsh vegetation appears in the wettest floodplain areas. In total, 250 species have been recorded, of which 12 are rare. The shallow waters support a rich submerged and floating vegetation of *Charophyta*, *Potamogeton*, and **Myrtophylium** spp.

Fauna   There are records of 23 species of mammals, and 140 species of birds. Mammals include boar *Sus scrofa*, hare *Lepus tolai*, steppe polecat *Mustela eversmanni*, weasel *Mustela nivalis*, red deer *Cervus elaphus*, roe deer *Capreolus capreolus*, and Siberian ibex *Capra sibirica*. Birds include pheasant *Phasianus colchicus*, red-crested pochard *Netta rufina*, and coot *Fulica atra*, and rarer species such as white-tailed eagle *Haliaeetus albicilla*, mute swan *Cygnus olor*, and great white heron *Egretta alba*. The lake is a wintering ground for around 60,000–70,000 wildfowl of 98 species, including whooper and mute swan *Cygnus cygnus* and *C. olor*, pochard *Aythya ferina*, and pintail *Anas acuta*. There is a rich zoobenthos with over 150 species of molluscs, oligochaetae, gammaridae, and chironomidae, an important food source for the bird populations. Fish include zander *Stizostedion lucioperce* and introduced carp *Cyprinus carpio*.

Cultural Heritage   No information

Local Human Population   There is a fishery for zander and carp.

Visitors and Visitor Facilities   A health resort is located on the lakeshore by the hot springs at Aksu.

Scientific Research and Facilities   Research has been focused on wintering wildfowl, including regular winter counts, as well as on game birds such as pheasant. Limnological research continues and there is a special research ship.

Conservation Value   No information.

Conservation Management   The reserve consists of nine individual units, ranging in size from 5 ha to 11,584 ha, and including shoreline elements and an aquatic section consisting of a 2 km lakeside strip. The other units are located on the northern and southern shores of the western and eastern ends of the lake, respectively, with one section of 5 ha on the northern shore. In addition, there are two areas on the slopes of the Terskey Ala Tau: Dzhaty-Oguzsky and Tyeploklyuchevsky. Commercial fishing is controlled.

Management Constraints   Changes in the forest cover of the surrounding mountain slopes may produce changes in the rate of inflow into the lake.

Staff   No information

Budget   No information

Local Addresses   State Committee for Forest Economy of Kirġhizia, Issyk-Kul'skiy r-n, S. Anan'evo

References
Bannikov, A.G. (Ed.) (1969). *Nature Reserves (Zapovedniki) in the Soviet Union*. Publishing House, Kolos, Moscow. Pp. 475–80.

Bannikov, A.G. (1974). *Around the reserves of the USSR*. 2nd Edition. Publishing House Mysl', Moscow. 235 pp.

Borodin, A.M. and Syroechkovski, E.E. (Eds.). (1983) Zapovedniki SSSR. Moskva 'Lesnaya Promyshlennost'. Pp. 214–15.

IUCN (1987). *Directory of wetlands of international importance*. IUCN, Gland., Switzerland and Cambridge, UK. 371 pp.

RAMIT ZAPOVEDNIK (STATE NATURE RESERVE)

IUCN Management Category   I   (Strict Nature Reserve)

Biogeographical Province   2.36.12   (Pamir-Tian-Shan Highlands)

Geographical Location   Lies on the southern slopes of the Gissarsky Mountains, approximately 200 km north-east of Dushanbe and 250 km south-east of Tashkent. Approximately 39°N, 69°E

Date and History of Establishment   October 1959

Area   16,139 ha

Land Tenure   State

Altitude   The highest point is in the north at 3,195 m; the lowest is in the south at 1,176 m.

Physical Features   The reserve lies in the upper reaches of the Kafirnigan River basin, and features river terraces, medium slopes and a higher area. It is triangular in shape and bounded to the north-west by the Sardan-Miena River, to the east by the Sorbo River and to the north by the Surkhab and Ushrut rivers, all of which have deeply dissected valleys with steep slopes. Soils are a cinnamon-coloured mountain type.

Climate   Mean monthly temperatures range from −1.8 °C in January, to 14.7 °C in July, with 210 days below freezing point and snow cover lasting from late-November to mid-March. Total rainfall is estimated at 1,500–1,000 mm. Rapid changes of temperature occur, with the maximum at 38 °C, and minimum at −30 °C.

Vegetation   Three vegetation zones are present: mountain steppe (1,300–1,800 m), mountain forest steppe (1,800–2,800 m) and uplands (2,800–3,200 m). The reserve is important for its groves of nut-producing species, such as walnut *Juglans regia* and pistachio *Pistacia vera*, and for fruit species such as cherry *Cerasus mahaleb (Prunus mahaleb)*, *C. pontica*, *Prunus divaricata*, apple *Malus* sp., and *Amygdalus buharica*. Other trees include *Rhus coriaria*, *Populus* sp., and *Betula* sp. Herbs include *Tulipa*, *Iris* and *Fritillaria*.

Fauna   Mammals include hare *Lepis tolai*, marmot *Marmota caudata*, forest dormouse *Dryomus nitedula*, vole *Microtus juldaschi*, rat *Rattus turcetanicus*, crested porcupine *Hystrix cristata*, wolf *Canis lupus* (V), red fox *Vulpes vulpes*, brown bear *Ursus arctos isabellinus*, beech marten *Martes foina*, snow leopard *Panthera uncia* (E), and ibex *Capra ibex*. Birds include Himalayan snowcock *Tetraogallus himalayensis*, dippers *Cinclus cinclus* and *C. pallasii*, hawfinch *Coccothraustes coccothraustes humii*, golden oriole *Oriolus oriolus*, blue whistling thrush *Myiophonius caeruleus*, Himalayan accentor *Prunella himalayana*, and Siberian ruby-throat *Luscinia calliope*. Reptiles include lizards such as *Agama* sp., skinks *Ablepharus* spp., and whip snakes *Coluber rhodorhachis* and *C. ravergiesi*.

Cultural Heritage   No information.

Local Human Population   No information

Visitors and Visitor Facilities   No information

Scientific Research and Facilities   Include development of methods to protect of walnut and fruit tree forests and research into ecosystems of the Gissarski mountain range.

Conservation Value   No information.

Conservation Management   No information.

Management Constraints   Introduction of red deer *Cervus elaphus* is a problem.

Staff   No information

Budget   No information

Local Addresses   Tadzik SSR, Ordjonikidzebadsky District

References

Bannikov, A.G. (Ed.). (1969). *Nature Reserves (Zapovedniki) in the Soviet Union*. Publishing House, Kolos, Moscow. Pp. 497–9.

Bannikov, A.G. (1974). *Around the reserves of the USSR*. 2nd Edition. Publishing House, Mysl', Moscow. 235 pp.

Borodin, A.M. and Syroechkovski, E.E. (1983). *Zapovedniki SSSR*. 'Lesnaya Promyshlennost', Moscow. Pp. 218–20.

SARY CHELEKSKIY ZAPOVEDNIK (STATE NATURE RESERVE)

IUCN Management Category   I   (Strict Nature Reserve)
                                              IX (Biosphere Reserve)

Biogeographical Province   2.36.12   (Pamir-Tien-Shan Highlands)

Geographical Location   Occupies the north-eastern slopes of the Chatkal'skiy Range in Osh oblast'. The reserve is surrounded by the Chatkal'skiy Range and its spurs on all but its south side which borders Fergana Valley. The main farmstead is in Arkit Village. Lies 60 km from Karavan Village, the centre of the district, and 130 km from the nearest railway station at Namangan. Approximately 41°47′N, 71°54′E

Date and History of Establishment   Established as a state nature reserve in 1959 by order of the Kirgiz SSR Council of Ministers. Twinned as a 'cluster reserve' with Chatkal'skiy State Nature Reserve in Uzbekistan. Designated as part of Chatkal Mountains Biosphere Reserve in April 1978.

Area   23,868 ha. The area of the biosphere reserve component is given as 23,900 ha in the nomination.

Land Tenure   State

Altitude   Ranges from 1,200 m to 4,247 m

Physical Features   Lying on the southern spurs of the Chatkal Range, the greater part of the reserve comprises a high moutain basin protected to the north, west, and east by mountain ridges. The higher mountains have rocky spike-like summits, with ridges separated by narrow and deep gorges. Where the mountains are lower, the peaks assume a soft cupola-like character. Within the reserve lies the moutain lake Sary-Chelek at about 2,000 m, 470 ha in area and 245 m deep, and a further six small shallow lakes. The central and lower region is strongly dissected and covered by nut-fruit forests, which owe their origin to the favourable microclimate, a reflection of the local relief. The western Tien Shan is a zone of high tectonic activity.

Climate   Due to the protection afforded by the surrounding mountain ranges, winters are relatively mild with plenty of snow, and summers are warm and wet. Mean temperature in January is −7.2 °C, but temperatures may drop to −27 °C. Mean temperature in July is 21.3 °C, rising to a maximum of 38 °C. Frosts occur from late-September, to the end of April. Annual precipitation is relatively high at 930–1,100 mm or more, with 42% falling in spring, 30% in winter, 20% in summer, and 8% in autumn. The snow cover lasts from the end of December to mid-March; it is 900–1,000 mm thick in forests and 500–600 mm thick in open areas.

Vegetation   Forests cover 8,229 ha, meadows and steppe 8,022 ha, rocks and screes 4,902 ha, and water bodies 601 ha. The flora comprises 1,071 plant species including 32 species of trees, 80 shrubs, and 886 grasses, typical of the entire south Kirghiz protected forest. The alpine forests are diverse, with representatives of the north and south such as relict walnut *Juglans regia*, fir *Abies semenovii*, spruce *Picea schrenkiana*, and grape *Vitis silvestris*. The subalpine belt stretches from 2,100–2,200 m to 2,500–3,000 m, with juniper woodlands and spruce-fir replacing meadows in lower regions.   At lower altitudes, nut-fruit forests predominate with walnut covering 50% of the reserve. Associates include apple *Malus* spp., prangos *Prangos pabularia*, pear *Pyrus* spp., and an understorey of *Prunus divaricata*, *Abelia corumbosa*, *Exochorda* spp., and juniper *Juniperus* spp.

Fauna   A total of 42 mammal species (including five which are naturalised), 157 species of birds (including 118 nesting species such as golden eagle *Aquila chrysaetos*, lammergeier *Gypaetus barbatus* and snowcock *Tetraogallus himalayensis*), five species of reptiles, two species of amphibians, and five species of fish have been recorded.   The fauna is best represented in the forest belt, the most charcateristic species being wild boar *Sus scrofa* and roe deer *Capreolus capreolus*, the latter present in large numbers. In autumn, brown bear *Ursus arctos* frequents the nut-fruit forests. The fauna of the alpine and subalpine belts is distinctive and includes snow leopard *Panthera uncia* (E), lynx *Lynx lynx*, ibex *Capra ibex*, and argali *Ovis ammon*. Ermine *Mustela erminea* and stone marten *Martes foina* are ubiquitous.

Cultural Heritage   No information

Local Human Population   The nearest town is Namangan, 70 km to the south.

Visitors and Visitor Facilities   More than 10,000 people visit the reserve and its museum annually.

Scientific Research and Facilities   The flora and fauna are currently being surveyed and the ecology of individual species of large mammals and birds investigated. Special attention is being given to the structure of the vegetation, the biological features of the main species of fruit trees and shrubs and other commercially valuable species, and methods of conservation and reafforesting the mountains with nut-forests.   As part of an international research programme, this district may serve as a natural control for monitoring background levels of pollution. Biotic and abiotic parameters are measured periodically and include dust content, sulphur dioxide, mercury, lead, cadmium, arsenic carbohydrates, and litter decomposition rates. Research has been carried out since 1977 by the Natural Environment and Climate

Monitoring Laboratory and since 1980 by the Middle Asia Research Institute. Facilities include experimental plots, a climatic station, and accommodation for scientists. The museum has a good collection of specimens.

Conservation Value Together with Chatkal'skiy, the reserve is representative of the western Tien Shan and supports a diverse flora and fauna. Many plants are of socio-economic value. The reserve is also important for scientific research and tourism.

Conservation Management The reserve is at present zoned. All farming activities in the core area ceased in 1960. There is some environmental education work.

Management Constraints Before the creation of the reserve, selective logging of the forest, grass cutting and grazing of cattle were practised. There is no local participation in management decisions taken by the reserve authorities. Management is limited to fire protection and enforcement measures. Serious problems arise from recreational activities, unorganised tourism, the thoroughfare through the reserve, and construction work on the banks of Sary Chelek Lake.

Staff 105 with 20 administrative, control and resources management staff and 5 researchers.

Budget No information

Local Addresses Sary-Chelek Reserve, p/o Arkit, Dzhangi-dzhol' District, Osh Region, Kirgiz SSR 716705

References
Anon. (n.d.) *Research Publication of the Sary-Chelek Reserve*. No. 1–4.
Bannikov, A.G. (Ed.) (1969). *Nature Reserves (Zapovedniki) in the Soviet Union*. Publishing House, Kolos, Moscow. Pp. 481–5.
Bannikov, A.G. (1974). *Around the reserves of the USSR*. 2nd Edition. Publishing House Mysl', Moscow. 235 pp.
Borodin, A.M. and Syroechkovski, E.E. (1983). *Zapovedniki SSSR*. Moskva 'Lesnaya Promyshlennost'. Pp. 215–17.
Pryde, P.R. (1984). Biosphere reserves in the Soviet Union. *Soviet Geography* 25: 398–408.
Rovinsky, F.Y., Cherkhanov, Y.P., and Chicheva, T.B. (1983). *Background monitoring in Sary-Chelek Biosphere Reserve*. USSR State Committee for Hydrometeorology and Control of Natural Environment. USSR Academy of Sciences Natural Environment and Climate Monitoring Laboratory. Moscow. 7 pp.
Yanushevich, A.I. and Chichikin, Y.N. (1960). The Sary-Chelek Reserve. In: *The Reserves of the Soviet Union*. Kolos Publishing House, Moscow.

TIGROVAYA BALKA ZAPOVEDNIK (STATE NATURE RESERVE)

IUCN Management Category I (Strict Nature Reserve)

Biogeographical Province 2.36.12 (Pamir-Tian-Shan Highlands)

Geographical Location Situated in the south-western part of Tadzhikistan near the border with Afganistan on the fluvial plain of the Vaksh and Pjandzh rivers. The reserve stretches for 40 km along the Buritay Hills and southern part of the Aktay Range-Hodzha-Kazian Hills. It is approximately 200 km from Alma-Ata. Approximately 37°15′N, 68°30′E

Date and History of Establishment Established as a state nature reserve in 1938.

Area 49,700 ha. In the early 1940s the reserve was reduced by 5,000–7,000 ha, but increased to 52,000 ha the following year. In 1976 it was again slightly reduced.

Land Tenure State

Altitude Ranges from 320 m to approximately 1,000 m. The banks of the Pjandzha and the Vaksh rivers are 320–325 m above sea level; the Kashkakum Desert lies at 530 m, Buritay Hills at about 1,000 m; and the Hodzha–Kazian Hills rise to 550 m.

Physical Features Geomorphologists distinguish six terraces in the Vaksh River Valley, three of which lie within the reserve. There are small rises and falls, as well as the old river beds with lakes, on the first terrace. The second terrace is 1.5–2m higher than the first and has not been flooded by the waters of the Vaksh River for a long time. The third terrace lies 3–4 km from the river on the border of the reserve. It descends steeply to one of the largest lakes of the reserve, Lake Dar′ya-Kul′. The sands of Kashkakum Desert lie to the south on the left bank of the river. The first and the third terraces, and in some places even the fourth terrace of hills, lie on the right bank of the river. Flooding is common on the left bank, leaving many former river beds and alluvial soils of varying thicknesses. The upper terraces of floodlands, which evolved as a result of lowering of the river's erosion base, are covered with sand and clay. The southern ranges of the Aktau Mountains are situated on the right bank of the River Vaksh. Floods usually occur in July and August when snow and ice melts in the mountains. Water level rises to 2–2.5 m, and sometimes up to 4–4.5 m when the lower terrace is flooded. The last large floods occurred in 1956, 1958, and 1959. Now the water level is controlled by Nurekskoy and Baypazinskoy hydroelectric power stations. Approximately 40 lakes (former river-beds) up to 5–6 m deep are scattered in the Vaksh Valley. The waters of these rivers are slightly mineralised. Soils are alluvial and saline, due to the high water table which lies only 0.8–3.0 m below the surface.

Climate Conditions are sharply continental and dry. Mean annual temperature is 14 °C–17 °C; mean temperature of the coldest month (January) is 2 °C–0 °C and of the hottest month (July) 28 °C–32 °C. The highest temperature in July is 46 °C–48 °C. Temperatures are above freezing point on 250–310 days per year, and above 10 °C on 200–250 days. Summer begins in May and lasts until mid-September. Strong, dry western winds with sand storms are characteristic. Autumn sets in at the end of September. Annual precipitation is about 200 mm. Humidity ranges from 40% to 25%–30% in spring~summer, in autumn it is drier, and in winter it reaches 70%–80%.

Vegetation Comprises riverine forest, with poplars *Populus prunosa* and *P. diversifolia*, tamarisk *Tamarix hispida*, and oleaster *Elaeagnus angustifolia*, reeds *Imperata cylindrica* and *Saccharum spontaneum*, and some liquorice *Glycyrrhiza glabra*. The aquatic flora includes *Scirpus* spp., *Myriophyllum* spp., *Potamogeton pectinatus*, *P. crispus*, and *P. perfoliatus*, and *Naja* spp. Saline areas of solonchak soils contain saltwort *Salsola richteri* and some ephemeral vegetation.

Fauna Mammals include jackal *Canis aureus*, hyaena *Hyaena hyaena*, Bactrian deer *Cervus elaphus bactrianus* (E), goitred gazelle *Gazella subgutturosa*, and Bokhara sheep *Ovis ammon bocharensis*. Avifauna includes whooper swan *Cygnus cygnus*, gadwall *Anas strepera*, tufted duck *Aythya fuligula*, goldeneye *Bucephala clangula*, goosander *Mergus merganser*, pheasant *Phasianus colchicus*, striated scops owl *Otus brucei*, stone curlew *Burhinus oedicnemus*, black-bellied sandgrouse *Pterocles orientalis*, and little owl *Athene noctua*. Reptiles include Central Asian monitor *Varanus griseus caspius* (V), Lebetina viper *Vipera lebetina*, Central Asian cobra *Naja oxiana* (E), and little carpet viper *Echis carinatus*.

Cultural Heritage No information

Local Human Population At the beginning of the century the Vaksh Valley was one of the most sparsely populated and scantily explored regions of Middle Asia. Kishlaks (villages) were far away from each other. Intensive agricultural exploitation of land in the valley began in the 1930s and the population increased accordingly.

Visitors and Visitor Facilities No information

Scientific Research and Facilities Work has been concentrated on building up stocks of Bactrian deer, gazelle, pheasants and overwintering, migratory birds. 'Turgai' vegetation has been studied. There are equipped laboratories.

Conservation Value No information

Conservation Management The nature reserve can be divided into four ecological zones, each requiring specific management regimes. The southern part of the reserve comprises the Vaksh Valley which contains the only wilderness. The northern part is a wetland complex, which can be managed for scientific and experimental purposes. The Pjandzha River area experienced many fires and, therefore, serves for research into the effects of fire and regeneration. Experiments on the reintroduction of several faunal and floral species have been carried out in hilly areas.

Management Constraints Increasing levels of pesticides in the water, due to unregulated farming in neighbouring areas, is a problem.

Staff No information

Budget No information

Local Addresses Tadzhik SSR, Kumbangirsky District, Dusti village

References
Publications relating to research undertaken in the reserve are issued by the Academy of Sciences of Tadzhik SSR.

Bannikov, A.G. (Ed.) (1969). *Nature Reserves (Zapovedniki) in the Soviet Union.* Publishing House, Kolos, Moscow. Pp. 432–7.
Bannikov, A.G. (1974). *Around the reserves of the USSR.* 2nd Edition. Publishing House Mysl', Moscow. Pp. 233–4.

Borodin, A.M. and Syroechkovski, E.E. (1983). *Zapovedniki SSSR*. 'Lesnaya Promyshlennost',
Moscow. Pp. 220–1.

GEOGRAPHICAL INDEX

TAXONOMIC INDEX

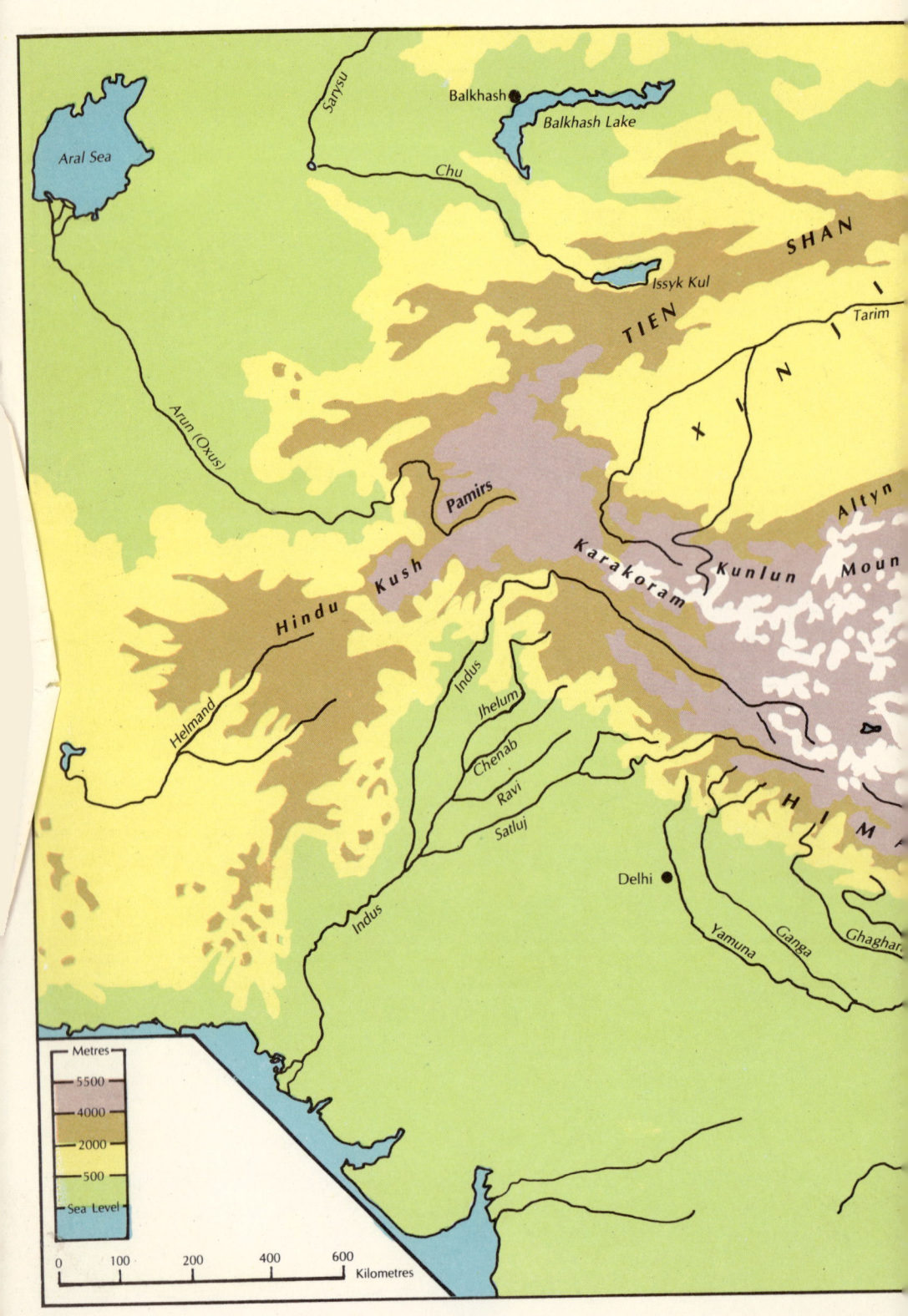